# The Sword and the Scepter

# The Sword and the Scepter

## THE PROBLEM OF MILITARISM IN GERMANY

Volume III:

**THE TRAGEDY OF STATESMANSHIP —
BETHMANN HOLLWEG AS WAR CHANCELLOR
(1914-1917)**

## By GERHARD RITTER

Translated from the German by HEINZ NORDEN

 **University of Miami Press**
Coral Gables, Florida

Translated from the first edition published originally under the title *Staatskunst und Kriegshandwerk:
Das Problem des Militarismus in Deutschland.
Dritter Band: Die Tragödie der Staatskunst Bethmann Hollweg als Kriegskanzler (1914-1917)* by
R. Oldenbourg Verlag, Munich, Copyright © 1964
by R. Oldenbourg Verlag, Munich.

ISBN 0-87024-182-6

Library of Congress Catalog Card No. 68-31041

Editorial Consultant for this volume:
Dr. H. W. Koch, University of York, England

Designed by Bernard Lipsky

Manufactured in the United States of America

# Contents

# The Sword and the Scepter

# Preface

TO ATTAIN scholarly stature, a study of the relation of politics and war in the First World War today must be based on the broadest research into the original documentary sources, including the masses of material still unpublished. This means that one must go to the archives and depositories. Only in this way can one gain insight into the countless individual interrelationships that must be known if one is to understand the course of political events and do justice to the acts of commission and omission of leading statesmen and soldiers, their successes as well as their failures. War—and especially modern mass war—means an enormous intensification in political life. Its concatenations began to extend over the entire globe at an early stage. In consequence, our own account has inevitably swelled in breadth, quite bursting the limitations that were observed in the first two volumes.

It was my original plan to carry the story to 1945 in this third volume and thus to conclude it, but this soon proved to be impossible. I have had to reserve the conclusion for a fourth volume, for which my researches have already been largely completed. That volume is to cover the following main themes: (1) The problem of a negotiated peace in the fall of 1917 (the papal peace initiative) and the supreme army command; (2) Ludendorff's policy of conquest and the dictated peace of Brest-Litovsk; (3) the frantic determination to achieve victory that marked the March offensive of 1918; (4) the collapse of the empire and the end of the traditional Prussian military system; (5) the Reichswehr and the Weimar Republic; and (6) the armed forces under Hitler and in the Second World War. In the present state of source research, the final two chapters can be little more than exploratory, but they are meant to round out the total picture.

It may seem surprising that the present volume does not at least carry the account to the end of the First World War; but the reasons are more than adventitious. As I seek to show in Chapter 11, the year 1917 represents a great turning point in world history; but more than that, it marks an incisive juncture in the problem of German militarism. Bethmann Hollweg's fall in July 1917, engineered by the generals, was the outward sign that they had achieved virtually unlimited political power. Hence the figure of the first war chancellor was bound to become the focal point of this book.

For the first time Bethmann Hollweg's policies in their relation to the conduct of the war are here illuminated from every angle, using the original documentary material and scrutinizing every last detail. It is essential to know all the mounting problems that faced him, the opposition with which he had to cope, the tangled threads of destiny. In this way alone can one really do justice to his actions as a statesman and his struggles with the military, and transcend the facile catchwords with which Bethmann Hollweg has been commonly treated by many German historians.

The basic concept of the present book, the result of many years of study, was already fixed in 1961, when the Hamburg historian Fritz Fischer published his well-known book, *Germany's Aims in the First World War*. This work utilizes an immense mass of source material from German archives and I have naturally had to consider it. I got a great many details from it myself, especially from the central archives of the German Democratic Republic in Potsdam, to which I have had no access. Its basic thesis is that Bethmann Hollweg, hitherto always shown as a pusillanimous compromiser and appeaser, was actually a practitioner of power politics with ambitious ideas of conquest, and hence a kind of precursor to Adolf Hitler; but this argument has convinced me no more than it has the great majority of professional historians in Germany and elsewhere. This misinterpretation may survive in the popular prints, but it is unlikely to carry much weight in the world of scholarship. For that reason alone it did not seem worth my while to freight this book with protracted polemics, especially since Fischer deals with but one aspect of German war policy rather than with our theme, the relation between politics and war. At the same time it seemed essential, indeed unavoidable, to show in my Notes, from the original documents, the numerous instances in which Fischer's account is based on arbitrary misinterpretations of his sources. Only in this way can the danger be stemmed of allowing an incorrect historical picture to become fixed.

In the main text of my book I have therefore limited myself to presenting my own views and offering the evidence for them. I have endeavored to steer clear of both apologetics and carping ex post facto criticism. Free of the national-liberal tinge that marks the accounts of most of my predecessors, as well as of the radical reversal of that bias that has become discernible since 1945 (as in the case of Fischer), I have tried to analyze the source material with the greatest care and cautiously to feel my way into whatever situation prevailed at the time, to the end of coming as close as possible to historical reality.

Nothing could be more precarious than the trade of the historian of the recent past. He is virtually crushed by the mass of his source material. If he is selective, he readily falls victim to the danger of merely picking evidence for a preconceived theory. If he pursues completeness and universality, his work threatens to turn into a mere documentary assemblage, instead of becoming a lucid, multidimensional projection of events in which light and shadow are fairly apportioned. The dilemma of the creative historian rarely grew as tangible to me as it did in the arduous work on this volume.

True, that labor was enormously stimulating and exciting as well. The tragedy I had set myself to describe was not, after all, confined to Germany. The spectacle is repeated with virtually every nation involved in the war—statesmen entangled, more or less helplessly, in the inexorable exigencies of war, the resistless pressure of passion unleashed in what is called public opinion. It was my special purpose to describe German war policy, not in isolation, but within the framework of history as a whole—insofar as that can be accomplished at this early date. So far only American foreign policy is all but completely documented in private as well as official publications. The great archives in Paris and London are still closed to scholars. Should that change—and after all August 1, 1964, will mark a full half-century since the First World War broke out—many details in the picture I project may have to be corrected or supplemented. I must say, however, that I do not expect any great surprises.

As for the record of military policy, the official documents for Germany and Austria-Hungary are now available in their entirety. It was never my intention to evaluate them exhaustively in any sense. I merely wished to acquire enough knowledge to project a clear and reliable picture of these policies and of the leading political and military personages concerned with them.

I commenced my source studies directly following my retirement in 1956, in part from microfilm secured from the National Archives in Washington (especially the important German document series *Weltkrieg 15 geheim*), in part by consulting the original documents in the Vienna archives, where I was granted the widest latitude and assistance. Subsequently, when the captured German documents had been returned from Britain, I also made special research trips to Bonn and Koblenz. I secured copies of further material from the Record Office in London.

In these efforts I enjoyed the devoted and skillful help of certain candidates for the doctorate, from among the last such generation under my care. Wolfgang Steglich spent several months in 1956 at work in Vienna, with financial support from the German Research Council, carrying out commissions for me as well as collecting source material for his own studies. Working in the Potsdam Central Archive in preparation for his book on Bethmann Hollweg as Reich Chancellor during the period from 1909 to 1914, Günther Zmarzlik took advantage of the opportunity to get me voluminous and important documentary material, which is likely to benefit my fourth volume even more than this one. Karl Heinz Janssen was kind enough to place at my disposal the entire documentation he had accumulated from the Munich, Stuttgart, and Karlsruhe archives, as well as from the papers of the Württemberg premier, von Weizsäcker, for his book about the military policies of the German federal states. He unearthed numerous items that were of unusual value to me. Klaus Schwabe made a number of important items from the papers of Hans Delbrück available to me. His long dissertation on the political attitude of German academics in the World War, which I hope will soon be published, forms an important supplement to my own work. In addition to the papers of major political and military figures I was able to scan at the federal archives in Bonn, I had the privilege, through the good offices of the Max Planck Institute of History at Göttingen, to study a comprehensive memorandum from the papers of Reich Minister of the Treasury von Roedern. Other sources made available to me are credited in my Notes.

To my surprise, many of the documents I had collected from the political archives of the German foreign ministry appeared in print while this book was in the writing, in a Paris publication, *L'Allemagne et les Problèmes de la Paix,* Vol. 1, 1914-1917, which P. Renouvin at once dispatched to me. Through the courtesy of his coeditor, M. Baumont, and the research worker, J. Grunewald, I received Volume 2 in proof in time to be useful to me in completing the final chapters of this book.

In working on the problems of American policy, I enjoyed valuable and generous support from Arthur S. Link, biographer of Woodrow Wilson, who sent me Xerox copies of all the chapters in the fourth volume of his great work that were relevant to me. More than that, he promptly sent me copies of all the letters from the papers of President Wilson and Colonel House for which I asked. I am also indebted for help and advice from General van Overstraeten, Professor Willequet, and Professor Ganshof in Belgium. Thanks are of course due to the many librarians who aided me, not least in the case of the Freiburg University Library, for whom nothing was too much. Financial support for journeys, copying services, and payment of assistants from the German Research Council and the Freiburg Scientific Society is gratefully acknowledged. Not least I wish to express my gratitude for the tireless assistance of K. Schwabe and G. Lauruschkat, without whom I could not have carried out this exacting work.

Freiburg
May, 1964                                                            GERHARD RITTER

# ONE

# The Period of the National Political Truce and of Brimming Faith in Victory (1914-1915)

# 1

# The Chancellor and the German Patriotic Dream (1914)

T HE GERMAN PEOPLE were convinced at the time of the outbreak of the Great War of 1914-1918 that it was launched as a surprise attack by their enemies on the peaceful heart of Europe. Such was not the case. Nor was it in turn an offensive war launched by the Germans, aimed at achieving a kind of hegemony. In other words, it is wrong to view it as having been provoked by the Germans who, in an access of muscle-flexing and political ambition, challenged their neighbors in order to gain, by force of arms, the great-power status of which they had so long dreamed.

It is true that in the Age of Imperialism neither the Germans nor other great nations were lacking in dreams of power and awareness of their own strength. As has been documented in earlier parts of this work, there were saber-rattling extremists, chauvinists, and militarists aplenty in Germany.[1] Yet it would be misguided to view German public opinion, in its bourgeois aspects—to say nothing of the working-class social democrats—as having been dominated by such extremist sentiments even before 1914. Nationalist passions did of course swiftly erupt once the war had broken out, together with a taste for conquest—among the Germans as with all the nations embroiled; but in the German case, this was not by any means the "logical" continuation of a German prewar imperialist spirit.

It is very difficult to determine with any precision just what was in the mind of the average German patriot who prated so much about the need for a German "rise to world power" before 1914. We may say with considerable assurance, however, that the notion of a German "hegemony"—whether on the European continent, the high seas, or the world in general—played a very minor role in the prewar German public prints. Voiced much more frequently and eloquently was a desire for equality among the powers of the world.

We have seen that this goal found its sharpest expression in the naval policies of the Tirpitz era; and we have minced no words in laying bare their political dangers and military futility. Yet it is unfair and misleading to characterize these policies as a form of cold war, bound to find its natural continuation in a hot war;[2] for this projects the notion of a deliberate militarist policy pursued by the German government, out to destroy British sea power at all costs, even by the hopeless adventure of a great naval war.

Berlin was not as blind as all that. Down to the very last there was extreme reluctance to engage in war with Britain. The German battle fleet had indeed been built as a defensive force rather than for purposes of the offensive, even though the Germans hoped to be able to exploit its strength in their diplomatic bargaining for equality. This bubble was soon punctured when the Germans realized that the British had no good reason to tremble before the German navy. It should be borne in mind, however, that to use massive armaments for purposes of political maneuvering and the achievement of equilibrium rather than for war is a staple of political life—today more than ever before.

Germany in the Age of Imperialism did strive for equality among the world powers, indeed, wished to become a world power itself. This was not a clearly formulated goal—it was a simple expression of German pride, of the natural self-assertion of a dynamic nation. The imperial government yielded to these ambitions by engaging—especially under von Bülow—in a busy and capricious foreign and colonial policy; and by pursuing powerful naval rearmament, which remained entirely unilateral until 1912.

Yet these policies encountered swiftly rising difficulties, stemming from the natural limitations imposed on a centrally situated continental country. Germany slid into a whole series of dangerous foreign-policy crises, isolating itself alarmingly. This was the "encirclement" by ententes and military alliances that troubled all politically aware Germans from 1911 onward. Only a government of adventurers could in such a situation have afforded to provoke war, to "reach for world power." The risks would have been all the greater, for the top military authorities had just then grown fully aware that German armaments on land were grossly inadequate for a two-front war, while the German battle fleet had little hope of winning a decisive battle against Britain. (See Volume II, Chapter 8, Part 1, especially pp. 157f., and Chapter 9, Part 3.)

There was no essential change in this situation prior to 1914, despite the great German arms bills of the final prewar years. On the contrary, Moltke, the chief of staff, was profoundly worried in the summer of 1914, as we have seen, because he knew that within a few years Zukhomlinov's strengthened Russian army and the French defense acts of 1913 would knock all the strategic plans of the German General Staff into a cocked hat and render a successful two-front war completely impossible. Did he then, in desperation, opt for preventive war? And did Chancellor Bethmann Hollweg follow his lead?

In the second volume of this work we carefully examined the sparse evidence in favor of the view that the German chief of staff did entertain ideas of preventive war; and we found no clear-cut proof that Moltke's conduct during those crucial days of late July 1914 was motivated by any considerations other than purely military-technical ones. Bethmann Hollweg himself was anything but an adventurer,[3] but to this day we have no documentation of any kind that would acquaint us with his inner thoughts during the July crisis. His closest associates, however, have unanimously testified to the fact that he was deeply troubled by Russia's steadily rising power, and the growing hostility between Germany's Russian neighbor and Germany's Austro-Hungarian ally, holding out the prospect of more and more menacing Balkan conflicts. His unconditional pledge of German armed aid to Austria in the event of conflict could be scarcely explained but by a certain fatalism that regarded an armed clash with Russia as inevitable sooner or later. We have not hesitated to characterize this fatalism—and Bethmann Hollweg's associated blindness to the true character and narrow limitations of Austrian policy—as culpable before the bar of history.[4] Yet all this does not alter the fact that German government policy in July 1914 was basically defensive rather than aggressive in character, even though the Germans repeatedly urged the Austrians to proceed against Serbia with swift military measures. For in the German view this Serbian war too was purely defensive, warding off mortal danger, rather than an aggressive act for the conquest of Slavic soil.

Of course it is easy to suggest after the fact that the preservation of the Danubian monarchy as a great power was not worth such enormously high stakes, indeed to ask whether to preserve it was even possible in the long run, and whether Austria as an ally did not increase the risk rather than bring added strength; but posing the question in these terms, the historian soon grows aware that he totally fails to comprehend the period in point. In 1914 no German statesman could have asked himself such a question, if only because he would have thereby forfeited all respect in the eyes of the German people, and of the German-speaking Austrians as well. It would have meant violating a solemn commitment, and he would have appeared not merely as a weakling and a coward, but as an outright traitor to the German cause. Even the breach of 1866 had never created so deep a division as to let the Germans in the Reich look on idly while the "sister empire" (the maintenance of which even Bismarck had declared to be a European imperative) fell to pieces. To say nothing of the fact that Russian domination of the Balkan peninsula, possibly including even Hungary, was then still regarded as an intolerable threat to Central Europe.

Behind these nationalist considerations, and the fear of losing the last reliable ally in Europe with Austria, there was an even deeper German motive—the natural assertiveness of a great power, the "thirst for prestige." There was to be no passive acceptance of continuing Serb activism, culminating in the assassination of the heir to the Austrian throne, that would deprive Austria of its status as a great power. Nor was Germany to lose face by being intimidated into reneging on its pledge of armed aid, from fear of Russia. At the time, this drive for power and self-assertion was so universally taken for granted in Europe as to be beyond discussion.

There were no reasons of vital self-interest why Russia should have allowed itself to become the protector of the Balkan Slavs, becoming on that account embroiled in a life-and-death struggle that. swiftly led to perdition. It was done purely for the sake of prestige; and it was solely for the purpose of enhancing its prestige as a continental power that France allied itself for better or worse with the czarist empire, widening the Balkan war into a major European conflagration. The Italians were driven to entering the war purely by ambition—they did not wish to miss their "hour of truth." By means of huge annexations of foreign territory, pledged in advance by treaty and far transcending the Italian ethnic area, they wished to attain to the status of a true great power. The British, lastly, were not merely or even primarily defending the security of their island against Germany—they were fighting for their moral and political prestige, for their position as a world power, for their mastery of the sea. Germany's decision to preserve the territorial integrity of the Dual Alliance lay along precisely the same lines. It is true, of course, that mere force of arms was neither a sufficient nor an appropriate means for solving the nationality problems of the Danubian state.

For the rest, the only distinction between German policy and the policy of Germany's rivals lay in the fact that the former was so overwhelmingly dominated by military considerations. This was not altogether unlike Russian policy, but it went much further. As we have seen and traced in detail, it was, in the final analysis, the fear of the professional soldiers that their settled offensive plans would become obsolete that wrecked the efforts of European diplomacy to contain the Serbian crisis by peaceful negotiation and political compromise and achieve a settlement between St. Petersburg and Vienna. Responsibility for the failure of the German political leadership at the crucial juncture, the night of July 30, lay primarily with the abject dependence on the plans of the military. This was more than mere weakness. It stemmed from Germany's predicament. It was Germany alone that had to count on a two-front war, that had to anticipate any aggressive designs of its adversaries if it wished to prevail.

How could Bethmann Hollweg, the "civilian," have accepted responsibility in imperial Germany for foiling delicately poised campaign plans, the success of which, his military advisers told him, depended entirely on the elements of surprise and lightninglike rapidity? But then, would a Bismarck have accepted the affront of a campaign plan that bound him hand and foot in a political sense and would unquestionably bring Britain on the scene against Germany, thus creating a three-front war? It is hard to envisage his falling in with such a scheme. We noted before that there was a serious flaw in the structure of the Bismarckian Reich, failure to insure political preponderance over the military (see Volume II, Chapter 7). In the July crisis of 1914, this deficiency was for the first time to exact a fearful toll.

If this flaw had already existed in peacetime, why should we expect it to have improved in wartime? The World War of 1914 is the first instance of "total" war, i.e., of a modern mass war waged with every resource the people can muster. In terms of the mobilization of manpower, it went far beyond what had ever been seen before, exceeding even the gloomy prophecies of the aged Moltke (Volume I, p. 215). It could not have been waged at all but for an almost inconceivable mobilization of war propaganda for the purpose of inciting nationalist passions, maligning, degrading, and slandering the enemy, preaching an airy faith in victory, and also inculcating hatred. Our earlier discussion (Volume II, Chapters 1 and 2) has already shown why the two parliamentary democracies in the West were better equipped than the imperial German bureaucracy to stir the masses with war propaganda and to keep them stirred up. We shall discuss further how this was done and on what scale. Obviously sober statesmanship, mindful even in mid-struggle of the need for a new, sound, just, and durable peace, was completely lost sight of in the maelstrom of passions in those countries. Did Germany stand a better chance to keep its reason?

Apparently only if the imperial German and royal Prussian bureaucracy were headed, as in Bismarck's day, by a statesman of stature, a man so great that his moral and political authority would overshadow all military hostility and jealousy. In wartime too he would have to hold in check the swirling passions of nationalist ambitions for power, the imperialist, chauvinist, and militarist sentiments intoned by journalists and party leaders, while winning and keeping, most importantly, the faith of the broad masses struggling at home and in the field—their faith in his reason and political skill. But all that would be possible only if the sovereign, representing the embattled state, remained loyal to him, backing the nation's trust in the Chancellor's government by his own popularity. Both these elements had been part and parcel of the Bismarckian Reich. Did such a situation still prevail in 1914?

The first question to ask is whether this Chancellor, whose foreign-policy calculations had been so utterly mistaken during the July crisis, who had shown himself so helpless against the military professionals—whether he was even capable of finding a political line of his own and then sticking to it in the face of the military leaders. It has long been the custom to judge

Bethmann Hollweg's leadership qualities very unfavorably, to attribute the failures of his policy to defects in his personality. Fairness seems to us to dictate that we should first inquire into the difficulties of his situation and the limitations of his power, before turning to the flaws in his character.

How far did Bethmann Hollweg's authority extend in wartime? That is perhaps the most important question. And on what did his authority rest?

In the end it rested solely on the confidence of his imperial master. There was neither a Reich cabinet with independent ministerial responsibility, nor a Reichstag majority, as in states under a parliamentary system, that had summoned him to office as "our man." Yet Bethmann Hollweg constantly needed a majority in the Reichstag to vote the war credits and pass emergency laws. In other words, he could survive only if a majority of the people's representatives gave him their confidence. To gain this confidence and to hold it amid the turmoil of an essentially hopeless war that was consuming the people's substance was a very difficult task, all the more so for a high imperial official who was not supposed to be a man of the people, and indeed was not.

The task became all but insoluble in the face of an open conflict between the patriotic aspirations of the embattled people (or at least of the journalists and politicians who determined "public opinion") and the sober realization of the statesman that complete victory was unlikely, indeed beyond reach. To confess one's doubts in such a situation meant to commit political suicide. To suppress them and make a pretense of confidence meant to deceive the people, which was bound to have fateful consequences someday, when victory really proved unattainable. To speak only with the greatest caution, allowing one's doubt to shine through occasionally, meant weakening one's authority and shaking the people's confidence even more. It was not really true that the Chancellor, as the Kaiser's confidant, was independent of party life and public opinion. In point of fact, they constantly kept him in turmoil and trouble, shunting him from pillar to post, from one emergency solution to another compromise. An embattled nation, sharing in the war down to the lowest rungs in the ladder, simply cannot be governed by authoritarian methods.

What, then, in terms of public opinion, did the constitutional support he enjoyed by authority of the crown mean to Bethmann Hollweg?

It must be admitted that William II stuck with Bethmann Hollweg with astonishing loyalty and tenacity down to July 1917. He shielded the Chancellor from a cabal that incessantly conspired in many ways against "Bethmann Hollweg the failure" from the first day of the war, as we shall yet see. This circle enjoyed and sought many connections at court and with the Kaiser's closest military entourage. The Kaiser repeatedly refused to receive delegations from the rightist parties that sought to agitate against Bethmann Hollweg. He severely told off the crown prince when he sought to act as intermediary for the cabal.[5] The Kaiser dropped Bethmann Hollweg only when the Reichstag majority deserted him, while at the same time Hindenburg and Ludendorff threatened to resign unless Bethmann Hollweg were dismissed.

The Kaiser must thus have entertained a profound confidence in his chief minister, to which Bethmann Hollweg responded with an unshakable loyalty of his own and a preparedness to defend his sovereign against any form of public criticism. William II probably sensed that the earnest and conscientious Bethmann Hollweg stood head and shoulders above the courtier and flatterer Bülow in an ethical sense. The Kaiser had never forgiven Bülow his "betrayal" of 1908. In the present situation he probably knew that with Bethmann Hollweg's dismissal he would be entirely at the mercy of ruthless bullies of the stripe of Tirpitz and Ludendorff.[6] It was a prospect to trouble him all the more since he himself was anything but a daredevil and man of action. According to Tirpitz he said as early as the spring of 1915, half in despair, that he had never interfered with his advisers, had indeed never done anything, yet now realized that it was he who would have to pay the piper. Perhaps this was no more than a passing outburst, but it does afford a glimpse into the Kaiser's state of mind.

What moral and political weight did the Supreme Warlord's confidence in his Chancellor carry with the nation—especially in view of the fact that the Kaiser's own authority was anything but intact? William II was never really able to overcome the severe crisis of confidence into which he slid on account of the *Daily Telegraph* affair in 1908. Part of the story is indeed that he was not equal to the exacting demands of his imperial office. It is true that on occasion he voiced sounder views (and probably took better decisions) than many of his military advisers, principally because he was not unsophisticated enough to share their naive and often blind faith in the superiority of German arms. Yet his intelligence was not enough to make up for his lack of a truly sovereign will and of a character inured to self-discipline. At bottom he was rather helpless in the face of the great challenge—a task indeed to daunt anyone—of maintaining a sound balance between military and political authority, which might have kept German war policy on an even keel. His ever-astonishing and often grotesque diatribes served only to conceal a deep anxiety and inner insecurity. At no time was he in any sense the leader of his people in their hour of deepest need. He was unqualified for expert judgment and top command in military operations, if only because he lacked the necessary application. One learns with dismay from the reports of various eyewitnesses how he spent his days at supreme headquarters with trivialities. Time and again the Chancellor vainly sought to induce him to undertake useful work in Berlin or Potsdam. His character was simply not equal to the grave responsibilities of a "Supreme Warlord." He was constantly torn between conflicting moods. A few examples will serve to illustrate this.

On August 21, 1914, bad news was received at headquarters in Koblenz. The Russians had invaded East Prussia. The Kaiser was in a bad mood and strolled for hours in the castle grounds with the chiefs of the naval and military cabinets, according to Admiral von Müller.

> In the end he sat down on a bench and said: "You too sit down! " The bench was very short, hence we fetched another. Said the Kaiser: "Do you already hold me in such contempt that none will sit beside me? " It was more than a mere phrase. He saw himself as shunned, because his policies had led to large parts of his country being overwhelmed by the enemy.[7]

The following day there was news of victories in Lorraine that put him in a jubilant mood. Whenever that happened, his entourage worried about the childish boasts he was likely to voice before dinner guests—about huge piles of corpses at the front, and the like. After a tour of the front during the March offensive in 1918 he declared over a glass of champagne: "If a British negotiator now came under a flag of truce to plead for peace, he would first have to kneel down before the imperial standard, for this is a victory of monarchism over a democracy." When Colonel House, President Wilson's confidential adviser, called on him in the winter of 1915-1916 with an offer of American mediation, he declared: "I and my cousins George and Nicholas shall make peace when the proper time has come."[8]

Count Roedern, at the time secretary of state for Alsace, tells of the Kaiser's return from a troop inspection in the Vosges Mountains, during which Generals Gaede and Falkenhausen had filled his ears with complaints about the lack of patriotic spirit among the Alsatians. Arriving at the railway station in Strasbourg, where Roedern had gone to receive him, the Kaiser immediately launched into a blustering tirade, audible to all the bystanders. Fine things he had been hearing about the Alsatians! Well, all their leaders would have to be eliminated—shooting them was the only solution. The Alsatians with their repellent, tight-lipped faces were far worse than the Lorrainese. This went on over dinner on the special train. The vicar general of the bishop of Metz should be strung up from the cathedral spire, he told Count Roedern and Governor Dallwitz. "Keep hanging them and shooting them," were his parting words, "never mind the clergy and the deputies! " Neither the Kaiser himself nor his entourage took such diatribes seriously. When Roedern worriedly inquired of cabinet chief Valentini whether His Majesty was really dissatisfied with the administration of Alsace, the reply was: "Nonsense! The Kaiser was merely making another grandstand play before his generals."[9]

That was precisely the trouble. In the end, those who knew him no longer took him seriously. Despite the fact that the Kaiser was possessed of a nimble and versatile intelligence, his peculiar personality had never grown to full manhood. He had no more than the outward manners of a ruler, lacking the requisite strength of character and true dignity. Small wonder that unlike his grandfather William I, whose intellectual attainments were far less pretentious, William II swiftly vanished into the shadows behind his advisers in wartime. Neither his Chancellor nor his generals were able to find any real support in him. Hence they limited their reports to him to the bare essentials—which he himself bitterly resented.[10] They could never be certain that the Kaiser would really stick to a decision wrung from him with considerable difficulty.

His sovereign's trust therefore did little to buttress the Chancellor's authority before the people. The confidence of the federal princelings meant even less, for some of them at least, as will be shown, simply swam with the tide of impassioned public opinion. In memorials and occasional speeches, they were prone to proclaim Pan-German goals of their own, eager to secure to their dynasties the greatest possible share in the generally anticipated war booty. Almost from the first day of the war this caused the Chancellor serious embarrassment.[11]

We shall yet learn of the gravity of this danger. Count Hertling, for example, the Bavarian premier, had his hands full to protect the "weak-kneed" Chancellor from the wrath of the king of Bavaria. The situation was very different with the higher echelons of the state governments, with whom Bethmann Hollweg had been working for many years in the federal council. There he enjoyed continuing support; and because he could always count on this body, Bethmann Hollweg convoked the foreign affairs committee of the federal council no less than fifteen times, to consolidate his support from the state governments.[12] This committee had actually been created by Bismarck, but never attained the slightest importance while he was in office. Unfortunately this tactic availed Bethmann Hollweg little. Under the constitution, the federal council did embody the federal sovereignty; but in practice it was simply composed of officials utterly dependent on their governments and without any political momentum of their own—indeed, a purely administrative rather than a political agency.

In general Bethmann Hollweg also found support among his Prussian fellow ministers, whom he repeatedly assembled in council to deliberate major questions of Reich policy; but the dualism of Reich and Prussia, mightiest of the federal states, which had been characteristic of the Bismarckian era, greatly complicated the disposition of the Polish problem (and indeed all eastern issues) during the war. More than that, it had a disastrous effect on domestic politics. Caprivi had actually come to grief on this dualism, the irreconcilable conflict between liberal Reich policy and the arch-conservative Prussian Junker diets and ministries. For Bethmann Hollweg too this was a constant source of trouble. No sooner did he try to lay hands on the Prussian three-class franchise, to preserve a cohesive national front, when he called forth the bitter hostility of the traditional Prussian elements that ultimately helped bring about his fall.

The Chancellor's biggest and most difficult wartime problem was his relation to the supreme army command, the *Oberste Heeresleitung,* usually abbreviated to *OHL.* Everywhere and at all times, victorious generals swiftly draw popular enthusiasm, for they can show solid successes for everyone to see. Statesmen can scarcely win such laurels so long as the war continues. Thus their popular authority always has its limits, and they have a hard time prevailing over popular military heroes. As we have seen earlier (Volume II, Chapters 1 and 2), this was no different in England and France. It was indeed the hostility of the supreme army command that brought about Bethmann Hollweg's fall. For the time being, however, no danger threatened him from that quarter.

The swift German advance through Belgium and northern France by mid-August aroused wild enthusiasm at home and raised high hopes among the politicians; but it faltered too soon to bring any extraordinary measure of popularity to the supreme army command. Moltke's sudden withdrawal as head of operations after the failure of the Marne offensive was at first camouflaged to the outside, but could not long remain hidden and weakened public confidence in the top military leadership. This was all the more true since Moltke's successor, General Falkenhayn, was for the time being able to do little more than skillfully and decisively bring to a halt the withdrawal of the German army on the right wing, preventing it from being outflanked by the enemy.

Thus neither the initial OHL nor its immediate successor were able to figure seriously as political rivals to the Chancellor in the sphere of public opinion. One might have anticipated that this would be true of Tirpitz as well. Oceans of propaganda had been devoted to building up the great German battle fleet, favorite creation of the Wilhelminian Reich. It had been vaunted as the surest war deterrent for the British. Now it had not only failed in this purpose, but its whole structure had been proved a fallacy. The test of strength at sea never came, and the British troop transports to France, like the long-range blockade of the North Sea, took place with virtually no interference. What a dreadful disappointment! Yet Tirpitz's peacetime prestige as a "strong man" was not so easily shaken in nationalist circles. Tirpitz himself, of course, was not at a loss for arguments that were to justify his naval policy, despite everything. It alone, he insisted, was responsible for Britain's more peaceable attitude toward Germany since 1912. Had there been but two further years of peace for the German naval act to have taken full effect, the British would not have dared risk war! [13]

The utter incompetence of German diplomacy in mastering the July crisis, so ran the Tirpitz line, together with the fateful invasion of Belgium had combined to drag Britain into the war, even though it was already half in the mood for a settlement; and now the war had to be fought with inadequate naval resources. As early as August 2 Tirpitz, with Moltke, began his campaign with the Kaiser for the total rout of the German foreign ministry, and indirectly of the Chancellor (see Volume II, p. 272). He carried it on by every means available to him, notably the influencing of public opinion, though very carefully, without exposing himself, and preferably through intermediaries between himself and the rightist parties and the crown prince.[14] It was only after his dismissal in March 1916 that Tirpitz emerged openly as opposition leader.

What initially helped Tirpitz was the deep-rooted distrust of the "Anglophile" Chancellor entertained by the extreme nationalists of the German Navy League; and also criticism of the German diplomatic performance in July 1914, which seems to have spread especially in officer circles and among many representatives of the Berlin intelligentsia, after Britain's entry into the war made the fearful gravity of Germany's situation amply clear.[15]

To complain of the "incompetence" of the foreign ministry had long been the fashion among the higher officer echelons. Bethmann Hollweg's open admission of August 4 that the German invasion of Belgium was a breach of law seemed to Tirpitz and the nationalists clear proof of his weakness. Above all, these circles were the source of stories that the disappointing passivity of the German fleet was attributable to the Chancellor, whose Anglophile and liberal prejudices had persuaded him to go easy on Britain, and who was unable to break away from his long-standing illusion that the British could be reconciled and won over for peace.

Obviously this was a malicious slander. Tirpitz tried in vain during the war and even more so afterward to blame others for the failure of the oft-predicted great battle at sea to materialize. It is quite plain today[16] that Tirpitz himself, especially in the crucial first weeks of the war, never dared to suggest to the Kaiser the risk of a great and decisive naval battle near British home waters—and it could have been precipitated in no other place. It is true that he was constantly pressing the chief of the admiralty staff for "greater activity," but concretely he proposed nothing bolder than a naval battle near Heligoland—if the British ventured thither, which of course they would not do. He also urged "expanded reconnaissance, possibly using the entire fleet," in the hope of encountering only smaller units of the British fleet. Lastly he suggested a foray by the German high seas fleet against the Channel entrance or the Thames estuary, so brief in duration that the German ships could begin withdrawing into Heligoland Bight no later than noon, before the British North Sea fleet could arrive; but Tirpitz proposed such action only when the 4th and 5th (reserve) squadrons should have been completed, i.e., not then and there, in August 1914.

The chief of the admiralty staff, the chief of the high seas fleet, and the chief of the naval cabinet all regarded these plans as senseless, dangerous, and technically unfeasible. And Tirpitz's own notes clearly show that he was prepared to risk the fleet, not in certainty of naval success, but only for the sake of prestige. Under no circumstances must the navy now remain idle, else no naval appropriations would be forthcoming after the war (to Pohl, September 16, 1914). This led to highly unedifying debates, growing sharper and sharper in tone, between Tirpitz, who figured at supreme headquarters only as an adviser, and those actually responsible for running the navy. Things soon reached the point where Tirpitz appeared even to the admirals as a perpetual malcontent and impractical dogmatist.

Even Moltke and Falkenhayn, the war minister, however, were irked by the navy's inactivity, especially its inability to interfere even in the slightest with British troop transports across the Channel, and they occasionally gave drastic vent to their ire. Falkenhayn, at one point, remarked that if the navy were unable to strike it would be better to use the crews on land! [17] Thus Tirpitz found himself under the necessity of defending the inactivity of his fleet arm against the generals, a very painful predicament for him.

The whole thing was a purely military quarrel, and Bethmann Hollweg had no reason to meddle in it. By his own testimony he never heard anything about a formal request to the Kaiser to authorize the great naval battle.[18] It is true that in the early days of August and again after the hapless engagement near Heligoland on August 28 he said to Pohl, chief of the admiralty staff, that Germany must have a great navy when peace was concluded. Tirpitz at once interpreted this as opposition to any active use of the navy, from an Anglophile readiness to negotiate. Actually, Pohl, like Bethmann Hollweg, was primarily concerned with the risk that the German coast would be at the mercy of the British, once the German navy had been destroyed to no good purpose.[19]

According to the admiralty chief, the Chancellor told him on August 8 it was "urgently desirable" that Germany for the time being practice restraint in naval warfare against the British, since Lichnowsky, the German ambassador, had told him on the basis of his final conversations in London that Britain wished to extricate itself from the war as soon as possible, a disposition that should not be discouraged by bloodshed. When Pohl advised Bethmann Hollweg that it was not possible to halt naval warfare, Bethmann Hollweg dropped his demand, not without some anxiety, it would seem. While this is noteworthy as a sign of the Chancellor's uncertainty in matters of military policy, of which we shall hear more, it had no effect whatever on the course of events. Nor did it lead to any estrangement between Pohl and Bethmann Hollweg. Down to February 1915 the two men, together with Müller, chief of the naval cabinet, worked together in full harmony.

We see therefore that at the outset of the war there was no real struggle over military or political issues between Chancellor and naval command. This was to occur only from 1915 on, over the question of submarine warfare. Tirpitz offered a prelude to it in his well-known interview with the American journalist Karl von Wiegand, given on November 22 and published on December 22. Indirectly and without the slightest official authorization, he there announced a German submarine blockade clear around England. Allegedly this was done to sound out American opinion. Actually it was meant to commit German policy on this naval strategy.

In a political sense, this was a very clever method[20] for arousing new hope among the German public for a decisive role of the navy, hope that was soon to grow wildly exaggerated. It was to gloss over disappointment in the battle fleet—at a time when no really effective German submarine fleet existed as yet! Tirpitz himself was in this way resurrected from semiobscurity as a grand figure on the political stage; and indeed it was noted at the end of the interview that Tirpitz was generally accounted as Bethmann Hollweg's most likely successor as Chancellor. This looked as though Tirpitz were throwing down the gage of battle; but if such was the intention, it failed. The Kaiser was angry over the failure of his battle fleet and the unfavorable outcome of the naval engagement at Heligoland and would have little truck with Tirpitz, whom he blamed for having built the wrong vessel types. Indeed he discussed the question of Tirpitz's dismissal at some future date with the chief of the naval cabinet.[21]

Thus Tirpitz too did not as yet represent an immediate danger to the Chancellor, busy though he was in undermining the Chancellor's moral and political authority. Bethmann Hollweg had still less to fear, for the time being, from the two generals who alone had the good fortune to become popular heroes by virtue of a great military triumph, Hindenburg and Ludendorff.

Their fame, swiftly growing to legendary proportions, can be understood only against the background of frustration on the western front and at sea. In their profound disquiet, the people clutched at these supposed geniuses, whose stature was regarded as beyond doubt after the tremendous success at Tannenberg and the subsequent swift expulsion of the enemy from East Prussia. Here in the east, at least, there seemed to be the prospect of bursting the intolerably oppressive enemy encirclement.

Had these two popular heroes made common cause from the beginning with Tirpitz and the Pan-Germans, Bethmann Hollweg's domestic enemies, they would have decisively strengthened opposition to the Chancellor in the early war years and obscured his political authority completely. Fortunately for Bethmann Hollweg, they were nonpolitical professional soldiers. Ludendorff, moreover, possibly mindful of Bethmann Hollweg's important share in pushing through the great defense act of 1912-1913, seems at first to have harbored no distrust of Bethmann Hollweg's political attitudes. This feeling was strengthened by the Chancellor's own zealous efforts to maintain good relations with eastern headquarters. As is still to be discussed, Bethmann Hollweg himself had boundless confidence in the military gifts of the victor of Tannenberg.

Ludendorff's attitude was probably dominated by the conclusion that Bethmann Hollweg might be his ally in his fight with Falkenhayn and for strengthening the eastern front. He may have thought that only the Chancellor's support might someday push him into top command of the army. In any event, Ludendorff's praise of Bethmann Hollweg grew as his quarrel with Falkenhayn deepened. In view of the later conflicts, it is surprising to read his defense of the Chancellor against the nationalist opposition, in a letter to the Königsberg journalist Wyneken, December 21, 1915.

> It is easy for a man who does not have full responsibility [as was true of Ludendorff too] to speak up and make demands, but one must sympathize with the situation of the responsible leader. In my view it would be premature to demand binding decisions [on peace with annexations] of him even now. The Chancellor may be slow in reaching decisions, but he will reach them, and in my opinion they will be on the strong side. . . . I know how much confidence he has in the field marshal [Hindenburg]. Hence I am fully reassured in that direction. Unfortunately there is unrestrained agitation against the Chancellor in many places. There is far too much ulterior ambition among us. New men would scarcely be any better, and probably worse in many respects. To the outside any change will signify a loss of power, and even "dynamic" men won't make it. Success at arms is what counts.

Even when the controversy of 1916 over submarine warfare broke out, the general stuck by the Chancellor, found words of high praise for him at meetings of nationalist opposition leaders, and strongly criticized anti-Bethmann Hollweg intrigues by the conservatives.22 "Heaven knows," he wrote to Wyneken then, "I'm far from satisfied with everything the Chancellor does and could wish he followed his impulses with greater vigor"; but Bethmann Hollweg, he went on, was not responsible for all that happened. From the domestic point of view, this everlasting talk about peace aims might be justified, but to the outside it was harmful. In the end only "success could decide whether a measure was wrong or right. That we cannot yet judge. It is easier to criticize than to act, as I know from much experience." There was no one to replace Bethmann Hollweg. Falkenhayn Ludendorff resolutely rejected.

> We are not edified by our prewar policies, and they might be better even now, but they have after all done fairly well. Let me put a counter-question: Will the foreign ministry be satisfied with the conduct of the war? I think it was Moltke who once said that politics begins when victory has been won and the enemy beaten. Well, has the conduct of the war opened the way for politics? This too one must clearly realize, to appreciate the Chancellor's difficulties.[23]

Thus Ludendorff, while the military running of the war was not yet in his hands. He could then still appreciate the limitations to foreign policy in total war, while the battle rages and the issue remains in doubt. Later on he no longer had this vision. Bethmann Hollweg was always reproached by his opponents with "allowing the reins to slip from his fingers," with failing to set those large war aims that would lift the people's spirits and inspire them to the most extreme efforts. In April 1915 Count Reventlow made such charges in an article, and Bethmann Hollweg noted in the margin that in theory there was justice to the demand that the statesman should set the soldier's task. Yet since the failure of the great offensives in east and west, Germany had no alternative but the defensive, and the question of how this was to be effected was purely technical in nature.[24]

What indeed was the concrete task of the German political leadership in a war such as this one? Could it do anything else but stimulate the popular war mood without allowing it to run rampant? Should it not endeavor to confine explosions of blind passion and violence that were bound to prejudice the peace to come? Should it not preserve internal unity and the party truce as long as possible in the interest of the national front, supporting the fighting forces by organizing the economy for war and marshaling money and material resources? Should it not, lastly, seek to recruit new allies and do all in its power to prevent states from joining the ranks of Germany's enemies?

This was precisely the line of Bethmann Hollweg's war policy. The only question is whether he was the right man, able to carry it out consistently.

Reading his wartime speeches in the Reichstag today, one clearly senses that despite his often exaggerated charges against the policies of Germany's enemies and his polemics centered on speeches by enemy leaders, Bethmann Hollweg deliberately avoided lapsing into fanatical preachments of hatred and political free-for-alls. Yet these war speeches were inspired by powerful and persuasive patriotic sentiment and doubtless fulfilled their task of keeping up the nation's courage and hope. Apparently their effect was enhanced by

Bethmann Hollweg's firm, virile, lucid, and animated delivery.[25] They were of tempered militancy, but never inflammatory in effect.

Their special warmth stems from a passionate endeavor to perpetuate as long as possible the sense of national unity, beyond all differences of class and party, that had arisen in the early weeks of the war. As we know, late in 1914 this goal led the Chancellor to place a ban on the public discussion of war aims, and later to attempt to reform the franchise in Prussia.

There can be no doubt that this was more than a mere tactical expedient to persuade the left parties to keep on approving appropriations to meet the cost of the war. On August 4 the Kaiser had said: "I have no more use for political parties—for me there are only Germans"—without a doubt the most effective words he ever uttered. Bethmann Hollweg was wholly in accord with them, indeed had actually formulated them. He was profoundly dismayed as he saw the conservatives respond with chilly silence on August 4, excluding themselves from the newfound sense of national unity.[26]

The democratic deputy, Haussmann, said to him in deep concern on October 4 that unlike Bismarck in 1870 Bethmann Hollweg would not bring home a great Reich from this war. "No," said the Chancellor, "but we shall bring home national unity and thus a nation. That is what we have become in this war. A new age will dawn after the war. Class differences have receded as never before."[27]

It was the social democrats who clung to the idea of a purely defensive war far more firmly than any of the other parties. On this account alone the national front could be preserved only so long as the government rejected chauvinistic war aims, or at least refused to commit itself publicly to such aims. This was the starting point for the difficulties Bethmann Hollweg in the end was no longer able to master entirely.

They were heralded in the very first wartime Reichstag session, when the social democrats, in order to avoid provoking a conservative challenge, were compelled to omit a passage in their declaration which expressly rejected a war of conquest. The Kaiser's own words in his speech from the throne: "We are not driven by lust for conquest," instantly encountered rightist opposition.[28] Those same days were already witnessing the first differences between the Chancellor and the military.

As early as the night of July 30-31, i.e., before total Russian mobilization was on record, Moltke had Major von Haeften draft an imperial "Proclamation to My People," which he persuaded William II to sign on the morning of July 31, long before the declaration of war on Russia. Bethmann Hollweg, who had not been consulted, blew up. At first he held up the proclamation, declaring it to be superfluous. Ultimately, however, on August 15, he allowed it to be published in an edited version.[29]

Another draft by Haeften followed the next day. Addressed to the Poles, it was to be dropped by the millions from an airship over the towns of Russian Poland, to which it promised national autonomy. Moltke was highly indignant when Bethmann Hollweg struck out the pledge of independence and delayed the decision. "The Chancellor does not know to this day whether we are at peace or war," he said. Haeften succeeded in having the foreign ministry approve his draft. Under Secretary Zimmermann remarked that if the war were won, Poland would have to serve as a buffer state! But the Chancellor shared the grave political doubts of the Prussian minister of the interior, von Loebell, and his Reich counterpart Delbrück against the creation of an independent Poland; nor was he swayed by Haeften's statement that the proclamation was not binding, since it was to be signed by a fictitious "High Command of the Allied Armies." In the end, however, Bethmann Hollweg gave way when he was reminded that in 1866 Bismarck did not hesitate to unleash Hungarian and Czech rebellions by means of pledges he had no intention of keeping.[30]

This incident is characteristic of Bethmann Hollweg's political attitude. He was irked over the fact that the military had invaded his own sphere of authority. He delayed a decision, consulted advisers, pondered the matter a long time from every angle, and ultimately found a compromise. Cautious and conscientious, he was slow to make up his mind and lacked a sure political instinct. These are the qualities with which he had to meet the tremendous outcry for expanded German power voiced by German public opinion directly after the first victories over the French and even more vociferously after the triumph of Tannenberg, a tide that threatened to sweep the German government along resistlessly.

Germans of today can look back only with dismay, after having passed through two disastrous wars in a generation, on the abrupt change from the idea of a purely defensive war to that of a war of conquest that then took place in Germany. Not that the entire German nation was implicated in this change, but it did involve wide strata of the middle class and especially the intelligentsia. It almost seems as though the Germans had suddenly become intoxicated in anticipation of victory, turning a blind eye to their desperate plight. We shall yet have to deal with the question of whether and in what measure this sudden eruption of exaggerated hopes of victory, of dreams of power raised to the level of absurdity and even brutality, actually worsened that plight, by seemingly confirming the worst anti-German charges from abroad and providing grist for their mill, thus threatening to rule out the last chance of a negotiated peace.

Beyond any doubt the extreme militarism that had already struck root in Germany, by virtue of the Prussian tradition, was enhanced to the ultimate degree by the impact of the Great War, with its challenge to survival and its encouragement of victory at any price.[31] Thus the problem of German militarism, around which this work revolves, here reaches its climax; but to resolve this problem it is simply not good enough to keep pointing at the Prussian militarist tradition, nor to attribute to the German people a particularly violent "imperialist" character. The historian who never transcends the shallow catchwords of the popular press has missed his profession.

The psychological background to the so-called "war aims movement" was formed precisely by the German people's unshakable conviction that they were taking the field in 1914 as victims of a malicious surprise attack, a systematic encirclement by envious rivals, especially Britain—in other words, that this purely defensive war had been forced on them. It was a naive conviction, greatly oversimplified by legendary concepts of history, the kind of myth, if you will, that seems to inspire all popular movements. Yet it was more than a mere journalistic contrivance. It was indeed a natural consequence of Germany's increasingly precarious isolation in the world since the turn of the century. Was it not the irreconcilable enmity of France, Germany's traditional arch-foe, that had driven that country into a military alliance with Russia? Was not this, in turn, responsible for the fact that Germany had to fight the war as a two-front war, and on the wrong front? And was this not also the reason why the might of the huge Russian empire, which had waxed so rapidly since 1909, posed a perpetual menace to central Europe?

It was quite natural, indeed inevitable, that the advances of German armies deep into enemy territory should have aroused hope in Germany. Now that the bloody issue had been precipitated, the oppressive menace that had held down Germany's political role for so long should be ended once for all, the encircling ring of Germany's enemies should be burst asunder, and Germany's borders should be made more secure than they had been heretofore. True, for the nonce no one had any real idea of how Britain's island realm too could be vanquished, since it had become clear that Tirpitz's battle fleet would avail nothing, while the submarine had not yet reached a stage of development as a major offensive weapon.

The demand to exploit the successes achieved on land grew all the more urgent. This meant creating safety zones at Germany's borders, and also, if possible, better bases on the coast of Flanders and northern France for winning a naval war against Britain. Not even the military experts were alive to the fact that border shifts had become of only limited military importance in an age of mass war, modern transport, and aircraft. How then should politicians and journalists have been aware of it? And neither Germans nor French nor Italians nor Russians appreciated that the great sweep of nationalism in the nineteenth century had rendered all the continental nations highly sensitive to territorial losses and border shifts, let alone infringement of their sovereignty; and that therefore the political effects of such changes, instead of providing military security, merely served as additional impediments to enduring peace. This would have been a statesmanlike conclusion, but in 1914-1918 it was rarely encountered even among statesmen. In time of war emotionalism usually outweighs reason.[32]

For the same reason, the idea of "guarantees" readily assumed the form of expansionism. This is seen with particular clarity in a memorandum which the deputy Matthias Erzberger, later to originate the peace resolution of 1917 and negotiate the 1918 armistice, sent to many German government agencies and also the Chancellor on September 2, 1914. Erzberger was an extremely hard-working politician, steadfast only in his Catholic convictions, for the rest a mere opportunist who had to have his hand in everything and took himself with great seriousness.

The main goal Erzberger professed was to secure Germany's future against further danger of war—but he immediately coupled this with the additional goal that "Germany's military sovereignty must be secured throughout the continent of Europe for all time to come." Hence Belgium, "won at the cost of so much blood" [sic], must be placed under German military authority (to be clarified constitutionally), as must be a French coastal strip from Dunkirk by way of Boulogne to Calais, as well as the Channel Islands, so that Germany would have free access to the high seas.

Furthermore, the cession to Germany of Belfort would be desirable, newly justified by the French invasion of Upper Alsace, and the acquisition of the entire Lorraine ore basin around Longwy-Briey as well. Erzberger called this "a reasonable demand by German industry," thus coupling massive material interests with patriotic politics. He was himself an executive of the Hamborn pit owned by the Thyssen interests, whom he persuaded to submit a series of petitions late in September in which the acquisition of the Lorraine minette ore basin was justified on the one hand by claims for compensation of losses the company had sustained in France, and on the other hand as a patriotic need—Germany, poor in minette ore, would thus be freed of its dependence on Swedish ore supplies. The German steel industry would then be enabled to outstrip Britain completely and forge ahead even of American industry. In other words, not merely continental but world dominance would thus be established. The Germanization of Lorraine, moreover, would be greatly facilitated by such a measure.[33]

But Erzberger was eager to extend German military rule and economic integration to the eastern reaches of central Europe as well. Russia was to be cut off from Germany as well as from the Baltic and Black Seas by a belt of buffer states. This was to be accomplished by "liberating from Muscovite thralldom" the non-Russian peoples of Russian Poland, Lithuania, and the Baltic provinces and turning them into semiautonomous states under German military suzerainty and also possibly into members of a customs union with

Germany. Austria was to proceed in similar fashion with the Ukraine, and Rumania with Bessarabia. The whole complex was to become a German-led federation, avoiding outright annexations that would only create internal difficulties for Germany.

Erzberger's political fantasies reached their height in his projection of ambitious colonial plans for Africa. Germany was to create a great Central African colonial empire, to include the Belgian Congo and French Congo, Nigeria, Dahomey, and the French West Coast. Italy was to get Tunis, if it stuck by Germany, while Austria would get Egypt. In this way conflict between these two powers and France and England was to be perpetuated. Lastly, enormous reparations were to be paid, not only to pay for war damage suffered by Germany, but also to place the Reich budget on a sound basis and institute much technical and social improvement, which Erzberger assiduously outlined.

Ignoring the more fanciful details such as the disposition of Egypt and Tunis, one would have to say that in its general outlines Erzberger's plans accorded with what many run-of-the-mill German patriots envisaged as the reward of victory at the time when German arms were at the height of their success in France. The Pan-Germans, led by the activist attorney Class, as well as the business leaders and intellectuals he mobilized, went a good deal farther in their demands. Class would have annexed Belgium and all of northern France from Belfort by way of Toul to the mouth of the Somme, to be "dictatorially" administered as a Reich province, in which the populace, however, would not enjoy German citizenship. Toulon would be turned into a German naval base. Virtually the entire European continent would be economically integrated under German leadership. The western and north-western borders of Russia would be pushed back to the limits of the seventeenth century. Above all, the French and Russian territories to be conquered were to be purged of their non-German inhabitants and replaced by German settlers.

A program worked out by Duke Johann Albrecht of Mecklenburg, president of the German Colonial Society, went even farther in this direction. He would have even driven the Walloons out of Belgium, leaving them to "their British and French friends." As for Africa, he would have divided it up among Germany, Turkey, and Spain, all except Cape Province and the former Boer states. Bethmann Hollweg had the police seize Class's pamphlet and sought by every means to prevent it from being distributed. He pleaded with the duke of Mecklenburg not to allow his program, which was already in print, to become public, since both the German workers and foreign countries would regard it as the representative utterance of a German prince, with disastrous effects.[34]

But what were Bethmann Hollweg's own ideas concerning war aims? He realized full well that the war had not arisen from a surprise attack by Germany's enemies, but from a conflict over power and prestige among the major European powers. From one of his last confidential letters to Valentini, written on December 3, 1917, we get a hint of how his share of the responsibility weighed on him. The conflict with Ludendorff that had led to his own fall was only a "passing vexation. . . . The thing that eats at one's soul is that one wasn't able to avert this global disaster. But on that only God rather than men should sit in judgment."[35]

Feeling that way, Bethmann Hollweg was bound to cast about for "positive" war aims that would help him to have done with brooding over the disaster and enable him to face the future with some measure of hope. This was indeed a need shared by the whole German cultural community, whose members strove desperately to imbue the senseless struggle with deeper meaning. The power conflict was idealized in terms of Germany's "spiritual mission." Germany was destined to win victory over "the West" for its lofty ideals. It was idealism pitted against materialism, a truly moral society against a mere collective, freedom as responsible action in the service of society against individual selfishness camouflaged as liberty, manly courage and love of country unto death against cowardly pacifism—or, as Werner Sombart put it with repulsive bluntness, the hero against the shopkeeper. In the final analysis, it was also a case of true Occidental culture against Muscovite barbarism.[36]

These polarities seem contrived and dubious to us today, but on the whole they were politically harmless. It is a fact that modern civilized nations cannot tolerate participation in war without seeking to justify themselves and mobilize their intellectual defenses. Witness Germany's enemies, who put up with the war only because it was put to them as a kind of crusade for democracy and freedom against tyranny.

All of this was of only very limited value to a politician like Bethmann Hollweg. As a responsible statesman, he could view his actions as justified only if at least one thing were attained at the conclusion of the great struggle: a better over-all situation for Germany, which must be protected against a recurrence of the dreadful crisis through which Bethmann Hollweg had lived in July 1914. He had to insure above all that there would be an end to the dual pressure from west and east, to the everlasting threat of irreconcilable French hostility whenever a quarrel broke out in Europe.

Virtually every German politician voiced such sentiments during the early months of the war, and it is not surprising that the Chancellor was beset from many sides at Koblenz and Luxembourg headquarters. The members of his staff, however, were by no means all infected with the annexationist contagion. On August 28, at the pinnacle of German military triumph, the minister of the German colonial office, Solf, wrote to the foreign ministry of his horror over the annexationist mania that seemed to have suddenly laid hold even of moderates. They seemed to believe that Germany would lose the war unless it got the ports on the coast of Flanders. Yet it was virtually certain that the war would not enable Germany to do as it pleased in the world. Solf was convinced that territorial aggrandizement in Europe could not do Germany the least good. The only certain result would be to make Britain far less inclined to approve Germany's acquisition of additional colonies from France and Belgium. Besides, what would Germany do with Belgium and parts of France? Germany had had enough trouble with Alsace-Lorraine, nor was the experience with the Danes and Poles within the Reich in any sense encouraging.[37]

Two months later the Prussian minister of the interior, Loebell, sounded an even more urgent warning against exaggerated hopes of victory among the people and against the flowery dreams of a greater Germany to come that were now being peddled by political ignoramuses and feature writers. The government had a duty, he said, to provide timely information lest the country give itself over to false hopes and dreams that were bound to be bitterly disappointed. Loebell's was the voice of conservative Prussia, which stood in mortal fear of still more Slavic elements on Prussia's eastern borders and regarded the break with Russia as a most undesirable interlude. He wanted to see everything avoided that might later on stand in the way of peaceful, if not friendly relations with Germany's eastern neighbor; for he ruled out any possibility that Germany would vanquish Britain by force of arms. The war would not relieve Germany of the burden of rivalry with Britain on the world scene. Hence the Germans urgently needed to be on good terms with Russia in the future and should not allow themselves to be maneuvered into permanent anti-czarist hostility by Austria, such as might result from annexation of Poland, for example.

Even if Russia were vanquished now, it could not forever be kept in subjection. Indeed, it should someday become Germany's strongest card in the diplomatic game against Britain. Hence Loebell would have liked to avoid all territorial aggrandizement in the east, apart from certain border rectifications in East Prussia in the direction of the Niemen and Narev, which he described on one occasion as "necessary," but on another merely as "desirable." Germany must at all costs avoid the imposition of arbitrary solutions, in violation of the immutable facts of history. It was not Germany's destiny to rebuild Europe, but simply to define its own vital needs. Tempting prizes, such as coal and ore fields near Germany's present borders, might have to be foregone.

What was necessary was to eliminate the continuing menace to Germany from the direction of France, and this could be accomplished by strategic improvement of Germany's western border. This might mean keeping Belfort, holding open the approaches through Belgium, and exacting a war indemnity that would "shackle France economically for as long as possible, keeping it from financial commitments elsewhere that would redound to Germany's disadvantage"; but that had nothing to do with Francophobia. On the contrary, among Germany's enemies France was the country that had, relatively speaking, "taken up arms against Germany from the noblest motives, a fact not lacking in historic tragedy." Yet the issue in the present war was the hard clash of interests rather than questions of morality.

Loebell discussed the Belgian question in a similar spirit. Germany, he said, needed a border that "would put the key to France in our hand, if possible." This meant annexing the territory on the right of the Meuse, which should be done by Prussia rather than choosing the ill-starred form of still another "Reich territory." The annexation of Belgium, whether open or covert, would become an issue only if the British were to refuse stubbornly to make peace. In that event, the Belgian occupation should be continued as a means of exerting pressure on Britain, and Germany's boldest ambitions in respect of Belgium might then form the basis for hard bargaining for peace.[38]

Another possibility was to surrender to the Dutch the part of Belgium not annexed by Germany. The Dutch, after all, had been masters of Belgium until 1870. They would have to pledge a close association with Germany, of course. To bring the Belgian coast and the fine port of Antwerp under German sovereignty, thus gaining direct access to the high seas, was most tempting, but would mean complete annexation of all Belgium, precipitating a fight with Britain to the bitter end; but quite evidently, Loebell did not regard this as a vital war aim. "What we not merely should have but must have is unconditional freedom of the seas," as well as a solid and unfragmented colonial realm that would be economically productive and possibly even self-sustaining, harbors that could be defended, and freedom of action vis-à-vis the British colonial empire, This was to be achieved by the cession of the great French and Belgian colonies in Central Africa rather than North Africa. Like Solf, Loebell wanted large territorial gains only overseas, not on the European continent.[39]

Our interest in the demands put forward by these two ministers lies in the fact that they probably represent rather precisely what patriotic German politicians at the outset of the war expected the peace to bring at the very least.[40] But how did Bethmann Hollweg himself envisage the upshot of the war?

He considered this directly after the outbreak of the war and discussed it with one of his closest colleagues, Minister of the Interior Delbrück, before his departure for headquarters at Koblenz. From that vantage point, in a directive of September 9, he developed to Delbrück a bold plan for replacing the world markets that might be lost in the struggle with Britain by the

creation of a great common market of the continental states. This encourages
the suspicion that Bethmann Hollweg was prepared for a protracted war with
Britain that could not initially be settled by force of arms. It is probable that
the British declaration of war brought the basic insecurity of Germany's
"world position" forcibly to his mind—how deeply the German economy was
intertwined with the world, yet how easily it could be blocked by virtue of
Germany's military and geographic situation! The remedy was to be a
"central European economic union through common tariff agreements, to
include France, Belgium, Holland, Denmark, Austria, Poland, and possibly
Italy, Sweden, and Norway," under German leadership, with only ostensible
equality of the members, though there would probably be no constitutional
head. [41]

It is this plan that represents the original and surprising element in
Bethmann Hollweg's war aims program. It demonstrates how deeply he must
have been concerned with the possible complete loss of Germany's world
position in the conflict with Britain. [42] What is not clear, however, is whether
he was thinking of a genuinely voluntary union of the European national
economies, or whether he was envisaging something in the nature of an
enforced pact. In support of the former view, he was forever speaking of
"trade treaties," even with vanquished France, of a closer customs union with
Austria-Hungary, and of the voluntary adherence of the Netherlands—which
would, of course, also have had to apply to Italy and the Scandinavian states.

On the other hand, Bethmann Hollweg also strongly emphasized Germany's economic leadership claims, declaring expressly that France was to be
rendered economically dependent on Germany by virtue of the trade treaty
to be concluded with it. Belgium, moreover, was to become a German
province, in the economic sense. When Delbrück registered strong reservations, Bethmann Hollweg wrote, on September 16: "Such a union probably
cannot be achieved by an understanding stemming from common interest,
but only on the basis of a peace to be dictated by us by virtue of our political
superiority. This aspect will probably also carry weight on the Austrian side
of the problem"—creation of a closer Austro-German customs union within
the larger union. This again smacks of imposed unification, though it may
mean no more than that a victorious Germany was bound to become the
focal point of any new European economic order. [43]

However that may have been, Bethmann Hollweg certainly knew that the
transition from a national to a European market system marked a radical turn
that would meet stubborn resistance on the part of the traditionally oriented
large employers' organizations as well as the upper echelons of government
economists. For that reason Bethmann Hollweg wanted the plan worked out
without publicity in the ministry of the interior. The groups concerned were
to be consulted "as little and as late as possible," and even other government

agencies (except for the foreign ministry) were to be excluded as long as possible—a policy which Delbrück zealously observed.

Delbrück himself was rather concerned about the Chancellor's plan. He thought its success would depend entirely on the success of German arms and the outcome of the economic war with Britain. He was also convinced that there would be strong domestic opposition. Yet he was strongly impressed. Only a tariff-free Europe, he wrote, would in the future be in a position to "face the powerful productive potential of the trans-Atlantic world with sufficient authority. We should thank God that the war gives us the occasion and opportunity to abandon an economic system that is about to pass its prime." All the same, the new system could be. put into effect only with the support of a liberal majority, including the social democrats, rather than through the rightist parties. In any event, the government must pursue a liberal course, including modification of the three-class franchise in Prussia. "Our responsibilities to the country require us to make the attempt, as a hostage to the war, to pave the way for reforms in social democracy in the direction of nationalism and monarchism."[44]

We see that both Chancellor and interior minister initially took the central Europe project very seriously and staked great hopes on it. Unfortunately consultations with various Reich and Prussian agencies soon yielded such a wealth of differences of opinion, objective difficulties, and economic and constitutional problems that early in October, during a visit at headquarters, Delbrück persuaded the Chancellor to postpone further work on the issues involved. As will yet be shown, they were not revived until the winter of 1915-1916.

A new directive Bethmann Hollweg dispatched to Berlin on October 22, 1914, in pursuit of peace preparations no longer discussed the great economic union. It merely voiced the desire that Germany might find substitutes in France and Russia for the loss of world markets. This was to be accomplished by making the French economy dependent on Germany, mainly by the cession to Germany of the Longwy-Briey ore basin, with the result that France and Belgium would henceforth have to secure their ore supplies from Germany, thus reducing their competitiveness. This effect might be enhanced if the French steel tariff could also be fixed.

As for Russia, a long-term trade treaty especially favorable to Germany was to be concluded, under which Russian customs duties would be reduced. Lastly, "in the event of victory over England" [sic], certain economic advantages should be secured there too—say, in the areas of patent law, colonial tariff policy, and economic concessions to large-scale enterprise in the Orient. England should be kept from instituting a protective tariff system, which would pose financial obstacles to the introduction of a system of universal military service that might be a possible threat after a lost war.

All this sounds much more modest than the grand perspectives of early September. Bethmann Hollweg did, however, cling with greater tenacity to certain aspects of the military-political program of September 9, of which the project for a central European union was but a part. His explicit reflections are especially important because they constitute a highly intimate expression of his views, hidden from the public, an official directive in preparation for possible peace negotiations. The defensive character of this approach was expressed in the very first sentence.[45] The general aim of the war was to be "security for the German Reich from the east and west for the foreseeable future. To this end France must be weakened to the point where it will not be able to rise again as a great power, while Russia must be pushed back from the German borders and its rule over non-Russian satellite peoples broken."

The second of these two demands was not yet spelled out here. The first, the weakening of France, was to be accomplished in the main by means of a large war indemnity, payable in installments, which was to prevent the vanquished foe for the next fifteen to twenty years[46] from spending any considerable means for arms. There is no mention, however, of any arms prohibition or limitation, of the kind subsequently imposed on Germany at Versailles. Coupled with the war indemnity demand was a demand for a trade treaty that would render France economically dependent on Germany, turn it into an export country for Germany, and eliminate British commercial competition in France. This treaty was also to provide "financial and industrial freedom of action, so that German enterprise could no longer be treated in a fashion different from French."

As we have already seen, this was to be a stage preliminary to the great over-all goal of a European economic union or common market. This, however, as Delbrück had already remarked, was really incompatible with any severe weakening or financial strain of the French economy. Territorial demands were limited. It was explained that the ore basin of Briey had to be ceded in any event, because it was required to meet the ore needs of German industry, as stated in representations to the Chancellor by representatives of the heavy industry of the Rhineland. Almost to the day of his fall, Bethmann Hollweg clung to this annexationist demand. He did not think it would weigh heavily on France, which had sufficient ore deposits in Normandy; and besides, the Briey pits had been largely in German hands even before the war.[47] As to whether Belfort was to be ceded, together with the western slopes of the Vosges[48] and the coastal strip from Dunkirk to Boulogne, that was to be a matter for military judgment.

This coastal strip, i.e., French Flanders with Dunkirk, Calais, and Boulogne, inhabited in the main by Flemings, might be apportioned to Belgium, if that country came under German suzerainty. Bethmann Hollweg rejected Belgian annexation outright, but neither did he wish the status quo restored.

Like most Germans, including the basically anti-annexationist Loebell, he merely wanted to keep the gateway through Belgium to France open. To this end the barrier fortress of Liège together with Verviers was to be joined to the Prussian Rhineland province, while a border strip of Luxembourg province was to become part of the Grand Duchy of Luxembourg, which was in turn to become a German federal state, possibly enlarged also by the "corner around Longwy." Whether Antwerp too was to be annexed (with a corridor to Liège) remained open, and there was no mention of annexing the Flemish coast—though there was mention of a German right to occupy ports of military importance, and above all that all of Belgium was to come under German suzerainty. Outwardly it was to remain a state, but it should be downgraded to satellite status, its coast placed at the disposal of the German military, and the whole country turned into a German province in the economic sense.

In this way the Chancellor hoped to gain all the advantages of annexation for Germany, without the insurmountable domestic difficulties. "Qualified agencies will have to judge the value of this position with respect to Britain." Naturally Belgium would be taken into the central European union, which we have already discussed, but this union Bethmann Hollweg wished to extend to the Netherlands also, though without military coercion and without changing the military obligations and way of life of the Dutch. What Bethmann Hollweg envisaged was a mutual defense alliance that would leave the Netherlands outwardly independent, but in fact would make the country, including its colonies, dependent on Germany. Possibly they might be given Antwerp, on condition that the Germans had the right to occupy the fortified city and the Schelde estuary. Lastly, there was also brief mention of German colonial gains (as is true of all similar German documents of the time), following the prewar trend toward a cohesive Central African colonial realm.

The content of this war aims program, heralding further demands to push Russia away from the German border, clearly shows that at the height of German armed success Bethmann Hollweg too had given up the idea of pure defense and was looking for guarantees of future security by a thoroughgoing reshuffling of power in central and western Europe rather than by certain local border rectifications. To what extent he was here following his own bent rather than outside pressures is a question that cannot be unequivocally answered. We are almost certainly not justified in asserting, on the basis of Bethmann Hollweg's subsequent attitude on the question of war aims, that his directive to Delbrück did not accord with his innermost convictions. There is no proof of that whatever, and the general situation did after all fundamentally change directly after September 9.

On the other hand, could Bethmann Hollweg, as a leading statesman at the pinnacle of German victory, even begin to formulate a program of war aims

that stood not the slightest chance of prevailing against the will of the nation,
i.e., the Kaiser, the military commands, and the overwhelming majority of the
political parties represented in the Reichstag? For example, it is self-evident
that Bethmann Hollweg had to lay stress on the incorporation of Longwy and
Briey, if only for the reason that he could not do without the support of
German heavy industry, as expressed chiefly through the national liberals in
the Reichstag. Among other things, he needed that support for his domestic
reforms, including revision of the Prussian electoral laws.

Bethmann Hollweg's correspondence with Delbrück shows that he often
had to contend with absurd demands on the part of the Kaiser, "who kept
reverting to the notion that territory to be annexed from Belgium and France
should be evacuated and treated like military colonies, i.e., be distributed in
the form of homesteads to deserving veterans and noncoms."[49] Bethmann
Hollweg stood a good chance of forestalling such narrow-minded military
thinking, but to go before a nation dreaming of power and conquest with
nothing better than a program of restoring the status quo would have been
unthinkable at the time.

In the light of these considerations, we are entitled to the surmise that
Bethmann Hollweg looked on his program of September 9 as the highest
attainable measure of moderation, in the event that France were swiftly and
decisively subjugated and peace negotiations begun at once. He must have
believed that it was feasible and seriously desired to put it into effect. In any
event, for many months he had Reich agencies work on various aspects of the
plan, with the cooperation of financial and economic experts. We can only
guess what was in his mind.

That he wished to keep down France for good and push Russia eastward is
plausible for reasons we have already discussed: There was to be an end to the
intolerable pressure of continental "encirclement." Yet did not the destiny he
now mapped out for Belgium fly in the face of his own solemn declaration
before the Reichstag on August 4, 1914, when he said that Germany would
seek to make amends for the wrong it had done Belgium as soon as its
military goal were attained? [50] By December 2 Bethmann Hollweg had
already delivered another speech before the Reichstag, with particular oratorical brilliance. In it he retracted his admission of wrongdoing, citing Belgian
documents recently found in Brussels and immediately published that seemed
to lend substance to the charge that Belgium had been violating its obligations
as a neutral power in favor of the Entente ever since 1906.[51]

Publishing these documents was a highly effective piece of propaganda to
justify the changed attitude of the German government before the public—
but it was no more than that. The true reasons must be sought in the area of
military considerations. Bethmann Hollweg had already allowed that to show
in late August, in a discussion with Tirpitz, when the latter developed to him

some rather farfetched plans for attacking Britain with a newly organized "marine division" in Flanders. If Tirpitz's report is true, Bethmann Hollweg announced his intention to annex a Belgian strip north of Antwerp, as well as Liège and Namur. Only South Belgium was to survive, as a buffer state.[52]

In some manner, the Belgian Channel coast was to be utilized for the improvement of the German naval situation vis-à-vis Britain. It was apparently up to Tirpitz to say how this might be done, for on January 8, 1915, the Chancellor asked him what goals should be envisaged in Belgium, "first from the point of view of the navy, and then quite generally from the point of view of Germany's future position as a world power."[53] As was to be expected, the grand admiral demanded annexation of the coast and of the Belgian fortifications as the minimal goal, better yet of the whole country—else the war must be considered lost. It was true that in its "nautical configuration" the coast did not meet all naval requirements, but for the time being it would have to do—since Tirpitz's earlier hopes for the conquest of great French ports on the Channel coast had not been realized. Thus, instead of securing objective military information, Bethmann Hollweg's inquiry[54] elicited no more than a political shopping list. The very inquiry, by the way, was calculated to strengthen the admiral's claim to be consulted in political matters.

The Belgian coast with its insignificant ports (except for Antwerp) was indeed quite inadequate for mounting a major attack on Britain or for launching submarine campaigns on a large scale.[55] The military argument for German border security in the west was far more plausible. Bethmann expressed himself on this subject quite bluntly, in a confidential discussion with the leaders of the moderate Reichstag parties on May 13, 1915. The situation in Belgium, he said, had completely changed since August 1914. The German invasion of Belgium had created unprecedented resentment. "Provided the military situation permits, we must see to it that Belgium will never be in a position to do us harm. We must prevent it from becoming a dependency of France and Britain, in a military, political, and economic sense. How we are to do this is another question. Belgium must become a satellite, not of Britain, but of ourselves."[56]

Well, the invasion of Belgium could not be undone, he went on. It had exacted torrents of blood, and the many precipitate and brutal "reprisals" on the part of German troops, had caused great bitterness.[57] It must be anticipated that Belgium would not again expose itself to such great danger, but would abandon its neutrality and join the camp of the Western powers for good. In effect this would mean that in the event of a new conflict enemy armies would begin their advance directly on the German border at Aachen, gravely threatening the industrial region on the Lower Rhine, the main source of Germany's economic power. Adding the fact that many and perhaps most

Germans then looked on Belgium, established as a state only in 1830 (and neutral from the outset), as a rather synthetic construction without much historical stature,[58] one can almost understand Bethmann Hollweg's endeavors to "render Belgium harmless" in one way or other. Virtually the entire German intelligentsia, including such outspoken liberals as Max Weber and Friedrich Meinecke, initially shared this attitude.

Yet it was unfortunate that Bethmann Hollweg committed himself in this way at the outset, for this wholly negated the character of the war as one of pure defense—a contention already rendered dubious by the invasion of Belgium. This was true not only abroad, but among the broad masses in Germany itself. Even more important, it was plain from the first day that Germany would never bring Britain to the peace table so long as it retained control of Belgium, whether as a satellite state or a Reich province. But since Germany could not hope to impose peace on Britain by force of arms (nor seriously entertained such a hope until the start of unlimited submarine warfare in 1917), the Belgian war aims were little more than a wishful dream—unless Germany were prepared and equipped to wage war against Britain for an unlimited time.

Thus the unsolved "Belgian question," in the final analysis the evil heritage of the hapless Schlieffen Plan, became the curse of the entire German war policy. Bethmann Hollweg himself was ill at ease over the whole matter. "Belgium is a horrible problem," he wrote on November 10 to the Württemberg premier, Freiherr von Weizsäcker, a wise political leader who was close to him. "All one can do is to pick the least bad solution among all that are possible."[59] In his uncertainty he kept on consulting more and more experts and advisers.[60]

At year's end the foreign and interior ministries presented him with a comprehensive memorandum, the result of much common consultation. It concluded that there was no solid guarantee of good behavior on the part of Belgium, except through harsh military and economic repression, which was bound soon to lead to conspiracies and rebellion. In the event, it would be shrewder and even more humane to advise the Belgians at once that they would lose their independence and to govern the country more or less dictatorially, with the prospect that it might someday become a direct Reich province on good behavior.

Germans who knew Britain well, like the Hamburg business leaders Albert Ballin and Max Warburg, pointed out emphatically that Belgium's situation had been occasioned by Germany's violation of its neutrality. Its annexation would bring hatred on Germany throughout the world and render peace with Britain impossible. They counseled restoration of the former monarchy, on condition of close economic ties with Germany and preferably (in Warburg's view) through trade treaties rather than a customs union. Legation Councilor Riezler, finally, Bethmann Hollweg's confidential adviser, tried for a compromise between annexation and freedom, coercion and understanding; but it served only to highlight the difficulties inherent in the problem rather than holding out any hope of solving it.

Bethmann Hollweg himself rejected annexation from the outset as a grave blunder, and was not deterred in this view even by the long report of the two Reich ministries. He made this quite clear to the Bavarian premier, Count Hertling, who had to negotiate with him concerning certain exuberant annexationist plans put forward by his king and the grand duke of Oldenburg. Belgium, said Bethmann Hollweg, would be a burden on Germany rather than an asset.[61]

On December 6 he was Hindenburg's guest at eastern headquarters and asked General Max Hoffmann, chief of operations and probably the shrewdest among the General Staff officers there, how he envisaged the peace. Hoffmann claims he replied that Bethmann Hollweg should first of all proclaim publicly that Germany would forego annexing even a square foot of Belgian soil; for Britain would be totally unable to put up with a Belgium under German control. "You are the first soldier to give such an answer," Bethmann Hollweg replied, obviously startled. "I entirely share your view, but if I were to say so before the Reichstag in Berlin, the public reaction would simply sweep me out of office."[62]

Two days later he was talking in Berlin with the spokesmen of German industry, the so-called war commission, namely the Pan-German-minded deputy Stresemann and the former Krupp director Roetger. Bethmann Hollweg wanted them to soft-pedal their war propaganda and wished to explain his policies to them.[63] He expressed himself with the greatest caution on the future of Belgium, using vague and noncommittal terms, but spoke all the more emphatically of France.

It was his urgent desire, he said, to spare that enemy as much as possible; and he regarded the question of ceding the north coast as highly controversial. He would prefer not to gain a single square foot of foreign territory; and if the German General Staff demanded the annexation of territory in the Vosges for military reasons, he was prepared to offer southern Belgium in exchange, to make it less insulting to the French. Indeed, he was almost sorry for France, which was Germany's most decent and chivalrous enemy. France's guilt was far smaller than that of Germany's other enemies, yet it was France that would have to pay the piper, since Germany could expect indemnities from neither Russia nor Britain. No, there should be no annexations of French territory at all, or at best only very small ones. France might have got over the loss of Alsace-Lorraine, "the wound of 1870," but to commit a new mutilation now would only perpetuate the unnatural coalition Germany was now facing. He regarded it as his bounden duty to prevent precisely such a coalition for the future.

These utterances are of the greatest interest. Quite naturally they have a rather different ring from the war aims program of September 9, for the Battle of the Marne had miscarried in the meantime, bringing havoc in its train; and on November 19, as we shall yet discuss further, Falkenhayn, the chief of staff, had bluntly told the Chancellor that the German army was no longer capable of winning total victory on all fronts.

It is noteworthy that only now did there emerge the kind of thinking one might have expected at once from a statesman, in contrast to a soldier, namely that enduring peace could not be maintained by sheer force alone but must be accepted as tolerable, perhaps even "just," by the nations of Europe—the very thing, in other words, that the peacemakers of Versailles failed to put into practice in 1919.[64]

The question is whether some of the war aims that have been discussed could be considered tolerable and to hold out the hope of a durable peace: degrading France to the status of a German economic dependency and a second-rate power, turning Belgium into a German satellite, dictating by force of arms a peace that would create a German-dominated continental economic union. One can scarcely reach any conclusion other than that Bethmann Hollweg, exposed to the pressures of military and political concerns and economic demands, was not sufficiently endowed with the sure political instincts and sovereign willpower of the great statesman. Beset by hopes, fears, and petitions, he was not able to identify and pursue long-range goals that were both attainable and in keeping with political wisdom.

But having said that, one must immediately add that it would have taken an unusual measure of political self-assurance to find the proper goals in the wake of such great successes in the field, especially in a world torn and stirred by the passions, cares, and ambitions of modern mass war, still further deepened in the present century over the last. We are accustomed to admire Bismarck's statesmanship on account of the moderation with which he concluded the German civil war of 1866 by a conciliatory peace with Austria and its South German allies, contenting himself with confirming Prussian preponderance all the way to the Main river in no uncertain terms, by broad annexations, and by deposing a number of dynasties in North and Central Germany. He did not display the same wisdom in the struggle against France in 1870-1871. Indeed, we know today that he went so far as to foment public demonstrations in favor of annexations, even though these were initially supported by only a few extreme nationalists like Treitschke.[65]

We know also that these annexationist goals prolonged the war for a full five months after the surrender at Sedan, during which nationalist passions in France rose to the boiling point. Yet Bismarck himself was inwardly uncertain whether he should conciliate the vanquished foe by generosity or humble him by taking away two provinces that had long since become thoroughly French but would greatly improve Germany's border in a military sense.

What finally decided Bismarck were purely technical military considerations, as was shown in Volume I, pp. 257f.—in other words, the same kind of motivation that played a leading role in Bethmann Hollweg's Franco-Belgian plans. Essentially the decision was taken at the outset of the war and hardened in public demonstrations; and everyone is aware today that it prevented enduring peace between France and Germany and thus became truly fateful.

It is well to bear all this in mind when condemning Bethmann Hollweg's September statement, which never meant anything more than a first, strictly confidential and highly tentative draft—an argument rather than a decision. As our further discussion will show, it is simply untrue that this memorandum formed the basis for Bethmann Hollweg's entire war aims policy, to which he clung in all essential points right down to the day of his fall.

It was quite an accomplishment for the Chancellor to free himself of illusions so soon after the failure of the great offensive in France, even though he did not immediately abandon all hope. It is easy to say in retrospect that Germany would have had reason to rejoice, indeed to regard it as a great success, had it been able to retain and perpetuate the status quo in its war against half the world. In a confidential message to the foreign ministry on November 24, 1914, Bethmann Hollweg already allowed this insight to transpire quite plainly, as we shall see. In 1919 he doggedly defended himself against the charge that it was his duty to have informed the German people at once about the gravity of the situation. He testified before the parliamentary committee of inquiry that he had been consistently attacked in public during the war on account of his pessimism, because in confidential talks with party leaders and politicians he never made any secret of his grave view of Germany's situation. Had he spoken in such a vein in the Reichstag, Germany would have collapsed at once, he added with much agitation. "Hence I kept up my courage, which was my duty to the people and to the army. I spoke in hopeful and confident tones, but I never painted a golden future."[66]

One might add that a public renunciation of final victory was bound to have had serious consequences in German foreign affairs as well, notably among neutral nations like Rumania and Italy that were then kept from joining the ranks of Germany's enemies only by the success of German arms, or like Turkey and Bulgaria, drawn to the German side only by respect for that success. The inner cohesion of the multination state along the Danube, Germany's Austrian ally, would have been gravely jeopardized by even an official hint that no victorious conclusion of the war was in sight. By comparison it seems far less important that of course any admission of this kind so early in the war would have meant political suicide for the German statesman making it. The people simply would not have tolerated him. Nor can their refusal to resign themselves after so much bloodshed and so many great military achievements and partial successes be simply put down as an imperialist delusion.

All the nations that locked horns in the great struggle of 1914 were alike in their striving for total victory and world power, in their relentless pursuit of military destruction of the enemy. To posterity the resultant hopeless entanglements and mortal enmities, the millions upon millions of victims sacrificed for the sake of highly dubious war aims, can only appear as a ghastly tragedy. In Germany this tragic and ultimately hopeless course of events was soon seen as such by both the leading statesman and the chief of the supreme army command, General Falkenhayn, who succeeded Moltke in mid-September. Both men suffered under the burden of their knowledge.

# 2

## Policy and Strategy in the First Year of the War; The Roles of Bethmann Hollweg and Falkenhayn up to the End of the Polish Campaign

Part 1

## The Question of an Eastern or Western Front After the Battle of the Marne

I T WOULD SEEM that no relation of mutual trust ever developed between Falkenhayn and Bethmann Hollweg. Falkenhayn, then minister of war, took a particularly outspoken part in the vehement controversy over the formal declaration of war that caused a rift between the generals and the Chancellor in the early days of August 1914 (Volume II, p. 270). This may have rankled with Bethmann Hollweg all the more, since otherwise Falkenhayn showed himself to be much more objective and reflective during those agitated days than Moltke, who was in a highly nervous state.

Falkenhayn's biographer[1] describes him as something of the ideal type of Prussian officer and aristocrat in appearance. He was tall, handsome, and resilient, physically and intellectually vigorous, born to be an "authoritarian," nimble and bright, yet always self-assured and disciplined. His aloof dignity often made people uneasy, as did his chilly temperament and penchant for sarcasm. His correspondence and military reports are brief and to the point, their clear and objective argumentation a welcome contrast to the verbose and abundant reports from the pen of his Austrian colleague, Conrad von Hötzendorf, characterized by a brimming stream of ideas and often vehement political bias, rather than the sure and calculating aim of the expert.

As war minister, Falkenhayn had first attracted attention in the Reichstag on the occasion of the Zabern affair, when he had aggressively defended the army, attracting as much antipathy from the public as he did approval and sympathy from the Kaiser. In ambition he was probably not far behind Ludendorff. At certain critical times, such as at Ypres in the fall of 1914 and

Verdun in 1916, Falkenhayn exerted a fateful influence by making it difficult for Ludendorff to break off in time an operation that had miscarried.

Yet unlike Ludendorff Falkenhayn was always objective in judging Germany's chances of victory; and at heart he was never given to overestimating himself. When he was recalled from the highest army office in 1916, he accepted the change with a stiff upper lip and continued to do his duty brilliantly as commander of an army (rather than an army group, as might have been expected). In contrast to his successor, he never put on the injured air of the great captain who has been wronged.

He gained few friends among his professional colleagues. In the General Staff he was accounted a kind of outsider, for he had not gone through Schlieffen's "school," having served in various capacities in China from 1896 to 1903. This, however, had broadened his political horizon and given him a certain worldliness uncommon in the German officer corps. He had, in this way, also preserved a certain aloofness in respect of the strategic concepts of the Schlieffen school.

His closest and most intimate colleague, General Wild von Hohenborn, himself a Schlieffen disciple, wavered in his estimate of Falkenhayn's military ability. On the one hand, he admired his chief's calm authority and firm presence in times of crisis ("a hell of a guy! "), and also found a good deal of dash in Falkenhayn's military and political ideas. On the other hand, he was under the impression that "as soon as it comes to General Staff work proper, Falkenhayn quickly reaches the limits of his capacity."[2]

To the older generals Falkenhayn, at fifty-three, was rather too young for his high post, particularly since in the beginning he combined in his person the offices of war minister and chief of staff. Nor did Falkenhayn enjoy the good fortune of having his authority confirmed at the outset by a great military victory. The greatest damage to his reputation, however, stemmed from the fact that he was very soon embroiled in bitter conflict with Ludendorff and Ludendorff's staff, whence the most hateful judgments of his character and military ability began to emanate. The only reason, it was maintained, why he refused to send enough reinforcements to the eastern front was envy of the success and glory that had come to that illustrious pair, Hindenburg and Ludendorff. These stories have continued to exert their effect to this day in the military literature on the First World War and to tarnish his image.

The aspersions were beyond any doubt undeserved. Falkenhayn was not lacking in jealousy and personal resentment of the self-willed and assertive Ludendorff, which still further poisoned relations between the two headquarters, but these sentiments assuredly did not govern his strategic decisions in 1914-1915. He was guided purely by objective military considerations, which he set forth in his memoirs with consummate and impressive precision.[3] Even those who may not find all his arguments completely convincing can scarcely doubt his sincere and serious efforts to arrive at decisions based on the facts.

Compared with the slow-moving Bethmann Hollweg, on whom the chancellorship weighed heavily, Falkenhayn appeared to General Wild von Hohenborn almost in the light of an urbane and ruthless reprobate, a judgment that certainly highlights the extreme contrast between these two men. Apparently the chief of staff displayed a certain condescension toward the Chancellor from the very beginning.[4] Bethmann, on his part, always endeavored not to allow his judgments to be governed by personal resentments. He was probably right when he said of Falkenhayn: "He is not a great man, but doubtless he is competent." Bethmann Hollweg also complained that Falkenhayn had no men of stature on his staff, a remark that applied principally to Major General Tappen, chief of operations, whom Falkenhayn had taken over from Moltke.[5]

The Chancellor always acknowledged the courage and energy with which Falkenhayn, at the most dangerous moment during the Battle of the Marne, took the trailing reins from Moltke's hands, preventing the crisis from burgeoning into full-fledged disaster. Initially, it would seem, he was kept fully informed of the military situation by the General Staff, without attempts to gloss over anything.[6] Yet according to a later note,[7] from October onward he lamented his failure to receive any clear information on how the war should be continued after the failure of the great offensive in the west.

Despite the great victory at Tannenberg and the ensuing expulsion of enemy forces from East Prussia, the situation in the east had greatly deteriorated because of the total collapse of the Austrian offensive in Galicia and the advance of powerful Russian units through Poland toward Upper Silesia. Yet much scope was left for a superior German strategy to score important successes in a war of movement. In any event, major reinforcements from the west seemed urgent.

Soon afterward the pathetic failure of the second Austrian offensive in Serbia also created a military and political situation that seemed to call for intervention by German troops there. The northwest corner of Serbia at least needed to be taken, to secure an open line to Bulgaria and allied Turkey, the way to which was now almost entirely blocked to war transport by Rumania. In the long run, this was the only way in which Bulgaria too could be won over as an ally; and effective support from Turkey was not possible otherwise.

Bethmann Hollweg was not at all prepared to leave decisions in such major questions of military policy simply to the generals, particularly in the light of the experiences he had undergone with the military during the July crisis. He insisted that no step of fundamental importance must be taken without his approval.[8] Falkenhayn, on his part, soon grew very niggardly with his information, surely because he was himself still grappling with the decision of whether to break off offensive operations in the west finally, burying all hopes of outflanking the enemy there.[9]

On November 8, under the impact of the menacing Russian advance in

Poland, Falkenhayn was considering attacking the Russian right flank by a surprise strike from Thorn in the north, even if this meant leaving East Prussia, Poznan, and Silesia unprotected for the time being. He contemplated using a very strong group of twelve army corps for this purpose, half of which he hoped to be able to draw away from the western front. He expected to direct this operation in the east himself, and had he been able to execute his plan as a surprise attack, it might have inflicted so devastating a defeat on the Russian main force that the Central Powers need not have feared any grave danger from the east for some time to come.

Unfortunately Falkenhayn clung to the view that operations in the west must first be concluded with a resounding military success, to wit the straightening of the enemy salient at Ypres, a goal he thought could be attained within two weeks at the most. The following day Ludendorff urgently asked for reinforcements, in order to insure the success of an offensive already drafted by Hindenburg's staff and aimed in virtually the same direction as Falkenhayn's own plan. Falkenhayn indicated that he would be able to dispatch four combat army corps from the western front within two weeks; and he raised no objections to the operation prepared at Poznan headquarters beginning at once, without awaiting the reinforcements from the west. Owing to the element of surprise, this action did indeed register a major initial success, while Falkenhayn had to accept the bitter disappointment of seeing the Ypres offensive, carried out at the cost of enormous bloodshed, becoming hopelessly mired in the mud of Flanders. By November 18 there could no longer be any doubt that it had failed.

At supreme headquarters this failure was quite generally regarded as disastrous. Evidently it dealt a serious blow to Falkenhayn's state of mind, undermining his confidence.[10] In the face of such unexpectedly strong resistance in the west, he was doubtful whether he could take responsibility for withdrawing large troop contingents from there, a decision not made easier by the fact that on November 14 the German artillery had only a four-days' supply of ammunition left! He was skeptical, moreover, whether the commitment of additional units in the east at the height of the muddy season would really bring decisive success.

In the meantime the offensive in the east, launched with inadequate forces, was halted and finally stifled by vastly superior Russian forces at Lodz. Appeals for help from the east grew more and more insistent, and on November 18 Falkenhayn called off the attacks at Ypres and ordered the eastbound transports prepared. He had no illusions, however, that these reinforcements could do more than plug gaps, without being able to precipitate any major decision. He communicated this conclusion to Hindenburg in no uncertain terms the very same day, to the bitter frustration of Poznan headquarters.

At the same time he sought out Bethmann Hollweg (who had been among those putting pressure on Falkenhayn[11] ) for a political discussion. During its course he made his own sense of military frustration quite plain. He bluntly told the Chancellor that unless either France or Russia were blasted out of the ring of Germany's enemies, there was no hope of any German victory that might lead to a "decent peace." He himself was prepared to grant highly equitable peace terms in the west as in the east. From the military point of view, he would ask for no territorial acquisitions, merely for war indemnities. Whether Germany's eastern border required minor rectifications would have to be studied. In the west it would be sufficient to raze the fortifications of Belfort. In distinction to earlier discussions, he now gave importance to neither the western slopes of the Vosges nor the Bassin de Briey before Metz. An understanding must certainly be sought with France, after the war at the latest.

So far as we know, this was the farthest that war aims had hitherto been cut back by the military side; and Bethmann Hollweg must have been rather surprised. In a report to Under Secretary Zimmermann of the foreign ministry he ironically compared Falkenhayn's terms with the sweeping annexationist demands urged on him just then by the rightist parties and the representatives of German heavy industry: Stinnes, Kirdorff, Thyssen, and Hugenberg, and their ally, the economist Professor Schumacher.[12]

What was even more astonishing was that Falkenhayn had proposed that Bethmann Hollweg seek to negotiate a separate peace with Russia through diplomatic channels, even though he must have known quite well that the powers of the Entente had, on September 4, signed a solemn undertaking not to conclude any separate peace:

> The psychological moment for taking up contact with Russia [Falkenhayn said] will have come when Hindenburg succeeds in beating the Russians so decisively during the course of the operations now in progress that they will be in no position to undertake anything further against us this winter. When that happens, I am agreeable to certain overtures being made from our side, in full agreement with Vienna, of course, since otherwise there would be serious danger of Austria deserting us.[13]

This noteworthy step was crucial to Falkenhayn. He stubbornly clung to this demand, against all political and military objections. He continued the war with Russia henceforth not for the purpose of "destroying" the enemy—which he considered impossible, in view of the continuing strain in the west—but with the sole aim of making him receptive to a separate peace, by inflicting heavy blows on him. "Victories in the east," he wrote to eastern headquarters on November 26, "that are won only at the cost of our position in the west are worthless."14

This was no signal for capitulation, for the war was to be continued as a single-front war until victory was won; nor should it be regarded (as it has often been) as deliberately "going easy" on the Russians. It did, however, mean deliberate renunciation of total victory, at least on one of the fronts, and was thus at odds with traditional General Staff views of the nature of true war. The incident succeeded in putting the breach between Falkenhayn and Hindenburg's staff beyond repair.

What was Bethmann Hollweg's response to Falkenhayn's representations? He was at first deeply suspicious that they constituted an attempt by the general to shift the blame for any unfavorable outcome of the war to the diplomats. Nevertheless Bethmann Hollweg agreed with Falkenhayn's estimate of the over-all situation, i.e., he too doubted that "military subjugation of our enemies is still possible, so long as the Entente sticks together."

Yet his report to the foreign ministry plainly bespeaks his uncertainty of what was now to be done. He engaged in a long and complex evaluation of all foreseeable alternatives, dangers, and hopes, in an effort to avoid paralyzing pessimism in respect of the future. For Bethmann Hollweg the statesman, with his strong sense of responsibility, this reluctance is as characteristic as are his frequent doubts and reservations.15 He concluded that the war would probably continue for a long time until universal exhaustion set in and that it would end in a draw. Even such an issue, however, he would be "inclined to view as a success for Germany, for it would demonstrate to all the world that even the strongest hostile coalition could not bring Germany to its knees, a fact likely to promote peace and betterment." To the people, of course, this would certainly seem a poor reward for such immense sacrifices.

Bethmann Hollweg, in other words, found that the situation was indeed grave though not desperate; and for that reason he felt he could not ignore the continuing importunities of the chief of staff for a separate peace with Russia. What he did doubt was that the czar was prepared for negotiations, even should Hindenburg win another victory, which was still very much in doubt at this moment, when strong Russian forces were advancing on Silesia and there was heavy fighting around Lodz. At the very least, Bethmann Hollweg thought, the greater part of Poland should be in German hands as a hostage. He was also concerned about the kind of peace terms Germany's allies might put forward, and what the danger was that an unsuccessful German peace initiative in Russia would be interpreted by the entire Entente as a sign of weakness, with the result that any inclination on the part of France to make peace would vanish.

Bethmann Hollweg was ready in principle to take up contact with Russia, but apprehensive and uncertain how this could be done. He sought the advice of his diplomatic colleagues. When a few days later the king of Denmark (through the Hamburg shipping magnate Ballin and his Danish friend, State Councilor Andersen, another shipper) sent an offer to the Kaiser to extend peace feelers to London and St. Petersburg, Bethmann Hollweg at once fell in. He carefully arranged matters in such a way that any semblance of a German initiative was avoided, and he also first secured the formal assent of the Vienna court.[16]

What Bethmann Hollweg could not know was that in those very days Czar Nicholas had talked to the French ambassador Paléologue about a plan for the future dismemberment of Germany, Austria-Hungary, and Turkey, under which it was taken for granted that the military power of the two Central Powers and their Turkish ally would be destroyed absolutely. This plan certainly did not reveal the slightest inclination to peace.[17] We shall be hearing more of it.

Bethmann Hollweg too was skeptical. Under Secretary Zimmermann was more than skeptical. He summarily rejected the idea of a separate peace with Russia. Peace with the czarist empire was out of the question, he held, until a real victory had averted the danger of Pan-Slavic expansionism, i.e., until the Russians were ejected from Poland and Galicia and brought to their knees. Greatly underestimating French determination to fight on, Zimmermann held that Germany ought to content itself with holding the line now attained in France and hurl all its might eastward. If this were not enough to liberate Poland and Galicia right now, Serbia at least should be completely subjugated, seriously compromising the prestige of the czar as the protector of the Balkan Slavs.

If the czarist government were then in a mood to talk about a separate peace, this should be "facilitated by fair terms on the part of Germany, possibly restoration of the territorial status quo and payment of a moderate war indemnity in the form of a loan." But to enter into peace negotiations with Russia now, before a clear-cut military decision had been achieved, and then to strike the main blow against Britain and France—that seemed to Zimmermann not only a betrayal of Germany's allies, but of the very meaning of the war, which had been begun to banish the danger in the east for all time.[18]

Thus Falkenhayn's political view that Britain and France were Germany's true and most dangerous enemies was opposed by a precisely opposite view, a conflict that ultimately stemmed from the paradoxical nature of this war, which was begun with the fronts reversed. A military quarrel was soon superimposed on this political issue, when the Chancellor journeyed to Hindenburg's headquarters early in December to seek advice and information.

There he encountered a great deal of resentment of the chief of staff, which had already taken the form of a sharply worded written exchange in

November, leading in turn to vain efforts at conciliation by the Kaiser. The generals were indignant that Falkenhayn had first pledged to dispatch strong reinforcements for the drive on Lodz, only to delay them then for weeks on end, finally sending them piecemeal and much too late. The most recent attacks in Flanders were considered utterly misguided, and the chief of staff's abilities were mercilessly dissected with the arrogance peculiar to the self-willed Ludendorff and his assertive and sarcastic chief of operations, Hoffmann. Indignation rose even higher when Falkenhayn's peace notions transpired through Bethmann Hollweg. Ludendorff, inured to an as yet unbroken faith in annihilation of the enemy as the true goal of war, and firmly convinced that such a victory could be won over the Russians if he were given enough troops, regarded such peace notions as more than heretical. To him they were criminal.

Nothing is known about the details of his discussion with Bethmann Hollweg; but the fact is that Bethmann Hollweg carried away a deep impression of the military qualities and organizational resources of the eastern army command,[19] while Ludendorff and Hoffmann conversely were impressed with the Chancellor's political shrewdness and henceforth regarded him as an ally against Falkenhayn.[20]

Bethmann Hollweg was now indeed himself quite doubtful of Falkenhayn. A discussion with him in Berlin seems to have caused only more bad blood. Falkenhayn insisted that the high hopes of victory voiced by Hindenburg and Ludendorff (as reported by Bethmann Hollweg) were illusory. The army was now nothing more than a "shattered weapon" with which decisive operations could no longer be conducted. The Germans could count themselves lucky if they succeeded in maintaining themselves on all fronts.[21] By such talk Falkenhayn completely forfeited the Chancellor's confidence.

Bethmann Hollweg promptly moved to the offensive, probably on the advice of Hindenburg. He negotiated with Lyncker, chief of the military cabinet, and von Plessen, the adjutant general, in an effort to get Falkenhayn relieved as chief of staff and restricted to the office of war minister; but he encountered determined resistance, for the two generals at the court knew the Kaiser's predilection for his current chief of staff and his distaste for Ludendorff. They also shared the Kaiser's lively approval of Falkenhayn's peace plans.[22] Indeed, on December 9 Lyncker effected Falkenhayn's formal appointment to the post of chief of staff, which he had hitherto held only in an acting capacity.

The only result was that eastern headquarters now took up the fight in earnest. Late in December Ludendorff seconded Major von Haeften, head of military intelligence in Poznan, to supreme headquarters at Charleville as liaison officer. Haeften was to attempt first to change Falkenhayn's mind in the direction Hindenburg and Ludendorff wanted, i.e., to win him over to the idea of a great winter offensive on the eastern front.

To this end Haeften handed Falkenhayn a report on the eastern operations containing high praise of Ludendorff's work—which the chief of staff instantly blue-penciled. Indeed, he took the whole mission in bad grace and gave Ludendorff's emissary a good dressing down; but he did hold up a directive to Hindenburg he had drafted the day before, in which he rejected as completely hopeless a plan put forward by General Conrad for "destroying" the Russians in an Austro-German dual offensive, the Germans attacking from the Narev, the Austrians from the San. Falkenhayn, probably quite correctly, did not credit the Austrians with any further offensive power, and he regarded the whole plan as fantastic. The encirclement contemplated for the Russians was far too wide and they could easily escape by retreating into the vastnesses of their empire.[23] He gave much higher priority to driving the enemy out of East and West Prussia, which the Russians had meanwhile reinvaded. This would create the basis for negotiating a separate peace without venturing on a major offensive that was bound to fail in the wintertime. The urgency with which he regarded peace negotiations is shown by the fact that since early December he had inquired almost daily at the foreign ministry about the progress of the Andersen mission in St. Petersburg and London! [24]

Having been rebuffed by the chief of staff, von Haeften repeatedly appealed to the Chancellor between December 28 and January 1, citing Generals Groener and Wild von Hohenborn, Falkenhayn's closest and most important associates, as now favoring a shift of the center of gravity to the east. Chiefly at issue was the disposition of four and a half excellently trained and equipped army corps, newly organized as a reserve force. Falkenhayn wanted to use them to revitalize the western offensive.

The objections of Wild, the quartermaster general, to this use were based in the main on military considerations. He argued that the eastern front currently offered much the greater chance of success. Further, the ability of sorely pressed Austria to hold out, as well as support for Turkey and the attitude of Bulgaria and Rumania, would depend on increased German activity in the east. These political arguments were supported by Bethmann Hollweg who for two months had been vainly asking for a German strike in Serbia, most recently at a discussion with Falkenhayn and Ludendorff on December 27 in Berlin, in which agreement was reached that such an offensive should be launched sometime later on. The plan had fetched up on the stubborn objections of Conrad von Hötzendorf, as will be shown further on.[25]

Haeften recommended that Falkenhayn be replaced by Ludendorff, and on January 1 the Chancellor once again proposed this change to Plessen. This time Plessen agreed to a change, but he wished to bring back Moltke, since the Kaiser did not like Ludendorff. On January 3 Bethmann Hollweg tackled the Kaiser in person, voicing constitutional arguments to avoid seeming to "meddle in military affairs," which was always taboo with the Kaiser.

Combining the offices of war minister and chief of staff in one person, he said, might cause trouble in the Reichstag, particularly because Falkenhayn did not enjoy too much confidence among the public, among thoughtful political circles, and, to his certain knowledge, among a large proportion of the army. People had their eyes fixed on Ludendorff, who had given such a brilliant display of his talents.

The Kaiser immediately agreed to the separation of the two offices, which had already been recommended to him by the crown prince and the crown prince's chief of staff; but he reaffirmed his personal confidence in Falkenhayn and declared he "would never appoint Ludendorff chief of staff, because Ludendorff is a dubious character, devoured by personal ambition. What were Ludendorff's great accomplishments? He had proposed certain strategic operations to him, the Kaiser, which H. M. had then authorized and recommended" [sic]! [26] After consulting Lyncker and Plessen, the Kaiser agreed to have Quartermaster General Wild von Hohenborn replace Falkenhayn as war minister—but Hohenborn was to remain at headquarters. Hohenborn was accounted a mere tool of Falkenhayn, not altogether fairly, as his opposition to the western offensive and his papers show.

Bethmann Hollweg was not satisfied, but characteristically preferred to "adjourn the matter" for the time being, allowing the military on their part to impress the Kaiser with army distrust of Falkenhayn. In a letter to Wahnschaffe he remarked that Ludendorff stood no chance just then, while other candidates like Beseler, Gallwitz, Below, and Knobelsdorff also came up against difficulties of one kind or another. He did not feel it was his task to condemn Falkenhayn out of hand, Bethmann Hollweg added. Criticism of Falkenhayn's work would have to be based on expert knowledge and intimate familiarity with its details; and then, it was always easy to criticize after the fact.

It would seem, he continued, that Falkenhayn too often left the initiative to the enemy and above all failed to grasp the moment in time when the scene of decision passed from the west to the east. Perhaps his personal ambition and a resultant lack of serious-minded objectivity were contributory factors. Army resentment was probably caused in the main by Ypres—"a situation, by the way, for which the army high commands are said to share the blame"—and by the protracted inactivity on the western front. In Bethmann Hollweg's view, this latter charge was unjustified, because everything now depended on holding the Franco-Belgian territorial gains by purely defensive methods and with the smallest possible losses, while the main impact was shifted to the east.

"In the east," Bethmann Hollweg went on, "it seems to me that intrigue by Ludendorff plays a part. Personally, the man doesn't make an altogether straightforward impression on me. Another thing I don't like is his wheedling on the telephone, about which you [Under Secretary Wahnschaffe in Berlin] told me the other day. I am not in a position to force the immediate recall of Falkenhayn. Nor am I all that much convinced of his inadequacy. I could take responsibility for such a step, moreover, only if I were supported by well-argued military opinion; and that is precisely what is lacking." Bethmann Hollweg advised Hindenburg of this lack by letter.

It will be seen that Bethmann Hollweg had by no means slipped into a state of utter dependence on Ludendorff. The reason why his testimony is so crucial to our over-all theme is that it illustrates the extraordinary difficulties confronting a statesman in the face of the technical complexities of modern war—and a war on several fronts at that—when he is at serious pains not simply to leave the conduct of military operations to the generals. We must admit that the Chancellor's judgment of the situation and of his military opposite number was strikingly objective. Yet the element of decisiveness was ultimately lacking in his judgment.27 As always in such cases, he sought advice from experts.

Plessen was supposed to make inquiries for him among the corps commanders, but what was elicited in this way is unlikely to have been very helpful to Bethmann Hollweg. On January 5, 1915, he personally wrote to Colonel General von Moltke, only to receive a most disappointing reply three days later. Moltke showed himself quite poorly informed about military matters since his departure. He was out of touch with front-line thinking, and his proposals for breathing new life into the western front were not far short of fantastic. He was also full of barely hidden resentment of his successor. He thought Ludendorff too young to be chief of staff, describing him as ambitious and self-willed and given to running his head against the wall, though at the same time very able. He suggested that Ludendorff become quartermaster general or chief of operations, say under Colonel General von Bülow, whose abilities Moltke had always overestimated.28 The letter told Bethmann Hollweg nothing new, and soon afterward he voiced his opposition to Moltke's return to office.

Hindenburg and Ludendorff grew all the more active. For a moment it seemed as though they were prepared simply to ignore Falkenhayn's command authority over them and the eastern front. Without even consulting him they made German divisions available to General Conrad on January 6, 1915, for purposes of a winter offensive in the Carpathians, a project of which Falkenhayn thought very little and which indeed came to a halt soon enough, despite enormous sacrifices.

Although this was in open defiance of verbal understandings that had been reached only a few days before between the two staff chiefs in Ludendorff's presence, Falkenhayn accepted the fait accompli. He did take advantage of it in a way that was evidently meant to rid him of his most dangerous rival and adversary. An "Army of the South" was formed of mixed German and Austrian troops under General von Linsingen, with Ludendorff appointed his chief of staff on January 8, suitable tribute being paid to his great achievements.[29]

Hindenburg immediately appealed directly to the Kaiser to give him back his quartermaster general—and he had every reason, for we now know that without his adviser he was virtually helpless in a military sense. Indeed, Lieutenant Colonel Hoffmann, who at first had to replace Ludendorff, was secretly the field marshal's severest critic. In letters to his wife, he showed the utmost contempt for Hindenburg, whom he described as a military ignoramus, the hollow idol of the unsuspecting masses.[30] On January 11 Falkenhayn met with Ludendorff, but this meeting only deepened the breach beyond repair. At Haeften's insistence Hindenburg drafted another direct petition to the Kaiser the next day, in which he bluntly demanded Falkenhayn's dismissal—in a form quite unprecedented in Prussian military history. He put an ultimatum to the Kaiser, i.e., he threatened to resign himself.[31] This was the first in what was to become a whole series of such threats. Even then Hindenburg felt absolutely secure behind the glamour of his legendary fame. Major von Haeften communicated the content of this petition to the Chancellor at once; but before the original was dispatched, Hindenburg once again consulted Hoffmann and Ludendorff. They concluded that the ultimatum went too far and persuaded Hindenburg to send instead a categorical declaration that he refused to cooperate with Falkenhayn in any way.

Hindenburg proposed to the Kaiser and the Chancellor that Moltke be recalled to his former office. At the same time he instructed Haeften to advise Bethmann Hollweg that supreme headquarters must on no account be shifted to the east as the operational center. This must be avoided at all costs, since it would seriously prejudice a successful issue. Ludendorff on his part added that he had no objections to Moltke's appointment, since for the time being no decision was to be sought in the west, to which Moltke would presumably confine his activities; but in addition to Wild as quartermaster general, Moltke should have the capable Colonel Groener as chief of operations.

All this did not sound as though Hindenburg and Ludendorff had much confidence in Moltke's abilities; but Hindenburg let it transpire that Moltke was the only man who held out reasonable assurance of good relations with eastern headquarters. At bottom Hindenburg was even then endeavoring to capture supreme command of the German army. "Once operations in the east are concluded," he added, "there is the possibility that Lieutenant General Ludendorff might be appointed quartermaster general in the west, in the event additional operations might still be in order there" [sic]. Poznan was certain that Russia would be finally vanquished as soon as eastern headquarters got its additional army corps.[32]

On the day Hindenburg drafted his second direct petition to the Kaiser, with its threat of resignation, and had it communicated to the Chancellor, Falkenhayn appeared in Poznan in person, to receive reports of the local situation from the commanders of several armies stationed on the eastern front, and to discuss the disposition of the newly organized army corps with the high command. A calm discussion with Hindenburg proved impossible, however, for no sooner were the two alone when Hindenburg, invoking his seniority as a general, told Falkenhayn that the army had no confidence in him and challenged him to ask to be relieved.

Falkenhayn rejected both insinuations—the declaration of lack of confidence being again unprecedented in Prussian military history—and Hindenburg announced that he, as field marshal, would ask the Kaiser to dismiss him. All the chief of staff could do was discuss future plans for the eastern armies with Lieutenant Colonel Hoffmann (who was, incidentally, accounted the leading spirit at eastern headquarters). Hoffmann unfolded designs for a winter offensive in East Prussia at great length to Falkenhayn, whose response was distinctly reserved. Nor did Falkenhayn say very much about his own intentions.[33] The controversial question of how the new army corps were to be used remained open.

Unabashed, Ludendorff now declared that the war was lost if Falkenhayn stayed on. His attitude and that of Hindenburg had come perilously close to open rebellion. Major von Haeften had already, at their direction, made the rounds of a number of higher headquarters on the western front, to whom he explained the situation in the east according to the gospel of Ludendorff, including the great expectations of victory entertained in Poznan. Haeften had come back with highly welcome declarations from leading generals that more troops could well be spared on the western front, to be dispatched eastward. Haeften also had long discussions with Colonel von Marschall, a section head in the military cabinet, whom Bethmann Hollweg regarded as Falkenhayn's chief supporter.

The arch-conservative inner circle was now mobilized as well. The well-known deputy, von Oldenburg-Januschau, was let loose upon the crown prince, to win him over to Ludendorff's view and have him intercede with his father in that direction. The crown prince did so, only to be sharply rebuffed by the Kaiser, who also received Hindenburg's letter with marked disfavor. Bethmann Hollweg learned of this, but still thought Hindenburg had actually threatened to resign. He promptly advised Valentini that Hindenburg's resignation would create a political crisis. He, Bethmann Hollweg, would not answer for it. This was on January 14, 1915. Two days before, he had already refused Hindenburg's request that he criticize Falkenhayn to the Kaiser's face—since the Kaiser was in no position to form an opinion of his own about military operations. As a matter of fact, Bethmann Hollweg did not again report to the Kaiser in this matter, and apparently did not even tell him that Hindenburg, after initial hesitation, had agreed to take on Falkenhayn's job himself—but only with Ludendorff as chief!

On January 15 a graciously worded order-in-council went to the field marshal, begging him to stay at his post even if Falkenhayn were to remain as chief of staff. The desired effect was not wanting. The aged general, deeply touched at this sign of imperial favor, gave up all thought of resigning. There was no slackening in the cabal against Falkenhayn, however. The next step was to persuade Colonel General von Moltke to communicate in a critical vein directly with the Kaiser. Moltke did so on January 17, but his message was ill-considered. Instead of cogent criticism, he indulged in generalized charges, for which he gave no evidence; and he simply emphasized the necessity of now seeking the great decision in the east.[34] So indignant was the Kaiser that he apparently threatened to dismiss Moltke from the army altogether, and Plessen was able to arrest this thunderbolt only at the last moment and with the greatest difficulty.

Even more ill-starred was an attempt to bring the empress into the picture. Von Haeften again played the middleman and was dispatched to Berlin for that purpose. On the train he tried, together with Oldenburg-Januschau, to win over Colonel von Marschall to the idea of appointing Ludendorff as chief of staff, which von Marschall, however, emphatically rejected.[35]

The empress received von Haeften late in the evening of January 18. He described Falkenhayn to her as an ambitious plotter who begrudged the field marshal his great victories; and he told the empress what Hindenburg had told him to tell her as he left: "Tell Her Majesty that this quarrel will yet be the death of me." The field marshal, von Haeften added, was indeed in such a state of distraction that he was unable to direct operations with his customary vigor. Empress Augusta Victoria immediately drafted an appropriate letter to her husband, which was somewhat reworked by Household Minister von Eulenburg. With remarkable courage, Major von Haeften, despite Moltke's warnings, undertook to deliver this letter to the Kaiser himself and to elaborate on it.

Reaching supreme headquarters, von Haeften learned that the four new army corps had meanwhile been placed at the disposal of eastern headquarters; that Ludendorff had been allowed to rejoin Hindenburg; and that, while Falkenhayn was staying on as chief of staff, his second office of war minister had been taken over by Wild von Hohenborn. The Kaiser had every reason to believe he had done everything he could to calm down tempers at Poznan; and General Wild had strictly enjoined all the officers at supreme headquarters from indulging in any criticism of the chief of staff.

Haeften, however, still convinced that eastern headquarters would be very far from satisfied, decided to go through with his mission nevertheless and to present the Kaiser with a request for several further divisions from the western front for the winter offensive in the east, in addition to the four new army corps. The result was as might have been expected. The Kaiser was furious at this continued insubordination, slammed his fist on the table, emphatically objected to having his womenfolk dragged into the controversy, and declared that of rights Hindenburg should be court-martialed for his machinations.

Colonel von Marschall, the Kaiser went on, who had only just returned from Poznan, had received the impression that Hindenburg was a weary old man at the end of his tether. Hindenburg had inveighed against Falkenhayn's allegedly misguided operation on the Aisne, but when challenged, he had been quite unable to say what was wrong with it. Nor was he able to mention a suitable successor to Falkenhayn, who was an outstanding officer.

The Kaiser was quite unwilling to consider either Falkenhayn's dismissal or the dispatch of still further troops for the winter offensive to be launched from East Prussia; nor did he share Ludendorff's expectation of great successes. When Haeften ventured to plead that the Kaiser instruct Falkenhayn not to quarrel with Hindenburg henceforth, the monarch flew into another rage. Haeften was shown the door, and an investigation was ordered, to see whether there were grounds for a court-martial. Plessen, however, again intervened, and Haeften got off with a transfer to the replacement command at Cologne. He was not even permitted to return to Poznan to report to his principals.

Thus the quarrel among the top military men ended on a note of high drama. By and large it was Falkenhayn who won the day. The commitment of the four new army corps to the eastern front did not really mean a concession to Ludendorff's importunities—or at least that was not the only reason. It would seem that in the end the General Staff itself grew uncertain. There was no point along the western front that offered any chance of a success for an offensive at the moment; and the wavering front of the Austrian ally never ceased to call for relief in the form of offensive action directed against the Russians rather than the Serbs.

Eastern headquarters was confident that such an offensive would mark the turning point in the war,[36] but Falkenhayn never shared this belief for a moment; and later on he was to give way to serious doubt about the whole decision to risk Germany's last major reserves of four new army corps (which he described as among the best Germany ever had in the war) for an offensive of purely local character. It is true that the Germans, in the so-called Battle of the Masurian Lakes, did at first succeed in ejecting the enemy completely from East Prussia and in taking large numbers of prisoners; but the offensive reserves of the German troops were also completely spent in the winter hardships of February 1915, and the attack was continued for a much longer time than the supreme command wanted. As for the great reserve that had been made available, it largely perished in the forests of Augustov, as Falkenhayn bitterly remarked.[37] It might have accomplished far more in the great summer offensive of 1915—indeed, it might then have carried the day.

Even so, Falkenhayn was not dislodged from his post, though Ludendorff remained the key man in the eastern command, as adviser to Hindenburg. The conflict between the two generals had deepened into bitter enmity and it was one of the tribulations of the chief of the supreme command to realize that the Chancellor was to all intents and purposes on the side of his opponents. It was a serious question whether in such circumstances any fruitful cooperation between the political and the military leadership was still possible at all.

## Part 2

# Austria and the Defection of Italy

COOPERATION between the political and the military leadership would have been utterly impossible if there had been anything deeper to the quarrel than mutual distrust between the two leaders, doubt on either side as to the competence of the other; but in fact the bickering between Bethmann Hollweg and Falkenhayn during the first year of the war shows not the slightest sign of a fundamental conflict between state and army, between politics and "militarism."

The Chancellor did not and could not dream of damping the zeal of the military for political considerations; nor did the chief of staff show the slightest inclination to exaggerate the military chances and achievements of the army and on that account to insist on unrealistic war aims and total annihilation of the enemy. On the contrary, Falkenhayn was the first and most consistent advocate of easing Germany's plight by making peace on moderate terms through diplomatic channels with at least one of its enemies, Russia being his first choice, though he hoped that France too might someday be ready. As for the idea of "total victory," he thought that unattainable, even on the eastern front.

What made him hard to bear for Bethmann Hollweg was his pride and arrogance, of which we shall hear more further on; but Falkenhayn was never a "militarist" in the narrow sense of blind pugnacity. Indeed, at bottom both Chancellor and chief of staff held out firmly against the nationalist, militarist, and annexationist furor of German public opinion. Unfortunately, the fact that they were both enlisted on the same side of this issue was overshadowed by their mutual distrust. The chief of staff, moreover, was far better able to hide his doubts about the fanciful victory expectations nourished by the press and the party leaders. His mask of the chilly and reserved professional soldier protected him against irksome questioners and importuners.

So well did it protect him that his name figured repeatedly in the plots of the anti-Bethmann Hollweg cabal, and also among the ambitious younger General Staff officers like Colonel von Seeckt, as the "strong man" who would someday snatch the reins from Bethmann Hollweg's feeble hands.[38] This led to a great deal of talk that aroused even the Chancellor's suspicions; and early in 1916 even General Wild thought Falkenhayn capable of entertaining the ambition to become political generalissimo someday. All this was nothing more than surmise. As a matter of fact Falkenhayn always held aloof from the Tirpitz-led political cabal against Bethmann Hollweg; and as for the complaints and petitions submitted to him by the Pan-Germans, he simply filed them unanswered.[39]

This must be kept in mind, if one wishes to understand why Bethmann Hollweg and Falkenhayn were able not only to continue to collaborate despite the serious blunders of the winter of 1914-1915, but indeed to work quite closely together at times.

A contributing factor may have been that the indifferent success of the Battle of the Masurian Lakes acted as something of a cold shower in eastern headquarters. Such, at least, was the impression the Chancellor gained during a visit on March 4, 1915. Hindenburg, he reported to Valentini,[40] had expressed himself in the gravest tones: It had become impossible to gain anything more than partial successes against the Russians; a decisive turn was out of the question. According to another report, Hindenburg actually counseled that peace be concluded.[41] It seems certain that he joined the Chancellor in inveighing against the totally unreasonable war aims propaganda of the Pan-Germans and their cohorts, while he wasted not a deprecatory word on Falkenhayn.

That Bethmann Hollweg himself was at the time very far removed from indulging in exaggerated expectations is shown by a statement in which he unburdened himself to Valentini. The Germans were daring the fates with their certainty of victory. They had been so corrupted by braggadocio over the last twenty-five years that they would probably lose all heart, if grandiloquence were now to be curbed. The only thing that might help would be to pass the dispatches from supreme headquarters through the hands of some sensible editor.

The Chancellor took advantage of the chastened mood at eastern headquarters to persuade Ludendorff to prepare a pessimistic report on the situation on the eastern front for Field Marshal Conrad. It was to help make clear to the Austrians that they had every reason for purchasing Italy's continued neutrality at the cost of territorial concessions, for that country's entry into the war might well lead to a military disaster. Early in February Bethmann Hollweg had asked Falkenhayn to work on Conrad along similar lines; but Falkenhayn had already been doing so on his own initiative ever since he had heard the first rumors of danger from the Italian side; and he kept on exhorting Conrad tenaciously and with much political skill. Here, at least, there was direct cooperation between statesman and soldier—though unfortunately it did nothing to improve personal relations between the two men.[42]

The situation of the Central Powers at the end of this first winter of the war gave ample grounds for pessimism indeed. The full measure of what the political and military leaders then accomplished and withstood can be gauged only when one appreciates the enormous burdens that weighed them down.

The great German reserve force on which so much hope had been staked had been frittered away in the cruel winter battle of the Masurian Lakes. The supreme command was almost surprised that the great Anglo-French offensives that began in February and March 1915 did not achieve a breakthrough despite the enemy's enormous numerical superiority, at least 6 to 1 in the Champagne, according to Falkenhayn,[43] and 16 to 1 at Lille. This demonstrated that in the era of the machine gun and modern trench warfare the defensive was far stronger than had been envisaged.

Disillusion over the failure of the Austrian army was all the greater. After failing in its offensive thrusts, it had all it could do to hold the Carpathian ridges against the Russian onslaughts and displayed symptoms of serious demoralization, especially among the Czech troops. More and more German formations had to be sent in to stiffen the front.

With the Anglo-French assaults on the Gallipoli peninsula late in February, the Balkans were thrown into confusion. Rumania's attitude, in particular, grew more and more uncertain; and since the Germans had knowledge of mutual aid agreements between Italy and Rumania, the news that Italy might move over into the enemy camp had a most alarming effect. At the same time more and more urgent appeals for help came from Constantinople, where the ammunition supply was virtually exhausted. The repeated defeats the Austrians had suffered in Serbia meant that the Danube route continued to be barred, and German supplies could not reach Turkey. This led to many arguments between Bethmann Hollweg, who pressed for swift intervention in Serbia, and Falkenhayn, who declared himself unable to comply, even though he thoroughly understood the emergency.[44] With every further setback to the military prospects, political friction between the two allies increased.

Relations had deteriorated quite badly within only a few weeks of the start of the war. The illusory war plan agreed on between Moltke and Conrad before 1914 (see Volume II, pp. 243ff.) now took its toll. Germany really had had no right to pledge the appearance of substantial German forces on the eastern front within a matter of weeks. Yet Conrad had built his great initial Galician offensive—which itself probably exceeded the capacity of his forces—on the assumption that the Germans would very soon ease his position by a powerful thrust from the north to Siedlce.

This thrust failed to come off, of course, as was to be expected in view of the situation in East Prussia. Indeed, Conrad was so informed even before he embarked on his operation, which ended in utter disaster long before the six weeks were up that Moltke had specified. Outraged and disappointed, Conrad put the whole blame on the disloyalty and selfishness of his German allies.

The tone of his letters shifted from initial exuberance over German-Austrian cooperation to spiteful distrust and bitter recrimination. His pride was hurt by the fact that his own troops, their morale severely shaken by defeat, were able to hold the front only on those sectors where the Germans had reinforced them. The Germans naturally claimed a voice in tactical questions, and this led to continual friction.

There was not a hint of gratitude for German aid. In December Falkenhayn asked Conrad to join in a campaign to open the Danube route, but Conrad declined. Not for anything, he told his adjutant, would he allow the Germans to achieve preponderance on the Russian front by transferring Austrian divisions away from there. Let them send their own divisions to Serbia! To Count Stürgkh, his liaison officer at German headquarters, he described the Germans as Austria's "secret enemies" and Kaiser Wilhelm as "a clown." Falkenhayn and the Chancellor, he said, were capable of betraying Austria behind its back.[45]

All this, of course, had its political repercussions. As early as September 8, Count Berchtold moved heaven and earth to call the attention of the Kaiser and his Chancellor to Austria's grievances about the German army command. Indeed, he arranged to let it transpire to the German foreign ministry by several routes, though in somewhat roundabout fashion, that Austria might well conclude a separate peace. Why had not the Germans simply evacuated East Prussia all the way to the Vistula if they seriously intended helping Austria? —thus ran the complaint that issued from headquarters at Teschen. Could it be, remarked Conrad, because the Kaiser valued his hunting grounds at Rominten in East Prussia more highly than his Austrian allies? Count Tisza charged the German government with having provoked the wretched war in the first place by its promises to Vienna, and then exacerbating it by its invasion of neutral Belgium, which in turn brought Britain into it and caused the neutrality of Italy and Rumania. It was all Germany's fault.

In the light of all this it is not difficult to imagine General Conrad's reaction when the German chief of staff asked him to urge his country to offer concessions to Italy. His first response was that Germany should rather seek to break the enemy circle by ceding Alsace to France (January 7, 1915).

This was a proposal, by the way, that had occasionally been voiced right within the German foreign ministry.[46] Conrad thought it monstrous that Austria should be expected voluntarily to surrender portions of its soil, in order to keep Italy from openly going back on its treaty of alliance—Italy, the hated and despised arch-enemy of the Hapsburgs, against which Conrad had so often vainly preached preventive war (see Volume II, pp. 229ff.)! Conrad was convinced, moreover—and probably rightly—that such a policy would merely cause the Italians to raise the price.

Of course Conrad's influence on Austrian foreign policy must not be overestimated. The numerous and voluminous memoranda with which he flooded the Austrian foreign ministry were evidently not taken very seriously there. In studying these exchanges one notes, above all, how Conrad's military as well as moral authority kept declining as the war wore on—there were no glorious victories to sustain it. On the contrary, Conrad had increasing trouble in warding off political criticism in the face of continuing disasters and defeats, for which he sought to blame inadequate prewar armaments.[47]

In Austria, indeed, the relation of politics and war developed in the opposite direction from Germany, where it began with an almost meticulous mutual respect of the respective jurisdictions, only to lead ultimately to complete military control. In Austria, on the other hand, no one seemed initially interested in questions of jurisdiction. Count Berchtold thought nothing of intervening in the sphere of the army high command, by way of the emperor's military chancellery;[48] and Conrad never hesitated to meddle in political affairs, even when, unlike the negotiations with the Balkan states, they did not touch military interests at all.[49] By the time Hindenburg and Ludendorff in Germany were summoned to the supreme army command, having utterly obscured the Chancellor's authority by the almost legendary glamour of their names—by that time Conrad's star had virtually set.

In the matter of Italy there were no disagreements between the Austrian chief of staff and the Austrian foreign ministry. Confidence was at a low ebb in the Ballhausplatz, the seat of the foreign ministry; indeed something like panic reigned there when the second Serbian offensive failed disastrously, and again when the Bukovina was evacuated before an attack by light Russian forces.[50] As early as November Berchtold was inclined to consider an American mediation offer Colonel House had made by the Austrian ambassador, Dumba.[51]

By December a very moderate peace program had been worked out, probably at Berchtold's behest. In the event of what was called "minimal peace," only limited demands were to be made even of Serbia, while Russia would be ceded East Galicia (Ruthenia) and the Bukovina, subsidiary provinces that had long been more trouble to Austria than they were worth. Russia was also to be granted free maritime access to the Mediterranean.[52]

A report submitted by section chief Count Forgách on January 10 went even farther. In it the military situation was described as so hopelessly mismanaged and the danger that threatened from Italian and Rumanian intervention so great, that every effort had to be made to reach peace quickly, even at considerable cost. Forgách hoped that the status quo might do, possibly with the surrender of the Bukovina, so long as Przemysl had not yet fallen, but he thought South Tyrol would have to be given to the Italians, to induce them to play the role of mediators.

The Germans, of course, would object strenuously to a status quo peace, since the people—though not their worried government—still entertained fervent hopes for victory. All that was completely illusory. Above all, the unfortunate issue was, politically and militarily, entirely Germany's fault. It was German policy that had kept Austria from throwing in its lot in time with Bulgaria and Turkey rather than Rumania. Germany had forced the Austrian command against its better judgment to throw its main forces against Russia rather than Serbia and had then sent reinforcements far too late. It had misguidedly insisted on forging ahead in the west, where it had abysmally failed against France, managing only to shoot up the Belgian fortifications—with the help of Austrian mortars! Its invasion of Belgium had brought Britain into the war, thus pushing Italy to the brink of defecting from the Triple Alliance. In short, Germany was the cause of the whole misfortune. It must now be content to end the war unconquered and with a passable peace treaty—if not, there would be a disaster beyond imagining.

This Austrian diplomat was willing to sacrifice South Tyrol, not to buy Italian neutrality and thus continue the war, but merely to recruit Italy as a mediator. This feeble stance by the Austrian foreign ministry cost Count Berchtold his job. Count Tisza, at the time the most powerful and dynamic of all Austro-Hungarian statesmen, succeeded in having him recalled on January 10. Berchtold's successor, Baron Burián, a Hungarian, would not hear of any offers of territorial concessions. The German emissaries who tried to bring him around all complained of his stubborn and dogmatic attitude.

For months on end there was a bitter struggle between the allies. On the German side, the southern state governments were vehemently, indeed passionately involved. Bavaria was traditionally sympathetic to the Austrian cause, but after the Austrian failures in September 1914 the Bavarian premier, Count Hertling, was bitter in his condemnation of the "aristocratic slovenliness" in the running of the Austrian army. He also shared the indignation of his Württemberg colleague, Freiherr von Weizsäcker, over Austria's stubborn refusal to yield South Tyrol to Italy.

When Berlin organized a mission to Vienna, headed by Prince Wedel, the former governor of Alsace-Lorraine, in an effort—vain, as it turned out—to persuade Emperor Francis Joseph to give way, Bavaria strongly supported the endeavor, by sending along Count Podewils. Weizsäcker had always been very reserved, if not pessimistic, about German chances for victory; and for a time he tried to get up a delegation from all the federated German princes to visit Francis Joseph. He kept urging that Berlin exert unremitting pressure in Vienna and demand concessions also to Rumania, so that this country at least would be kept out of the war.[53]

Actually, such pressure was not necessary. The German Chancellor was well aware of the danger threatening the Central Powers from Italy's entry into the war on the other side. Indeed, if anything, he overestimated the threat, which he considered nothing less than mortal. Only this can explain the astonishing fact that he considered ceding certain Prussian territories to Austria in compensation, if there were no other way of persuading Vienna to surrender South Tyrol. He actually managed to have the Prussian cabinet adopt a contingent resolution to that effect. At the session of February 17 he asked that the Kaiser empower him *in extremis* to offer Emperor Francis Joseph "border rectifications" in the Upper Silesian counties of Lubczyce and Pless. What this meant was the surrender of some of the proudest conquests of Frederic the Great!

No conclusion was reached on this matter; and on February 20 a plan for a handwritten message from the Kaiser to the emperor was temporarily shelved. Almost directly afterward Erzberger made another proposal to the Chancellor. Erzberger had been working hard for peace, in Rome with Pope Benedict XV, and also as assistant to Bülow, who was special emissary to the Quirinal. Erzberger wanted the Polish coal region of Sosnowiec, east of the Upper Silesian border, given to Austria in return for South Tyrol.

The Chancellor agreed and in another Prussian cabinet session on February 27 gained authorization to make such an offer. If this did not work a cession of Silesian territory was to be proposed, though only if the supreme army command regarded Italian entry into the war as intolerable and was prepared to "recommend" the Silesian cession as a last resort, i.e., to share the political responsibility. This actually happened, and the Kaiser, on March 6, signed the letter submitted to him. It never had to be dispatched, for the Sosnowiec offer proved to be good enough. Vienna gave way at almost the instant when the Kaiser, "in a mood of depression," gave his signature. The Austrians said they were prepared to cede South Tyrol.

The incident was kept a highly classified secret and was only recently brought to light. It is surprising in more than one respect. It shows the Chancellor endowed with amazing vigor and tenacity in pursuit of his policies.[54] It shows him wielding unexpectedly great personal influence, not only on the cabinet, including the minister of war, who was at first most vigorously opposed, but also on the Kaiser. It shows, lastly, how close the collaboration then was between Bethmann Hollweg and Falkenhayn—though also how close these two men were to desperation; for it would have been an act of desperation to make such a deal with Austria, purely by cabinet decision, over the heads of the Silesians and without consulting the legislature. It was only natural that Ludendorff, acting also on behalf of Hindenburg, vigorously protested to Zimmermann at the foreign ministry early in March, when rumors of the proposed deal reached his ears. Actually, he was disinclined to take them seriously.

Certainly the German offer made it easier for the Austrian government to decide to yield. Yet it was not the pressure from Berlin that was crucial, nor the blandishments held out from there. The critical Austrian cabinet session of March 8 shows clearly that it was fear of the military threat, which Falkenhayn kept emphasizing again and again,[55] and which Conrad too painted in the gloomiest colors for his government in early April. "Italian intervention in the war," he said, "will render our military situation completely untenable, and probably Germany's too. In a political sense, such an eventuality would undoubtedly mark the destruction of the monarchy."

Even so, however, Conrad did not believe that the concessions would have any practical result, and he therefore advised Burián to seek peace with Russia immediately in any event. Russia could well be granted "sole and undisputed title to the Dardanelles and the Bosporus," which the western powers would undoubtedly begrudge it. The situation would change radically "if Russia made peace with the Central Powers, or at least one of them [sic]. . . . Russia could then strike out for the Bosporus with Constantinople and the Dardanelles, either from the Black Sea or by marching through Rumania and Bulgaria." Austria would probably have to be prepared to surrender Eastern Galicia all the way to the San and Dniester, receiving in return a free hand from Russia to proceed against Serbia and Montenegro. Germany's eastern borders would remain unchanged, but a sense of loyalty required that it should be asked for its approval "at the outset." The Austrian chief of staff made it clear enough, however, that he thought even a separate peace with Russia conceivable and desirable.[56]

This type of amateur diplomacy, dashed off on the spur of the moment on the basis of casual whims, is typical of Conrad von Hötzendorf in the role of politician. But Burián too scarcely impresses one as a statesman of stature. He seemed rather at the end of his wits when he inquired of Bethmann Hollweg on April 20 whether a swift peace with Britain, involving the evacuation of Belgium, might not free German troops for the front against Italy. Bethmann Hollweg had to point out to him that there could scarcely be a less favorable juncture for a peace bid to Britain than the moment when Italy was threatening to defect to the Entente camp.[57]

As we know, Austria's readiness to sacrifice Southern Tyrol already came too late. From mid-March on, Sonnino's negotiations with Vienna had been nothing but a deliberate subterfuge. As for Germany's offer to Austria, Grey knew about it and the Silesian plan as well—which is more than the Austrian foreign ministry could boast—and he used it to offset Russian opposition to Italy's outrageous territorial demands along the Adriatic.

We need not here discuss the question of whether more success might have been achieved had the Austrians shown themselves to be conciliatory at an earlier stage. What happened is that nationalist sentiment in Italy simply swept aside the reservations of the liberal "neutralists" and the pacifist mood of the socialists. Government and chamber were compelled to declare war, not on the basis of whether more territory was to be gained here or there, but because the people insisted on not standing aside in the hour of decision but on playing their part in the rivalry among the great powers.

It is also a fact, however, that the Central Powers could not even begin to equal the schedule of annexations the western powers held out to Italy as the prize of victory in the secret pact of London, signed on April 26. It comprised all of South Tyrol to the Brenner line, Gorizia, Trieste, Gradisca, all of Istria and the Istrian isles, Dalmatia to Cap Planca and most of the Dalmatian isles, the port of Vlonë and the island of Sazan and part of the Albanian coast—i.e., according to Allied estimates 200,000 German-speaking Tyroleans and more than three-quarters of a million South Slavs. The offer further included the Dodecanese islands, a substantial share in the contemplated carving-up of Asiatic Turkey, and expansion of Italian colonial possessions in Africa, in the event the Allies were able to expand theirs at German expense.[58]

In terms of foreign policy, the situation of the Central Powers was thus even more hopeless than their statesmen knew at the time. In the very days when Conrad proposed to tempt the Russians into a separate peace by the offer of free disposal over the Straits, the western powers reached agreement with Russia that would give that country full sovereignty there. Constantinople would become Russian, together with both shores of the Straits, to the Enos-Midia line on the European side and to the Sakaria river on the Asiatic side. The Russians would have the right to establish fortifications, and they would get the islands in the Sea of Marmara as well as the islands of Imroz and Bozcaada which dominate the southern approach to the Dardanelles. There were further agreements on carving up Turkey in Asia in thorough-going fashion.[59]

The czarist government did not even dream of entertaining the idea of a separate peace. On the contrary, because of the insecurity of its internal situation and the failures of its armies, it kept asking for assurances of continuing active support by its western allies and for evidence that their glittering hopes for the future were justified, so that the war zeal of the Duma parties might be maintained. Russian Foreign Minister's Sazonov had as early as August 7, 1914, suggested a special treaty binding the three Entente powers not to make peace separately, and such an agreement was actually concluded in London on September 5.

Only nine days later, soon after Tannenberg and the liberation of East Prussia, Sazonov had presented the British and French ambassadors with a set of war aims that included the cession to Russia of the lower course of the Nieman and Eastern Galicia, and the accession to Russian Poland of Eastern Poznan, Southern Silesia, and Western Galicia. Alsace-Lorraine and possibly parts of the Prussian Rhineland and the Palatinate were to go to France, certain border regions to Belgium, and Schleswig-Holstein to Denmark. Hanover was to be recreated as an independent kingdom and the Danubian monarchy cut up into three parts. Bosnia, Herzegovina, Dalmatia, and Northern Albania went to Serbia and the German colonies were to be divided up among the victorious powers.

Essentially this was the program Czar Nicholas personally explained to French Ambassador Paléologue on November 21, as we already know. The czar had added, however, that the Hohenzollern dynasty would have to forego the imperial title and surrender East Prussia, at least in part. These discussions did not lead to a formal treaty, but the war aims that formed their substance gained much greater momentum than all the eloquence of German orators and journalists.

On September 20 Sazonov's comprehensive program was unanimously approved by the French cabinet; and the reports of the Russian ambassador in London showed clearly that the British government differed only on details, chiefly the question of the left bank of the Rhine. In the main, however, there were no divergences of opinion on the war aims question among the Entente powers. Prussian militarism, the alleged threat to the freedom of Europe, was to be destroyed, German power and pretensions were to be thrown to the ground before there could be peace. This was the unchanging London response to repeated American mediation efforts. Perhaps never before in history was the power of crude oversimplification, of political mythology, if you will, manifested in so sinister a fashion as in the First World War.

In the face of these closed enemy ranks, against this determination to destroy Germany, little significance attaches to Germany's painful, devious, and repeated gropings for some chink that might be widened into disagreement among its enemies, so that some neutral power might propose mediation with some hope of success. Certain attempts were launched in St. Petersburg and London—through the Danish shipping magnate Andersen, Mme. Vassilchikova of the czarist court, the banker Mankiewitz, the Hessian relatives of the czarina, and other intermediaries—but they came to nothing, as did the picaresque efforts of the German legation in Berne to establish contact with opposition groups in the French chamber through venal agents and journalists.[60] Even an attempt to insure Rumania's continued neutrality through territorial concessions, a course initially urged by German diplomacy in Vienna and Budapest, was doomed to failure; for the Rumanians had long since covered themselves by a secret treaty with Russia that promised them gains no Austrian diplomat could rival.[61]

In sum, by the spring of 1915 the Central Powers had no alternative. They had to resort to arms again, and they were bound to score major successes if they wished to master the dangers now menacing them on all sides. Since the main threat lay in the east, it was here that the bulk of the German army had to be committed.

## Part 3
# Military Victory and Political Failure in Russia

FALKENHAYN was very reluctant to change fronts. He continued to be convinced that the ultimate decision must fall on the western front, and that the time for attempting it was growing short; for sooner or later the appearance of a great new British army (the so-called Kitchener Army) with much strengthened equipment and armaments was in prospect. With its arrival, the preponderance of Germany's enemies on the western front would grow overwhelming.

A new army reserve of fourteen divisions had been created by reorganizing the army and withdrawing one infantry regiment from each existing division; and with its help it was hoped to be able to mount a large-scale offensive operation. That it would have to be located in the east was dictated by the emergency that prevailed in the spring of 1915. To Falkenhayn's personal credit, he allowed his strategic decision to be influenced neither by Conrad's insistence on reinforcement of the wobbly Austrian front in the Carpathians and the Bukovina, nor by his equally strong insistence that the hated Italian foe, now that he had at last entered the war, be suitably "chastised," nor by the old, fantastic plan for a double envelopment of the Russians from East Prussia and East Galicia, which Conrad now served up again.

Falkenhayn stuck to his guns. All available forces were to be kept together for the great breakthrough at Tarnow-Gorlice, which was brilliantly planned and executed, not least owing to the work of Colonel Seeckt as chief of staff to General von Mackensen. The result was a tremendous military success. The Russian front was completely smashed and the enemy driven back to the Rokitno marshes in a whole series of integrated thrusts and enveloping actions.

The author took part in this great campaign and witnessed the fall of Warsaw and the conquest of Eastern Poland and Lithuania; and those who passed through this experience will clearly remember even today the enormous lift it gave to German spirits. There was a sense of relief after the hopeless slaughter of trench warfare. Anguish and frustration gave way to rising new hopes of victory. By and large, this was to be the last great success at arms vouchsafed the Germans in this war. Within a few months, Falkenhayn had attained what he set out for, and more. The enemy was pushed back and weakened to such an extent that there was no further immediate danger to German and Austro-Hungarian territory. Rumania was so terrified that it dared not stir. All of Poland, Lithuania, and Galicia had been cleansed of the enemy, and a much shortened and on the whole straight front line of trenches had been created, reaching from the Gulf of Riga to Chernovtsy.

Discredit was cast on this astonishing victory only subsequently by military historians, in the familiar controversy over the question of whether it might not have been possible to win an even greater victory that would have decided the war. Russia, it is held, could have been forced to its knees, its fighting power destroyed rather than merely paralyzed. To that end Falkenhayn should have directed his blow, aimed early in July at the northern flank of the Russian army, not by way of the Narev and Bug, but from the Niemen by way of Kaunas and Vilnyus, as Ludendorff desired.

Falkenhayn's rejection of this far more sweeping enveloping maneuver is held by his critics to be responsible for the fact that the campaign was after all less than completely successful.[62] These critics are, of course, partisans of Ludendorff, who once again bitterly resented the failure to follow his own bold plans. His views were expressed to the supreme army command through his field marshal, in an exchange of almost insubordinate acerbity, with Falkenhayn replying in the same vein.[63]

The very nature of this controversy probably precludes a clear-cut answer, and we cannot deal with its technical military aspects here; but it must be mentioned that on this occasion too Falkenhayn ignored Ludendorff's wishes, not from personal animosity, but for weighty and objective considerations,[64] stemming mainly from his responsibilities as supreme commander of both fronts. Heavy attacks in the west loomed with certainty in the immediate future. They would urgently necessitate the transfer of large reserves from the east; and this limited both the available time and the number of troops, which even so did not run to much more than half the Russian strength.

As a matter of fact, it took considerable nerve to carry out the eastern offensive unswervingly, despite a major French attack in July, a German numerical handicap on the western front of 600 battalions, the entry into the war of Italy, against which Austria was able to establish only a feeble defensive front, and the increasingly critical situation of Turkey. Faced with such an array of problems, Falkenhayn deliberately limited the goals of his campaign and refused to stake everything on a single card. This was rational calculation rather than "military nihilism."[65]

It is certainly true that Falkenhayn distrusted Ludendorff's ambitiousness and activist temperament. For this he had good reason, not only from the experiences of the preceding winter with its great plans gone awry, but from Ludendorff's summer operations in Lithuania and Courland, which consumed great resources and about which he had consulted no one—his purpose had been purely "empire building."[66] As we shall see, this undertaking was to have major political repercussions, but strategically it was a mere sideshow, at times actually getting in the way.

But Falkenhayn also apparently distrusted Ludendorff's military estimates, i.e., his judgment as to the possibilities of enemy counteraction in the face of enveloping attacks. Falkenhayn was probably right. It can be shown that on more than one occasion, especially in the winter of 1914-1915 and the spring and summer of 1918, Ludendorff's boundless drive to make the impossible possible clouded his judgment and substituted wishful thinking for realism.[67] It is almost an occupational hazard of higher generalship that it imperceptibly slips from intrepidity to the blind and headlong pursuit of victory. A year later Falkenhayn himself was not to escape this danger altogether, in a somewhat different form.

Bethmann Hollweg followed the new quarrel between eastern headquarters and the chief of staff with much concern. He was in friendly correspondence with Hindenburg throughout the year,[68] but found it regrettable that eastern headquarters felt impelled to lose no time in airing its differences with Falkenhayn in public. He also deplored insinuations that an envious Falkenhayn begrudged Hindenburg his great successes. Both sides, he felt, had lapsed into the error of excessive brusqueness. "Falkenhayn's merits," he wrote, "are being acknowledged more and more, though he nowhere commands trust. He will never be able to get rid of Ypres." Bethmann Hollweg did what he could to assuage public opinion.[69]

In the political sphere he continued to be on good terms with Falkenhayn. The prestige of the chief of staff had been steadily rising during the course of the successful campaign; but this did not mislead Falkenhayn into overestimating his military achievements. On the contrary, from the very beginning he urged that the victory be exploited for purposes of a peace offensive in St. Petersburg. As early as June 3, right after Przemysl had fallen, he proposed that the czar be offered an armistice, in view of his grave military plight. The offer was to include an Adriatic port for Serbia.

While refusing to savor his military triumph over Russia, Falkenhayn still insisted that the real issue must be pursued in the west. Bethmann Hollweg had to talk him out of the misconception that a separate peace was to be had almost at will, and in this he was helped by the latest unfavorable news from the czarist court, transmitted by State Councilor Andersen. The Chancellor realized that a separate peace was probably completely beyond reach, and even a general peace at best obtainable only on the basis of the status quo. "Whether we shall have to follow that path," he said, "will be exclusively up to military judgment."

He was not directly rejecting the status quo as a basis for peace, it will be seen,[70] but he did hint that its acceptance would be regarded throughout Germany as a capitulation, gravely reflecting on soldier and statesman alike. Yet the contact in St. Petersburg was continued. Bethmann Hollweg did not abandon hope that the Russians might come to their senses, if the offensive continued to make progress, an eventuality for which he formulated a proposal of his own. He realized, however, that the offers by the Entente, of which he apparently knew, could not be bettered by Germany "even if we completely ignored our two allies." Actually he used a number of intermediaries in the course of the summer to let the czar know that Germany was prepared to offer very moderate peace terms. According to Russian sources, in July he even proposed a Russian-German condominium in the Dardanelles, which were to be demilitarized, as well as a huge reconstruction loan.[71]

It is certain that Bethmann Hollweg was no more carried away than was Falkenhayn by the flood of annexationist demands that swept over Germany in the summer of 1915, in the wake of the great successes of German arms, and that found expression in countless petitions and memoranda from intellectuals, politicians, and patriotic groups. On June 16, having had somewhat more encouraging news from the czarist court,[72] Bethmann Hollweg expressly cautioned the chief of staff against excessively exuberant victory statements at the top. These, he pointed out, would merely have a deterrent effect on any Russian inclination to talk peace. The Russians were concerned lest unlimited occupation of their soil would compel them to fight for their lives to the bitter end.

Two days earlier Bethmann Hollweg had written Falkenhayn at length why he could under no circumstance agree to the annexation of Russia's Baltic provinces as a war aim, also asking that the chief of staff set his face against any such ambitions voiced in military circles. The admonition was far more in point with Ludendorff than Falkenhayn.[73] The Baltic regions, Bethmann Hollweg declared, were undesirable not only politically, but also militarily, on account of their exposed geographic situation. It was a complete illusion to regard these regions as being German in character. Latvians represented by far the greater part of the population and would constitute a most unwelcome revolutionary element. Germany needed neither Baltic ports nor large agricultural areas. Above all, Germany must incur Russia's permanent hostility by cutting off its sole ice-free access to the sea—this would necessarily lead to renewed conflict and render illusory any effort to split Russia away from Germany's other enemies after the successful conclusion of peace. That was why even Bismarck had held that Germany should consider the question of the Baltic provinces without any hint of nationalist sentiment and indeed never lay hands on them.[74]

Thus nationalist acquisitiveness was certainly not to stand in the way of peace with Russia. This was true of the Polish question as well. As early as December 1914 Hindenburg had called for the annexation of a Polish buffer strip,[75] to protect East Prussia from another Russian invasion and bring the strongly fortified Narev line under German control. In the light of what happened late in 1914 this need seemed self-evident in informed German circles, turning up even in anti-annexationist statements, such as von Loebell's.

This question grew acute after the whole of Poland had, in fact, fallen into German hands. Falkenhayn inquired how the Chancellor envisaged that country's future. Bethmann Hollweg replied on August 4 that in the event of a separate peace with Russia, Poland would remain Russian, except for strategically necessary border rectifications that were not specified.[76] In the event Russia would surely grant the Poles a large measure of autonomy. If the war were to end in some other way, "though still with Russia greatly weakened" (a curiously cautious way of putting it! ), there would either be the creation of an autonomous kingdom of Poland, closely tied to Germany or Austria by alliance or military convention, or the greater portion of pre-Congress-of-Vienna Poland would be combined with Galicia into a state under Austrian suzerainty. In that case the border rectifications required for Germany's security might have to be rather more generous, though on no account were they to amount to a fourth division of Poland.

Such was Bethmann Hollweg's first Polish program, which can scarcely be described as savoring of a "dictated peace."[77] In confirmation of this view, the Chancellor simultaneously emphasized that the way to a negotiated peace with Russia must be kept open as before, despite impassioned and bellicose statements in the Duma, which had in the meantime persuaded the chief of staff to abandon all hope of peace. Bethmann Hollweg, on his part, held that St. Petersburg might still see the light, once all hope had waned that the Allied attack on the Dardanelles would carry Constantinople, Bulgaria had been drawn over to the German side, and the impending major Anglo-French offensive in France had failed. What the military administration must at all costs avoid was to turn the Poles into Germany's enemies.

Thus the Chancellor clung to his hopes for a negotiated peace with Russia rather longer than did the chief of staff. Late in June, by way of Sweden, he took up contact again, this time with a hint about the threatening defection of the Poles. This was in marked contradistinction to the policy of his Austrian allies.[78] Initially Vienna and Budapest had emphatically urged a swift peace and declared themselves willing to offer moderate terms. In mid-July Prince Hohenlohe, the Austrian ambassador in Berlin, gave a horrified report about the flood of annexationist demands that had boiled up in Germany in the wake of the successful Polish campaign.

But with the fall of Warsaw, Hohenlohe himself seems to have caught the contagion of conquest. He implored the Chancellor to seek an understanding with Britain—just how this was to be done he left open—and to exploit the "fantastic" victories in the east as probably the last chance to break once for all Russian influence in Europe and Russian meddling in the Balkans. Let him detach the Baltic provinces, Poland (which, of course, was to go to Austria), and a Ukrainian border strip, which together with Eastern Galicia and the Bukovina was to form a new Austrian crownland that would exert a strong attraction on the Russian Ukraine. Hohenlohe promised his foreign minister to do everything to prevent a separate peace with Russia that would be unfavorable to Austria. Such a peace might indeed find favor in Berlin, he added, because Bethmann Hollweg, whom he described as indecisive and lacking in energy, was likely to lose his nerve.[79]

Hohenlohe's fears were groundless, for in the end all the efforts in St. Petersburg failed. The Russian diplomats liked the German proposals and the czar himself was timid and war-weary and reluctant to break off entirely the contact he had made through the king of Denmark; but he felt himself firmly bound to his western allies by the September treaty and allowed himself to be persuaded by his military entourage that the retreat of his armies from Poland, Lithuania, and Courland was not really decisive. These countries were not really part of Russia; and the deeper the enemy penetrated eastward, the worse his situation would grow.

Thus it can be asserted that in Russia at least continuation of the war that was to mark the doom of czarism was essentially the fault of Russian militarists. (Direction of the war, incidentally, was soon to be taken over by Nicholas II in person.) Yet a portion of the blame must go to the liberal bourgeoisie with its impassioned patriotism and Anglophilia, which raised a loud outcry in the Duma and criticized the defects of the czarist system, intimidating the czar. Perhaps the decisive vote was cast by the Russian foreign service, which voiced fears that Russian defection from the alliance would draw the lasting hostility of the western powers, thus making Russia dependent on Germany in foreign affairs.[80] In any event, on August 11, 1915, a Russian cabinet session presided over by the czar resolved (and immediately made public its decision) that Russia would not even respond to an enemy peace offer, no matter how enticing, until victory was won.

The die was now cast. True, the great Russian campaign had not brought final victory in a military sense, but it certainly did bring considerable relief to the Central Powers. In a political sense, however, all the hopes that had been staked on it had come to nothing. Perhaps they had never been anything more than a drowning man's frantic grasping at a straw.

One can scarcely avoid a sense of horror today when one looks back on the deep gulf that yawned in the summer of 1915 between the grave worries for Germany's future weighed on both the responsible statesman and the leading general and the tide of victory expectations and demands that resistlessly inundated the country. In those very June days when Bethmann Hollweg was warning the German chief of staff against plans for annexation in the Baltic (probably ignorant of the support he was thereby lending to Falkenhayn's own strategic views on Ludendorff's plans of conquest), the Pan-Germans staged a meeting of extreme annexationists in Berlin, under the leadership of Berlin university professors.

Very probably this congress marked the high tide of the annexationist movement. It organized a petition to the Chancellor that ultimately commanded 1,347 signatories, including 352 professors, many of them bearing illustrious names. It took its place beside a similar but earlier one, jointly sponsored by the great employers' organizations. Both quickly became known abroad and had their share in drawing the utmost odium on "German militarism," not least owing to the demand they put forward that the people in the regions to be annexed should be either expropriated or expelled en masse.

The movement put Bethmann Hollweg in an extremely difficult position. He declined to receive a delegation that wished to hand him this brainchild of the "intellectuals." Later, when a countermovement was organized under the aegis of the historian Hans Delbrück, for the purpose of helping Bethmann Hollweg with extremely moderate peace resolutions, the Chancellor refused any official support to this group too, indeed, avoided even a private discussion with Delbrück, in fear that his precarious position might be still further undermined.

Delbrück was the only bourgeois publicist of stature who found the courage to oppose this Neo-German Bonapartism openly. This brought him into such disrepute in nationalist circles that the German crown prince wrote his father, asking that this "disloyal character" be promptly expelled from the university.[81]

Bethmann Hollweg himself thought he had no choice but to display the most radiant confidence in victory in his Reichstag speeches, while mentioning his war aims ideas only in the most cautious, deliberately obscure, and ambiguous phraseology. The last thing he wanted was for any hint of his efforts to achieve a separate peace with Russia to reach the public.[82] In late March Count Hertling had written him from Munich that rumors along such

lines had aroused widespread indignation. Hertling recommended that Bethmann Hollweg summon the so-called foreign affairs committee of the Federal
council, to advise the federated governments of the Reich government's war
aims. Behind all this stood the king of Bavaria whose ambition it was to
become king of Belgium and who had publicly spoken of claims of the
Wittelsbach dynasty to the Rhine estuary. What he really wanted was to
intercede with the Kaiser at the head and in the name of the German princes,
to the effect that "things cannot go on in this fashion"—in other words, that
the "weak and incompetent" Chancellor would have to be dismissed.

It was the grand duke of Oldenburg who had incited him in this direction.
The grand duke was an ardent follower of the Pan-German line. Hertling had
been able to foil the plan for the time being only by promising to make
emphatic representations to the Chancellor himself. This he did, but in a very
moderate form; and as we know,[83] Bethmann Hollweg declared before the
committee of the federal council on April 7 that Germany must seek to guard
against future Belgian hostility by means of "guarantees"; that it must also
endeavor in the event of victory to secure war indemnities and certain
improvements in the strategic frontiers in west and east, as well as a German
colonial "empire" in Africa.

Bethmann Hollweg, however, stuck to a deliberately vague terminology
and reemphasized that the war was purely one of defense and was not waged
in pursuit of a conquest. Count Hertling was content—his heart was not really
in his campaign against so-called "rotten peace" and he was much influenced
by his friend, Count Lerchenfeld, his Berlin delegate to the federal council.
Lerchenfeld had long since buried any hope of a victorious peace and held
that Belgium would inevitably have to be handed back unconditionally. In
mid-June Hertling went so far as to intercede warmly with the foreign
ministry and the Chancellor in favor of a peace offer to the czar, by way of
the king of Denmark, on terms highly favorable to Russia.[84]

Thus the Chancellor actually received support against his enemies from the
South German movements, Freiherr von Weizsäcker also being wholly on his
side, though this did very little to alter the grave threat under which he
constantly lived. As early as the spring of 1915, the precarious party truce
was in danger of collapse, for the right was insisting on an unequivocal
declaration in favor of a peace of conquest and annexation, while the left as
strongly urged a public declaration foregoing any such aggrandizement.

It took all of Bethmann Hollweg's tactical skill to persuade the social
democrats not to give too open expression to their peace wishes in the
Reichstag on March 10; but he could not keep a certain distrust from
spreading among them concerning his ultimate aims, and this took the form
of thirty left-wing deputies absenting themselves from the vote on the war
appropriations.[85] It was even more difficult to cope with the rightist opposi-

tion, particularly because the already existing controversies were complicated by the issue of submarine warfare on merchant shipping, which had begun in February. The sinking of the great British liner *Lusitania* on May 7 by a German U-boat marked the opening gun in the protracted diplomatic conflict between Germany and America which ended by bringing America into the war. Even in its initial phase, it brought down a storm on the Chancellor's head, because he refused to respond instantly with the "mailed fist."[86]

In the event one can but admire the skill with which Bethmann Hollweg, in his Reichstag speeches of May 28 and August 19 with their inspiring patriotic note, temporarily checkmated his nationalist opponents. On the evening of August 20 there were actually street demonstrations supporting him! Yet Bethmann Hollweg, in his public statements on war aims, never really went beyond the formulation he had used repeatedly before—he called for "reliable guarantees and securities for Germany's future."

On Poland's future too he did not, on August 19, go beyond the minimum dictated by the failure of his peace efforts—he had to say something to make Germany's role as "liberator" seem meaningful. What he did say was that he declined to compete with Russian "blandishments," but hoped that German occupation of a Poland freed of the Russian yoke would serve to end the ancient quarrel between Germans and Poles and "lead that country toward a happier future, in which it could cultivate and develop a national life of its own."[87]

This was the note on which the first year of the war ended. The top German statesmen and soldiers were agreed not only that it had not brought a decision, but that the chances for a German victory had alarmingly declined. By the spring of 1915 Falkenhayn no longer seriously believed even in the possibility that "reliable guarantees and securities" could be gained in Belgium.[88] Yet not a hint of such thoughts could be allowed to transpire in public.

# TWO

# The Period of Frustration and of Disintegration of the National Unity Front (1915-1916)

# 3

# Balkan Warfare and Balkan Policy in the Latter Part of 1915

ON SEPTEMBER 22, very soon after the conclusion of the great Polish campaign, the major Anglo-French offensives Falkenhayn had long expected began, in Artois and Champagne. They would have commenced before, but for the unexpectedly slow pace of organization and equipment of what was called "Kitchener's Army" in England. Even so, by summer the troops arrayed on the western front against Germany were numerically far superior to the Germans, 150 divisions against 100. They had strong reserves at their disposal, according to a German estimate of August 24 no less than thirty-seven French and at least fourteen British divisions.[1]

There were moments of supreme tension and danger during the fall battle. The German generals in the field complained that the supreme army command too long ignored their warnings, ordering available reserves to be committed too late, thus exacting unnecessarily heavy German losses in averting a breakthrough. General Wild on his part muttered about blunders by the front-line generals and had trouble in assuaging the apprehensions of the Chancellor, whose distrust of Falkenhayn's competence was fed new fuel.[2]

Falkenhayn's closest collaborators, however, found that he had never displayed more magnificent generalship than at this critical juncture. His swift grasp, energy, and unshakable calm enabled him to keep control of a potentially chaotic situation. Personal danger never deterred him from investigating a threat on the spot. From the political point of view, an even more important factor was that the convulsions on the western front and the enemy's crushing numerical superiority never swerved him from his total strategic concept. He had often been charged with bias in favor of the western front, but he now clung with iron resolve to the plan of first rendering the eastern front tenable. The great operation to clean up the Balkan problems, subjugate Serbia, and open up the Danube route to Bulgaria and Turkey had had to be postponed time and again. Now at last it was to be carried out.

Political and military action in wartime ultimately form a single entity. In theory the two components can be neatly delimited, but seldom in practice. All this became clearer at this point in the course of the war than at any other. As we have seen, Bethmann Hollweg had repeatedly, in the winter of 1914-1915, urged a strike against at least the northeast corner of Serbia, the Negotin panhandle, possession of which would have given the Central Powers a clear southeastward route for coming to Turkey's aid. At the same time, such a success would have gone far to make up for the repeated defeats Austrian armies had suffered in Serbia, while also deterring Rumania from entering the war, and supporting German diplomatic efforts in Sofia for a military alliance with Bulgaria and in Athens for continued Greek neutrality. At times there was also the thought that the subjugation of Serbia and its complete elimination from the political stage might foster any Russian inclination toward a separate peace.

Neither the foreign ministry nor the Chancellor met with serious opposition on the part of the chief of staff, who on March 16 had explicitly told Foreign Minister von Jagow it was quite untrue that he, Falkenhayn, was reluctant to proceed against Serbia. What was lacking was simply the necessary military resources. It seemed at first quite hopeless to gain the cooperation of General Conrad, who was much too concerned about his shaky Carpathian front to authorize troop transfers from there. Feasibility studies of a Serbian campaign showed, moreover, that small sorties made in those trackless and thinly settled highlands would accomplish little against the strong and highly competent Serbian army, especially in the winter.

It really needed Bulgarian cooperation to attack the Serbs from two sides. Only during the time that Constantinople seemed to be in mortal danger from the Allied Dardanelles campaign did Falkenhayn briefly show himself more amenable to foreign ministry desires to strike even without Bulgarian aid. On his part, he urged the foreign ministry to redouble its efforts for a military alliance with Sofia and for unimpeded munitions transit across Rumania. He intervened autonomously in these negotiations with the help of German military attachés, and he placed military reports and evaluations at the disposal of the foreign ministry for use in the foreign capitals. Indeed, since the early summer of 1915, an increasingly complex web of diplomacy and military effort had been spun, to the end of maintaining, if not strengthening, the position of the Central Powers in the Balkans, despite Turkey's sore plight, Italy's entry into the war, and the more and more ardent Allied wooing of Greece and Bulgaria.

We scarcely need follow the details of this game here.[3] In the end it was success on the battlefield that told. It was the impressive German victories in Poland and Austria's successful defense against the Italians on the Isonzo rather than diplomatic representations that persuaded Rumania to remain neutral and foiled Allied efforts in Sofia and Athens.

On the other hand, there were serious differences of opinion among statesmen and generals at the top on how the victories on the Russian front should be exploited. Bethmann Hollweg, ever concerned with the fate of Turkey and the possible political and economic effects of its collapse, urged the supreme army command to execute the attack on Serbia with all speed as early as the first breakthrough successes late in May and again early in July; but Falkenhayn stuck to the strategic principle of never allowing dispersal of his forces to jeopardize the successful impact of the main thrust. He was convinced that a Russian defeat could not fail to have its effects in the Balkans; and he thought that the difficult Serbian campaign might perhaps be dispensed with, if the Rumanians could be compelled to open up the munitions route to the southeast, either by a show of military strength or by economic sanctions.

The foreign ministry, anticipating highly unfavorable political effects from either measure through its knowledge of the situation in Rumania, was opposed. Von Jagow instead resorted to an expedient that is almost reminiscent of the cabinet diplomacy of the eighteenth century and that also met with Falkenhayn's approval. An attempt was to be made to blast this slippery Serbian enemy out of the hostile coalition by a tempting peace offer. The kingdom of Serbia was to remain intact, only the Negotin panhandle being ceded to Austria and certain contested territories to Bulgaria, for which Serbia was to be compensated by full title to Montenegro and North Albania.

Initially the Austrians, depressed by their earlier defeats in Serbia, were won over to this plan. General Conrad hoped it would give him the forces he needed to launch the campaign of vengeance against Italy he so ardently desired. A Greek intermediary was briefed; but the Serbs would not listen to such overtures—quite naturally, for if any enemy of Germany had reason to look on the war as a people's war for survival it was Serbia. To the Serbs this was no cabinet war! In time the Central Powers were to repeat this experience on every front.[4] Yet, as we shall see, the idea of a negotiated peace with Serbia was to emerge again soon, in September.

All in all, German Balkan policy too gives an impression of close and methodical cooperation among military and political agencies, even though friction was not altogether absent. Late in July, long before the Russian campaign had ended, its political fruits began to mature. Bulgaria abandoned its reserve and let the Germans know it wanted to negotiate in the matter of an alliance. These negotiations began on August 3 and ended on September 6 with a treaty of alliance and a military convention drafted by Falkenhayn.

Bulgaria was persuaded to sign the latter only by being promised large territorial gains at the expense of Serbia, in excess of its losses in the Second Balkan War, and even so only after the Turks, by their amazing military prowess, had all but foiled the Allied Dardanelles campaign.

German diplomacy also succeeded in securing the continued neutrality of Rumania and Greece, so that the campaign against Serbia could at long last begin. We are not here concerned with its success, nor with the impressive military achievements of the participating German and Bulgarian troops and their leaders, though mention must be made of the unceasing friction with the Austrian command that resulted. Conrad jealously insisted on supreme command, though the failure of his offensive in Volhynia meant that he could supply only two and a half divisions instead of the six he had promised, compelling the Germans to almost double their contingent to eleven divisions.

In the end Conrad went back on all his pledges and unceremoniously pulled out of the fighting front to pursue cheap triumphs in Montenegro. He was almost totally uninterested in opening the Danube inland seaway and was concerned only with thrusting toward the Adriatic, to inflict maximum damage on his arch-enemy, Italy. It proved extremely difficult indeed to reconcile the opposing interests of the participating powers in the Balkans and get them to join in a single undertaking. The special character of the Balkan campaign made it almost impossible to distinguish between political and military decisions. Every time Bulgarian interests were favored—by pointing the attack in certain directions or at certain targets, for example—there was a risk of driving precariously neutral Greece into the arms of the Entente. Every time Greek or Turkish wishes were considered, the Bulgarians grew resentful. In October this led to a serious clash between Falkenhayn and Bethmann Hollweg, a quarrel that throws a sharp light on the view the chief of staff took of his constitutional position.

Just before the campaign began, the foreign ministry had once again tried to bring the Serbs, who now saw themselves facing a grave threat from two sides, to a separate peace table, this time through the mediation of King Constantine of Greece. Since the Second Balkan War, his government had been tied to Serbia by a defensive alliance. Greece was, indeed, under very strong pressure from the Allies, who not only threatened to starve out the country but had been landing more and more troops in Salonica, ruthlessly ignoring Greek neutrality.

King Constantine was outspokenly pro-German and had a hard stand in preserving his country's neutrality. The German political leaders wanted to make it easier for him by encouraging him to serve as a mediator in Serbia's interest. Early in October 1915 Bethmann Hollweg asked Falkenhayn privately whether there were any military objections to advising Serbia confidentially to withdraw its troops to North Albania and thence to embark on peace negotiations.

The general expressed strong opposition and learned only later that the foreign ministry had already instituted steps in Athens aimed at mediation. On October 11 he protested vehemently to the Chancellor in writing:

Your Excellency knows that I never meddle in matters that are not my official concern. The present matter, however, is one that may have a baleful influence on our strategy and in any event touches it directly. To decide it against the advice of the chief of staff of the field army and institute it without his knowledge, means to endanger the country's military interests, which in wartime are supreme. It is my duty to protest this procedure in the strongest terms. I must at the same time request Your Excellency to be good enough to advise me what steps are being taken to preclude a recurrence.

Protest, reprimand, and challenge could scarcely have been worded more brusquely; and Bethmann Hollweg's reply, a handwritten draft of which survives, was equally abrupt. There had been sound political reasons for the step taken in Athens, which in fact long antedated the discussion with Falkenhayn. The general had no way of knowing that "there was not the least possibility of untoward effects on the conduct of the war. It was a purely political matter and entirely my responsibility." Hence there was no need whatever for protest, and "I see no reason for going into the point raised at the conclusion of Your Excellency's letter."

Falkenhayn apparently came back the same day, in a communication that has not been preserved. He must have pointed out that Bulgaria, only just won over as an ally with considerable difficulty, was likely to regard the German step as a betrayal of its interests and thus become alienated. The Chancellor promptly rejected the argument. In one paragraph of the draft of his reply which was subsequently crossed out he maintained, not very convincingly, that the question discussed with the chief of staff in person and the diplomatic initiative in Athens had nothing to do with each other.

His rejection of military criticism was extremely blunt:

I am quite unable to concede Your Excellency the right to criticize this matter, nor can I make the details of the conduct of foreign affairs dependent on Your Excellency's approval. My endeavor to maintain constant liaison and agreement with Your Excellency in all questions touching on Germany's struggle for survival has been so amply demonstrated that I am reluctant to engage in a controversy over jurisdiction likely to precipitate a conflict that could not but do harm to the common cause.

Bethmann Hollweg proposed that further face-to-face discussion should take the place of pointed written exchanges but apparently no such discussions took place. In any event, on October 17 Falkenhayn sent a harshly worded reply:

> In my view it is not only the right but a supreme duty of the chief of
> staff of the field army to oppose by every means at his disposal any
> measure—including any political measure—which in his view is calculated
> to exert an unfavorable influence on our military situation. . . . The chief
> of staff of the field army can comply with this obligation only when the
> head of the government keeps him continuously informed on all mea-
> sures that might conceivably affect the military situation. Should this
> lead to irreconcilable conflict, the arbitration of His Majesty must be
> invoked since the political leadership has no precedence over the mili-
> tary so long as the aims of the war have not yet been attained.

Unless Bethmann Hollweg agreed with this view, he, Falkenhayn, would
promptly bring about a full clarification of the question, for entirely objective rather than personal reasons.

Thus the delicate question of political precedence over the military became an issue right during the war. As we know from Volume I, Chapter 8,
Part 3, it had earlier on divided Bismarck and the elder Moltke, precipitating
serious conflict. Bethmann Hollweg, on this occasion, avoided turning it into
a bone of contention. His concluding reply of October 18 was couched in
conciliatory terms: Chancellor and chief of staff indeed enjoyed the privilege
of each opposing measures taken by the other which they thought ill-advised—but not without prior personal discussion. Had Falkenhayn voiced his
objections orally, he, Bethmann Hollweg, could have readily reassured him.
As it was, his protest amounted to a mere assertion, and as such it constituted
intervention beyond his jurisdiction.[5] As for any obligation on his part to
keep the chief of staff continuously informed on political matters, Bethmann
Hollweg simply ignored this aspect. He could have scarcely disputed the point
with objective arguments, for clearly political and military issues were inex-
tricably intertwined in this Balkan campaign. Hence Falkenhayn's bridling,
despite its pointed tone, was scarcely a declaration of military independence
from political direction, nor a claim to political power along Ludendorffian
lines, but nothing more than a vigorous assertion of fully shared responsibility
on Falkenhayn's part. All the same, the very fact of the quarrel and the
brusqueness with which it was fought plainly show that there was a very
strong element of tension between these two men, despite their cooperation.

Actually, the clash resulted in Bethmann Hollweg taking steps to meet
Falkenhayn's political concern. On the same day on which he wrote his
second reply to Falkenhayn he asked Jagow to make efforts toward reconciling Bulgaria and Greece. This was possible only if the Bulgarian government
were ready to renounce certain territories lost to Greece in the Second Balkan
War, especially Kavala. There were protracted negotiations on this question
with the German diplomatic representatives in Sofia and Athens, in the
course of which the German military attaché in Bulgaria, Lieutenant Colonel

Massow, proved much more optimistic than the envoy, Michahelles. Falkenhausen, the military attaché in Athens, also sent the chief of staff optimistic reports, and Falkenhayn proposed to the foreign ministry that he have a go at promoting a military agreement between the two Balkan countries.

Unfortunately, with the progress of the offensive in Serbia, it soon developed that Bulgaria's territorial claims grew to a level unacceptable to Greece, and the German diplomatic initiative was slowed down. Falkenhayn himself was much influenced by his Bulgarian colleagues as well as by Massow's reports; and above all he was worried about losing his valuable Bulgarian ally. Hence he was more inclined to meet Bulgarian wishes than was the foreign ministry. Yet he carefully avoided any dictatorial demeanor in this matter, along lines Ludendorff would probably have followed. He even swallowed purely military counterarguments from the lips of the foreign ministry representative, Treutler—arguments supported by General Wild. He agreed that Massow was something of a dreamer, and he refused to support Massow's efforts to thwart Michahelles's designs and possibly even to supplant him. In other words, Falkenhayn may have had his disagreements with Bethmann Hollweg, but he did not waver in his loyalty.[6]

Nothing came of Greco-Bulgarian reconciliation; and as for Bethmann Hollweg's efforts on behalf of a negotiated peace with Serbia, they met with stubborn opposition on the part of Austria. As the troops of the Central Powers penetrated more deeply into Serbia, Vienna's former readiness to make peace on moderate terms faded more and more. Late in September Count Tisza was still talking about a mild peace; late in October he was already talking about carving up Serbia.[7] At the outset of the campaign Baron Burián declared that Austria had no desire whatever to annex the Serbian kingdom, which might possibly be joined to Montenegro. By late October he favored deposing the Serbian dynasty and placing the country under King Nikita of Montenegro—though first of all there would have to be unconditional surrender, without any pledges for the future. Ten days later he was no longer prepared for even such an offer, preferring that both Serbia and Montenegro should continue separately, greatly diminished in size and cut off from the Adriatic.

These shifting plans were a cover-up for the continuing uncertainty about Austrian war aims. Austria and Hungary were as much at odds on this question as they had been at the time of the declaration of war in 1914. Jagow and Bethmann Hollweg vainly exhorted them that the cause of the Central Powers required a swift end to the Balkan campaign. A demand for unconditional surrender would only drive the Serbs into a war of desperation. On the other hand, peace with Serbia would cut the moral ground from under the British in Salonica, besides making a powerful impression on the whole Entente, which would have to conclude that the Central Powers did desire peace and were quite capable of breaking up the enemy coalition by separate peace treaties.

This might bring far-reaching consequences. The strong need not fear the "semblance of weakness." Why should not Serbia be granted access to the Adriatic by ceding it North Albania and Montenegro? Why should the misguided effort to create an independent Albania (as Burián wished) be repeated? Jagow emphasized more than once that the Germans deserved the lion's share of the credit in this campaign, but that they had not taken the field to revenge General Potiorek's defeats in Serbia. What Germany wanted was a sensible Balkan settlement. Falkenhayn too vainly pressed for the immediate formulation of peace terms, so that the war might be more speedily terminated.

But Tisza for the nonce no longer wanted any form of peace with Serbia; and Burián's pigheadedness brought the German diplomats to the verge of despair.[8] He could not be persuaded to give up his Albanian schemes nor was he amenable to appeals to set peace terms for Serbia. Ultimately the whole discussion lost point, for despite its total defeat Serbia did not surrender but moved the remnants of its army—still 140,000 men at that—into Montenegro and Albania, whence they were transported to Corfu and later Salonica, which the Austrians were quite unable to prevent.

By mid-January the Germans were up against the fact that the Austro-Hungarian cabinet had officially decided on carving up Serbia between Austria and Bulgaria, i.e., to wipe it off the map completely. Only Tisza dissented—he frowned on large-scale annexations of Serb territory. Germany had to accept the situation for the time being, unless it wished to add another bone of contention between the two allies; and next to the Polish issue, the question of Serbia was the most complex of all, as well as the most urgent. But as Jagow wrote Falkenhayn, Germany was certainly reserving its position when it came to settling Serbia's fate.[9]

Berlin was also deeply concerned about Austria's treatment of Montenegro, against which it alone had been waging war. In mid-January, Montenegro pleaded not merely for an armistice but for peace. Bethmann Hollweg saw the possibilities of the event from the point of view of his over-all policy. It was the first time a member of the great anti-German war alliance had opted out, and its treatment was thus bound to become a paradigm of the peace policy of the Central Powers. If this small country were spared and made a friend, this would, in Bethmann Hollweg's view, leave a strong impression almost everywhere. For example, Montenegro might be compensated elsewhere for the cession of Mount Lovchen, which commanded the Bay of Cattaro—the Austrian General Staff was obsessed with the strategic importance of this bay. Such an exchange would serve as a bait for peace moves throughout the Entente countries, especially in Russia, which was bitterly disillusioned about Britain. For a great power like Austria to offer concessions to so small an enemy meant no great sacrifice. If on the other hand Montenegro were strangled, this would feed fuel to the flames not only of enemy but also of Pan-German propaganda. The enemy camp would point to the destruction of Serbia and the strangulation of Montenegro as an earnest of what was in store for any power overwhelmed by the Central Powers or seeking to make a separate peace with them, while the example of Austria would inspire the Pan-Germans to offer opposition to any attempt at negotiated peace—which meant opposition to Bethmann Hollweg himself.[10]

The Chancellor made the most emphatic representations to this effect to the Austrian ambassador, refusing to allow himself to be sidetracked by references to Montenegro's irreconcilable hostility. These objections were particularly unconvincing since only a short time before Baron Burián had been willing to elevate King Nikita to the dignity of rulership over a combined Serbia and Montenegro! But Bethmann Hollweg made no impression whatever on the Austrian envoy; and in formal terms Germany had no voice in the matter. In Jagow's words, what Burián wanted was to leave Montenegro mutilated, "a barren heap of rocks, incapable of sustaining life." Jagow foresaw the most serious consequences; but here again the vanquished foe evaded the strangler's grip. King Nikita fled the country, leaving no one behind with authority to conclude a peace. Bethmann Hollweg was horrified at the news. He found it beyond belief that Austrian diplomacy was too dense to build golden bridges for a defeated enemy who wanted peace.[11]

Thus in both cases, Serbia as well as Montenegro, peace by force was planned rather than actually put into effect. The plans, however, are of great historical importance. They show that the Prusso-German camp was not the only one where certain forces were unhesitatingly ready to exploit military victory for aggrandizement, heedless of world opinion and the possibility of lengthening the war. Austria went even farther in this direction—with the difference that its case was based largely on the armed achievements of others! In Burián's view, "the total disappearance of one of the belligerents from the battlefield" would be far more effective than any readiness to reach a peaceful understanding.[12] This was typically militarist thinking.

Burián was indeed under political pressure from the direction of his chief of staff, Conrad von Hötzendorf, who had been besieging him with political aides-mémoire since November, together with oral inquiries for which he set the stage with further voluminous memoranda. For this soldier there was only one solution to the Balkan problem, a very simple solution: annex all of Serbia and Montenegro and as much of Albania as possible. All the alternatives were mere half-measures that would soon exact their toll.

To restore Serbia, even with a greatly diminished territory, would mean the loss of Austria's status as a great power, and thus the loss of the war. The

South Slav question must be solved by uniting all the Serbs, Croats, and Slovenes under the banner of Austria. He advocated this view at a time when the Austrian army, although it had advanced to Kragujévač, had failed in encircling the Serbian main force and was dependent for victory on the support of German and Bulgarian troops. As early as November 5, Conrad took it for granted that Austria should have the exclusive right to occupy Serbia after the war and that Germany must be prevented from interfering with Austrian policy in the Balkans.[13] Germany, he insisted, was quite capable of sacrificing Austrian interests to others.

On November 26, with Serbia subjugated, Conrad demanded urgently that the dual monarchy's war aims in Serbia, Montenegro, and Albania be promptly formulated. He thought Albania should be carved up among Greece, which was to get South Albania as a reward for its neutrality (and at the same time be put at loggerheads with Italy!), Bulgaria, without whose help the Austrians could not have conquered the country, and Austria-Hungary. To this report Conrad appended a map showing the new borders, together with another, showing the mutilation of Montenegro, if that country's outright annexation were not feasible. In that eventuality, however, Conrad wanted Montenegro "integrated" as a satellite of the Danubian monarchy.

Two days later he demanded the immediate extinction of Serbia and its ruling dynasty, anticipating that such a fait accompli would make a terrifying impression on Greece and Rumania. When the Serbian conquest had been completed, Conrad, on December 18, 1915, began to speak very assertively in the name of the Austrian army and navy, who did not wish to be placed in a disastrous war situation a second time by Austrian diplomacy, which had so often in the past shown itself to be weak-kneed. He impatiently reproached the political leadership with having no clear war aims and asked for the most intimate and direct contact between it and the generals, for otherwise the war could not be successfully waged, in either Serbia or Poland, nor could conquered territory be properly administered. The army must know what it was supposed to be fighting for.

In his reply Burián was at pains to convince the rabid annexationist Conrad that the government too pursued "the greatest possible increment in power and security" as its war aim. Yet in midwar the government could not publicly commit itself to conquests it might not be able to retain when peace was concluded. This was as true of the South Slav question as it was of Poland, on which Germany's position was not yet unequivocally clear. Burián said he was not aware of having stinted in his political briefings of the high command, and he shared the view that this den of Serbo-Russian agitation must be destroyed and never allowed to rise again. "It is clear that Serbia and Montenegro must come under our military and political supervision"; but no definitive decision could as yet be taken on the modalities. He wished to see Albania continue intact, though "under our effective protectorate."

Burián did indeed plan to extend Austrian political influence all the way to the Strait of Otranto and thus expel Italy from the entire east coast of the Adriatic. He wished to implement the protectorate by annexing the entire coastal region of Montenegro and the Sanjak of Novibazar, thus securing a direct connection with Albania twice over. This plan, of course, anticipated that the Austrians would continue to be able to advance deep into the south; and it was communicated to the Austrian chief of staff only late in January 1916, and to the German ally not at all.[14]

Burián showed his correspondence with the chief of staff to the Hungarian premier, Count Tisza, eliciting a very comprehensive memorandum that included an impassioned protest against the annexation of Serbia. It would shift the population mix in the dual monarchy in an intolerable way, i.e., threaten the unequivocal dominance of the Magyars in their half of the realm and their good relationship with the Croat people. The entire structure of the monarchy would be deprived of what had, since the settlement of 1867, been one of its strongest pillars, and the way would be paved for its disintegration.

But Tisza's protest was also directed at the dangerous illusion that Austria-Hungary was able to set war aims entirely as it saw fit. The success of Austrian arms had so far been purely defensive, and the best that was in sight was a negotiated peace, i.e., a compromise peace, rather than one imposed by force. The monarchy was "territorially saturated" even now. Large-scale annexations could serve only to enhance the existing centrifugal forces to a dangerous degree. Besides, they would be very difficult to put into effect, would form a serious obstacle to peace, and would contravene the cabinet decision of July 19, 1914.

Unfortunately, Tisza's own peace program was formulated in such a way that it too seemed attainable only by a "dictated" peace—cession of large eastern regions of Serbia, which had been promised to Bulgaria; assignment to Albania of all regions inhabited by Albanians; the cutting off of Montenegro from the Adriatic coast; Hungarian annexation of the northeast corner of Serbia. Tisza's settlement would have left one or two vest-pocket states that could not survive without Vienna's goodwill. They could be kept in line by favorable trade treatment that could be withdrawn at any time, as well as by political and military conventions.[15]

At Tisza's request, the joint Austro-Hungarian cabinet discussed this program on January 7, 1916. Colonel General Conrad participated, having been at pains to send each of his fellow participants a comprehensive memorandum beforehand.[16] As before, he regarded all the protectorate schemes as useless and dangerous compromises. Tisza's objections he disposed of as Hungarian particularism; and he would hear nothing of the survival of Montenegro, even in mutilated form. If King Nikita were to sue for peace, he would first have to surrender unconditionally.

Conrad realized, on the other hand, that Austria no longer had the military resources to subjugate Albania. Hence he stuck to his partition plan, so that at least North Albania would come under firm Austrian control—with Bulgarian and possibly Greek help! He admitted that if the war aims were too ambitious they might later on have to be pulled back, but that was no reason why they should not be formulated even now. The Italians must at all costs be driven from the eastern shores of the Adriatic, Russian Poland must become Austrian crownland, undivided, if at all possible. He committed himself to fight with every means at his command against any German intervention in Balkan politics or any acquisition there. He naively assured Tisza that according to his intelligence reports he anticipated no insurmountable objection on the part of the Entente governments against the annexation of Serbia. Serbia had always been a problem country and the Entente would be glad to see it go.

Conrad did not prevail entirely with his proposals in the joint cabinet meeting, which decided to proceed against Montenegro and Albania according to Burián's plans. Against Tisza's advice, Serbia was to be totally annexed. Its remaining territory, after cessions to Bulgaria, Albania, and Hungary that were already agreed upon, was to embrace only one and a half million people, one-third of all Serbs, two thirds of whom would come under the Austro-Hungarian Empire, but all this was to remain secret, since any peace with Russia must not be allowed to come to nought on that account. The official communiqué was couched in rather general terms.

It did not deter Conrad from continuing his opposition. When King Nikita left his country, Conrad again urged that Serbia and Montenegro be liquidated at once and for all time, by open proclamation. "Surely the Entente do not wish to add a single day to the duration of the war on account of their Balkan protégés," he wrote Burián. On the contrary, only resolute action and absolute confidence in victory could make any impression in these circumstances. For outward appearance, a referendum on joining the dual monarchy might be held in Montenegro. Burián called the plan farcical, but Conrad refused outright to fight for the creation of an Albanian protectorate. He said he would not take responsibility for dispatching crack units to a country they would subsequently have to evacuate.

Burián's reply reflected the situation that prevailed in Austria. Rather than invoking the arbitrament of the aged Emperor Francis Joseph, he preferred to resort to wheedling. Of course he lacked military judgment, he said, and could exercise no influence on the decisions of the army high command; but he would be particularly gratified if it were possible to make military progress in Albania and thus facilitate the attainment of the government's long-range aims. He was at considerable pains, moreover, to persuade the chief of staff of the advantages of a protectorate over all of Albania; but the only result was that Conrad reiterated his bitter complaints about Austria's misguided Balkan policy since 1908. Conrad ended with the equally bitter admission that the Austrian army and navy were quite unable to effect the occupation of Albania all the way to Vlonë, as Burián wanted.

In the course of February 1916 the Austrians did after all advance in Albania to the Durrës-Elbasan line, in the vain hope of capturing the remnants of the Serbian army that had escaped thither; but this advance quickly led to a bitter quarrel with Austria's Bulgarian ally, who wished to secure a substantial share of West Serbian and Albanian territory as well. There was an actual clash with Bulgarian forces near Elbasan and a cabinet crisis in Bulgaria. It was only owing to Falkenhayn's intervention that the difficulty between the allies was papered over in March. An agreement was made delimiting the respective occupation zones of the belligerent powers.

As time went by, it became more and more clear that Germany, by taking part in the war in the Balkans, had stirred up a hornet's nest of opposing ambitions among its allies and now stood in danger of frittering away its precious fighting resources for interests that were not its own. Right down to March Falkenhayn clung to the plan of launching a major offensive against Salonica with his Balkan allies, and possibly even the agreement if not the aid of King Constantine, to expel the growing concentration of Anglo-French forces there and thus perhaps win Greece as an additional ally; but technical difficulties, notably the question of how to get supplies across the trackless and railless Serbian highlands, proved insurmountable, or at least bade fair to take far too much time, as Seeckt, the highly competent chief of staff of the German offensive army, had already explained in mid-January.

In the end Falkenhayn concluded that the fate of Germany would, after all, be settled in France rather than in the Balkans. He concentrated every possible fighting resource on the western front, in a last desperate effort to break out of the frozen stalemate before Britain's great new offensive army could launch its assault. Preparations for the battle for Verdun now got underway, while the Balkans were left to the Balkan peoples themselves and to Austria, on the premise that the large Allied force in Salonica could only serve to weaken Entente striking power in the west. Gallipoli had been abandoned in the meantime, eliminating the main threat to Turkey. If Salonica were taken, there would only be further bitter quarreling among Austrians, Bulgars, and Greeks. Any advance of the forces in Salonica in the direction of Bulgaria could be fended off largely by the Bulgarians alone, on account of the mountainous character of their country. On the other hand, as Falkenhayn later recorded, the Bulgarians were bound to cling to their alliance with Germany, because of the constant pressure on them.[17] Politically as well as militarily, these were valid arguments.

# 4

# Plans for *Mitteleuropa* and the Polish Question in the Winter of 1915-1916

THAT THE subjugation of Serbia, originally planned in July 1914, was now achieved, that the focus of unrest that had kindled the First World War was for the time being extinguished, was, of course, a matter of considerable satisfaction to the Central Powers; but it did not notably lighten the gloom of the over-all situation. The tremendous preponderance of enemy strength in the west remained, together with the oppressive prospect that it might greatly increase even further in the course of the summer to come. As Karl Helfferich, who became German minister of finance early in 1915, reports, Bethmann Hollweg had long been skeptical of the political value of Germany's military successes. Beginning in April 1915 he time and again discussed with Helfferich the need for taking advantage of any peace possibility, on the basis of the status quo, if nothing better was to be had.[1]

Count Lerchenfeld reported to Munich late in October 1915 that the foreign ministry was considering openly inviting Germany's enemies to the peace table as soon as the Serbian campaign was concluded. True, this might be interpreted as a sign of weakness, but there was no real danger to Germany, whose forces stood deep in enemy territory. In the event the bid were declined, the people would back the government all the more; for its willingness to make peace would then be clear beyond all doubt.

At the same time, any peace tendencies in the enemy camp would only be strengthened. True, Germany would have to forego annexations, and Belgium, in particular, would have to be surrendered; yet even there Germany might be able to gain certain military guarantees and "full indemnity." Germany, moreover, could count on the return of its colonies and the cession of "French and British areas in the Congo." In a military sense, Germany could scarcely expect much more than to hold its positions. An advance on Paris or Calais was out of the question. In the east it might be possible to take Riga, but that was about all. Even General Falkenhayn now agreed that Belgium might have to be surrendered.

These were represented as the purely personal views of Minister Count Wedel, who acted as the foreign ministry spokesman. Presumably they were meant as nothing more than a trial balloon, launched to sound out the federated governments; and when Hertling reacted with consternation, the story was virtually retracted and described as purely speculative.[2] But clearly Bethmann Hollweg that fall seriously considered that with the conclusion of the Serbian campaign and the successful defense in the west the time might have come to present a peace offer.[3] In a note of November 10, War Minister Wild von Hohenborn records that Bethmann Hollweg touched on the matter in a Prussian cabinet session, eliciting Wild's vigorous opposition. Bethmann Hollweg also expressed concern that leading social democrats had reported incipient popular war weariness.[4]

Late in November Bethmann Hollweg discussed peace possibilities with Falkenhayn as well, in a vein that left Falkenhayn with the impression that he was ready to make an overt peace offer to the other side. The general sent him a worried letter the next day, rejecting the notion that Germany had the alternative of offering peace or continuing to fight until the enemy's will was broken. "This is no longer the kind of war with which we are familiar. In a very real sense, it has become a struggle for survival for all the belligerents." Germany must stick it out to the end, be it good or bitter, whether it wanted to or not.

In such a struggle the side that came out with peace offers without very certain signs that one of its enemies was prepared to yield displayed pernicious weakness, no matter how carefully the proposals were worded; for such offers merely served to weaken the people's and the army's will to carry on, while strengthening the enemy side. This would be an "ineffable misfortune," and no domestic considerations could justify it. Bethmann Hollweg declared that this was a misunderstanding. All he had wanted to say was that Germany was prepared to support any peace tendencies to be found among its enemies, and that it would not deliberately nip such aspirations in the bud—by excessive annexation demands, for example.[5]

Obviously Bethmann Hollweg had to engage in a desperate and perilous balancing act between the persistent annexationist demands of the bourgeoisie and the peace yearnings of the socialist masses. Early in December a Reichstag session impended, for the purpose of authorizing new war appropriations. The social democratic leaders, alarmed by the general dissatisfaction with the food situation among the masses and the increasing activities of their extreme radical and left pacifist followers—there had actually been small street demonstrations against the war in Berlin! —were resolved to put questions on this occasion that would show their unequivocal opposition to any policy of conquest, thus forcing the Chancellor to offer a similar declaration. This, they hoped, would have a favorable effect abroad.

Reading the report Scheidemann made about his long confidential discussion with Bethmann Hollweg on this question on December 4,[6] one gains the impression that the Chancellor was glad to fall in with the social democratic declaration. What he was greatly worried about was the opposition of the bourgeois "war aims majority," and he diligently searched for an innocent-sounding formulation to which the socialists might agree. On the other side, the bourgeois party leaders besieged him to drown out any harmful impression of incipient weakness by a firm show of confidence in victory and by standing up strongly for German "vital interests." They felt the people needed reassuring, while the social democratic question in the Reichstag was likely to create the impression abroad that Germany might be beginning to crumble.[7]

It was indeed a daunting situation for a statesman who was staking everything on keeping together and sweeping onward a national front that was slowly disintegrating. Nor was it made easier by sharp opposition, on the part of the war minister and the chief of staff, to any public display of German readiness for peace, while at the same time these two men gave only the vaguest answer to the crucial question: How long would Germany's reserves of manpower, food, and raw materials enable it to "stick it out"—in a war that Falkenhayn had but recently once again described as a "war of attrition," without any certainty of military success? [8]

In such circumstances it would have been a miracle, had the Reichstag session of December 9, 1915, run along the accustomed lines of a "demonstration of national unity"—even with the Chancellor's renewed display of his astonishing capacity for obscuring rather than bridging political chasms by statements that seemed to be pregnant with meaning but ultimately committed him to nothing. The nationalists, including even his critics at imperial headquarters,[9] were enchanted by the note of unshakable confidence he struck, while the left was appeased by his declaration that Germany would not prolong the war by a single day merely to gain territory that might be used for bargaining purposes. Yet Bethmann Hollweg avoided any formal and open statement foregoing annexations, while he expressly rejected a German peace offer as premature. To top things off, Dr. Spahn, leader of the centrist party and spokesman for the bourgeois majority, did his best to foil the effect of the social democratic interpellation, putting further difficulties in the way of that party's adopting a moderate nationalist line.

Thus annexationist sentiment continued to exert powerful pressure on German policy in late 1915; but now that a victory in the Balkans had been shared with Austria and Bulgaria, German peace hopes shifted at least to some extent in a different direction that may have struck the government as less perilous. This was the goal of a "Union of Central Europe."

There had always been trends in that direction. The spark of "Great Germany" (i.e., a Germany including Austria) had never quite died away, even after 1866, least of all among the German-speaking Austrians, who longingly eyed the German Reich in their precarious situation vis-à-vis the Slavs. On the German side too, companionship in arms had from the outset created much sympathy for the Austrian "brethren," despite the many grave disappointments that attended fighting "shoulder to shoulder" with the motley multinational Danubian forces, poorly armed and trained, and given to swift disintegration.

On both sides there was a swift flowering of political pamphlets calling for closer and enduring ties between the two empires. In Austria the movement was fostered especially by the Sudeten Germans (i.e., those inhabiting the fringes of Bohemia), by Viennese historians, led by Heinrich Friedjung, and by German-minded social democrats like Karl Renner. In Germany there was actually a formal organization, and support was given by many trade associations and well-known college professors, some of them of Austrian antecedents.[10]

Perspectives quite often transcended the borders of the two empires, along lines set by Bethmann Hollweg himself as early as September 1914. As we have seen, he proposed that the loss of German world markets be compensated by the creation of an economic union that was to embrace virtually the whole continent. These hopes received new impetus when the Danube route was opened to Bulgaria and Turkey. It seemed now that the vague utopian dreams of German publicists prior to 1914, projecting a great commercial route from Berlin to Baghdad, were a step nearer to realization. Turkey's audacious projects for undermining Britain's position as a world power in the middle east, zealously supported by Germany and mentioned by Bethmann Hollweg in his first Reichstag speech on December 9, lent further momentum to such fancies.

The well-known book by Friedrich Naumann, *Mitteleuropa,* marks the high point of this movement. It appeared in the fall of 1915, precisely at the right time to become the German wartime best seller.[11] There were a number of reasons for this tremendous impact. Naumann was a writer of great skill and stature and he knew the multinational state on the Danube inside out. He was also a great idealist who foresaw a glorious future for Germany. Before the war he had tried to soften the entrenched hostility between the nationalist right and the socialist left by means of a new national-social movement. Now he sought to purify German nationalism by blazing new trails.

With fiery rhetoric, inspired by true liberal convictions, he sought to persuade his fellow countrymen that the time had come to form a great community of nations in Central Europe, embracing in addition to Germans West and South Slavs, Hungarians, and possibly Rumanians. A whole series of smaller peoples was to aggregate around the solid and enduring core of the Austro-German alliance, but this was not to become an empire ruled from the center but a somewhat nebulous "superstructure" with common federal institutions; for only if *Mitteleuropa* were a federal community with common institutions would it be able to withstand the pressures from the great world empires in east and west. In the era of modern large-scale enterprise, whether in business or politics, particularism was a thing of the past.

Much of Naumann's book was devoted to showing the great economic advantages that would accrue from the creation of a common Central European *Lebensraum*. To be meaningful and enduring, however, such a community required a complete change in the thinking of the participants. They had to grow out of their narrow and unrealistic nationalism with its defiant arrogance. They needed to have an understanding of the feelings and interests of other peoples. Mutual distrust must give way to mutual aid and sympathy. In this way alone could the crucible of war give rise to a fairer, freer, riper future for Europe and Germany.

Beyond doubt this high moral note, this appeal to the great cultural traditions which the West shared, this voice of reason and goodwill amid the insensate passions of the war, account for the book's great appeal to countless Germans at the time (including, incidentally, the author). Here at last was a voice of calm reason and goodwill, a guidepost to positive war aims—more than the defense of the native soil, less than the rape of other nations: the tempting challenge to reshape the future of Germany and Europe. It was a challenge that confronted Germany with great tasks; but in return it promised far better security than was offered by Bismarck's Dual Alliance with its constant threat from the direction of the Balkans. Not the least of its attractions was that it would belatedly heal the painful wound inflicted by Bismarck on Germandom by the "Little German" solution of excluding the Hapsburg realm from the German national state. If Naumann's objective were attained, the dreadful sacrifices and bloodshed of the war would take on deeper meaning.

Those who lived through this period are tragically aware in retrospect today that Naumann's *Mitteleuropa* movement was from start to finish nothing more than a will-o'-the-wisp. We have already seen the realities of "front-line comradeship" between the armies of the two empires. At the time only the highest military echelons knew all the facts. The truth is that if the idea of a federated Central Europe rising above all the special interests of the non-German Danube nationalities had ever stood a chance of acceptance, time had long since run out. Nationalist sentiment, as well as the disintegration of the Hapsburg Empire, had progressed too far to be stemmed by mere counterpropaganda.

Despite all the agitation on the part of Naumann and his supporters in Austria and Hungary, his plans aroused nothing but distrust among all but a vanishingly few Poles, Czechs, Magyars, Bulgars, and South Slavs. Those plans were widely considered camouflage for German expansionism. Czech émigré publicists like Masaryk and sympathizers like Seton-Watson did everything in their power to stamp Naumann as an imperialist and *Mitteleuropa* as the latest form of Germany's drive for world power. As a countermove representatives of the Allied governments convened economic conferences in Paris in March and July 1916, and agreement was reached there to continue intensifying the blockade and to carry on economic warfare even after the conclusion of peace.

Nor were the expected voices of radical nationalists lacking in Germany, crying out that Naumann's ideas meant falsifying and endangering Germany's "mission" in the world. Lastly, the continuing intensive debate among economists and business leaders showed that even an Austro-German customs adjustment and economic union would encounter enormous practical difficulties and unbridgeable economic differences. More and more the idea of *Mitteleuropa* drifted away on a sea of words.

Bethmann Hollweg had already had a similar experience when he charged Delbrück with the mission of having the appropriate German federal agencies study the problem of an Austro-German and Central European customs union (see p. 30, above). It is remarkable—among other things for the great influence of public opinion on his policies—that he was not permanently deterred by these difficulties, but reverted to his plan in the fall of 1915 and even initiated negotiations on it with the government in Vienna.

Apparently it was none other than Falkenhayn, the chief of staff, who gave the first impetus, in a discussion with the Chancellor on August 28, which he immediately confirmed in writing. In view of the danger of a long war of attrition, he proposed a long-term close defensive alliance between the German Reich, Austria-Hungary, Bulgaria, and Turkey. This alliance, however, would also have to set itself economic and cultural goals; and it might later be expanded by the adherence of Sweden, Switzerland, and possibly even Greece.

In Falkenhayn's view, such an alliance would have a deterrent effect on Britain, which would then have to give up hope of ever being able to exhaust Germany and its allies. Solution of the difficult Polish question might be made easier. Falkenhayn assured Bethmann Hollweg that he did not wish in any way to meddle with the political sphere; but he took his plans sufficiently seriously to ask and obtain the Kaiser's immediate approval.[12]

The full measure of his political concept is not easy to fathom. Bethmann Hollweg, who was at great pains to achieve agreement with the chief of staff on so important a question, kept complaining about evasive and contradictory answers when he pressed for the proposals to be concretized. The Chancellor's principal objection was that the existing war alliances with Austria and Turkey—the one with Bulgaria was only just being signed— already marshaled the joint political, military, and economic resources to the limit that was at present attainable. There was no practical prospect of expanding this alliance by the accession of the neutrals Falkenhayn named, nor would these additions be of advantage to Germany, except for Sweden.

On September 5 Bethmann Hollweg expressed himself with profound skepticism on the subject of a future program of long-term treaties of alliance. These doubts came rather unexpectedly, in view of his "September Program" in 1914. Hitherto such treaties, he said, had brought Germany either nothing but bitter disappointments, as in the cases of Italy and Rumania, or more loss than profit. As we see, the victory hopes of the early war weeks had long since vanished, giving way to stark realism. Bethmann Hollweg did not quite say that Germany's alliance with Austria was a liability, but this is what he must have had in mind, when he recalled Bismarck's *cauchemar des coalitions.*

Falkenhayn replied that he was not really concerned with long-term treaties. What he wanted was the political impact of a great Central European grouping of states, for its effect on the war. This was probably a rationalization, for in truth Falkenhayn had no valid arguments with which to counter the Chancellor's political objections. Puzzled questions were asked inside the foreign ministry—Which political adviser had put Falkenhayn up to this scheme? [13]

After several fruitless talks, Bethmann Hollweg did get to the bottom of it on October 15, and what he found was a far-reaching plan for the future. Political necessity, according to Falkenhayn, would force Germany to stick with Austria-Hungary. Russia was lost for good as a potential ally, while Britain would be deterred from another war only if it saw itself face-to-face with a Central European bloc. The core of such a bloc had to be formed by the two major Central Powers. Attached to them, if possible, should be the Scandinavian countries, Holland, Switzerland, Turkey, Bulgaria, and perhaps still other Balkan countries. Germany's bonds with Austria-Hungary must be indissoluble, for a victorious Austria, quite possibly strengthened by the annexation of Poland, would give no aid to Germany in any future war, indeed might turn against Germany.

The two Central Powers were to form a union in which Germany had the leadership role, while Austria-Hungary would have to surrender its sovereignty in part. Since Austria would never do so voluntarily, it must be compelled, no later than at the time of concluding peace. Falkenhayn found examples of such federation in the old Germany as well as the new, and in the United States of America. According to a note by Wild he envisaged the Danubian monarchy's relation to the German Reich much like Bavaria's to Prussia. The Kaiser was to be president of the federal union, operating with a kind of senate, presumably composed of representatives of the federated states.[14]

A military convention would be of value only if Germany dominated Austria-Hungary in such fashion. Indeed, such a convention would be worthless and even dangerous between equals. Germany had nothing to learn from the Austrian army—which Falkenhayn described as a "corpse"—while the Austrians had much to learn from Germany—that is, if the slovenly Austrians could rouse themselves to that end. This was likely only if Germany kept Austria under close surveillance, imposing remedies for deficiencies. Otherwise the Austrians would only corrupt the German army—or they might gain a really efficient army and pose a danger to Germany in another war. In no circumstances should Germany enter into a union with Austria other than in a role of domination.

This was curious reasoning indeed! Like most General Staff officers, Falkenhayn was convinced that the current war would be but a prelude to other wars—he had ceased to believe that the war could be won. Germany would have to establish the best possible starting position for such future wars. That meant a federal union of states on the European continent, which would secure for Germany a better breadbasket than the Dual Alliance of 1914, besides giving it a clear-cut role of political leadership. Only when these two requirements were met by means of political and economic treaties could there be any question of military agreements.

But how was this to be accomplished? The discussions with Bethmann Hollweg in mid-October took place against a background of irritation already known to us from the exchange about Bulgaria and Greece (Chapter 3). In the sequel, on the subject of *Mitteleuropa*, the chief of staff struck a different tone, but his basic attitude was the same (letters of October 30 and November 4 and 7). It became quite plain that he regarded the creation of the great federal union as a primary task for German diplomacy. Not until then could the military make its move, but the program for that eventuality was extremely radical. The Kaiser was to have supreme command over both armies. The Austrian army was to be under German command even during large peacetime maneuvers. Universal military service was to be applied uniformly, weapons were to be the same, German drill was to be adopted. There was to be a common General Staff under German leadership to work out war plans, and officers were to be mutually detailed to certain academies. In other words the Austrian army was to be Prussianized.

This meant a total reversal of the *Mitteleuropa* idea into a militant, not to say militaristic institution. It corresponded rather closely with Ludendorff's ideas. In a letter to the historian Delbrück, Ludendorff was just then calling for a strong *Mitteleuropa* from Scandinavia to Turkey as a necessity. Austria would have to be upgraded with an iron hand, militarily and economically.[15]

Falkenhayn, however, did not share Ludendorff's annexationist designs, especially in the east. Indeed, he was reluctant to tell the Chancellor in detail even what "strategic border rectifications" he thought necessary for military reasons in Belgium and around East Prussia. He was afraid this might lead to a fourth partition of Poland. He would say no more than that rather little was really necessary. Above all, such discussions were premature while the war was still in progress. "I wish the Chancellor wouldn't bother me with such rubbish," he remarked to Wild with some annoyance.

Understandably, Falkenhayn looked down on the allied Austrian army with a mixture of resentment and arrogant contempt, born of the disappointments it had caused him from the outset. How then could he have imagined for even a moment that a powerful federal union could be reared on such an ideological base? Could he have seriously believed that the Austrians, at the end of a jointly fought war, would allow themselves to be persuaded or coerced into military subordination to Germany? And did he think that an alliance based on such subordination and coercion would exert the slightest attraction on neutral states?

Apparently Falkenhayn had not seriously thought out the political aspects of his great plan, but had simply tossed it off in a mingled mood of wishful thinking and impatience, arrogantly leaving the question of ways and means to "the politicians." This, at least, was the light in which his closest collaborator, General Wild von Hohenborn, viewed the matter. There was always a certain flair to Falkenhayn's plans, he remarked, but the conscientious homework was lacking.[16]

Falkenhayn's *Mitteleuropa* scheme was echoed in grossly exaggerated terms in a private letter Colonel von Seeckt wrote to a friend at the time, a sad sidelight on the political dilettantism that prevailed in General Staff circles. What is more, Seeckt went on to use the occasion for an attack on the Chancellor. He was much too slow-moving and pessimistic, with no confidence in himself or the Reich. He was certainly not the kind of modern Bismarck needed for the establishment of a new German sphere of dominance extending from the Atlantic Ocean to Persia. That called for "a cool-headed yet fiery leader, a man with faith in himself, his people, and his sword. Could this today be anyone but a soldier? For me there is only one man with the ability to lead and formulate such a program, Falkenhayn."[17]

Falkenhayn had indeed gone to great lengths in firing his younger associates with enthusiasm for his political ideas. In truth, however, the man who was being so vocally touted as the leader and strong man was by no means as certain of his cause as it seemed at first blush. He turned a deaf ear when the Chancellor tried to tell him how unrealistic his plan was. Later on he admitted that this was probably true, only to express doubt whether in that case any close and enduring association with Austria made sense. If Germany were to strengthen Austria in a military and territorial sense, there would soon be a struggle for dominance. Falkenhayn, in other words, stood firm in refusing any negotiations about a military convention.

This caused considerable difficulty for Bethmann Hollweg's policy line; for the Chancellor, in the meantime, had become much more deeply involved in *Mitteleuropa* plans than might have been expected from his aloof attitude on September 5. The reason was that the *Mitteleuropa* issue had in the meantime become closely intermingled with the question of Poland's future. This, the most delicate of all the questions in the east, had just then reached a stage where a solution could not be long postponed. It overshadowed Germany's whole relationship with Austria. On the other hand, Berlin had recently heard some voices in Vienna suggest that the Polish question might be solved within the larger framework of a *Mitteleuropa* union. Before we turn to this approach, it is essential to review briefly the whole background of the Polish question since the beginning of the war.

As early as August 1914, with the troops scarcely yet in motion, Austrian diplomats were in a panic lest the German military anticipate them with a proclamation to the people of Poland.[18] Count Burián, at the time still in retirement, during a discussion held as early as August 12, advocated the view that in the event of victory over Russia, Austria would have to restore the kingdom of Poland and attach it to the Hapsburg monarchy in some fashion. On the same day Count Berchtold sent a long message to his ambassador in Berlin, for transmission to the German government. It would be intolerable, he said, if Germany were to create both a Polish and a Ukrainian buffer state, as seemed to be its intention, according to reports from reputable German sources. A newly independent Poland would inevitably attract Galicia, which Austria would be in a far worse position to prevent than Germany would be to prevent the defection of its province of Poznan.

There was but one practicable solution for Austria: Poland must be integrated with Galicia in some appropriate constitutional way. To avoid a disproportionate weakening of the German element on the hither side of the Leitha line within the Austrian Empire, Galicia thus enlarged would have to quit the Austrian federal council. This would give the German element in Austria the same kind of preponderance enjoyed by the Magyar element in Hungary.

Germany, on its part, would gain the advantage that the Austrian government would be able to keep Polish irredentism from infecting Poznan. If

Poland were to become independent, this could scarcely be stopped. Indeed, such a state would become a hotbed of French and Russian intrigue directed against the Central Powers. A Poland integrated with Galicia, however, would remain loyal to Austria from fear of Russia, indeed, would adhere to the Austro-German alliance, despite Germany's Polish policy. Accompanying the message were fanciful plans for the creation of a new Austrian province, Ruthenia-Ukraine, grouped about Lvov, together with a proclamation addressed to the Polish people, to be made public on the occasion of the fall of Warsaw. Even an administrator for the new Polish-Galician region was named, Bobrzynski.

All this makes exceedingly curious reading. It will be seen that Austria embarked on its great Galician offensive not only with very great expectations but with equally clear-cut plans of conquest. It must be kept in mind, of course, that the political unrest that was rife among Austria's Galician subjects provided a powerful motive.[19] The views presented in Berlin at the time on behalf of the Austrian foreign minister did not greatly change under subsequent Austrian governments.

The German foreign minister, von Jagow, was incautious enough on August 15 to voice his general agreement with the Austrian ideas to Ambassador Szögény in general terms, though he cautioned against precipitate action; but Count Berchtold was eager to exploit the occasion and expressed his warmest gratitude the very next day. A start must be made immediately, he said, in organizing the administration of Poland—which was then still a long way from being conquered! The rise of a radical socialist independence movement in Poland must be prevented. What was meant, of course, was the formation of a Polish legion under Pilsudski.

To that end, Berchtold went on, General von Colard, accompanied by the former Galician governor, Bobrzynski, would proceed at once to Cracow and thence to Kielce in Russian Poland. He requested that the German government immediately turn over to these gentlemen administration of those parts of Poland to be occupied by German troops! After the fall of Warsaw, they would make that city their headquarters. The Germans were, of course, free to assign a liaison officer to General von Colard, so long as German troops were in occupation. The Austrians, in other words, were laying claim in advance to territory yet to be won by the Germans. Szögény was charged with the task of gaining their agreement.

The reply was what might have been expected: For military reasons alone, the German government would wish to install its own governor and officials in Warsaw. The task of the most immediate urgency, moreover, was to defeat the Russians. Vienna at once sent a new directive, in which the German intention was deplored. The czar of Russia, it claimed, had just publicly pledged full independence for the kingdom of Poland, which was to be combined with Galicia and the Polish districts of Prussia. (Strictly speaking, this was not true.[20]) There was thus grave danger that Poland might turn pro-Russian, and on that account, assurances about the future of their country must be given to influential conservative circles in Poland as soon as possible. According to intelligence received in Vienna, these circles were currently most sympathetic to the idea of Poland joining Austria-Hungary, while the thought of a prolonged German occupation was abhorred even more than a return to Russian overlordship.

The "better elements" in Poland must, therefore, receive assurances as soon as possible from the Germans too that their occupation would not last long, and that after the war Poland would have an independent national administration within the Danubian monarchy. German troop commanders and officials should be confidentially briefed along these lines and encouraged to "enlighten" influential Polish circles appropriately. It would be best if an Austrian governor with a troop contingent were to be dispatched to Warsaw (which the Germans still had to take).[21]

It might be thought that such naive presumption would have been decisively put down in Berlin. The German foreign ministry did indeed send a formal note in which it declined to turn over administration of territory occupied by the Germans to Austrian officials, so long as such territory supported a German front line. The result was that henceforth there was mention only of joint administration of the various occupation zones; when Austria's newly appointed ambassador Prince Hohenlohe remonstrated with Under Secretary Zimmermann on August 23 that the Poles would scarcely be inspired to fight the Russians with complete dedication by the prospect of ending up under Prussian rule, Zimmermann did not argue. He said he would advocate assurances to the Polish people that the occupation of their country by German troops was to be considered only a temporary measure. No one within the German government, it will be seen, thought of a Polish conquest on behalf of Germany. At the same time, however, any assurances that Poland would be left to Austria were avoided.

Count Tisza in Vienna meanwhile saw to it that the heady wine Count Berchtold was serving himself was suitably watered. During a discussion with Count Stürgkh on August 19 he made it clear that on no account must the acquisition of Poland be allowed to upset the balance between Austria and Hungary within the dual monarchy. Such an accession was bound in any event to alter its structure incalculably. He urgently warned against making any pledges to the Poles at this time. In the event of such a large accession, Hungary would have to reserve the right to claim a counterbalance by the incorporation of Bosnia, Herzegovina, and possibly Dalmatia as well.[22]

This was not tantamount to an absolute Hungarian veto; and since Polish national committees had meanwhile been established in Cracow and Lvov, for the purpose of organizing a Polish legion to fight against Russia, the joint Austro-Hungarian cabinet decided on August 20 on Bobrzynski's motion that a proclamation to the Polish people should be issued after all at the earliest possible date, either directly before or after the entry into Warsaw. The Germans were to declare that they desired no annexation of Polish territory, but came only as liberators, while the Austrians, in case of victory, were to hold out to the Poles the prospect of association with the Danubian monarchy. Tisza, however, prevailed in having this pledge proclaimed, not by the emperor, but, less bindingly, by the Austrian commander-in-chief, through the agency of a cavalry detachment to be dispatched to Warsaw.

Berlin at long last did prick up its ears and began to offer objections. The German foreign ministry sent word that Jagow's initial assent to the "Austro-Polish solution" had been purely tentative and that any final decision would have to be very carefully considered. Actually, Jagow had from the beginning insisted on protection of Germany's very substantial economic interests in the Polish market. This was now reiterated, and an interest in Polish industry and coal mining was hinted at. Zimmermann further expressed doubt that the Poles would be as eager to embrace Austrian allegiance as Vienna seemed to believe.[23] For the time being, vague and noncommittal pledges to Poland should be enough, he said on August 28. Until Russia were beaten—the Battle of Tannenberg was still raging!—there should be no written commitments.

Thus German policy opted for dilatory treatment of the Polish problem, nor were the Germans swayed by representations that the Austrians needed a cooperative Polish populace on the left flank of their Galician offensive. At the same time, there was a clear hint that German public opinion might someday very well demand German territorial acquisitions in Poland, which created considerable irritation in Vienna; but the Austrians had no choice but to yield, for the popular uprising for which they had hoped and which they had fomented failed to materialize, while the great battle in Galicia soon took a highly unfavorable turn. Even Hohenlohe thought it best to wait and see whether the Austrians or the Germans would carry the day over Russia. Vienna did pride itself on having averted one eventuality it feared: Germany's proclamation of an independent Poland as an autonomous buffer state between Germany and Russia.[24]

What interests us particularly about this whole exchange is that it plainly shows that from the first day of the war the Polish problem drove a dangerous wedge into the relationship between the two allies. Their power interests clashed quite unequivocally here. Despite many incidents,[25] this was of little practical importance so long as Poland remained unconquered. The problem became extremely acute, however, as the great summer offensive of 1915 advanced toward Warsaw.

Both General Staffs, Austrian and German, now pressed for clarification of future plans for Poland, so that these might be taken into account, as the country was occupied.[26] We already know Bethmann Hollweg's answer of August 4.[27] At that time he had not yet made up his mind which of the possible solutions to the Polish problem was "least unfavorable" to Germany, being convinced that there was none without some risk. If Russia were prepared to negotiate a separate peace, Poland might be returned, except for some border rectifications. If not, an autonomous Poland must be created, associated either with Germany or Austria. Either course carried difficulties and implied certain separations which must, however, not be allowed to reach the level of a fourth partition of Poland.

This statement highlights the German dilemma about the Polish question. It was entirely plausible, even to Falkenhayn,[28] that it should have been treated in dilatory fashion, so long as hope for a special peace with Russia had not been entirely extinguished. Yet even after August 11, when the last hope was wrecked, there were difficulties with every conceivable solution. After the event, critics repeatedly asked why the whole insoluble problem of Poland was opened up in the first place, instead of everything simply being left as it was. In his comprehensive memorandum of September 2, 1915, Jagow acknowledged that this would have been the lesser evil.[29] He argued, however, that the huge Russian empire with its inexhaustible manpower, potential for industrial growth, and its trend toward expansionism was a constant worry and nightmare to Western Europe and must be pushed farther eastward. For once the war were over, there would be an end for good to traditional Prusso-Russian friendship based on dynastic ties. The wedge which Poland constituted between East Prussia and Silesia would pose a mortal danger to Germany, once Russia had rearmed on a grand scale—always the great fear of the German General Staff! Everything pointed to the likelihood, moreover, that czarist autocracy would soon end in revolution. Such a revolution could scarcely avoid realizing Polish autonomy, which had been promised even now; and a Russian-supported Poland hostile to Germany was bound to become a center of anti-German and anti-Austrian irredentist propaganda.

These were not considerations that could be ignored with impunity.[30] Since Germany would never be able to eliminate Russia as a great power, nor dare ever again count on Russian friendship[31]—German war policy being then based on the notion of a continuing threat to Germany's central position—it was not implausible to try to lessen the Russian danger by the creation of a Polish buffer state. This might serve also to improve the exposed military position of Germany's eastern provinces, which had played such an important part in the elder Moltke's deployment plans, and always made it so immensely difficult to protect Germany's eastern borders. Bethmann Hollweg's enemies reproached him with trying to erase the impact abroad of Germany's invasion of Belgium with a Polish "liberation."[32] Actually, such illusory hopes played no part in Jagow's line of reasoning—indeed, he expressly rejected them as foolish.

Military considerations were soon added to the political. Even under Moltke and Waldersee, the General Staff had seriously considered the idea of encouraging a Polish insurrection against Russia in the event of a two-front war, and indeed the establishment of an independent kingdom of Poland under the Prussian crown. Even Bismarck had not closed his mind to the possibility of the re-creation of Poland in one form or other in the event of war.[33] The Poland manifesto of August 1914 (see Chapter 1) was apparently an echo of these traditions. Falkenhayn had initially upheld it, and at this very time was calling for efforts to get the majority of the Poles to come out openly on the German side—by which he meant adherence to his *Mitteleuropa* union. A goodly number of Polish recruits, he said, thoroughly drilled over the winter, might by the spring of 1916 reinforce the German army more nearly to the Russian level.[34]

We shall have occasion to see later on that this military argument was taken vigorously by Ludendorff the following year and helped accelerate the proclamation to the Polish people, which Bethmann Hollweg in September 1915 had rejected as utterly unrealistic.[35] He was strongly influenced by the importunate Austrians who were very eager to see their wishes, originally voiced in the summer of 1915, realized now, directly following the occupation of Warsaw. Baron Burián made a special trip to Berlin to that end, presenting his plans to Bethmann Hollweg once again at great length on August 13, 1915. For purposes of scaling up his demands, he pretended that Austria regarded taking over responsibility for Poland as a heavy burden that events had nevertheless rendered unavoidable.

He had already asked for an immediate proclamation to the Polish people, a demand to which the Chancellor yielded only in the most noncommittal terms. Nor was there any change in the arrangement under which a German rather than an Austrian administration was established in Warsaw. The Austrians did, however, secure a very advantageous division of responsibility for the over-all administration of Poland and succeeded in being most effectively represented in Warsaw, both diplomatically and militarily.[36]

On the main issue, the question of Poland's future, Bethmann Hollweg, according to his own notes, expressed himself with great reserve, putting forward many arguments against an "Austro-Polish solution." Poland's entry into the Austrian federal council would consign the German-speaking Austrians to impotence, which could be quite intolerable to Germany. Germany could not surrender its large industrial interests in the part of Poland it had conquered. The Germans wanted no immigration of Poles and Jews from the east. In accordance with Ludendorff's wishes, the Suwalki district would have to be severed from Poland, and there would have to be a number of strategic border rectifications. Certain crownlands in Poland would have to be open to the resettlement of Poles from the border regions falling to Germany.[37]

All the same, the Chancellor had no effective reply to Burián's argument that a protracted occupation of Poland, conducted with marked benevolence, could not end with a simple return of the territory to Russia.[38] Yet he stuck to the position that Germany rejected the idea of an independent kingdom of Poland, as well as the integration of Poland with Germany. Burián, of course, immediately chose to interpret this as approval for association with Austria. He repeatedly urged that Germany annex Lithuania and Courland west of a line running south from Riga—in other words compensate itself for the loss of the Polish prize.

Vienna had offered a similar proposal as early as 1914. Bethmann Hollweg's answer is quite remarkable. As in his letter to Falkenhayn of June 14 which we already know (see p. 69, above), he insisted that Germany must not squeeze Russia in the Baltic beyond all reason. This would merely sow the seeds of future wars. Riga, he said, seemed a dubious gain to him. He did admit that Germany could not forego certain acquisitions in Courland and Lithuania, to improve its border strategically; but this was nothing new and merely a more precise identification of the desired border rectifications. He asked the military side how extensive they were to be and soon afterward, on September 11, stated that they should be limited to the minimum that was strategically necessary, since any substantial increment in Polish and Jewish population elements would be harmful to Germany, while their reduction by expatriation would be possible only within narrow limits.[39] Clearly, he never contemplated expulsion of the whole population, but only limited resettlement measures that were to make room for German peasantry expelled from Russia.

To carry on the negotiations, Bethmann Hollweg asked Burián for a written report on how Vienna envisaged the association of Poland with the Austro-Hungarian union. He also evidently charged Jagow with preparing his report on the Polish question of September 2, with which we are already familiar. This report did not comport with the Chancellor's thinking in all its parts, for in its final section it recommended the establishment of an autonomous Baltic duchy under a German prince, which could not possibly have corresponded to Bethmann Hollweg's views at the time.[40]

On the other hand, he almost certainly agreed with Jagow's arguments against a Poland associated with Germany. It would harbor an almost unmanageable irredentist movement, especially along the Vistula. Above all, Prussia's eastern provinces would be heavily infiltrated by Polish and Jewish elements. The Austrians stood a better chance of preventing this than the Germans, if the matter was embodied in a treaty with them beforehand. The crucial objection, however, was barely hinted at. Polish-German association could be enduring only if it were possible to reconcile Prussian and Polish nationalism. This was altogether improbable, in the light of the bitter nationalist struggle of the preceding decades, the persistent anti-Polish attitude of the German government and its administrative organs, to say nothing of the geographic abutment of the two nations.

Since a wholly independent Poland was not in the German interest, and a fourth partition of Poland did not seem possible or desirable, Bethmann Hollweg came to share the view that the Austro-Polish solution might in the end be the one "least unfavorable" to Germany, provided it was staged with the proper guarantees respecting German interests. He may also have shared Jagow's view that in the long run it would be scarcely feasible to keep this prize of victory from the Austrians. But he was ill at ease over the whole matter, and this was the reason why on September 11 he did after all give serious consideration to Falkenhayn's *Mitteleuropa* plans, which he had rejected but a few days earlier. In sharply modified form, they were to facilitate solution of the delicate Polish problem.

Apparently a Poland under Austrian control was intolerable for Germany unless the alliance between the two Central European powers was secure for all time. Otherwise the German eastern border would be completely embraced by Austro-Polish territory, posing a serious military threat to Germany. In an economic sense, Germany would be cut off from its entire eastern trade; but in the midst of such considerations, a 100-page "memorial" from German Austria reached the Chancellor's hands. Written by the well-known Austrian historian and publicist Heinrich Friedjung with a number of his sympathizers, it had been sent to leading political personalities. It left so strong an impression on Bethmann Hollweg that he had it submitted to the Kaiser and subsequently received the author for a discussion.[41]

It is something of a puzzle why Bethmann Hollweg took this work so seriously, for the Friedjung circle, composed of renowned Viennese professors and writers, had virtually no political influence. Indeed, their *Mitteleuropa* notions were emphatically rejected by both prime ministers of the dual monarchy, Counts Stürgkh and Tisza, each of whom was jealously intent on maintaining his political autonomy. What seems to have struck Bethmann Hollweg was the suggestion that this juncture, when Vienna was making its annexationist ambitions in respect of Poland so plain, should be exploited for purposes of tying the Hapsburg monarchy more firmly to Germany—by means of a military convention that would serve to improve the Austrian army system, and by gradual rather than abrupt amalgamation of the two countries' tariff systems.

The Chancellor very probably welcomed Friedjung's advocacy of far-reaching integration of German and Austrian army systems after the war—by treaty, in the form of a close alliance with mutual guarantees of territorial integrity, rather than by force, as Falkenhayn envisaged it. Here was authority he could cite when next he negotiated with Burián concerning Poland's future. Jagow, moreover, and above all the Viennese ambassador Tschirschky—who was apparently in contact with the Friedjung circle—also thought the time propitious for exploiting the Polish question in order to strengthen the alliance with Austria and render it more enduring.[42]

Anticipating Falkenhayn's support for strengthening the military alliance with Austria, Bethmann Hollweg sent him the foreign ministry's Poland memorandum of September 2 nine days after that date, making reference to Friedjung's pamphlet, and asking for recommendations how this closer integration could be combined with Germany's military demands, to be put forward specifically on account of Poland—presumably this meant the border strip.

Bethmann Hollweg must have been brought up short when he encountered the staff chief's stubborn opposition of which we already know. Falkenhayn would have nothing to do with any military agreements until a political and economic *Mitteleuropa* had been created—even though the Chancellor told him at great length of the technical difficulties in the way of even an Austro-German customs union.[43] Bethmann Hollweg got a better reception from war minister Wild von Hohenborn, who agreed that Polish association with Austria was in the circumstances the solution least unfavorable for Germany, and who also supported the military convention Bethmann Hollweg wanted. But General Wild, falling in entirely with eastern headquarters, wanted voluminous annexations in the east—Kovno, Grodno, Ostrolenko, Plosk, the Warta line, also Courland and Lithuania, by way of compensation for the Austrian gains as well as from annexationist motives.[44] This was much more than the Chancellor liked.

Thus Bethmann Hollweg's position was not exactly easy when it came to resuming negotiations with Burián on the Polish question, the more so since Falkenhayn had told him he anticipated that leaving the major part of Poland to Austria would cause a power shift about which he was not at all enthusiastic.[45]

In Austria too there were great difficulties, indeed, even greater ones, when the joint cabinet of the two constituent monarchies met on October 6 to consider how liberated Poland might be integrated into the Austrian Empire.[46] The debate quickly showed that the task was impossible without completely upsetting German preponderance in the Austrian half of the empire, indeed, without breaking up the dual monarchy, already weakened by internal tensions.

A Polish populace of eighteen millions or even twenty, including West Galicia, could not be governed at the level of a remote and subsidiary province, as Hungary might govern a satellite Croat state. The Poles would certainly demand and obtain a full and equal share in the central government and parliament in Vienna. Here the various constitutional dodges set down in a memorandum by Count Stürgkh at Burián's request would be of no avail. Burián himself sensed that Stürgkh's proposals would sound illusory to the Chancellor and asked for certain changes to make them at least outwardly more palatable in Berlin. Nothing, for example, was to be said about the knotty question of defense.

But Burián was quite alone in his optimism that somehow a formula would be found that would satisfy both the German-speaking Austrians and the Poles. Count Stürgkh himself voiced the gravest forebodings and said that apprehension in German-speaking Austria was growing. Minister Koerber said that the duality principle would be jeopardized in any event. Count Tisza rejected any binding pledges to the Poles, to say nothing of a triad principle, and announced that Hungary would put forward major compensatory claims. The war minister, Krobatin, rejected any association with Poland outright. The whole debate was pointless, he said, for Poland was not to be had. In the end, Burián had to resume his German negotiations without any clear-cut cabinet instruction or support.

The crucial interview with the German Chancellor took place in Berlin on November 10 and 11. The very detailed Austrian minutes[47] show that at bottom the gulf between the two statesmen was unbridgeable. Bethmann Hollweg ardently advocated a close long-term alliance between the two Central Powers that would lead to uniform military organization, and a mutual preferential tariff with progressively lower customs barriers. Burián said he was basically in favor of a closer alliance but would not commit himself in any way, especially in military matters. Austria must maintain the fullest autonomy in respect of its decisions and institutions, and account must be taken of its financial weakness.

Burián was very hesitant in the matter of a customs union as well, and insisted that the impending renewal of the settlement between Austria and Hungary must come first. He seems to have been mainly concerned with securing from the Chancellor assurances that Germany was willing to forego ambitious war aims in the west and to leave Russian Poland to Austria. He did not, of course, say so openly, but it was clear that he thought Bethmann Hollweg was pursuing altogether chimerical plans in Belgium—trying to square the circle, so to speak. He expressed his vexation when Bethmann Hollweg told him German public opinion would not stand for the country getting no territorial gains to speak of out of the war, after so much bloodshed, while Austria grabbed all of Poland, with certain unwelcome side effects for Germany.

As he had done before, in August, Burián tried to divert the German

appetite to the Baltic, and again without success.[48] He displayed irritation
when Bethmann Hollweg criticized Stürgkh's memorandum about Polish
association with Austria and expressed concern over the tremendous Slav
preponderance that might loom in Austria—which he declared to be totally
without foundation. Indeed, he insisted—though he clearly knew better—that
the German-speaking Austrians were not worried on that account.

The interview, in other words, did not lead a single step beyond the
position on August 13, despite formal assurances that the two participants
were pursuing the same aims.[49] The only tangible upshot was a promise that
the German alliance plan would be committed to writing; and such a document was indeed dispatched to Vienna two days later. It constitutes the most
unequivocal evidence to be found anywhere among official war documents of
Germany's willingness to enter into a *Mitteleuropa* type of alliance.

The Dual Alliance of 1879 was to be deepened into a thirty-year pact that
went far beyond defense against Russia, each country guaranteeing the
integrity of the other. Additional long-term agreements, covering political,
economic, and military matters, were to be concluded. It all had a strong ring
of confidence in the future; but when one studies the document more closely
one notices that caution predominates over confidence. The delicate problem
of a military pact, for example, is simply passed over, to be "reserved to
discussion between the respective military establishments"; and as we already
know, the German General Staff could not be budged from its refusal to
engage in such negotiations.

The concrete agenda was limited to proposals for a customs union, and
even in that area stressed the difficulty of reconciling an Austro-German
preferential tariff system with the two countries' existing European trade
treaties, insofar as these included a most-favored-nation clause. Germany, in
other words, was not prepared to limit its access to other markets merely for
the sake of the limited Austro-Hungarian market. Indeed, Germany was
interested in a trade treaty with Austria only if that facilitated Austro-
German trade by reducing Austrian import duties. This, it was stated, must
provide the principal recompense for any German renunciation of Russian
Poland.

This is the only passage in which Poland's future is even mentioned in the
document, which states emphatically that Germany could conclude such a
treaty only if it prevented the progressive Slavization of Austria and restored
to the German-speaking element the position of leadership that was its due in
Austria's interest as the eastern march of the German-speaking peoples.

The demand was well-founded. What could be Germany's interest in tying
itself even more closely to the Danubian monarchy, if the accession of Poland
were to turn it into an essentially non-German Magyar-Slav state?[50] On the
other hand, it was equally clear that Vienna could not accept such conditions.

Had the Hapsburg dynasty and its supranational bureaucracy been foolish enough to try to organize the monarchy as Germany's "eastern march," their Slavic subjects would have risen in rebellion and the monarchy would have disintegrated. Even without the accession of Poland, dominance of the German-speaking element was a thing of the past and could not have been restored by a military alliance with Germany. As for Austrian industry, it was still far too weak and backward to stand up to German industry in free competition—not to mention the sharply divergent interests of Austria and Hungary. There was no willingness on that side to forego a protective tariff wall against Germany, hence even the customs union never had any real chance to get off the ground.

Further developments which we need not follow here in detail, soon confirmed that. The Chancellor displayed much confidence in the prospects of his project when explaining his plan at executive sessions of the German federal council.[51] But the Austrian government's official reply of November 24 to the German program of November 13 expressed little more than a readiness in principle to allow the economic experts to discuss the possibility of a customs union. Even this was hedged in with many reservations. Above all, Austria and Hungary would themselves have to reach agreement on the subject. As for economic compensation for Germany's foregoing Russian Poland, Austria expressly rejected the whole idea. All war gains should be divided up among the allies under an equitable formula. The reply concluded with a detailed rejection—marked by a note of irritation—of any German efforts aimed at safeguarding Austria's alleged character of a German "eastern march." This was quite superfluous, it was declared.[52]

Actually, even the tariff talks were a long time in materializing. First the Austrian and Hungarian governments had to discuss the renewal of their treaty of state, and these negotiations dragged on from January 1916 to late February 1917; there was much more talk there of raising than of lowering duties on German goods, for both governments stood in fear of the superiority of German industry. It was not until late April 1916 that the German foreign ministry at last prevailed in getting at least preliminary talks started between German and Austrian officials. These, however, got nowhere. Only subsidiary technical questions were discussed.[53]

Even before these talks had begun, the *Mitteleuropa* idea had been squelched at the political level.

We have already seen that with the successful conclusion of the Serbian campaign—i.e., the turn of the years 1915-1916—Burián and the Austrian high command were insistently pressing for large-scale annexations in Serbia, Montenegro, and Albania. If the war indeed ended in victory and Vienna were able to cash in on these plans, which Germany could not effectively oppose, and if Austria were also to unite Russian Poland with Galicia, what then would become of Germany's ally? How much substance was there to the repeated assurances of Burián the Hungarian that the political role of the German-speaking element within the Hapsburg monarchy was in no way menaced, hence no special measures to protect it were needed? And would German public opinion stand for the war ending with such an immense and unfairly one-sided expansion of Austro-Hungarian sovereignty?

It was only natural that such thoughts should turn up first among the generals. As early as October, in a letter to Zimmermann, Ludendorff had demanded that Poland not be allowed to fall to Austria, but be organized as "a more or less independent political entity under German suzerainty."[54] In his letter to Hans Delbrück, already cited, he called for a policy of "divide and rule." There should be an autonomous czardom of Poland, minus Suwalki, with other parts, as many as possible, to go to Prussia. "These will be our breeding places for the manpower needed for further eastward struggle, which will inevitably loom."[55]

Colonel von Seeckt, whose predilection for political soap bubbles we already know, saw salvation in outright annexation of at least the greater part of Poland. This was to be turned into a Prussian province of "South Prussia," as in the second and third partitions of Poland in 1793-1795. Such a province might enjoy a certain provincial autonomy and home rule, but it must be thoroughly pervaded by the Prussian state mentality. This would never succeed under Austrian auspices; and as the experience of Galicia showed, Poland would then never become a dependable bulwark against Russia.[56]

We find not a hint of such annexationist notions in Falkenhayn. Nevertheless, his experiences in the Serbian campaign and afterward had destroyed his faith in Austria's reliability as an ally. On January 23 he told the Chancellor he had reached the conclusion that to leave Poland to Austria-Hungary was too great a risk, from the military point of view. Even a military pact would not remove the potential danger. He said he now thought that some form of Polish association with Germany short of membership in the federal structure of the Reich would be relatively the best available solution of the problem.[57]

These views were well-received in the foreign ministry. On February 16, in a confidential letter to Ambassador Tschirschky,[58] Jagow enumerated the selfsame objections to the Austro-Polish solutions discussed above, describing the establishment of a Polish state firmly tied to Germany as the most acceptable solution in the end, despite the dangers and difficulties it carried. Poles and Polish Jews, however, would not acquire German citizenship or the right to immigrate into Germany.

Though this matter was not yet to be discussed with the Austrians, Burián soon sensed the change in the German attitude,[59] and pressed in turn by General Conrad,[60] he proposed to the Chancellor, in a long private communication late in February, that the Polish question now required speedy clarification.[61] His argument was the increasing political activity of the Polish population. In the long run, he said, the administrative agencies in the two occupation zones would not be able to maintain the required strict neutrality on the question of Poland's future. This was a hint bound to make an impression in Berlin, for the German governor general in Poland, General von Beseler, was complaining increasingly that Austrian military and civilian agencies were agitating for the Austro-Polish solution.[62]

At the time Bethmann Hollweg was deeply involved in a political crisis occasioned by the issue of submarine warfare. He was, furthermore, disinclined to resume the "academic" discussions about Poland while the Battle of Verdun still raged. He postponed the talks until April, though like Jagow he had abandoned the Austro-Polish solution by late February.[63] For him this was the inevitable consequence of the failure of his *Mitteleuropa* plan. Not until after his long Reichstag speech of April 5 did he signify his readiness for new talks with Burián, and these took place on April 14 and 15. There were some hard clashes, and the idea of *Mitteleuropa* was definitively buried.[64] It was quickly apparent that there was no way of bridging the conflicting interests of the two allies in the Polish question, and the negotiators parted without having reached agreement.

Of course Bethmann Hollweg was right in his concern that the multination Hapsburg state would be quite incapable of "digesting" so great an increment in its Slavic population. Yet his statements show that he was at least equally worried by the German public response to Austria's acquisition of all of Russian Poland, while Germany got no major territorial gains. Such an eventuality was bound to reinforce German annexationist demands elsewhere, notably in Belgium and in the Baltic—and in both areas this would have been most unwelcome to Bethmann Hollweg.

He knew, on the other hand, that the Austrians would not be easily persuaded to forego the acquisition of Poland. Hence, in a tactic typical of his political style, he had considered and asked Falkenhayn's opinion on a compromise even before the talks with Burián began. This would have provided for a division of Poland between the two allies, rather along the lines of the then-existing occupation zones. The larger share, falling to Germany, would become a grand duchy of Warsaw, outside the German federal union, yet closely tied to Germany politically, militarily, and economically. This would spare Germany the necessity for large-scale annexation of Polish territory, which General Beseler had described as essential, if Poland were to become Austrian—all the region to the west and north of a line from the Warta river by way of Modlin near Warsaw to the Niemen, with some three million Poles and eastern Jews, whose integration into Prussia the Chancellor found quite unacceptable—"we would find it quite impossible to pursue a sound policy in Poland under such circumstances."

Bethmann Hollweg was well aware that such a rump Poland would be an ill-favored structure, if only because the Poles in the newly formed grand duchy would at once strive for reunion with their fellow countrymen in the Austrian area and Galicia. In any event, the whole thing would be taken as a fourth partition of Poland, which Bethmann had always been at pains to avoid. His attempts to move the border of the new grand duchy as far south as possible did not help matters; nor was his proposal to summon the Austrian Archduke Charles Stephen to the throne of the new grand duchy in order to satisfy the ambitions of the court at Vienna anything more than a feeble compromise. Bethmann Hollweg himself was convinced that any new Polish dynasty would have embraced Polish nationalism by the second generation.

Falkenhayn remarked at once that the southward shift of the border would be very hard to push through and, for that matter, would avail Germany little. Nevertheless he accepted the proposed partition plan as a provisional solution, as did the Kaiser. Falkenhayn, however, made certain proposals of his own, which he thought would improve the plan, though they were even more impractical—similar constitutions in the two parts, which might have a "federal council" of their own. Falkenhayn had long since given up any hope of securing army replacements from Poland.[65]

Clearly, Bethmann Hollweg's partition plan was no more than a makeshift solution against the eventuality of Austrian recalcitrance. The ultimate goal would always have to be the creation of a grand duchy of Warsaw embracing all of Russian Poland. It was therefore decided not to mention the partition plan in the talks with Burián, but to demand all of "Congress Poland" (i.e., the part apportioned by the Congress of Vienna), in the anticipation that the other side might perhaps after all remain content with the southern part of Poland, thus placing the odium of a fourth partition on its shoulders.[66]

Could there be more telling proof of the erosion of the alliance than these truly devious tactics? Surely Burián was right when he emphasized strongly during the talks that the creation of a new Polish kingdom associated with Germany would be quite unacceptable to the Hapsburg monarchy. It would render Galicia ungovernable as a province of Austria and sooner or later would lead to its loss. The Poles would never forgive Vienna for having given them up to the Prussification they hated. They would do everything in their power to enlist Russian aid to reunite them with the Poles under Austrian and Prussian sovereignty.

With his characteristic frankness, Bethmann Hollweg admitted that these would be his convictions too, if he were a minister of Austria; but since he was not, he had to be guided by German interests exclusively. Burián, however, would not acknowledge such an interest. The alleged autonomy of the new buffer state would be a mere fiction, he said. Prussia-Germany would simply be compelled "to keep down the Polish populace by force of arms.

Such a state, with a restless and dissatisfied people, was scarcely suited to serve as a military bulwark against Russia. Indeed, as a buffer state it was bound to carry the seeds of further complications and future wars." If, as the Chancellor expressly declared, the Prussian policy of Germanization of Poznan and West Prussia was to be continued, there was scarcely an alternative to the new state becoming an outpost of German power, held by main force.

Both the Central Powers, in other words, were incapable of entertaining a policy under which Poland would have been truly "liberated." Germany could not do so, because it was necessarily afraid of adding to the danger already posed by the salient of territory, inhabited by non-Germans, that projected deeply into its eastern regions. Austria could not, because an increment of twelve to fourteen million Poles threatened to complete the disruption of the multination Austrian state, while an autonomous Poland was bound to lead, sooner or later, to the defection of Galicia.

On the other hand, both allies would be threatened by the same danger if Russia carried out the liberation of Poland after the war. The newly recreated kingdom would become even more of a bone of contention between the former partition powers, just as in the eighteenth century, but, in the age of modern nationalism, with incomparably worse consequences. There was in fact no satisfactory solution to the Polish question. In the end, it was the course of the war rather than the will of the Central Powers or of Russia that settled the destiny of Poland. Nevertheless, talks on the subject between Vienna and Berlin continued endlessly after April 1916, and the conflict between the two allies kept on deepening.

Once again Bethmann Hollweg successfully resisted Austrian efforts to channel the German desire for tangible war gains northward, in the direction of the Baltic. Yet it is noteworthy that he was less determined and put forward other reasons than he had voiced before. There was no more talk about Russia's natural need for possession of a free port on the Baltic coast. Instead, he said that the Baltic countries, poor in natural resources, provided no adequate substitute for Poland, and that Russia was far less likely to surrender them than it would be to surrender Poland.

About the only explanation is that the Chancellor had succumbed to the pressure of public opinion and the military establishment. Eastern headquarters, i.e., Ludendorff, had in the meantime established a very active administration in conquered Courland, where everything pointed at Germanization to come. Thanks not least to the work of Ludendorff's own publicity men, his efforts were vigorously supported in the German press. During the winter of 1915-1916 virtually the entire cultured and politically engaged German bourgeoisie was dreaming of the "liberation of the land of the Teutonic Order" and its German-speaking inhabitants, or at least demanding a strengthened border defense for East Prussia.[67]

As we have already seen, even Jagow was swept up in this propaganda wave (see p. 106, above), while War Minister Wild von Hohenborn supported the agitation for the annexation of Courland and Lithuania (p. 108). It was difficult enough to resist the pressure for annexations in the west, but it seemed almost impossible to stanch the pressure in the east for any length of time, let alone permanently. Bethmann Hollweg did, however, make efforts to contain it. On January 20 he wrote Hindenburg that Germany had to count on having to return to Russia the region to the east of the Memel line, which meant the main part of Lithuania east of Kovno and Grodno and the Niemen fortifications. Hence he wished to countenance no anti-Russian nationalist propaganda among the Lithuanians and even less the White Ruthenians. Only the Lithuanian areas directly abutting East Prussia were to be annexed, i.e., the areas of the so-called Niemen and Narev lines, which the generals had time and again described as indispensable to rectifying the border. The people there could be more easily amalgamated with the East Prussian population if there were as little nationalist propaganda among them as possible. As for the rest of Lithuania, Bethmann Hollweg wanted to see it merged into a greater Poland movement, in other words gravitating toward Poland rather than Germany.[68]

But it was not until the talk with Burián on April 14 that a clear-cut turn toward plans of conquest in the Baltic began to emerge. Bethmann Hollweg told Burián that Germany wished to annex outright only about 24,000 square miles with two to three million people (Suwalki, about 4,800 square miles, Courland and the Kovno district, about 8,000 each, and Grodno and Vilna,[69] about 3,200). This was certainly not all the territory Germany had occupied, but it was a "border strip" of respectable width. Bethmann Hollweg was putting into more precise terms what he had hinted at only vaguely in his Reichstag speech of April 5: "History never returns to the status quo in the wake of such tremendous events." Proceeding on the principle of nationalism,[70] Germany

> cannot voluntarily surrender to the mercies of reactionary Russia the peoples between the Baltic and the Volhynian marshes whom it and its ally have liberated, whether they be Poles, Lithuanians, Balts, or Letts. . . . Russia must not be allowed a second time to deploy its armies along the unprotected borders of East and West Prussia. It must not again, with French money, use the Vistula region as its entryway to unguarded Germany.

Bethmann Hollweg took a dangerous step with this speech—a step away from the reserve he had practiced so far and in the direction of the powerful annexationist trend of the time. Quite evidently he was trying to keep all his options open—he said nothing in public about the size and character of the guarantees for Germany's eastern border, whether they were indeed to be exacted by annexation or rather by the creation of buffer states. As before, on December 9, there was even a statement that Germany was prepared to sit down at a table with the statesmen on the other side to examine the possibilities of peace, if only the enemy forewent his openly declared war aim of destroying the power of Prussia once for all. Germany was not waging war to destroy foreign nations but to secure itself against further attack in the future. "Unlike 1870, when all Germans took it for granted that the reward of victory would be territory and the establishment of the Reich, Germany had, at the time of the outbreak of the war, but a single aim: to defend and maintain itself. . . . Germany's sons are bleeding and dying for Germany, not for a patch of foreign soil."

Bethmann Hollweg was still clinging to the defensive character of the war, in principle. Yet at the same time, and for the first time, restoration of the status quo was unequivocally rejected, not merely in the east. True, there was no mention of the annexation of Belgium, but the structure of the Belgian state was to be fundamentally altered. The Flemish people must not again be abandoned to Gallicization. Their national character must be protected and developed, as a basis for good-neighborly relations between the two countries, and as part of the system of guarantees that had been repeatedly demanded.

The whole tone was more one of martial resoluteness than of readiness for peace. The result was that the right applauded wildly while the moderate left grew uncertain of the Chancellor's political line. Had he really changed course, or was he merely yielding to the pressure of public opinion, without actually believing in the kind of victory that would enable Germany to expand its borders? Actually, Bethmann Hollweg did not for a moment dream of allowing annexationist demands to jeopardize any chance for a general negotiated peace or a separate peace with Russia, as was to be shown soon, in the summer of 1916.[71] But of this the public knew nothing.

Bethmann Hollweg's attitude becomes understandable only in the context of the severe political crisis to which he was being subjected at the time on account of the submarine warfare question.

# 5

# The United States and the First Two Submarine Warfare Crises in 1915-1916

Part 1

## Origin and Start of the War on Commerce with Submersibles (Spring of 1915)

T WAS GERMAN submarine warfare on merchant shipping that constituted the prime point at which the clash between the country's statesmanship and military thinking was made most fatefully clear. This conflict was
an almost classic paradigm of the basic theme of the present work, the
problem of militarism in Germany. It is probably not saying too much to
contend that the ultimate triumph of the military over the objections to
unlimited submarine warfare maintained by the leading German statesmen
marks the turn toward Germany's inexorable perdition. Bethmann Hollweg
fought it stubbornly in the first two submarine crises of 1915 and 1916, only
to succumb the third time round, in January 1917. Henceforth the generals
were to prove themselves consistently the stronger in the race for public
approval—even though the hope they had staked in the U-boats was to prove
illusory in a matter of months.

Here we already impinge on the second phenomenon that rendered the
U-boat controversy so memorable in a historical sense: More than any other
event of the war, it demonstrated the irresistible power which public opinion
with all its prejudices, passions, and myths can exert in a modern mass war,
even within the purely military sphere. Unlimited submarine warfare against
merchant shipping had early on turned into a popular myth—the myth of the
only certain path to victory, the myth of a "miracle weapon," kept from
being used vigorously and in time only by the pusillanimity and possibly even
Anglophilia of that chronic failure and sob sister, Chancellor Bethmann
Hollweg. It was this myth much more than the tohubohu about war aims and
annexations that undermined the political truce of 1914, disrupted the
nation's fighting morale, and spread distrust of its leadership.

Perhaps the oddest thing was that once launched on its political career this myth lashed back on the military. First to have its clear-headed technical vision clouded was the admiralty, drawing the whole naval officer corps down after it. Later on, after the beginning of the year 1916, even that clear-headed realist, Falkenhayn, was blinded. In retrospect it is utterly baffling that technically trained naval officers should have ever viewed so hazardous and indeed almost frivolous an undertaking as submarine warfare on merchant shipping as a warranty of victory in the struggle against British world power—or at least that they should have assessed its chances of success as sufficiently high to justify risking war with America.

It was Commander Bauer, in charge of the German submarine force, who took the first step, on October 8, 1914, with a request that the newly created British mine fields blocking the Channel be answered by unlimited submarine warfare on merchant shipping. The request met with serious objections, first at fleet headquarters, and then even more so within the admiralty itself. There was doubt that such a campaign would work sufficiently well, and reluctance to commit so gross a breach of international law. Surprisingly, these reservations gave way to confidence in success within a matter of weeks, even though the number of German submarines suitable and available for operations in British coastal waters was ludicrously small.[1] Germany then possessed no more than twenty-one U-boats, of which twelve were obsolescent, fueled with kerosene rather than diesel oil, and incapable of long-range operation. By Bauer's own calculations, only one-third of the remainder, i.e., a grand total of three submersibles, could be put into action at the same time. The others were either in the dockyard for repairs or en route to or from the scene.

Late in December Bauer submitted a plan for blockading Britain, a plan that contemplated no more than four blockade stations: on the east coast, the eastern part of the Channel, the Bristol Channel, and the Irish Sea—each permanently manned by a single submarine, with extended breaks during inclement weather. In the view of Chief of the Admiralty Staff Pohl, while this would not actually starve out Britain, it should incline the country toward peace in a very short time![2] That view, however, was initially based, in curious ignorance of the facts, on seven rather than four blockade stations, on the premise that half of the twenty-unit U-boat strength could be in active service at a given time.

As it turned out, even Bauer's plan soon proved far too optimistic. The bulk of the imports on which the British economy really depended entered the western rather than the eastern ports. Ever since April 1915, however, German U-boats could no longer be dispatched through the Channel, which had been made virtually impenetrable to them by minefields, nets, submarine traps, and surveillance vessels. They could reach the Irish Sea only by sailing around Scotland and the Orkney Islands, virtually doubling the length of the approach, to 1,400 nautical miles. Since these vessels could scarcely make twenty knots, and only a little more than ten when submerged, while their range was limited, they had to spend so much time coming and going, even in favorable weather free of storms and fog, that they could spend only a few days on station.[3]

The western approach to the Channel with its ports had become virtually inaccessible, and after some modest initial successes, all efforts to sink British troop transports en route to France failed. Similar failures attended attempts to harass the big British colliers en route to France, although a special flotilla of small boats, the so-called Channel Fleas, was stationed along the Flemish coast. The most irksome effect of the lengthened approach was that only one out of every five German U-boats could be in action at a given time, while the other four were either en route or in drydock, repairs often dragging on over many months, on account of the high rate of attrition.

During the first two years of the war, this situation did not materially change. By October 1915 combat losses—no fewer than twelve units! —and the establishment of additional squadrons in the Mediterranean and Baltic had reduced the number of big U-boats available for use against Britain to eight. By February 1915 this figure had again risen to twelve and by April to seventeen.[4] The German admiralty itself had said in January 1915 that at least six to seven U-boats would be necessary to blockade the British west coast alone. By March 1916 it turned out that only two to three units could be committed simultaneously on this sea front.[5]

The British west coast was 600 nautical miles long, the whole coast 1,700 miles; and on a single day in September 1914 no fewer than 100 steamers were observed to enter or leave the Firth of Forth.[6] Sea traffic on the west coast was naturally far heavier; hence it was quite unrealistic to speak of an effective blockade—indeed, not even the main ports could be really barred. The German navy was well aware of this, but counted on the shock effect on neutral shipping of sudden sinkings. It told the Chancellor that no serious protest by the neutrals was to be anticipated, if only for the reason that after the first few sinkings without warning, neutral shipping would entirely shun the British coast.[7]

This proved as illusory as, for example, the hope that sporadic Zeppelin bombing raids on London would engender war-weariness in Britain, when in actual fact they merely aroused indignation, effectively fed fuel to enemy propaganda, and occasioned heavy German losses without any military gain. The illusion that air raids on civilian populations at the level of brute terror can lead to political upheaval was, of course, even more thoroughly exploded on both sides during the Second World War.

The sinking without warning of commercial and passenger shipping by submarine torpedoes thus becomes the first symptom of the degeneration of modern war into total war, in which a steadily increasing role was to be played by terror weapons meant for destroying the enemy economy and demoralizing the enemy nation's fighting spirit. The use of such weapons is always a sign that there is not enough power to destroy the enemy's military forces. The German navy resorted to submarine warfare on merchant shipping because its battleships and armored cruisers were capable only of guarding the coast of Germany and keeping the Baltic open, not of destroying British sea power. The British had even earlier begun to bar Germany from world trade, because the British land forces too were incapable of precipitating a decision. They did this in violation of international law, i.e., the London declaration of maritime law of 1909 (which they had never ratified); and in the course of time, despite all the protests of the neutrals, their action was elaborated into a complete trade and hunger blockade, with surveillance of all sea traffic destined for Germany, even by way of neutral ports. Hence the German campaign against merchant shipping had ample legal justification, as a reprisal.[8] Britain's outright blockade of the entire North Sea, which it declared to be a theater of war, was as much an act of force as Germany's declaring British coastal waters a war zone.[9] Yet legalistic arguments did not alter the fact that war on merchant shipping was viewed throughout the world as atrocious and inhuman and brought the Germans the reputation of being truly barbaric militarists. This was true even among well-meaning neutrals like the Scandinavians and the Dutch, who were at first reluctant to believe that Germany could be seriously contemplating such acts of violence.[10]

The German retort that the deliberate starving of a nation by total blockade was, if anything, even more inhuman had some effect; nor was there from the very outset any dearth of protests against the blockade, though they were virtually without effect. Indeed, the blockade not only limited neutral maritime commerce but subjected the neutral nations to more and more irksome and humiliating British control measures.[11] But the German argument was not as effective as it might have been, for despite these measures food imports to Germany from the continental neutrals, especially Holland and Scandinavia, never entirely ceased. Until 1916 they actually increased considerably over the final peace years, in certain categories like meat, butter, cheese, salt herring, and eggs, sometimes to several times the prewar volume. These increases were at the expense of Britain, whose imports from those countries declined in proportion. These sources of German food imports did not begin to dry up until late 1916.[12]

Even less of an impression was made by the second German argument— that the Germans, to stand any chance of surviving the bloody battles in France, had to cut the unending stream of arms shipments from America to Britain. Initially, at least, these deliveries were not very voluminous, because the United States had no large-scale war industry.[13] It was widely known, moreover, that the most important shipments, of troops and arms to France, were so well protected that they were virtually immune to submarine attack.

As for the third German contention, it was almost beyond argument. Under the traditional law of sea war, merchant ships could be stopped and searched, and "contraband" could be seized. The ships might be required to enter port and could be sunk only as a last resort and after the attacking naval vessel had taken the crew and passengers aboard. These provisions dated back to an era that knew only the large heavily armed cruiser as the effective unit in war on ocean-borne commerce. Light and vulnerable submersibles could obey them only at great risk, if at all.[14] That was not absolutely true. It was shown in practice that even submarines could conduct effective war on merchant shipping by the rules of what was called cruiser warfare—except that the ships would always be sunk without prior search, though only after being hailed and stopped—by voice or warning shots. The crew must be permitted to take to the lifeboats, which, of course, would save their lives only if the sea were calm and visibility at least fair.

Despite constant reiteration by the German admiralty and fleet command that effective submarine warfare meant unrestricted sinkings by means of torpedo, U-boat commanders used this method far less frequently than traditional cruiser methods. This was for the simple reason that they usually could not carry more than six or seven torpedoes, at most ten. Periscope marksmanship, moreover, was highly inaccurate, especially in heavy seas, the average rate of misses being 58 percent![15] Besides, U-boats under water were often far too slow to approach their targets in time.

By late 1916, cruiser-type sinkings accounted for no less than 400,000 tons a week. German admiralty perspectives at this time did not go beyond raising this figure by about one-half, to something like 600,000 tons, by unleashing unrestricted submarine warfare.[16] It was for the sake of this increase—later, it is true, substantially exceeded for some months—that Germany provoked war with America in 1917.

It is only against the background of these hard technical facts that a clear and accurate picture can be drawn of the conflict between government and navy on the issue of submarine warfare. The facts were strictly withheld from the public, as military secrets, especially the small number of submarines in action, with the result that the most fantastic ideas circulated. Even the Chancellor and the foreign ministry were given only very sketchy information. In February 1916 Bethmann Hollweg asked the admiralty staff to give him precise figures on the number of large U-boats that were available for action against Britain, both immediately and later on. The admiralty refused outright to provide this information on the ground that it alone was responsible for the technical adequacy of the new weapon and its "full success against Britain." It took an extended and stubbornly conducted written exchange to persuade the admiralty to present the Chancellor personally with certain data, which greatly dismayed him, despite their strongly optimistic bias.[17]

A representative of the *Reichsmarineamt* (naval office) made statements to the federal council at the time that were quite evidently calculated to arouse exaggerated hopes within the government. Without giving any breakdown, he spoke of 203 submarines, "large and small, available for action, under construction, and being tested." The number "available for action" was given as fifty-four. Only direct questioning by the Chancellor elicited the fact that some of the fifty-four units, "large and small," were being used for training purposes. That only two or three were stationed off the west coast of Britain was studiously concealed.[18]

The German navy had myriad other opportunities to confuse the Reichstag deputies—to say nothing of the press—and nourish exaggerated hopes, by lumping together units, whether large or small, that had only just been ordered, with others that were on test or in drydock, or being used for training purposes, or intended for other maritime stations, or reserved as auxiliaries for the armored fleet, or built as torpedo carriers or minelayers. None was allowed to know that every large U-boat was two years abuilding, while the trial period took another quarter-year.[19]

Thus it was not easy even for the responsible political leaders to gain a clear picture of the potential threat to merchant ships from submarines, which had never been tested in war prior to 1914. Reality merged into wishful thought. The surprise successes of the U-9 and U-21 against four ancient and ill-guarded British cruisers in September 1914 created a storm of enthusiasm for the "miracle weapon." But such successes were far between and served to whet the navy's appetite for further and greater successes against merchant ships. As early as October individual U-boat commanders proceeded to sink merchant ships on their own, when they were unable to find any enemy warships—however they still stuck to the rules of cruiser warfare.

By early November Admiral Pohl had overcome all his scruples and pressed for neutrals. What gave him a pretext in international law as well as the outward occasion was the British declaration that the entire North Sea was a war area. But behind it all there was also the restless military ambition of a naval officer whom Tirpitz was forever reproaching with the inactivity of the great battle fleet.

It was Tirpitz's interview with Wiegand, already mentioned in Chapter 1, that poured more oil on the fire when it was published in late December. Thenceforth the question of submarine warfare was no longer a naval problem for the experts to judge, but a political issue of the first order, with everyone having his say. A "U-boat movement" quickly came into being, far transcending annexationist circles and unleashing even stronger passions. Again the academic superpatriots were in the forefront with plans and petitions to the Chancellor and the navy on how to starve Britain into submission. Some of the most renowned names at the University of Berlin were among them.[20]

Bethmann Hollweg's initial reaction to the admiralty demand late in November was concern over the possible indignant response of the neutral nations, which would serve only to worsen Germany's military and economic situation so long as it had not yet achieved a clear victory on the continent. This was detailed in an official reply by the foreign ministry of December 27, which took considerable care to avoid the impression that consideration of Britain or of international law played any part in the Chancellor's decision.[21] It did say cautiously that the torpedoing of neutral vessels was not entirely compatible with generally accepted international law, but it was also at pains to state in conclusion that it was considerations of military and political opportunity that determined the government's attitude. For that reason, U-boat warfare was not roundly rejected but only postponed until such a time as the war on the mainland was going better for Germany, and the intervention of such neutrals as Italy and Rumania had become less probable.

We see again that the Chancellor, as in July 1914, was in danger of being run into the ground by the impatient military men, in whom he put far too much trust, and of being diverted from his chosen course by public opinion. Throughout January he managed to withstand Pohl's rising importunities, but at a chancellery meeting on February 1, 1915, in which Interior Minister Delbrück, Under Secretary Zimmerman, and General Falkenhayn took part, he yielded at last. There is only a sketchy record of this fateful talk, but the evidence is clear that Bethmann Hollweg was at the time under unusually heavy pressure from public opinion.

Returning to Berlin from headquarters, he found everyone in public life swept up by enthusiasm for the miracle weapon, including many Reichstag deputies. What was worse, he heard malicious rumors to the effect that he, the Chancellor, was bringing on Germany's downfall, because he was preventing vigorous action, from Anglophile prejudice. Yet as he admits in his memoirs, the crucial element in his decisions was not the shock of this experience but the impression of absolute confidence made on him by the German navy.

He must have asked himself more than once whether he, the man of everlasting doubt and hesitation, might not be standing in the way of an outstanding opportunity for victory. Apparently it was Admiral Pohl who was chiefly responsibile for persuading him that the risk of certain neutral nations entering the war against Germany was not as great as Bethmann Hollweg believed it to be. If they were told in advance that their merchant ships would be in danger of being sunk without warning in British coastal waters, they would be deterred—certainly this would be true, once they had lost the first ship!

After all, they had allowed themselves to be intimidated by the British declaration that the North Sea was a war zone—even though this was little more than a statement on paper. According to German admiralty intelligence—actually of highly dubious value—the Scandinavian countries were anticipating U-boat warfare with something akin to impatience. Thus neutral maritime trade with Britain would cease and the island would be virtually blockaded. If Germany struck immediately, before the wheat crop from Argentina could reach Britain, that country's grain reserves would be exhausted within six weeks. Any further delay would be fatal.

When Bethmann Hollweg objected that surely a fleet of twenty U-boats was insufficient, Pohl replied smartly that the navy had made every technical preparation and was certain of success. The Chancellor probably could not conceive of the possibility that this might merely be a frivolous boast. In any event, he did not see through the Navy's game, especially since the admiral failed to tell him that he himself did not know how small would be the number of U-boats that could be in action at a given time.

Bethmann Hollweg had no clear idea of the practical problems involved in a war on merchant shipping; and he failed to inquire what would happen if neutral vessels continued to make for Britain, and to take precautions against that eventuality. And what would happen if British vessels sailed under neutral flags, or if neutral crews and neutral goods were carried in British bottoms? And how could one distinguish between the proper use of flags and their misuse, etc.? When Bethmann Hollweg expressed concern for the food supply for the Belgian people, which was being maintained by imports from America, Pohl seems to have satisfactorily reassured him that the seaway around Scotland and through the North Sea would remain open to the Americans.[22]

Falkenhayn's qualms too were stilled when Pohl boldly assured him that the U-boats would seriously hamper enemy troop transports across the Channel. Bethmann Hollweg delayed his approval of an appropriate proclamation until the next morning, and the text was then agreed on by the admiralty and the foreign ministry. It declared the waters clear around Great Britain and Ireland, including the entire Channel, to be a war area, in which after February 18, 1915, all enemy merchant ships would be sunk, no responsibility being assumed for the lives of crews and passengers. It further warned neutral shipping of the risk incurred in those waters, by virtue of accident or misidentification. A foreign ministry opinion from the pen of Privy Councilor Kriege simultaneously sought to justify the whole action under international law as a reprisal measure.

None of those responsible for it could have dreamed at the time of the ultimately disastrous consequences this step was to bring. Yet high German naval officers were quite well aware that it was taken precipitately. Admiral von Müller, chief of the naval cabinet and ordinarily Bethmann Hollweg's loyal ally, thought that the Chancellor's sudden change of heart—of which he learned only subsequently—was sad proof of his inadequacy.[23] He was furious that Pohl's ambition should have resulted in such haste, and he was almost certainly correct in his assumption that Pohl, whose term as chief of the admiralty ended on February 1, 1915, when he was appointed to head the fleet, wanted to leave office with credit for having pushed through the U-boat campaign.

For that reason Pohl had simply confronted his successor, Admiral Bachmann, with a fait accompli. Bachmann was by no means in agreement but had grave doubts of the wisdom of mounting a great blockade with so few boats and without any finished naval bases in Flanders or elsewhere. The severest critic turned out to be Tirpitz, Pohl's rival and opponent, who felt he had been ignored in the crucial consultations. In both official and confidential letters he had always expressed doubts of whether the number of vessels and the state of preparedness were sufficient to strike at this time.

But this had not kept Tirpitz from agitating in public with every resource at his command. Indeed, on January 27, 1915, he used the same arguments on the Chancellor, in an attempt to allay his worries about the neutral nations, that Pohl advanced a few days later.[24] As the only witness present, moreover, he offered not a word of opposition when Pohl, on a yacht trip on February 4, 1915, in the harbor of Wilhelmshaven, abruptly tackled the Kaiser with the Bethmann-approved proclamation, exacting the monarch's signature virtually without anything resembling consultation. Tirpitz's subsequent criticism of Pohl served him as an alibi, but this did not keep him from making common cause with Bachmann in demanding that the war on merchant shipping, once decided on, be conducted in the most extreme form, and in bitterly opposing any relaxation.

There was soon serious occasion to reexamine the validity of the decision of February 1. First of all Admiral Pohl, now heading the fleet, had to note and report to his successor, Bachmann, that not nearly as many submersibles were available as he himself had assumed when he issued his directive as chief of the admiralty staff on February 2. The heavy blow with which he had planned to open the campaign—the blow that was to frighten the neutrals— could not be struck at all; and immediately, even before the new campaign had begun, a storm of neutral protests rained down on Berlin from all sides, including Scandinavia, but most sharply of all from Washington. The note transmitted by the American ambassador on February 12 was formally polite but very strongly worded, indeed tantamount to an ultimatum. The United

States government, it said, would hold the German government strictly accountable for any loss of American lives and property.

All this did not look as though the neutrals would allow themselves to be deterred from trading with Britain. Instead, what now loomed was a break with the United States. So far this risk had not bulked large in the German deliberations, for Wilson was firmly believed to be a man of peace; and at this juncture, when Italy's neutrality was being so hotly contested, the risk of a naval conflict with that country was scarcely less acute. Bethmann Hollweg was in a serious quandary. The grandiose proclamation of a naval blockade around Britain could no longer be withdrawn, unless the German government were prepared to forfeit the last shred of prestige abroad and throw away its authority at home. The Chancellor essayed a compromise. The German foreign ministry drafted a reply promising that ships under neutral flags would not be troubled further, if they could be identified as neutral and if they carried no contraband. The German government further guaranteed that merchant ships flying the American flag would not be attacked at all for the time being—but only in the firm expectation that there would be no further misuse of that flag by British ships.

This was patently a half-measure. In practice there was no guarantee that the American flag could always be unmistakably identified by periscope, and there was even less certainty that there would be an end to the misuse of national flags. On the contrary, all vessels nearing the British coast might well hoist the American flag, though the German navy's view of this risk was soon to be proved exaggerated. Actually, during the early war years most American cargoes were shipped in British bottoms, since the American merchant fleet still lagged far behind. Wilson's threatening note, however, spoke not merely of ships but of American lives and property; and it was loss of American lives that was soon to give rise to severe conflict. Clearly it was very difficult for Germany to extricate itself from the adventure in which it had become embroiled on erroneous premises.

Nor did the admirals want such a thing at all. They had counted on initially including isolated neutral vessels among their sinkings, indeed had wished for such an eventuality,[25] expecting that it would exert a wholesome shock effect. They were quite unwilling to abandon the venture, on the contrary, were more determined than ever to see it through with a will, despite the secret doubts we know they harbored concerning the adequacy of their arms resources. On the other hand, everyone at supreme headquarters realized that a breach with America and Italy at this juncture, when the great eastern campaign was in preparation, would have incalculable consequences, affecting even the attitude of Turkey and the Balkan countries.

Falkenhayn was particularly sensitive to these dangers and wished to avoid any possibility of a break with the United States. As for the Kaiser, he loathed the idea of warfare against merchant ships, with the accompanying drownings of civilians. It violated the code of chivalry and was incompatible with traditional Prussian concepts of honor. He inveighed against Pohl, claiming that the admiral had taken him unawares with the proclamation of February 4. Nor did the chief of the naval cabinet share Pohl's misconceptions, and Bethmann Hollweg therefore had firm backing in his stand against the naval activists.

At Falkenhayn's suggestion, Bachmann and Tirpitz were asked to report by wire to the Kaiser, then at Lötzen, "in what measure they were prepared to guarantee that Britain would be forced into a conciliatory attitude within six weeks after the start of the new campaign against merchant shipping"—which was the time limit Pohl had always claimed. In their reply, a product of extreme cunning, the two naval men said they were convinced that this time limit would apply, "provided it were possible to use every available power resource with the greatest vigor from the very outset." What "power resources" were meant—possibly the great battleships? —and what was meant by a "conciliatory attitude" on the part of Britain—these questions remained open. Tirpitz subsequently interpreted the latter as a return to the principles of the London declaration on maritime law.

The Kaiser thought the reply full of ifs and buts. The admirals nevertheless succeeded in having the answering note to Wilson, dispatched on February 16, couched in rather sharper terms. It now no longer mentioned a "guarantee" by the German government of the safety of American vessels. Instead there was merely an assurance, already included in the foreign ministry report of February 4, that U-boat commanders were being instructed "to avoid forcible action against American merchant ships, insofar as these were identifiable as such." There was a bare hint at the end that Germany would gladly forego the new style of war on merchant shipping, provided Britain were ready to abide by the London declaration and make possible the legitimate importation of food and raw material into Germany.[26]

This was completely beyond attainment. As Prime Minister Asquith put it in the House of Commons on March 1, 1915, "We would not dream of letting our efforts [to maintain dominion of the seas] be strangled in a web of legal technicalities."[27] His Majesty's government also immediately rejected a mediation proposal the United States government transmitted to London and Berlin simultaneously on February 20. The proposal called for a cessation of the new German campaign against merchant shipping and of offensive minelaying, in return for which the British would permit food imports to Germany, their distribution to be supervised by American agencies.

The German foreign ministry heaved a great sigh of relief. But Tirpitz and his faithful henchman Bachmann displayed a typically militaristic response. They opposed acceptance as a "sign of weakness." In return for German renunciation of unlimited submarine and mine warfare, they called for totally unacceptable counterdemands, such as release of interned German merchant ships to bring in food under neutral flags. There were agitated scenes between them and the political leaders at a session presided over by the Kaiser, during which Tirpitz, by Müller's testimony, was extremely tactless and rambunctious.

A remarkable feature of this meeting is that the Kaiser, perhaps impressed by Tirpitz's vehement opposition, for the first time showed signs of wavering. The Chancellor, he said, would have to accept the fact that the entire German nation was clamoring for the U-boat campaign. In the end, however, he took Admiral von Müller's advice and decided in favor of Bethmann Hollweg. The American note was answered affirmatively, though in addition to food a safe-conduct was demanded for animal feeds and industrial raw materials.[28]

In the event, all the tumult was fruitless, for Britain was unwilling to allow dominion of the seas to be wrested from its hands so easily. London refused the offer. There had been so much pulling and hauling on the German side in the meantime, however, that the time limit of February 18 had passed without the solemnly proclaimed campaign being initiated. The admiralty staff was able to issue combat orders only on February 20, for the time being limited to the North Sea and the English Channel, where the Germans thought they were reasonably safe from encountering American and Italian vessels. Furthermore, a safety zone was staked out for sea transports from the Scandinavian countries to Britain, within which ships under neutral flags were on no account to be attacked. Two days later the western coastal waters were also declared open for attack, though the German submarine commanders were sternly admonished to exercise the greatest caution in respect of American and Italian ships. For purposes of recognizing the American passenger liners that plied these waters, pictures and sailing schedules were circulated among the U-boat men. In addition, they were assigned escorts drawn from experienced merchant officers of the North German Lloyd and the Hamburg-American Line.

The Chancellor had clearly prevailed over the naval command in the essentials of his policy. He may have believed, or hoped, that the great venture had now been rendered comparatively harmless. This was soon shown to be a grave miscalculation. At the same time, the admirals' hopes for a stunning initial success that would impress the whole world promptly turned to water. As was to be expected, the merchant tonnage sunk by the few U-boats cruising around Britain remained very modest. Five thousand ships entered and departed British ports during the month of March, and of these only twenty-one were sunk. Neutral shippers abandoned their initial attitude of watchful waiting, and their crews went back into service, at bonus pay.

The U-boat danger did not seem all that great, especially since, for reasons already mentioned, sinkings without prior warnings were the exception in practice rather than the rule, while there proved to be ample scope for evading the submersibles or destroying them. In a military as well as an economic sense, virtually nothing was achieved. The political effect, on the other hand, was all the greater—and it was negative all the way.

The campaign did immediately provide the British government with the occasion and pretext for a serious reprisal measure. Early in March announcement was made of a tightening of the maritime blockade under which German exports as well as imports were to be completely cut off. As for the neutral nations, they were thrown into the greatest agitation when, in the very first week of the campaign, some neutral vessels were sunk without prior warning. Not very many were involved—one each from Norway, Holland, Greece, and Sweden—but the effect was indignant protest rather than deterrence; and it took considerable effort and sizable indemnities to assuage the trouble. There was one crisis after another within the German foreign ministry. These constantly intensifying European tensions, at the very time of the Herculean struggle to keep Italy and Rumania neutral, were so intolerable to the Chancellor that he requested the admiralty on May 6 in sharp words to "prevent further attacks by our U-boats on neutral vessels at any cost, in accordance with the understanding reached." Bachmann gave a most insolent reply—he was unaware of any such understanding, and "any further limitation on U-boat attacks would be tantamount to a cessation of the whole campaign."

This answer arrived just after the greatest maritime disaster of the war had occurred—one that was to have the most far-reaching political consequences. On May 7, south of Ireland, a German U-boat had sunk the huge British passenger liner *Lusitania,* pride of the Cunard Line, without warning. The ship carried 1,257 passengers, including 440 women and 129 children, and a crew of 702. She sank within twenty minutes, carrying 1,198 people down with her, including 120 American citizens. The occurrence of this terrible event at the very beginning of the German U-boat campaign constituted beyond doubt a misfortune that years of German diplomatic effort were never able to undo. It seems almost beyond belief today that the German public failed to comprehend this in the least. On the contrary, the sinking was celebrated—quite widely even in the leftist press—as a great German U-boat triumph.[29]

The wave of U-boat mania and Anglophobia was still rising; and as always, the modern mass media with their thoughtless lack of vision had their eyes fixed solely on the success of the day.[30] The diplomatic consequences of the disaster, moreover, were slow to develop to their full strength. President

Wilson's first *Lusitania* note of May 15, made public immediately, did carry a sweeping protest against the sinking of peaceful merchant ships without prior warning and sharply insisted on the right of American citizens to travel freely throughout the world; but it studiously avoided a threatening tone.

It demanded that the act of the U-boat captain be condemned; and this, of course, the Kaiser could not possibly do, since the *Lusitania* was a British— i.e., an enemy—rather than a neutral vessel, and the German captain, in sinking her, had not acted counter to his instructions. Not only had he not been forbidden to sink passenger ships, but on the contrary, a directive from Bachmann had actually enjoined him to do so, since it was bound to make the greatest impression of all.[31] The German navy, in other words, was eager for the shock effect rather than shrinking from it, though from a military viewpoint the sinking of passenger vessels made no sense unless they transported troops or also carried a cargo of munitions—as, incidentally, was established later on in the case of the *Lusitania.*[32]

These circumstances doomed any understanding over the *Lusitania* case from the outset, especially if further passenger ships were to be sunk during the negotiations. Bethmann Hollweg realized that he must prevent this at all costs. Yet how could he prevail when he did not succeed in halting even the sinkings of neutral freighters, which continued throughout the month of May and included even American vessels? Late in the month Bethmann Hollweg decided to appeal for Falkenhayn's help. At headquarters in Pless, he had the foreign ministry representative, von Treutler, make representations to Falkenhayn to the effect that the United States was close to breaking off relations with Germany. If America were to join the enemy camp, there would be consequences among the European neutrals, and there was a chance that Holland not only would not oppose but would actually join a transit of enemy forces with the purpose of rolling up Germany's western front from the back.

This cleverly contrived warning had the intended effect—even though it doubtless exaggerated the danger. Falkenhayn, however, insisted that Tirpitz and Bachmann must be given a chance to state their views to the Kaiser and had them summoned to Pless by wire. The audience took place the very next day, May 31, Falkenhayn joining the Chancellor in demanding that the U-boat campaign be waged in such a way as not to give rise to political conflict. The admirals said that in that case there was no alternative to ending the whole campaign, which they well knew to be impossible, in the light of German public opinion. The wavering Kaiser agreed and said that the Chancellor would have to assume responsibility for such a cessation.

Unfortunately, the Chancellor himself was not present; but once again, as on February 28, when the American mediation proposal was under discussion, Cabinet Chief von Müller saved the day. He prevailed with a proposal that Bachmann be charged to work out a new directive to the U-boat commanders, together with the Chancellor. This was done the following day in Berlin. The U-boat captains were instructed to attack only if they were absolutely certain that the target was an enemy ship. In case of doubt, they must sooner let an enemy merchant ship pass than sink a neutral vessel.

The Kaiser's verdict was ambiguously worded, but Treutler and von Müller interpreted it to mean that attacks on large passenger liners, whether enemy or neutral, would henceforth have to cease. In a talk with Bachmann in Berlin on June 2, the Chancellor sought to confirm this, only to encounter sharp opposition from the chiefs of both the admiralty staff and the high seas fleet. Bethmann Hollweg refused to argue the point further with the admirals and instead appealed directly to the Kaiser through Treutler.

The Kaiser realized that further sinkings of liners would be intolerable, at least during the diplomatic exchanges over the *Lusitania* case; and on June 6, over the head of the naval command, he issued the appropriate order to Bachmann, as drafted by Müller.[33] Tirpitz and his henchman in turn petitioned the Kaiser directly to revoke the order, using arguments characteristic of their militarist approach. Not only would the order mean virtually foregoing the whole U-boat campaign, but since it could scarcely be kept secret, it would be interpreted as an apology for the sinking of the *Lusitania.* Germany's enemies, the neutral nations, the German people, and the German navy could only interpret this as a dangerous sign of weakness.

The whole question of military prestige was here placed above political considerations, no matter how compelling. At the same time there was the hint of a threat to make the order public—which would have been an easy thing to do for Tirpitz with his manifold resources. The final sentence of the petition, moreover, threatened the resignation of the two admirals. They were not in a position to assume responsibility for the Kaiser's order, they said. The resignation of the universally admired Grand Admiral Tirpitz would have been calculated like nothing else to bring to the boiling point public agitation over the U-boat question and against the political leadership—including not least the Kaiser himself.

The incident is highly significant for the development of German militarism in the war. For these high naval officers their naval undertaking had become an end in itself, a pure matter of prestige. The statesmen would have to accept this rather than deciding on their own what was needed.[34] The admirals laid claim to their own political responsibility and had the audacity to put their resignations to the sovereign in the form of an ultimatum, in the manner of cabinet ministers. It was a first in the history of the Prusso-German officer corps—but the Kaiser was to see many repetitions of it in the course of the war.

On this occasion his reaction was one of indignation. His reply was unmistakably sharp: "My order stands, and shall hold the chief of the admiralty and other military superiors to strict account for putting it into effect and maintaining its secrecy. Whatever political consequences there may be are the Chancellor's responsibility." Factually, the accuracy of this statement is beyond question, though it does give a hint that the Kaiser himself was unwilling to carry that responsibility. When Tirpitz and Bachmann next offered their resignations, these were brusquely rejected. The Kaiser's marginal notes on both their letters show how strongly he reacted to the unprecedented character of the incident: "No! At a time like this, this is a felony. ... These gentlemen must obey and stay. This is a regular military plot! Tirpitz is behind it! "

Outwardly, however, there was no sign of German readiness to moderate U-boat warfare. Germany's answering note to America of May 28, drafted in full agreement between government and navy, contained not a word along such lines, but on the contrary sought to justify the sinking of the liner on the grounds that it had been armed as an auxiliary cruiser and was transporting Canadian troops (later shown to be untrue). The *Lusitania* was further charged with carrying a cargo of arms and, like all British ships, had allegedly been instructed to ram U-boats. This in turn elicited a refutation from the other side, and thus the exchange of notes continued through the summer, always under the full glare of publicity. Rather than a true exchange of views, this was at bottom no more than a propaganda skirmish, conducted for its political effect on world opinion. To perceive the true political forces and purposes behind it, we must first take a look at the situation of the United States and the attitude of Wilson and his advisers.

## Part 2

# The Problem of American Neutrality and the Submarine Campaign in the Summer and Fall of 1915

ONE OF THE STAPLES of German propaganda on behalf of the submarine campaign was to counter American protests with charges of moral hypocrisy—i.e., bias on the side of Germany's enemies motivated by massive economic interest—as well as of dogmatic pacifism. These charges were directed primarily at President Wilson, whom many Germans even today regard as a hypocrite and unworldly doctrinaire, if not an outright deceiver. This continuing hatred of Wilson is based also on the exaggerated hopes the Germans pinned to his mediation as the debacle of 1918 approached, hopes that were to be bitterly disappointed at Versailles.

All war propaganda, of course, uses stereotypes; but in America too

Wilson's memory was tarnished by American revisionist criticism of shattered illusions and insincere neutrality.[35] Not until the last few decades have American historians, by their immense research and profuse publications, made it possible to tell the true charges from the false or exaggerated ones with any precision, to distinguish achievement from failure, and to gain deeper insight into the historical backgrounds and motivations of United States policy under Wilson.

As is true of all questions of grand policy, it has become abundantly clear that here too the actions of responsible statesmen were governed by the real interests of their country—what is called *raison d'état*—rather than by their personal inclinations, and even more by force of circumstance, from which statesmen can seldom escape to anything but a limited degree. In matters of foreign policy the American president was then and still is today much more a law unto himself—especially in time of crisis—than most of the heads of government in Europe; but his power rests entirely on favorable public opinion at home and on the success of his party.

Thus the American president is in particularly large measure a reflector of public opinion, with all its prejudices, and he must avoid anything that would alienate him from the people and harm his party.[36] Woodrow Wilson was a highly self-willed man, sensitive, reared on puritanical principles, and inclined to autocratic airs. He was slow and conscientious in his thoughts and decisions, and for these reasons alone, he was given to solitary decision taking, often withdrawing from the world to his study for days at a time and drafting his statements himself on the typewriter. Yet his policies did not at all express merely his personal whims but were always governed by the moods and interests of his country. Even his pacifist ideology, which seemed so dogmatic and unrealistic to most Europeans, was American to the core, ultimately the upshot of the centuries-old special situation of the American continent, beyond the quarrels of the European powers.

Nevertheless, once America's entry into the First World War was settled, Wilson understood much sooner than most of his fellow countrymen that the era of isolationism was over for good. He proclaimed it to be America's mission to secure peace everlasting, and this was to be the ideology on which America's new role as a leading world power was to be based. It was a thrust into the unknown and unfamiliar, and in the end American public opinion deserted him over it.

It was quite understandable that the Germans should have charged from the outset that Wilson's policy was not really one of neutrality, mentioning with deep resentment the arms shipments that passed continually from the United States to Britain and France. This was, in fact, held up to the American ambassador, Gerard, at his every encounter with German officials. The facts that international law did not prohibit such shipments and that

German arms firms had made a great deal of money from such shipments in earlier wars did not lessen the dangers of this trade to Germany. The American State Department argued on legal grounds that the United States would not be observing neutrality if it refused such shipments to the British, who were inadequately armed, in contrast to the well-armed Germans; but this was anything but convincing to the Germans.

It is well-established today, nevertheless, that Wilson made serious efforts to preserve his country's neutrality without formally violating international law—not without many inner qualms and much struggle with his advisers and associates. Indeed, Wilson earnestly strove to keep his country out of the war, in keeping with its isolationist traditions. He tenaciously fought for this goal as late as February and March 1917, after the Germans had proclaimed absolutely unlimited submarine warfare. Wilson by no means moved with flying colors from this traditional policy to the "new diplomacy" of an embattled world power. He did so only with grave reservations and after long inner struggle, moved by many motives, the ultimately crucial one being the U-boat campaign.

Inwardly, by political conviction, Wilson was, of course, never neutral but wholeheartedly on the side of Germany's enemies. Like the great majority of his fellow countrymen, Wilson had his roots in the British cultural tradition; and since the German invasion of Belgium, he was firmly convinced that the Entente was fighting for right and against wrong, for the principle of good against that of evil. As did all Americans of Anglo-Saxon origin, Wilson viewed German militarism as the embodiment of the principle of evil—that and imperial autocracy, of which the Western democracies, owing not least to the Kaiser's bluster, entertained highly exaggerated ideas. In Wilson's circle it was really only the radical pacifist William Jennings Bryan, Secretary of State until early June 1915, who was truly neutral in sentiment. All the others—his legal counsel, Lansing, soon to succeed Bryan, the American ambassador in London, Walter Hines Page, and above all Wilson's closest adviser, Colonel House—were ranged so unequivocally on Britain's side that they made Wilson appear a moderate and a true neutral. There is an overwhelming wealth of private and official testimony to that effect.

Familiarity with this evidence is essential to an assessment of the practical political importance of the early mediation efforts Wilson launched from August 1914 onward. It was his ambition to make peace in Europe as a neutral mediator, in order to enhance his country's political prestige; but at the outset he had no clear idea of the war aims of either the Entente or Germany, and only the vaguest notions of his own of what the future world peace should be like.

Directly after the outbreak of war, Wilson offered his good offices as a mediator to both sides, but this was scarcely more than a polite gesture, which not even House took seriously. On the urging of Bryan and other middlemen, these offers were repeated as early as September, this time through the ambassador in Berlin, Gerard, in rather amateurish form.[37] It goes without saying that the Allies were quite unwilling to allow anyone to meddle with their conduct of the war until there had been some decision at arms. For the time being, therefore, they rejected any American attempt at mediation.

By the same token, Berlin was extremely reticent, expecting little good from so markedly pro-English a mediator—at least until the last spark of hope for a favorable or at least tolerable issue of the war had been extinguished.[38] It is quite true, moreover, that at this time Wilson feared nothing more than a German victory, which in his view would change the course of American civilization, prevent any improvement in international morality, and compel the United States to transform itself into a militarist state.[39] His adviser, Colonel House, warned him of the Kaiser's alleged intention of extending German hegemony to South America. He held that the only proper attitude for the United States to take was to maintain absolute faith in Germany's ultimate defeat and not to be swerved by German military successes.[40] House, however, *was* afraid of a total victory by Russia, which might upset the balance. Thus the Bethmann government had some good reasons for shrinking from a general peace conference under American mediation and for preferring to stake its hopes on disrupting the Entente by separate peace negotiations.[41]

House undertook his own first major effort at mediation during a trip to Europe he made late in January 1915 at Wilson's behest. He had been encouraged by assurances from the German ambassador, Count Bernstorff, that the German government would respond favorably to his offer, though statements by Lord Grey in London struck a more reserved tone. According to his memoirs, Bernstorff, a diplomat of notably "Western" stamp, overestimated both House's peaceable orientation and his willingness to oppose British violations, as well as his understanding of Germany's critical situation.

House shared Wilson's repugnance to the war and his ambition to serve as a peacemaker, but he was in doubt from the outset whether the United States could take responsibility for bringing about peace before Germany was completely defeated and prepared to abandon its militarism.[42] He was concerned, furthermore, lest the Entente governments consider his peace mission a hostile act and he sought to reassure the Russian and French ambassadors on that score. All he was trying to do, he said, was to bring out before the world the "unreliable and traitorous aspects of Germany's false peace representations."

Grey was highly apprehensive of Colonel House's trip. Britain's allies regarded it as a German-incited maneuver to split up the Entente. Were Grey to enter into negotiations, he could not, without endangering Anglo-American friendship, reveal to the Americans the full scope of the aggressive war aims to which the Allies had in the meantime committed themselves. If he did so, he would also be undermining Allied cohesion.

He therefore assured the Allied governments that Britain would not dream of allowing the peace maneuver instigated by Bernstorff to swerve it from resolutely carrying on the war, nor would it be tempted into any agreements that fell short of satisfying all the Allies. These assurances were successful in gaining their approval. In the event the Central Powers were to signify their readiness for peace through a "negotiator with plenipotentiary powers," the Allies would listen and then consult on the peace terms that were to be "imposed" in direct negotiations with the enemy. In other words, the Entente would be graciously willing to accept the capitulation of Germany and its allies, proffered by Colonel House. There was no hint that there might be any bargaining.

To Grey's infinite surprise, his apprehensions were quickly shown to be quite baseless. The American mediator was not deterred from his trip by hints dropped to him by the British ambassador, Spring-Rice, concerning French and Russian expansionist ambitions. Nor did he, once he had arrived in London, display any opposition to far-reaching wishes by the British dominions for the acquisition of German colonies. Quite evidently he was far more concerned with gaining the trust and friendship of the British than with terminating a war he too viewed as a crusade by democracy against militarism.

House was reluctant to allow himself to become embroiled in discussions of concrete war aims and border changes, subjects on which he was willing to state only his own private opinions. While his principal, Wilson, did wish to make peace, he wanted on no account to be drawn into the conflicting ambitions and national interests of the European powers, nor did he wish to share responsibility, let alone give any guarantees for a peace settlement.

Thus the House-Grey talks about the peace problem ranged for the most part over the broad perspectives for the future. The British minister spoke of a world organization to secure a durable peace, which would have to be created after the war, lest there be a repetition, without prior mediation efforts at a European conference, of such hapless events as the precipitate war declarations of July 1914. This was the first stimulus for what was subsequently to become the League of Nations. House's immediate reaction was hesitant and evasive,[43] but Wilson was soon to take up the proposal with enthusiasm, making it one of the main goals of his policy.

House on his part unfolded plans for general disarmament and nationalization of the munitions industry, which was widely credited in America with warmongering. He also pressed for international agreements to insure "freedom of the seas," i.e., the inviolability of all maritime commerce even in wartime and the abolition of the right of prize on the high seas. He envisaged that Britain, thus freed of all concern for its imports—since its ports were so numerous and scattered as to make a total blockade impossible—would be able to forego "dominion of the seas" and restrict its navy to mere coastal defense, while Germany could abandon submarine warfare, if its maritime commerce were not impeded. The United States, on its part, would be relieved of all concern for the health of its rapidly growing overseas trade in wartime. In the end this grand design became Colonel House's main concern, though it was never made clear how and when "freedom of the seas" should come into existence. House contemplated a congress of all the powers, including the neutrals, presided over by Wilson and independent of any peace conference.[44]

Clearly, this American brought with him to Europe much goodwill for world pacification, but very little understanding of the depth and irreconcilability of prevailing differences. Grey was extremely shrewd in his negotiations, giving the impression of personally sympathizing with House's proposals, though he made no commitments whatever. He was even less willing than his fellow cabinet members to surrender in wartime the principle of Britannia ruling the waves in return for uncertain treaties, nor was he willing to lay aside the hunger blockade weapon against Germany. As for the German government, we have already noted that it declared on February 16, and again on February 28, that it was prepared to forego submarine warfare if Britain permitted imports of food and raw materials by sea. We have also seen that the German admirals, backed by public opinion, were opposed to this concession. They insisted that the U-boat was their only weapon for bringing Britain down.

For the rest, Berlin awaited House's arrival with the same apprehension that had prevailed in London. On the one hand, a falling-out with the Americans was feared, on the other hand that they might exact a curtailment of war aims that would arouse a storm of indignation throughout Germany. Hence Zimmermann, not unlike Grey, had thought it wise to warn House in advance, by writing him on February 3, when he was in London, that the German government would scarcely be able to defy public opinion by accepting a demand for payment of an indemnity to Belgium, which the Entente had put forward.[45]

Colonel House did postpone his journey to Berlin, counter to the urgent entreaties of the American ambassador in Berlin, Gerard;[46] but this was mainly on other grounds. Grey and the Allied governments had made representations to him that Germany's military situation must first have grown far worse, before one could begin to negotiate with it. When he did at last set out in mid-March, he realized full well—and was confirmed in this conviction by

French Foreign Minister Delcassé during a stopover in Paris—that he was quite unable to present to the Germans anything like an Entente offer to bargain. Not even the return and indemnification of Belgium would necessarily bring peace, nor would restoration of the status quo, against which the Russian and French ambassadors had protested even before House's departure from America.

In his talks with Zimmermann, Jagow, and Bethmann Hollweg, House therefore did not even bring up Belgium, but was content to submit his grand design for establishing "freedom of the seas," which naturally met with prompt, if theoretical approval.[47] For the rest, House was astute enough to discern the moderate and peaceable spirit of the Chancellor and his political associates, as well as the deep gulf between them and the military. What impressed him perhaps most was the constant danger these men faced from public opinion with its unrestrained war aim demands. The total impression he took back home with him concerned the great risks of arousing national ambitions in wartime, engendering exaggerated hopes of victory. This was bound to tie any government's hands. He now viewed France rather than Germany as the main obstacle to an understanding.[48]

In the meantime the U-boat campaign had destroyed all illusions of getting Britain and Germany to agree on a common formula for "freedom of the seas." The sinking of the *Lusitania* abruptly conjured up the danger of an open break between Germany and the United States.

The American public was thrown into an indescribable state of tumult. So great and universal was moral indignation that the former German colonial minister Dernburg, who had hitherto conducted pro-German propaganda in the American press with much skill and success, had to leave the country in a hurry, for none any longer dared publicly defend the German cause. Even the German-Americans were now effectively silenced. Wilson himself was publicly attacked as a coward, when an incautious phrase—to the effect that America was "too proud to fight"—aroused the suspicion that as a radical pacifist he might be capable of ignoring the national interest. He had no choice but to vent the general wrath by a very strongly worded protest to the German government.

But Wilson gave a great deal of thought to formulating this protest, on which he put in long hours with his advisers. In the end, he avoided any direct threat. All his associates, not merely the pacifist secretary of state Bryan, realized that for the time being a diplomatic break with Germany, let alone entry into the war, was simply not feasible; for despite all the moral ferment, the vast majority of Americans were very far from ready to abandon their traditional isolationism and meddle in the European war.

Public opinion, moreover, was far from settled with respect to the British too. Criticism of British methods of naval warfare, notably the hunger blockade and the arming of merchant ships, was by no means limited to Americans of German and Irish descent. Further west, indignation over the *Lusitania* incident steadily declined. There were many voices—later on joining for an attack in the Congress—that inveighed against Americans traveling on British ships in the war zone, let alone an arms-carrying ship, when the Germans had warned against precisely such a thing. This, they held, was merely calculated to draw the United States into unwanted military conflict.

Bryan too wanted to see such journeys prohibited or at least warnings issued against them. In this he did not prevail with Wilson, who regarded it as a cowardly surrender and who was always zealously intent on preserving his country's prestige—for which he preferred the moralizing term *honor.* In a curious but typically American way, national ambition and morally founded pacifism were blended in Wilson. Many critics, in America and elsewhere, are of the opinion even today[49] that Wilson's claim to unlimited freedom of travel for his fellow countrymen in wartime and in naval war zones constituted an expansion of neutral rights not justified under international law. But the president was never as much interested in legal questions as in moral and political ones. He regarded U-boat warfare, sinkings without warning at the cost of innocent lives, as downright inhuman and contemptible. He was quite unwilling to tolerate it and rejected all reference to the technical difficulties that faced submersibles and made it impossible for them to wage war on merchant shipping along traditional lines. His notes addressed to Berlin demanded that the new tactic be completely abandoned. It is true, of course, that there were political as well as moral motivations behind these demands.

The reason for Wilson's stubbornness and resolution was not that he did not shrink from armed conflict, but, on the contrary, because he feared that continuation of the U-boat campaign might someday constrain him to resort to arms, for the sake of America's commercial interests as well as of "honor." This becomes quite clear from the fact that only a few days after the *Lusitania* sinking, encouraged by messages from Colonel House in London, he repeated his previously unsuccessful offer to bring about an agreement under which the Germans would abandon their U-boat campaign, while the British would cease interfering with food imports to neutral ports in Europe.

For a moment it did seem as though the British government, under the impact of the sinkings and the first German gas attacks in Flanders, was more inclined toward such an agreement than it had been in February—this, at least, was how Colonel House interpreted Grey's cautious statements; but the effort once again remained fruitless. To the British, the danger to their own imports from U-boat warfare did not yet seem great enough to persuade them to give up their policy of cutting off Germany from world trade; while the German government did not display instant readiness to lay down its only weapon against Britain, solely for the sake of food imports. In any event the

Germans, as before in February, demanded that raw materials be included and that the enemy forego arming his merchant ships. In return, Germany was prepared to abandon gas warfare, a terrible innovation dating from the spring of 1915.[50] This reply made it much easier for Grey to decline the American proposal.

All that was left to Wilson to do was to try to persuade the German government to abandon U-boat warfare by vigorous protests that yet must not take on the form of an ultimatum. This explains the curious form of the second *Lusitania* note of June 10, which the president personally drafted on his own typewriter. It is perhaps one of the most characteristic pieces of evidence for his political mentality and his gifts as a propagandist and rhetorician. With lofty pathos, bound to make a deep impression in America, it proclaimed the august and sacred rights of humanity, compared to which the question of whether the *Lusitania* was armed and carrying munitions (which was denied) appeared trifling. Yet the note did not go beyond a moral appeal to the German government, avoiding language that might be interpreted as threatening. It asserted with great firmness the right of American citizens to travel unharmed through the war zone even on belligerent merchant ships, but at the same time offered America's good offices in any attempt to reach an understanding with the British government on changing the character and conditions of warfare at sea.

Small wonder this note set off a great round of speculation in Berlin on what Germany might expect of America. Bernstorff had dropped hints to Colonel House that he personally was an uncompromising opponent of U-boat warfare. Following a talk he had with the president on June 2, he reported to Berlin that unless Germany succeeded in calming agitated American public opinion by a conciliatory reply, Wilson would be hard put to avoid breaking off relations. To reinforce this report, Bernstorff dispatched an expert, Meyer-Gerhard, to Germany. Naturally, Bethmann Hollweg and Jagow took full advantage of it in their struggle against the admiralty for effective limitation of U-boat warfare; but its usefulness was soon blunted by further dispatches from Bernstorff, reporting that public concern in America was rapidly abating.[51] Secretary of State Bryan, moreover, did his part by confiding to the Austrian ambassador, Dumba, that Wilson's sharply worded notes should not be taken at face value, since they were mainly aimed at assuaging American public opinion. Vienna promptly retailed this news to Berlin, where it left a strong impression.

But Bryan resigned early in July, having been unable to prevail with his policy of peace at any price.[52] A diametrically opposite policy was pursued by his successor, Lansing, who was determined that America should join the Allied cause, as soon as popular opinion were ready and the war turned against the Entente. He saw imperial Germany as the sworn enemy of democratic freedom throughout the world—an enormously dangerous enemy who must in no circumstances be allowed to win. Only active American intervention was likely to prevent this eventuality.

Lansing believed that German agents were busily at work everywhere, sowing discord among the democracies to prepare the ground for German world dominion. If the Allies were defeated, it would be America's turn next. Even now Lansing professed to discern manifold efforts on the part of Germany to establish its power and influence in the countries of Central America. America would have to forestall these efforts, by the purchase of the Danish West Indies, for example. His apprehensions occasionally led Lansing into rather grotesque phantasmagorias of the future—postwar imperial Germany joining with monarchial Russia and Japan to carve up the whole world, a process in which Western Europe, Africa, and possibly the two Americas would fall to Germany, while Russia would grab Scandinavia and Western and Southern Asia, and Japan the Far East, the Pacific, and possibly the west coast of North America.[53]

Yet despite these fanciful notions, Lansing had the coolest head among all of Wilson's advisers. His power politics were least inhibited by moral considerations and pacifist impulses. Only for the moment was he constrained to content himself with strong words and intimidation—his hostility to compromise with Germany, the great enemy of the free world, was unswerving. Colonel House was calmer and more objective in his judgment of German policy, which he knew to be inwardly divided from his Berlin visit. He did not think that either the Chancellor or the German foreign ministry had been swept up into militarism.

But House was not an uncompromising neutralist either. He felt that the United States government must not display weakness but firmly envisage the possibility of becoming involved in the war, for which it must arm in time. If American diplomacy adopted a firm tone, this could only strengthen the peace forces in Germany; and if the German militarists prevailed and forced a rupture, America's entry into the war might very well shorten it and thus exert a useful effect. The only intolerable eventuality would be a German victory.

Obviously German diplomacy had every reason to exert its influence in the direction of reducing tension in the summer of 1915, even though there was as yet no immediate danger of war with the United States. Count Bernstorff actually anticipated a positive gain from German abandonment of submarine warfare, a victory for those American groups that were demanding that arms exports be halted and that Wilson should intervene on behalf of peace— meaning United States pressure on Britain to lift the hunger blockade and enforce "freedom of the seas." This was to lead to a great peace initiative by the neutral powers—in other words, a negotiated peace.[54]

Equally obviously, this was pure illusion. Arms exports were an integral and increasingly important part of the vast rise in foreign trade the war had vouchsafed the United States, suddenly and greatly expanding its national income, after a serious business recession before the war.[55] Any attempt to prohibit arms exports would have failed because of the opposition, not only of powerful industrial interests, but also of the Anglophile sentiments of the majority of the American people. The trade restrictions that British blockade measures imposed on American exporters were growing more and more irksome. The blacklists of firms suspected of trading with Germany and the checking of American business records right on American soil were felt to be humiliating and a blow to national pride, and protest was on the rise.

In an economic sense, all this actually counted for little against the immense profits that flowed from war trade with France and Britain. The danger of German U-boat sinkings without prior warning was resented all the more because the theoretical immunity of neutral shipping was of little avail to the Americans in practice—both for travel and exports they were largely dependent on British and French bottoms. Above all, since Britain did not dream of voluntarily foregoing its naval blockade of Germany, and since the anti-German alliance was for the time being firmly resolved not to enter into peace talks until Germany had been clearly defeated in a military sense, America would have had to use force against its British friends to fulfill Bernstorff's hopes and expectations. The country was not resolved on this goal, nor were its military resources equal to the task, as everyone knew. An arms embargo alone would not have been sufficient to achieve it and was out of the question in practice.

The political leaders in Berlin took a long time realizing all this—and probably never did altogether. What was clear by the summer of 1915, however, was that submarine warfare, rather than seriously threatening British imports, involved Germany in growing American animosity; and even though this had not yet led to war, it threatened grave harm to Germany's moral and political standing on the continent, especially in the Balkans. Bethmann Hollweg therefore insisted that Germany's reply to Wilson's second *Lusitania* note must at all costs contain clear-cut concessions, even though he was unable to secure complete cessation of submarine warfare, in the face of opposition from the admirals as well as public opinion. The struggle for these concessions was an extremely painful process; and as Bernstorff correctly perceived, it was foredoomed to result in nothing better than compromises.

Wilson insisted that American lives be protected, on neutral as well as Allied belligerent vessels; but no U-boat could have searched every ship for American passengers and crew members before sinking it. Embarking passengers in frail lifeboats at sea, moreover, was no assurance of survival. Hence such a concession was simply not feasible, as the German naval command documented by statements from experienced U-boat officers. Even to spare passenger vessels generally, including small ones, created problems. They were quite capable of being used for arms shipments and as troop transports, while many freighters also carried passengers.

Actually, the danger to American passengers was not nearly as great as was believed in America, because, by imperial rescript of June 6, U-boat commanders were enjoined from sinking large liners (see p. 133, above). Not least with a view toward German public opinion, however, this order had been held in such strict secrecy that even Ambassador von Bernstorff did not know of it until late August. As we have seen, in the course of the summer, U-boat commanders took to foregoing torpedo attacks whenever possible, proceeding instead by the law of prize, although in much abbreviated form; but the naval command, forever concerned with the safety of its ships and the full exploitation of their technical capabilities, insisted that the submarine campaign was pointless but for sinkings without prior warning and exaggerated the dangers that threatened submersibles from abuse of flags, U-boat traps, and armed merchant ships.[56]

In the beginning, therefore, all the Chancellor's efforts failed to secure agreement with Admiralty Chief Bachmann and his master, Tirpitz, on a conciliatory note, answering Wilson's. In the end, a solution was found, with the aid of the American ambassador, Gerard.[57] The Americans were offered safe-conduct for a certain group of specially marked and previously announced passenger liners plying between America and England. This pledge was given in the "confident hope" (rather than "on condition") that they would carry no contraband. Assurances were also given in the answering note of July 8 that "American ships will not be hindered in the exercise of legitimate sea passage [i.e., if they did not carry contraband] nor will the lives of American citizens traveling on neutral ships [i.e., other than British] be imperiled."

In Gerard's view this represented a practical compromise well-suited to overcome the current political tension and guarantee the safety of American transatlantic passengers, without German abandonment of U-boat warfare. At home Bethmann Hollweg's note was a success too, in that even his nationalist opponents found it both shrewd and firm; for it failed altogether to comply with Wilson's demand for a condemnation of the *Lusitania* disaster, indeed, in a dramatic passage, held the British responsible, because of their policy of having their merchant ships attack U-boats. Had the German U-boat commander warned the *Lusitania*, he would have certainly been rammed.

Well, the answer may have pleased the Germans, but from the American point of view it was most unfortunate, and its tone set the compromise proposals completely at nought; for Wilson could only conclude that the Germans proposed to continue sinking, without prior warning, large British liners not covered by special agreement. Indeed, he was bound to suspect that the Germans, by the agreement they proposed, wanted to persuade him indirectly to legitimize this inhuman form of warfare.

This he rejected indignantly in his note of July 21, thus eliminating Gerard's compromise as well. Even so, however, Wilson still avoided any unequivocal threat. Indeed, he invited the German government, in terms almost of warmth, to fight with him for "freedom of the seas," offering to mediate appropriate agreements between the British and German governments as their "common friend." He was evidently determined to come to the aid of the German "peace party," as Gerard and House called it, although he was also impressed with the fact that sinkings without prior warning had virtually ceased during the preceding two months. Hence he expressly declared willingness to acknowledge as legitimate, in view of the technical difficulties of the new U-boat weapon, the simplified kind of "cruiser warfare" now being practiced. Wilson, in other words, seemed to be groping for an understanding and to be quite unwilling to pursue the *Lusitania* issue for the time being—not even the question of an indemnity.

Bethmann Hollweg was able to breathe more freely and accept with equanimity the inevitable howls of rage in the German press over Wilson's third *Lusitania* note. But the bone of contention—the basic difference of opinion over the *Lusitania* case—had only been buried, not eliminated, and every new liner incident would rekindle American distrust and indignation. Nor was German navy opposition stilled, even though the Chancellor zealously sought understanding and cooperation, to a degree that today seems surprising. Bethmann Hollweg acted as though he were dealing with coeval cabinet colleagues, whose assent he had to woo, beg, and even implore.58

Bethmann Hollweg wanted to avoid the impression abroad that the German political leadership was permanently at odds with its navy and that it had no influence on naval strategy.59 More importantly, the German admiralty also enjoyed the solid support of the U-boat front that extended from right to left, the Pan-German and rightist parties having molded it into an opposition movement against Bethmann Hollweg. Led by the deputies Count Westarp, Freiherr von Zedlitz, Bassermann, and Spahn, they besieged the Chancellor with representations based on information obtained from the Reich naval office.60 They had wide control over the German press and organized national demonstrations against any limitation on U-boat warfare, a campaign in which the great industry associations were as prominent as the German intellectuals.

This opposition made itself unmistakably felt during the discussion on whether Germany should take up Wilson's positive proposals and offers in his third *Lusitania* note. The discussion was set off by a brilliant report by the treasury minister, Helfferich, on August 5. On the one hand this document set forth the unfavorable economic and financial effects of a break with America; on the other hand, it pointed to the possibility of German-American collaboration in the fight for "freedom of the seas," as offered by Wilson.

In Helfferich's opinion, Germany should forego U-boat sinkings without prior warning, at least for the time being, and limit itself to the law of prize (which Wilson had acknowledged) until its situation on the continent had improved in a military sense, while in the meantime it would become apparent whether the American president were seriously prepared and able to force Britain to let up on German imports.[61] Naturally the Chancellor, like Admiral von Müller, was in agreement with this proposal. But the U-boat chauvinists, probably secretly warned by the Reich naval office, instantly sounded the alarm in the nationalist press, and apparently Bethmann Hollweg, afraid of public protest, did not at once dare support Helfferich's plan with the Kaiser.

Instead, he first tried to win over Tirpitz, for he knew that Tirpitz, like Admiral Pohl, head of the fleet,[62] had meanwhile been assailed by doubts of whether the modest results of U-boat warfare against Britain actually warranted the risk of a break with America. But Tirpitz could scarcely be expected to put his popularity at risk. Like the whole naval leadership, he had long since become a prisoner of the myth he had created. If the risks inherent in a war on merchant shipping along the western coast of Britain were indeed too great, then the U-boat fleet should be inconspicuously shifted to the Mediterranean; but as for sinkings without prior warning, that principle must on no account be touched.

Before the issue could be decided, another perilous incident took place. On August 19, off the south coast of Ireland, a large British freighter with passenger accommodations, the *Arabic,* was sunk by a torpedo hit without prior warning, the U-boat commander having either not recognized or failed to credit the vessel's character as a passenger carrier and having believed that he was about to be rammed. Forty-four people lost their lives, including two Americans.[63] The incident dramatically illustrated how uncertain were the measures taken after the sinking of the *Lusitania* for safeguarding passenger steamers and American lives.

Evidently there was but one method for the effective prevention of such dangerous incidents, the general abandonment by Germany of sinkings of merchant ships without prior warning. Unfortunately, the German admiralty would have to wait until the U-boat concerned returned to its home port on September 2 before learning details of the sinking. The Chancellor was unwilling to wait as long as that. He at once reminded the fleet command of the previously issued secret injunction against sinking large passenger ships without prior warning; and at a meeting at Pless headquarters on August 26, presided over by the Kaiser,[64] he tried to have the scope of the order expanded. Henceforth no passenger ships at all, not even small ones, were to be sunk without prior warning and disembarkation of passengers and crew into lifeboats. The order was to be communicated to the United States government at once, together with an offer to accept arbitration in the *Lusitania* case and a plea to Wilson to proceed with the measures he had proposed in London for softening the blockade.

Bethmann Hollweg naturally met with bitter opposition from Tirpitz and Bachmann to such a "sign of weakness." They balked at any disavowal of present German tactics and were also against urging Britain to return to the London declaration on maritime law. Bachmann thought it would weaken the legal basis for Germany's U-boat campaign rather than bringing Germany any advantage. Falkenhayn strongly supported the Chancellor, declaring that a break with America must be avoided at all costs, even the restriction or abandonment of submarine warfare. Six months of that campaign, he pointed out, had not harmed Britain to the point of persuading it to yield, nor was this to be expected.

Despite this unequivocal statement, no decision was reached immediately, for once again the Kaiser was assailed by doubts, while Bethmann Hollweg's followers—Envoy von Treutler, Admiral von Müller—were hesitant and cautious. The Chancellor was furious and said afterward that he could not forever dance on a volcano on account of the U-boat issue. He claimed that he had been "encircled on every side" in the meeting, but added that unlike the encircled Russians, he would never surrender or accept this setback. Already the navy was boasting to the Americans that the German foreign ministry could do as it pleased—the navy would continue doing what it thought right. Bethmann Hollweg swore he would not leave Pless until the Kaiser had endorsed his plans. The maximum concession he was prepared to grant was to communicate the new order to Washington only "in confidence." This was a political question, not a naval matter, and the admiralty should keep its nose out of it.

We see here one of those rare moments when the Chancellor, usually cautious and slow-moving, openly lost his temper, asserting his will and even more, his responsibility. Bypassing the admirals, he subsequently had his way with the Kaiser, first in a private audience and then in an exchange of wires with Berlin.

On August 27 Ambassador Count Bernstorff received wired instructions to advise the United States government confidentially that German U-boat commanders had been ordered to sink passenger ships, whatever their size, only after prior warning and with human lives safeguarded. The imperial rescript to the navy to that effect was issued three days later, but the admiralty had already "recommended" to the chief of the high seas fleet not to use U-boats further for the time being; and on August 31 the Kaiser asked the fleet command to "consider" not even stationing U-boats off the British west coast any longer for the time being. An objection by Admiral Pohl was curtly rejected; and von Müller did not even dare present Pohl's letter of resignation to the Kaiser.

Opposition by Bachmann, the chief of the admiralty staff, was equally unavailing. He submitted a long letter directly to the Kaiser, protesting Bethmann Hollweg's procedure. The only result was that he was relieved of his post, to be replaced by Admiral von Holtzendorff, who was closer to Bethmann Hollweg's position and thought to be opposed to Tirpitz. Tirpitz himself submitted his resignation for the second time, and his only reward was forfeiture of his role as regular adviser to the crown in matters of naval policy. For the time being at least, he was restricted to his administrative duties as head of the Reich naval office. Bethmann Hollweg had scored a complete victory over the admirals. It was a safe prediction, of course, that henceforth Tirpitz would stir up opposition to the Chancellor even more fiercely than before.[65]

But for the moment the way was open for a new naval policy. Very soon after Tirpitz's rebuff, Bethmann Hollweg submitted to the Kaiser for decision a new memorandum from Helfferich, together with a countermemorandum from the admiralty staff. William II approved Helfferich's recommendations, with which we are already familiar, straight down the line. The admiralty staff was commanded to report just how many merchant ships had actually been sunk without prior warning since July 1, and how many after having been stopped and searched. As we know, this was a very delicate question for the naval authorities. It might well have uncovered some remarkable surprises, but in the event it seems not to have been followed up,[66] perhaps because the first act of the new admiralty chief, von Holtzendorff, was to change course completely. Upon assuming office he remarked that the submarine campaign had so far completely missed its aim. He not only strove for clearer and more precise directives to the U-boat commanders, but on September 18, on his own responsibility, without advising Kaiser or Chancellor, issued a secret order to the effect that during the next few weeks, i.e., during the continuing crisis over the *Arabic* case, there was to be neither outright submarine warfare nor submarine attacks on merchant ships off the west coast of Britain and in the English Channel, even under the law of prize, while in the North Sea war on merchant shipping must be solely under the law of prize.

Thus the danger of still another unexpected incident involving American vessels had been effectively banished and Helfferich's proposals implemented in fact. Diplomatic negotiations could now be concluded in an air of calm.

In the course of the month of September, Count Bernstorff did succeed in reassuring the United States government and American public opinion. Complete success did not come until he was authorized to offer indemnification for loss of American lives and a formal reprimand to the U-boat commander who had sunk the *Arabic*. Until that time there had been some massive American threats that had deeply impressed the ambassador, who reported more than once that a diplomatic break might come at any moment and that all America was bitterly resentful.

Actually, Secretary of State Lansing, as he relates in his own memoirs,[67] realized full well that the *Arabic* case was even less suited to offer a casus belli than the *Lusitania* affair. It had failed to whip up the war spirit in America; and Lansing knew that the president might well dismiss him if he drove the Germans into war with the United States by a show of intransigence.

Lansing also knew quite well how Count Bernstorff himself felt about the U-boat war, and he got what he wanted without too much trouble. On two occasions the ambassador went beyond his instructions in order to reassure the Americans. Instead of advising the United States government in confidence of the Kaiser's order to the U-boat commanders, as he had been told to do for reasons of German public opinion, he made it public at once; and he carefully edited the statement he had been given, so that it carried a direct rather than a veiled condemnation of the torpedo attack on the *Arabic*. Thus both men, Lansing and Bernstorff, exceeded their formal authority in order to reach a settlement as quickly as possible.

After such great efforts, submarine warfare was thus brought back to a far less dangerous stage. True, the American goal of having it conducted entirely along the lines of cruiser warfare, again voiced by Lansing, was met only for the time being and in the main danger zone. The *Lusitania* issue had only been postponed, not settled. Once again, the "volcano" had become quiescent, for how long only the future could tell.

## Part 3

# America Emerges from Isolationism; The Second U-Boat Crisis in the Winter of 1915-1916

ALTHOUGH U-BOAT warfare had been completely halted for the time being, the fall and winter months of 1915-1916 saw the determination of the Western powers strengthen rather than weaken. The failure of the great breakthrough attempts in Artois and the Champagne (see Chapter 3), far from discouraging the British, set them to rearming with a will. In January 1916 conscription was introduced in Britain, at first only for unmarried men, but after May for all young men.[68] Lloyd George built up a great British arms industry. The blockade against German trade was steadily tightened, despite continuing American protests and mediation efforts. In February 1916 a special blockade ministry was created, headed by the ruthless activist Lord Robert Cecil.

The British radical chauvinists, nevertheless, kept on complaining that the government was not applying the blockade stringently enough. As early as May 1915, Asquith's liberal war cabinet had had to admit a few conservatives to stay in power; and Lord Grey, at heart a moderate, had to maneuver with great care to avoid being compromised by his talks with Colonel House; for the British looked down with chilly contempt on the Americans with their perpetual complaints about violations of neutral rights and their pacifist moralizing. "The clatter of the president's typewriter," Lloyd George wrote later, "hid no mortal storm." These neutrals, he added, were doing a flourishing business, but shunned their share in securing liberty.[69]

President Wilson and his adviser Colonel House grew more and more alive to the danger that their constant and vain efforts to halt both the British blockade and the German U-boat campaign were eroding their moral authority. At the end of the war, Wilson admitted to himself, America might find itself without friends. On the other hand, some U-boat incident might sweep America into the war against its will; and it would then be compelled to wage a mere campaign of vengeance, rather than playing the role of arbiter and helping Europe attain a just and enduring peace, the world a better organization of the powers.[70]

Guided by such considerations, Wilson decided in the fall of 1915 to follow House's advice, abandon his policy of absolute neutrality if necessary, lead his country out of its traditional isolationism, and actively intervene in the war; but this was not to be the course desired and envisaged by Lansing, i.e., a simple move into the camp of Germany's enemies for the purpose of hastening their victory. What Wilson proposed was the convocation of a congress of all the belligerents, at which a "reasonable"—i.e., moderate—peace was to be negotiated. America would announce that it would declare war on the side that would resist such a settlement. Which side that would be was to emerge from talks in Berlin, Paris, and London.

The curious inconsistency in this plan was that House and Wilson did not for a moment contemplate taking the German side against their British friends, but were from the outset determined to side with the Allies. They did not, of course, wish to be party to the kind of annexationist peace envisaged by the French and Russians, but rather to come to the aid of Grey's relatively moderate policy. They hoped that an offer of American aid would tempt the British cabinet into agreeing to immediate peace negotiations on the basis of the Anglo-American proposals rather than insisting on a fight to the bitter end; and that Britain would be able to persuade its allies to join in such a step.

As for the Germans, threats rather than inducements were to persuade them to yield to these proposals. What the whole scheme amounted to in practice was that Germany, with American prompting, was to submit to the will of its enemies, though the peace was to be negotiated rather than imposed, while both sides were to relinquish their more extreme war aims. Wilson's own real war aim—at the time his only one—was to preserve the world from never-ending new wars, i.e., from further attacks by German militarism. That was how he saw it. His chief instrumentalities were to be disarmament and a league of nations, an idea he now took over from Grey and proclaimed to be part and parcel of the American program. In any event, an attempt was to be made to break off the war before it was fought to the end. Wilson and House thought this was the only chance of making peace on moderate terms.

But was there indeed such a chance? In January 1916, Wilson dispatched Colonel House on a second tour of Europe. House assured the diplomats of the Western powers that Germany would of course reject the terms and they could thus firmly count on America's entry into the war on their side. When Count Bernstorff, worried about Lansing's latest threatening steps,[71] assured Colonel House before his departure that he would be welcome in Berlin, this in turn worried rather than pleased the colonel. If the Germans showed themselves to be conciliatory, this might embarrass American diplomacy before its British friends. What Colonel House was chiefly concerned with was the attitude of the Allies.

To inform himself, Colonel House did, however, pay a visit late in January to Berlin, where he had long talks with Bethmann Hollweg, Jagow, Zimmermann, and the German colonial minister, Solf. He did not put forward any proposals for peace negotiations; nor was he able to report anything more than general impressions from Britain, where he had initially encountered much chilly reserve. He did gain the impression that the British cabinet was divided. At present the Entente did not think peace possible; for on the basis of the existing military situation the Germans would make demands which the Entente, not having been vanquished, would be unable to entertain.

This could be interpreted either as a rebuff to German proposals as hopeless, or as a challenge to a kind of surrender and a plea for peace. Bethmann Hollweg had little choice but to assure House that he had always sought to remain on good terms with Britain and the United States, that he deeply regretted the conflict with Belgium, whose neutrality he had by no means violated as airily as London seemed to believe, and that he greatly desired the restoration of peace. But he could not formally "plead" for peace, he added, since Germany, after all, had not been defeated.

Bethmann Hollweg went a step further and said that for Germany enduring peace meant assurance of not again being threatened from the direction of

Belgium or Poland. According to House he nevertheless expressed willingness to evacuate France and Belgium, provided France paid a war indemnity, which the American at once rejected as unacceptable—although he appreciated that the offer represented a considerable concession. Indeed, Bethmann Hollweg could not possibly have gone further without gravely imperiling his political position—at this time of another full-blown U-boat crisis.[72]

Seven weeks later, when he had finally succeeded in ousting Tirpitz and in once again preventing a declaration of unlimited submarine warfare, Bethmann Hollweg almost importuned the United States government through its Berlin ambassador to take up the task of peace mediation at last, appealing to its humanitarian sentiments, and also citing the terrible slaughter at Verdun. On March 18, he actually offered to dispatch a special envoy to Washington to this end. By way of German terms, he mentioned only the return of all Germany's colonies and the payment of an indemnity in return for the evacuation of North France. He was vague about Belgium, but did hint that he was ready to relinquish "most of it," leaving garrisons behind only for a limited time. By Bethmann Hollweg's account, these were terms the American found quite acceptable. But details of this confidential talk immediately leaked from Washington into the British press, compelling the Chancellor to suppress them in the German press and to prepare a denial, in order to forestall new German storms of indignation.[73]

House's over-all impressions were like those he had received the year before. The conflict between civilian and military authority in Germany was greatly limiting freedom of political action. He described the Chancellor as well-meaning, but of only limited capacity, and felt that he would not be able to stay in office for much longer—unless America took effective action against the British blockade. He saw unlimited submarine warfare coming, and for that reason alone redoubled his efforts to win over the Allies to his peace plan, before it was too late.

But this time too he encountered chilly reserve in Paris. Briand and the secretary general at the Quai d'Orsay, Jules Cambon, listened politely to the offer of American aid in the event of great military setbacks, but they did not dream of trimming their military and political plans accordingly, displaying the "very high spirits" House had anticipated.[74] The British political leaders, who tended to be quite cold-blooded in their judgments of French military achievements and prospects, were rather in doubt whether Briand entertained the same genuine confidence in victory as the chauvinist Poincaré.[75] But war hysteria had long since become the controlling power in the French chamber, where any hint of a negotiated peace was scored as criminal *défaitisme*.

In consequence, Cambon, in the presence of Briand, rejected House's offer of American peace mediation outright, as impracticable. So ardent were the colonel's efforts to win French confidence for himself and his president, however, that at the end of the talks his opposite numbers gained the impression (which they passed on to the French foreign service) that on account of the U-boat issue the United States was virtually certain to enter the war before the end of the year.

House kept assuring the Frenchmen that Wilson wished the war to end favorably for them and was prepared to help them to that end, diplomatically and even militarily, whenever they might find it useful or necessary. Alsace-Lorraine was to be theirs—though Germany was to be compensated in Asia Minor, for Turkey would, of course, have to disappear from the map. In the face of such zeal, displayed by their American friend, the French had little reason to entertain the idea of a negotiated peace, which appeared to them as premature, superfluous, and altogether undesirable. The more unfavorably the war went for the Allies, House assured them, the stronger would be American friendship.

Far from disappointed by his failure in Paris—on the contrary, elated at having met with such trust from the French leaders—House returned to London, where he once again became entangled in curious illusions. Actually, no one there took his mission quite seriously, least of all the American ambassador, Page, who welcomed House with a flood of reproaches about the colonel's and the president's policy of naiveté and studiously absented himself from House's talks with British ministers. All the same, the British cabinet was by no means unanimous in rejecting a negotiated peace outright. Grey earnestly wanted to see an end put to the mass slaughter as soon as possible. Reginald McKenna, chancellor of the exchequer, whose adviser was John Maynard Keynes, feared Britain might suffer financial disaster if the war lasted much longer. Walter Runciman, president of the board of trade, was particularly keenly sensitive to the U-boat danger.

But they were all equally doubtful that Wilson the pacifist was actually prepared to take part in the war; and they were apprehensive about the consequences of American intervention for peace at a moment when Germany was threatening a major offensive on land and at sea. Grey said the people would break his windows if he entertained such an idea, and he feared even more for the cohesion of the war alliance. Except for the possibility of alienating Wilson completely, Grey might not have been willing to talk with Colonel House at all.

Throughout the war, perhaps the greatest obstacle to negotiations was an instinctive feeling among the belligerents that once they sat down around a table, no power in the world would be able to send its soldiers back into a hail of bullets or mount a new, bloody offensive, merely for small gains here or there, or border rectifications and the like. So much blood having already been shed, neither the British nor the French were willing to call it quits before the final destruction of German militarism, which, by universal conviction, was threatening the security of the "free world."

This was time and again unequivocally reiterated in the public statements of British statesmen:[76] and even the liberal press was fond of envisaging just how the free world was to be made secure. Germany must be reduced to the status of a second-class power, while Austria-Hungary and Turkey must be completely carved up. Colonel House's broad perspectives—a league of nations, general disarmament, and freedom of the seas—no longer had much appeal in London. At the urging especially of Lloyd George, House had to at last overcome his scruples in getting American policy embroiled in the territorial disputes of the European powers.

What House did, in concert with Grey, was to draft a kind of war aims program, intended to constitute the minimum demands to be made of the Central Powers. The thing was done in a very loose and noncommittal form. All that Grey stated in writing was that House personally expected terms not unfavorable to the Allies from the contemplated peace conference. Enumerated among such terms were the restoration of Belgium, the return of Alsace-Lorraine to France, indemnification to Germany by possessions outside Europe, and "access to the sea" for Russia.

A smaller circle of British cabinet members met on February 14, and in these talks further terms were mentioned which House acknowledged to be "reasonable"—the restoration of Serbia, independence for Poland, Italian-speaking regions of Austria to be ceded to Italy, an end to the arms race, and guarantees against renewed military aggression. The draft Grey prepared on February 22 with House's assistance further gave House as authority that President Wilson was prepared to issue invitations to a peace conference as soon as Britain and France felt that the time was ripe. Should those two countries accept the proposal, while Germany either balked or behaved "unreasonably" at the conference, the United States would "probably" enter the war against Germany. If, on the other hand, the Allies delayed accepting the offer, or the war went so badly for them that American aid would be pointless, the United States would "probably" lose all interest in Europe.[77]

This formless memorandum was anything but a binding treaty of state, and the concluding threat to the Allies little more than a phrase. Grey apparently never took it quite seriously. Like other British and French diplomats, Grey regarded Colonel House as a rather naive American campaign manager, intent on improving Wilson's reelection chances by allowing him to appear in the role of peacemaker. Jules Cambon laughed scornfully at the memorandum. In his memoirs, Lloyd George insists it forfeited its political weight when Wilson, after having instantly agreed to it, inserted one more "probably." The sources do not support this. The change played no part at all in the London talks. Actually there was no willingness there to take part in any peace conference Wilson might convene. The so-called "Grey-House memorandum" was elevated to the status of a serious peace effort only in the later war literature.

Grey, in his memoirs, charged the Germans with having passed up a favorable chance for peace at the time, especially considering the subsequent imposed peace of Versailles.[78] But he ignored the fact that the German government never learned of this chance, indeed, that it never really existed in practice. Wilson and House waited in vain during the ensuing four months for the British and French governments to declare the time ripe and to request American intervention. They kept pressing for it, Wilson going so far as to deliver encouraging public speeches.

Actually, the British cabinet never formally approved the memorandum, nor did Grey even dream of recommending its acceptance to France and Russia—he actually passed it on only to Paris. He explained that Britain's heavily engaged allies must be allowed to use their own initiative in instituting peace talks. Lloyd George, later on, was furious that American war aid had not been secured as early as 1916 by accepting the American offer, for which he blamed both Grey and Wilson—the latter for insisting on "probably" in place of a firm assurance.

But even Lloyd George himself, when he was at the helm, did not lift a finger in the direction Wilson expected. Why did he fail to do so? Ultimately, there is perhaps but one explanation for the attitude of the British cabinet. Things were allowed to drift, because the continental Allies were known not to want a negotiated peace, indeed not even peace talks, so long as only Germany had won military victories and its armies were still deep in enemy territory. What the Allies wanted was victories of their own.

In the long run, little was to be expected of American war aid, as House himself bitterly acknowledged; and the Europeans hoped to dispose of Germany long before it could come into play, when Kitchener's Army would at long last set foot on French soil and a thunderous Battle of the Somme could be launched. In any event, they were in no mood to allow Wilson to meddle, for they feared that his pacifism and conciliation would merely serve to cut down the prizes of victory.

If the Americans wanted a share in securing the free world, as was considered to be their moral duty, why all these peace offers and conferences? Now that the submarine campaign had again been intensified since March, did they not have ample reason to strike? Such a course of action was hinted at to the United States government more than once, and America's Anglophile diplomats like Page were certainly in favor of it.[79]

In retrospect, it seems a profound tragedy that this second mission of Colonel House failed. We see here exemplified the hopelessness of any effort to halt, by diplomatic means, a modern mass war, once it has been unleashed and before it has run out of steam. We already know that the leading German statesmen, including even the Kaiser and his chief of staff, were far from confident in victory, despite all the German successes on the battlefield, and desired nothing more than a prompt negotiated peace, if it could have been had at anything even approaching acceptable terms; but even had they been able to hold the German annexationists and chauvinists in leash and put forward as a basis for negotiation the kind of *Verzichtfrieden* (broadly: status quo peace) House and Grey envisaged, they would have been quite unable to have Alsace-Lorraine disgorged, unless Germany had first been totally and manifestly vanquished. Grey himself knew this,[80] just as he knew that France would never forego this triumph, unless its doom were sealed. Hence, in the end, there was no alternative to fighting on to the bitter end—whether or not the Americans intervened. More millions of human lives had to be sacrificed. Obviously the risk involved in the submarine campaign had grown much greater for Germany than it was the year before. Any new incident might now instantly trigger war with America.

For the Chancellor, the blow he suffered around the turn of 1915-1916 was all the more serious. In his fight against the admirals, he now lost the support of the chief of staff, which he had so far enjoyed. At the conclusion of the victorious Balkan campaign, Falkenhayn was obviously at a loss in deciding what might now be done to bring the war to a tolerable conclusion in the course of the new year. He gave much thought to the problem and held many consultations,[81] and during the Christmas days summarized his findings in a long memorandum.

His judgment of the situation on the side of Germany's continental enemies was highly optimistic. Falkenhayn thought that sooner or later popular resolve and the power to resist would collapse in both Italy and Russia; and France too he considered to be strained virtually to the limit. Only Britain's will to fight on was, in his view, unbroken, while British manpower and material resources had scarcely been tapped. Britain must therefore be the main German target; and since Falkenhayn was able to argue persuasively that an offensive on the British sector of the Flanders front was unlikely to bring a decision, militarily or politically, nothing was left but unlimited submarine warfare, which the admiralty virtually guaranteed would soften Britain up before the year was over. If this indeed came true, America's entry into the war would become much less crucial, and it might be postponed or even prevented by diplomatic means. In any event, it would be a long time before the military effects were felt. Now that the Serbian campaign had been victoriously concluded, there was no further mention of the effect of America's entry on Italy, the Balkan countries, Holland, and Denmark—of which Falkenhayn had been so deathly afraid in 1915.

Falkenhayn's confident tone was traditional for official General Staff papers. From today's perspective, nevertheless, his report reads like a declaration of military bankruptcy. Falkenhayn thought that a resumption of the great offensive against Russia would be completely unpromising, because there were no tangible targets. If the Germans took St. Petersburg, they would be lumbered with a metropolis, without precipitating a military or political decision. To march on Moscow would mean being sucked into a vacuum. The only rewarding targets were Odessa and the Ukraine; but their conquest was feasible only if Rumania participated, and the General Staff had long since, for many reasons, rejected the idea of forcing that country to join the Central Powers.

Conrad von Hötzendorf, of course, had urgently recommended an Italian offensive (which he ultimately mounted, with Austrian troops alone, and with disastrous consequences); but such an offensive, in Falkenhayn's view, would never end the war. Italy was but a secondary theater of operations and of little concern to Britain. Similarly, nothing of any great importance could be expected of adventurous Turkish plans for invading Egypt across the Suez Canal, or Iraq, Persia, and India; and even less from attacks on Salonica.

There was one thing Falkenhayn's memorandum did not say, though its author was soon to make it known during talks with the fleet command. He entertained serious doubts about the staying power of Germany's allies, and his confidence in German morale was also fading. He was of the opinion that the war would have to be brought to a close before the beginning of the winter of 1916-1917.[82] To achieve this goal on the eastern front was not feasible, among other reasons, because this time the General Staff would be quite unable to withdraw the main reserves from the western front, as it had done in the summer of 1915. Even now, at the turn of 1915-1916, Germany's enemies enjoyed a very considerable numerical superiority on the western front, notably owing to their large army reserve, which Germany lacked.[83]

Very well, if there was no chance of seeking an issue in the east or south, what were the prospects in the west? The vain French and British thrusts during the preceding fall had served to show that a frontal break through the enemy lines was a hopeless undertaking. In any event, Germany's lack of substantial reserves forbade such a thing. What the Germans could scrape together was enough for only a limited offensive with limited goals. Falkenhayn wanted to see it pointed at a target the French would not wish to lose at any cost, for reasons of prestige, the fortress of Verdun—or rather, its ruins. Falkenhayn hoped that the French armies would be bled white here, without compelling Germany to make similar sacrifices. And since French resources had long been strained to the limit, the Verdun offensive was to lead to a swift French collapse, thus "sending Britain's finest blade spinning from its hand." Another possibility, according to a line of reasoning put forward by Falkenhayn later on, was that the British might commit their Kitchener Army prematurely to the French front, where it would be frittered away in mere defensive action.

So obviously uncertain and speculative was this plan that one can regard it only as a last and almost desperate resort in a hopeless situation. As a soldier, Falkenhayn was not content simply to wait and see what the other side would do, but he had long since lost the chance of defeating them in open battle; hence he had to content himself with inflicting as much damage as possible at the enemy's most sensitive point. Unable to vanquish the foe, he wanted to bleed him white.

Not only Falkenhayn's personal authority as a strategist hung on this project, but, so far as could then be seen, the fate of the whole war, and therefore of Germany. That is the reason why Falkenhayn tenaciously clung to its execution beyond all reason. Yet he was not blind enough to stake everything on the Verdun offensive.[84] He wanted to see unlimited U-boat warfare set going at the same time, uneasy though he probably was about it and lacking in complete confidence that it would work. Indeed, he did not hide his doubts in his memorandum. In it he spoke of a "shadow" that darkened the glowing picture of the future painted by the navy: "A prerequisite is that the navy is not in error. There is insufficient experience in this area; and such experience as we have is not exactly encouraging."

Yet in Germany's imperiled situation, it would be militarily irresponsible, he added, to ignore the judgment of the only qualified experts and forego the use of so effective a weapon because of the possibility of dangers to come; and once having made up his mind to chance it, he responded to the Chancellor's political reservations with the greatest asperity—perhaps because of his own residue of inner uncertainty. In February Bethmann Hollweg asked Falkenhayn for a formal opinion on the question of unlimited submarine warfare. The chief of staff replied that it was

> the only weapon capable of inflicting an immediate blow on Britain in its vitals [in other words, not merely on its mainland front] . . . . Judging from the official declaration by the chief of the admiralty staff, I regard the effectiveness of this weapons system as demonstrated. In consequence, our strategic leaders have no right to forego U-boat warfare; and if that is true, our political leaders too cannot claim the right to prevent the strategic leaders from using a weapons system necessary for achieving victory. [85]

The brusque language probably stems from Falkenhayn's feeling that during these months he was not merely head of the supreme army command but indeed in charge of the entire war. He felt absolutely certain of his hold on the Kaiser in all matters military. He was quite frank about this toward Captain Widenmann, Tirpitz's scout and confidant (see Volume II, pp. 173ff.), and he seems to have been flattered when Tirpitz, in a meeting on

January 5, shrewdly addressed him as "His Majesty's expert adviser for the whole conduct of the war" on whom, in consequence, also devolved responsibility for use of the U-boat fleet.[86]

In his discussion with Widenmann, Falkenhayn hinted that to his mind the whole question was military. He is quoted as having said that it was a basic mistake to submit military matters to the Chancellor, especially statistics:

> Military questions are no concern at all of the diplomats. They will have to be satisfied with a simple yes or no from the military agencies. Diplomats interpret everything in their own favor and entertain reservations. That is the great difference between a soldier and a diplomat. The soldier is used to action. The diplomat is unable to proceed to the action stage, even when he has decided to act.

Widenmann immediately remarked that Falkenhayn must have reference to Bethmann Hollweg's timidity and lack of firm resolve, which the chief of staff let pass without comment. If Widenmann's report can be trusted, the great military triumphs of the preceding year had served only to accentuate Falkenhayn's arrogance and harden his insistence on his prerogatives. Once he had been skeptical of the information given him by the navy; but now, ever since the war ministry talks early in January with Tirpitz and Holtzendorff, he had become credulous and uncritical, allowing himself to be impressed by navy figures and speculations about Britain's shipping losses and economic plight. Strictly respecting navy jurisdiction, he asked few questions even when he was presented with the most implausible data on German U-boats supposedly available against Britain.[87] He accepted them without a murmur.

Bethmann Hollweg was bitterly disillusioned when it turned out that henceforth he would have to face the joint opposition of army and navy on the U-boat question. In the first flush he feared the Kaiser would now be unable to hold out against his military advisers. A confidential note of January 10, 1916,[88] intended solely for his immediate associates, throws a revealing light on his inner struggles: Falkenhayn's demand seemed to him a mere gamble, he said, with German survival as the stake. Naturally he was determined to resist such a life-and-death chance.

But here again Bethmann Hollweg's destiny, evident throughout the war, stubbornly asserted itself. The politicians could not match the risk the military was willing to take with an alternative that might have offered greater certainty of success. Could the war be terminated by the winter of 1916-1917 without ruthless U-boat warfare? There was no guarantee of such an issue, only hope, at best vague conjecture. The Chancellor did not even think that American entry into the war had already become inevitable. All he was sure of was that there would be a diplomatic rupture and that German food and raw material imports by way of neutral countries would be completely cut off.

If intensified submarine warfare was indeed unavoidable, he speculated, must not Germany at the very least first sound out Britain quite unequivocally on its possible readiness to negotiate, hinting at the impending resumption of U-boat pressure? Yet at best what could such a course achieve except a thin peace made even more unpalatable to the people by navy assertions that except for the Chancellor's intervention Germany could have forced Britain to its knees? Even worse, any German bid for peace negotiations would probably fail and Britain would only exploit it to heighten anti-German sentiment throughout the world, which would in turn react adversely on German morale. "If these dangers are indeed excessive, as I believe them to be, the U-boat campaign will mark the end of the story, regardless of who happens to be Chancellor."

The Chancellor was sounding a note of deep resignation, indeed almost of desperation; but he allowed none of this to show before the chief of staff. On January 8 he told Falkenhayn that in his view U-boat warfare was a last resort. "It represents such a sharp challenge to the neutral nations that if it fails Germany will be done for." He authorized the necessary military preparations, but no announcement must be made until the diplomatic negotiations with America had been successfully concluded, and it certainly could not begin before March 1.[89] As always when he faced crucial decisions, Bethmann Hollweg was playing for time. Yet, as we shall see, during the ensuing weeks he roused himself to offer strong opposition to the military. It was not an easy task.

True, the army-navy front was not quite as united as it seemed at first. Admirals von Müller and Capelle inclined toward caution and Holtzendorff was not as sure of himself as he pretended to be, while War Minister Wild vacillated in his judgment.[90] Nevertheless, they besieged Bethmann Hollweg and the Kaiser with oral and written arguments. More than that, in their efforts to sharply intensify U-boat warfare, with the possible removal of all restrictions on passenger liners and neutral vessels, they had the support of public opinion, which was clamoring more and more loudly for such a course.

Since the third *Lusitania* note and the *Arabic* case, the parliamentary leaders of the nationalist right, Count Westarp and Bassermann, and Spahn, the centrist leader, had kept urging Jagow and Bethmann Hollweg, Falkenhayn and Holtzendorff, to take a strong U-boat line.[91] In the press too they called for brusque rejection of American intervention. American mediation proposals were described as mere "traps," the German replies criticized as "appeasement." There was a furor over the whole mission of Colonel House in Berlin—he was supposed to have brought an "ultimatum" in the *Lusitania* matter. The rumor mill was fed by the bustling deputy, Erzberger, foreign ministry commissioner for propaganda abroad, who was fond of making a show of his inside knowledge. On this occasion, however, he was quicker than his colleagues to grasp the fact that for the time being the prospects of a successful U-boat campaign were slight.[92]

The conservative opposition sought also to influence the crown prince, through County Councilor von Maltzahn, his political adviser. In the process, Prussian Junker apprehension of reform of the three-class franchise, already announced by Bethmann Hollweg, played a not insignificant part. Early in February the conservatives considered tabling a vote of no confidence in the Reichstag and forcing the issue to a head. In the event, this was not done. Instead, in the Prussian diet, where the conservatives were sure of a majority, their leader von Heydebrand on February 9 pushed through a resolution in the expanded ways and means committee, calling on the speaker to warn Bethmann Hollweg against appeasing the Americans. This was to be done in a solemn declaration that was also handed to the press.

By this action, however, the Prussian diet was clearly exceeding its authority; and Bethmann Hollweg at once took advantage of the incident to explain to the Kaiser that these Prussian reactionaries were laying impious hands on his imperial command power and diplomacy, an incursion against which he, the Chancellor, had to protect the sovereign. On February 12, the *Norddeutsche Allgemeine Zeitung* published a government declaration along such lines. Holtzendorff and Tirpitz were officially instructed not to hand out classified military information to parliamentary deputies, and both were further admonished to avoid with the greatest care any discussion of intensified submarine warfare with the press and leading political figures. Bethmann Hollweg summoned the conservative leaders in the Prussian diet, who found themselves under the necessity of beating a retreat. Late in March Bethmann Hollweg also succeeded in forestalling a political coup in the Prussian upper chamber.

But where the Prussian diet had failed, the German Reichstag was to succeed. Heydebrand, Westarp, Bassermann, and Spahn worked like beavers to bring about a joint declaration by all the bourgeois parties in the Reichstag declaring unlimited U-boat warfare to be the only possible military solution and insisting that such a policy be adopted. The declaration was drafted on February 16 and presented to the Chancellor by a deputation representing all the political parties to the right of the progressive. An extended debate ensued, in which the centrist deputies Spahn and Gröber distinguished themselves by their militancy. This was the first endeavor by a Reichstag majority—the "war aims majority" of 1914-1915—to exert direct influence on the conduct of the war. During this discussion Bethmann Hollweg seems to have limited himself in the main to rejecting the declaration as an unwarranted interference in the affairs of the military high command. He seems to have doubted the political wisdom of revealing to civilians the unvarnished truth about the weakness of Germany's U-boat arm.[93]

Bethmann Hollweg was, of course, quite well aware that behind the conservative opposition lay a desire to undermine his position and if possible to oust him. There was much talk about such plans in federal council circles too. Indeed, several of the federated governments confidentially offered to come to the aid of the Chancellor by a vote of confidence in the federal council.[94] He did not take advantage of this immediately, but he did intervene vigorously when the Reich naval office, through a Captain Löhlein, tried to lobby for its war policy within the federal council, using exaggerated U-boat figures.[95] Prince Hohenlohe, the Austrian ambassador, was another to be deeply worried that the Chancellor might yield to the U-boat-mongers or give way to Falkenhayn or some other general. He successfully sought authority from his government to protest unlimited U-boat warfare and a possible break with America. Early in March Hohenlohe reported that Tirpitz no longer envisaged Falkenhayn as Bethmann Hollweg's successor, but the Bavarian Count Hertling. Hohenlohe thought that in the long run Bethmann Hollweg's position would become untenable.[96]

All this was rumor, without a real basis. It is true that the leaders of the four major Reichstag parties tried to circumvent the Chancellor in early March and appealed to the war minister to get them an audience with the Kaiser—almost certainly with the intention of warning him against his Chancellor; but General Wild indignantly rejected the request and immediately notified Bethmann Hollweg.[97] The Chancellor had long since taken the possibility of such efforts into account; and he interpreted Falkenhayn's arrogant and aloof attitude to mean that the general thought of himself as the next chancellor.[98]

Here, in fact, Bethmann Hollweg was wrong. Falkenhayn greatly disappointed the conservative cabal, in that he refused to take up contact with it and indeed disallowed any outside influence at all on the decisions of the General Staff.[99] As before, he kept hands off political intrigues. In the end even Ludendorff maintained his allegiance to Bethmann Hollweg, criticizing the conservative effort to bring him to fall. Bethmann Hollweg, Ludendorff said, was an excellent Chancellor, while Falkenhayn, with whom the conservatives wanted to replace him, was quite undeserving of trust.

Ludendorff was both irked and worried about Falkenhayn's *rapprochement* with Tirpitz on the U-boat question, fearing that Tirpitz would now support his rival's candidacy for the chancellorship.[100] This is probably the explanation for Ludendorff's favorable estimate of Bethmann Hollweg, who was generally considered "soft" in the army as in the navy.[101] Even so, no general would then have dared urge the Kaiser to drop his principal adviser.

The continuing chauvinist pressure and petitioning—including still another document signed by professors at the University of Berlin—nevertheless had highly unfavorable political results. They precluded the only appropriate decisions: to forego either U-boat warfare altogether, or at least sinkings without prior warning; and thus German policy once again drifted into dangerous half-measures.

Late in February Bethmann Hollweg drafted a comprehensive report, which is certainly one of the most impressive documents of his chancellorship. It was intended to enable the Kaiser to take a clear-cut decision in the wretched U-boat matter, and especially to counter the proposal for unrestricted warfare with that weapon with telling arguments.[102] Bethmann Hollweg imperiously swept aside the shifting speculations of the navy and its economic experts on possible sinkings and the British tonnage plight. These, he said, were far too uncertain to serve as the basis for a major political decision. He barely hinted at the grotesque lack of realism in the notion that a country like Britain could be starved into submission by a dozen submarines:

> Whether in convoy or not, a certain number of ships are bound to reach Britain through the wide meshes of our U-boat blockade and mine barriers, possibly by way of France. Even without considering present stockpiles, a tolerable rationing system would mean that Britain's bread grain needs would be met by four or five medium-sized ships a day. Above all, if the British yielded [with America standing in the wings!], it would be tantamount to a public admission that German sea power had destroyed British dominion of the seas. Surely Britain would sacrifice its last man and its last penny before agreeing to such a surrender!

In the face of such confident statements, how much value attached to the admirals' assurances that Britain could not possibly hold out longer than half a year or even four months? [103]

With the same clarity the Chancellor set forth the political consequences of a break with America, which the military of late—including even the supreme command—took so lightly. He was concerned that such a break would not only draw increasing hostility from the neutral nations but greatly strengthen the enemy war potential—and further, shake the confidence of Germany's allies and even of the broad masses of the German people in their leaders.

Every word of these predictions and apprehensions was subsequently found to have come true; but the most burning question of all could not be answered with assurance: how the war could be brought to an end without starving Britain out—which was virtually impossible in any event. Bethmann

Hollweg acknowledged that there was no easy answer, but he did allow for the possibility that further military setbacks on the mainland and the failure of the hunger blockade of Germany might cause Britain to become war-weary, perhaps even in 1916. For the first time, the goal of a negotiated peace on the basis of a stalemate was here hinted at in an official document.[104] Actually, no other goal was possible, short of surrender.

Bethmann Hollweg, however, would have forfeited any chance of prevailing over the military with his report, had he drawn the conclusion that U-boat warfare should be completely relinquished. Once again his only resort was "the way of the diagonal," in the face of the high feelings, wishful thinking, and dreams of victory that dominated the army, the navy, the Reichstag parties, and German public opinion. In the final section of his long report he gave his ideas on how a break with America might be avoided without completely foregoing use of the "miracle weapon." In addition to cruiser warfare by the law of prize, as well as mine warfare, there still was the possibility of sinking *armed* enemy ships without warning anywhere at sea, and also unarmed enemy freighters within the naval war area of Great Britain and Ireland.

Unfortunately, if such a policy were carried into effect, there remained the possibility of renewed diplomatic conflict with America, triggered by untoward incidents. Bethmann Hollweg minced no words about this aspect. Such difficulties could arise from mistaking unarmed for armed ships, passenger ships for freighters, or neutral for enemy vessels, or even when American crew members serving on enemy merchant ships lost their lives in sinkings.

To avoid such confusion, the Chancellor called for precise directives to German U-boat commanders. Large liners on regular schedules, moreover, were to be spared for the time being even if they were armed, to avoid another *Lusitania* incident.[105] After the experience of the preceding year, however, it could scarcely be expected that such directives and restrictions would completely prevent new incidents; and this proved to be true soon after the beginning of the new intensified U-boat campaign.

Bethmann Hollweg himself probably never really believed that there was a foolproof method. He was not even sure that the Americans would not protest the sinking of armed merchant ships without warning. If the Americans did break with Germany over the question of armed merchant ships, he concluded, this would be "a fate we cannot escape." To yield on this point merely to appease one of Wilson's whims "would be incompatible with our dignity and would be tantamount to outright renunciation of the U-boat arm."

All this sounded like whistling while passing a graveyard and was rather out of keeping with the Chancellor's cast of mind, as was to be shown soon afterward on the occasion of the *Sussex* crisis. It was no more than a compulsory hostage to the demands of the military, who sorely beset the Chancellor with their insistence on intensifying U-boat warfare. In early January he had already told Admiral Müller that he felt himself in a similarly dreadful situation vis-à-vis the military to that of July 1914. If Germany put unrestricted U-boat warfare into effect, he said, "all the remaining neutrals would join hands in rising against us, the mad dog among the nations." He was seriously considering resigning, he added.[106] In Müller's diary one can clearly trace the Chancellor's rising concern as he watched the Kaiser succumb more and more to the combined pressure of the General Staff and the admiralty.

On the very day when he drafted his report, February 29, the U-boat campaign had started up again, by imperial rescript; and the policy he described as politically acceptable—barely so—was not much different from the directive the navy had issued on February 11. The U-boat squadron stationed at Pola had reported a sharp increase in the arming of enemy transports in the Mediterranean, with the result that U-boat successes in the war on merchant shipping were steadily declining. Without consulting the Chancellor, the naval high command had thereupon persuaded the Kaiser to authorize a resumption of U-boat warfare along the west coast of Britain, together with a first step toward its intensification. Armed merchant ships were to be attacked and sunk without warning, as soon as they were identified as such.

Admiral Scheer, chief of the high seas fleet, newly appointed late in January and known to be of particularly aggressive temper, had so worded the order that enemy merchant ships were to be spared only in exceptional cases and no longer searched at all. The Chancellor and Jagow had not been able to prevent this, and they decided not to protest, except for insisting that passenger ships be exempted. Yet it developed almost at once that the naval command was far from content with this initial "intensification," which it described as a mere half-measure. It pressed for dropping all the remaining restrictions in the immediate future. Bethmann Hollweg's report aimed at preventing at least this.

Emplacing guns with trained crews on merchant ships was, of course, an act of war that put a different face on the campaign against merchant shipping, the more so when these merchant ships were expressly empowered and encouraged to attack U-boats, as was indeed done in a directive from the British admiralty.[107] A German U-boat had seized a copy of this order on board an armed merchantman, and the foreign ministry sent facsimile copies to all the neutral nations, together with a declaration, dated February 8, that announced intensification of the merchant shipping campaign.

Even in the United States many acknowledged that armed merchant ships taking aggressive action must be accounted auxiliary naval cruisers and expect to be so treated. Hence they demanded that British freighters loading in American ports should be unarmed. Washington, like Berlin, was subject to the pressure of public opinion, which was highly volatile in America. Chauvinistic American congressmen hostile to Germany had forced Secretary of State Lansing to take up the still unsettled *Lusitania* issue again; but by early February, after hard bargaining, Count Bernstorff had succeeded in reaching agreement with Lansing on the wording of a German declaration apparently acceptable to the latter, even though it did not formally acknowledge the illegality of the sinking.[108]

At that very moment the German announcement of intensified U-boat warfare of February 8 reached Washington, where it aroused profound concern, further deepened by the fact that not even Bernstorff was told that large passenger liners were strictly exempted, even when they were armed. Any prospect of finally settling the controversy over the sinking of the *Lusitania* promptly went by the board.

It was not the only hope to go. There were pacifist as well as chauvinist trends in the United States; and besides hatred of Germany, fired by Anglo-French atrocity propaganda, there was also much bitter criticism of the British blockade of the Central Powers, especially in the business world. Senator Stone publicly charged the president with having violated American neutrality to Germany's prejudice on twenty occasions.

Yielding to such sentiments, Lansing had sent a lengthy note to London as long ago as October, in which the forcible limitation and obstruction of neutral maritime trade was condemned as being in violation of international law. January saw a movement in the Congress—in Wilson's own Democratic party at that—which urged that British merchant ships be disarmed and insisted that American citizens be forbidden to travel on belligerent vessels.

Lansing and Wilson—the latter already necessarily concerned about his reelection in the fall of 1916—were deeply troubled. They recognized that a U-boat commander could scarcely be expected to abide by the rules of cruiser warfare, approach a ship on the surface, and issue a warning, when he had to anticipate that his ship might be destroyed by a salvo at any moment. To meet this objection, Lansing sent a confidential message to the Allied governments, proposing a so-called modus vivendi, an agreement with the Germans. They were to discontinue sinkings without warning, on condition that the Allies disarm their merchant ships. This was rejected in Paris and London, but when it became known in America through a press leak, the plan initially found enthusiastic support there.

Intensification of U-boat warfare in February ruined this new chance of a rapprochement between Germany and America too. It is true that in an objective sense Lansing's proposal pointed in the same direction as German protests against the aggressive arming of merchant ships; but for that very reason it aroused political suspicions as being only another German trick, and objections grew.

Wilson now intervened and forced his secretary of state to withdraw the offer, so to speak, in favor of a declaration that any attack without warning on a vessel carrying American citizens would be considered a breach of international law and of Germany's solemn pledges, whether the ship was armed or not. Using all his oratorical skill, Wilson defeated the congressional opposition that wished to forbid travel on armed ships and in the naval war zone. He described such an injunction as incompatible with the dignity and sovereignty of the United States. In practice, moreover, he could have scarcely detained armed British ships, on which the large American export trade was dependent.

Thus tension with America once again rose to a level that caused Bethmann Hollweg to be fearful of any further intensification of U-boat warfare. His position was further imperiled by the fact that the Kaiser had become very unsure of himself under the continuous representations made to him by both the defense arms. On March 3, strongly impressed with Bethmann Hollweg's report, he expressed himself as completely convinced by it; but the next morning Falkenhayn made another military report and succeeded in changing his mind.

The Kaiser summoned Bethmann Hollweg, Falkenhayn, and Holtzendorff for the evening of March 4, and this joint meeting turned into a highly dramatic showdown between political and military authority. Bethmann Hollweg brought all of his persuasive skill into play, using the full weight of his arguments and his personality to turn the Kaiser back again and making it quite clear that he would have to resign if the generals and admirals prevailed. He spoke with much fire and cleverly topped Falkenhayn's pessimistic outlook with a deliberately optimistic attitude.

He could not agree, he said, that Germany was unable to endure another winter campaign. On the other hand, America's entry into the war would prolong the struggle until Germany was utterly exhausted. He had no doubt whatever that at the very least the enemy wished to destroy the dynasty and Germany's position as a great power; but he had faith in Germany's staying power and ultimate victory, since in the long run the enemy coalition would crumble. He brought up Frederic the Great and the Seven-Years' War, which seemed hopeless at the time, yet was brought to a conclusion that laid the basis for Germany's position as a great power. For the first time he sounded the note of "sticking it out," the slogan that was to be so frantically accentuated later on.

By Bethmann Hollweg's own testimony, the attitude of Falkenhayn was correct. He spoke with cool objectivity. His strongest argument was that Britain would bargain only after defeat, which was undoubtedly true and from which he drew the only conclusion possible for a soldier: Germany could not avoid the risk of unlimited U-boat warfare, and in view of all things there was no time to lose.

If Falkenhayn was unwilling to admit that the risk was hopeless until it had been so proved in action, this was no more than the military counterpart to the thinking of his civilian opposite number. Bethmann Hollweg refused to accept military adventure, so long as there seemed to be a single spark of hope left for a peace of political compromise. The whole debate, therefore, may serve as a classic example of the natural conflict between sword and scepter. In reading the transcript one cannot fail to sense the tragic fact that both men were vainly struggling to extricate themselves from a hopeless entanglement.

Tirpitz had been quite deliberately kept away; but had he been present, the Kaiser might after all have followed the military counsel to commence unlimited submarine warfare at once. Holtzendorff did not share the grand admiral's powers of persuasion; and when he was questioned as to the number of available U-boats, he seems to have responded rather uncertainly and evasively. The Chancellor was unable to get the issue unequivocally settled, but he did succeed in having the date of commencement and—as he thought—final decision postponed until early April.

As a matter of fact, that past master of compromise Admiral von Müller had already the night before recommended delay to the Kaiser as a way out of his uncertainty. In the meantime, at the behest of the Kaiser, the neutral powers were to be given further information in a diplomatic note about Germany's quandary in the U-boat question, in order to create a better climate of acceptance for the German strategy. This was essayed by a round-robin note on March 8, though Bethmann Hollweg thought the gesture pointless.[109]

Working closely with Admiral von Müller, the Chancellor shrewdly and vigorously took advantage of the reprieve to get rid of his main adversary, Tirpitz. To this end he used inflammatory newspaper stories by Count Reventlow, which enraged the Kaiser, who saw them as interfering with his privileges as supreme warlord. To familiarize the Kaiser with the propaganda practices of the Reich naval office, Bethmann Hollweg also showed him the exaggerated reports to the federal council by Captain Löhlein, which have already been mentioned. Navy public relations activities were now transferred entirely to the admiralty, a deliberate snub to Tirpitz, who was already offended because he had not been invited to the crucial recent headquarters meetings. On March 12 Tirpitz submitted his resignation, which was at once accepted.

When Bethmann Hollweg, on March 5, wrote his report to Jagow about the controversy with Falkenhayn, his hands were trembling with agitation.

This is understandable, for his whole power and position as the political leader of the Reich had been at stake; and for the first time he had had to threaten to resign, even that threat not achieving an immediate clear decision.[110] The chief of staff too was deeply upset and depressed, for his whole authority as the chief military leader, which he had believed to be unassailable, had failed in the test.

During the ensuing days, moreover, the news from the Verdun front was all bad. The offensive, launched with great confidence, had bogged down; and what had been meant to be the decisive battle threatened to degenerate into a hopeless slaughter of such proportions that Falkenhayn had to consider breaking off the engagement.[111] The Chancellor meanwhile held an impressive press conference on March 13, in an effort to explain his attitude and foil the slanderous allegations of his enemies.

Two days later, the foreign affairs committee of the federal council supported his plan for limited U-boat warfare, to avoid risking a break with America. The committee fully endorsed his policy and voted him the confidence of the federated governments.[112] As Count Lerchenfeld reported to Munich, the demands of the German navy were meeting with sharp opposition in federal council circles.

It was clear, however, that the grand admiral's fall would cause a strong public reaction and spur the Chancellor's enemies to redouble their efforts. Prince Hohenlohe reported to Vienna that signatures to petitions of protest to the Kaiser were actually being solicited in public places. One such petition, carrying 30,000 names, was handed in by the Pan-German historian Dietrich Schäfer.[113]

Conservatives, national liberals, and centrists were laying the groundwork for a formal Reichstag resolution in favor of unlimited U-boat warfare, and some of their drafts reached the press. Had such a resolution been adopted, it would have marked the first time that the Reichstag had sought to intervene directly in the conduct of the war. In view of the attitude of the left and even some of the centrist deputies (including Erzberger, who was now zealously supporting the Chancellor's position), as well as of the national liberal party caucus, it is uncertain whether such a resolution could have commanded a majority.

Yet the very fact of a public debate on the U-boat issue on the floor of the Reichstag was bound to bring incalculable political consequences at home and abroad, as shown plainly in the tumultuous session of March 24, when the split among the social democrats into two hostile wings came out into the open and fist fights almost broke out on the floor.[114] It threw Bethmann Hollweg into a terrible quandary, for he could not take the risk of putting forward in broad public his most important argument—the absurdly small number of U-boats available against Britain—without drawing a charge of treason.

The Chancellor vainly sought to make this clear to the party leaders in secret talks on March 18, when he told them that war with America and the whole world would mark Germany's downfall: "They will club us to death like a mad dog! "115 But the politicians remained recalcitrant; and Bethmann Hollweg tried, through official press releases, to attack the resolution as meddling with the authority of the high command and threatening the political truce. Above all he sought to have the U-boat debate shifted from the floor of the Reichstag to the main committee.

In this objective he ultimately succeeded; but in these nonpublic executive sessions he was now constrained to lift the veil of secrecy from the true U-boat figures. He persuasively argued the political consequences of a German-provoked war with America, and the hopelessness of any prospect of starving out Britain with the means available to Germany. Tirpitz's successor Capelle loyally supported him by giving the figures—apparently unvarnished—on actually available U-boats, conceding the inadequacy of the volume of tonnage sunk, and even admitting that the German Zeppelin raids had only slight military value.

The sessions were long and tension ran high. Pale and bent, chain-smoking cigarettes, the Chancellor seemed nervous and exhausted, close to physical collapse; but he stuck it out and convinced most of his listeners that his approach was governed solely by a deep sense of responsibility. Following his presentation, the social democrats Scheidemann and David declared that further attack on the government would be irresponsible; and the deputy Müller-Meiningen of the progressive party described the announcement of U-boat warfare as a big bluff.116

The end result was a compromise, probably first formulated by Erzberger, on which all the parties, including the majority wing of the social democrats, were able to agree. The Reichstag resolution actually adopted contained only a request to the government "to grant the widest possible scope in the use of the U-boat arm requisite for the assertion of Germany's naval role in negotiations with other states [i.e., America], while observing the legitimate interests of neutral countries." This was little more than stating the obvious.117

But if the Chancellor really believed he had now banished the danger of a conflict with the United States, this was soon to be proved a fallacy. Even during the discussions with the Reichstag committee, new points of issue with America came to the fore. Predictably, the "intensified" U-boat campaign begun late in February turned out to be a most unfortunate compromise. The world learned nothing of the limitations that were to distinguish it from war on merchant shipping with no holds barred; and since Admiral Scheer's directives to the U-boat commanders were meant to conceal rather than emphasize these limitations, there was soon a spate of new "incidents." Armed and unarmed merchant ships, and even passenger ships, under neutral as well as belligerent flags, were sunk without warning.

By early April there had already been four cases in which American lives were either lost or endangered. The most serious of these incidents was the torpedoing of the French steamer *Sussex* on March 24. Of the 325 passengers on board no fewer than eighty were reported killed or injured. There was indignation throughout the world, which was convinced that the Germans had now abruptly initiated unlimited U-boat warfare without prior announcement, despite all the earlier pledges and agreements. In consequence, the danger of war with America increased still further.

Secretary of State Lansing thought that the long-awaited time had come to take his country openly into the Allied camp. He proposed an immediate break in diplomatic relations with Germany to the president. Colonel House too counseled that this new German "challenge" be accepted, lest America lose credit at home and abroad and thus any chance of influencing the shape of the peace to come.[118] Wilson himself still hesitated.

His stubborn adherence to a policy of neutrality was characteristically expressed in a kind of appeal for help wired to Grey on April 6. Would it not be far better now to put into effect the steps toward mediation discussed with House in February rather than to break with Germany and thus prolong the war almost indefinitely? —an idea the British must have found hard to comprehend. The bid was, of course, futile; and on April 20 the German government was handed a sharply worded note, still short of an ultimatum with an actual time limit, which Wilson had barely been able to prevent, in long consultations. There was, however, the unambiguous threat that America would break diplomatic relations with Germany, unless the German government immediately abandoned its current methods of submarine warfare against liners and freighters. This note marks a historic turning point. Once for all it committed American policy to the abandonment of neutrality if the Germans continued or resumed sinking merchant ships without warning. Further negotiations on this point had now become pointless.

Berlin was deeply depressed. If the government yielded to so naked a threat, new domestic trouble could be foreseen. The Chancellor might well be compelled to resign and Tirpitz might have to be recalled. (Tirpitz, in fact, announced that he was submitting a new imploring report to the Kaiser and vainly requested an audience.) Bethmann Hollweg thought at first that Germany could not possibly give way to America without further ado;[119] but he met with such uncompromising firmness on the part of the American ambassador, Gerard, that he abandoned all hope of compromise. During the Easter days, April 23-24, he held talks in Berlin with Holtzendorff and the ministers Capelle and Helfferich; and fortunately he found the navy representatives less defiant than might have been expected.

Capelle, formerly one of Tirpitz's closest collaborators, was shrewd enough at last to admit the plain fact that already most of the sinkings by far were being effected by artillery fire from U-boats on the surface, after prior warning, and that these successes might well be further increased by strengthening U-boat guns. In March, "intensified" U-boat warfare had increased tonnage sunk only 60,000 over February, and this was certainly not worth picking a fight with America over. Apparently even Holtzendorff was converted with surprising speed. He clung to the view that Britain could not be beaten without unrestricted U-boat warfare and that a break with America was not a major military threat; but he admitted that it would greatly worsen Germany's economic plight and immeasurably prolong the war, thus increasing the all-or-nothing risk to Germany, which was not worth a few hundred thousand tons of enemy shipping.[120] Thus the Chancellor prevailed in having a directive sent to the fleet on April 24, to the effect that until further notice war on merchant shipping was to be conducted solely by the law of prize. Scheer, chief of the high seas fleet, defiantly responded to this admiralty order by recalling all U-boats detailed to the campaign—in other words, by simply calling it off.

Bethmann Hollweg still faced the touchy job of winning over the Kaiser to his policy of appeasement and overcoming the impassioned opposition of the chief of staff, who on March 10 had made another dramatic personal appeal to the Kaiser, pleading for unrestricted U-boat warfare. At the outset, Bethmann Hollweg's task seemed not all that difficult. At a conference with Holtzendorff and Falkenhayn on April 26 at Charleville the latter once again opposed the American demands, but he also offered a compromise proposal that had virtually no chance of acceptance.[121]

The Kaiser seemed at first resolved to avoid a break with America at all costs; but his attitude changed in a matter of days, after Tirpitz's comprehensive new memorandum had reached him. By then Admiral Scheer had stated that continuation of the U-boat campaign by the law of prize was a hopeless undertaking he would not entertain, while Falkenhayn had made new representations: The Verdun offensive had been initiated on the understanding that unrestricted U-boat warfare would stalemate Britain in the foreseeable future. If this were not so, continuation of the offensive would be pointless and Germany would be reduced to mere defensive action, a strategy that was bound to lead to ultimate defeat.

There is no reason to doubt that these were Falkenhayn's honest convictions. Yet manifestly it also represented an effort to shift responsibility for the failure of the great, bloody Verdun offensive (which was already then essentially a fact), and indeed for the failure of the whole war, to the shoulders of the political leadership, i.e., the Chancellor. Bethmann Hollweg was bitterly disillusioned when the Kaiser at once adopted this line of reasoning and on Sunday, April 30, told him at a morning audience that continued diplomatic relations with America would bring Germany "nothing positive. You have a choice," he said, "between America and Verdun."

The strain was too great for Bethmann Hollweg's humane temperament. The next morning he desparingly told Valentini, chief of the Kaiser's civil cabinet, that he saw his position as intolerable and untenable, in view of the continuing attacks on him by the military and by major sections of the misled nation. He thought he would have to give way to Falkenhayn.[122] Valentini got the impression that Bethmann Hollweg had suffered a complete breakdown and considered a recommendation to the Kaiser for a change in the chancellorship, with Falkenhayn succeeding Bethmann Hollweg and Hindenburg becoming chief of staff, since Bethmann Hollweg seemed to him no longer equal to his difficult role.

But Valentini clearly underestimated Bethmann Hollweg's political resilience. Rather than giving way, Bethmann Hollweg had even the day before moved heaven and earth to change the Kaiser's mind. On Sunday afternoon he had summoned Jagow and Helfferich by telephone and wire from Berlin to help him. Both at once wired him data supporting his position. In a report of his own, Bethmann Hollweg emphatically rejected the imputation that he bore any responsibility for the failure of Verdun. How a break with America could be avoided was a purely political question, as was the effect of U-boat warfare on Britain. It was strictly up to the General Staff to decide whether the Verdun offensive should be broken off for local military reasons. The political justification advanced was based on erroneous assumptions and was therefore inadequate. As Chancellor he rejected any responsibility for such a decision, which was bound to be very damaging for Germany's over-all situation.

It is doubtful whether these notes were submitted to the Kaiser at all, for by Sunday night—apparently without the knowledge of the Chancellor—Admiral von Müller once again interceded with the Kaiser in his role as conciliator. Speaking also with the authority of Capelle and Holtzendorff who, according to his own testimony, were outraged by the Kaiser's latest change of mind—indeed, able to cite a memorandum Holtzendorff had given him[123]—Müller spoke in the name of the naval high command and consequently succeeded at once. He was left with the impression that the Kaiser ultimately dreaded the thought of "having America on his neck."

Judging from his remarks to Valentini, Bethmann Hollweg apparently learned of this latest turn only on the afternoon of May 1, 1916, when he got the Kaiser's approval for another audience for the American ambassador, Gerard, which he had sought for days. He had invited Gerard to headquarters, so that the American might personally brief the Kaiser about his president's attitude, on which for the moment no details were ascertainable by normal diplomatic channels. It was an unusual step, not unattended by a certain risk, in view of the Kaiser's character, but it met with complete success.

The reception took place in an atmosphere of goodwill, the ambassador being able to explain the American side of the U-boat controversy at length and refute the Kaiser's often primitive objections without arousing his ire. [124] Directly afterward the Kaiser decided to approve an answering note to America drafted by the German foreign ministry, in which intensified U-boat warfare was relinquished. To appease German public opinion, the note began with massive charges against the British blockade policy and its American support, but it ended with a declaration that henceforth, even in the British war zone, merchant ships would not be sunk without warning and the saving of human life, provided no attempt was made to escape or offer resistance. There was an appended clause, however: The German government now expected that America would redeem its pledge made in the third *Lusitania* note of July 23, 1915, to support the principle of freedom of the seas with the Allies, in other words, to insist on a revision of the British blockade policy. If this were not done, Germany reserved full freedom of action.[125]

This was precisely in keeping with the proposals Helfferich had offered in August 1915, and was indeed included at his behest. The domestic effect was excellent, for it made the German note appear as a generous and temporary concession rather than a surrender to American threats.[126] In terms of foreign policy it was foredoomed to failure, since the American government was neither willing nor able to force an abandonment of the British blockade policy. The only consequence was that Wilson, in a new note on May 10, 1916, protested the German reservation: The American government could in no way allow its insistence on respect for neutral rights and the laws of humanity to become dependent on the success of diplomatic negotiations with any other belligerent power.

Here was another disappointment for German policy. In foregoing intensified U-boat warfare Germany was doubtless motivated in large part by the expectation and hope that this might persuade President Wilson to persuade London in turn to take a step favorable to Germany—if not a revision of the blockade policy, then possibly the peace table. On April 11 Count Bernstorff had reported a confidential talk with Colonel House, in which the American had mentioned Wilson's intention to make peace in a matter of months. [127] The German foreign ministry had at once eagerly responded to the hint. During Easter the Chancellor, in several discussions with Gerard, had tried to explain that he could not hope to win over German public opinion, then at fever pitch, to a peaceful understanding with America, unless that country did something to counter the British blockade policy. Much as he had already done on March 18,[128] he strongly emphasized that his government was ready to make peace at any time, on liberal terms which, however, he was unwilling to spell out until there was a sign of willingness to negotiate.

Bethmann Hollweg discussed the problem further in numerous talks with

Gerard at Charleville, and apparently the American, like Colonel House be-fore him, held out the prospect that President Wilson would by late summer offer the belligerents his good offices in bringing about peace. Probably all that stood behind these promises was the fact that Wilson and House still had not buried their hopes, already known to us, that someday the "Grey-House memorandum" of February might take effect. Bethmann Hollweg, however, knew nothing of the content of this memorandum and its minimum peace terms.

Had he known the true sentiments of Germany's enemies and of the American mediator, he might not have gone as far as he did with the Ameri-can ambassador in Charleville, which was to invite House for further talks in Berlin and to make plain once again his hopes for Wilson's peace efforts. [129] Count Bernstorff learned about this from Gerard's report, via Colonel House, at once drew renewed hope, and counseled that U-boat warfare be not merely restricted but discontinued for the time being.

Bethmann Hollweg was more skeptical. The German people, he remarked, were full of the deepest animosity against America and would believe in its sincerity as a mediator only when Wilson did something to change the British blockade policy. He must first bring the British to the point where they showed a willingness "to talk peace with us, even though but unofficially for the time being," or else the situation would become untenable. But Colonel House would be most welcome in Berlin at any time, he said on May 6. [130]

There was no answer to this invitation, and the American note of May 10, which the Chancellor left unanswered, disappointed his hopes of gaining America's mediating help by way of an understanding with Britain, as he wished. Yet he never abandoned his efforts in that direction until late in the year. They were facilitated by the fact that U-boat warfare in British waters was virtually at a standstill for many months on end; Bethmann Hollweg also counted on Wilson's desire to appear in the role of peacemaker in a reelection year. The course of House's mission in March 1916 had already made it clear to Germany how vanishingly small were the chances of success.

The *Sussex* crisis, by the way, was concluded only after a last serious run-in at Charleville headquarters. On the evening of May 1, the Kaiser had reached his decision in a talk with the Chancellor alone, without once again summoning Falkenhayn and the admirals—on the grounds that he already knew their views, in truth probably to avoid still further agonizing discussion. The next day the chief of staff submitted his resignation, a step which but shortly before he had described to Tirpitz as "unsoldierly."

Apparently Falkenhayn too was at the end of his hopes, politically as well as militarily. He felt that the Chancellor had circumvented him and swept him aside, and that the Kaiser, who only two days earlier had given him his assent, had left him in the lurch a second time. When the Kaiser begged him to stay, however, he did not insist, from a soldierly feeling, as he put it, that he could not publicly oppose an imperial order already issued. There followed a brief, pointed exchange with Bethmann Hollweg on the U-boat issue, which ruled out any hope of agreement. Thus the political cooperation between the two men was at an end. Neither forgave the other this quarrel.

# 6

# Failure of the Verdun Offensive; The Austrian Front Crumbles; The Fall of Falkenhayn

H
OW DEEP the rift was between Bethmann Hollweg and Falkenhayn was soon shown in a characteristic clash over the question of war censorship, which late in May 1916 gave rise to stormy debates on the floor of the Reichstag. They showed the world that the period of the patriotic party truce was drawing to a close, while the deep conflicts between right and left on matters of foreign and domestic policy were pushing to the fore.

The Chancellor's major Reichstag speech of April 5, discussed at the end of Chapter 4,[1] had already been affected by these tensions; and to maintain at least an outward semblance of political unanimity in the Reichstag, he had been compelled to adopt certain ambiguous formulations. In the ensuing debates there was a storm of complaints about hardships and abuses of every kind, all the parties agreeing only on their objection to press censorship and the prohibition of public demonstrations.

The left wished to demonstrate openly for prompt peace, international reconciliation, and domestic reforms. The right wished to cast off all restraints to annexationist propaganda, support for unrestricted U-boat warfare, and opposition to a Chancellor it described as "slack." These opposition tactics sought to draw a line between military and political censorship. The former was loyally approved, the latter attacked all the more vehemently.

Traditional Prussian militarism assigned the right of imposing censorship on the press exclusively to the replacement commands, an authority that was legally part of the "state of siege." These commands were purely military authorities, over which the Chancellor and the foreign ministry had influence only through general directives to the head censorship office of the replacement General Staff rather than by direct order; for under Bismarckian tradition the generals were under the direct authority of the emperor.

This situation gave rise to constant friction between the civil and military authorities. The military commands and the General Staff were naturally inclined to slap prohibitions and censorship on the leftist rather than the rightist press. Bethmann Hollweg, on the other hand, was mainly concerned with suppressing as long as possible the hapless press debate on war aims and the U-boat war, to maintain the so-called party truce. Hence his "political" censorship kept on arousing the resentment of the rightist parties.

In the event, Bethmann Hollweg was particularly irked when, during the censorship debate in the Reichstag late in May, he learned that Falkenhayn, the chief of staff, had told the Reich association of newspaper publishers that he regarded as harmful any limitation on freedom of the press that did not serve the ends of the war. This was meant as a reply to a petition to the Chancellor by the association, asking that press censorship be eased. A copy had been sent to Falkenhayn.

It was, of course, improper for the chief of staff to issue any such statement at all without first consulting the Chancellor, and the press at once exploited this for its own political purposes in campaigning against the Chancellor; but from the exchange on the matter between Chancellor and chief of staff it must remain doubtful whether Falkenhayn was aware of the political implications of his action.

In any event, Falkenhayn seems to have had no objective differences with Bethmann Hollweg on the censorship issue. Like War Minister Wild von Hohenborn he believed that war aims should be publicly debated only at such a time as the government might be able to intervene with positive declarations—in other words, when the peace had been secured. The unwonted sharpness with which the Chancellor protested the general's meddling with his jurisdiction is therefore all the more remarkable. He actually had a direct complaint to the Kaiser drafted, the wording of which he pointed up in his own hand.[2]

It is almost certain that his extreme irritation derived from the fact that his enemies on the right were at this time attacking him in the most vicious way. The press being open to them to only a limited degree, they exerted themselves without restraint in clandestine and often anonymous pamphlets and memoranda, privately reproduced and mailed to thousands of addresses. Often they were distributed even in the trenches.

These pamphleteers did not shrink from the crudest slanders and imputations. On June 5 Bethmann Hollweg fought back in a spirited Reichstag speech that probably represents his most outstanding oratorical achievement. He pilloried two particularly ignoble specimens in this malicious campaign,[3] but at the same time he appealed for public support with a passion unprecedented from the lips of a high imperial official. Perhaps this is the closest he ever came to becoming a people's tribune and orator. He implored the nation to drop the ancient, poisonous distrust of the democratic left's patriotism, but to drop also the revolutionary slogans that issued from the left, pitting class against class. He appealed for militant national unity.

The powerful impression he left was not confined to the left. Neither in the Reichstag nor in the press did anyone venture to defend the pamphleteers. Apparently even Falkenhayn felt it necessary to make a show of disavowing them. To the great surprise of the war minister, and despite his running correspondence with the Chancellor on the censorship issue, he sent the embattled Bethmann Hollweg a telegram of congratulation for his successful attack on the "wild-eyed annexationists and rabid U-boat zealots."[4]

Even some of the conservatives now backed away, for they feared that further attacks on the Chancellor would put them out of favor with the Kaiser, to whom they reasserted their loyalty, through an emissary, von Kessel. Some of them sought a personal rapprochement with the Chancellor and with Valentini, and for the time being at least the stridor of the opposition was moderated.[5]

A contributing factor was that the Kaiser himself was bitterly resentful of hints by the pamphleteers and rumormongers that he shared responsibility for the "spineless" Reich policy, and that he discouraged U-boat and Zeppelin attacks on Britain on account of his blood ties to the British royal family and his fortune of 500 millions in the Bank of England.

Other malicious rumors circulated in the navy. The foreign ministry was said to be unhappy over the German success in the Battle of Jutland, because it prejudiced discussions already under way with Britain concerning a humiliating peace. The crown prince himself gave credence to this nonsense and said so to his father's face. The Kaiser flew into a rage and fired the crown prince's political adviser, County Councilor von Maltzahn, one of the most rabid Pan-German opponents of Bethmann Hollweg.[6]

But about this time Bethmann Hollweg's supporters at last succeeded in getting an anti-annexationist movement off the ground. A national committee for a German peace was established under the leadership of Prince Wedel, a former governor of Alsace-Lorraine. The impetus had been given by Reichstag deputy Erzberger, and there was support from official circles.[7]

All this did not keep the Pan-German propaganda campaign against current government policy from continuing all through the summer, publicly as well as clandestinely. The leaders of the movement went so far as to try to enlist Bavarian particularism in their attacks on the hated Chancellor. They took advantage of Bavarian resentment of the Reich food administration, established in the spring of 1916 under the East Prussian, von Batocki, who exacted increased deliveries from Bavarian agriculture, which caused much outraged fuming in Munich beer halls and coffee houses.

As the result of a meeting of the Pan-German union in Munich in July, a petition was dispatched to all the federated princes, asking them to take action against current Reich policy which, by refusing to initiate unrestricted U-boat warfare, was charged with prolonging the war; the crushing burden of interest on war loans was ruining state finances, which were dependent entirely on direct taxation. The petition did not fail to mention that only large war indemnities and the annexation of farmland, forests, mines, industries, railways, etc., could ease the German financial burden. There was also a direct appeal to the king of Bavaria, signed by various Bavarian politicians and celebrities, but actually inspired by Count Reventlow, asking the king to lend new laurels to the house of Wittelsbach by vigorous intervention to "save" Germany.

This document was presented to King Louis III on August 5 by a delegation of rabid Pan-Germans. The king was clumsy enough to allow himself to be drawn into a debate on the subject, which caused great embarrassment to his prime minister, Count Hertling. Hertling saw his own position threatened and successfully called on Cardinal Archbishop Bettinger to help him fend off the campaign of incitement. He had a great deal of trouble resisting navy importunities to enlist him against Bethmann Hollweg's policies. Ultimately Hertling once again availed himself of the foreign affairs committee of the federal council, ostensibly to challenge the Chancellor, but in reality to support him; and as always, he found vigorous support on the part of von Weizsäcker. In the sessions of August 8-9, when it was learned that the German U-boat fleet had grown by only seven units since March, it was decided to leave the Pan-German appeal unanswered.[8]

Despite all of Bethmann Hollweg's efforts, the united political front of 1914 was steadily crumbling. It is noteworthy, however, that in the demonstrations, petitions, and memoranda mounted by the anti-Chancellor cabal the demand for large-scale annexations was sounded less vocally than the call for unrestricted U-boat warfare. It was quite plain also that the Prussian conservatives were worried about domestic political reforms.[9]

The military situation during this summer was indeed little calculated to revive hopes for peace with victory and territorial aggrandizement and to elicit a popular response to such Pan-German proclamations. On the contrary, the war had entered a stage where for the first time the specter of defeat seemed to appear on the horizon, however distantly; and if the Chancellor, during these months, was methodically working for a change in the supreme command, he was motivated by nothing less than fear that the fortunes of war were taking a disastrous turn.

His doubt of the chief of staff's military competence had sharply risen by virtue of the enormous losses in the Verdun offensive. Late in August Falkenhayn disputed the Chancellor's contention that the whole operation had been a miscalculation. He denied that he had ever believed it would incline France toward peace "any more than would any active war operation." His particular goal had been

> on the one hand to paralyze France for the further course of the war by bleeding it white if it chose to commit its army at Verdun, and by causing internal repercussions if it relinquished that fortified position; and on the other hand to provoke Britain into committing its full resources prematurely. Both of these goals have been attained, although not precisely to the degree that had been anticipated—that almost never happens in war—but still to an appreciable degree.

France had lost a good quarter-million veteran soldiers more than Germany before Verdun. What would have happened, Falkenhayn asked, if this army had intervened along the Somme or elsewhere, and if Britain, instead of commencing its Somme offensive late in June, had done so only in August, by which time Germany had been under the necessity of depleting its reserves in the west to an extraordinary degree to bolster the eastern front, which had begun to buckle because of the failings of the Austrians? [10]

This was not an alibi. We know from Falkenhayn's Christmas memorandum that he never believed a breakthrough at Verdun was possible, nor even that this fortress could be taken. He was out to inflict the greatest possible military and psychological damage on the French foe. He admitted that French resistance was "unexpectedly" strong, implying that he had underestimated it. The French had been able to throw many more reserves into the fray than he had thought possible, and they held out with great tenacity.

But Falkenhayn seems to have greatly overestimated French losses, compared to the German. It is certain that the forty-seven infantry divisions the Germans committed at Verdun suffered far greater attrition than the French infantry, which outnumbered them two to one and was rotated at the front far more quickly.[11] In retrospect, the only possible judgment is that the Germans mounted the Verdun offensive from the beginning with forces that were far too thin to gain a really decisive success. (It was for that reason too that it had been staged on only the east bank of the Meuse, which was too narrow a front.)

Apparently this was done because the chief of staff viewed the Verdun offensive only as a complementary operation that might make possible a breakthrough elsewhere. He hoped especially to force the British to strike prematurely, enabling him to meet them in a powerful counteroffensive, using all his reserves, rather than having to rest content with mere defensive action.[12] In view of the small size of the German reserves this was certainly a gamble, based on an overestimate of German capabilities and an underestimate of those of the enemy.

But the great British "Kitchener Army" had long been a nightmare to the German supreme command; and the great battle of the Somme did show the terrifying offensive effect it was able to exert, owing mainly to its enormously strong ordnance and fresh manpower resources. Falkenhayn can scarcely be blamed for anticipating the main danger to Germany on the western front, especially its British sector, rather than in the east. He was doubtless right when he argued before the Chancellor late in August that unless Rumania were provoked to intervene—which he thought dependent on very different factors—it did not ultimately matter in the least whether the German forces stood on the Dvina or the Aa, on the Berezina or the Niemen, on the Stokhod or the Turiya. On the other hand a retrograde movement in the west would almost certainly shake the entire front there; and when that happened, the most brilliant successes in the east would be of no avail.[13] Nor could Falkenhayn possibly foresee that the Austrian front in Volhynia, adequately manned and well-secured, would cave in as completely as it did early in June, the exigency that overturned all his plans for the western front.

Thus the Verdun offensive was by no means an ill-considered venture as such but part of a far-sighted strategic plan; military criticism has been directed at its execution rather than its planning, mainly at the fact that Falkenhayn allowed the offensive to continue far too long, when his first doubts as to whether it should not be broken off dated back to late March. He was never quite able to refute the censure that in this question he had allowed himself to be swayed too strongly by the bravado and technical objections of General von Knobelsdorff, chief of staff of the crown prince's army group, thus helping to bring about a terrible bloodbath without end.

It is an oversimplification to try to explain this failure on the basis of ambition and unwillingness to admit error, as Falkenhayn's detractors have done. An operation like that at Verdun, embroiling vast forces on both sides, could not simply be broken off overnight without risking dangerous reverses. Falkenhayn, however, should have foreseen this contingency; and the fact that he was deceived and ignored the prior warnings of experts[14] suggests that his military judgment was uncertain.

He did, by the way, repeatedly issue orders from early April onward to discontinue the major offensive in favor of smaller attacks on a limited scale, to the extent that these were essential to improve the German positions; but until late August he did not really prevail, being apparently swayed too long by Knobelsdorff's fear that French counterattacks would hurl the Germans back to their starting positions once their action slackened. On the other hand, Falkenhayn was clearly not in a position to withdraw larger units from the Verdun sector for use on the eastern front or in the battle of the Somme, in the face of the menacing force the French had concentrated at Verdun.

It may indeed have been a fundamental mistake to shift the main impact of German fighting power back to the west, after the highly successful eastern offensive of 1915. Should Falkenhayn not have moved against St. Petersburg, Moscow, òr Kiev in the spring of 1916, sweeping Rumania along by main force, if necessary? But then, the offensive capabilities of Germany's Austrian ally had long since vanished; and such an operation would have meant denuding the western front of reserves altogether. In view of the greatly increased Anglo-French striking power, moreover, it would have entailed the gravest risk of a breakthrough in the west.

The history of the First World War published by the former Reich archives is highly critical of Falkenhayn and concludes that as early as the fall of 1914 he should have used civilian manpower to construct a strongly fortified defense line far behind the western front—Nieuport-Lille-Maubeuge-Metz-Strasbourg-Upper Rhine. This shortened front would have made powerful forces available for the subjugation of Russia.[15] But regardless of the military merits of such a policy, the political historian can be under no doubts that in a political sense it would have been wholly unfeasible. Only in 1918 could it be considered, as a last resort.

Had Falkenhayn followed Conrad's wishes in the spring of 1916 in strengthening the Austrian army in the Tyrol or setting the Isonzo front in motion with the help of German forces, he could also very probably have won great "victories" in Italy that would have made an impression. As we already know, he declined this opportunity, not merely from military considerations—that Germany must not scatter its efforts on subsidiary theaters of war, so long as its rear was not secure in both east and west—but also because he distrusted his Austrian allies. He doubted the strategic ability of the volatile Conrad, and he questioned the fighting quality of the Austrians.

Falkenhayn, moreover, for very sound reasons, did not believe that Italy, entirely dependent on the Entente powers, could be decisively eliminated from the war; and he thought that advancing the front line from the Alpine slopes into the Po valley would be disadvantageous from a military point of view.[16] The Italian campaign was therefore virtually nothing more than a welcome opportunity for General Conrad and many Austrians to "have it out" with their hated neighbor; and no German chief of staff could take the responsibility for shedding German blood for the attainment of such a goal.

It is noteworthy, however—throwing a sharp light on the relation of war and politics in Germany—that Falkenhayn seems never to have discussed this question with the Chancellor, even though political considerations played an important part in the General Staff's stand. By August 1916, in any event, Bethmann Hollweg did not yet know that in the preceding December Falkenhayn had urgently tried to dissuade his Austrian counterpart from his offensive plans against Italy, and that Conrad undertook his belated and foredoomed strike from the Tyrol in May 1916 against repeated German warnings. Indeed, the timing of this operation had been communicated to the German General Staff only at the last moment.[17]

It was certainly unfortunate that owing to the differences between the two chiefs of staff the military forces of the Central Powers were split between two offensives in the spring of 1916. True, Austrian divisions could scarcely have averted the disaster at Verdun; and despite the diversion of six divisions thrown against Italy, the Russian front, in the judgment of both German and Austrian generals, remained adequately manned.[18] But Conrad had withdrawn precisely his best German-Austrian troops from the Russian front for his operations; hence the great offensive launched by the Russian general Brusilov early in June met with a wretchedly inadequate defense.

In the sector of Rovno-Lutsk, held by the fourth Austrian army, where the Russians had actually planned only a diversionary action, they achieved an unexpected success. By noon of the second day of the offensive they had taken 40,000 prisoners, and the routed remnants of the Austrian regiments scattered into the forests. The crumbling morale of the Austrian army was, of course, one result of the conflicts within the multinational state. The Czech and Ruthenian troops especially were said to be going over to the enemy in droves when the heat was on; but on this occasion, by the testimony of an Austrian diplomat at Teschen headquarters—of whom more anon[19]—the leadership deserved the lion's share of the blame.

The Austrian forces were headed by Archduke Frederic, long since known to be incompetent. He and his officers had neglected virtually everything that might have contributed toward troop training and discipline. The Lutsk sector of the front had been quiet and was extremely well-equipped, and it had turned into a kind of luxury resort in the Volhynian marshes, with hunting and gaming taking the place of military exercises. The front was pierced so swiftly that the troops fled in wild panic, allowing no time or opportunity for rallying them to launch effective counterattacks. All that the command could do was to try to plug the holes in the front as well as possible with reserves brought up in a hurry. By the end of June 200,000 men had been lost. Gradually the retreat extended to the entire eastern Austrian front. The severest setback was suffered by the army of the south, which moved back all the way to the Carpathian passes in the course of the summer and relinquished the Bukovina to the Russians, thereby encouraging the Rumanians to enter the war.

These unhappy events marked a turning point in the fortunes of war, spoiled the relationship between the Central Powers, and sealed Falkenhayn's own doom, as they did later on for Conrad von Hötzendorf. Only three weeks after the beginning of the Brusilov offensive, an Anglo-French artillery barrage of unprecedented intensity rained down on the western front. The author, then an officer in the front lines, was a witness to this desperate struggle of exhausted troops amid the shell holes and rubble heaps along the Somme.

One reads with consternation today that on June 29, only five days after the Anglo-French artillery barrage had begun and more than three weeks after the Russian breakthrough at Lutsk, Ludendorff bitterly complained to the foreign ministry that Falkenhayn had not given him six divisions in May to help take Riga, a failure Ludendorff attributed entirely to personal jealousy. He added that he regarded these six divisions, made available for service in the east only with the greatest difficulty, as a reserve entirely at his discretionary disposal.[20]

The incident glaringly illuminates Falkenhayn's desperate position in July 1916. Besieged from all sides with urgent requests for more troops, he could no longer give any thought to higher strategic considerations. He was compelled to shift from one expedient to another, living from hand to mouth, so to speak. Naturally his critics now assailed him on every hand, for he was scraping the bottom of the barrel and was unable to provide anyone with the reserves so urgently needed. Supreme command of the army turned into a dreary and painful business shuttling exhausted divisions and regiments to and fro.

It was at this point that Bethmann Hollweg too abandoned faith in Falkenhayn's star. This can be seen plainly from his confidential letters to cabinet chief Valentini from mid-May onward. Very poorly informed on military matters, he regarded the collapse of the Volhynian front as stemming from the lack of integrated command on the eastern front.[21] Looking back on Falkenhayn's work since the fall of 1914, he now found that the "second supreme command" had made virtually every possible mistake. He adopted Crown Prince Rupprecht of Bavaria's criticism—shared by virtually all the generals on the western front—of the failures and military crises at Ypres in 1914, at Arras and in the Champagne in 1915, and now at Verdun. It was the supreme command that had been to blame every time, for failing to heed the warnings of the army commanders, whose staff chiefs were then made into scapegoats.

If Falkenhayn stays, we shall lose the war—thus Rupprecht had written. Bethmann Hollweg himself had listened to what he now knew to be erroneously optimistic estimates of Russian and French fighting power. He inveighed against Falkenhayn's opposition—still to be discussed—to the creation of a single eastern high command under Hindenburg. "This resistance has continued right down to the moment when it may be too late, despite the streams of blood already shed. Where does incompetence stop and criminal culpability begin? " Jagow too later on spoke of "the crime of Verdun."[22]

Bethmann Hollweg's letters were written in a mood of deep gloom and discouragement. "I am depressed and desperate," reads the final sentence in a letter of July 4. Valentini was quite right in urging the Chancellor not to throw in the towel prematurely and in advising him not to play spokesman for the ever-disgruntled generals—"Let them be man enough to state their own case if they are dissatisfied." The importance of a unified command on the eastern front should not be overstated nor criticism of Falkenhayn exaggerated—"It has taken the enemy two years to integrate offensive action, and it is doubtful whether anyone else could meet the current crisis in any other way." The military situation must not be viewed in too gloomy a light, and one should not allow oneself to be swerved by public criticism of Falkenhayn, which notoriously tended to hysteria.

All these arguments can scarcely have convinced the Chancellor. In terms of running the war, it was most important to see to it that the public did not lose confidence in the supreme command. He was bound to conclude that sooner or later, in view of the steadily worsening war situation, the time would come when the authority—or rather the myth—of Hindenburg would have to be thrown into the balance. If that were done first on the threatened eastern front, it would greatly facilitate a subsequent change in the supreme command; and the sooner it was done, the easier it would be for the political leadership to justify before the public any meager peace Hindenburg might have to conclude.

Such reasoning is already embodied in a confidential wire Bethmann Hollweg addressed in late June to General Lyncker, couched in terms intended for a personal report to the Kaiser:

> The name Hindenburg [he said] is the terror of our enemies and electrifies our army and our people, who have boundless faith in him. I view our situation gravely. Our manpower resources are not inexhaustible, and the mood of the people is depressed by food shortages and the way the war drags on. But even should we lose a battle, God forbid, our people would accept such a setback under Hindenburg's leadership, as they would a peace over his name. If this is not done, the duration of the war and its changing fortunes will be chalked up against the Kaiser by the people. We must take these imponderables into account.23

Such thoughts were quite common among the politicians in the summer of 1916. Deputy Erzberger, always with his ear to the ground, tried as early as May to win over highly placed personages at headquarters to the view that Hindenburg should replace Falkenhayn, to restore popular morale, which was badly shaken, especially in Saxony. "Even the Kaiser can afford to lose the war, with Hindenburg at the head—it would simply show that he had done everything possible. To lose the war without Hindenburg would mean the downfall of the dynasty."

The Württemberg minister Varnbüler voiced similar sentiments about the same time; and even the shrewd and calculating Weizsäcker remarked in discussion with Bethmann Hollweg in June that "neither he nor the Kaiser would survive military setbacks unless Hindenburg's strength were used to the full."[24] There was a steadily growing sense of disquiet over the issue of the war that was now giving rise to a call for Hindenburg as the savior in need, endangering Falkenhayn's political position.

There was, however, another reason of immediate urgency why Bethmann Hollweg favored expansion of Hindenburg's command authority. Lamentably, the Hapsburg state was beginning to disintegrate and its military leadership to break down. News from Vienna about Austrian morale kept getting worse. In mid-July Berlin learned of a report submitted by the Austrian envoy in Bucharest, the later foreign minister Count Czernin, who predicted the complete defeat of the Central Powers and their allies with "mathematical certainty," if the war were long continued. Their victory was declared to be an "impossibility," and Czernin recommended that a peace at substantial sacrifice be concluded as soon as possible, though during a phase that was favorable to the Central Powers, which he hoped might occur.[25] The German ambassador in Vienna was able to dispel German fears that Austria would sign a separate peace, although there was much private intrigue and anti-German sentiment in that city; but even he was unable to say how long the country's military resources would hold out.[26]

The failure of the Austro-Hungarian front, especially the loss of the Bukovina, had left a very bad impression in Bulgaria, where it was feared that Rumania would now strike. King Ferdinand and Crown Prince Boris had been pressing since mid-June for a unified German high command in the east, preferably under Hindenburg. This would at one stroke restore flagging confidence, while at the same time dampening Rumanian enthusiasm for entering the war. They demanded that the Austrian commander-in-chief, Archduke Frederic, resign.[27]

A more important development was that such ideas were now voiced in Austria itself. On July 23 Bethmann Hollweg had a talk with the Hungarian opposition leader Count Andrassy,[28] which showed him that confidence in the army leadership had completely vanished in Hungary. The Austrian command no longer enjoyed the slightest prestige anywhere. It was considered nothing but a "morass." This was a reference to the notorious "hen coop" at Teschen headquarters, whither General Conrad, newly married to a Viennese society lady who had divorced her husband on his account, had taken his wife. She in turn had assembled a circle of officers' ladies, giving occasion for various entertainments and more ladies' salons. There was no end of gossip about all this among the Austrian Catholic nobility and the officer corps.

But Andrassy also rightly complained that Conrad not only left the political leadership uninformed but engaged in outright intrigue against it. Above all he criticized Conrad's military failures in Italy; and he was horrified by the disaster in Volhynia. "All of Hungary, the people as well as the army, would account it a real blessing if Field Marshal Hindenburg were entrusted with command of the entire eastern front." Count Tisza shared this view, Andrassy said, as did Count Burián. With the survival of the monarchy at stake, formal reservations and questions of etiquette must not be allowed to stand in the way. Andrassy, however, no longer believed in victory and did not altogether rule out the possibility of disaster. He hinted at the possibility that Austria might seek a separate peace with Britain or Italy.

The unfavorable impression this discussion made on Bethmann Hollweg was confirmed several weeks later when he visited Vienna at the invitation of Emperor Francis Joseph and his government, to discuss the Polish problem. [29] Many Austrians, he reported, despaired of the country's ability to fight on and were prepared to accept even the most humiliating peace. Others were boiling with indignation over their high command. "Its authority has been completely undermined, with the emperor, the people, and the army in the field." There could be no doubt of this, from his talks with Burián, Tisza, Stürgkh, and the diplomat Prince Montenuovo. These gentlemen had declared to him quite openly that the widening of Field Marshal Hindenburg's authority (extended in the meantime to a major share of the eastern front) brought a sigh of relief from army and people. The only regrettable thing was that the Germans had for so long heeded Conrad's opposition.

Bethmann Hollweg's reports agreed entirely with the bitter criticism of the army high command and the chief of staff personally expressed in secret dispatches by the section councilor, Ritter von Wiesner, the Austrian foreign ministry's "Questenberg" at Teschen headquarters. [30] Wiesner insisted that Conrad's pet project, the Italian campaign, carried out against the wishes of the emperor and the warnings of Archduke Eugene, commander of the southern front, was a failure from the start. In his planning work the chief of staff lacked seriousness, thoroughness, and responsibility. He required military supervision, and more than that, in the political field, something akin to guardianship.

Motivated by vanity and neurotically hypersensitive, Conrad, according to Wiesner, was incapable of self-criticism and of cooperating with others. He was much too strongly influenced by political resentment and wishful thinking, which often led him into inspired but fantastic notions. Hence the German General Staff must be allowed to exert a decisive influence on the conception and execution of Conrad's operational decisions. "Independent decisions on his part must be precluded as a matter of policy"; everything must be resolved by agreement between the two high commands.

The Austrian high command, in Wiesner's view, bore part of the responsibility for the disastrous failure on the eastern front. It should have long since removed the commander of the fourth army, known to be incompetent. Nor should it have tolerated the scandalous state of affairs that prevailed there, as we have already heard. Unfortunately, the high command dwelt in an ivory tower and had no real contact with the troops. It was nothing but a paper-shuffling office, an old-fashioned military debating society.

As shown by the example of the first, second, and seventh armies, Austro-Hungarian regiments were effective only when they were closely conjoined with German troops, officered in part by Germans, trained by Germans. The Germans were entirely justified in insisting that the reserves they made available so generously should fight under German rather than Austrian command. There was no reason whatever to impute self-seeking reservations to them. The two general staffs must be compelled to work together intimately, not merely by means of occasional conferences, as had hitherto been the case. The time had come for major decisions on military policy, and this was possible only if the two heads of government were involved.

In view of all these factors, it is readily understood why the German Chancellor pressed so hard for a unified high command on the eastern front under Hindenburg, to prevent any recurrence of such hapless events as the disaster at Lutsk. It also becomes understandable why he did not take Conrad's opposition too seriously and suspected that Falkenhayn's reservations were motivated by personal jealousy of Hindenburg; but whether he was right remains questionable. Poor cooperation between commands is a traditional weakness in coalition warfare, a natural consequence of the failure of the national interests of the partners to coincide entirely. It is the task primarily of political rather than military authority to strike a political balance.

Even a unified command under Hindenburg could have scarcely prevented the ill-conceived campaign against Italy—Conrad, after all, simply failed to heed the repeated warnings of the German supreme command. It should have been the job of the German government to intervene, but as we have heard, it was not briefed at all by the military; and it failed to perceive the magnitude of the danger, since even German generals on the eastern front did not recognize it in time. Only a few days before the Lutsk breakthrough, the German Colonel General von Linsingen, commanding the army group there, had given an optimistic review of his sector of the front.

It is a general truth that despite occasional front-line inspections by high staff officers, army group commanders are far too remote from the everyday realities of warfare to form accurate judgments of the efficiency of the troops at the front. Nor do they exert much influence on it. Even the higher troop commands find that difficult to accomplish and can do so only over longer periods of time, for troop efficiency and morale are not dependent entirely on the minimum of military training front-line troops can conduct. What after all could German generals have done to remedy the deep-seated rot in

the Austro-Hungarian army—inadequate equipment even in peacetime, deficiencies in training and in the replacement and supply systems, slack and
slovenly administration, the shortage of qualified leadership and training personnel following the terrible losses of the very first war months, the demoralization in the wake of so many failures and defeats, and above all the canker
of many tongues and nationalist clashes in the army?

To imagine that the Hindenburg mystique could put all this right, that his
supposed strategic genius could decisively better the situation on the eastern
front, was at bottom a very naive notion. The scope of higher strategy was
severely limited in trench warfare. Once the war of movement had come to a
halt in the east as well, the strategic tasks of an army group command consisted essentially—with some exceptions—of shifting reserves to places where
they were most urgently needed, or at best of deciding whether this front
sector or that should be held or relinquished. All the combat decisions as
such, the tactical phases, were up to the divisional staffs, or at best the army
and corps commands.

Viewed from this realistic perspective, the heated controversy that flared
up at imperial headquarters in June over putting Hindenburg in top command
in the east had very little military significance, though in a political sense it
was all the more important. In effect such a unified command, embracing all
the Austrian troops on the Russian front as well, would have had only the
virtue that decisions on committing reserves and forming main points of
resistance would have been speeded up, since there would have been no more
need to concert the two high commands; but even that goal was attainable
with any degree of assurance only if either the Austrian high command were
reconciled to playing a kind of subsidiary role as an auxiliary to its German
counterpart, or Hindenburg himself were made responsible to Teschen headquarters, which would have meant that Conrad von Hötzendorf would have
become nominally commander-in-chief of the German armies in the east.

Both politically and militarily, one alternative was as bad as the other. If
Hindenburg were made responsible to *both* high commands, the situation
would have been made far worse rather than improved. An added complication was that the reserves available in the east had long since become inadequate to plug the holes that kept opening up. Falkenhayn alone was in a
position to decide to what extent German divisions could be spared from the
hotly contested western front. His already superhuman job grew more difficult in the precise degree that the power of his capricious subordinate Ludendorff increased—to say nothing of the worry that Ludendorff's well-known
propensity for conquests in the Baltic area would make it impossible to shift
German troops in time to Volhynia and the Bukovina.[31]

In fact, Ludendorff was not merely capricious—he was filled with a deep
loathing of his rival and superior, Falkenhayn, for whose fall he worked with

every resource at his disposal. He was in constant touch with the foreign ministry (especially Zimmermann), by letter and telephone. It is quite clear that he was among the Chancellor's advisers in Bethmann Hollweg's many-pronged efforts to undermine Falkenhayn's credit with the Kaiser and under-line the political urgency of putting Hindenburg in supreme command.[32] It was asking a great deal of Falkenhayn to support expansion of Hindenburg's eastern headquarters jurisdiction before the Kaiser and the Austrians.

Actually Falkenhayn tried to persuade Conrad on July 12 and again a week later to have Austria's entire Russian front—which was laced with many German troops, as a kind of "whalebone"—placed under the unified com-mand of the German Field Marshal von Mackensen and his chief of staff, von Seeckt[33]—within the framework of the Austrian high command, of course. Both these officers had gained high renown in the campaigns of 1915 in Poland and Serbia, and both were intimately familiar with the situation in Volhynia and Galicia. In a military sense this was an excellent and clear-cut solution to the command issue. Seeckt himself had suggested it, in the belief that in this way a heavy counterattack on Rovno might still be mounted.[34] In face-to-face discussion Falkenhayn had also proposed the alternative of Prince Leopold of Bavaria, still with Seeckt as chief of staff.[35]

Conrad, sensing that his power would be greatly curtailed, vetoed both plans; but Bethmann Hollweg too withheld his approval. He promptly wired General von Lyncker that "our people will not appreciate Hindenburg being once again sidetracked in favor of a second-rank general." He proposed in-stead that Hindenburg be named in place of Mackensen, gaining the cautious support of the war minister, who was reluctant to lose Falkenhayn's trust and thus his own standing at headquarters.[36]

It was von Lyncker, chief of the military cabinet, who on June 25 under-took to discuss Bethmann Hollweg's views with Falkenhayn—though without mentioning that the Chancellor was behind it! The discussion was limited to the question of command over the entire German and Austrian eastern fronts, Lyncker pointing out that the appointment of anyone except Hindenburg would be regarded by the public and the army as stemming from jealousy of Hindenburg's glory. Falkenhayn was impressed and agreed to reconsider the matter.

He did state, however, that political moods and sentiments could not set aside military reservations, which he set forth with complete objectivity. It would be impossible, he said, to make the new commander-in-chief answer-able to both the German and the Austrian high commands. He also expressed doubt that the time had come when Hindenburg and Ludendorff could be spared at the Courland front.[37]

That same day Falkenhayn went to the Kaiser and told him that many voices favored putting Hindenburg in command. There was much to support this view, he added, especially the temper of the German public; but then he put forward his military counterarguments, with which the Kaiser at once strongly fell in. The job to be done on the southeastern front, he said, did not call for a top-ranking general like Hindenburg. Let the Austrians see how they made out alone, supported by German troops. He was, of course, dissembling. His real opinion is revealed in something he said to General von Plessen: "We would then have a king in the west [Falkenhayn], and one in the east [Hindenburg], and before you know it, I would be out of the picture." He was as worried as ever about Ludendorff's ruthless power drive.

The anti-Falkenhayn group at headquarters set a regular conspiracy afoot to change the Kaiser's mind. Valentini and the diplomat Baron Grünau persuaded Lyncker to suggest to the Kaiser—who was once again wavering—that even federated princes like the king of Bavaria might soon besiege him with demands for putting Hindenburg in charge. He was urged to heed other voices among his military entourage, for example to have a private talk with War Minister Wild. The group was unanimous that the Chancellor must on no account intervene in this matter, essentially one of military command.38 That would only provoke the Kaiser.

Efforts at headquarters in this direction continued methodically. Bethmann Hollweg was hopeful that Louis III of Bavaria might indeed put in a word, perhaps even demand outright that Hindenburg replace Falkenhayn;39 but when the king paid a visit to supreme headquarters late in June, he seems to have shrunk from such intervention—or at least failed to change the Kaiser's mind.40

At Bethmann Hollweg's behest the envoy von Treutler again held discussions with Lyncker and Falkenhayn. This was during the days when the full fury of the Somme offensive was unleashed, and it was apparently suggested to the chief of staff that in view of this new danger he should unburden himself of responsibility for the eastern front; but Falkenhayn was afraid that a divided authority would only make troop shifts from east to west more difficult, should they become necessary.

In the end, on July 2, Falkenhayn yielded, purely from tactical-political considerations, according to the verbal testimony of Lyncker. A letter from Jagow to Treutler had stated that there was widespread indignation in Berlin that Falkenhayn, allegedly from personal jealousy, was preventing Hindenburg's appointment to top command. To silence these voices, Falkenhayn, together with Lyncker (who once again carefully refrained from naming the Chancellor as his instigator), persuaded the Kaiser to sanction a request to the Austrian high command asking approval for giving Hindenburg command of the entire eastern front. The inquiry, however, was worded to avoid any impression of great urgency.41

William II gave way with great reluctance and flew into a rage at the suggestion that he should consider public opinion in Berlin. This he described as a form of abdication. It meant that Hindenburg was taking his place, as tribune of the people.[42] So great was his agitation that he promptly announced he could no longer bear to have Treutler, liaison man with the foreign ministry, about, even though he acknowledged that the man was able and had done good work. He had Treutler relieved. His entire entourage noted his mood of deep depression.

These events carry profound significance. They show that the Kaiser was more sensitive to what was going on than his Chancellor. A political turn of great importance was taking place. The authority of the crown, and with it the old monarchial order, were about to pale once for all before the gloriole that encircled the two popular heroes of Tannenberg. The Kaiser's freedom of action, and the Chancellor's as well, were being circumscribed by the need for taking uncontrollable popular opinion into account.

But more than that, the Kaiser undoubtedly stood in dread of the ruthless Ludendorff in the role of his principal military adviser. When on July 4 the Austrian, as expected, sent word through the German liaison officer General von Cramon that they would deeply resent the appointment of Hindenburg as commander-in-chief east, rejecting it out of hand, the Kaiser was clearly relieved. He promptly vetoed Lyncker's proposal that he appeal directly to Emperor Francis Joseph, since neither Archduke Frederic nor Conrad deserved the slightest consideration; and when Lyncker advised placing Hindenburg at least in full charge of the German forces in the east, the Kaiser grew rude and said that he was not minded to allow himself to be deposed. Indirectly but quite clearly his boasts and frantic efforts to play the absolute master reveal that he was afraid in his heart of Ludendorff. As he put it on July 22 to Valentini: "Hindenburg does only what Ludendorff tells him to do, and Ludendorff will do what I tell him to do."[43]

By contrast, Bethmann Hollweg, as we have already seen from his letters to Valentini, was most unhappy that the "big issue" had been rejected and that he was powerless to intervene directly. Probably at no other time did he sense so deeply the quandary of his official position, which burdened him with ultimate political responsibility for the war's outcome without granting him any direct influence in the sphere of military command. He found the situation quite intolerable:

> I see us running the risk of drifting toward perdition. My responsibility as such compels me to act. Many people, including even highly placed officers, expect me to intervene. Yet I have to tell myself that I should probably spoil everything if I did intervene. And so I must keep my hands in my lap. The situation is thoroughly rotten and in the long run untenable.[44] . . . How can one calmly carry on while one sees the coun-

try hurtling toward the abyss, not from objective causes but by virtue of personal ambitions? Is not part of the blame mine? Can I be of any use at all in my office, if I keep silent in the face of such things?

Falkenhayn's yielding had been to no avail. Bethmann Hollweg continued to believe that he was acting from selfish motives and spoke of the "dreadful responsibility" Falkenhayn was taking on himself. "Germany and history will call him and the Kaiser to account." Exhortations kept arriving from Hindenburg's headquarters to "keep working for the 'big issue.' " The two generals prevailed on Helfferich, who happened to be visiting them in Kovno, to telephone Bethmann Hollweg on July 4. The absence of a unified command, he said, went beyond the limits of responsibility that could be accepted in so dangerous a situation. The two were actually close to submitting their resignations, but Helfferich did not dare pass on details of their opinion of Falkenhayn's military performance.

The very next day Ludendorff felt called upon to report to the Reich chancellery that he had only just learned that the situation at certain threatened positions had improved, by virtue of troops having been dispatched there. He cited as typical evidence for the lack of a unified command that he had heard about this only within the hour.[45] On July 5 General Hoffmann drafted a report which the field marshal was to send to the Kaiser or his adjutant general. Bethmann Hollweg, to whom General Eisenhart-Rothe had been dispatched as a courier, counseled against sending the message in its original form.[46] Doubts had come to the Chancellor whether it were really advisable to change chiefs of staff in the middle of the battle of the Somme, and whether this were the right time to summon the "heavenly twins" from the eastern front to Charleville. Might it not be enough for the time being to "surround Falkenhayn with some competent men"? [47] Efforts continued to be made, however, to shake the Kaiser's confidence in the efficiency of his chief of staff, by relaying adverse criticism from high troop commanders on the western front. Much store had been set, in this connection, in Crown Prince Rupprecht of Bavaria and General von Below of the Somme front; but both reneged when it came to the crucial moment.[48]

Meanwhile the situation grew more and more critical on the eastern front, especially its southern wing; and the Austrian high command's pleas for help got more and more frantic. By mid-July even the foreign minister, Count Burián, repeatedly appealed to the Chancellor for German reinforcements to the southern army. Bethmann Hollweg transmitted the appeal to Falkenhayn with a recommendation that it should be granted only on condition that the Austrians should at last show themselves amenable to the Germans' demand for a unified high command. To that end he offered diplomatic assistance. He no longer spoke of placing the entire eastern front under Hindenburg, however, but only of extending Hindenburg's authority to the south, the army groups of Prince Leopold and Linsingen. This was a compromise Falkenhayn himself had proposed to the field marshal on July 8, in order to meet his demands and at the same time dampen Ludendorff's ardor. Hindenburg had agreed, but not Conrad.[49]

The quest for a compromise continued and Bethmann Hollweg hoped to be able to reach an understanding with Falkenhayn, after which the two of them would compel Austrian agreement. Initially the chief of staff was skeptical and balky. Germany was simply not in a position to make available sufficient troops to reoccupy the Bukovina, as Burián wanted. Hence hard-and-fast conditions would serve only to increase tension between the two headquarters. Strengthening the Austrian front would serve a purpose only if the Austrians themselves were to make a beginning of holding their front. Since June 10 twelve German divisions, a sizable army, had gone down the drain in the gaps the Austrians had allowed to open up. Instead of crying for help Vienna should be trying to raise the morale of its various nationalities.

Bethmann Hollweg bade Falkenhayn to come to a meeting in Berlin on July 18,[50] at which the chief of staff appeared with the brusque remark that he had only a few minutes' time. The situation at the front was bad, critical, "soft as a pudding"—the vernacular seemed to him sufficient answer to the Chancellor's inquiry. He was apparently at pains to let Bethmann Hollweg know he was well aware that he was facing an opponent working for his downfall by every possible means. But after a rather sharp exchange Falkenhayn did enter into a calm discussion of various matters, including the command question.

He had just tried in vain, in a personal discussion, to win Conrad's approval of the compromise already mentioned; and he now sought to present the Austrian's military objections to the Chancellor, objections with which he said he was compelled to agree. Placing the army group of Linsingen under Hindenburg, he said, would create a weak "seam" between the German and Austrian spheres of command at the most exposed location. German headquarters, moreover, would be inclined to point any retreat toward the northwest rather than the southwest, as the Austrians would have it. The Austrian high command would feel "dispossessed" and resentful; and a mere change in the spheres of command would be of only theoretical rather than practical value.

Nor could a Hindenburg in supreme command cure the canker of treason among the Czech and Ruthenian regiments, or remedy the lack of reserves. Falkenhayn had actually just reached agreement with Conrad and Ludendorff on the only practical step that could be taken at the moment to bolster the tottering eastern front, methodically mixing the units in such a way that Austrian divisions were shifted to Hindenburg's front, while German divisions went to Galicia in return.51 Falkenhayn added that he would not dignify with any response the reproach that he was motivated by personal enmity against Hindenburg and Ludendorff. If Conrad were to agree to the creation of a unified command in the east, so would he, Falkenhayn; but he would not do so against Conrad's opposition.

There is no reason to doubt the sincerity of these arguments. They convinced General Lyncker as well, who declined to join Falkenhayn's opponents in undermining the Kaiser's trust in his chief of staff.52 Falkenhayn himself must have begun to sense, however, that his military authority was ebbing away. To avoid disaster at the borders of Rumania, he did after all dispatch aid to the Austrians in the Carpathian mountains—indeed, he sent a crack unit, the so-called Alpine Corps. He had Cramon further sound out Teschen on whether a feasible solution of the command issue might not be worked out.53

In time the moral authority of the Austrians suffered so greatly because of further disasters at their front that their opposition to a German high command slackened noticeably. There was another breakthrough at Lutsk and Brody, and Turkish troops actually had to be summoned to stiffen the Galician front.54 Cramon's reports and an urgent wire from the Chancellor on July 21 persuaded Falkenhayn to try another compromise. Let Hindenburg take command of the entire Austrian front in the east, south of the Pripet, including the Linsingen army group, while surrendering his German troop command, i.e., becoming answerable to the Austrian high command—with the proviso that the latter would act only in agreement with the German supreme command. Both commands would thus have the benefit of Hindenburg's tested counsel for operations all along the eastern front.

The idea was brilliant. In a formal sense it harked back to the earlier German proposal of placing the entire Austrian front under German command, only that Hindenburg now replaced Mackensen, as Bethmann Hollweg had wished.55 It offered Falkenhayn the additional advantage of relieving him of continual competition with a "commander-in-chief east." Hindenburg, moreover, would have to show the world what he, the renowned captain, could do with Austrian troops.

Nevertheless there is no reason to attribute the whole project to personal jealousy on the part of Falkenhayn. It was in fact based on a proposal by Groener which had been endorsed by the political section of the General Staff under Colonel von Bartenwerffer (later on Ludendorff's right hand), because it would put Ludendorff where his ruthless energy would be most useful.56 Further, the change would make it easier to loosen the grip of eastern headquarters on the reserves in the north and make them available for the Galician front.

Above all, according to Cramon in Teschen—with whom Falkenhayn was

in constant telephone communication—it was the only form of German command over the Austrian front to which Conrad was prepared to assent, since
in a formal sense it left the prestige of the Austrian high command untouched. Even Emperor Francis Joseph expressly approved. Ludendorff, with
whom Falkenhayn at once discussed the plan by telephone, did object, but
Hindenburg stated that he would abide by any imperial order to that effect.
Bethmann Hollweg's close entourage, on the other hand, fumed and was
convinced that German public opinion would bitterly resent placing its national hero under Austrian jurisdiction.

The issue was finally brought to a head by the Kaiser's decision to take
part personally in the discussions with the Austrians. Bethmann Hollweg had
unloosed a hail of telegrams on him. He emphasized the danger threatening
from the Rumanian side, cited Hungarian and Austrian dissatisfaction with
Teschen headquarters, and reported urgent demands for putting Hindenburg
in charge on the part of not only the Bulgarians but prominent Austrian
politicians and generals, the South German states, and German public opinion.[57]

What made the strongest impression on the Kaiser was a dispatch, passed
on by Bethmann Hollweg on July 22, from Ambassador Tschirschky on a
discussion with Andrassy. The gist of it was that if there were such a strong
demand for Hindenburg even in Austria-Hungary, why should it not be possible to prevail over Conrad's objections? The Kaiser was persuaded at once
to set out for talks with the Austrians at Pless, but en route he had second
thoughts, which Jagow, Lyncker, and Wild did their best to overcome. Without asking his permission, they summoned Bethmann Hollweg to Pless in
turn, and he had already arranged that Hindenburg and Ludendorff should be
invited.

As soon as the imperial party arrived on the evening of July 25, a kind of
race developed between Falkenhayn, who wished to leave for Teschen early
the next morning for preliminary talks with the Austrian high command
along the lines of his proposal, and Falkenhayn's enemies, who persuaded the
Kaiser to bid the chief of staff to await the Chancellor's personal report.
Bethmann Hollweg arrived shortly before eleven o'clock that night and in an
immediate audience put it to the Kaiser that Hindenburg must at all costs be
made commander-in-chief of the whole eastern front. The fate of the house
of Hohenzollern was at stake, he insisted. If he had to conclude a disappointing peace, he could do so only with Hindenburg, not without him. In effect
this was already a covert demand for Falkenhayn's relief.

Falkenhayn was now instructed to sound out Teschen along the lines
proposed by the Chancellor, which he did, with negative results, as was to be
expected. The Chancellor and his confidants were convinced that they were
dealing with a prearranged plot by the two staff chiefs; and according to

notes left by Valentini, Bethmann Hollweg had a long, serious, and highly agitated interview with the Kaiser, "whom he spared nothing." According to the Chancellor's own report, he argued against Falkenhayn "with unparalleled vehemence."

Archduke Frederic and General Conrad were summoned to Pless for the next afternoon. The Kaiser, much wrought up, remarked with irritation that he was now expected to "square the circle." The Chancellor was no less upset, and on the next morning (July 27) he told Admiral von Müller in confidence that things had reached a stage where Germany might have to ask Wilson to mediate on the basis of a German surrender of Belgium. In the meantime headquarters east had arrived, and there was a sharp exchange between Falkenhayn and Ludendorff in the presence of the Kaiser, who sided with Ludendorff. He is said to have told the chief of staff not to keep interrupting the field marshal and at the last he declared: "I want to tell you one thing, I'm not leaving here without having straightened out this affair. That much I owe my people."[58]

In the evening the Austrians came for a conference, which was made easier by the simultaneous receipt of bad news from the Austrian front. Archduke Frederic, a man of small caliber but considerable charm, had already shown himself less obstinate than his chief of staff in Teschen. Nevertheless the meeting even now was unable to go beyond a compromise. Hindenburg was to take over the entire front from the Baltic to the second Austrian army (the army group under Böhm-Ermoli in the region of Tarnopol). He was to remain under the German high command, which was to reach agreement with the Austrian high command on orders to the groups south of the Pripet.

In substance this agreement accorded rather closely with Falkenhayn's first compromise proposal of July 8. Yet the manner in which it was reached represented a bitter disappointment to the German chief of staff. He felt pushed into a corner by the fact that Hindenburg and Ludendorff had been summoned for consultations on a matter that was solely within the competence of the supreme command. They had had their initial talk with the Kaiser alone, moreover, and he had been called in only later. Deeply hurt, he considered submitting his resignation and stayed away from the dinner tendered the Austrian guests, having in consequence to accept the fact that the crucial meeting took place without him. It was the first plainly visible step toward depriving him of power.

The new agreement was little more than an ostentatious measure to reassure the German public, though it was greeted with great hopes on all sides, even in the countries allied with Germany.[59] So little did it achieve real unity of command on the eastern front that almost immediately a number of highly complex additional agreements had to be concluded in order to bring about tolerable cooperation between the two high commands and preserve their freedom to commit their sparse reserves at the various fronts.

As Falkenhayn had predicted, there were prompt clashes between headquarters east and the German supreme command, for the chief of staff found
it quite impossible to reach agreement with so ruthless and self-willed a
subordinate as Ludendorff on the apportionment of reserves and on troop
shifts.60 From the outset Ludendorff was manifestly intent on precipitating
conflicts, which he carried straight to the Kaiser, confident of the Chancellor's support and sure that he would sooner or later be called to replace
Falkenhayn.

When his requests were rejected or met only after what he thought was too
great a delay, he had the field marshal appeal directly to the Kaiser, which
was a quite unprecedented procedure. He would also complain to the chief of
the military cabinet that the chief of staff was "unwilling to heed my earnest
admonitions and seems incapable of dispensing with half-measures." He
would either ignore orders to dispatch units to other sectors where serious
danger threatened, or carry them out only with the greatest reluctance and
after repeated pleas.

He was, of course, primarily concerned with the protection of his own
front sectors; but on August 9, on the receipt of intelligence that Rumania's
entry into the war was imminent, he had Hindenburg sign a direct appeal, in
which the Kaiser was "implored" to dispatch at once four or five divisions
from the western front for a strike into the Bukovina—as though such a thing
were even conceivable while the Battle of the Somme was raging! At the
same time he refused to detach even a single division of his own to reinforce
the Austrian army of the south under Archduke Charles, heir to the Austrian
throne. Indeed, Falkenhayn had to reconcile himself to a further weakening
of that army, from which General Conrad withdrew a division to counter a
particularly massive Italian attack on the Isonzo.

Ludendorff and Hindenburg, in other words, were already seeking to function as the Kaiser's immediate advisers, in supreme command of the army,
putting forward proposals and demands that went far beyond their jurisdiction and endeavoring by every means at their disposal to check or circumvent
Falkenhayn's influence over the Kaiser. They were in constant close touch
with General von Seeckt, chief of staff to Archduke Charles, in an effort to
mobilize Seeckt's influence at supreme headquarters against Falkenhayn. Indeed they went out of their way to voice their criticism of Falkenhayn and
his chief of operations, Tappen, with the result that doubt and secret opposition began to stir among the younger officers even in Falkenhayn's own
staff.61

When General Groener visited Falkenhayn at headquarters in mid-August,
he found the chief of staff seriously affected in body and mind by all these
troubles. He was impressed with Falkenhayn's sincerity when he was assured:
"You may believe me, I am pondering the maps day and night, to find
available troops." In his memoirs Ludendorff himself later admitted that until

he first visited the western front in the fall of 1916, he had no idea of the desperate severity and danger of the struggle there. Perhaps he really did not realize in August 1916 that he was asking the impossible of the high command. Yet he was not merely out for divisions, but for the fall of his hated rival. As before, in the winter of 1914-1915, every resource was marshaled to that end, including political intrigue, and even the empress was once again enlisted.[62] Even in the purely military question of committing reserves, Bethmann Hollweg was formally requested to intervene with the Kaiser along the lines Ludendorff desired.[63]

The Chancellor did indeed soon take an active part. On August 15 his agent, Baron Grünau, reported to him that the Kaiser wished to see Russia made more amenable to peace by vigorous military action. The trouble was that Falkenhayn apparently could not make up his mind to break off his ill-starred Verdun offensive at last. On the contrary, only the day before he had reached agreement with General Knobelsdorff on a new attack on Fort Souville, outraging the crown prince and Schulenburg. Some thirty divisions would now again be tied down and "Herr von Falkenhayn will be able to say that he is unable to spare any divisions from the west." Grünau added that in his own view the only possible explanation was malice or lack of resolution on Falkenhayn's part.

This report was palpably biased and distorted the true situation, an example of the type of rumor then circulating among Falkenhayn's enemies at headquarters.[64] But Bethmann Hollweg took it seriously and reacted with a comprehensive report of his own to the Kaiser—already known to us in part—in which he drew a vivid picture of the decay within the Danubian monarchy, described the contempt in which Conrad and Teschen headquarters were held, and emphasized the great pressure being exerted by politicians in Vienna and Budapest to have Hindenburg made commander-in-chief over the entire eastern front.

Bethmann Hollweg's main point was the urgency of shifting the full weight of German military operations to the eastern front. "Every single man who can be spared [in the west] should be committed at the scene where the final issue of this world struggle now impends."[65] This was an attack on Falkenhayn, whose strategy was at the outset criticized as fallacious—though indirectly and with a certain reticence. Bethmann Hollweg's memorandum was received at headquarters coincidentally with a direct report from Hindenburg and Ludendorff, in which they protested in writing and in almost threatening terms against a repeated order to make a division available for transfer.

Falkenhayn now set about defending himself vigorously. He demanded that the Kaiser enjoin further direct reports of this nature, instructing Hindenburg to route them through official supreme command channels; but the Kaiser no longer dared. He did reject the field marshal's protest, in a private communication couched in friendly terms, emphasizing that "supreme head-quarters retains exclusive responsibility for its directives." Even this was enough to set off a new storm at headquarters east and unleash an open attack on Falkenhayn, aimed at bringing about his downfall.

The opening gun was another direct missive to the Kaiser on August 19, in which Hindenburg claimed he had received totally inadequate support for his front. He rejected out of hand—and doubtless wrongly—supreme headquarters' argument that replacement troops were needed much more urgently by the army under Archduke Charles on the Rumanian border, against which the main impact of the Russian offensive was now being plainly directed. At the same time Hindenburg sent a wire to the chief of the military cabinet, in which he threatened his resignation unless the Kaiser immediately granted him an audience in the presence of only Lyncker and Ludendorff, i.e., excluding Falkenhayn. Ludendorff too sent in a resignation, which was to be submitted, however, only after Hindenburg's final decision. Baron Grünau was informed of all this by telephone, and he immediately passed on the information to Bethmann Hollweg by wire. Grünau, indeed, kept bombarding the Chancellor with reports from headquarters that were strongly biased in the direction of headquarters east.[66]

The Chancellor promptly responded with a wire to Lyncker, stating that he had heard of Hindenburg's threat to resign and would have to present to the Kaiser immediately his views on the political repercussions of such a step. He arrived in Pless almost at once, on August 21, intent on convincing the Kaiser that Falkenhayn no longer enjoyed the confidence of the army. But the trip was a disappointment to him. The Kaiser had meanwhile, in gracious but unmistakable terms, declined the audience Hindenburg sought. The threat of resignation he simply swept aside: "Your Excellency continues to have my trust . . . but surely will accord me, at this stage of severe tension facing me, your fullest support in easing my task of leadership in a war of unexampled ferocity. I shall therefore regard your inquiry as disposed of."

Incredible as it may seem, Hindenburg still did not let up. On August 20 he responded with another long document full of new complaints about Falkenhayn, and maintaining his own views of the situation at the front; but all this was done so ineptly, harping on petty details about troop shifts and lacking any broad perspective, that it miscarried completely and failed of its intended effect even on Bethmann Hollweg, who indeed was quite unhappy about it.

On August 21 Falkenhayn replied in a long memorandum to the Chancellor's criticism of August 16 which the Kaiser had given him to read. This document can scarcely have failed to make a strong impression on the Chancellor. It was a surpassingly skillful defense of Falkenhayn's strategy since the beginning of the year, couched in firm, clear, and virile language. It was also a scathing indictment of those "laymen, including many in field gray up to the highest ranks . . . who believe it sufficient to settle where the next strike is to be made and then shift surplus forces to that point." These people were simply incapable of appreciating the desperate German situation, how limited was the scope for leadership by virtue of exhaustion of resources on all fronts, and the mischief instigated by misleading catchwords like "decision in the east" and "decision in the west."

Few will dispute today that Falkenhayn was amply justified in his rebuke to his adversaries in the Hindenburg camp, and that he deserves high credit for his unswerving refusal to endanger the gravely threatened western front in order to plug holes in the eastern front—which could never have made up for a possible collapse of the German front on the Somme.[67] The Kaiser, at least, was convinced. The Chancellor dared not at this moment ask for the removal of the chief of staff.

Even Lyncker and War Minister Wild, both of whom had supported Hindenburg as commander-in-chief on the eastern front, now proved balky. They firmly disputed that Falkenhayn had forfeited the confidence of the army and was being unfavorably judged by the real experts within the General Staff. Unable to rest his case on the criticisms of younger officers in the operations division—reported to him by Colonel Bauer, one of the most radical Ludendorff adherents—and unsure of sufficient support from the crown prince of Bavaria and the duke of Württemberg, the Chancellor had to depart on August 24, having failed in his purpose.[68] The Kaiser sent a negative but friendly private letter in response to Hindenburg's last appeal. Falkenhayn once more managed to retain the Kaiser's favor.

It was not to last long. Three days later imperial headquarters was advised by telephone that Rumania had declared war on Austria-Hungary. Although not really unexpected, the news struck like a bombshell. The Kaiser at first lost his head completely, considered the war lost beyond hope, and concluded that Germany would have to sue for peace. It took much reassurance on the part of his entourage to restore his spirits. This was naturally done with constant references to Hindenburg as the only possible savior in need. Valentini kept working on Lyncker, who was finally convinced that a change in command was inevitable and so advised the Kaiser, together with Plessen, the adjutant general.[69]

The war minister, Wild, once Falkenhayn's loyal supporter but long since wavering, also replied to the Kaiser's inquiry as to the staff chief's strategic competence in terms that inclined to criticism rather than praise, noting that his interlocutor had already inwardly decided against Falkenhayn.[70] By the afternoon of August 28, the decision had been all but made; and when Bethmann Hollweg, Hindenburg, and Ludendorff appeared at Pless castle the next morning, summoned by Valentini and Lyncker, it remained only to ratify formally the appointment of a new supreme command.

According to notes by Plessen and Lyncker, the Kaiser did not have an easy time of the decision, nor could it be justified by purely military considerations. Falkenhayn was in no way responsible for Rumania joining the enemy camp. He had expected this to happen rather later, but he never had any doubts but that the continuing Austrian defeats and retreats fed fuel to Rumanian belligerence, especially since the Allies were offering that country the most outrageous territorial annexations as bait.[71]

It was for that reason that Falkenhayn, against Ludendorff's stubborn protest, had assigned by far the greater part of the German reserves on the Carpathian front to Archduke Charles rather than to the armies under headquarters east; but as shown in his letter to the Chancellor of August 21 he also realized that the Rumanian decision was based far more on the general war situation than on closing individual gaps in the Austrian front. The only thing that would have made a real impression in Bucharest would have been a successful strike to regain the Bukovina; but since the Austrians had lost more than half a million men since early June on the eastern front alone, two-thirds of them prisoners and "missing," the necessary resources were simply not available at the crucial time. To his credit, on the other hand, Falkenhayn had prevailed in the commitment of Turkish divisions in Galicia and in getting Bulgaria to agree formally to intervene against Rumania, if that country entered the war—which was soon to prove extremely useful.

All that could not undo his fate. What was alone decisive was that the Kaiser needed a political scapegoat at this moment of disaster (which he overestimated); and Falkenhayn was the sacrificial goat. In the eyes of the people, moreover, a savior was needed. It was in that role that Hindenburg was summoned with his nominal assistant but actual master, Ludendorff. The decision was one of the weightiest the Kaiser ever took in the spheres of war and politics. As we have seen, it was Bethmann Hollweg who pressed him for it by every means, and thus the historic responsibility was primarily his.

At least one officer at imperial headquarters perceived how momentous this decision was, Colonel von Marschall, Lyncker's most important associate in the military cabinet. He confessed to Groener on the evening of August 28 his fears that Ludendorff "in his boundless pride and ambition will wage war until the German people are completely exhausted, which will saddle the monarchy with the blame." He added that he had set down his views in a memorandum, since he could not assume responsibility for the change in command.[72]

His words were prophetic. The strongest stricture on Bethmann Hollweg's gifts as a statesman is that he failed to see the future with the same clarity, despite his gnawing doubts about Ludendorff, and that he believed blindly that the glory surrounding Hindenburg's name could be used as a cover for a compromise peace. This was to be his own downfall, for neither Hindenburg nor the German people were prepared to accept a "peace of renunciation" of the kind Bethmann Hollweg pursued—indeed, quite the contrary. His policies therefore drifted once again into a murky atmosphere of insincerity and half-measures. It is true, however, that Bethmann Hollweg's illusions were shared by virtually all the German politicians of the time. The appointment of a "third supreme command" was greeted with a storm of enthusiasm, and the Chancellor was showered with congratulations.[73]

In order to pass fair judgment, it is necessary to note that he was no more entirely free in settling this matter than in any others concerning the war. The pressure of public opinion was stronger than his will and his insight. There was an almost obsessive quality to the notion that the war must not be brought to an end without first having another go with that presumed genius, the hero of Tannenberg.

It was the same kind of obsession that later dictated the desperate venture of unrestricted U-boat warfare. On both occasions the means employed to bring salvation led Germany even deeper into perdition. This would have been difficult to foresee with certainty; and to convince the public of it would have been quite impossible. There are few historical examples that demonstrate with such clarity how inhumanly difficult it is to surmount and master the natural conflict between statesmanship and war. We have closely followed Bethmann Hollweg's zealous endeavors not to lose the reins in running the war. He had had many clashes with Falkenhayn on this issue, and in the end had always managed to prevail. Henceforth a stronger will wrested the reins from his hands.

Within our historical presentation as a whole, Falkenhayn's fall and the seizure of power by the "third supreme command" marks an epoch. With the rise to the pinnacle of the military hierarchy of Ludendorff, a ruthless man of will and a soldier first and last, the problem of militarism in Germany gains a new aspect.

# THREE

Rise of the
Supreme Command
to Political Supremacy
(1916-1917)

# 7

# The Poland Manifesto
# and Its Failure

A S NOTED by Admiral von Müller, Bethmann Hollweg, on the day the
new command was appointed, was "dissolved in bliss over Hindenburg's personality."[1] But before the month of September was over
he already had evidence that the new "chief of staff" was only a
figurehead who pliantly covered everything held to be right by Ludendorff,
the real head of the *Oberste Heeresleitung* (OHL), the supreme army command. Hindenburg's signature was no more than a mere matter of form.
Bethmann Hollweg had also come to appreciate that the change of cast,
rather than softening the conflict between political and military authority,
had deepened it to an immeasurably greater degree than had been the case
under Falkenhayn.

This was dramatically illustrated by Hindenburg's reply to a request put
forward by the Chancellor on September 28 that a desire voiced by leading
Reichstag deputies be met by delegating a qualified General Staff officer to
appear before the next session of the budget committee, for the purpose of
briefing its members on the war situation. It was bad enough that the Kaiser
rejected this request as "unwarranted parliamentary interference in the command power"; but Hindenburg (i.e., Ludendorff) gratuitously added: "Confidence in me has been widely expressed, and I expect that my favorable view
of the situation will meet with the same confidence and strengthen optimism."[2]

It also became clear very soon that even the authority of Hindenburg's
name, despite wide approbation in Austria, was not strong enough to overcome the internal tensions within the war alliance. During the final days of
his tenure Falkenhayn had tried to go beyond the July 27 reorganization of
the command in the east and establish by treaty a position of supremacy for the

German emperor and his General Staff over all the armed forces in the alliance. In "all common affairs relating to the conduct of the war" his was to be the final decision, as a rule on the basis of prior understandings with the various high commands. A desire for such a convention had been voiced by Enver Pasha of Turkey, King Ferdinand of Bulgaria, and officers in Austrian high command circles.

Falkenhayn seems to have been mainly motivated by a desire to tie the Bulgarians even more closely to German military leadership, especially in the event of a Rumanian campaign; to put an end to the perpetual quarrels with General Conrad over points of military concentration; and above all to prevent any repetition of so misconceived an Austrian operation as the Italian campaign of May 1916. Archduke Frederic was won over to the plan, but Conrad von Hötzendorf objected strenuously, indeed threatened to resign, since he regarded a German supreme command not only as utterly impracticable, but incompatible with Austria-Hungary's status as a great power. Emperor Francis Joseph was less sensitive and had a counterproposal worked out that would have amounted to something like a supreme war council of the allied powers.

These negotiations were not yet concluded at the time of Falkenhayn's fall, but the new supreme command did not hesitate a moment to continue them; and it did quite soon, on September 6, succeed in securing written agreement among the four allies, which formally granted the German emperor a "supreme war leadership." Before taking any important decision, however, he had to listen to the individual high commands and reach agreement with them in principle. The "supreme leadership," moreover, was limited to general strategic planning. Thus the whole scheme had formal rather than practical significance.

To top it off, Conrad had insisted on adding a secret clause relating to his sphere of authority: In all operations and negotiations protection of Austro-Hungarian integrity was to have equal importance with that of Germany; and if the Austrian high command found itself unable to accept the "proposals" (mind you, not directives! ) of the supreme war leadership, the two monarchs were to confer. Thus acknowledgment of the special national interests of the Danubian monarchy within the alliance was carefully preserved.[3]

Despite all the generous German armed aid they enjoyed, the Austrians retained their profound apprehension of German preeminence. At Teschen headquarters the Germans were thought quite capable of bartering away Austrian interests to an unlimited degree at the peace table, indeed even while the war was still on.[4] There were widespread complaints of German arrogance and tactlessness. The Germans on their part were increasingly worried about the signs of internal decay in Austria, nor were they by any means certain of their allies' loyalty, once the situation had become critical. Reporting such sentiments to his minister, Prince Hohenlohe thought it wise to add that for the time being, with Austria owing Germany two and a half billions in war debts, there was no alternative but to cling to the alliance "until we can again stand on our own feet." He thought that a continuing close relation between the two countries was desirable but by no means "the best and only policy."[5]

The recipient of this report, Count Burián, tried on his part to make the best possible capital for the Hapsburg state out of the German alliance. Since July he had pressed for an agreement that all "war booty" taken by any of the allied powers in any theater of war would be divided up in a fixed proportion favorable to Austria—he had in mind about one-third. This was to apply to war indemnities as well. There were protracted negotiations on this matter.

The Prussian war ministry took the position that subsequent division of war booty was not feasible;[6] but Count Burián stubbornly insisted on prompt agreement about a quota for at least the war indemnities, apparently fearing that at a later date Austria might draw the short end of the bargain. He combined this with a demand for a "solidarity agreement," under which the two powers should bind themselves not to evacuate occupied territories until their enemies returned whatever territories they had taken.

This might have obliged the Germans to continue the war indefinitely, to restore to their ally the extensive regions he had lost—East Galicia, Bukovina, Gorizia. This Bethmann Hollweg steadfastly rejected, against incessant and ultimately almost threatening pressure on the part of Burián and his Berlin ambassador. He did, however, promise an equitable division of any war indemnities that might eventuate, in proportion to each ally's expenditures and subsidies to other allies.[7] This was a pledge Germany could well afford to make, since its war effort was incomparably the greatest and its subventions to its allies were enormous. The entire debate was at the time purely theoretical, indeed quite unrealistic, and it is understandable only in the context of the discussions then taking place about the future of Poland and the general war aims of the Central Powers, of which more anon (Chapter 8, Part 3).

In the face of such internal tensions to which the alliance was being subjected, it comes as a surprise that the OHL thought the time opportune not only for concluding a military convention with Austria-Hungary, which Falkenhayn had vigorously rejected only the year before on the ground that Germany should first bring its ally completely to heel, but also for initiating a complete political reorganization of the Danubian monarchy. To this end the Chancellor was given a report from a German liaison officer with the second Austrian army concerning a discussion with its chief of staff, Bardolff, who had unfolded a fanciful plan to him.

Under it Conrad von Hötzendorf and Archduke Frederic were to be "removed" from office and the heir to the throne, Archduke Charles, would be proclaimed supreme commander. He would then, "over the head of the aged emperor," put into effect the alleged political testament of the assassinated heir, Francis Ferdinand. This provided for dividing the dual monarchy into six viceroyships, grouped by nationalities, each under an archduke who would rotate every five years. German would be the language of government and command, and there would be an over-all "Chancellor."

Astonishingly enough, Ludendorff took this pipe dream with sufficient seriousness to present it in an official communication over Hindenburg's signature to Bethmann Hollweg. He did not identify himself with its contents, but stated that it was Germany's "inescapable duty" to help Austria-Hungary "put its house in order." Attached to the document, but not preserved in the files, was a military convention, probably also drafted by Bardolff, which apparently went a long way toward adapting the Austro-Hungarian military system to the German model.

The Chancellor had no choice but to tell the OHL as tactfully as possible that the whole scheme was amateurish and unrealistic and to propose direct negotiations with the Austrian high command at Teschen concerning a military convention, which indeed he welcomed as such. He did not neglect to mention that Austria might resent any German efforts to meddle with its internal affairs, might indeed respond by going back on the alliance and concluding a separate peace, even at considerable sacrifice.8

To Ludendorff, the headstrong activist, this probably seemed another example of "weak-kneed German diplomacy." How primitive were his and Hindenburg's notions of the character of the alliance was shown again a few weeks later. Following the proclamation—still to be discussed—of a kingdom of Poland to come, to exclude Galicia, Emperor Francis Joseph had promised his Galician subjects expanded home rule, as a kind of substitute for their exclusion from the new state, thus seeking to avoid political unrest. This act of appeasement was all the more necessary since it was precisely in Galicia that the Polish nationalist movement had had its inception in 1914.

But German headquarters was indignant that the German government had not been informed of this step beforehand. Indeed, there it was viewed as an openly hostile act, an attempt to outmaneuver German Polish policy in Warsaw. The Kaiser called the Austrian edict "scandalous," and his frenetic wire to the Chancellor on November 6 showed clearly how completely he had succumbed to the influence of his new military advisers, even in political questions. Hindenburg, he said, was outraged by Burián's double-dealing. The Germans would have to refuse to deal with him any longer and force his resignation.

Bethmann Hollweg tried vainly to calm the waters and make the Kaiser understand that such steps would be deeply resented in Vienna, indeed regarded as an insult to the aged emperor. The OHL replied on November 7 in deliberately provocative tones that Austria's action demonstrated a flagrant disregard of German power and purpose which could not be allowed to go unanswered. German diplomacy had already made far too many tactical compromises. "Our unwillingness to intervene in the internal affairs of Austria before and during the war has burdened our conduct of the war at every step. If we continue to shun such intervention where our vital interests are at stake it will mean giving up any hope of stiffening Austrian policy, and the question arises as to why we are fighting for Austria at all." How did the Chancellor envisage future relations with Austria? "In a military sense, I must insist that this question be completely clarified."

Not even at the height of his differences with Falkenhayn had the Chancellor been addressed in such tones. He, the responsible political leader, was being subjected to a cross-examination by the military concerning his policies. Quite naturally, he at once rejected this arrogant meddling, firmly and courteously. The OHL's criticism was objectively unfounded, he said. "Since His Majesty has entrusted me with political leadership, for which I alone bear the responsibility, I must repudiate your reproaches." Attempts to curtail Austrian sovereignty would not only be futile but would mean subjecting the relation to intolerable strain. Such relationships between Austria, Britain, and France as had not been destroyed by the war might in this way be actually strengthened, quite possibly giving Austria an important advantage in any peace negotiations. This latter observation served only to unloose new indignation at headquarters.

Here was the first open clash between statesmanship and war under the Ludendorff era. It was to be only the first of many more. Through the mediation of Baron Grünau a settlement of sorts was achieved. Hindenburg blandly assured Grünau that the last thing he had wanted to do was to meddle in political questions—but in wartime they were often hard to distinguish from military questions.[9] The new OHL was indeed not only incapable of making such distinctions but unwilling to do so. Only a few days later it carried its criticisms of the Chancellor's policies to the broad public, in a form considered wholly improper and contrary to tradition even among high military officers, who were horrified.[10]

It was above all the diplomats of the foreign ministry who were put in an impossible situation by the constant danger of political explosions at headquarters. The minister, von Jagow, Bethmann Hollweg's most loyal associate and unflagging counselor, drew the consequences and resigned late in November, actively helped along by Ludendorff, who had long been in friendly correspondence with his successor, Zimmermann.[11] Bethmann Hollweg probably hoped that this established relationship and the new minister's robust and rather jovial nature would ease his relations with Ludendorff and the parliamentarians of the right; but the new man was also much worried about

OHL cooperation, especially because no high-ranking diplomat of standing had been posted to headquarters since Treutler's withdrawal. The Kaiser wanted none—it "made him nervous," he said. He preferred to surrender to the influence of the generals without interference, interrupted only by the occasional visits to Pless of the Chancellor and Zimmermann.[12]

It is scarcely surprising in the circumstances that in many important matters the military influence so often won out over the political, Ludendorff, the ruthless driver, over Bethmann Hollweg, the hesitant worrier. It was noticeable during the very first weeks of the Ludendorff era, when the long-smoldering Polish problem came to a head.

We heard in Chapter 4 that the negotiations about Poland's future between the Chancellor and Burián in April 1916 brought no agreement and were broken off inconclusively. Germany was quite evidently far less concerned with resuming them than Austria. Bethmann Hollweg long shrank from committing himself in the touchy Polish issue through a proclamation to which there were so many possible political objections, most of them put forward by his domestic opponents, the Prussian conservatives, but some shared also by the Prussian cabinet.

An added element was that the German occupation authorities, under the shrewd and moderate governor general, Beseler, had begun to win a measure of trust among the Polish population, or at least its upper classes, while the disastrous failures of the Austrian armies on the Russian front had naturally shaken confidence in the moral and political authority of the Danubian monarchy. Hence Germany could afford to wait, while the Austrians grew increasingly impatient as they lost more and more ground and the Polish nationalist movement, once set loose in Galicia, champed at the bit. Another reason why Germany kept hesitating to proclaim the restoration of a kingdom of Poland was that from July onward the news from Stockholm—where Germans were still meeting with Russians—spoke of increasing war-weariness within the czarist empire, holding out at least the possibility of a separate peace. The Germans were reluctant to spoil such a chance.

We need not here trace in detail the various negotiations between Vienna, Berlin, Warsaw, and Lublin that resulted from this situation in the summer of 1916.[13] Although Bethmann Hollweg only hesitantly followed the recommendations of Governor General Beseler for cautiously easing the reins of government in Warsaw in favor of the Polish nationalist movement, Burián repeatedly complained of alleged and real pro-German propaganda in the German zone of occupation. Until late July Vienna stuck rigidly to its demand for an "Austro-Polish" solution, nor was it swayed by certain territorial concessions on the German side. Burián kept repeating at great length, indeed verbosely, his arguments for annexation of Poland by Austria, with which we are already familiar. Not even the German proposal of Archduke Charles

Stephen, known to be pro-Polish, as a candidate for the throne of a Polish state associated with Germany found favor in Vienna. Emperor Francis Joseph in particular would have no part of it.

Gradually, however, certain Austrian diplomats and generals realized the embarrassment of a situation in which Vienna asked for exclusive possession of a Poland, no square mile of which it could have retained without German help. Both the military and the political representatives of Austria with the governor general in Warsaw, Colonel Païc and Baron Andrian, now urgently besieged Conrad and Burián with pleas that the humiliating and dangerous inferiority of the Austro-Hungarian army on the eastern front could be remedied only by establishing a large Polish army with the support of the nationalist movement, including even its radical democratic wing under Pilsudski. Païc thought that no fewer than 300,000 to 500,000 men could be mobilized for the Central Powers in a free Poland; but in return Austria might have to accept the relinquishment of Congress Poland to the Germans, and possibly even the loss of Galicia: "Better to lose Galicia than the war! "[14]

Undoubtedly this was a gross overestimate. In Beseler's sober judgment, voiced at about the same time, the creation of a Polish army would in any event take a great deal of time and money; and the envoy, von Mutius, added skeptically that it might not even come to pass, in view of the strong aversion by the rural populace to military service. Even so a Polish army could come into being only after the creation of a Polish state, and only through the initiative of Polish nationalists.[15]

Conrad von Hötzendorf, bowed down by the military disaster, was won over to Colonel Païc's plans. Without German aid, he wrote to Burián on July 12, Austria was lost in any event, and if the war were won the Germans were certain to have their way. If Vienna were now amenable to German desires in Poland, it might in return gain support for its goals in the Balkans. He himself counted on a quarter-million Polish soldiers by the summer of 1917, if an agreement on Poland were reached no later than September.

Thus the military objective, the hope for Polish recruits—Sazonov in the Russian Duma spoke contemptuously of "cannon fodder"—which had for some time disappeared from the discussions, came back to the fore.[16] By the spring of 1916 Falkenhayn had stopped counting on them; but after the tremendous Austrian losses on the eastern front he thought that despite all the political and military objections an attempt at least had to be made to tap the Polish replacement reservoir.

This might best be done by creating German "Polish legions" from all of Poland, incorporating the existing Austrian "Polish legion." Should this prove impossible, the Polish legions should be drawn from the German occupation zone alone. Falkenhayn, in other words, had only a volunteer force in mind rather than a conscripted army; and he may have been partly motivated by the fact that the Austrian Polish legion, under German command on the Styr sector, had recently given a good account of itself.

He submitted his proposal on July 19 to Bethmann Hollweg,[17] who the year before had taken a more skeptical view of Polish recruitment, completely rejecting forced conscription by the occupying power as contrary to international law; but in view of the current critical military situation he at once assented to Falkenhayn's proposal for volunteer enlistments. He was most gratified that Conrad as well as Falkenhayn had now set about overcoming the Austrian foreign ministry's stubborn opposition to German plans in Poland and sweeping aside Burián's "Austro-Polish solution" once for all.

Austria's continuing appeals for help on the eastern front, moreover, could be used to exert political pressure. "Our Austrian allies must appreciate," Jagow wrote to Vienna on July 17, "that it won't do to ask and accept help from the strong brother in time of need, only to pick his pockets in return, once the danger is over."[18] There were, furthermore, foreign policy reasons for hastening a German proclamation. By mid-July it had been learned from concededly old Russian press dispatches that a proclamation by the czar impended. Going beyond Grand Duke Nicholas's noncommittal pledge of 1914, it would announce the creation of an autonomous Polish state. If the Central Powers wished to achieve anything with their plans, they would have to act beforehand. Sazonov had actually obtained the czar's approval in early June for such a proclamation, which the Western powers had long desired, not least from fear of a possible Polish-German army; but the reactionary Stürmer cabinet subsequently canceled or at least suspended this action. Sazonov, moreover, lost his post as Russian foreign minister on July 20 and was replaced by Stürmer, who changed the czar's mind.[19]

This turn of events, however, did not immediately transpire in Berlin and Vienna; and under pressure from the military Burián was at last, after long hesitation, forced to change course. Late in July he assented to a plan for a Polish "buffer state."[20] It was to be a sovereign hereditary monarchy, associated with both Central Powers rather than Germany alone. It was very strongly emphasized that both countries would have to enjoy complete equality of treatment in political, economic, and military respects.

From the German point of view this was thoroughly unsatisfactory. Indeed it was sharply at odds with a memorandum then drafted by Beseler, which set forth the German point of view in a particularly impressive fashion. It demanded absolute unity for the new monarchy, as a German protectorate, which meant that Austria would have to relinquish the occupation zone it had been administering. The kind of condominium being proposed by Burián would indeed have led necessarily to unending friction and jealousy, seriously diluting the two powers' influence on the new state.

Unlike most of his colleagues, Beseler was not obsessed with military considerations. The Polish question was to him mainly a political problem. He thought that recruitment of volunteers would be a hopeless project if it were tried before the new Polish state were created. Indeed, he held that precipitate and deficient organization of a Polish army in the rear of German front-line troops represented a real danger. The only useful Polish army would be one based on universal military service, and such a regular force could be organized only after the Polish state had become a reality. It was unlikely to be available before the war ended, and only preliminary steps could be taken now. Falkenhayn was impressed and stated on his part: "The organization of a Polish army should be considered only when we are sure what will happen to that country politically." It was for that reason that he was pressing for the creation of an autonomous state with military ties to Germany, though he was not on that account willing to forego immediate volunteer recruitment.21

He did not cling to even this position after the failure of Bethmann Hollweg's attempt to swerve Austrian policy from its feeble compromise proposal by personal talks with Burián in Vienna (on August 11-12). The Chancellor extracted no more than a few concessions in the matter of annexing a German "protective strip" on the East Prussian border and in a few other border questions. It was agreed that "an independent kingdom of Poland in the form of a hereditary monarchy based on a constitution" should be promptly proclaimed but brought into being only after the war. Until that time the present occupation administration, sharply divided into two separate zones, should be preserved, while later on there would be a kind of condominium, in that the new Poland would be specifically enjoined from pursuing a foreign policy of its own. It was to figure nominally as an ally of the two empires but would be required to submit to them for approval any treaties with other countries.

True, the new kingdom was to have its own Polish army, but the preparatory work for its organization and for the entire military system was to be handled by a mixed German and Austrian military commission. There were no further written clauses covering the future status of this army, except that "Baron Burián will support the position that supervision and top leadership of the army should be unified and fall to Germany." Thus not even Germany's position of military leadership was unequivocally fixed, nor was there any agreement concerning economic integration, i.e., Polish incorporation into the German customs area.22 Each country promised the other that no part of its own traditionally Polish territories must go to the new state.

This was perhaps the worst possible solution to the Polish problem, for it awakened hopes, only to dash them at once. Not even the old quarrel about which of the two countries should exercise a protectorate over Poland was settled. It would seem that this Vienna agreement disillusioned Falkenhayn completely about the Poland proclamation, the immediate military utility of which he already knew to be highly questionable.[23] According to his memoirs, he protested immediately afterward and asked for a postponement. According to a wire Bethmann Hollweg dispatched to Vienna, his reservations were also founded in military considerations—with a strike against Rumania impending, the situation was far too uncertain for a solemn proclamation to the Poles. This objection appealed not merely to Bethmann Hollweg, but to Ludendorff, and in the end even to that insistent backer, Burián.[24]

The Chancellor himself had gone to Vienna for negotiations only reluctantly, thinking them essentially hopeless, in view of what was known about Burián. When his apprehensions were confirmed and the generals were no longer pressing him, his zeal for the project probably flagged even further. Germany had little interest in a Poland that would be under a divided military administration even after the proclamation and prevented from entering into an economic union with Germany. Bethmann Hollweg was manifestly relieved when, on August 15, he received a wire from the Kaiser (presumably at Falkenhayn's suggestion), which enjoined him to keep the Vienna agreements strictly secret, lest there be interference with possibly approaching negotiations with Russia about a separate peace. At the same time the Kaiser urgently desired that such negotiations be promoted by every possible means. Falkenhayn, it was said, was of the same opinion.[25]

Falkenhayn at any rate took up the matter at once and persuaded the foreign ministry to propose to Vienna that the contemplated action be once again postponed. At a Prussian cabinet meeting he let it be plainly known that he was at bottom reluctant to tackle the creation of a Polish buffer state. Dealing with the Polish problem was not really in the German interest, though in the circumstances it could not be avoided. The solution now envisaged, i.e., establishment of an autonomous Poland at the end of the war, closely integrated with Germany in political, military, and economic respects, did seem the best way out and was perhaps the only reasonably acceptable solution to the Polish question. He could have scarcely expressed himself with greater caution.[26]

He also mentioned his hopes for a separate peace with Russia. In view of Sazonov's resignation and the increasing emphasis on the forces of reaction, it was not impossible that the Russian government might incline toward peace. The dispatches arriving from Stockholm indicated that Russia could not stand up to a third winter campaign. One of his remarks was particularly eloquent in showing his deep concern not to spoil such chances and in revealing his painful political quandary. "I am not in the fortunate position," he said, "of being able to choose between east and west. I must seize upon the first opportunity to disrupt the Entente." [27]

Bethmann Hollweg's hope that Russian militancy might be waning was not unfounded. There had been a report as long ago as early June about discussions which the German industrialist Stinnes had had in Stockholm with one of Stürmer's confidants on the possibility of a separate peace. The Russian minister seemed seriously interested in making peace. Even more striking was the fact that the liberal vice-president of the Duma, Protopopov, had expressed himself in similar terms early in July in talks with the well-known German banker Max Warburg. Protopopov had said that Russia had enough of war and was unwilling to make further sacrifices for Britain. He had even sought contact with the German envoy von Lucius.

By mid-August there was more news about Stürmer's war-weariness and his alleged intention to summon Bodkin, known to be an Anglophobe, to the Russian foreign ministry.28 The German foreign ministry lost no time in exploiting the bridgehead of pro-German diplomats in Scandinavia for further probings in St. Petersburg, and it also recruited paid agents for propaganda and intelligence purposes. There could be no question that war-weariness was rapidly spreading among the broad Russian masses, after the hecatombs of the most recent offensive, in which the Russians were thought to have lost about a million men; nor was there any doubt but that Russia's economic difficulties were growing, while military discipline was crumbling.

Reading the reports and diary entries by the French and British ambassadors dating back to the fall of 1916, one gains the impression that the Russian Revolution of March 1917 had long cast its shadows before it. Berlin knew about this but was unable to estimate the effect of these symptoms of attrition on policy at the top and therefore remained very cautious in its judgments.29 There was good reason for such reticence. The Allied representatives in St. Petersburg were profoundly distrustful of the policies of Stürmer, whom they despised, indeed hated. Wherever they sensed peaceful tendencies among the upper classes in St. Petersburg, they saw German machinations at work; and they did everything in their power to warn the weak and pusillanimous czar against them, and against his ministers as well.

Every advantage was taken of Russia's far-reaching financial and military dependence on the Western powers. It is true, however, that the archconservative Stürmer government was under constant threat from liberal-democratic opposition in the Duma, among whom the leader of the "Cadets," Milyukov, was most prominent as a chauvinist and Anglophile superpatriot. It soon transpired in St. Petersburg that there had been talks in Stockholm between German politicians and Protopopov, bringing a storm of criticism down on him—indeed, sensational press reports stamped him as a kind of traitor.

The Russian government did not dare disengage itself from the Western powers even though it sensed plainly that the war had undermined the crown's authority. Had it tried to pull out, it would have forfeited its standing at home and abroad. Czar Nicholas possessed neither the insight nor the personal authority with his own people to admit the fact of defeat and endeavor to make peace in time. He was tied to his allies hand and foot.

Nevertheless, Russian resistance was visibly ebbing away; and in retrospect we may well ask whether Germany might not have waited with greater calm and patience for the processes of disintegration to make themselves felt at the front as well rather than stirring up Russian nationalism once again by proclaiming a Polish state associated with Germany—to say nothing of bringing on a new and terribly dangerous foe by initiating unrestricted U-boat warfare.

If there was any German statesman who instinctively inclined to such a policy of watchful waiting, it was certainly Bethmann Hollweg. Yet his political vision was no more capable than was the military vision of the General Staff of foreseeing with any degree of assurance the impending internal collapse of the czarist empire, of basing a calculated risk on this foresight, and of taking decisions accordingly.[30] And unhappily he himself had held the stirrup for a man now at the head of the army, who was impatience personified, to wit, Ludendorff.

Ludendorff was the prime mover in getting the faltering Poland project off the ground again, though he was not the only one. He also exerted a crucial influence on its further course. On August 18 Burián voiced an anguished protest against the delay, but it found only a feeble echo in Berlin and could not drown out the reservations voiced to Bethmann Hollweg during these days by conservative politicians and ministers opposed to a kingdom of Poland. The voice of the new OHL, however, carried far greater weight.

For Ludendorff, to be sure, the Poles were of interest only as a potential source of military recruits. In running occupied Courland and Lithuania he had shown himself distinctly anti-Polish, and Beseler's policies as governor general, aimed at a German-Polish rapprochement, were excoriated at headquarters east as soft and sloppy; but even Ludendorff realized that if he wanted to gain Polish manpower for German war purposes the establishment of a more or less autonomous Polish state under German sovereignty was essential. He had wanted such recruits ever since September 1915, since the "Austrian mess," and again since Brusilov's breakthrough in June 1916, indeed most urgently after the latter two disasters; but this did not keep him from insisting that the Polish state be sharply curtailed in territory. When he was summoned to the OHL he immediately sought an understanding with Beseler and initially worked in concert with him.[31]

The rapidity with which the OHL, barely in office, managed to prevail over the political objections of Kaiser and Chancellor in the Polish question is amazing. By September 12, when hopes for a separate Russian peace had not yet been extinguished by any means, Bethmann Hollweg advised the governor general that there was now nothing to prevent the proclamation from being issued. Another remarkable aspect is the speed with which Ludendorff's delusion that a large quota of military manpower could be gained from occupied Poland vanquished the sober realism of Beseler and his associates.

On August 23, even before he had taken office, Ludendorff had insisted to the Chancellor that a postponement of the proclamation—to which he offered no objection—must on no account delay Polish recruitment. It was at this time that Baron Lerchenfeld learned through the foreign ministry that Ludendorff was after enforced levies in the occupied Polish territories, which horrified Beseler, all of whose plans would have been knocked over.[32]

If this report is true, Beseler's fears of the excessive demands by the new high command on the eastern front may explain why, in a long memorandum of August 23, he suddenly showed himself less averse to volunteer recruitment than he had been earlier that month. Without relinquishing his views in principle, he now spoke of preliminary work looking toward the formation of Polish units, which he estimated initially at three divisions numbering 30,000 men. Apparently he was seeking Ludendorff's support in his efforts to push through the Poland proclamation. His only hope of interesting the Poles was that instead of enforced levies, he would prevail with volunteer recruitment, along the lines of the Polish legion the Austrians had established.[33] It would seem that Ludendorff ruthlessly seized on this dubious expedient, following a talk he had with Beseler at Pless on September 2.

This was the first major political intervention by the new OHL, made possible by its direct influence on the Kaiser. This was immediately expanded by an effort to exploit the new supervisory authority over the allied armies, embodied in a treaty on September 6, for purposes of pushing the Austrians completely out of the administration of occupied Russian Poland without the intervention of political authority. On September 2 General Conrad had inquired how the German OHL envisaged the establishment of a Polish army. He himself proposed that there should be either enforced recruitment following a proclamation about Poland's future, or extension to the German zone of occupation of volunteer recruitment for the Polish legion—which would, of course, have brought the Austrians strongly to the fore.

Hindenburg responded on September 11 with a demand that the division in occupation administration must first be eliminated, meaning that the Austrian zone, run from Lublin, would have to be absorbed by Germany's Warsaw-centered government general. Only in this way would it be possible to bring a unified Polish national army into being. He left it open whether this was to be achieved by levies or recruitment.

Beyond any question this flew in the face of the Vienna agreement negotiated by Burián and Bethmann Hollweg; and Conrad rightly emphasized that the whole matter was one for the politicians. But while Conrad at once transmitted the exchange to Burián, the German OHL simply ignored its foreign ministry, answering the Austrians' political objections with arguments of its own, often pitched in a highly dramatic tone. Austria, it was declaimed, could confidently "leave to His Majesty the Emperor of Germany the lofty task of instilling a spirit of militancy into the Polish people"; otherwise the OHL would prefer to see no proclamation at all, nor would it wish a mixed military commission to consult. It would then be better if the two occupation powers pursued their separate ways in raising Polish troops. The date of this document was September 30.[34]

Burián, of course, vigorously supported the Austrian high command in rejecting these sudden demands, which simply knocked the Vienna agreement into a cocked hat; and since Conrad too stood firm, Ludendorff was under the necessity of asking the Chancellor's diplomatic aid, which Bethmann Hollweg gave him, although he must have known that it would give offense to Austria and meet with rejection. Nothing could have more clearly illustrated the weakness of his position vis-à-vis the new OHL.

Bethmann Hollweg made no bones before the Austrians about the fact that he was acting solely at the insistence of the OHL who, in view of the military situation, were unable to abide by the Vienna agreement and had to insist on unification of the two occupation zones, so that the establishment of a Polish army might be accelerated. Burián indignantly rejected this imposition, even though Bethmann Hollweg echoed the OHL threat that Germany would proceed on its own in its zone. On October 18 Prince Hohenlohe complained to Zimmermann at the foreign ministry in unusually sharp terms about these "absurd" demands. As he put it later, he said he suspected that the Wilhelmstrasse was sometimes "not quite in its right mind." After all, surely it was not in the German interest to go out of their way to engender intolerable irritation and resentment in Austria-Hungary. Even if the Austrians were to swallow hard now, the consequences might be quite serious at the peace table—a subtle hint at negotiations for a separate peace!

Zimmermann's reply was extraordinarily illuminating. The demand originated with Ludendorff, he admitted, and Bethmann Hollweg had been informed of it only at the last moment. Asked why the Chancellor bowed to such tactics, Zimmermann shrugged his shoulders. Surely Hohenlohe knew that decisiveness had never been one of Bethmann Hollweg's fortes. Now, besieged on every side, he was even more likely to seek shelter behind the rugged figure of Hindenburg rather than opposing proposals that came from that quarter. Perhaps Hohenlohe would care to make vigorous representations to the Chancellor directly and warn him not to allow himself to be coerced by the military authorities, for that was now the danger, with Ludendorff having so important a voice. He, Zimmermann, had already on more than one occasion brusquely rebuffed Ludendorff's intervention.[35]

In sum, the responsible political head in Germany, supported in the Reichstag only by the left,[36] was virtually powerless before the supreme military command, which he needed to protect him against the furious attacks of his nationalist opponents. It was an altogether unnatural state of affairs that could not last long.

Ludendorff was now determined to stake everything. If the Austrians would not relinquish Lublin, let them leave the creation of a Polish army entirely to the Germans. They could have a nominal part in the "mixed military commission," but without any real voice. To this end he invoked the Vienna agreement, which provided that "supervision and top direction of the Polish army were to be unified and in German hands," from which he chose to conclude that its organization too must be the exclusive concern of the German OHL. This created a serious predicament for Bethmann Hollweg, who could not very well dispute the dual character of the agreed protectorate. In a rather tortured communication to Vienna he argued that he had refrained from insisting on more precise written formulations only to spare the prestige of the Austrians, who wished to figure as co-founders of the Polish state. Burián, however, had assured him verbally that in settling military questions in Poland he wished to appear solely in the role of *Kompaziszent,* which might be rendered as "sympathetic bystander." Conrad, of course, denied that this implied foregoing all active participation. Hence no agreement was reached on this question as well.[37]

Meanwhile the Austrian high command took a step that created great consternation in the German camp. It reorganized the Polish legion, formed in the Austrian occupation zone, into two regular divisions, to be called "Polish auxiliary corps," allowed them the Polish national colors, and requested that Hindenburg relieve them from front-line duty to effect the reorganization and permit them the recruitment of volunteers in the German occupation zone as well.

There can be no question that Conrad was simply responding to an emergency. The legion had long since become restive and demanded that it be granted special status; but by seeking to reorganize it as the core of a future Polish national army and immediately publicizing this step, the Austrians gave the appearance of trying to undercut their ally in Poland and anticipating if not actually sabotaging his efforts to create a Polish volunteer force.

The German OHL, in any event, took this view of the matter;[38] and it was not content simply to protest. Preparations were immediately made to initiate recruitment in the German occupation without further delay, if necessary even before the proclamation of a new Poland. Beseler fell in with this venture and thus abandoned his original Polish program completely, though not without some qualms. Ludendorff's ruthless determination overcame all his resistance.

Bethmann Hollweg, on the other hand, was not unhappy that over all these conflicts the proclamation to the Poles receded more and more into the distance. Rightist opposition to the new Polish policy line now intensified, especially on the part of the conservatives. To some extent they were appeased by impressive addresses which General Beseler delivered in October before the Prussian cabinet, party leaders in the Prussian diet and the Reichstag, and even members of the Prussian upper chamber; but this did not overcome conservative dislike of a policy that was basically friendly to the Poles, nor did it allay fears that a Poland manifesto might become an obstacle to a separate peace with Russia.

An important element was that early in October more favorable news arrived from Stockholm, calculated to confirm the Chancellor and the foreign ministry in their view that delay was urgently indicated.[39] Protopopov had been appointed minister of the interior, and the former prime minister Kokovtzov, personally close to Bethmann Hollweg, together with former minister Giers, known to be pro-German, had been summoned by the czar, suggesting that they might be under consideration for cabinet posts. The Swedish foreign minister Wallenberg offered to mediate and actually discussed possible peace terms with the Russian envoy Nekludov—he warned urgently that a Poland proclamation at this juncture might jeopardize the chances of a separate peace.[40] Bethmann Hollweg thereupon persuaded the Kaiser to authorize another postponement, on October 2, and grew convinced of the probability that Russia might enter into peace talks before winter. He was indeed at the height of his hopes for a separate Russian peace.

But the OHL kept on pushing, together with Beseler and the Austrians. The army people wanted a conference of the two high commands, at which Austria would be compelled to forego its occupation administration, leaving Poland virtually to the Germans. The Chancellor, of course, knew in advance that such a meeting would fail, and hence had little taste for it. His reluctance was deepened by his fears that Burián would again revert to his old demand of using Poland as a hostage to regain the regions of East Galicia and the Bukovina, which Austria had lost.

On October 10 Bethmann Hollweg embodied all his arguments into a letter, in which he frankly tried to make clear to the OHL the enormous responsibility it would be shouldering in continually urging haste. He did not gloss over the tenuousness of his peace hopes, nor did he discount the possibility that the Russians might, in separate negotiations, reconcile themselves even to the loss of Poland and other territories.[41] But he concluded nevertheless that a manifesto was bound to provide new ammunition to the Russian war party against the partisans of peace. One reason for the tremendous responsibility involved, he said, was that German public opinion firmly believed there was a chance of peace. If these hopes were shattered in the wake of a premature Poland manifesto, public sentiment was likely to overreact in a manner that might be disastrous to the conduct of the war, a danger that would be enhanced by Austria's increasing unfitness in the field. The Prussian cabinet shared the grave fears which Reichstag and Prussian diet deputies had voiced at Beseler's briefings, to the effect that the chance of peace with Russia might be foiled. The deputies had not been receptive to the idea that the gradual establishment of a Polish army was an urgent military necessity, before which all other considerations must give way—Beseler had mentioned a training period of eight months. In sum, while there were doubtless substantial advantages to the establishment of a Polish state, they would be far outweighed if this measure resulted in actually delaying peace.

It was a stern exhortation. Bethmann Hollweg accentuated the apprehensions among the deputies and ministers, who were neither as strong in their feelings as he made them appear, nor as unanimous; but did he really believe his representations would persuade a man like Ludendorff to drop or even temporarily postpone the Poland plan? Evidently not, for while he insisted that the conference with the Austrians proposed by the OHL would undoubtedly precipitate the manifesto and initiate recruitment immediately, he avoided an outright refusal to convene such a meeting. On the contrary, he said he was in basic agreement that it should be called, merely asking for reconsideration of the OHL position. What was Bethmann Hollweg really after?

It seems to us that this document throws an unusually sharp light on the relation between the political and military leadership in the Bethmann-Ludendorff era. The statesman instinctively sensed the menace inherent in the resistless energy of his military counterpart; but he could not prove beyond doubt that Ludendorff was deluded in his expectations—even though he knew that some of the experts had very different ideas about the prospects for Polish recruitment[42]—nor, being dependent on what Germany's enemies might do, could he marshal political arguments that were convincing beyond doubt.

All he could do was to weigh both sides of the case with the greatest care—and that approach was foredoomed when it was pitted against a cold, ruthless, determined, and unhesitating driver like Ludendorff. Bethmann Hollweg had neither the outward authority nor the inward assurance to prevail against a popular hero in an all-out fight. Unlike his opposite number in uniform, he was unwilling to stake everything on a gamble. What he displayed here was the same inner insecurity that was soon to be reenacted in the much more important controversy over unrestricted U-boat warfare.

Bethmann Hollweg could have scarcely expected that he could persuade the OHL even to reconsider its decisions seriously. It is likely that his letter, rather than outlining a practical program, was meant in a way to salve his own conscience.[43] As was to be anticipated, Ludendorff's reply airily swept aside the Chancellor's political objections. From the intelligence available to him, he believed neither in a Russian move toward peace nor in the sincerity of Swedish mediation offers. Peace would come only by the overwhelming strength of German arms, which would signal to the Entente beyond any question Germany's determination to win victory. In this endeavor full utilization of Polish manpower by no means came last, and it must not be further delayed. Yet recruitment would be an empty gesture unless the two occupation administrations were unified. If Austria were unwilling to agree, Germany must go ahead alone and leave no doubt among the Poles concerning Austria's attitude. It would then no longer be a matter of "agreeing" to any manifesto, even if Burián should press for it.[44]

Just what Ludendorff meant by this threatening language remained rather obscure. Did he plan to recruit or simply conscript soldiers in the German occupation zone even without a manifesto? "We must act in Poland," he wrote at the time to Wyneken. "There is no pat solution. Everything is a question of power, and we need manpower."[45] In any event, he insisted on the conference with Conrad and Burián; and it actually took place on October 18 in Pless, Beseler participating.[46]

In a sense what happened there was preordained in that the German side, at a preliminary meeting the day before, had agreed, on a compromise, despite Ludendorff's grandiloquence, against the event that Burián would be unyielding. If the occupation administrations could not be amalgamated entirely, there should nevertheless be a gradual process of unification, by means of an Austrian delegation to be dispatched to Warsaw, as Beseler proposed on October 18.

More important in a political sense than the compromise—which ultimately prevailed—was the fact that promulgation of the manifesto was now finally agreed on, "as soon as possible." It was to be followed by "prompt" recruitment in both occupation zones. Thus Bethmann Hollweg's political objections—which Burián did not share, by the way—simply fell to the ground; but he himself was in part responsible, for while he had reiterated these objections at the outset of the preliminary discussion, emphasizing that the Poland manifesto was bound to "slow up" the chances of peace, he had added that prior to the victorious conclusion of the Rumanian campaign such chances were probably nonexistent, so that the manifesto might even so be acceptable right then.

It would seem that in the meantime his hopes for a separate peace with Russia had indeed again sharply declined, while he maintained a private reservation to. relinquish the "buffer state," should new possibilities of negotiations with St. Petersburg open up.[47] At any rate, he allowed the generals to have their way for the moment; and surprisingly, he displayed a great deal of reserve, if not outright passivity, during the conference. In the preliminary discussion he had remarked that if the decision was for the Poland manifesto, despite the weighty political counterarguments, it could only be on military grounds; and if these were inescapable, political considerations would have to give way. It sounded like a surrender to the military, but apparently betokened only a chilly reserve. Quite possibly he had already lost political interest in the Poland manifesto.

In the main session he allowed the generals to argue their case for unified occupation administration without taking much part—it was after all not his affair. Although he did not really share their illusions on the matter of recruitment, oddly enough he let their discussion of it pass with little comment. In the preliminary discussion he had mentioned that in Berlin the prospects for voluntary recruitment were not viewed very optimistically. Why, then, did he not insist that this central point be clarified, especially by Beseler and his associates? One suspects an ulterior motive behind this reticence. Let Ludendorff find out for himself, he may have thought, how far he will get with his headlong pressure! If, counter to expectation, the experiment succeeded, well and good. If it failed, the damage would not be excessive; and perhaps such a failure, with the discredit it would bring, would show the generals that they were not infallible.

Whether or not such thoughts passed through his mind, he allowed the generals to display their rhetorical techniques to the full without bestirring himself, so to speak. Hindenburg's arguments were informed with the patriarchal warmth and patriotism of one whose intentions were of the best, even though he did not have all the details at his fingertips. Ludendorff spoke with the pointed self-assurance of a soldier acknowledging only military considerations and anticipating "final victory" by spring, if he got his Polish recruits. Beseler was full of wishful thinking and spoke of four or five volunteer divisions—no longer merely three. Ultimately, he thought, a million men could be raised!

Surprisingly, the only realist among the generals on this occasion appears to have been Conrad, who remarked dryly that a Polish army could be had only if there were a Polish state. If soldiers were wanted, a king or regent would have to be installed, together with a Polish government able to raise an army. Naturally he elicited only horrified disagreement on every side. Even in the political opinion of the Chancellor, it was much too early to create an independent kingdom of Poland; but he did not feel that this was the time to argue fruitlessly with the Austrians about the future shape of Poland, and such things as "condominium" or German "preponderance," important as all this seemed to the generals. In the end everything depended on how the war was going. He knew there was not the slightest chance of agreement between himself and Ludendorff, who had instantly responded to his letter of October 10 with impossible annexationist demands, including Grodno, Kovno, Lithuania, and Courland.

No sooner were they taken than the decisions at the conference lost interest for Bethmann Hollweg. He was now concerned with a far more important project that Burián broached to him directly after the conference, a plan for a peace offer to the enemy powers, with which we shall deal in the next chapter. The Chancellor responded with such enthusiasm to this suggestion that he was willing to see such a peace manifesto go out in a matter of days. By comparison, a Poland manifesto would simply be a nuisance, since it was bound to anticipate the peace terms in part and arouse resentment in Russia.

This objection was voiced especially at sessions of the foreign affairs committee of the federal council on October 30 and 31, when the Chancellor drew a picture of the situation in Russia, much as he had in his letter of October 10 to Hindenburg. He spoke of the very strong pressure from the OHL that compelled him to proceed with undue haste.[48] Indeed, Hindenburg and Ludendorff, while they allowed Bethmann Hollweg to persuade them to agree to the peace action on October 26, insisted that it must on no account delay the Poland manifesto and the recruitment that was to follow in its wake.[49] Thus, after the brief negotiations in Vienna, a date of November 5 was agreed on and the wording of the manifesto was likewise settled. At the last moment, the OHL tried its best to water down the political concession, but Burián refused to go along.

Made public on the agreed date, the manifesto to the Poles was kept in such general and cautious terms that it could have only a limited political effect. It actually did not go beyond promises, without taking any firm step toward the realization of a Polish state with its own government. On October 22 a delegation of Polish notables had called on the Chancellor to put forward a moderate program, but these wishes were not fulfilled, and Bethmann Hollweg gave them only noncommittal assurances.

It goes without saying that a Polish state that did not even include the ancient royal city of Cracow and was limited entirely to those territories that had formerly been Russian could not possibly satisfy Polish nationalist aspirations. The manifesto nevertheless made a very strong impression throughout the world and especially in Russia, where it had long been feared that the Germans would ultimately succeed in alienating the Poles from Russia. St. Petersburg was deeply chagrined that its own plans for a Poland manifesto, postponed time and again, had now been anticipated. There was considerable indignation, especially among the liberal opposition, and the incipient conflict between the Duma and the Stürmer government was accentuated.

There could be no further thought of a separate peace, and those who had said that such negotiations would not be prejudiced were effectively refuted; but Bethmann Hollweg, reproached for this before the Reichstag committee of the whole on November 9, defended himself with assurances that Russia was even so nearing the end of its strength and would soon have to sue for peace.[50] This, however, was still to take some time. Yet it can scarcely be said that the Poland manifesto prevented an earlier peace, or delayed it. When the Stürmer government fell on November 24, it was for quite different reasons. Part of the reason was the growing revolutionary unrest in exhausted Russia. In any event, czarist foreign policy underwent no change, indeed, was even stiffened, so far as Russian adherence to the Western Alliance was concerned.

What did happen is that the German manifesto moved the Polish question further into the sphere of international policy. The Western powers now began to interest themselves in the fate of Poland. Wilson especially, under the influence of Colonel House and the émigré, Paderewski, was won over to the Polish cause. He tried to organize a food relief campaign for occupied Poland; and in his great peace speech of January 22, 1917, he said that any new European settlement would have to include the restoration of a united, independent, and autonomous Poland.

Hence the German step did in the long run considerably aid the Polish cause. So far as the hopes of the Central Powers were concerned, it was a complete failure, in every sense. There was some initial success in further alienating from Russia certain portions of the Polish people, notably an upper stratum of city notables, landed proprietors, and members of the higher clergy, whose loyalty to the occupation powers was somewhat improved. The belated Russian Poland manifesto, issued by the revolutionary Lvov-Kerensky government on March 29, 1917, did not essentially alter this attitude, which was indeed reinforced by the impression that chaos prevailed in Russia. What did not happen was what General Beseler had looked for. The Polish people never put their full trust in the Central Powers, especially Germany. On the contrary, the Polish nationalist movement as a whole fell out more and more with the German occupation authorities, of whom it ultimately became the mortal enemy.

There were many reasons for this. Inevitably, the German regime was harsh. With the growing military dilemma of the two Central Powers, there was no alternative to squeezing the country by requisitioning food and raw materials, closing factories, etc., which brought on the hostility of the peasants and urban workers. The latter were even further antagonized by a labor draft that was sometimes enforced with unnecessary ruthlessness. Polish industry was severely handicapped by being cut off from the Russian market; and Austrian opposition foiled the close economic integration with Germany the Germans wanted.

These effects were intensified with the fading of any hope for a victory by the Central Powers, which had still seemed quite realistic after the subjugation of Rumania late in 1916. It was only natural that the hopes and sympathies of Polish patriots turned more and more toward the West after America's entry into the war and the great new French and British offensives on the western front in 1917. It had become plain even before that the German regime, run mainly by conservatives and monarchist officials, was by its whole nature unable to maintain close liaison with the rising nationalist and democratic forces in Poland and to understand their aspirations. In that respect, Austria, with a civil service staffed by Poles and Galicians, had the better of it. The German policy was too authoritarian for that, and even Beseler could never make up his mind to treat the Poles as proper allies rather than as a subject people—there would, of course, have been a serious risk in wartime.

Least of all was Beseler able to sympathize with the newly rising movement of democratic Polish nationalism, which predominated by far in Austria's Polish legion (now renamed the auxiliary corps). The popular hero of this movement was the partisan leader Pilsudski, a militant socialist from the Polish gentry, who long before 1914, with the clandestine support of the regional Galician government, had waged an underground struggle against the czarist regime for a new Polish republic. The whole underlying irreconcilable character of the conflict was most tellingly shown by the fact that the Germans succeeded for only a very short while in enlisting Pilsudski's cooperation with the "state council" Beseler had organized. Ultimately, on July 22, 1917, he was arrested and thus turned into a martyr of Polish democracy.

Pilsudski's arrest was connected with his secret participation in sabotaging German recruitment, of which we shall yet hear. Here we touch on the ultimately crucial cause for the political failure of the Central Powers, the utter failure of their military policy.

The great miscalculation was that the proclamation of freedom for Poland was followed almost immediately, on November 9, by the scheduled call for a volunteer army, on the insistence of the OHL, a point on which Bethmann Hollweg like Beseler had concurred.[51] Ludendorff's sole motivation for the manifesto was thus made abundantly clear to one and all: exploitation of Polish manpower resources for war purposes. The effect was to stifle any politically favorable sentiments among the broad masses of the people. It was enhanced by the fact that recruitment was handled by German rather than Polish agencies, and Pilsudski's popular nationalist movement was virtually challenged to engage in obstruction and secret sabotage. The recruitment campaign turned out to be a complete failure. Only a few hundred volunteered in the course of November, most of them unfit for frontline duty. By late April the number had risen to only 4,700.

This was a bitter disappointment for Ludendorff; but instead of realizing that the precipitate action on which he had insisted was a mistake, as Conrad had predicted, and that something akin to a Polish state must first be established if there were to be a Polish army, Ludendorff closed his mind even further to the demands of the politicians, and by his obstinacy completed the ruin. At heart Ludendorff deeply despised the Poles. He insisted on "results," i.e., recruits, before he was willing to see political concessions made to them in return; and he regarded any other policy simply as "weakness." Thus he became a stumbling block in the way of any gradual establishment of a Polish state; but the Austrian high command was no less willful.

To train and organize Polish volunteer units, it would have been essential to use a cadre of Polish officers and noncoms. These were actually available among Austria's Polish auxiliaries, and they were indeed to be so employed, under an agreement between the two general staffs of November 11. The Austrian auxiliary corps was even shifted to the German occupation zone, though the jealous General Conrad refused to allow it to be detached from the Austrian army and come under German command; for the manifesto of November 5, instead of ending the rivalry between the two allies in the Polish question, had served only to deepen it. Neither General Conrad nor Baron Burián had really buried the idea of an "Austro-Polish solution." They did all they could, under the continuing condominium, to draw the Poles over to their side. General Beseler rightly suspected that Vienna's representatives at Warsaw were engaging in obstructionist tactics against his regime. Baron Andrian's reports to the Austrian foreign ministry bristled with hostility, and make startling reading indeed.[52]

Emperor Francis Joseph had died on November 21, 1916, and four weeks later Burián was succeeded by Count Czernin; but this radical change in the Austrian government made little difference. In early January 1917, the Germans pushed their claim for a monopoly on the administration and protectorate of occupied Poland, but encountered vehement resistance on the part of Czernin, with whom Bethmann Hollweg, on January 6, had a personal discussion, without effect. The two statesmen simply left Poland's political future open, and only the German claim to military leadership was reaffirmed. Soon afterward the joint Austro-Hungarian cabinet, over the opposition of Tisza (who was willing to let the Germans have Poland in return for economic concessions), agreed that the problem should be kept completely open, in the hope that at the peace table overwhelming German preponderance might be avoided by negotiation—in effect, with the help of the Entente.[53]

Czernin did soon afterward admit that an "Austro-Polish solution" could not be attained in practice, but he did not formally relinquish it, any more than had Burián before him. The difference was that Czernin was less concerned with incorporating Congress Poland with Austria than with holding on to it as a bargaining counter that might be traded for other gains, for example in Rumania. Even so Poland remained the everlasting bone of contention between the two Central Powers it had been before, with unending diplomatic friction following in its wake.

The results were, of course, disastrous in the military sphere. Opposed to any strengthening of German power in Poland, Conrad obstructed, if not sabotaged, the creation of a Polish force by holding back his Polish auxiliary corps. Yet Ludendorff shared responsibility for this refusal. Late in November, after protracted negotiations between Beseler and the Austrian governor in Lublin, General Kuk, the wording of an oath to be administered to the Polish troops had been settled. Avoiding mention of either of the two emperors, it put forward in their place the "Polish fatherland" and its future king; and it also included a pledge of loyalty-in-arms to the forces of Germany, Austria-Hungary, and their allies "in the present war."

The German OHL stubbornly refused to approve this formula and insisted instead on a wording that would mention the German Kaiser as "supreme warlord" and pledge armed allegiance to Germany forever. This opposition continued even after Bethmann Hollweg and Czernin had come to terms on January 6, agreeing that if the OHL approved the Beseler-Kuk oath, Emperor Charles of Austria would direct the transfer of the Polish auxiliary corps and acknowledge German supreme command over the Polish army. The OHL refusal amounted to outright sabotage of the whole military organizing effort, indeed Germany's whole policy in Poland, which Ludendorff himself had promoted so precipitately. Quite evidently he had lost interest by now. In December he had allowed it to transpire that in the circumstances the OHL would prefer to forego a Polish army and go out for workers rather than soldiers.

The controversy over the wording of the oath dragged out over many months,[54] an almost grotesque response in the light of the ridiculously small number of Poles who were to swear it. While it remained unsettled, the state council formed of Polish notables on January 14 was unable to make any progress whatever in its efforts to create a Polish army; but Ludendorff remained recalcitrant. "If the Poles wish to come with us," he said, "they will also do so with this oath [putting them under the Kaiser]. Let the Poles show once for all whether they really wish to come our way. They must be told unmistakably that ours is the power to command, not theirs. We have yielded more than enough, now let them do their part. Later on, I suppose, we shall have to play a different tune." Here was militarism pure and simple.

It was not until late in February that Ludendorff finally signified his willingness to subscribe to the Beseler-Kuk wording—but only if the Austrian occupation authorities were withdrawn from Lublin and the 7,000-odd soldiers with Austrian citizenship (for the most part Galicians) were withdrawn from the Polish auxiliary corps. Such terms could not even be seriously considered; but at precisely this juncture Conrad von Hötzendorf lost his post as Austrian chief of staff. His successor, General von Arz, was an ardent supporter of the alliance with Germany and an admirer of the German army system; and he searched for a compromise.

Since Czernin refused to allow the auxiliary corps to be cut up, Ludendorff, in order to avoid taking over into the German forces its 7,000 Austrian citizens sworn to allegiance to Emperor Charles, agreed to a proposal by General Arz that the whole corps be moved to the front as part of the Austrian army. Among the Poles in Warsaw this "sidetracking" created indignation. The state council protested and demanded vigorous action looking toward the creation of a Polish national army under its own leadership. It actually threatened to resign. For the first time this resistance met with success. After protracted negotiations, the Polish auxiliary corps was withdrawn from Austrian political and military jurisdiction and at last placed under the command of General Beseler. The question of the oath and of the citizenship of its Austrian members was not resolved.

By now, however, it was too late to use the corps for purposes of building up a serviceable Polish national army. Revolution had broken out in Russia; the czar was overthrown and a radical Poland manifesto issued. The former Polish legion had now been idling in garrison duty for a year, turning into an undisciplined mercenary horde, sometimes looking like nothing better than a gang of thieves, looters, and war profiteers rather than a military force of any consequence.

Under the impress of the Russian revolution with its front-line mutinies, this process of disintegration only progressed still further, a development giving all the greater concern since beginning in the spring of 1917 unrest, looting, strikes, and student rebellions were spreading in the countryside. This would have been the critical time to score successes with volunteer recruitment. The Polish state council was actually prepared to cooperate to this end and agreed to issue a new call for volunteers on April 22, 1917; but Ludendorff protested its promulgation, unwilling to yield in the matter of the oath unless compelled to do so by a compact between the two emperors.

Discussions about such a compact dragged on until June 18. On that same day Czernin confirmed an agreement—still to be discussed—concluded on May 18 in Kreuznach at Ludendorff's urging, under which Austria formally renounced its condominium over Poland (without really dropping the idea). Not until June 29 did the text of the imperial settlement arrive in Warsaw, and thus the matter of the oath was finally laid to rest.

Unfortunately this solution could not undo the neglect and mishandling of the months before. The state council had after all made its call for volunteers public in May and opened a far-flung network of recruiting offices; but the results by the end of June were unimpressive, no more than about 2,000 men. The new recruiting offices, moreover, their activities apparently influenced by Pilsudski, aroused the suspicions of the German occupation authorities, who were sure they were secretly recruiting partisans; and during the course of the summer most of the offices were disbanded.

What was even worse, most of the Polish soldiers refused to swear the oath, and there was no choice but to intern them. As already suggested, the reason lay partly in the agitation spurred by Pilsudski, who had withdrawn from the state council under protest on July 3; but the growth of republican and anti-German sentiment also played a part, as above all did the OHL's endless delay in the decisive step and the conflict between the occupation powers. Officers and men of the Polish auxiliary corps did not wish to be torn asunder by distinctions in the oath for Galicians and non-Galicians.

The presence of the auxiliary corps now became a mortal embarrassment to the German occupation power, and efforts were made to get rid at least of the Austrian citizens. Late in August, after weeks of negotiation, the entire corps, except for a small cadre for new formations, was transferred to Galicia. There, with infinite effort, it was restored to a reasonable condition; and toward the end of the year it was shifted to the Austrian front.

Bethmann Hollweg was no longer Chancellor at the time of this inglorious end to an undertaking launched with such great hopes by Beseler and the OHL. The debacle merely served to confirm his skepticism, which had deepened as the revolutionary decay of the Russian front grew more and more plain after the summer and new prospects of a separate peace in the east thus opened up. In May 1917, in common cause with Ludendorff, though from very different motives, the Chancellor had once again delayed a further step in Polish national self-administration, the installation of a regent, as demanded by the Warsaw state council and favored by Beseler. He did not wish to commit himself prematurely to a fait accompli that might make peace more difficult.

Actually his influence on the course of events in Poland was not overly great, if only because soon after the Poland manifesto he was beset by far greater troubles. He found it more and more difficult to maintain his position against the bitter hostility of Ludendorff and of his domestic enemies. Repeatedly, in November 1916, he cited to critics of the Poland manifesto in the legislatures and the federal council the enormous pressure on the part of the supreme command, to which he had had to yield. Thus he sought the protective cover of Hindenburg's authority for his Polish policy; but this did not keep his enemies from charging him with unpardonable weakness toward the Poles, and decrying the Poland manifesto of November 5 as the kind of blunder typical of a feeble, unrealistic, and humanitarian policy. (Tirpitz went so far as to call it a form of suicide!) As always, the East Elbian Junkers opposed any serious review of the policy of "Germanizing" the eastern provinces of Prussia, inhabited by Poles. The only concession by the Prussian cabinet was an announcement in February 1917 that existing emergency laws directed at the Poles would be eased.

The precipitate Poland manifesto and the subsequent delay and sabotage in its implementation are clearly to be laid at Ludendorff's door. The failure, nevertheless, became one of the chief items in the bill of indictment his militarist enemies laid against the allegedly incompetent Chancellor.

# 8

## A Peace Offer
## by the Central Powers
## and the Break with America

Part 1

## Germany's Relation with America
## in the Summer of 1916; Belgian Peace Feelers

I N NO OTHER sphere was the influence of the new militaristically minded
German supreme command as baneful as in German-American relations
and the question of U-boat warfare that lay at their heart.

Throughout the year 1916 one can observe how Bethmann Hollweg
sought zealously, indeed desperately, to extricate the country from a murder-
ous war that was growing more and more hopeless. There were peace feelers
of every kind, sometimes aiming at a separate peace with one enemy or the
other, sometimes seeking a general negotiated peace that would leave neither
victor nor vanquished. Neither in Russia nor in France were any tangible
possibilities for a separate peace turned up, despite the continuing peace
feelers via Stockholm, with which we are already familiar, and the expendi-
ture of many millions for the purchase of a press outlet and the organization
of an opposition group in France. The only remaining hope was that Wilson
and his friend Colonel House might serve as mediators. An approach to the
main enemy, Britain, that might promise success was possible only through
them.

We have already seen, in Chapter 5, Part 3, how eagerly Bethmann Hollweg, in the period after March 1916, took advantage of negotiations over
U-boat warfare, not only to convince American diplomacy of his goodwill in
seeking an understanding, but also to push it into a peace initiative of its own.
He expended enormous energy, against the opposition of the military and the
nationalists, to secure cessation of intensified U-boat warfare after the *Sussex*
incident. His closest associates at the time were deeply impressed with his
personal achievement in the struggle against Tirpitz and his ilk. "He has saved
Germany," Jagow told the deputy, Haussmann. "He has really grown into his

world role," Riezler told Jagow, adding that the public should be apprised of Bethmann Hollweg's personal achievement.[1]

Yet how hopeless was Bethmann Hollweg's situation! Month after month, repeatedly encouraged by optimistic reports from Bernstorff in Washington, he looked for the American president to take some action either to ease the British blockade of Germany or to bring about a negotiated peace. And indeed, until late May Wilson and House continued their efforts to interest London in the mediation proposals laid down in the so-called Grey-House memorandum of February 22 (see Chapter 5, Part 3, above).

When all the letters and dispatches to Grey brought no results, Wilson, on May 27 before an American pacifist group, delivered a notable speech that for the first time acquainted the world with his ideal of a negotiated peace, a peace of understanding—views he was to reiterate on many occasions in the time to come. There was to be self-determination for all nations, big or small, enduring world security from aggression and breach of international law, and the creation of a league of nations to stabilize world peace.

All this was quite deliberately tailored to the British mentality, but the echo in the British press was almost as unfavorable as that in the German press. The British were indignant that Wilson, instead of openly siding with the enemies of Germany, had said that the controversy over the causes and aims of the war was not America's affair. Wilson was deeply hurt, but even more depressing news came from Paris. France, it was said, was totally uninterested in any peace mediation efforts, for never again, now that half the world was in league with it against Germany, did it stand so excellent a chance of bringing Germany to its knees.[2] The great ideologue of peace was profoundly disillusioned. He had his first inkling that the Western powers, just like Germany, were simply fighting for power goals and were by no means the selfless defenders of peace against autocracy and militarism he had thought them to be. Wilson never quite got over this disillusion.[3]

Tensions between him and the British grew over the trade blockade and ship searches, in which the British showed increasing ruthlessness. During the long breathing spell in the U-boat campaign in the summer of 1916, resentment in American business circles reached new heights. As on a previous occasion, this led to irritable diplomatic exchanges with Britain, and the president was at times so put out that he seriously considered whether it might not be better to follow German urgings and support the German desire for an "armistice looking toward peace," even against Britain's will.[4]

But America was growing rich from Allied trade, and America's economic interests made it impossible for Wilson to risk a diplomatic break with Britain, as did his ideological ties with Western Europe. His closest advisers, Colonel House and Secretary of State Lansing, warned him of the risks of any public mediation offer that had not first been approved by the Entente. What if the Germans accepted and the other side balked? America would then either have to join the German camp openly, when it actually hoped for its defeat, or display its impotence to all the world. The American ambassador in London, Walter Hines Page, confirmed these ideas in a flow of reports. No one in Britain wanted a "premature" peace, before the total victory in which everyone believed was achieved. The president's very speech before the peace group had made him suspect and unpopular among the British, as had Colonel House's various special diplomatic missions.[5]

But these difficulties could not repress Wilson's ambition to become the world's benefactor and peacemaker. Nevertheless, all through the summer and fall he remained completely passive in the peace question, if only to avoid endangering his reelection on November 7 by a diplomatic failure. Bernstorff failed to appreciate, moreover, Wilson's calculation that a great worldwide appeal for peace prior to November 7 might be interpreted as a mere election maneuver and thus might do harm to his moral authority.

Thus Bethmann Hollweg, pining for some peace action on Wilson's part, was put to a long test of patience. This was even harder for him since apparently some of his closest diplomatic advisers did not see quite eye to eye with him. Zimmermann and even Jagow were highly skeptical about any mediation effort emanating from America. They thought Wilson too naive and pro-British, unlikely to be truly neutral, and given to playing the "chosen protector" of whatever he thought just and fair, chiefly perhaps the status quo; and if the Germans declined to entertain his proposals, he would openly join the enemy camp.

Judging from the content of the Grey-House memorandum of February 1916, these fears seem to have been well-founded, for it provided for holding the threat of war over Germany's head at the outset. In a directive to Bernstorff on June 7, in any event, Jagow instructed the ambassador to try to prevent President Wilson from approaching Germany with a "constructive" mediation proposal. This sounded very much like a rebuff—and it was indeed based on the premise that should the war continue to go favorably for Germany, peace on the basis of the status quo, without qualifications, would be unacceptable to Germany, among other things in the Belgian question.

But must it be concluded that Jagow would have, in any circumstances, rejected peace that restored the status quo in Belgium? In the light of his general approach this is unlikely, for he immediately expressed doubts of Germany's ability to bring about a solution in the Belgian question that would be in accordance with its interest. Jagow nevertheless was apparently not prepared to drop without further ado Germany's oft-repeated demand for realistic safeguards for its security, most recently reiterated in Bethmann Hollweg's Reichstag speech of April 5. Even more than the Chancellor, moreover, Jagow was taking into account the strong aversion of the German public to Wilson as a peace mediator.[6]

Bethmann Hollweg shared the foreign ministry view that Wilson's intervention in the details of peace negotiations should be prevented. Let Wilson limit himself to convoking a conference of representatives of the European powers. The Chancellor clung tenaciously to this view down to January 1917. He was afraid that to bring in Wilson as a mediator would mean in effect that Germany would be placing itself entirely in his hands; for an international peace conference, once met, could not be easily disbanded in order to resume hostilities.

Bethmann Hollweg was not much impressed by the German people's aversion and distrust of Wilson. That would be allayed, he thought, once Germany's predicament became still more serious.[7] Late in July, with the war going badly in both east and west, he seriously considered asking Wilson for a peace initiative on the basis of German willingness to restore Belgium, i.e., apparently dropping the much-discussed issue of guarantees and safeguards.[8] Queried by Bernstorff, he dispatched a clarification of the directive of June 7 on August 18, which struck a completely different tone. It was true that Germany could not be expected to commit itself in advance to any concrete peace terms, in return for accepting mediation. But Bernstorff was to do everything possible to encourage a Wilson effort that would initiate peace negotiations among the belligerents. Beyond this, the Chancellor, in contrast to Jagow's draft, was also willing to approve a general peace conference with neutral (i.e., American) participation, if it were held in the wake of successful discussions among the belligerent powers for the purpose of settling general questions of international law and affairs like freedom of the seas and disarmament, on which Wilson laid such stress.[9]

Bethmann Hollweg was primarily intent on bringing the belligerents to the conference table, as he had always been. All else was to be settled only then, in the expectation that immoderate demands on both sides would automatically abate, once the end of the cruel struggle moved tangibly close and any continuation of the slaughter purely for purposes of conquest became difficult. He hoped, in a manner of speaking, to exclude the delicate Belgian question by limiting himself initially to a general declaration that Germany had never intended to annex that country and desired to come to terms on future relations with it in direct negotiations with King Albert. A prelude to such negotiations had already taken place in deepest secrecy in the winter of 1915-1916 between the Bavarian Count Törring, brother-in-law to the king, and his confidential adviser, the Belgian sociologist and politician, Professor Waxweiler.[10] The two had met repeatedly in Zurich. These discussions had brought no immediate practical results; but they had shown that King Albert was seriously interested in a negotiated peace.[11]

In his war diaries,[12] Albert I is shown as a statesman of incorruptible detachment and independence of judgment, utterly free of hollow patriotism and sentiments of hatred, highly critical of the military capacity of his allies, whose confidence in victory he was always inclined to view as mere bluff. He had great respect for the achievements of the German army. He believed that the war would continue indefinitely and end in general exhaustion without any clear-cut victory, unless peaceful negotiations terminated it in time. He was very jealous of his government's autonomy and always refused to have the remnants of his army, which could be replenished only from volunteers escaping across the Dutch border, absorbed into the British or French forces. Convinced that Belgium would be soon forgotten unless it retained troops of its own, he vigorously resisted allowing his regiments to be bled white by participation in the kind of pointless and partial offensives the British and French generals kept on launching. His greatest fear, moreover, was a grand Anglo-French offensive for the forcible reconquest of Belgium, since it would merely transform the country into a heap of rubble.

Grandiose catchwords like "saving European culture from the barbarians" or "fighting for justice" made not the slightest impression on him. *"Sauver la civilisation,"* he noted dryly, *"ce serait chercher résolument à faire la paix dans une Europe encore saine."* He was proud of never having violated his obligations as a neutral; but he was bitterly disappointed with the results of this policy of neutrality and had become convinced that a small country like Belgium could avoid being trampled down as a battlefield only with the help of strong military power. He thought that Germany was ultimately stronger than France with its domestic instability, and in a letter to Count Törring and according to a note the count made on January 5, 1916, he was inclined to seek German protection.

Judging from Törring's note he was prepared to forego Belgian neutrality and conclude a kind of military alliance with Germany that would give that country the security of its western borders Bethmann Hollweg desired and offer Belgium protection against being overwhelmed in the event of another war. The cities of Liège, Namur, and Antwerp were to be "defortified" and garrisoned with only light Belgian forces—but no Germans. The king proposed that French border fortifications like Givet, Maubeuge, and Condé be occupied as German bases. The rail lines leading to them might come under German control, to be used at any time for troop and supply transports. Thus Germany would be taking over military protection of Belgium's southern half, while the defense of the northern half would fall to the Belgian army. A defensive agreement might provide for cooperation between the two armies in certain contingencies.

In place of a direct customs union, a revision of the existing tariff was proposed, and Belgian social legislation was to be accommodated to the German. In addition Belgium would agree not to take part in any trade agreement directed against Germany. A condition was that Belgium would retain full autonomy in all domestic affairs and that its existing territorial limits would remain intact. There was no mention of either German or Belgian war indemnities. The Belgian emissary did mention, however, that Germany might indirectly provide a kind of indemnity by purchasing part of the Congo colony—at a high price, since King Albert was reluctant to forego it. The Belgian desire for an exchange of territory with Holland—the right bank of the Schelde in return for a Belgian enclave—appeared only as a side issue. The main purpose of such a bargain was apparently to make the treaty popular.[13]

All in all this was a concrete settlement proposal unequaled by any other peace feeler. The German response was on the positive side; and in its final version the original demand for dividing the country into Flemish and Walloon administrative districts was dropped. The remaining differences did not really relate to increased German security but rather to concretizing the military protection King Albert desired.

The German bill of particulars did not include the right of permanent occupation, but an option to that effect, presumably against the event of war, in which it might indeed become essential. There was a pledge, however, that this right would be exercised sparingly, "according to circumstances"; but Germany, of course, wanted protection not only against France but also against Britain, and thus a firm demand was put forward covering the possibility of a base on the Belgian coast, perhaps in the Zeebrugge-Bruges-Ostende triangle. The occupation of French border fortifications was rejected as "unsuitable."[14] To make the new point palatable to Belgian pride, it was proposed that the harbor facilities in question be leased by Germany on a long-term basis.

The Congo was not mentioned. All territorial questions, including the colonies, were to be settled in the light of the over-all relationship between the two countries, possibly a disguised way of saying that Germany would forego any annexations. Belgian indemnity requests were not dealt with. Indeed, a counterdemand may be read into the proposal that Germany should be granted, without payment, 60 per cent of the shares of a new company that would run the Belgian main rail lines and the port facilities of Antwerp. In place of the original customs union, the request was now for Belgium to accommodate itself as closely as possible to the German tariff system, in ways to be further negotiated. As for the Belgian-Dutch territorial exchange, the German government was for the time being not yet ready to commit itself to such a thing.

It is impossible to say whether Bethmann Hollweg would have insisted on all these points in further negotiations,[15] for the talks had to be broken off before the final German draft could be discussed. King Albert repeatedly emphasized that he would enter into no agreement that violated the sovereignty of his crown, i.e., the autonomy of his country and the integrity of Belgian territory, and there is no reason to doubt this. The reason he wished to reach an agreement with the Germans was to avoid satellite status with respect to the Western powers, which he called *inféodation*. For that reason he refused, in July 1916, to enter into a customs union with France, as well as a military treaty with the two Western powers that would have required him to introduce conscription.[16] But of course he did not wish to become a German satellite either. It is not certain but by no means impossible that the proposed mutual alliance could have been cast into a form that would have avoided even the semblance of such a thing. The king evidently thought that it could. The Western powers, on the other hand, could not possibly have accepted such a settlement, unless they had clearly lost the war. Thus there was a strong touch of unreality to these secret talks with the German government.

This is why they failed, not because the German demands were excessive.[17] The Entente leaders had got wind of the talks in February and began besieging the king in visit after visit. He was at odds on this issue, moreover, with his ministers, of whom at best three inclined toward a negotiated peace.[18] The rest were more or less radical nationalists, some of them actually annexationists, who put all their faith in the Western powers. All the same, the Belgian cabinet in January 1916 had declined to join the London pact of September 4, 1914, which would have required their country to stick to the Allied side to the bitter end. At the time negotiations had been going on for weeks about a public declaration by the Allied powers that pledged Belgium full restoration of its independence and territory, a generous indemnity, and participation in the peace negotiations to come. This "Declaration of Sainte Adresse" of February 14 made a strong impression in Belgium and thus served as a well-aimed counterblow against any efforts at a separate agreement with Germany.[19]

The king had been maneuvered into a hopeless and indeed perilous position.[20] He sent word through his emissary, asking the Germans not to press him at this time; but he did not simply give up his efforts. As a first step he promised to take part only as an observer in an economic conference scheduled in Paris for March, at which a permanent economic boycott of the Central Powers was to be prepared. He did not, moreover, propose that the talks be ended, only that they be adjourned until early May. He hoped that both Russia and France would become further exhausted in the course of the summer, and thus more amenable to peace than they were now. He would then consider reorganizing his cabinet with members who were less ardent nationalists and agreeing to a negotiated peace, to be confirmed by the parliament. This would be easier if Belgium were permitted to supplement its defensive treaty with Germany with a "reinsurance treaty" with other powers who would agree to protect Belgium against possible German intervention in violation of the defensive treaty. This point, however, does not seem to have been made as an outright demand.

All these plans betokened an astonishingly high measure of confidence in the success of German arms—the Verdun offensive had just commenced—together with serious doubts that the Entente would stand firm. Obviously Bethmann Hollweg's government could not afford to have this contact broken. Even if King Albert should be unable to unshackle himself from his alliance with Britain, it was extremely valuable to Germany to keep in touch with the only head of government in the Western camp who basically favored a negotiated peace rather than a victory of annihilation. From the very outset clerical go-betweens were available for this purpose, for Pope Benedict XV took a particularly lively interest in the fate of Belgium. The connection with the pope ran for the most part through the Bavarian premier Count Hertling and the centrist deputy Erzberger, both of whom had been tending this line for the Chancellor ever since August 1915. [21]

In April 1916 Rome dispatched a new offer to the German foreign ministry to arrange negotiations with King Albert. Asked for his views on the matter, Count Törring recommended pursuing it but limiting any German statements to the Vatican on peace terms to generalities. [22] He went further and proposed that the peace terms themselves be once again cut back. Belgium should be offered an indemnity and a "limited" army, not merely a militia. He also rightly noted that a Channel base would provoke bitter opposition on the part of Britain. Ways should be sought for making it possible to occupy and secure the coast—i.e., against the event of another war—without immediately and prominently revealing such an intent. This was sage advice, though it was unlikely to forestall Entente resistance, even had it been followed.

Erzberger eagerly took up the suggestion from Rome, which had been communicated to him late in April by the papal chamberlain Gerlach, an intimate friend. He discussed the matter in person with the Chancellor, who stated formally that he would accept "any mediation by the Holy See in the Belgian question, as in questions of peace generally," and that he was prepared for a new exchange of views with King Albert. Contact with the king was then actually established through clerical go-betweens; but late in May he advised Rome that he could do nothing until he had reached agreement with his ministers "to make it clear to the Entente powers that unhappy Belgium desired to reach an understanding with the Central Powers." On July 24 Gerlach reported: "An emissary from the king of the Belgians visited and said he was strongly in favor but could not reach agreement with his government." Things never got beyond that point. [22]

Down to the spring of 1917 the Germans tried repeatedly to keep in touch with the king. According to his former adjutant, General van Overstraaten, contact was made in early October 1916 by two different routes, advising the king that the German Chancellor had been in "semiofficial" touch with the

British and Belgian governments since May. On the German side an offer of general peace negotiations was made on the basis of full restoration of Belgian independence, indemnification for Belgian losses, and under certain circumstances even the return to France of the Longwy-Briey area, in which King Albert was to serve as mediator. Informed of this by the American food commissioner, Hoover, the British cabinet at first hesitated to reject such an offer, or so at least Brussels believed; but in the end Lloyd George, supported by *The Times,* roundly declared that Britain could not waste time talking idly about peace at a time when the full force of its military resources was only beginning to assert itself.

The Belgian government thereupon thought it wisest not to compromise itself by mediation and dispatched the foreign minister, Baron Beyens, to dissuade the king from receiving the Belgian intermediary, M. Philipson. On October 10, following his discussion with Beyen, Albert I noted in his diary that in addition to Lloyd George, Briand had also opposed the Philipson mission, refusing permission for the Belgian to go to La Panne, where the king then resided. The intermediary could probably be written off, he added.[24]

It was a very curious incident; and it will be possible to form a judgment concerning the reliability of the information about it only when its source provides further details. One would want confirmation, particularly, that the German offers really went so far, and also precisely what was the authority of the Belgian intermediaries. That they did make certain efforts is beyond doubt, and it is at least highly probable that they somehow acted at Germany's behest. In December Bethmann Hollweg was still trying to enlist King Albert as a mediator, this time through the Spanish envoy in Brussels, Marquis Villalobar.

The king of Spain had ambitions to become a peacemaker;[25] and as long ago as July 1 the marquis had been ordered to make representations to King Albert, who had rejected this intervention as ill-timed and who apparently did not want Spanish mediation in the first place.[26] The contact late in December got no further—the Chancellor thought that the Spaniard went about it in a clumsy fashion.[27] Bethmann Hollweg in consequence decided not to repeat the experiment when efforts to persuade him to do so were made late in February 1917 by Hertling, who had received a settlement proposal from an unnamed Belgian source, amounting in effect to almost complete acceptance of the German terms put forward by Count Törring the year before.

Even earlier, in January, the Holy See had made renewed mediation offers, through the papal nuncio in Munich; but these no longer stood any chance of success in the totally changed situation then existing, directly after the Entente had rejected the public peace offer of the Central Powers, and just before the declaration of unrestricted U-boat warfare.[28] Efforts to come nearer to a negotiated peace through Belgian mediation nevertheless continued throughout the year 1917; we shall yet have to discuss this, together with the very independent attitude of King Albert toward the open German peace offer of December 1916, which put him sharply at odds with the Allies (see Part 4 of this chapter).

Count Hertling's eager participation in these mediation efforts was in keeping with his general attitude since the spring of 1916. He had been rather startled when he first heard in the late fall of 1915 that the foreign ministry in Berlin was thinking of peace negotiations in the near future (see the early part of Chapter 4). Early in May 1916, following the failure of the Verdun offensive, Hertling, like Weizsäcker, relinquished hope that the war could be brought to an end satisfactory to Germany in time—in time, particularly, to remedy the food crisis that bore down more heavily in Bavaria than elsewhere.

Hertling grew so concerned over the course of events that he kept pressing through Lerchenfeld in Berlin for a meeting of the foreign affairs committee of the federal council, where he might be briefed—and possibly reassured—about the situation. His representative wrote him on May 6 that he had been more or less doubtful of victory ever since the Battle of the Marne, but that there seemed to be no reason for absolute despair at the moment. If the German navy could only be kept from further folly—i.e., if America could be kept out of the war—and if there were no crop failure, Germany could still last a good long while.

This observer, however, also thought that Germany should make peace before the food situation made this mandatory. "I should have done so as long ago as November 1914, on the basis of the status quo . . . but what would the German people have said? Now I don't see how peace can come until one side or the other becomes exhausted." He did, however, arrange for Hertling to come to Berlin and call on the Chancellor, who told him that he too was always keeping his eyes on peace, now more than ever before, and was doing everything he could to keep the navy under control and America out of the war. [29]

Count Lerchenfeld was one of the shrewdest statesmen and observers of the scene in the war years. He had concluded quite correctly that the Chancellor's peace policy was utterly dependent on his ability to keep U-boat warfare at a standstill. He also had a surprisingly lucid and accurate judgment of the general chances for a negotiated peace. On July 24 Hertling sent him a proposal to be used with the Chancellor, which anticipated the latter's ideas even down to certain details. An open peace offer was to be made to Germany's enemies as soon as possible.

Germany's situation, Hertling wrote, was bound to grow continually worse, by virtue of economic problems and exhaustion of manpower reserves. Germany must not hesitate much longer to bring the war to an end. As soon as the great offensive on the Somme began to slacken, the psychological moment might arrive for Germany to propose peace negotiations, without waiting for a "first step" by the enemy. The proposal should be transmitted through neutral channels, with the pope, Sweden, and Holland perhaps all acting at the same time. In view of the complexion of the war map and the lack of success attending the enemy's offensives, Germany could afford such a step much better than the other side. Germany need stand in no fear of a gloating foreign press.

The statesmen on the other side knew only too well that Germany was very far from the end of its strength, and this was a point that must be emphasized. In the light of the public mood in their own countries, they could not simply reject so solemn and public an offer—if they did, it would have a profound effect on morale. Once the belligerents met at the peace table, it would be very difficult to reignite the terrible war—the people would take care of that. Of course Germany must reveal its peace terms only when the bargaining was under way. The starting position was favorable, particularly since Britain was bound to be apprehensive that the German U-boat fleet would grow. [30]

These considerations were quite similar to those that gave rise to the actual peace offer of the Central Powers of December 12, 1916. It was in Hertling's letter, however, that they made their first appearance, at least so far as the diplomatic source material now available is concerned. Count Lerchenfeld's comment of July 27 is noteworthy. Except for the fact that the Austrians had meanwhile suffered complete failure on the eastern front, he said, Germany's enemies might well have had the war "up to here," following the failure of the Somme offensive. For the time being the impression that the Central Powers were invincible had been destroyed, and it would take a great deal of doing to make up for setbacks and losses in the east.

There was no foreseeing at the time, late July, that some of the lost ground would soon be regained, in the subjugation of Rumania. Lerchenfeld himself was doubtful of prognostications based on the mood of the people in the enemy camp. It was true, he said, that the nations were sick of war, but as with us, there was a firm conviction among our enemies that they must stick it out, unless all was to be lost. Lone voices of reason could not prevail against the strength with which this conviction had been inculcated. Hence peace was not a question of terms. Even if Germany were to offer to return Poland, Belgium, and North France tomorrow, it would be of no avail. The enemy was determined to see Germany beaten. Lerchenfeld concluded that he did not know how long this madness would last.

The only hope was the defection of one of the enemy countries, in particular France. The war spirit was certainly not yet waning there, but the manpower shortage was beginning to hurt, both in the field and at home. Helfferich was among those who agreed with these views, according to Lerchenfeld; but for the time being there was nothing to do but to "grit one's teeth." Should signs of weakness appear in France, a hint should be promptly given to French peace circles that Germany was ready to "build golden bridges." This was bound to happen—Germany was ready for it. This was true in respect of Russia too, despite all the Reichstag declarations about Polish independence; but there it stood little chance of success, for Russia was too immobile and the masses were inured to hunger.

Were these judgments correct? Before tracing Bethmann Hollweg's peace efforts from August 1916 onward, and especially following the change in the supreme command, we must review the peace prospects in the enemy camp. Unfortunately we can do this but imperfectly, so long as the London and Paris archives are not opened up.

## Part 2
# The Problem of Peace and the Allied Governments

WAR-WEARINESS and a longing for peace were on the rise among the nations in the summer and fall of 1916, especially on the continent. So strong were these sentiments in Russia, in the wake of the huge losses suffered in the summer offensive and the growing economic crisis, that the first symptoms of disintegration began to appear in army and government by the end of the year. The disappointing setback in Rumania only made matters worse. As we have already seen, the representative assembly, the Duma, far from pressing for peace, redoubled its patriotic zeal and took out its rage and disappointment on the government, which it charged with incompetence. Military failure, in other words, while not immediately dampening war ardor, did lead to revolutionary unrest.

The czar could not have dared to enter into peace negotiations of any kind without being called a traitor. As late as the spring of 1917 he assented at once to an extravagant war aims program, brought to him by a special French envoy, Doumergue, on the occasion of a diplomatic conference in St. Petersburg. It provided for a French border on the Rhine, and to keep Russia in the war conceded it any westward expansion of its border it might desire. Nicholas II's last letter to Poincaré, thanking him for Doumergue's mission, was written a week before his abdication. [31]

In France a similar contrast could be discerned between the suffering and embattled people's longings for peace and the political attitudes of their parliamentary representatives and their executive. Count Lerchenfeld had indeed spoken the truth. The terrible bloodshed at Verdun and on the Somme had exhausted the French armies and their reserves—the class of 1918 actually had to be called up in 1916! [32] The people were fearful of being bled still further. They shrank from a third war winter. There was a severe labor shortage. Prices kept on rising, while wages remained stationary. The masses were growing restive and the socialist party was being split by the defection of a radical pacifist group—whom the French called *défaitistes,* a synonym for traitor—from the *union sacrée* of the political parties. All these developments had their parallels in Germany. In France, too, many inveighed against an allegedly soft and passive government and called for a "strong man."

A difference was that in France there was bitter criticism of the allegedly incompetent generals, whose prompt dismissal was demanded after every military setback. More importantly, the parliament insisted on intervening more and more in purely military affairs, creating an ultimately intolerable situation, as described in Volume II, p. 27. After the Battle of Verdun, the Briand government saw itself compelled to institute secret sessions of the chamber and the senate in which the high command had to reveal many military secrets and submit to a veritable barrage of curious questions and critical attacks, the latter mounted especially by ambitious rivals and political intriguers.

Yet in all these attacks few voices were raised against a continuation of the frightful slaughter—on the contrary, there was virtual unanimity in demanding still greater military effort. Bleeding from a thousand wounds, France gave an unexampled object lesson of the demoniac character of modern mass war with its unrestrained political passion, its heroic will to victory, its patriotic pride—but also its deadly hatred. To avoid being swept into the abyss by these passions, successive French governments, including that headed by Briand, who in his heart of hearts probably favored moderation, had no choice but to give ground. Yet Briand, unlike Bethmann Hollweg, chancellor to an emperor, never, so far as can be seen, tried to damp down the fires or to evade their grip; for Briand was at bottom only a functionary of the parliament, aware that the chauvinist president behind him, Poincaré, was watching him with eagle eyes for signs of defeatism, as were his parliamentary rivals in the chamber.

Briand's special gift was a fiery oratory that appealed to patriotic sentiments. He used it to unleash storms of enthusiasm in the chamber when two representatives of the extreme left dared on September 19 to bring up the immensity of the sacrifices France was being compelled to make, compare them with the far lesser contributions of its allies, and demand a negotiated peace instead of incalculable further bloodletting.

Briand's whole tactic against this "defeatism" amounted to nothing more than an appeal to naked hate—hatred of the Germans who had suddenly, in 1914, under a plan long premeditated, leaped at peaceful France's throat, and were now carrying off women and children and old men, brutally mistreating them. To make peace with Germany would be humiliating and dishonorable, a denigration of the memory of France's dead. A negotiated peace, moreover, would serve only to perpetuate the German danger.

Combined with this warning was a highly effective appeal to national pride: France, the protagonist of freedom and justice in the world, source of the noblest and most admirable ideas civilized mankind could boast, must emerge "enhanced" from this great ordeal. Even now it was facing the victory to come "with radiant countenance . . . its brow transfigured by an aureole of glory," etc., etc.

Delivered extempore, this speech was Briand's greatest oratorical triumph. In the judgment of his biographer it established his reputation abroad. The chamber was afire with enthusiasm and resolved, 421 to 25, to have the masterpiece posted all over France. [33]

There can be no doubt that Briand completely won over what is called, in modern democracies, "public opinion," i.e., the spokesmen on the home front—or at least the great majority of them. The French premier's speech had been delivered in response to a challenge laid down by the deputy Brizon, a radical "loner," much like the German communist in the Reichstag, Karl Liebknecht. Brizon was supported by only a small group of sympathizers. He belonged to an international faction of extremist socialists who had been meeting about this time in Switzerland (more precisely in Zimmerwald and Kienthal in the canton of Berne) under the leadership of Lenin to call upon proletarians of all nations to demonstrate against continuance of the slaughter.

For the nonce this faction remained politically impotent in France, but during the course of the winter the majorities at French socialist congresses in favor of continuing the *union sacrée* and participating in the government began to decline. A number of opposition papers circulated among the working class and petty bourgeoisie—sheets like *Bonnet Rouge, L'Eclair, L'OEuvre, Les Nations, La Tranchée Republicaine*—harping on all kinds of abuses brought on by the war; but beyond giving voice to grievances, they offered no program for peace, and among opinion leaders they stood in the odor of being in the pay of the Germans, which was almost certainly true in some instances.

The secret hopes of the disaffected centered on the former premier Caillaux. Responsibility for Caillaux's fall in the summer of 1914 rested principally with his wife; and ever since he had been burning with impatience and ambition to return to power as leader of an antimilitarist opposition, if not indeed as a peacemaker. This had brought him into contact with dubious international adventurers and German agents; but he had proved incapable of outlining a positive program as leader of an opposition group.[34]

As in Germany, the patriotic majority strongly favored annexations, a trend that was fostered by heavy industry, again as in Germany. The *Comité des Forges,* principal spokesman for French industry, proclaimed in mid-July that the coal deposits of the Saar would be indispensable to the French steel industry, once the ore deposits of Lorraine—the return of which was taken for granted—came under French control again. Indeed the statement went on to say that for economic reasons further territorial acquisitions on the left bank of the Rhine would be desirable.[35]

When the Belgian government discussed its desire to annex Luxembourg with the French foreign ministry early in 1916, it came up against one French motivation for such war aims. Philippe Berthelot, deputy chief of the political department (which he later headed), declared roundly that the question raised by Belgium would have to remain open for the time being, since France itself was under the necessity of expanding eastward. "Our capital lies too close to the border," he said. "We must seize the opportunity to place it farther away—in other words, we must resume the policy of Louis XIV. It is not enough to reunite Alsace-Lorraine with France. To prevent a recurrence of the events of 1914, we need at least part of the Palatinate." The question of whether Luxembourg might not also have to be annexed had not yet been settled. [36]

This was quite in keeping with the views then being held by the whole French government. In July three committees, instituted by Briand, began to work on the preparation of peace terms. One was to study the financial consequences of neutralizing the Rhineland, another the exploitation of occupied mines and factories, the third France's "legitimate claims" to the left bank of the Rhine, from the historical and diplomatic point of view. The result, embodied in a report by the minister Léon Bourgeois, was discussed at a meeting Poincaré held on October 7 with Briand, Freycinet, and Bourgeois and was subsequently submitted to the two chamber presidents. There was initial hesitancy, with a view to France's allies, to call for neutralization or even annexation of the whole left bank of the Rhine immediately; but it was agreed that prolonged occupation was essential at the very least, as a kind of guarantee for payment of reparations. Further, adherence *(Anschluss)* of German-speaking Austria to Germany was to be prevented, after the dissolution of the Hapsburg Empire. [37]

Clearly, the Versailles peace terms were in the making years before the fact. In November Briand expressed himself even more plainly, in a draft for a directive to his London ambassador, Paul Cambon, dispatched to him in somewhat changed form on January 12, 1917, and according with a formal decision by the French council of ministers. The return of Alsace-Lorraine was to be insisted on, not within the "mutilated" borders of 1815, but the older ones of 1790, including Landau, Homburg, and Tholey. The Saar region was to be added. Whether Luxembourg would become French or Belgian was still left open. The return of Alsace-Lorraine should not be counted as a territorial gain for France, but merely as the restoration of an old legitimate claim. *Bon's esprits* in France wished to see the whole left bank of the Rhine annexed, as "a lost heritage of the French revolution." It was indeed needed as a French glacis or buffer zone *(Vorgelände)* in Richelieu's sense. Such an annexation would, however, probably be viewed as outright conquest and thus cause trouble; but since Germany must on no account be allowed a foothold beyond the Rhine, negotiations were necessary among the Allies, looking toward the neutralization and provisional occupation of the left bank of the Rhine. The original November draft actually spoke of two satellite states in this area, one under French protectorate, the other under Belgian. [38]

These were the terms entrusted to Doumergue for his mission to St. Petersburg, already noted—he was to secure the czar's assent to ease their acceptance on the part of the other Allies. The upshot was a secret treaty that was, for safety's sake, not immediately communicated to the rest. In fact, it met with opposition even within the French cabinet, because it left it to the czar to fix the western border of Russia, which held a potential danger to the future of Poland. [39]

There were still other demands contained in the original version of Briand's directive to Cambon. East Frisia with its islands was to fall to Holland, Heligoland to Britain, Schleswig with the North Frisian islands to Denmark. Poland's future was touched on but cautiously, but in any event the Polish regions of Silesia, Poznan, and the lower Vistula were to become Polish, as were the Polish regions of Austria, i.e., Galicia. "This would deprive Berlin of any cover [against Poland]." There was, of course, also mention of "sanctions" (not merely reparations) and indemnities, and of guarantees for their payment. Lastly, a permanent alliance of the victorious powers to secure the peace was put forward, along Wilson's lines. Briand regarded all this as modest and reasonable, calculated to restore the balance of Europe, and he anticipated that Britain would acknowledge the unselfish character of the French proposals.

Such, then, was the picture of Germany's future, as viewed through the eyes of the French government at the end of that year of terror, 1916. That Paris therefore wanted no part of American peace mediation becomes clear enough. Even in late May, when the French learned of the Grey-House memorandum and of Wilson's subsequent statements, they had responded with vehement opposition, characterizing peace negotiations at this juncture as a *désastre* for all mankind. Briand even saw danger in Grey's artless response to a peace feeler from Scandinavia, to the effect that the Allies could consider only an official offer by Germany. Briand would not hear of peace talks before victory was won. In his November draft of the Cambon directive he sharply rejected any neutral mediation effort as unwarranted intervention, put forward merely from self-interest or German-influenced intrigue.

Thus the prospects for the success of any German initiative toward peace were gloomy indeed. This gloom was deepened by the fact that in Britain too the thought of a negotiated peace showed no signs of prevailing.

The British situation differed from the French in that Britain, despite the cruel bloodshed in the battles of the Somme, had not depleted its manpower resources to the same degree. The British arms industry too had not yet reached its full potential. Lloyd George, the war minister, at any rate, looked on everything that had happened so far as only a beginning. On the other hand a much greater propaganda mobilization was required in Britain than on the continent. The British liberal tradition was still too strong to give way readily to war zeal and willing sacrifice—it was basically neutralist, insular, and antimilitarist. Apart from the almost insignificant Zeppelin bombing raids there was no direct threat to the home soil of the island kingdom. In October 1916 the House of Commons was told about huge mass demonstrations for peace that were taking place week after week in many industrial centers. [40]

All in all, however, British war propaganda succeeded surprisingly well. British liberals did swallow the slogans they were fed—the "war to end war," "German barbarism fighting its last battle," the "fight to set the world free"[41]—and the British masses displayed admirable patience and tenacity. Doubtless the U-boat campaign was an important element, for it raised British pride in dominion of the seas to white heat. The British, furthermore, regarded it as barbaric. Most essentially of all, it nakedly threatened their survival.

Even more amazing was the unswerving strength of character with which Britain's leaders clung to the idea of total victory, despite ever-repeated military setbacks, the seriousness of which they fully realized. None could have given a gloomier picture of Britain's predicament late in 1916 than Lloyd George in his memoirs—the unfathomable difficulties, the hopeless world situation. It is true, of course, that Lloyd George took recourse to such dark colors to set off his achievements as prime minister all the more. But Britain's serious position was certainly not glossed over in the writings of that time by other British cabinet members, like Chancellor of the Exchequer McKenna, President of the Board of Trade Runciman, blockade chief Sir Robert Cecil, and even Lord Lansdowne. All the military efforts of that year failed, even the gigantic offensive on the Somme. The great naval Battle of Jutland was at best only half a success. The Salonica campaign was such a failure that Rumania had to be left to face its doom unaided. An entire Anglo-Indian army fell into Turkish hands in the Mesopotamian desert at Kut el Amara. The food situation, while not yet critical, was becoming more and more difficult; and the rapidly rising success of the U-boats in the fall months boded ill for the future. War costs, swollen by aid to Britain's allies, had long since reached dizzying heights and were about to destroy Britain's ancient wealth for good. So serious had Britain's financial situation grown that it could not have been maintained at all without American aid, which put Britain into a state of oppressive dependence on the United States, sharpening still further the tension between the two countries stemming from the blockade question. [42]

Russia was palpably close to collapse, Italy teeming with political unrest and militarily ineffective, France determined to fight on despite its exhaustion. In the face of such realities, what importance could be attributed to the pledges of generals Robertson and Haig that next year offensive action in France and Flanders would be attended by better success, when no breakthrough had been achieved this year? In such a plight was it not really advisable to consider the offer of peace mediation Colonel House had transmitted in the spring, in the form of the Grey-House memorandum of February 22 with which we are already familiar? After all, it provided for American entry into the war, should Germany prove recalcitrant. Down to his resignation in December Sir Edward Grey never abandoned hope that in the face of the continental allies' increasing exhaustion, negotiations might still come about, in which his agreement with Colonel House might somehow come into play.[43] During the summer of 1916 reports kept reaching Britain from neutral sources—America, Holland, Spain, the Vatican, Sweden—that the Bethmann Hollweg government was seriously prepared to discuss peace, especially a separate peace with Britain.[44] Were such feelers to be rebuffed, indeed could they be in view of the American desire for peace?

Quite evidently it was the situation in St. Petersburg that most disturbed Grey. Sazonov, tested friend of the Entente, had fallen on July 23. We are probably not far wrong in assuming that this event provided the main occasion for the deliberations held by the cabinet's war committee in August for the purpose of clarifying British war aims. The government wanted to be fully prepared, should peace negotiations suddenly eventuate after all. The point of departure for these meetings was a voluminous report drafted at the prime minister's behest by "two eminent officials" of the Foreign Office and circulated among members of the cabinet without any comment by Grey—it was in fact officially considered by the cabinet only in 1917. Nevertheless, it apparently formed the basis of all further discussions of war aims, even with France. [45]

In contrast to similar French war aims formulations, the British document was not dominated by considerations of British security and power expansion. Britain had no territorial aspirations on the European continent and felt no threat to its insular safety. The chief element was the principle of nationalism, which was to give all the nations of Europe, big and small, gratification of their "national claims," security, and freedom to develop. Only in this way, the British felt, could a durable peace be insured, and this was Britain's main interest.

The authors of the document realized, however, that this noble principle could only be approximated, by virtue of the war aims commitments already entered into, especially with Italy, and because of the conflicting special interests and expansionist ambitions of the Allied powers. This applied even to the very first war aim, the restoration and indemnification of Belgium. Britain's special goal was not to allow the Belgian coast to fall once again into German hands under any circumstances. The country was therefore to relinquish its neutrality and conclude a permanent alliance with the Western powers, counter to the wishes then being voiced by King Albert, as we already know.[46] Belgium's desire to annex Luxembourg was to be granted, as was France's for the return of Alsace-Lorraine, without any discussion of the question of nationality and without a plebiscite. For strategic reasons the British were even prepared to assent to certain French "border rectifications," though these were not to assume any considerable extent and take the wishes of the people into account. The admiralty—whose views were entirely predictable—was to air its ideas on the future of Heligoland and the Kiel canal.

The British report was concerned with Germany's eastern border only to the extent of demanding the creation of a greater Polish "buffer state" under the Russian crown. It was to have free access to the Baltic and incorporate all the Polish-speaking areas of Prussia and Austria. Oddly enough, the British also wanted to incorporate the Czechs into Poland, holding that they would eagerly accept the "superior" Polish culture. The Serbs, Croats, Slovenes, and even the Montenegrins were to be gathered into a common state of South Slavia, to be established. The authors of the report hoped that this new state would reach peaceful agreement with Italy over Italian expansionist ambitions on the Adriatic coast, which were considered to be ethnologically unjustifiable.

Together all the newly created Slavic states would form a useful counterpoise to Russian as well as German hegemony. Only German-speaking Austria and Hungary would be left of the Hapsburg monarchy; and on account of both its weakness and the political desires of the majority of the people, this rump state was to remain dependent on Germany. Instead of allowing such a wretched construction to survive, however, it would be best to carry the principle of nationalism to its logical conclusion and let Germany absorb German-speaking Austria. This would greatly augment the South German Catholic element and weaken Prussian preponderance, which the report considered to be the root of all evil in the recent history of Europe. It would also be an important contribution to the democratization and demilitarization of Germany.

Austrian *Anschluss* might also serve to compensate Germany in some measure for the great population losses in Alsace-Lorraine, Schleswig, and Poznan. The Germans might in this way be more easily converted from their aversion to general disarmament, which the authors of the report considered the main goal for the postwar period. They anticipated, however, that the Germans would forego their superior army only in the event they had to accept a dictated peace; for their pride and all their hopes rested on armed might. This went far beyond the Pan-German circles, whom the German government had always disavowed, though without on that account—according to the authors—desisting from aggressive policies.[47] As for a league of nations to secure the peace, such a union would be useful only if America decided to take part and relinquish its isolation for good.

The question of a negotiated peace was briefly discussed. It might very well become inescapable if there were no clear victory. In that event there would probably be no alternative to ransoming Belgium from the Germans, so to speak, by means of concessions elsewhere. The only possible locations would be colonial territories, and Britain would thus be the chief sufferer. The Germans would be able to speak triumphantly of victory, even though they might have received only an installment on their ambitious goals.

This was probably intended as a warning. The writers of the report were afraid of easy compromise, should it come to negotiations—but they did not exclude the possibility of compromise; nor for that matter did the British chief of staff, Robertson, whose opinion Asquith also sought. Robertson was a soldier of uncommonly clear and calm judgment, even in political questions.[48] He was also, by the way, an admirer of the German army, and highly critical of the military efforts of Britain's allies. A taciturn and rather forbidding man, he was repelled by the very verbosity of the French generals. In order to anticipate the ever-nimble French, Robertson strongly favored prompt fixing of British demands to be put forward at the peace table.

To this end Robertson had submitted a report of his own on August 31, which even Lloyd George, for whom Robertson was in many respects a thorn in the flesh, described as "statesmanlike." Robertson, a traditional Englishman, was not concerned with any principle of nationalism but with the balance of the continental powers, the maintenance of British sea power, and keeping any strong power away from the Belgo-Dutch coast. In Robertson's view the balance of Europe required keeping a strong power in Central Europe, and that could only be Germany, not any Slavic state. Only in this way could Russia as a great power be contained.

Germany should therefore be kept strong as a land power, while being thoroughly weakened in respect of sea power. This latter objective, according to Robertson's report, might be achieved by returning Schleswig and possibly part of Holstein to Denmark, internationalizing the Kiel canal, and seizing the port of Kiel, the North Frisian islands, and the east coast of Heligoland Bight—in other words a very thorough amputation, the full volume of which the admiralty would decide.

On the other hand, Robertson too had no objections to the incorporation of German-speaking Austria into Germany when the Hapsburg state was dissolved, which he did not wholly favor. At least he did not object to a very close association between a Danubian monarchy reduced in size and Germany. The question of Alsace-Lorraine would have to be settled as France wished; but Robertson spoke only of territorial "portions" Germany was to lose and said not a word about strategic border rectifications.

Belgium was to get the grand duchy of Luxembourg and the left bank of the Schelde. On the subject of Poland's future Robertson was skeptical. Russia would probably have to be allowed to prevail; but he doubted that the Germans would ever be beaten badly enough to consent to cede the province of Poznan to the Poles, unless it remained part of the Reich under a German sovereign. The Germans were still less likely to let East Prussia be separated from the Reich by surrendering West Prussia.

Robertson discussed the future of the Baltic nations and the Middle East only cautiously, suggesting, however, that the present power constellation would not last forever. This was evidently meant as a warning not to give way too readily to the soaring ambitions of the Allies, mainly Italy and Russia. The colonial question caused Robertson much concern. Like the authors of the Foreign Office report, he suspected that the Germans might demand the return of their colonies in exchange for evacuating Belgium and relinquishing parts of Alsace-Lorraine and Poland. It was, of course, principally Britain and even more its Dominions that were interested in these colonies. If there were special negotiations there might well be strong differences with the Dominions; and this would probably mean that in the end only Togoland would remain in British hands as freely available for compensatory purposes. All this would have to be promptly clarified with the Dominions.

Obviously the British staff chief was thinking of peace negotiations with Germany even more seriously than the Foreign Office under Grey. Estimating the military prospects soberly, he did not think the day would come when Britain could simply dictate peace terms. For that reason he discussed at length the question of the kind of armistice that should prevail during the negotiations. He thought it would be wrong to continue the blockade during that period, but he ultimately consoled himself with the thought that the Germans would proceed ruthlessly if they were in Britain's position. The blockade would help shorten negotiations. "The hungrier the enemy is kept the better. After all, he probably has a bare sustenance." In sum, an armistice should not be refused, but it should be granted only on severe terms: immediate evacuation of occupied territories, immediate release of all prisoners of war held by Germany, "token" surrender of part of the German fleet.

Such were the thoughts of the least militaristically inclined among Britain's military leaders, the one who had the fewest illusions about the military situation and was perhaps least obsessed by hatred of the Germans. His view that Britain must prepare itself for negotiations with Germany and hold a program to that end in readiness was shared by Grey, who discussed the matter a few days later with the French ambassador Cambon, from whose lips he now heard the Paris government's intentions for the Rhineland, with which we are already familiar. Grey offered no immediate objection, except that he expressly acknowledged only the annexation of Heligoland as a British war aim.[49] Yet the British government remained strangely unresponsive to German peace feelers.[50] There was at least one member of the British cabinet who was bitterly opposed to any talk of making peace. This was Lloyd George, the minister of war and by far the strongest personality in the government.

To put an end to the talk of peace Lloyd George told a leading American journalist in an interview on September 28 that since Germany was determined to fight Britain to the bitter end, it would have its way. The struggle would continue until a knockout was scored. Let the whole world know that any outside intervention was out of the question. Britain had not seen fit to call in a mediator at a time when it was unprepared for war. Now that it was prepared, it would tolerate none until Prussian military despotism was destroyed for good. At the outset of the war the world watched the unequal struggle dry-eyed; let it now forego tears and weeping when the war was being brought to an end. The inhumanity of the impending climax would not be as great as the cruelty of ending the war while civilization remained under threat from the same enemies. Lloyd George described what he had seen on the battlefields of France and insisted that so terrible a slaughter must never be allowed to recur. Those responsible for these crimes against mankind must be punished so severely that they would never again be moved to repeat them.[51]

This interview had approximately the same effect on Lloyd George's international reputation as the famous chamber speech held shortly before had for Briand. Its blending of high moral tone with a kind of sportsmanship enormously enhanced the minister's popularity among the British masses. There too he now appeared as the embodiment of the "strong man" for whom public opinion clamored. The written protest of Sir Edward Grey, who saw the door to America suddenly slammed shut, remained fruitless,[52] as did the objection of liberal members of the House of Commons to this fighting spirit, which they regarded as "un-British." [53]

The Welsh firebrand unintentionally became the destroyer of liberalism by winning the day for a radical militancy based on the masses rather than on Parliament. The House of Commons, elected six years before, was no longer felt to be the true representative of the national will. British public opinion was no longer set by the speeches of the Right Honourables, but by appeals to mass rallies and street demonstrations, dominated by flaming patriotic oratory and preachments of hate.[54] Among the chauvinist wing of the conservatives, the so-called die-hards, Prime Minister Asquith, a typical liberal mediator by nature, acquired a reputation for softness and inaction.

The radical anti-German press, under the influence of Lord Northcliffe, did everything to deepen this unfavorable image. Asquith and Grey had no choice but to defend themselves publicly against any suspicion of harboring peaceful intentions. Asquith did so in the House of Commons on October 11, Grey at a press banquet on October 23, both of them with arguments with which we have long been familiar: the war must end only when Prussian militarism had been extirpated root and branch and the freedom of the world secured. Otherwise all the sacrifices would have been in vain. [55]

On November 9, at the Lord Mayor's banquet in London's Guildhall, Asquith expressly disavowed any thought of a separate Anglo-German peace. He mentioned rumors set afoot by German agents in Britain, to the effect that Germany was prepared to restore Belgian independence and grant that country indemnification in return for such a separate peace. Britain, in other words, could have peace at a bargain price if it declined to allow itself to be drawn even more deeply into the war by its allies for purposes of their war aims; but Britain, Asquith argued, was committed to the restoration of not only Belgium but Serbia as well. Above all, Britain was fighting for the common war aims of the whole war alliance, and the interests of its allies were also its own. The issue went beyond Belgium. What was at stake was to secure the freedom of the world. [56]

It was a sharp blow to the hopes of many liberals that Anglo-German understanding would be possible as soon as the German Chancellor could make up his mind to issue a declaration unambiguously in favor of the Belgian claims. The radical labor leader Ramsay MacDonald had tried to say so in the House of Commons on May 24, though he had left the crucial sentence unfinished. The speech had aroused great hopes in liberal German circles, all the same.[57] Apart from Snowden, however, MacDonald had few followers in the House of Commons. The highly popular labor leader Henderson unreservedly joined Asquith in his warnings against a premature peace of compromise, negotiated before victory was won. Such a peace would do violence to British national honor and legitimate claims. [58]

One would like to know more about the origin and background of the "rumors" circulating in Britain, according to which Germany was willing to relinquish any claim to Belgium. So far nothing more than scattered notes have been found on the subject.[59] Still, in the face of the fact that the British prime minister found it necessary to reply to them publicly and thus call attention to them, it is not easy to conclude that there was no substance to them at all. Even so, however, the Belgian question played no discernible role in the internal discussions of the Asquith cabinet about a negotiated or imposed peace, debates that grew very lively at times in the course of the fall months.

These talks were in continuation of the war aims debate begun in August. On October 4 navy minister Arthur James Balfour, ex-prime minister of a conservative cabinet and later on Lloyd George's foreign secretary and thus a man who carried considerable weight, submitted his views on war aims in writing.[60] Even though peace had not yet been secured, Balfour's war aims entirely predicated an imposed peace. By and large, his views accorded with the proposals put forward by the Foreign Office and by Robertson. Even more forcefully than Robertson, however, Balfour emphasized the need for maintaining Germany as a strong land power and enabling it to associate itself with Austria-Hungary, which Balfour wished to see preserved, following the detachment of its Slavic regions.

Germany, Balfour thought, would always be rich and densely populated, and thus would hold a potential threat. There was no point in trying to prevent this by force, to repeat Napoleon's fruitless experiment with disarming Prussia. A strong Germany would be able without difficulty to forestall Russian preponderance in Europe. Balfour was opposed to intervention in Germany's internal affairs, to postwar trade treaties imposed by force—which would be humiliating—and to war contributions. Reparations should be demanded only for damage done in Belgium, North France, Serbia, and at sea. If Austria was to lose its South Slav territories, it must be somehow granted continued access to the Mediterranean. The two Central Powers would of course have to disgorge all the non-German populations within their borders, including Alsace—Balfour estimated the total at more than twenty millions; but the Allied motto should be: Germany for the Germans, but only on German soil.

Balfour did not greatly depart in detail from the reports that had preceded him—they were evidently available to him. He voiced fears that Denmark would probably not wish to accept the return of Schleswig-Holstein without international guarantees, and unfortunately the region on both sides of the Kiel canal was German in language and sentiment. In contrast to the Foreign Office report, Balfour thought that Poland must on no account become a wholly independent buffer state. Like the ancient kingdom of Poland, such a state would only become an everlasting bone of contention among its neighbors; and why should Britain offer Germany security in its rear against Russia on a silver platter? The best solution would be an autonomous Polish state within the Russian empire, which should help in "Europeanizing" Russia. If possible, the Czechs should also be given a country of their own, bordering Poland, but not part of that country.

From the British point of view this was certainly a moderate program, but like all the other plans, it was feasible only in the event of Germany's total defeat. For that reason it was opposed by Balfour's former foreign secretary, Lord Lansdowne, a conservative who was accounted the real founder of the Anglo-French Entente and whose voice therefore carried particular weight.[61]

To Lansdowne total victory by the Allies seemed less than certain. In a long report on November 13 he painted the situation of Britain and its allies in very gloomy colors, all of his contentions carefully documented with up-to-date official military, economic, and political intelligence. Was the bloody struggle to be endlessly prolonged, he asked, without Britain and its allies carefully reviewing their war aims to see which of them might be dispensed with? He vigorously supported Robertson's proposal to prepare for a negotiated peace, while he regarded Lloyd George's "knockout" policy with deep skepticism. He was opposed to discouraging any effort that might lead to an exchange with the enemy on the possibility of a settlement. There was much news from neutral countries and indeed incidents right within Germany—of which Lord Lansdowne enumerated several—hinting at a serious disposition to peace on the German side, not least because of the German people's war-weariness. It would be very strange, he said, if the coming winter would not already bring soundings as to whether Britain were prepared to discuss peace terms or proposals for an armistice.

Lansdowne was foreseeing something like a peace offer on the part of the Central Powers, which was indeed made only four weeks later. England must be prepared. Lansdowne expressed agreement with the general formula Asquith had used in one of his speeches, that there should be no peace without adequate compensation for what lay in the past and adequate security for the future; but the world must not gain the impression that the Entente was vengeful, selfish, and intractable, that it regarded any attempt to rescue it from its blind alley as an unfriendly act. In this sense Lansdowne regretted Lloyd George's "knockout" interview, and even more Briand's superpatriotism, which branded the very word *peace* as subversive.

This warning was both objective and well-founded, and it left a deep impression within the British cabinet, whose members realized full well that Britain stood at the crossroads. Asquith asked the military and naval heads for an opinion on whether the war might not end in a draw. General Haig, the commander-in-chief, answered with little more than the usual expressions of military confidence, not without overestimating British successes and underestimating enemy morale. [62]

Sir William Robertson, on the other hand, had already submitted a report at Lloyd George's request, in which he expressed himself with admirable honesty and objectivity on the enormous difficulties facing the Allied command, avoided any predictions of a breakthrough on the western front, and maintained that as British chief of staff he had only limited scope for judging the future prospects in a modern war of coalition, in the course of which countless political and economic factors played a part. He advised that an end to the war should not be expected before the summer of 1918. Faced with the prime minister's new inquiry, he rejected in sharp soldierly terms any imputation of foregoing final victory, but stated frankly that still larger casualties must be anticipated and very much greater efforts would have to be made, unless the war were to be lost. The General Staff should also become more independent of politics.

Grey, the foreign secretary, reacted very uncertainly to these representations. He wrote that if the military authorities thought that Germany could be defeated and that a peace could be ultimately imposed on it, it would be precipitate to initiate negotiations now. The prospect of U-boat warfare had not yet been clarified. Britain's future depended on whether Germany could "bring us to our knees before military operations on land can bring Germany down." Even so, with the military and naval authorities believing that there was no more than a probability that the situation of the Allies would improve, negotiations should wait. If, on the other hand, they thought that there was not even such a probability, it would be better not to protract the war uselessly for another year but to end it on the best terms presently available.

This should be done, using mediation that was "not unfriendly," as soon as the generals foresaw a worsening of the situation. It would be particularly important to know what the appropriate authorities might have to say about the prospects of British mercantile shipping and the question of tonnage in general. This was quite plainly an evasion of the issue—let the soldiers bear the responsibility! Grey's own inclination ran more in the direction of a negotiated peace. His warning that sentiment and fine words should not be allowed to decide the issue was undoubtedly to be understood in this sense.

The position taken by Lord Cecil, who headed the blockade effort, was much more impressive. He too was under no illusions as to the gravity of the situation. Unless the utmost in effort were put forward, it might grow desperate, especially in the question of available tonnage. Things looked bad in the Allied countries, especially Russia. Nevertheless, "peace concluded at this time could not but be baleful. At best we could do no better than restore the status quo, with a great increment in German power in the east [Cecil did not mention Belgium]. Beyond that the Germans would be bound to note that peace had been forced on us by their U-boats; and it would be shown that Britain's insular position increased rather than reduced its vulnerability." The war, in other words, must be continued. [63]

The prime minister shared this view. Without encountering any opposition in the cabinet, he decided that the time for peace feelers had not yet come. It was the same attitude against which Colonel House's mediation efforts during the preceding spring had fetched up. But the die-hards, especially in the conservative party, men like Bonar Law and his friends, were not yet satisfied. Lord Cecil had already said that it would be necessary to wage the war along much sharper lines. Imports should be restricted, which meant lowering the standard of living. There should probably be compulsory labor service, and in any event, there would have to be large-scale industrial reorganization with partial nationalization, increased conscription, a greater share for the wealthy in the general burdens to be borne, the closing of certain ostentatious clubs, cuts in ministerial pay, and similar rigorous measures. To put all this into effect there was to be a cabinet committee of only three, in whose hands the actual conduct of the war would be placed.

Lloyd George, the war minister, seized upon this demand with fiery energy. He had recently returned in bitter disappointment from a trip to Paris he had taken in mid-November with Asquith for the purpose of putting more vigor and unity into the Allied conduct of the war and impressing the French with the gravity of the general situation. He had been dismayed by Briand's superficial optimism and predisposition to gloss over problems with rhetorical phrases, and also by the instability of domestic French politics. He now strongly pressed for tightening up the conduct of the war in Britain and challenged Asquith to do no less than to entrust him with the leadership of the committee of three, which was not even to include the prime minister. (We have already noted, in Volume II, pp. 52ff., that the British cabinet system did indeed provide objective reasons for such a reform.)

This challenge, of course, implied a personal vote of lack of confidence in Asquith, which was quite intolerable to the prime minister. The conflict, exacerbated by the personal intrigues of certain conservative leaders and deliberate press leaks, quickly blew up into a government crisis to which the Asquith cabinet fell victim early in December and which brought Lloyd George, long since touted in the press as a "strong man," to the helm. In Volume II, pp. 56ff., we discussed the "new style" of Lloyd George's war cabinet, composed of conservatives, liberals, and labor men, with Sir Edward Grey notably absent. The new cabinet took office on December 10, 1916, two days before the Central Powers launched their peace offer, an offer that was therefore already doomed before it was made.

Our account has shown that the British, in the fall of 1916, wrestled with problems and doubts quite similar to those facing the governments of the Central Powers. Like the third German OHL under Ludendorff, the British saw the way out of their troubles in the direction of an intensified rallying of every resource for the final struggle; and like the Germans, this is what they put into effect; yet they never even tried to end the cruel conflict by negotiation, oddly enough for the very reason that encouraged Bethmann Hollweg to make such an effort. As expressly confirmed by Lloyd George,[64] the

British were as well aware as was Bethmann Hollweg that once the belligerents sat down at the peace table, any resumption of the fighting would be inconceivable. As in the early summer of 1916, this was their crucial reservation, rather than concern that German demands might be excessive. Lord Cecil put it quite bluntly—even a restoration of the status quo would have been regarded as an intolerable German triumph. Again, oddly enough, it was the civilian ministers rather than the generals who cast the deciding vote in the fateful decision. No British general or admiral would have arrogated to himself the kind of independent political role claimed by Ludendorff in Germany.

## Part 3

# Postponement of U-Boat Warfare and Preparation of a Peace Offer (August to December, 1916)

WHETHER THE PROSPECTS were favorable or not, Bethmann Hollweg had no choice. He had to stake everything on bringing about peace negotiations as soon as possible, since they were probably the only means for preventing unrestricted U-boat warfare, and with it America's entry into the war. This was not a mere matter of stubborn naval ambition. Neither the German people nor the Kaiser could ever be expected to break off the war in the face of the great achievements and successes of German arms—in other words, to capitulate—until this last extreme weapon for the subjugation of Great Britain had been put to the test. Its application could be postponed, but it could scarcely be suppressed in the long run, once it was universally realized that there was no chance of winning final victory on land.

The German navy had of course been pressing all summer for the increased use of U-boats, especially Admiral Scheer, head of the fleet, whose self-confidence had risen still further after the Battle of Jutland, in which he had been the guiding spirit. Admiralty chief Holtzendorff appreciated the Chancellor's political quandary and searched for a form of U-boat warfare that would be as effective as possible without conjuring up new conflicts with America; but Scheer rejected all such efforts as half-measures. In his opinion limited warfare on merchant shipping, while it might appease public opinion and the government leaders, would never lead to real victory, hence would merely delay or prevent the only proper decision.

These differences gradually led to a serious crisis of confidence, and the naval officers afloat began to look on the admiralty chief as a man of indecision. At the height of the summer there were protracted discussions between the political and naval agencies on whether unrestricted U-boat warfare should not be initiated at least in the English Channel in order to cut off Britain's supply and transport lines to France during the battle of the Somme. Had Falkenhayn firmly insisted, the chances are that Bethmann Hollweg would have yielded for these limited waters.[65] But the chief of staff, deeply disturbed by the failure of his Verdun offensive and the mounting disasters on the eastern front, had enough sense not to provoke the additional risk of American entry into the war. On August 16 the plan had been dropped. Would the new OHL display similar good sense?

The U-boat question was among the very first the Chancellor discussed with the new men, following their appointment, at first on a somewhat confidential basis and subsequently in the presence of all the top military and political leaders. At this time, August 29-31, Hindenburg and Ludendorff were not yet fully oriented about the over-all military situation; and in the immediate wake of Rumania's war declaration they had to anticipate the possibility of deep new incursions into the southeastern front. Naturally they wished to wait and see how the situation would develop there, before accepting the risk of an American declaration of war.

The Chancellor cautioned them that America's entry into the war might very well persuade certain neutral nations to join the enemy camp, especially Denmark and Holland. Ludendorff was therefore minded to wait until the subjugation of Rumania would make it possible to spare enough divisions to secure the Danish and Dutch borders. He was not swerved from this stand by the pleas of admirals Holtzendorff and Capelle, who now for the first time called for unrestricted U-boat warfare without equivocation. They were manifestly under pressure from Scheer and his associates, but they also knew that the general situation was rapidly worsening, and they were greatly impressed by a new admiralty staff report that marshaled voluminous statistics in support of the view that this was the right moment to strike boldly against Britain's imports. [66]

Holtzendorff suddenly insisted that in view of the already difficult British food and economic situation, that country's resolution might be broken by the end of the year. Bethmann Hollweg, supported by Helfferich and Jagow, disputed this and succeeded in having the decision adjourned until the military situation came into better focus. It was a dubious success. In an effort to exploit Hindenburg's authority for his own end and confident that he would be able to work closely with the popular hero whose stirrup to power he had only just held, the Chancellor told the admirals that the OHL's estimate of the military situation must be an essential element in deciding the U-boat issue.

Ludendorff instantly took this to mean that he rather than the political leadership would have the last word and responsibility in this matter. The danger was increased when it was quickly shown that Hindenburg too only seemed to go along with Bethmann Hollweg and his political associates. Bethmann Hollweg had expressed the doubts of the latter that the navy would be able to circle Britain with a ring of iron so strong that it could not be pierced, thus forcing the enemy to his knees. Hindenburg on his part shared the illusions of the U-boat enthusiasts. "How happy we would be," he exclaimed, "if we could start the U-boat campaign at once!" He wanted to shorten the waiting period to a week or two.

When the Chancellor said at the end that he proposed to tell the Reichstag party leaders that all the appropriate authorities had carefully considered the question and were agreed that the decision in the U-boat question should be postponed and that even the field marshal had declared that developments in the Rumanian campaign must be awaited, both generals instantly objected. They insisted that the situation must not be made to look as though they opposed the U-boat campaign. Hindenburg went so far as to demand that the Chancellor should describe him as showing full sympathy for it, and he had to be talked out of this notion.

Following this talk, Bethmann Hollweg could be under no illusion but that the U-boat question, his central policy issue, had become more difficult for him rather than easier in the wake of the change in the OHL. Time was running out for his peace efforts.

There is some evidence that at this juncture his own opposition to unrestricted U-boat warfare no longer carried the absolute conviction that had hitherto borne him up. His subsequent conduct can scarcely be explained in any other way. It had first become apparent in the federal council committee session of August 8, already mentioned. Here Bethmann Hollweg had been among ministerial colleagues and federal representatives, whose discretion and sympathy he could implicitly trust. He had indeed then said that the chances of starving Britain out by cutting off its food imports were slight, since the British could use convoys escorted by warships, as they were indeed doing for their troop transports in the Channel, and as the Germans had long since done with their sea traffic to Denmark and Sweden. (Bethmann Hollweg had also on more than one occasion cited the inability of U-boats to operate at night as a reason for his doubts.) Yet on this occasion he did not entirely exclude the possibility of resuming unrestricted U-boat warfare. What he said was that it "could be considered only in February 1917 at the earliest, if at all." Apparently he did not wish to prejudice the chances of success by precipitate action, which might forfeit the prospects of peace in 1916—a very uncertain prospect, it must be said. [67]

Bethmann Hollweg displayed even greater uncertainty at a Prussian cabinet meeting of August 28, directly after Rumania's declaration of war, which clearly much disturbed him and struck a blow at his hopes for a separate peace with Russia. There was a real question, he said, whether this was not the time to shift to unrestricted U-boat warfare. Holtzendorff was pressing for it, and there was much to be said on that side, especially since one of the earlier main arguments, that Rumania (and, of course, Italy, even before that) could be kept out of the war, at least until after America's entry, had now been invalidated. True, the attitude of Holland and Denmark in such an eventuality was uncertain. On this point, however, Helfferich remarked that imports from Norway, Denmark, and Switzerland had slackened perceptibly since July. Holland was under severe pressure from Britain. If imports from neighboring countries were dwindling to nothing anyhow, one of the most important arguments against ruthless U-boat warfare would fall to the ground. The German harvest was bountiful—at this time the disastrous potato crop failure was not yet known—while the British harvest was poor. The Americans and Canadians had only slight surpluses, so that Britain had to obtain its imports mainly via the long sea routes from Argentina, India, and Australia. It was nevertheless doubtful whether Britain would reach the point of surrender within six months, as indeed it was whether Germany could hold out that long.

Bethmann Hollweg admitted he shared these doubts, but noted that there had been major changes since spring. The number of large submarines at the disposal of the high seas fleet had grown from seventeen to twenty-six; and the military situation on land had worsened considerably. A decisive victory by the German army was no longer in prospect, as it had been at Verdun. He concluded that "if we are to shift to unrestricted U-boat warfare, not a day must be lost." [68]

This was certainly a most surprising statement, considering the Chancellor's attitude at the big meeting held only three days later, which we just mentioned. What apparently happened is that he, like Helfferich, under the immediate shock of the Rumanian war declaration, felt the war on land was lost, especially since Austria-Hungary's prompt collapse had to be anticipated. This may have made him waver and consider that perhaps U-boat warfare must be tried as a last recourse.

This was in Berlin. Two days later, in Pless, he was able to push through the appointment of Hindenburg as chief of staff and held long talks with the field marshal. As we heard earlier,[69] he was greatly reassured, perhaps mainly because he caught something of Hindenburg's unshakable calm and confidence, even in the face of the Rumanian danger; and Hindenburg did not try to push the Chancellor into precipitate decisions. This may be the explanation for Bethmann Hollweg's swift change of mood.

Even so, however, he did not fight for an outright rejection of U-boat intensification, only for delaying the decision. He went so far as to say that if he were convinced U-boat warfare would bring a successful end, he would agree at once. What was essential was to present clearly the various factors that argued pro and con. As before, he remained deeply skeptical, though perhaps a little less so. One element may have been that the navy's technical arguments were now put forward by Holtzendorff and Capelle, both of whom had sided with the Chancellor in the spring crisis.

Twenty-six U-boats rather than seventeen meant that as many as five stations on the west coast of Britain could be permanently manned. During the coming winter a further respectable number of new and much improved U-boats were to go into service. The projection for February 1917 was forty to fifty units ready to be committed on the British sea front, and even larger numbers were in prospect for early summer.[70] There could scarcely be any doubt—and Bethmann Hollweg had none—of the correctness of the admiralty staff calculation, based on experience, that the Germans would be able to sink at least 600,000 register tons a month, once all restrictions were lifted.

A subject on which he reserved judgment concerned the political repercussions of such losses. A whole series of his old counterarguments had been struck from his hand; and above all his hopes had been dashed that an acceptable or at least tolerable peace might become possible even without unrestricted U-boat warfare, by new military successes on land or the departure from the opposing alliance of at least one of Germany's enemies. With such hopes waning even among the generals, to take the great risk appeared to be the last recourse from a truly desperate situation. Foreign Secretary von Jagow baldly projected the political consequences of this risk at the Pless meeting: "Germany," he said, "will be looked on as a rabid dog, and the whole world will gang up on us to restore peace at last."

Bethmann Hollweg, in other words, had to hasten to marshal all his resources to bring the war to an end by diplomatic means.[71] On September 2 he queried Count Bernstorff by wire on whether he viewed peace mediation by Wilson as possible or promising "if we pledge conditional restoration of Belgium. Otherwise must consider unrestricted U-boat warfare."[72] It was a kind of desperate cry that found no real echo. Bernstorff had always viewed the situation in America in too optimistic a light.[73] Otherwise he would have had to report not only that Wilson would not lift a finger until his reelection, but that his advisers were vigorously opposing any and all intervention. "There shall and must be no compromise peace with Germany," Lansing wrote in a memorandum at the time, and that meant no mediation effort. If the president did launch an effort that stood any chance of success, Lansing added, he would not participate. America's proper policy was to join the Allies as soon as possible and cast down the German autocrats.[74] But Bernstorff's response to the query from Berlin contained not a hint of such opposition. Wilson's mediation efforts, he wired back, were postponed until after the election but would go into effect immediately afterward. They were bound to be most promising even before the year was up. He hinted that

Wilson might swing into action even sooner, if the Chancellor personally suggested it.

The result was that the German foreign ministry, on September 23, drafted a directive to the ambassador, instructing him to ask Colonel House confidentially to suggest that the president send the powers a peace "challenge" immediately, without waiting for his reelection. The proposal was to avoid any specific territorial terms, and there must not be the slightest hint that Germany was behind it. The German navy, the directive continued, expected that its greatly augmented U-boat resources would bring swift success, in view of Britain's economic situation; it believed it would be able to force this main enemy to make peace within a matter of months, by unrestricted U-boat warfare. There was no time to be lost, since otherwise Germany would have to take "other decisions."

At imperial headquarters this carefully thought out and formulated draft was rewritten into something more like a threat than a courteous invitation. The changes were actually made by William II himself, on the basis of a counterdraft prepared by Ludendorff. It was the first time the supreme military authority intervened directly in diplomatic business; and the incident reveals the degree to which the Kaiser had already fallen under the influence of the headstrong quartermaster general.

The Kaiser went so far as to draft a communication to Ambassador Gerard in English, announcing unrestricted U-boat warfare in even more unvarnished language; and he grew indignant when Bethmann Hollweg tried to have the message withdrawn or at least delayed. In the end, despite all foreign ministry efforts, the Kaiser's version got to Wilson through House, reinforcing the American president's impression that the German government was trying to blackmail him into a peace action.

Ambassador Gerard had already advised the American press that all restrictions were about to be lifted from U-boat warfare, unless a serious peace effort got under way promptly.[75] The news created a sensation and fanned the flames of anti-German sentiment. Wilson's own desire to become a peacemaker, however, was probably strengthened, for like the Chancellor he was bound to wish to avoid the U-boat intensification and the American involvement in the war that would follow; but for the time being his attitude did not change. The peace action was in suspense until the election.

Meanwhile high naval officers[76] at headquarters were busy lobbying the OHL for immediate commencement of unrestricted U-boat warfare, since it was now generally accepted that Hindenburg would have the last word on the matter. Ludendorff on this occasion adopted a correct attitude, declining to accept the navy's judgment of the political consequences of such a step in circumvention of the Chancellor's authority. He seems, further, to have been suspicious of the technical data provided by the navy. Some of his staff officers, like Major Wetzell, chief of the operations section, and General Groener, chief of the rail transport section, strongly opposed ruthless U-boat warfare, for political as well as technical reasons. [77]

Even so the OHL position in these talks was that if the Rumanian campaign went well mid-October might be the right time to launch the U-boat campaign. Bethmann Hollweg was dismayed and insisted that the outcome of the unfinished peace action in Washington must be awaited. He enlisted Helfferich's aid and sent the envoy Kühlmann, just back from The Hague, to headquarters to report that the Dutch could mobilize more than half a million men in the event of war. [78]

But Bethmann Hollweg's concern was soon shown to be excessive. Hindenburg and Ludendorff wrote at once that they had never intended to settle the date of the U-boat campaign without the Chancellor and on the contrary highly valued loyal cooperation with him. The last thing they wished to do was to play politics behind his back, indeed, meddle in political matters at all. [79] All they had been considering was the military contingencies that might make it possible to open the campaign by mid-October.

Soon afterward, however, on October 5, Hindenburg did bring up the matter of jurisdictional demarcation between the generals and the politicians. Was the agreement of late August no longer in force? Had not the Chancellor, before the members of the Reichstag, emphasized the responsibility of the OHL in the decision on the U-boat question? Had he now changed his mind? Another dispute on the lines of authority seemed to impend in the very highest reaches of the government.

The exquisite courtesy of the field marshal's language, however, made it clear that for the time being he was not interested in an open struggle for power. He wanted only to avoid public responsibility for postponing the U-boat campaign, the opening of which was in any event indefinitely delayed by the Washington negotiations. Nevertheless, only a quarter-year later, Hindenburg did vigorously preempt a decisive vote in the U-boat question.

Bethmann Hollweg meanwhile took advantage of the occasion to limit the liability he had incurred by his remarks at Pless. He reaffirmed that the judgment of the military high command carried great weight in the U-boat issue, and that the Kaiser's decision on it flowed from his military command power, a view that suddenly replaced the OHL with the Kaiser; but since the decision directly affected Germany's relations with neutral states, it was also an act of foreign policy, for which the Chancellor was required to bear the sole and inalienable constitutional responsibility. Bethmann Hollweg concluded that even so the field marshal would surely agree that so incisive a step as unrestricted U-boat warfare could not be decided on without the Chancellor's participation.

The statement was intended to assert and maintain with the greatest emphasis the political leadership's claim to jurisdiction in the U-boat question. Since the OHL offered no objections, Bethmann Hollweg was quite justified in assuming its agreement.

Holtzendorff was not pursuing the goal of U-boat attacks without warning with the same zeal as Admiral Scheer and his associates. The issue simply remained in suspense; but the admiralty chief of staff did persuade the Kaiser —incidentally, at the suggestion of a front-line command! —that war on merchant shipping under the laws of prize, which Admiral Scheer had for so long discontinued, should be resumed on October 15, with certain precautions.

This was actually done, until the end of January 1917, and the tonnage sunk, in excess of 350,000 tons a month, was far greater than the chief of the high seas fleet had expected.[80] It is true that incidents involving loss of American lives continued, but it proved possible to settle them without major political conflicts. The whole U-boat issue now revolved around the question of whether war with America should be risked, for the sake of running up these sinkings to a still higher figure. The admiralty staff was of the opinion that two weeks of shock treatment entailing the ruthless sinking of all shipping would suffice to deter the neutrals completely from trading with Britain.[81]

Meanwhile the Reichstag parties saw to it that the Chancellor promptly lost his plenipotentiary power to decide the U-boat question, tacitly acknowledged by the OHL and to be exercised in common with it, but on his own political responsibility. Bethmann Hollweg himself was not altogether uninvolved in this unfortunate development.

Eager to shake off at one stroke the whole pack of his domestic enemies and calumniators, he employed very forceful words against Britain in a Reichstag speech of September 28. "Any German statesman," he said, "would deserve to be hanged, if he shrank from using against this enemy every suitable weapon that would really shorten the war." The entire tone of his speech, in fact, dismayed his social democratic followers; and it created an impression among all the parties that the Chancellor's opposition to U-boat warfare was no longer as determined as before.

This impression was deepened in subsequent secret meetings of the budget committee from September 29 to October 10, which revolved mainly around the U-boat issue. At these hearings Navy Minister Capelle, in contrast with statements he had made the preceding March, gave assurance that the number of U-boats and trained crews was now fully equal to sustaining unrestricted U-boat warfare for several months. He went so far as to make the bold assertion that the military significance of American participation in the war would be "zero."

The Chancellor himself stuck to the position that the question of when— and even whether—unrestricted U-boat warfare could be risked was still open;

but he firmly declined the role of an entrenched enemy of this radical form of warfare. "If it brings us even one day nearer peace, it will be done." The question could be settled only provisionally, on a basis of pure expediency. He left it to Helfferich, the youngest and ablest of his associates, to lead the out-and-out struggle against the U-boat zealots.

Helfferich too, however, showed a changed demeanor. Once again he mustered comprehensive and impressive statistics to show there was no assurance whatever that an unrestricted U-boat blockade would make the British amenable to peace in the foreseeable future; but like the Chancellor he admitted that conditions for such a blockade had become much more favorable than during the preceding spring. He too was at pains not to have his remarks interpreted as championing the case against U-boat warfare. The word *never* should not enter this issue, he said. "If we can wage U-boat warfare with good conscience, we must do so, and we must not wait another day."

Why were these sweeping concessions made to the U-boat zealots, concessions that merely served to confuse the deputies on the left? [82] Did the Chancellor really feel the pressure of the demonstrations and petitions to the Kaiser and the government that were then being sponsored by the great trade associations and Hamburg merchants? [83] Or was he merely anxious to keep his relation with the OHL on the fairly even keel it still enjoyed?

Another explanation seems far more plausible. Bethmann Hollweg may have wanted to assuage the despair that was spreading rapidly among the deputies. On every side, even among the parties of the right, a very gloomy picture of the military situation was being painted. The Battle of the Somme was still raging, as it had been for months, and it showed up the tremendous enemy superiority in matériel. Everyone could see that the multination state of Austria was rotting at the core and that the Austrian front was crumbling. The Rumanian campaign was only in its early stages and its issue was still uncertain.

Greatest concern was reserved for the rapidly rising problems of feeding the people and providing them with the necessities of daily life. There were complaints on every hand that the masses were increasingly restive, resentful, and war-weary. On the floor of the Reichstag the speeches retained an air of optimism, but it was a different matter in the secret committee meetings. There gloom was so intense that Bethmann Hollweg called together a small group of party leaders to brief them and hearten them with careful figures on relative military strength and industrial capacity.

The Chancellor, however, firmly declined to engage in a "policy of desperation" and to launch unrestricted U-boat warfare as a step along that way. Yet he could do little more than rouse the hope that Germany could "stick it out," that the enemy would not be able to break the German fronts. It was clear that victories on land could not bring the enemy to the peace table, certainly not in the west.

Faced with the situation as it was, the social democrats and most of the democrats (the progressive party)—the latter not without defections[84]—were willing to go along with the sticking-it-out policy, in the hope that Germany's enemies would tire in the end, realize that their efforts were hopeless, and agree to bargain. This, of course, was not good enough for the representatives of the right, who trembled for their annexationist goals. "Time works for the enemy," said the national liberal Stresemann.

They demanded the immediate launching of unrestricted U-boat warfare, and it was hard to meet their demand with an outright rejection of this hazardous expedient without risking the charge of being a traitor to one's country. Bethmann Hollweg's defense against such a charge was to speak of postponement rather than abandonment and also to cite the military necessity for delay, advocated by none less than Hindenburg himself. Bethmann Hollweg insisted he was in complete agreement with the supreme command.[85]

In so doing, he provided the key element that was to spell his doom in the subsequent development of the debate. The reason he had been able to muster a Reichstag majority for his rejection of U-boat warfare during the preceding March was that the centrist party under Erzberger came over to his side. On this occasion too Erzberger sought to support the Chancellor's policies—among other things, he spoke in favor of a separate peace with Belgium.

But Erzberger was outmaneuvered by the deputy Gröber who headed the party's nationalist right wing. Gröber offered a resolution behind which he hoped to unite the whole committee, in an understandable desire to bridge for one last time the right-left conflict that was growing more and more irreconcilable and thus to save the crumbling party truce. But except for a very few, the only unanimity centered on the popular hero Hindenburg, in whom all had unlimited faith.

Could the entire committee be prevailed on to extend this trust to the U-boat question as well? In its original version, introduced on October 6, Gröber's resolution amounted to a request for an "official opinion" from the supreme command, to which the following commitment was appended: "Should the OHL express itself as favoring unrestricted U-boat warfare, the Reichstag would see no reason for refusing its assent." What this meant was that the affirmative vote in the Reichstag was to encourage Hindenburg to come out for unrestricted U-boat warfare—even though, technically speaking, he was being asked only for an expert opinion! For the very first sentence of the resolution said: "The Chancellor alone is responsible to the Reichstag for the political decision in the question of unrestricted U-boat warfare."

Subsequently constitutional considerations seem to have dictated changes in the original version. Violence would indeed have been done to constitutional tradition, had there been such direct contact between the parliament and the military authorities, and had the Reichstag affirmed an official military opinion over the Chancellor's head; but the compromise version adopted on October 7 was most unfortunate. "The Chancellor alone," it reiterated, "is responsible to the Reichstag for political decisions affecting the conduct of the war"; but then it went on: "The Chancellor's decisions will necessarily be based in large part on the views of the supreme command. Should the decision be taken in favor of unrestricted U-boat warfare, the Chancellor would be assured of Reichstag assent."

There was no mention of what would happen if the Chancellor decided against unrestricted U-boat warfare. But the whole incident can be understood only on the premise that in such an event he would have had to count on Reichstag opposition, certainly on the part of those deputies who had voted for the resolution. Thus, in the central issue of his war policy, the Chancellor was not only tied to the vote of the OHL, but in effect obligated in advance to a positive decision on the U-boat question.

Actually, Deputy Gröber got his resolution accepted only within his own party—even Erzberger declared himself in agreement. On the floor of the Reichstag it got only a first reading, since the progressives and social democrats objected. Yet Bethmann Hollweg could no longer muster a majority without the centrist party, hence that party's stand meant in effect that his teeth were drawn vis-à-vis the OHL in political decisions. Centrist politicians later denied vigorously that this had been the intention—the real purpose was to reassure the hesitant Chancellor if he were indeed on the point of deciding in favor of U-boat warfare.

The element of truth in this was that no quarrel of any kind between Chancellor and OHL was being enacted at the time before the eyes of the Reichstag deputies, who probably could have had no idea of the grave political dangers their resolution held in the event such a conflict really occurred. Yet it is undeniable that the resolution did bring fateful consequences.[86] Had the Chancellor dared to challenge the OHL in the U-boat matter or postpone a decision still further against its will, he could have counted on the support of only the progressives and the followers of Scheidemann and David on the left—and not even that was certain. Crown Prince William seems to have grasped the situation instantly—or his adviser Maltzahn made it clear to him. In a letter he advised his father to dismiss the Chancellor at once, since the head of the government now enjoyed the support only of "Jews and social democrats who are puppets of America. . . . Throw him out! "[87]

Following the committee deliberations, the thing that weighed heaviest on many politicians, including some on the left, was a sense of being condemned to helpless passivity in the face of military events that exacted more and more sacrifice without ever reaching a clear-cut decision. In addition, the economic and political situation threatened to deteriorate month by month in Germany as well as in the countries allied with it. What on earth could be done to bring peace a step nearer, if there was to be no unrestricted U-boat warfare at all, or if it remained a risky venture with slim chances of success?

It was from such oppressive sentiments that the democratic deputy Conrad Haussmann on October 25 wrote the Chancellor a letter in which he urged him to offer the enemy peace negotiations quite openly—not in a Reichstag speech or newspaper interview, but through diplomatic channels. Haussmann pleaded that Bethmann Hollweg should not shrink from the charge of "weakness." If Asquith took such a step now, the world and posterity would acclaim him as a statesman. If the enemy rejected the offer, Germany would have the right and duty to expect its people to endure hunger, its army to put forward its supreme efforts, and the occupied territories to make new sacrifices in the crisis. The enemy's present game of deluding Germany with peace prospects would then be ended beyond any doubt. [88]

What Haussmann could not know when he was writing his letter was that this very same plan was already the subject of diplomatic talks between Berlin and Vienna, and that Bethmann Hollweg was pursuing it with the greatest energy, for the same considerations that motivated Haussmann. Part of the impetus came from news that had reached the German foreign ministry from Britain early in October. Lloyd George's famous "knockout" interview of September 28 had met with strong opposition in liberal circles. Other dispatches said that a fair peace offer would greatly embarrass British politics at this particular moment.

Even Grey's speech of October 23 was viewed by Bethmann Hollweg's associates, notably Riezler, as bearing a conciliatory tinge, since its tone was less vehement than before. The Chancellor thought this intelligence important enough to warrant a special session of the Reichstag main committee on November 8, to give him the opportunity for a public response to the speech. He sharply rejected Grey's German war guilt thesis, once again emphasized that the war was purely defensive in character, and declared that Germany was ready to cooperate with an international organization for the purpose of insuring permanent peace. His most important assurance was that Germany had never made the annexation of Belgium one of its war aims. All doubts about German intentions were certainly not cleared away by the Chancellor's speech; but he probably went as far as he possibly could in public to proclaim to the world that he was ready to reach agreement even on the question of Belgium. The rightist press, of course, protested vehemently. [89]

But Bethmann Hollweg was not willing to let it go at speeches, let alone wait for the American president to launch a peace action, now disappointingly overdue, despite the optimistic reports Bernstorff kept transmitting at times. [90] It was incumbent on the two Central Powers to venture on a diplomatic step of their own, if international peace talks were to eventuate in the immediate future. Baron Burián shared this opinion, which indeed he voiced to the Chancellor at the conclusion of the meeting on the Polish question on October 18, already discussed. [91] Bethmann Hollweg responded with alacrity. The suggestion fitted in with political plans he had been considering since the summer of 1915. So far, however, he had announced his readiness for peace only in Reichstag speeches, for fear that a formal peace offer through diplomatic channels would be viewed as a sign of weakness and strengthen enemy determination even further. There was no room now for hesitation and no time to be lost. In the Chancellor's mind everything depended on getting peace talks under way before the onset of a third winter of war, which the whole world dreaded. Within a week of his talk with Burián, he decided to act[92] and obtained the Kaiser's assent. On October 26 he went to Pless to secure the agreement of the OHL.

Apparently he succeeded without any major difficulty. The two generals were ready to abide by the Kaiser's decision, though Ludendorff declared at once that Britain would never be brought to the peace table by diplomatic means. That indeed may have been the hidden reason for his assent. In any event, he did not dispute the Chancellor's argument that a manifestation of Germany's willingness to make peace might mobilize the pacifists in the enemy countries, while a refusal of the offer would serve to strengthen the German fighting spirit.

Soon afterward, on the basis of gossip from German headquarters, some sources within the Austrian high command imputed still another motive to Ludendorff. He was speculating that all resistance to unrestricted U-boat warfare would fall to the ground, the moment it was demonstrated to all the world that the Chancellor's peace efforts had been in vain. There was no harm in waiting until that time, since troops to secure the Danish and Dutch borders would be available only when Rumania had been subjugated.[93] The story has the ring of probability.

The OHL, however, made its approval contingent on absolute avoidance of even a semblance that Germany was weakening. Not only was this to dictate the formulation of the offer, but the Polish proclamation was to come first and the Reichstag must pass and proclaim the introduction of universal compulsory auxiliary war service. Ludendorff thought these measures would impressively betoken German confidence and undiminished will to carry on the war. On the political side there were of course objections—from Vienna, too, and for very good reasons—and there was a lengthy tug-of-war as to what should come first, in which the OHL had its way in the end, much to the harm of the cause.

The Chancellor returned to Berlin from supreme headquarters on October 27, and late that very evening he presented his plan before the Prussian cabinet. As it was to be henceforth, his strongest argument for the peace offer was that the government must not "sit on its hands" *(ratlos dasitzen)* while the war continued without prospect of thoroughgoing German success. It must act to bring peace closer. A fair peace offer would also convince the neutral nations that the Germans were not the savage and reckless barbarians enemy propaganda pictured.

For reasons still to be discussed, Bethmann Hollweg was unwilling to make known in the offer itself the peace terms he envisaged as a basis for negotiations; but when Breitenbach, the Prussian deputy premier, questioned him; he did after all enumerate them to the ministers. Given to a circle of intimates in strictest confidence, the list is of the greatest interest because it probably reflects Bethmann Hollweg's innermost intentions more closely than any of the subsequent versions discussed with the OHL and Burián.

For France he proposed that part of the Briey basin be exchanged for certain communities in Lorraine and Alsace,[94] and that an agreement be reached on the question of colonies—in other words, the entire Lorraine ore region was no longer to be annexed. The future of Alsace-Lorraine as a whole was also to be the subject of negotiations. Belgium was to be restored, but would be required to cede Liège—although War Minister Wild, in the discussion, held that it was of no military importance—and also to enter into economic agreements that would protect Germany against a "boycott," evidently a reference to the notorious Paris economic conference of spring 1916. As for the Flemish coast, Bethmann Hollweg did not think it could be retained.

This was certainly a great climb-down from the September program of 1914. It even forewent the "securities and guarantees" that had been so much in the forefront during the preceding years. Nor was there any mention of dividing Belgium administratively between the Flemish and the Walloons. Russia was to cede part of Courland and Lithuania and recognize the independence of Poland. Of the German colonies, the Chancellor was prepared to give up Kiao-chow and the South Sea islands, but proposed that Germany work for the creation of a compact colonial domain in Africa, as before. Lastly, he still desired war indemnities, but not necessarily in cash. Economic concessions and trade treaties with the major powers might be substituted.

This was clearly a program of great moderation. It was in fact somewhat more modest than even the less concretely formulated terms that had been confidentially communicated to President Wilson late in January 1917. As far as the West was concerned, it came quite close to a straightforward restoration of the status quo.[95] Compared with the vast goals of conquest then being discussed and mutually pledged in Paris, London, St. Petersburg, and Rome, as we know, this German bill of particulars seems not only modest but almost tantamount to total renunciation.

Such a peace, Bethmann Hollweg said, would be indeed "meager," but he himself would not be disappointed, for he had always maintained that if Germany showed the world that it could not be vanquished, that its potential for growth could not be inhibited, and that it could successfully defend the achievements of 1870, "we should thank God." Remarkably enough, he found more support than opposition in the Prussian cabinet, though there was disappointment over the forfeiture of Belgium. Most of the ministers were doubtful of the chances of any peace offer. [96]

Three days later the Chancellor presented his plans to the foreign affairs committee of the federal council, convoked to this end at his express request on October 30-31. The program was quite similar, but on almost every point he left it open whether the desired goals—such as Briey, for example—could be actually attained. It was too early to speak of colonial questions, he said, and he was content with the established general goal that Germany should strive for a great Central African domain rather than frittering away its efforts. He was unwilling to commit himself on the indemnity issue, certainly not on whether it should be paid in money. Germany's actual costs could never be recovered, especially since any indemnity would have to be shared with Austria. He had never expected much along such lines. "If we stand up to the overwhelming enemy superiority and come out of it able to negotiate, we shall have won." [97]

Bethmann Hollweg refused to tie himself down to any "minimum demands." He doubted that any irreducible program would bring peace negotiations. It was almost impossible to establish, moreover, what was really militarily indispensable. From the German viewpoint Courland and the Dvinsk line were certainly desirable, but Germany might well be able to settle for something less, e.g., only part of Courland. In Belgium Falkenhayn had not thought Liège important, but insisted on the coast, which was beyond reach. Hindenburg, on the other hand, clung to Liège as absolutely essential. On the question of Belfort too Falkenhayn and Hindenburg held divergent views.

When he was pressed on the Belgian question by individual members of the council, as he had been by the Prussian ministers three days earlier, Bethmann Hollweg said that he would of course strive for as much assurance as possible that Belgium would remain a peaceful buffer, but only actual negotiations could show in what measure this would be possible. The generals wanted the fortifications razed, and this might be within the realm of possibility. They also wanted guarantees for a German right of passage in the event of war.

In the economic sphere security for German trade, especially in Antwerp, must certainly be bargained for; and there should also be a German voice in the Belgian rail system, possibly through the creation of a company in which German capital dominated. These were much the same terms Count Törring was supposed to have discussed with King Albert's emissary in January 1916, indeed, on which agreement had already been reached in part. What had happened was that some of the terms had been further cut down. Anticipating further objections, the Chancellor added that the general war situation was not now, nor was it likely to be, of such a character that Germany could envisage placing Belgium in a position of real dependence.

It is quite clear that at this point in time Bethmann Hollweg had not merely revised his program of September 1914–he had almost completely abandoned it. There was no more mention of holding France in subjection for a stated period of time. On the contrary, the Chancellor wished to meet this enemy with particular reserve, since he thought the likelihood of agreement with France greatest.[98] Only a small remnant was left of the "securities and guarantees" that were supposed to have been exacted of Belgium, and on this matter Bethmann Hollweg hoped to reach agreement with King Albert I. In fact, he was very outspoken on the Belgian question before the committee: "The glowing hopes we entertained in the years 1914-1915 are now probably beyond fulfillment. Unfortunately the war has not gone the way we had expected."

In a talk with Count Westarp in December 1916 Bethmann Hollweg had firmly declined to take the view that Belgium's future had to be regarded as part of an unending struggle with Britain. He was unwilling to believe that British enmity was irreconcilable and aimed at annihilation, and indeed he did not think that postwar Europe would be haunted by continuing war tensions.[99] He had, of course, long since abandoned the notion of a continental economic community to be dominated by Germany. His hopes for sizable acquisitions to "rectify" borders were now limited to East Prussia. He was not yet sure how much could be expected, but he was quite willing to make a distinction between what was "desirable" and what was really "necessary."

Like the Prussian ministers, the members of the federal council were persuaded that the contemplated peace action was necessary; but they did not at all like the idea that the Poland manifesto should come first, and they were even more strongly opposed to letting the peace offer go out without mention of concrete terms. This was without a doubt the weakest point in the whole plan, and as will be shown it led to differences with Vienna from the outset. Bethmann Hollweg said that it was his purpose to arouse indignation over the current war policies throughout the world, but if he was in earnest, he would have had to hold out for everyone to see a concrete framework of peace that would be acceptable to all. Simply to reiterate in general terms the German view that the war was defensive in character and aimed at "preserving Germany's honor, survival, and peaceful future" was not enough.

We already know, of course, that what the enemy governments envisaged by way of a peace program was quite incompatible with Bethmann Hollweg's plan. The Allied heads of government would not have been satisfied with even the greatest measure of moderation on the German side. What they wanted was surrender, not moderation. Peace terms were to be dictated, not negotiated. Lerchenfeld had seen this quite clearly. There was, in truth, no chance of an understanding between the two sides.

An altogether different question was whether a German peace offer might not set a powerful peace movement in motion in the enemy countries.

Shrewd advice on this matter was leaked to the Germans by the papal diplomat Monsignor Marchetti: Let the Central Powers, at the height of their
triumph over Rumania—which was having a depressing effect in the Allied
camp—issue a general declaration that they were willing in principle to restore
the status quo in France and Belgium and return national independence to
Serbia, without mentioning a word about guarantees or territorial changes
before sitting down at the peace table. It would be soon enough then. Such a
step would make the deepest possible impression not only among the neutral
nations but among the enemy nations as well. [100]

These were wise words, and it is tragic that they lacked any prospect of
being heeded. Neither at his own supreme headquarters nor in Vienna and
Sofia could Bethmann Hollweg have prevailed with Marchetti's proposal, even
though Germany desired the restoration of Serbia as much as Austria wanted
Germany to forego French territory and put Belgium back in order. Yet the
German peace offer was indeed meant to be more than a moral gesture—it
was to lead to serious negotiations. At the same time it was entirely predictable that such crucial German concessions at the outset would be interpreted
in the enemy camp as a sign of collapsing morale and weakness rather than of
magnanimity and a genuine desire for peace. At home the nationalists would,
of course, howl about a "cowardly surrender" of Germany's great military
achievements; and even the moderates would have serious reservations that
peace negotiations would be made intolerably more difficult, if Germany in
advance relinquished its major "hostages," the occupied territories, without
getting anything in return.

Bethmann Hollweg himself was assailed by such doubts, and Burián agreed
with him. [101] Both of them, in other words, balked at doing precisely what
the other side regarded as a primary precondition for negotiations, as will
soon be shown. Neither, for that matter, was entirely free in his decisions, the
German Chancellor even less than the Austrian minister. They were in the
same boat with Briand, Asquith, Protopopov, and their successors. They were
all prisoners of inflamed public opinion and impassioned popular nationalism.

The difference was that, unlike the German Chancellor, the other side did
not even try to bring all the belligerents to the conference table. We have
already seen how tightly the Entente governments were tied to each other by
treaties covering annexations and common peace negotiations. They were
forever worried that this cohesion might weaken and they looked on any
attempt by the Chancellor to say that Germany was ready for an equitable
peace as a splitting maneuver. The ties between Germany and Austria were
not nearly so close, and Germany's allies were as yet very far from resigning
themselves to defeat. Their implicit trust in the strong German arm by their
side—in other words, their reliability as allies—depended in large measure on
German willingness to help them retain occupied territory, regain that which
had been lost, and if possible conquer still more.

Not the least reason why Bethmann Hollweg declined to make concrete peace terms known together with his offer was the certain expectation that Germany's allies would present an all but endless list of war aims. The complex situation in the Balkans especially would make it very difficult to reach agreement. It would take a thick tome, he sarcastically remarked to the Prussian cabinet. He was in fact merely anticipating what happened later on on the other side at Versailles.

Before the federal council committee he gave still another reason. Any list of war aims would represent the maximum for Germany's enemies, the minimum for the Central Powers. It was "like trying to square the circle. . . . If we enumerate a long list [as public opinion and the OHL demanded] they will simply refuse. If we ask only a little, they will bargain us down still further." This was indeed the crucial sticking point. Whatever list of peace terms Bethmann Hollweg would have compiled would have been considered cowardly appeasement in Germany, while abroad it would have been decried as an expression of German militarist arrogance, making negotiations impossible. Despite the terrible bloodshed and increasing economic stringencies there was still far too much self-assertion and striving for power on either side to provide the framework for a negotiated peace, a "cabinet peace."

Thus Bethmann Hollweg's peace action was foredoomed from the start. Rather than being the product of political wisdom, it appears more in the light of an expression of conscientious statesmanship, aware of its responsibility before the judgment of history. This was indeed the Kaiser's immediate and enthusiastic reaction, when the Chancellor first reported to him on the plan. He wrote to Bethmann Hollweg that same evening of October 31: "Your plan to make peace is a moral act that is necessary to free the world from the pressure weighing us all down." 102

The Chancellor voiced similar sentiments on the eve of the proclamation at a confidential meeting with representatives of the federal states in the Reichskanzlerpalais. He said he felt it to be his duty to tell the people and the armed forces, at home and abroad, that Germany did not wish to let the war continue a day longer than necessary, merely for the sake of unrestrained conquest. "Who can foresee the future? " he continued. "Who dares to challenge fate in these cosmic events? Granted the chance that peace can be restored, we stand before God and our people with our conscience clear." 103

No doubt these words were spoken sincerely; but in the decision taken by Bethmann Hollweg the statesman, pressure of conscience was, of course, not the only motive, nor even the one that ultimately tipped the balance. As we already know, behind it stood the bitter necessity for making every possible effort to bring the war to an end without the risk of unrestricted U-boat warfare, i.e., without provoking American entry into the war and thus taking an even greater gamble with Germany's future. Added to this came the grave danger that Austria might soon collapse and even defect. Both of these risks dictated that German diplomacy act with the utmost expedition.

Bethmann Hollweg had originally planned to announce the peace offer publicly at once, on November 2, in the Reichstag, and he had had Jagow compose a draft on October 28, directly after the federal council committee meeting. But difficulties ensued with Burián and it became necessary to delay; for from the outset the Austrian minister was concerned not merely with bringing the war to an end, but even more with committing Germany to the diplomatic protection of Austrian interests at the peace negotiations.[104] We have already heard at the beginning of Chapter 7 of his insistent but vain efforts to push through a solidarity pact between the two Central Powers that would oblige Germany to stand on Austria's integrity, i.e., to help it regain its lost territory by force or negotiation. Along with these negotiations now came discussions concerning a common program of peace terms.

Burián had brought along such a program to Pless on October 18. Its first and most important point was the restoration of the 1914 territorial limits for all four of the allied powers. In practice, of course, this applied only to Austria and Turkey, and in both cases it was quite unrealistic. In return Germany was to get back all its colonies—which it did not even want—and acquire the Belgian Congo, while letting go completely of Belgium and France, "subject to security for legitimate German interests vis-à-vis Belgium."

In the main the program was concerned with reorganizing the east and the Balkans. It demanded for Austria "strategic border improvements" against Italy, Russia, Rumania, and Serbia; a new settlement along the Dalmatian coast, along lines we already know from Chapter 3, i.e., a protectorate over Albania and partial annexation of Montenegro; and restoration in totally mutilated form of Serbia, mainly to satisfy Bulgarian wishes. There was also mention of German border rectifications in Courland and Lithuania and of recognizing the kingdom of Poland, whose future relation with the Central Powers, however, was not discussed.[105] All in all the gains for Austria were far more generous than those for Germany, as Bethmann Hollweg was not slow to note.[106]

What galled him particularly was the proposed return of the Bukovina and all of East Galicia, and the demand for Italian border changes at a time when the Italians stood on Austrian soil; but that alone was not the reason for his rejection. He was simply sticking to his basic aversion to being tied down to any concrete program before peace talks had started, certainly to so unrealistic a program as the Austrians envisaged. Let each of the allies put forward and fight for his own program, once a conference was convoked, he remarked, asking for the very thing Burián was intent on avoiding.

This led to troubled and sometimes tempestuous talks. In the end Burián was persuaded that peace talks would never eventuate if so many terms were enumerated. But he stuck to his guns that an attempt should be made to combine into a single peace program the lists initially to be prepared by each ally for himself. It was hard to counter his argument that there must be no disunity among the four powers at the conference table; and thus a beginning was made in establishing official German and Austrian war aims inventories.

Bethmann Hollweg sent the first drafts to the OHL on November 4, asking for an opinion. What he was in effect doing was to concede the OHL a voice in a purely political matter. It seems a curious step—until we remember that he thought Hindenburg's authority indispensable to cover a "meager peace" before the court of public opinion and therefore needed the field marshal's approval. This, after all, had been the main political motive in summoning the popular idol as chief of staff.

The document he now dispatched to Pless contained essentially the same points he had already presented to the Prussian cabinet, slightly modified, to make them more palatable to the generals. Pride of place was now assigned to the "annexation of areas in Courland and Lithuania," but with the addendum that thereby "a sound north-south strategic border, to include the kingdom of Poland, should be created against Russia." This left the precise extent of the contemplated expansion open, while having the ring of some higher aim.

The restoration of Belgium was no longer expressly mentioned, only "guarantees in Belgium, to be fixed, if possible, by negotiations with King Albert." The fact that Bethmann Hollweg was really thinking of an economic deal that would forestall a boycott of German goods was glossed over, and annexation of Liège was held out in the event that acceptable "guarantees" were not forthcoming. There was a certain sharpening of the claims against France, in that there was no longer talk of exchanging parts of Briey for some communities in Alsace-Lorraine, but only a simple statement that Briey and Longwy were to remain in German hands, while the question of a "border regulation by means of a strip of Alsace-Lorraine" was reserved for the time being. [107] An eventual war indemnity or compensation was mentioned, but in terms that seem to have been kept deliberately vague.

Reading this program uncritically, one cannot possibly mistake its purely tactical intent, especially when one bears in mind the skepticism Bethmann Hollweg had expressed on war indemnities, military border rectifications, and the Belgian issue before the federal council committee only shortly before; but as expected, the program fell short of satisfying the two generals even in its modified form. They wished to see the "border rectifications" in the Baltic region more precisely specified and extending quite far into the east, to "a line extending from the Gulf of Riga west of Riga and passing Vilna on the east in the direction of Brest-Litovsk." In Belgium they asked for exploitation of the natural resources of Campine, economic union with Germany, seizure of the railway system, and the right of occupation. In return for this limited "surrender" of Belgium, Britain was to pay a war indemnity to Germany. France too was to pay a war indemnity and compensation—though these might be suspended—evacuate the occupied part of Alsace, and cede Germany the right to maintain "border fortifications" on the western slopes of the Vosges, beside giving up Briey and Longwy. A colonial settlement was to turn over the Congo to Germany, and Luxembourg too was to become German. Germans living abroad were to receive compensation. Except in certain details, the OHL agreed to the Austrian peace terms.

These were very considerable additions to the list. [108] At the conference table—if indeed there should be one and Bethmann Hollweg insisted on these claims—the effect would have been to make a negotiated peace impossible, or at least very much more difficult. That he ever had such intentions is more than unlikely, indeed, was expressly denied by Riezler, as will be shown further on. For the moment Bethmann Hollweg's concern was not the question of committing himself to a minimum peace program from which he would be unable to retreat. He had already rejected such a thing on principle before the federal council committee. [109] In his relations with the Kaiser, the Austrians, and sooner or later the Reichstag as well, he wanted to be able to point to OHL approval for a peace program the German public was bound to consider thin.

Thus he contented himself with expressly rejecting the totally unrealistic demand for an indemnity in return for "relinquishing" Belgium. [110] For the rest, he simply recast the document, tacitly including some further considerable moderations. [111] Still a third version was prepared for Austrian consumption. In it the territorial acquisitions, "border rectifications," and colonial questions were held in a generalized, vague, and noncommittal form—Briey no longer being even mentioned—Luxembourg was given the status of an "autonomous federal state," and restoration of Belgian sovereignty was expressly pledged. Also added were a series of measures against economic defamation of the Central Powers and for freedom of the seas and Danube shipping.[112]

Bethmann Hollweg, in other words, was quietly trying to moderate the war aims program once again, if only to avoid challenging Burián, who kept pressing for the relinquishment of Belgium. In Austria too there had been attempts meanwhile to reach an understanding with the generals in the question of peace terms. General Conrad, however, replied in such brusque militarist terms that by comparison the OHL demands seemed almost harmless. He did not succeed in changing Burián's earlier program to any great extent. [113]

On November 15 Burián came to Berlin for two days of talks with Bethmann Hollweg, Jagow, and Zimmermann, during which the form of the peace offer and the common war aims program were to be settled. The conflict between the two Central Powers emerged sharply. The Austrians tried for a program both powers would put forward in common, while the Germans vigorously resisted any such commitment. There was no agreement even on the particulars. Burián regarded German demands of Belgium excessive, while Bethmann Hollweg had even more fault to find with Austrian ambitions in the Balkans. Even so there was at least tentative agreement on the wording of the peace note, into which Ludendorff had already managed to inject a sharper warlike tone, ringing with confidence in victory. At Burián's behest it did, however, now hold out the prospect that the Germans would bring a full list of their war aims to the peace conference. [114]

The Germans balked for a long time, but in the end it was agreed that a common program would be prepared. Burián came prepared with a draft to that end. It never actually got on the agenda, because Bulgaria and Turkey were to be invited to participate; but these two countries, feeling safe behind the written pledges of territorial increments given to them in their treaties of alliance with the Central Powers, were in no hurry to put forward their shopping lists, though it was learned that these would be very long. Much time was lost in this fashion, and in the end Vienna began to grow anxious. By early December Burián realized that the whole peace action might well fetch up on the rock of a common war aims program and quietly dropped the idea. The Berlin decision remained on paper.

But the Austrian minister fought all the more resolutely in Berlin for the solidarity pact that has already been mentioned. [115] In the end the Chancellor was prevailed upon to give oral assurances that Germany would do all it could to restore to Austria-Hungary its prewar borders, on the basis of such enemy territories now held by the Central Powers—note well, not merely by Austria itself! But the Chancellor declined to be drawn into a firm commitment, and this caused deep resentment in Vienna and still further shook the relation of mutual trust between the two allies.

Even during the conference of November 15-16, the Germans were deeply mindful of the conflict of opinion and interest. This is plainly seen in a dispatch sent directly after the meeting and evidently in some way connected with it. [116] In it Jagow asked Count Bernstorff whether he could report if and when President Wilson was likely to launch efforts at peace mediation. "Question important to evaluate possibility of similar steps from another side."

Wilson had been reelected on November 7. In view of the difficulties in reaching a satisfactory agreement with the Austrians, the German government swung around and was once again inclined to await an American peace effort, before embarking on any steps of its own. Unlike Baron Burián, Bethmann Hollweg, following Bernstorff's earlier dispatches, banked on Wilson not meddling with the question of peace terms, in other words leaving Germany a free hand.

Not content with directives to the German ambassador, he tried to influence American policy more directly. On November 17 he granted an interview to a journalist of the Hearst papers; and on November 22 he had a talk with Joseph Grew, legation councilor to Ambassador Gerard, which left a deep impression on the former. Grew found the Chancellor in a very depressed mood, tired, and deeply disappointed over the continuing setbacks to his peace efforts, indeed embittered that "this total madness of human butchery" must go on and on, simply because the politicians could not see reason.

But the news from Washington was not reassuring. Bernstorff did report a talk in which Colonel House had assured him that the president expected to take steps in the peace question "as soon as possible, presumably between now [November 21] and the end of the year." Grew provided similar intelligence; but the Germans had been told time and again to surfeit that Wilson would swing into action directly following the election. Now new obstacles were mentioned: the recent sinkings of the *Arabic* and the *Marina* without warning; and the brutal measures in Belgium on which Ludendorff had insisted and under which civilians were deported to German labor camps for work in war industry—more about this further on. These incidents were said to have aroused world opinion to a pitch that made a peace action impossible for the moment. The plan was not abandoned, merely postponed.

Inside Germany it was hard to judge whether these arguments were real or merely a pretext. It is true that the Belgian deportations aroused deep resentment abroad. On the other hand, ever since Lloyd George's famous "knockout" interview Wilson had been doubly apprehensive that any peace action on his part would be rejected in London, and a failure would, of course, hurt his prestige. His friend Colonel House, in talking to Bernstorff, blamed Wilson's vacillation for the new delay, but actually even he was opposed to American peace action. As earlier in the year, he feared that the Germans might respond favorably while the British would refuse. This could mean either that America would be driven into the German camp and have to fight the Entente, or—if the Germans did launch unrestricted U-boat warfare—that America would have to enter the war against Germany, which was precisely what Wilson wished to avoid.

House, moreover, was opposed to any steps that would arouse resentment in Britain and France and entangle America deeply in the problems of peace in Europe. When Wilson showed him the first draft of his later peace note, he urgently advised further delay.[117] Lansing's attitude too was unchanged. He was very unhappy over Wilson's peacemaking ideas. The president, he wrote in a memorandum, still had not grasped the danger a victory by the "autocrats" held for the free world. Total victory must first be won. On December 8 he advised Wilson to break off diplomatic relations with Germany over the new naval incidents; and two days later, using approximately the same arguments as House, he warned him against any mediation effort whatever.[118]

Thus the president found himself entirely isolated in his thinking, even in respect of his closest advisers, and began to waver. Bethmann Hollweg, on his part, simply could not wait indefinitely. He had wanted to launch his offer before the onset of winter, the third one of the war, but winter was now well under way. The Austrians were increasingly restive. The young Emperor Charles personally interceded with William II and was dismayed to be referred to Hindenburg. He wired Burián that Germany seemed to have turned into a complete military dictatorship; but he did seek out the field marshal the next day, only to find that Hindenburg blamed the German foreign ministry for the delay. [119]

More important to Bethmann Hollweg than these importunities was the fact that the crowning success of the Rumanian campaign, the capture of Bucharest, impended immediately and might serve as an important psychological factor. He continued his preparations for his own peace offer side by side with his wooing of Wilson, keeping two irons in the fire, so to speak; but in the meantime the danger threatening Bethmann Hollweg's peace policy from the naval side increased. The navy men made continuing representations to Ludendorff, trying to draw the OHL over to their side. Captain von Bülow told the general that the U-boat campaign would "end in a morass," if there were further interference with unwarned sinkings. An American peace effort, he said, would merely serve the British as an excuse to drag out negotiations until imports from the new harvest had reached England and the strategic time for a blockade had been missed.

Ludendorff, on his part, like Hindenburg grew bolder in meddling with naval matters, being held in check only with the help of Admiral Müller, who persuaded the Kaiser to issue directives calculated to prevent further sinkings that would intolerably complicate the situation. Holtzendorff, chief of the admiralty staff, was at this time still sincerely intent on giving the U-boat campaign a form that would, if possible, reap successes without precipitating a break with America; but he was under pressure from the chief of the fleet, and since virtually all British merchant ships were now armed, waging U-boat war by the laws of prize grew harder and harder. During the preceding spring America had refused to discuss the legitimacy of sinking at least armed merchant ships without warning. Holtzendorff now urged renewed negotiations to that end. On December 9 Bethmann Hollweg gave his consent—at the very moment when it was finally decided not to wait for Wilson any longer, Bucharest having fallen three days before. [120]

There had been considerable difficulty at supreme headquarters before the decision could be taken. On December 8 the OHL, in the Chancellor's absence, made a last-minute attempt to win over the Kaiser to an abrupt change of course. New conditions were to be attached to OHL approval of the German peace offer, which was to be contingent on the government giving assurances that it was "likely to bring about the kind of peace Germany required." This, of course, was a formulation that lent itself to almost any interpretation and held out the prospect of complicated new discussions on war aims. In addition, the unrestricted U-boat campaign was to commence in January, seemingly come what may, since it was apparently not to be made dependent on any failure of the peace offer. What these demands meant was that the OHL, now that Bucharest had fallen, was no longer worried about its ability to defend the Dutch and Danish borders. It had lost all interest in the peace offer, which it now viewed only as causing an irksome delay in the launching of unrestricted U-boat warfare. With the Kaiser's help, the Chancellor was to be outflanked.

The Kaiser, fortunately, declined to play the game, giving the Chancellor an opportunity to state his position. Bethmann Hollweg at once left for Pless with Zimmermann and there, in a curt and firm note, rejected the generals' scheme. He secured assent to publish the peace offer of the Central Powers on December 12, using the agreed text. As we already know, however, there was one concession to Holtzendorff. Unrestricted U-boat warfare as such would not be launched, should the offer be rejected; but in that event Washington would be notified that Germany would find it necessary henceforth to treat armed merchant ships as warships, to be sunk without warning. A perilous step indeed! But even more dangerous for the Chancellor was the realization that his policies were beginning to be nullified by the military. [121]

With the peace offer to the enemy powers those policies entered upon their climactic crisis.

## Part 4

# Failure of the German Peace Offer; The Army and Navy Win Out in the U-Boat Question (December 12, 1916 to January 9, 1917)

THE GERMAN peace offer came at a point in time when a change of government was taking place in the three main Entente countries. In all three cases the change was aimed at hardening the war spirit. In Russia the Stürmer government, which had at times aroused such strong hope for a separate peace in Berlin, fell on November 23, to be replaced by a government headed by Trepov, whose foreign minister, Pokrovsky, was close to the uncompromising nationalists in the Duma. In Paris Briand had had to resign on December 7 under the continuing attacks of his rivals, especially Clémenceau, who charged him with lack of vigor. On the very day of the German peace offer, December 12, however, Briand was able to form a new government of "national concentration," which was confirmed in the chamber the following day, though its prospects for survival were not very high. Lloyd George's new "war cabinet" met in London for the first time on December 10—we have already discussed its background. This latter development was especially disquieting to Bethmann Hollweg. It reduced the chances of a negotiated peace still further.

On December 11 Bethmann Hollweg received a number of the federal premiers and delegates to the federal council at the chancellery to brief them on the impending offer. On that occasion he specifically cited the change in Britain in support of his appraisal that rejection was more likely than acceptance. In consequence he placed great emphasis on the domestic and moral motivations behind the offer—we have already heard about this [122]—and on the expected effect on the neutral nations and on pacifist sentiment throughout the world. Virtually all those present agreed with his analysis, but it was also stated that the Pan-Germans were bound to offer strong resistance to a negotiated peace and that in the event of rejection agitation for unrestricted U-boat warfare would burst all bounds.

Bethmann Hollweg's reply was that Germany's moral posture would greatly increase in neutral eyes if the offer were spurned. There would even be hope that expansion of U-boat warfare beyond the present limits—meaning of course the sinking of armed merchantmen without warning—might then be effected without precipitating a conflict with America. Even now, he added, tonnage sunk had reached very high levels, which could be still further increased. We can see how he envisaged a way out of Germany's threatening predicament; but this does not imply that the entire peace action meant nothing more to him than a diplomatic prelude to unrestricted U-boat warfare.

Nevertheless there was domestic resistance to the peace offer. During the ministerial conference of December 11, the premier of Baden, von Dusch, warned against treating Belgium "too gently," since this would create a furor throughout the country. In his Reichstag speech the next day the Chancellor adopted a resolute note of confidence in victory, to dispel any impression of a German spell of faintheartedness among the nationalists and militarists. He said that the German fronts were more secure than ever and even suggested that the German U-boats held out the specter of a hunger blockade to the enemy. This, of course, merely fed fuel to enemy propaganda, facilitating rejection even more than did the text of the peace note in the wording the OHL had exacted. No one is eager to accept peace from the hands of one who comports himself with the assurance of a victor.

The Kaiser, unfortunately, lent further force to this triumphant tone with a saber-rattling address to the troops at Mulhouse, which was instantly picked up in the press, evidently by the doing of the OHL, but to the Chancellor's horror. No displays of confidence, however, were able to lessen the distrust of the rightist parties in the "soft" Chancellor and his peace plans. The leftist parties and the centrists had all they could do to keep the opposition from debating the peace terms on December 12, which would have wrecked any chances the note might have had abroad.

The national liberals, led by Stresemann, protested in an open letter to the Chancellor against the exclusion of the Reichstag in the preparation of the peace note. They demanded immediate convocation of the main committee in order to discuss the peace terms, which the Chancellor refused. Zimmermann, the new foreign minister, whom the right was said to trust, was deeply disappointed at the attitude of the party leaders, when he met them in briefing sessions. To appease them he misinformed a press conference that Germany had dispatched the note solely to anticipate a most unwelcome peace effort on the part of Wilson. [123]

Yet Zimmermann himself was half-hearted in the whole matter. On December 15 he told Hertling in confidence—according to a note by the latter— that he hoped the German offer would not be accepted. The Bavarian premier understood this to mean, approvingly, that Zimmermann did not think an international congress to deal with the question of peace would be in Germany's interest. Hence we may assume that Zimmermann would have preferred either negotiations for a separate peace or intensified U-boat warfare, limited for the nonce to armed merchantmen. Two weeks later, at any rate, Zimmermann voiced such sentiments to a Bavarian diplomat, a peace note from Wilson having been meanwhile received. Zimmermann was afraid that international talks would delay a decision beyond the point at which the U-boat fleet could still be effectively committed. Like the Chancellor, Zimmermann hoped that a U-boat campaign against armed merchantmen could be launched without precipitating a break with America. [124]

In a sense Zimmermann was being more realistic than Bethmann Hollweg with his vain hope of international peace talks, mingled with many doubts even on his part. Actually, the differences between the Chancellor and his foreign policy chief were tactical rather than basic. Nevertheless, they had a rather unfavorable effect on the course of negotiations with Wilson, as we shall yet see.

Before that stage was reached, however, the whole peace effort was threatened from another side, the reckless annexationism of the generals and admirals. While waiting for replies to the German peace offer from the enemy powers, the navy and the OHL thought their best policy, in preparing themselves for any impending negotiations, would be to put together a minimum program of peace terms. In this way the first formal and official lists of war aims came into being, and they turned out to be a comprehensive catalog of continental and overseas objectives.

Not that Bethmann Hollweg had asked for any such thing. [125] All he had done was to ask Holtzendorff orally what strategic bases the navy might need elsewhere to defend a Central African colonial domain. [126] The navy responded with two memoranda (of November 26 and December 18) that went far beyond the Chancellor's defensive frame of reference. They set up a program that called for a whole system of bases, sally ports, and radio stations calculated to pose a serious threat to British dominion of the seas, and also to control and disturb world trade on all the major oceans. To achieve a fundamental improvement in Germany's constricted maritime situation, acquisition of the Flemish coast was declared to be essential, together with the coast of Courland with Vindava and Lepaya, the islands of Oesel and Mohn, and the Faroe islands, to secure egress into the Atlantic. In the Mediterranean Vlonë was to be annexed, elsewhere the Azores, Dakar with Senegambia, and Tahiti. Most of Germany's South Sea colonies were to be retained.

The OHL fully supported this program and on December 23 added one of its own, no less extravagant, fully equipped with maps showing the new frontiers of the German Reich that were contemplated. In both the west and the east they reached far beyond the goals discussed with Bethmann Hollweg early in November, always on the basis that the acquisitions required for German "security" would on their part have to be secured by advancing the lines still further. Beyond Longwy there were to be adjoining Belgian regions in the north. Around Luxembourg a ring of German territory was to be "absorbed." The Meuse crossing at Liège was to be secured by incorporating Givet in Belgium, annexing a "staging area" to the west of the Meuse, and keeping all of Belgium in a state of strict dependence. Germany's eastern border was to be screened against Poland by a wide buffer strip. The annexations in the Baltic area and Lithuania were to be protected by advancing the border with Russia eastward, encircling Poland in a wide arc, and leaving only a small line of actual contact between Poland and Russia itself. Lastly, Ludendorff also wished to "utilize" Rumanian Walachia in some form for Germany, perhaps along the lines of one of the ancient Roman provinces. He prevailed upon Hindenburg to add a remark about the Polish border question. "I cannot accept anything less than these demands," he said in imperious tones.[127]

It would have been a waste of time to quibble over such wishful dreams at a time when it was already clear that the enemy powers were quite unlikely to enter into any direct talks. Bethmann Hollweg curtly advised the OHL that there would have to be a discussion, and this took place at Pless on December 29, in an atmosphere of extreme ill-temper on both sides, for reasons to be discussed further on. To avoid an explosion, the discussion was essentially limited to the border problems in the west, the difficult questions of the east, on which there were strong differences of opinion, being deferred as "not yet acute." [128]

So, at least, Bethmann Hollweg himself described it in a confidential letter to Valentini. Beyond that, however, he apparently tried to avoid any commitment to a fixed war aims program by dilatory tactics. An inquiry dated December 31 showed that he had dismayed the OHL by remarking that Germany might not be able to retain Briey and that further discussions would depend on the developing war situation. Hindenburg demanded to know what Bethmann Hollweg's minimal territorial terms were in the event of negotiations at the present war situation. He wished to know the unconditional terms to be put forward even at the risk of prolonging the war.

But the Chancellor was undeterred. He referred Hindenburg to the exchange of telegrams early in November, which he still regarded as binding. In other words, he stuck to his own extremely moderate war aims program. For the rest, he said, politics was always "the art of the attainable." It was quite impossible to commit oneself rigidly to a minimum program before negotiations had started. An attempt must be made to disrupt enemy unity, and this might make it necessary to yield on one point in order to reap important benefits elsewhere. The instructions to German negotiators would include maximum rather than minimum demands. Beyond what point Germany would not retreat was a matter to be decided in the light of the total situation. If separating France from the Entente, or indeed the whole matter of making peace, were in jeopardy on account of the German insistence on Briey and Longwy, the problem would be solved in agreement with the OHL "as commanded by His Majesty." Bethmann Hollweg concluded with the statement that he could not possibly specify minimum terms now, since this question would not enter the acute stage for many months to come and none could foresee the situation that would prevail at that time. [129]

Envoy Riezler subsequently testified at great length before a Reichstag investigating committee on these dilatory tactics of the Chancellor, from discussions he had had with him. Bethmann Hollweg, he said, not only refused to take seriously "this imaginative catalog of war aims drafted by some nameless General Staff officer," but even refused to spend much time debating it. That would at best only result in a compromise that would still go too far, while binding his hands. "I know perfectly well that the moment I present a tangible chance for peace to the Kaiser I shall have my way with him." To be sure, he added, the OHL would inveigh against him, and the people would resent any peace concluded on unfavorable terms—"but peace will be made all the same." [130]

Even then, it will be seen, Bethmann Hollweg was convinced that any real agreement with the OHL on the war aims issue was practically out of the question; and he put his faith instead in the Kaiser's peaceful inclinations and confidence in him. If there had once been hope that Hindenburg's authority would serve to buttress a "meager peace," that had long since gone by the board. The Chancellor simply evaded any commitment about a peace program—but equally, he dodged an open struggle for power, which he, pitted against the idols of the crowd, would have been bound to lose.

In the long run, of course, Hindenburg and Ludendorff would not stand for such evasion. Three months later they succeeded in having the Chancellor, the foreign minister, and the chief of the admiralty staff join them in signing a war aims program that accorded entirely with their wishes and extravagant dreams. As will be shown further on, Bethmann Hollweg and his associates assuaged their political consciences by a mental reservation. They told themselves that the program would have real meaning only in the event the Germans won total victory, which they regarded as virtually out of the question. They were also convinced that if worse came to worst the Kaiser would not allow peace to fail because of excessive German annexationism.

Thus the door was left open; but the adoption of mental reservations and dilatory tactics suggests the direction in which things were drifting: toward the political hegemony of the generals.

Meanwhile the German offer to negotiate peace had, despite all its weaknesses, registered a strong impression abroad, even in the enemy countries. Initially it aroused hope and was certainly warmly welcomed in the neutral countries that were not outright anti-German: Scandinavia, the Netherlands, and Switzerland. As for the enemy countries, in the words of the Swedish foreign minister Wallenberg, the people in every one of them thought differently from their governments.

As Bethmann Hollweg had expected, the reaction of the war-weary masses was most clearly discerned in France. On December 13 Briand sternly warned the French chamber that the German offer was a piece of hypocrisy, intended to poison French public opinion; but three days later the league of socialist clubs in Paris and its suburbs passed a resolution by a very large majority, stating that it was the duty of the Allied governments not to reject the peace offer without first having taken note of the enemy proposals. The resolution also condemned conquest and annihilation as French war aims.

In Italy too demonstrations and unrest were anticipated, should the Allied rejection be couched in tones that were considered too brusque. This was why the foreign minister, Sonnino, expressed himself very cautiously about the German peace note in the Italian chamber of deputies. No one would be minded to reject negotiations, he said, if the note contained serious proposals in accordance with the principles of nationalism, humanity, and justice. Italy did not wish to subjugate or destroy any foreign nation; but the Allies must first reach agreement about their reply.

As everywhere else, the press in Britain was thoroughly in line with militant patriotism, hence deeply suspicious of anything that emanated from Berlin. Still, the liberal newspapers, especially, soon began to consider the peace offer seriously, and the government was warned from many sides not to put itself in the wrong by rejecting all negotiations outright and thus falling in with the secret desires of the Germans.

Aside from the neutrals, with America in the lead, Sonnino too warned against outright rejection, adding, however, that Italy would never assent to restoration of the status quo. Belgium desired consultations on a joint reply that would request Germany to state its peace terms, rather than rejecting the offer unconditionally. The Vatican made a similar proposal, adding that the papal secretary of state had reason to believe, on the basis of confidential reports from German and Austrian Catholics, that the German demands would be moderate.[131]

All this was considered by the British cabinet, with the result that Lloyd George's speech of December 19 at least avoided formally slamming the door on negotiations. He did say that the confident tone of the note and of the Chancellor's speech plainly showed that Prussian militarism with its arrogance was as alive as ever. This was what had long made Germany Europe's hated troublemaker; the real aim of the war was to exterminate Prussian militarism. To consider a peace offer with unstated terms meant to put one's head voluntarily in a noose, with Germany holding the rope. Lloyd George, nevertheless, said in conclusion that Britain would wait to hear what terms and guarantees Germany was offering.[132]

There are reasons for doubting that the British government was seriously prepared even to listen to concrete German peace proposals, let alone to discuss them; for in Paris even to listen to terms might have been interpreted as treason to the common cause.[133] Even so, however, had Germany at once taken the hint and at least held out the prospect that France and Belgium would be fully restored, also indicating a willingness to participate in an international peace organization, an international public debate would have been set off, even if there were no peace talks at the government level; and for the Entente governments such a debate might have become very embarrassing. Paris and St. Petersburg greatly feared such an eventuality.

Understandably enough, the Russians were in the greatest hurry to stifle all discussion by parliamentary action. As early as December 15, i.e., directly after the German peace note had transpired and following a bristling speech by the newly appointed foreign minister, Pokrovsky, the Duma resolved that the "hypocritical" German offer be categorically rejected, since it merely evidenced German weakness. More than that, the resolution rejected any thought of "entering into peace negotiations of any kind under present conditions." The vote was unanimous, for the radical left had been temporarily banned from the sessions a few days earlier. The Duma was digging its spurs into the sides of the people, so to speak, in an effort to revive the flagging Russian war spirit. There was indeed an element of frenzy to this resolution, for Maurice Paléologue, the French ambassador, was able to report to Briand that pro-German circles at court and the higher levels of the bureaucracy, industry, and the socialist parties had welcomed the offer of the Central Powers.[134]

As we have already heard, Briand had warned the French chamber two days earlier against the "poison" of the German offer; but he was unable to get a vote without first consulting with London. There Hardinge, under secretary of state in the Foreign Office, proposed a reply to the effect that German proposals were awaited; but the Quai d'Orsay thought this much too dangerous, since it might lead to discussions. Whatever Germany proposed, wrote Jaquin de Margerie, director of the political section, it could not be trusted. The only way to negotiate with such an enemy was to force him to accept one's own terms. This was on December 19. That same day Briand addressed the French senate to announce that there would be a joint reply by the Allies, rejecting the German offer, since it was fraudulent and a sign of waning power. Following a secret session, held at the instance of Clémenceau, the senate was curtly told on December 22 that "France cannot conclude peace with an enemy who occupies its territory."

This was a clear-cut commitment. Still, it took considerable effort to formulate the joint reply of the Allies. In agreement with the British, the French foreign ministry had taken on the job, but its drafts met with much opposition. The note of reply was to be aimed at the neutrals and the Allied peoples even more than at the governments of the Central Powers. Hence the rejection had to be justified with great skill and caution. [135] These difficulties were enormously compounded when a peace note from President Wilson (dated December 18 but becoming known only two days later) burst upon the scene like a bombshell.

It denied any connection with the German offer, insisting it had been planned long before. It took care not to offer the services of the president as mediator or to make any peace proposals of its own, since this might have been resented by the Allies as a form of interference. Instead, it did precisely what the German government was most afraid of and expected least: it called on the contending parties at last to state their war aims with greater precision. Perhaps they were not as far apart as was feared and agreement was possible. After all, both sides were declaring themselves in favor of the same ideals— protection of small and weak nations against coercion, securing a lasting peace through a single league of nations rather than rival power blocs, etc.

This conciliatory language, which put both sides on the same moral level instead of condemning the "aggressor," created much indignation in England and France. Wilson was undoubtedly in dead earnest. He refused to believe that conflicts in national interest were irreconcilable, and he wanted a negotiated peace to prevent the unrestricted U-boat campaign he foresaw with certainty otherwise, and by preventing it keep his country out of war. [136]

Wilson's closest advisers, however, were afraid that conciliatory manifestos would serve only to destroy friendship between America and the Entente governments. They did all they could to reassure the latter, advising them not to take the note too seriously. The Anglophile American ambassador in

London, Walter Hines Page, actually told Balfour that he regarded his president's "insulting words" as a bad error of judgment and warned against "buying a pig in the poke," as the Germans seemed to expect the Allies to do.

Lansing went so far as to almost sabotage the effect of the note. During a press conference he said that America already stood on the brink of war and now wanted to know what the war was really being fought over. The note, in other words, was anything but a peace note. Wilson was furious and initially considered dismissing Lansing; but in the event he forced Lansing subsequently to water down his statement. The American ambassador in Paris, Sharp, nevertheless cited Lansing in his efforts to do everything in his power to reassure the French.

He described the American note as nothing more than a tactical maneuver, launched for domestic political purposes. Lansing himself insisted to the French ambassador, Jusserand, that the president's sympathies were entirely on the side of France, and that he, Lansing, regarded all the French war aims as legitimate, including the return of Alsace-Lorraine, on which House and Wilson had not yet reached a final position. His advice was to tell the Germans that no negotiations were possible with a "military autocracy," only with a liberalized government, as indeed actually happened in 1918.

Lansing also said he had reason to believe that the Germans were already so discouraged that they would probably accept Allied terms. He expressed himself in similar terms to the British ambassador, Spring-Rice.[137] And indeed, despite their resentment over Wilson's peace initiative, the Allies worded their reply to him with the same care as in the reply to Germany. They had all the more reason for doing so, since the American note had been very warmly received by the neutral nations. The governments of Scandinavia and Switzerland actually expressed their satisfaction in official notes.

The reply to the Germans was handed to the American ambassador by Briand on December 30 and made public the following day. It avoided open invective (in which Briand's first draft had indulged), but in the sharpest terms represented Germany as the aggressor and lawbreaker who trampled human rights underfoot. It made reference to forced labor and deportations imposed on Belgium and sought to invalidate Germany's moral fitness for a negotiated peace. The German offer was described as a mere piece of legerdemain to confuse public opinion, an artfully baited trap to exploit the momentary favor of war, force a "German peace" on the world, and above all put the full blame for the horrors of war on the other side.

Peace terms were barely touched on—all violated rights and liberties must be restored; the rights of nationalities must be established (in a very general form, not binding on all the countries concerned); small countries must be guaranteed a free existence; general security must be effectively assured; the threat that had so long hung over the world must be irrevocably removed—

that, of course, meant "Prussian militarism," though the term was not used, nor, for that matter, was there any mention of "destroying" German power or of the certainty of Allied victory. What was solemnly asserted instead was that the Allied governments were sensitive to the "gravity of the hour" but completely at one in their attitude with their people.

Everything was done, in other words, to place the blame for the failure of the German peace initiative on Germany itself and to pillory the Germans as insincere. As for the reply to Wilson, that took a good deal more time, not being dispatched until January 10, 1917; for it proved very difficult to formulate the greedy annexationist demands of Britain's allies in terms that America would not find too objectionable.

The "nationality principle" espoused by Britain caused the Russians and French special headaches, for as Ambassador Jusserand wrote, it might well lead to malicious references to Ireland, where the British had just put down a Sinn Fein rebellion, to Poland, to the Boer republic, to India, etc.; but the trick was pulled off, in the main by glossing over the most extreme commitments and by surrounding the main demands with an aura of international law and morality.

The Central Powers and their two allies were described not merely as dangerous aggressors and conquistadors but as outright criminals. Every atrocity was enumerated, from the Belgian invasion and the horrible Armenian massacre the Turks had only recently staged, to the execution of Nurse Edith Cavell (still to be discussed), the Belgian labor deportations, the London Zeppelin raids, and, of course, the U-boat campaign against merchant shipping.

The Allies, by contrast, were made to appear as the saviors of humanity and international law, in complete agreement with Wilson's idealistic goals, but protesting vigorously against being placed on the same level with their adversaries, as though two groups of belligerents were facing each other with claims of equal merit. It was solely to secure law and freedom that they demanded, in addition to the restoration of Belgium, Serbia, and Montenegro, the evacuation and indemnification of France, Russia, and Rumania, a guarantee of territorial and maritime frontiers against unprovoked attack—neither being precisely defined— the return of "provinces snatched from their owners by force," the "liberation from foreign rule of Italians, Slavs, Rumanians, and Czechoslovaks," the liberation of unspecified peoples from bloody Turkish tyranny, and the expulsion of the Turks from Europe. There was no desire to "exterminate" [sic] the German people or to drive them into "political oblivion,"[138] but Europe was to be liberated from the brutal avarice of Prussian militarism.

In the whole Allied camp there was but one statesman who stubbornly refused to rebuff the hand proffered by Germany without further ado. It was the ruler of the country hit most severely, just then being brutally exploited by the German military administration: King Albert I of the Belgians. On December 19 and 20, 1916, he persuaded his cabinet to dispatch a separate Belgian reply to Germany and not to reject the German peace feeler until Germany's peace terms were known.

As we already know, the king was bitterly opposed to continuation of the war to an end that must in any event mean the ruination of Belgium. "Our war aim is not the same as Britain's," he noted in his diary on December 5. "We are not under arms to destroy Germany." Nor was he persuaded by Berthelot, a French diplomat dispatched to him, that the war, then not yet entered by America, was sure to end in total victory by the Entente. He believed instead that the end would come from general exhaustion, without either victors or vanquished.

On the other hand, according to his biographer, he thought he had reason to believe that Germany was prepared to restore Belgian independence, to forego the Congo, and to pay indemnifications. [139] He was not thinking of a separate peace at all—indeed, he told the British, who feared such an eventuality, that the Germans could not possibly evacuate Belgium until there was a general peace. He did, however, demand negotiations with the enemy, if not now, at the height of German military success, then as soon as possible.

He was dismayed to hear from Berthelot's lips that even if Germany offered France Alsace-Lorraine and more, no Frenchman, in Berthelot's opinion, would dream of laying down his arms. The king, of course, created quite a stir with his opposition in London and Paris, so much so that his ministers soon began to waver and to his deep chagrin accepted a compromise. An appendix was added to the Allied reply to Germany, in which the special position of Belgium, from the point of view of morality and international law, was underlined, though these statements amounted to little more than generalities, put forward for purposes that were left obscure. On the other hand, a separate Belgian statement was appended to the joint reply to the American peace note. In it there was no mention of the prospects of peace mediation, the fierce longing of the suffering Belgian people for settlement of the long war was stressed, and American aid in the country's salvation and restoration was solicited. [140]

By their replies to the German and American notes, the Allies had committed themselves to a clear-cut political line. They did not desire peace negotiations at this time, and they rejected Wilson in the role of mediator. They were ready to negotiate only once their military triumph was clearly established. Even the czarist empire, close to internal collapse, dared not deviate a single step from this line.

Unlike this united and straightforward attitude of the Entente powers,

German policy during the crucial weeks at the turn of the years 1916-1917 displayed a picture of complete uncertainty, disunity, and confusion. Bethmann Hollweg had labored long and arduously to elicit an American initiative toward a negotiated peace. Now that it had occurred, it was received in Berlin with suspicion, doubt, and concern rather than being welcomed as a step in support of the German peace offer. The rightist parties as well as the OHL were bent on viewing it as a game played with a stacked deck, in cahoots with England, in order once again to delay the onset of unrestricted U-boat warfare and thus save Great Britain from this threat. This was an almost direct reversal of the truth. Yet Hindenburg at once wheeled up his heavy guns. "For national reasons," he wired the Chancellor, "and in view of our strong military position we cannot entertain the proposition. To allow ourselves further delay would amount to a grave sin of omission, which we cannot justify in a military sense. These sentiments are shared by our armies, facing the foe. Officers and men expect that we will bring the full weight of our resources to bear, without fear or favor." [141]

For the time being, Bethmann Hollweg was still able to avert this crude attack. But the Kaiser as well as Zimmermann, his foreign policy adviser, were suspicious because Wilson, demanding in his note that war aims be stated, seemed to be meddling with the details of peace negotiations, despite his protestations to the contrary. This distrust epitomized the halfhearted and contradictory quality of German policy, as far as Wilson was concerned. He was summoned as a trusted middleman in getting peace negotiations started, yet he was never entirely trusted. The Germans did not really believe in his neutrality and thus were of two minds about his mediation. They expected him to bring the belligerents to the peace table without breathing a word to the other side about what Germany intended to propose.

Zimmermann, as we have heard, was afraid that the peace conference Germany proposed would actually take place, because there Germany would have to put its cards on the table, and because he was sure it would delay use of Germany's strongest reserve weapon, unrestricted U-boat warfare. Like Zimmermann, certain other statesmen close to the Chancellor, such as Helfferich, Solf, and Kühlmann, apparently thought that peace negotiations meant playing one enemy power against another, until one of them, possibly Russia, would have been maneuvered out of the enemy bloc. [142] Yet after the official declarations on the German peace note issued in Paris, London, St. Petersburg, and Rome, surely there must have been the gravest doubt that such a policy would meet with the slightest success. And could anyone in Germany seriously believe that Wilson would lend himself to such a tactic?

The president too realized that no progress could be made on the road toward an understanding among the governments by a public debate over loudly proclaimed war aims. On December 24 he therefore sent an additional communication to all the belligerents, advising them that their reply could be sent in confidence. Ambassador Bernstorff had learned this from Lansing's lips three days earlier. Lansing added that this meant that the contemplated peace conference could, on the basis of such confidentially communicated peace programs, come into being only slowly. Bernstorff took this to mean that the president wished to serve as a kind of clearinghouse for further peace steps. This, however, caused Zimmermann even deeper concern. Could it be that Wilson wished to prevent direct negotiations between the belligerents, so that he could personally intervene?

As we have seen, Bethmann Hollweg, who carried the whole burden of responsibility on his shoulders, took the American mediating role more seriously from the outset than did his associates, and also expected more from it. Yet no one had as much to fear as he from a discussion by the political parties of his war aims, once they were known in all their moderation; and they had to be very moderate indeed, to find any kind of international hearing. Such a discussion would have exposed and exacerbated the deep rifts in German public opinion. (In fact, since late in November the German press had been free to discuss the war aims issue, on the insistence of the political parties.) More than that, the conflict between the government and the OHL, hitherto carefully concealed from the public, would also be exposed; and because of the extravagant annexationist demands of both navy and army already described, this quarrel had just then almost reached the breaking point.

The Americans may have for the time being desired nothing more than confidential intelligence; but in the light of earlier experience, could any reliance be placed in the discretion of the State Department? It was widely known to be easily accessible to inquisitive journalists. It seemed reasonable to delay a reply to Wilson's peace note at least until Germany had received written and definitive replies to its own offer from the enemy powers. If, as anticipated, they were in the negative, Germany's reluctance to part with details of its peace terms prematurely would have been well justified. Such revelations would have been pointless, if the enemy rejected negotiations in any form; and in that event responsibility for the failure of the peace effort would clearly fall to the other side, even in Wilson's eyes.

On the other hand, it would be very awkward to say, no matter how politely, that Germany wished to discuss peace terms directly with its enemies, without the participation of America, which was to be summoned only after the war was over, to discuss the possibilities of insuring permanent peace through a league of nations organization. Yet that was almost precisely the way it was put in the answering note which Zimmermann on December 26 handed the American ambassador, Gerard, in the name of the German foreign ministry. Despite all the polite verbiage, it was in a sense a vote of nonconfidence; and it was quite inappropriate since Lloyd George's speeches of

December 19 must have told the Germans that their enemies did not dream of "buying a pig in a poke," but were determined first to wait and see what peace terms Germany might offer before sitting down at the conference table, as Zimmermann once again proposed. It was indeed doubtful whether they were prepared to sit down at the conference table in any circumstances.

Zimmermann formulated this precipitate reply after some wavering and only after consultations with Vienna. He subsequently justified this misguided step by arguing that Germany needed to anticipate enemy requests for its peace terms (a challenge already put forward by Lloyd George!) and could not allow Wilson to grab the initiative in the peace question. From his statements as a whole during these days we can only conclude that Zimmermann did not wish a general peace conference, nor did he want America to act as a clearinghouse. Like the German rightist parties and the OHL, he took the speeches of the enemy heads of state to mean that this only boded ill for Germany. It is doubtful that Bethmann Hollweg shared these views; but during these weeks, as we shall soon see, he was under the strongest pressure from the OHL, increasing his doubts and uncertainties. Hence he gave Zimmermann a free hand.[143]

He may not have become aware at once that he was thus departing from the policy toward America he had been following hitherto. At any rate, he was willing to revert to it at once when, soon after the note from the Entente government rejecting the German peace offer became known, new offers surprisingly arrived from Washington. Even then there was much talk in Entente circles that President Wilson resented the Central Powers having anticipated his peace note by one of their own. There can be no doubt that in the beginning he was irked, for his own endeavor was now under the suspicion of having been launched in support of the Germans.

Wilson's most recent biographer, A. S. Link, shows, however, that the views Bethmann Hollweg transmitted to him through Bernstorff and Grew gave Wilson profound satisfaction and actually tipped the balance in encouraging him to launch his own effort. He kept working on it ceaselessly, right down to the last day of January, always worried about unrestricted U-boat warfare which, in the light of all that had happened in recent years, would inevitably drive his country into the war, unless the last shred of American prestige abroad was to be forfeited. For Wilson personally this prospect was particularly galling, for he was proud of being a pacifist, and his reelection in the fall of 1916 was mainly due to the slogan: "He kept us out of war!"

This may account for the fact that he did not feel hurt by Zimmermann's rejection,[144] but on December 27 entered into a new proposal hatched out by his friend House and the German ambassador, Count Bernstorff, who was always prepared to work toward an understanding: Let the German peace terms be communicated in strictest confidence to Colonel House, for the president's personal information, rather than being dispatched to the Department of State. The president would then endeavor to bring about a peace conference, on the basis of this knowledge. According to Bernstorff, the Americans set little store by territorial reapportionments. What they wanted chiefly was agreement for their plans to secure the peace—disarmament, freedom of the seas, arbitration machinery, and a peace league.

Once again Bernstorff was optimistic. He did not think the Americans would insist on their own participation in the peace conference, but did believe they were ready to put strong pressure on the Allies to get such a conference going—and it would certainly have stood no chance to get going without such efforts. "With the exception of the Belgian question," he concluded, "the American government is likely to be more helpful than harmful to us, since the Americans have only just realized just what British dominion of the seas means." Bernstorff warmly recommended that Wilson's services as a mediator be used, though it was clear that he feared Berlin would be reluctant to do so.

This was at first not the case with Bethmann Hollweg. Bernstorff's dispatch reached him only on January 3, by which time the Entente's reply to the German peace offer had been received, ending all hope for a direct understanding with Germany's enemies. Apparently Bernstorff succeeded in communicating his optimism to the Chancellor. Here, after all, even after the failure of the German peace initiative, there might still be a way of coming closer to the desired goal, with the help of the American president, whose appeal the Allies had not yet answered.

In any event, Bethmann Hollweg himself drafted a reply to Washington that proved one thing beyond doubt: He was not out to provide a diplomatic pretext for unrestricted U-boat warfare but to prevent that contingency even at the last moment, if at all possible. At the very least, he was intent on saddling the other side with the blame for the failure of the peace effort, by offering concessions. His first draft included a list of peace terms that accorded by and large with the program he had sent the OHL on November 4. The draft did not take into account the OHL modifications and additions, but it was slightly sharpened in a few points. A new element, added with an eye to Austria, was a general demand for the territorial integrity of Germany and its allies; and there was also the briefest and vaguest mention of Austria's and Bulgaria's most important war aims.[145]

Bernstorff was to be empowered to communicate this list to House and Wilson on a strictly confidential basis; and he was to add that if a preliminary peace was concluded among the belligerents at a conference, Germany would agree, at a general conference (i.e., including the neutral nations), to support courts of arbitration and a peace league, as well as to search for ways in which limited disarmament on land and at sea might be achieved, in order to bring about freedom of the seas.

This meant complete acceptance of the House-Bernstorff proposals—except that German support of American ideas for peace was made contingent on fulfillment of German war goals in a preliminary peace. Bethmann Hollweg evidently hoped in this way to gain Wilson's support for Germany. This, however, implied a measure of faith in the sincerity of Wilson's neutralism, and even more in his understanding of the peace demands of the Central Powers. Without these prerequisites, i.e., if Wilson looked at the German list through British eyes and regarded it a sign of impossible arrogance and incorrigible militarism, it would have to be anticipated that Wilson would oppose the German plan; and in that event communicating the German list to him was bound to worsen rather than improve German-American relations.

We do not know whether these considerations or others persuaded the Chancellor to drop his draft in favor of another prepared by Zimmermann at the foreign ministry and presented to the OHL for approval. Things had indeed in the meantime reached such a stage that no important diplomatic document could be issued without Ludendorff's approval. This may have been the reason why Bethmann Hollweg forewent his own draft. The intolerable tension that had meanwhile developed between him and the OHL doomed it from the start.

Thus Bethmann Hollweg reconciled himself to the fact that an altogether different version, formulated by Zimmermann and approved by Holtzendorff and the OHL, was dispatched to Washington on January 7. There was no more talk of joining hands with America to work for a compromise peace. [146] Instead, American mediation was rejected even more brusquely than before. German public opinion made it thoroughly undesirable! Germany must not give an impression of weakness and the Germans were indeed convinced of their ability to bring the war to a victorious end, in both a military and an economic sense—which was almost certainly not true of the political leaders.

Peace terms could not be immediately disclosed, the note said; but Germany was ready and eager to cooperate in Wilson's peace league and the like. Such matters, however, were fit subjects for discussion only after the conclusion of an armistice. For the time being Germany offered to conclude an arbitration treaty, the so-called Bryan pact, with the United States, as a token of goodwill. Bernstorff was also to give assurances that German peace terms would be extremely moderate and that Germany did not wish to annex Belgium, but it did regard the question of Alsace-Lorraine as beyond discussion and would not tolerate a postwar economic boycott. The note closed with a kind of threat. If—as was to be feared from experience so far—Wilson saw no possibility of forcing the Entente to compromise by exerting strong pressure on Britain, unrestricted U-boat warfare would become a matter of absolute necessity. If Bernstorff knew any way how this could be done without courting a break with America, he was asked to wire instantly.[147]

The whole directive had been quite clearly drafted with a view to gaining the approval of the OHL (which successfully insisted on modifications[148]) rather than assisting the German ambassador in his negotiations with the Americans. Bethmann Hollweg's allowing it to be sent represented a very dubious concession. The Entente powers, three days later, made their own peace terms known, and the longer Germany balked at doing so, even on a confidential basis, the greater the likelihood that the Americans would regard the German peace offer as a mere sham.

In the meantime the Chancellor had lost the power of decision in the U-boat question as well. It was to be a profoundly fateful turn in the relation of sword and scepter.

As was to be expected, Ludendorff had immediately taken advantage of the news of Lloyd George's speech of December 19 to demand that U-boat warfare now be launched "with the gloves off." Among other things, the situation on the western front (which he had just visited) made this necessary, he said. Zimmermann was able to quiet him once more, insisting that cool-headedness was essential and that the enemy powers' formal answer to the peace offer must be awaited; but Ludendorff was no longer content with sharper measures against armed merchantmen, which had been agreed to before and were now again held out to him. "Without unrestricted U-boat warfare," he said on December 22, "we shall lose the campaign. My impressions at the western front have only served to confirm this." Last September the Chancellor had after all agreed that the OHL should settle the timing of the unrestricted U-boat campaign. Well, the time was late January. America was bound to join the war against Germany sooner or later. Hindenburg would be unable to accept responsibility for the success of the campaign, if the government continued to balk.[149]

Hindenburg confirmed this in his wire of December 23, already known to us, in which he characterized Wilson's peace note as a mere maneuver to help Britain by dragging out Germany's decision.[150] He too cited Bethmann Hollweg's assurances of the preceding September, though for the time being he was content once again to demand only that U-boat attacks on armed merchantmen be allowed. True, in the long run that was not enough. The only possible exceptions that might be discussed concerned the northern countries and perhaps America—provided this did not reduce the effectiveness of U-boat warfare. "I expressly reserve my position in this respect," he added arrogantly, insisting that preparations for unrestricted U-boat warfare be made now.

The Chancellor was thus confronted with a kind of ultimatum in this jurisdictional issue, the second time it had been made an issue since October.

Bethmann Hollweg of course stuck to the answer he had then given and insisted that the only expansion of U-boat warfare that was immediately possible was the torpedoing of armed merchantmen; but even in that event, a declaration to America, already prepared, could be dispatched only after a formal reply had been received from Germany's enemies. It was true that such a reply would probably be in the main negative, but it might leave a back door open, which the Germans must not slam shut. The impression must be avoided that the whole German peace offer was but a prelude to unrestricted U-boat warfare, as many voices in the neutral countries were already asserting, corroborated, alas, by the war whoops in the German press.

Bethmann Hollweg can scarcely have expected that this argument would make a strong impression on the OHL. For the generals the peace effort had indeed never meant anything more than a prelude to the U-boat war; but the Chancellor struck a notably conciliatory tone, in order to avoid an open conflict, if that were possible. It was for that reason that he concluded his telegram with a phrase that terrifyingly reveals his inner uncertainties: "To the degree that I am able to convince myself, along the lines of Your Excellency, that the advantages of U-boat warfare waged without any restrictions whatever outweigh the handicap of America joining our enemies, I shall be prepared to consider even the question of unrestricted U-boat warfare." Discussions on this subject, he added, could take place as soon as the German peace initiative had come to some kind of conclusion, perhaps by an answer from the Entente. Of course he, Bethmann Hollweg, would take the mood of the armed forces into full account.

Even though the Chancellor reserved the ultimate decision to himself, this was already half a retreat. The generals, in typically military fashion, were not slow to take advantage of the opening. On December 26 they responded with a telegram devoid of ifs and buts. "Our military situation," it said, "leaves no room for negotiations that would postpone a military measure once it is recognized to be necessary, thereby paralyzing the vigor of our strategy." The OHL therefore requested that U-boat action against armed merchantmen be authorized immediately, without negotiations with America, and that there be prompt discussions concerning intensified U-boat warfare, meaning of course unrestricted U-boat warfare. Public opinion, misunderstanding the Chancellor's declaration before the Reichstag committee, held Hindenburg rather than Bethmann Hollweg responsible for the decision in the U-boat question. Now that opinions seemed to be diverging sharply, this was no longer tolerable to Hindenburg:

> To preserve the position of the OHL I must state [it was not made clear whether such a statement was also to be made publicly] that while Your Excellency as Chancellor may claim [note, not "bear"!] exclu-

sive responsibility, I shall, as a matter of course, continue, with all the energy at my command and with the fullest sense of responsibility for the successful conclusion of the war, to support every effort in the military sphere that I consider to be necessary to that end.

This came perilously close to a declaration of war and caused the Chancellor to announce an immediate visit to Pless for the purpose of holding discussions. What Bethmann Hollweg did not learn was that Holtzendorff, chief of the admiralty staff, had meanwhile gone over to the other side—Holtzendorff who in recent months had time and again helped him to postpone unrestricted U-boat warfare and at the last had agreed to rest content with proceeding against armed merchantmen. On December 22 Hindenburg had received a message from Holtzendorff, accompanied by a voluminous report, in which an urgent recommendation was made that unrestricted U-boat warfare be commenced not later than February 1, 1917.

This so-called Kalkmann memorandum played a decisive part in the ultimate decision of the Kaiser and his military advisers. It endeavored to deflate the reservations, estimates, and calculations Helfferich had put forward in August, doing so on the basis of very comprehensive and careful estimates of British and world tonnage, of Britain's conservatively estimated food and raw materials stockpiles, and of whatever reserves might still be available. Despite the fact that the number and quality of large U-boats had meanwhile risen, the tonnage that might be sunk was still estimated at 600,000 a month, as at the beginning of the year. In other words, an increase by about one-half was held out over the results of the so-called "cruiser warfare" of November and December.

In the main the memorandum sought to prove that Britain would not be able to take countermeasures that would be really effective. It was not denied that American entry into the war would have unfavorable military and economic consequences; but these effects were trivialized as much as possible. 151 The chief argument was that Germany would have reached its goal long before American aid could become effective. Within five months the tonnage available to Britain would have been reduced by about thirty-nine per cent, creating an intolerable situation for that country. This was, however, on the premise that unrestricted U-boat warfare would commence instantly on February 1, 1917, without prior announcement of any kind, exerting a powerful shock effect on the neutrals and their ships' crews.

Torpedo attacks on armed merchantmen alone, it was maintained, would not suffice to bring thoroughgoing success. Many typically militarist arguments were made in the memorandum and in the accompanying letter to Hindenburg from the admiralty staff chief:

Germany must, while there is still time, change course abruptly and teach the neutrals the lesson that it does not lag behind Britain in willpower and the determination to prevail. To do otherwise would represent a grave danger, not only now but for the future. . . . Compromise and appeasement are least calculated to do away with the hate and resentment engendered by the war. An amiable attitude is no proper substitute for the imposition of respect. The world has always bowed to the success of the strong.

The experiences of 1917 were to show that this whole approach of the admiralty staff was a fearful miscalculation. Yet it would be wrong to condemn it as heedless adventurism, a term that might be applied to the earlier plans of the spring of 1915 and 1916; for it remains a fact that since then German technical capability had substantially grown, and thus the chances of success as well. Lloyd George, in his memoirs, shows that he took this possibility as seriously as anyone. According to him, President of the Board of Trade Runciman, in the session of the war committee of November 9, 1916, expected a complete breakdown of British shipping before June 1917; and soon afterward he stated that this eventuality might occur much sooner.

Admiral Jellicoe, head of the fleet, stated in writing late in October that he saw a serious danger that by the early summer of 1917 lack of tonnage might compel Britain to accept peace negotiations on unfavorable terms. In April 1917, after the figures of tonnage sunk had risen enormously, he told the American admiral, Sims, that the Germans would win the war if the British could not stop these losses quite soon, something they saw no way of doing.[152]

This, to be sure, was said from an ulterior motive. Jellicoe needed naval aid from the Americans and wished to keep their optimism down; but it is true that of every 100 large oceangoing ships then leaving Britain, twenty-five never returned. As Lloyd George put it, with sinkings at that rate Germany's expectation of being able to force Britain to its knees by August did not, in the circumstances, seem improbable.

We may assume that Lloyd George deliberately painted Britain's situation in gloomy colors for the purpose of making his own achievement shine forth all the more brightly, by contrast. Apparently he deserved the major share of the credit for the curiously long-resisted decision of the British admiralty in May 1917 to do what Bethmann Hollweg had predicted in 1916 it would ultimately have to do—adopt the policy of organizing ships into convoys, to be escorted and protected by naval vessels in the war zone. When that happened, U-boat sinkings declined as rapidly as U-boat losses mounted, and the successes predicted by the German navy failed to materialize.

There was no one in Germany in 1916, however, who could have foreseen this with absolute certainty, certainly not unless he was himself a naval expert—and the experts all stood against it. Holtzendorff seems to have been finally won over in mid-December, under the persistent pressure from Scheer and the arguments of his associates to support unrestricted U-boat warfare being opened up no later than February 1, 1917. This was at the time the German peace note had been dispatched—which everyone in the admiralty expected to fail. Holtzendorff knew as early as December 15 that the OHL too counted on that opening date.[153] Hindenburg expressly told him so on December 24. In the circumstances, it is very strange that by the end of the year Holtzendorff had not yet sent the admiralty memorandum to the Chancellor, but instead was content to demand that unwarned sinkings of armed merchantmen must begin by late December.[154] We shall soon see what was behind these tactics.

As things stood, Bethmann Hollweg's effort to settle the open quarrel between himself and the OHL by face-to-face talks was foredoomed. On arrival in Pless on December 29 he was received icily. More than that, Helfferich, vice chancellor and interior minister, who accompanied Bethmann Hollweg and who had a quarrel of his own with Ludendorff over the auxiliary service law, was rudely barred from the talks altogether. On this point the Chancellor forced a reversal.

The discussions as such seem to have dealt mainly with the preposterous OHL peace terms of December 23, which Bethmann Hollweg was trying to get modified by dilatory tactics, as we have already seen (Note 128, above). The generals put forward many complaints, some of them quite absurd, but including the contention that efforts were being made to push them aside in the U-boat issue.

This once again afforded the Chancellor an opportunity to assert his constitutional responsibility for political questions, while insisting that there too he sought complete agreement with the OHL. If that were not possible, the Kaiser would have to decide. Bethmann Hollweg as well as Helfferich once again voiced serious reservations concerning unrestricted U-boat warfare, though the admiralty staff memorandum was not discussed. Instead there was rather prompt agreement on the wording of the note that would announce to America the onset of intensified action against armed merchantmen, an announcement that was to be deferred until an Allied reply to the German peace offer had been received. Such a reply was expected in a matter of days, but at bottom it held no further interest for Ludendorff even then.

Directly after this session, Ludendorff conferred with the headquarters representative of the admiralty staff, Captain von Bülow, to whom he reported what had happened. Bülow noted that he urged Ludendorff to intervene with the Chancellor once more concerning the U-boat issue, but Ludendorff refused to act as the "front man" again, before the official talks Bethmann Hollweg had promised had taken place. He said that was Holtzendorff's affair. He, Ludendorff, had to husband his energy for a more important task. (Could he have meant ousting the Chancellor?)

The naval man thereupon told Ludendorff that the chief of the admiralty staff saw no possibility of winning the Chancellor over to the launching of unrestricted U-boat warfare; and while Bethmann Hollweg said no, the Kaiser's mind could not be changed either. Only if the OHL confronted William II with a clear choice between Bethmann Hollweg and Hindenburg would the Kaiser be forced to decide against the Chancellor. Ludendorff replied in some irritation that he would do what he thought necessary, with or without the admiralty staff. Bülow then said that even the smallest concessions to neutral countries in the matter of unrestricted U-boat warfare boded ill—he wanted to make sure that Ludendorff would not in any way bow to the diplomatists.[155]

The incident suggests why Holtzendorff was reluctant to submit the admiralty staff report to the Chancellor. He was convinced that only an OHL ultimatum would bring the desired end, and he was intent on bringing about such a confrontation. Only if all the services formed a united front before the Kaiser in insisting on unrestricted U-boat warfare would the Kaiser be forced to back down.

But it would seem that Bülow, if anything, overestimated the Chancellor's steadfastness in this now increasingly difficult question. Immediately after the discussion, according to a note made only ten years later by Freiherr von Lersner, a Foreign Office councilor posted to Pless at the time, Bethmann Hollweg voiced serious doubts about how much longer he would be able to prevent unrestricted U-boat warfare.[156] He seemed to realize that he could not prevail, except at the cost of an open break with the OHL, which he dreaded, for political reasons. The open hostility with which he had been received at supreme headquarters could leave him in no doubt that the two generals who owed their positions at the head of the army to him were now actively working for his downfall. He also knew that in any open power struggle the idol of the people was bound to prevail.

Two days later the Allied reply to the German peace offer was made known in Berlin. It dispelled even the last feeble glimmer of hope that Germany might reach an understanding with its enemies by direct negotiation. The Kaiser flew into a rage and said that in the light of such cynicism he would have to change *his* peace terms. There would be no more pulling of punches against France and Belgium. King Albert would never be permitted to return to Belgium. The coast of Flanders must become German.

Emperor Charles of Austria sent the Kaiser a wire along very different lines. The Allied reply, he said, was certainly unwelcome in its conclusions, but it did not exclude the possibility of spinning out the idea of peace. He was afraid that this link would be broken if the two monarchs now issued hurried proclamations to their armies, exhorting them to fight on. Let the Kaiser first launch at least one more diplomatic effort. The OHL, on the other hand, urged him to issue an order immediately, paying no attention to Austrian wishes.

It was up to Bethmann Hollweg to mediate between these conflicting tendencies. As a first step, he succeeded in bringing about consultations between the two Central Powers on the orders to be issued to their armies, so that this at least would not give rise to irritation; but further trouble loomed when Count Czernin turned up in Berlin on January 6 to discuss the Polish question as well as the reaction of the Central Powers to the Allied reply.

We have already seen, from the manner in which Wilson's latest mediation offer of December 27 was treated,[157] that there was no longer agreement even between the Chancellor and the German foreign minister. This discrepancy came out into the open during the talks with Czernin. The Allied reply, Zimmermann said, was so vicious that the German retort—which was to be sent to the neutral nations in token of Germany's position—must now ruthlessly unmask the Entente. Germany must reject the slanders vigorously, speak up sharply, point to the political atrocities committed by the Allies. That was what the German people expected.

Zimmermann, in other words, identified himself entirely with "indignant German public opinion," whereas the Chancellor thought that the effect of the Allied reply on the German public was of only secondary importance. What was important in his view was to deepen the impress of the German peace initiative among the neutrals. Fruitless polemics would bring Germany no nearer peace. What needed to be done was to issue a brief and objective correction of the slanders concerning German policy and strategy contained in the Allied reply. Germany must not slam the door on peace.

Czernin voiced similar sentiments—he too was unwilling to see the link, however tenuous, broken. In the end Zimmermann's draft was rejected and a new version agreed on. By and large it struck a calm and dignified note; but to the Allied charges that Germany was violating international law and the freedom of small nations it opposed precisely those countercharges the other side had feared and anticipated beforehand. It brought up the fate of the Irish, the destruction of the freedom and independence of the Boer republics, the subjugation of North Africa by Britain, France, and Italy, the Russian suppression of alien peoples, and lastly the unprecedented rape of Greece— forcible occupation, quelling of nationalist and royalist rebellions, overthrow of the government by means of a blockade. Germany, it was said, had already attained its purely defensive war aims, while its enemies demanded whole provinces and the humiliation and mutilation of Germany's allies.

At that time, around January 7, Zimmermann had already joined the camp of the generals in the U-boat question as well, in part under pressure from his friends among the Reichstag deputies of the nationalist right. Under Secretary von Stumm, on the other hand, shared the Chancellor's qualms, especially his greatest fear, that the prospect of American war aid would, despite economic exigencies, keep Germany's enemies, Britain in the lead, in the war until Germany was completely out of breath.[158] Bethmann Hollweg himself, as usual, sought to delay his final decision as long as possible; but the military side saw to it that he would be forced to decide, promptly and abruptly.

This time the impetus came from the navy, Ludendorff having again declined the role of "front man." By January 4 Holtzendorff had not yet apprised the Chancellor of his change of mind; and on that day the foreign ministry completed the agreed directive to be wired to Bernstorff, announcing that armed merchantmen would be mercilessly sunk.[159] The next day the admiralty staff chief suddenly visited Bethmann Hollweg and handed him a copy of his letter to Hindenburg of December 22, together with his comprehensive staff memorandum.

Holtzendorff seems to have reached his decision following a scene on January 4 with Captain von Levetzow, an emissary from Admiral Scheer, who roundly told him that his hesitancy had lost him the confidence of the navy. He said that there was in effect no naval leadership, the admirals feeling that Holtzendorff had deceived them. Once he had made up his mind, Holtzendorff immediately took a further step. On January 6 he wired Hindenburg that he would now appeal directly to the Kaiser, and on January 8 he appeared at headquarters where, in a most fateful turn, Admiral von Müller, chief of the naval cabinet, expressed agreement with him, as Capelle had already done.[160] In consultation with Ludendorff and Hindenburg, a plot was now hatched to take the Chancellor by surprise.

From the documents Holtzendorff had given him, Bethmann Hollweg must have concluded that all the military men had joined forces against him, as during the preceding spring, and that in view of the general war situation and the failure of his peace offer he would not be able to postpone the launching of unrestricted U-boat warfare much longer. This resigned conclusion was probably responsible for his approval of Zimmermann's previously discussed directive to Bernstorff of January 7, which in effect already held out the threat of unrestricted U-boat warfare.[161] He did, however, still manage to insert a final clause stating that possibly the ambassador might know a way of avoiding a break with America despite this intensification.

The Chancellor seems to have clung to this last glimmer and to Bernstorff's dispatch of December 27. In any event, on January 8 he had Holtzendorff summoned to the telephone and told him that he must still reserve to himself the diplomatic preparations for unrestricted U-boat warfare. He would arrive in Pless the next day and wire Bernstorff to hold up the note just dispatched, announcing unwarned attacks on armed merchantmen.

What Bethmann Hollweg sought to achieve was, of course, to prevent headquarters simply going over his head in settling the U-boat issue, the most important of his whole war policy. He was bitterly resentful of the military conspiracy being hatched in Pless, and his distrust of Holtzendorff personally had sharply risen. He told the admiral to his face that his whole proposal for an intensified campaign against armed merchantmen was nothing but a "U-boat trap" set for the politicians. The aim was to bring about war with America and then to expand it beyond all reason.

Holtzendorff on his part threatened immediate issuance to the U-boat fleet of the order to sink armed steamers unless the Chancellor agreed to have the note delivered in America. Apparently he was quite blind to the fact that the note, followed so soon by the launching of unrestricted U-boat warfare, was bound to be considered a German act of deception on the other side of the Atlantic. In the event, however, he did agree at least to delay his U-boat directive for another day.[162]

The two generals at once agreed with him, and the incident serves to illustrate their continuing uncertainty as to whether the Chancellor could really be won to the cause of unrestricted U-boat warfare. If it could not be done, Holtzendorff wanted at least to keep open the option of launching the partial campaign against armed merchantmen. Bethmann Hollweg's call drove the military men into a frenzy of action—the great decision must at all costs be taken before his arrival. On first meeting the Kaiser at noon the admiral had found him in very low spirits. Now the admiral girded himself not only to gain the sovereign's approval for the U-boat order but also to read aloud his letter to Hindenburg of December 22, of whose arguments William II had not yet taken note. Armed also with the Kalkmann memorandum and the endorsement of his demands—they were no longer mere proposals! —by all the military authorities, Holtzendorff hoped to attain his goal.

Thought was nevertheless given to a possible course of action, should the Chancellor remain obdurate; and there was agreement that in that event he would have to go. If he yielded, a further stay in office would be useful, for as Holtzendorff pointed out, Bethmann Hollweg enjoyed considerable confidence abroad; and the chances of keeping America out of the war might be slightly better than they would be if there were a change in the chancellorship. It must be observed that the whole plot was hatched in a most amateurish fashion, and was indeed ultimately executed in the same style later on in July. There were no real proposals as to who should succeed Bethmann Hollweg, the most impossible names being mentioned at random.[163]

The admiralty staff chief's audience went entirely as desired, the Kaiser being won over without a great deal of effort. He did, however, seem to sense that this military plan was not quite constitutional, and he tried to muster his courage for the coming showdown with Bethmann Hollweg by blustering talk. That night he remarked to Müller that U-boat warfare was a purely military matter of no concern to the Chancellor. For that matter, even a change of cast would not be the worst thing. The two admirals sought to talk him out of this, Holtzendorff obviously motivated by the thought that it would be better for the Chancellor to stay—provided he yielded! In order to pin down the Kaiser's approval in the U-boat question and equip him with arguments for the discussion with Bethmann Hollweg, Holtzendorff wrote a brief memorandum, dealing mainly with the political aspects and couched in highly effective terms. This he handed the sovereign the next morning.

But the agitated discussion everyone had feared never came about. When the Chancellor arrived in Pless on the morning of January 9, after a long and tiring night journey—he was also suffering from a stubborn case of bronchitis—he was received at the station by Admiral Müller, who at once told him that everything had already been settled. He added that he himself, hitherto always opposed to unrestricted U-boat warfare, had now like Capelle convinced himself both that it had become inevitable and that it stood an excellent chance of success.[164]

Müller's intention was to reassure the Chancellor, but apparently he succeeded only in destroying the last remnant of Bethmann Hollweg's composure in the U-boat question. Müller had been his friend, always ready to mediate, and with his defection the last military buttress of Bethmann Hollweg's opposition to U-boat warfare collapsed. As he reported himself, the long admiralty staff memorandum had already made quite an impression on him, reinforced by a communication from "a naval authority of the highest rank."[165]

The ever-active Helfferich, however, spent the entire night from January 8 to 9 studying the voluminous Kalkmann memorandum, and by four o'clock in the morning drafted a brief countermemorandum, which he wired to Pless immediately. He had no choice but to acknowledge the reliability of the admiralty staff's statistical calculations and projected sinkings. What he disputed was that the decision was as urgent as was maintained in Pless. He pointed out that America, on entering the war, was bound to redouble its efforts, which would in turn correspondingly improve Britain's situation. This would have scarcely been of much help to the Chancellor in his discussions with the generals; but the matter never did reach the discussion stage, for by 2:30 P.M., when Helfferich's long telegram arrived in Pless, the talks had long since ended.

The abbreviated OHL minutes on the course of these talks leave the impression that the Chancellor did not even seriously try to oppose Hindenburg's demands. Indeed, he seems at the very outset to have agreed to diplomatic preparations for unrestricted U-boat warfare, aimed at still keeping America out of the war, if possible, despite his skepticism that such an effort could succeed. According to this source he reiterated several of his well-known reservations, but on the whole he seems to have taken a favorable view of the chances of a U-boat campaign. At any rate, he admitted that these chances had materially improved since the spring. Nevertheless, U-boat warfare represented the last trump card. "It is a very grave decision, but if the military authorities regard it as necessary, I am not in a position to contradict them."

But the report Bethmann Hollweg gave to Valentini directly afterward paints a rather different picture of what took place. He said that he spent more than an hour presenting the weightiest arguments against intensified U-boat warfare, without getting through to either the generals or the admirals (with whom he seems to have had separate talks). He told Helfferich, on the other hand, that an argument put forward by Ludendorff greatly impressed him, namely that during the coming spring Germany's enemies were bound to launch a giant offensive on all fronts. In the west it would far exceed the momentum and artillery support of the Battle of the Somme. Not a day was to be lost if Germany's U-boats were still to be in time to paralyze the enemy's lines of supply and munitions. Otherwise the OHL could not take responsibility for the course of military operations.

To such arguments Bethmann Hollweg could not possibly respond with vague references to a continuing possibility that the American peace effort might be successful—it was in fact officially rejected by the Entente powers the very next day, with a program of peace terms that already foreshadowed the Treaty of Versailles. Still less could he bring up the latest confidential talks between Colonel House and Count Bernstorff, which were already known to the generals, together with the German rejection of January 7. [166] The Chancellor, in other words, had no further cards he might have placed on the table as an alternative to U-boat warfare. He could offer no tangible chance of a negotiated peace, no decisive successes by the armed forces. It was far more likely that Germany's allies would collapse before long and that Germany's own manpower reserves would melt away, right in the middle of what had come to be called the "turnip winter," when for the first time Germany's food shortage had reached the crisis stage.

No, Bethmann Hollweg could only reiterate his fears that America's entry into the war would prolong rather than shorten the war, reviving the flagging spirits of Germany's enemies, opening up new perspectives for their generals, substantially strengthening their economies and their military resources. All of this he did say to the generals, and in his frantic search for military arguments he even mentioned the outlandish possibility that Germany's enemies might starve out the Swiss to the point of allowing them transit across Switzerland—a notion Hindenburg actually described as holding certain military advantages. Yet without positive and tangible prospects for the future Bethmann Hollweg could not hope to make the slightest impression on Hindenburg and Ludendorff. They would scarcely have deserved to be called soldiers, had they been ready, at this late date, to forego the experiment of intensified U-boat warfare—unless the Chancellor could have proved to them by chapter and verse that the admiralty staff was guilty of miscalculating. That Bethmann Hollweg, by his own admission, was unable to do, any more than the generals could nail down the opposite case. As things stood, all the calculations were nothing more than estimates, conjectures, probabilities. If everything in normal warfare was uncertain, how much more so in a new and untested variation.

The so-called crown council that was convened at six o'clock in the evening to discuss the U-boat question was thus little more than a formality. Its real purpose was merely to concede to the Chancellor his constitutional voice in a decision that had already been taken—the launching of unrestricted U-boat warfare on February 1, without further negotiation or proclamation. The participants, including the three cabinet chiefs, stood surrounding the Kaiser, who was pale and distraught, one hand resting on a table, and who made it quite clear that he did not desire any real consultations. The Chancellor, Holtzendorff, and Hindenburg were merely afforded an opportunity to state their viewpoints with the utmost brevity. Bethmann Hollweg's remarks, nevertheless, went on for some time, and Valentini gained the impression that the Kaiser listened only with considerable impatience and rejection. He seemed to be waiting nervously for Bethmann Hollweg's concluding statement, to the effect that despite the reservations he had voiced, he could not advise the Kaiser to reject intensification of U-boat warfare against the recommendations of his military advisers, even though he formally disagreed with them. A few weeks later, however, William II told Count Roedern he had listened to the words of his Chancellor with deep emotion, feeling the deepest sympathy for this high-minded and conscientious protagonist. His three cabinet chiefs had received the same strong impression.[167]

Whether or not this is a true account, there can be no doubt that this meeting on the evening of January 9, 1917, marked the darkest hour in Bethmann Hollweg's political career. It meant the formal capitulation of political authority to the military in the most crucial issue of the First World War by far. For Bethmann Hollweg personally it was the prelude to the last act of his tragedy. For Germany it was a turn that not only tragically prolonged its grim struggle but made that struggle truly hopeless in a military sense, as will be shown. For the world it meant—as all the participants well knew—that the great power beyond the seas would now be inevitably swept into the war, torn from its traditional isolationism.[168] What the participants did not know[169] was that it ushered in a historic turn such as the countries of Europe had not witnessed in a millennium and a half. Europe, once the world's political center, became merely one of many scenes of action, a process that has taken on fully global dimensions since the Second World War.

Later on, after the failure of the great U-boat offensive, the thing that did the greatest harm to Bethmann Hollweg's reputation as a statesman was his failure to resign immediately when his policies were defeated by the military. Even Helfferich, his most loyal associate, was so indignant over Bethmann Hollweg's surrender that he at first avoided him and simply submitted his own resignation. This, however, was only a first impulse, and Helfferich let the Chancellor talk him into staying on. As for the Chancellor himself, his dominant reaction after the crown council session was deep disenchantment with the Kaiser, on whose steadfastness he had hitherto built all his plans. Admiral Müller found him in this mood in Valentini's rooms directly after supper. What had wounded Bethmann Hollweg most deeply was a gesture of the Kaiser he took to mean: Good heavens, is the man still holding back? William II, he said, had thoroughly spoiled the German people in the last twenty years, encouraging their vanity and chauvinism. Only the lowest classes had remained truly German. The Kaiser had done irreparable harm to his prestige and that of his dynasty.

But when Valentini advised him to submit his resignation in the circumstances, arguing that the future was even blacker than Bethmann Hollweg thought, the Chancellor instantly rejected this course of action. He had already given thought to it in the morning, following the talks with the military men. It was simple and tempting, he said, to resign in the face of irreversible decisions that had already been taken without him and to absent himself from the evening confrontation with the Kaiser; but after a long inner struggle he had resisted the temptation, and he now gave the cabinet chief his reasons, in much the same terms as those in which he often formulated them later on.

What he said was that to resign meant a kind of desertion, an evasion of his share of responsibility for the war's outcome. His personal fate did not matter, nor did he much care whether posterity would praise or reproach him. As for holding on to power, that was now less tempting a prospect than ever. Still less was he tempted by the role of opposition leader, at the head of the social democratic and progressive anti-U-boat faction, in a struggle against Hindenburg and the Reichstag majority. That would merely be "an adventure leading to disaster."[170] His resignation would not affect the launching of U-boat warfare in any way. On the contrary, Bethmann Hollweg was certain that once he went all power, in matters of domestic as well as foreign policy, would pass to the military juggernaut.

With U-boat warfare a settled matter, Bethmann Hollweg thought it his duty to do all in his power to help it gain whatever success might be possible and to refrain from all actions that might reduce its chances and aggravate even further Germany's domestic and foreign dilemma. His resignation, he thought, would be interpreted as a demonstrative act, an open protest that would bring harmful consequences, at home and abroad. At home the wreckage of the party truce would be completed and the conflict between right and left dangerously accentuated. The main danger was the effect on the social democratic working masses, who at this very moment were to be spurred to even greater efforts in Hindenburg's arms program. Such internal conflict would remain no secret to Germany's enemies, who would rejoice over it. Neutral distrust of German policy would be deepened, especially in America, and the last chance of keeping America out of the war would vanish. (It was quite true, of course, that Bethmann Hollweg was known abroad to be one of the "moderates," and the constant attacks on him by the Pan-Germans were closely followed there.) Everywhere in the world the Chancellor's retirement would diminish confidence in the success of the new U-boat weapon, especially among Germany's allies, who had long been worried about the strident German U-boat propaganda and the growing friction with America. It was quite possible that his disappearance from the scene would weaken confidence in the success of the new weapon and do further damage to the alliance, which had already been shaken in Sofia and Vienna.

These were certainly considerations that could not be ignored. There can be no doubt that they would weigh heavily in the mind of a conscientious patriot. At the same time it is hard to understand why conscience did not move Bethmann Hollweg, despite all his qualms, to implement his protest by resigning, if he were absolutely convinced that the U-boat campaign spelled Germany's doom and that the admiralty prognostications were illusory.

Our careful account has already made it clear that for many weeks he had no longer been quite sure of himself in this matter. He actually said as much to Helfferich. Hindenburg and Ludendorff were so very definite in holding that the immediate launching of U-boat warfare was essential to relieve the pressure at the fronts, and were so willing to take full responsibility for the military consequences. The chief of the admiralty staff, moreover, as well as the head of the fleet and the navy minister, Capelle, previously opposed, all predicted, indeed almost personally guaranteed, full success within a matter of months. Bethmann Hollweg thus had to ask himself whether he could, in all conscience, advise the Kaiser not to authorize the step.[171] Had the situation been different, he surely would not have waited for the crown council but would have sought a private audience, in a last-ditch effort to change the Kaiser's mind, threatening his resignation, if necessary. The fact that he did no such thing plainly underlines his inner uncertainty.[172]

Perhaps this demonstrates the limitations of Bethmann Hollweg's talents as a statesman. It is not unfair to suggest that in the end he was a typical intellectual, always beset by doubts, lacking the true statesman's infallible political instincts and unswerving will. But those who level such charges should be quite clear about the extraordinary if not superhuman qualities of character they expect him to have possessed. The crushing responsibility would have been his in the face of the opposition of virtually all leading military and naval experts, against the will of his sovereign, the Reichstag majority, and indeed the great majority of those politically active Germans who spoke out in public—and these included even social democrats. Against the weight of these opinions Bethmann Hollweg is expected to have followed solely his own personal insight, which could have been scarcely more than instinctive. This he is expected to have done in a situation that seemed to offer no recourse but a ruthlessly executed hunger blockade of Britain. It was not the first time, moreover, that he had been confronted with this decision, but the third. Bethmann Hollweg always took his political responsibilities with the greatest gravity, but his mental resources were not inexhaustible.

## Part 5

# The Break with America

ON JANUARY 16 the Chancellor told the federal council committee ruefully that he was reminded of the way things had been in July and August 1914. Once again the military men were in far too great a hurry, unwilling to allow efforts at political compromise to mature. Even before the Entente had re-plied to Wilson's peace initiative, a military decision had to be forced. The ostensible reason was the same as in 1914. Not a day must be lost, if technical preparations for the lightninglike launching of the wonder weapon were to be completed by the designated date. Ludendorff was totally unwilling to allow diplomatic negotiations once again to delay military action. Yet it was soon to become clear that neither the German government's attitude of reserve nor the brusque rejection of the Entente powers had deterred Wilson from spin-ning out the threads of his peace mediation effort. On the contrary, never did he pursue it so zealously as during the final weeks before the launching of unrestricted U-boat warfare, which he feared so greatly.

It seemed at first as though Bethmann Hollweg's hope might be fulfilled and an acceptable compromise reached with America in the U-boat question, namely an understanding about the sinking of armed ships without prior warning. On January 9 Bernstorff received a memorandum on the question, with the request to begin discussing it informally with Lansing.[173] The am-bassador did not learn until much later that the memorandum had meanwhile been rendered obsolete by the decision taken on January 9. He immediately warned against proceeding precipitately, lest this wreck Wilson's efforts on behalf of peace. Since the middle of the month he had had good reason to hope for an understanding. We have already heard, in Chapter 5, Part 3, that the question of arming merchant ships had aroused strong public controversy in America. Even Lansing and Wilson, by the spring of 1916, had not been altogether sure of themselves. This was now even truer, for the British were arming their vessels with bigger and better guns, served by well-trained artillerymen from the army and navy; and by denying coal to unarmed ships they virtually forced the neutrals to follow suit. This led to a highly agitated confrontation between Lansing and the British ambassador on January 18.[174]

Most importantly, throughout January the mood in the White House tended strongly toward peace. Returning from Washington to Berlin, American ambassador Gerard, on January 6, held a much-noted speech before the German-American chamber of commerce, in which he said that relations between the United States and Germany had never been better.[175] On January 4 Wilson eagerly told his friend, Colonel House: "There will be no war. Our country does not want to become entangled in this war. We are the only great white nation that remains remote from the war, and it would be a crime against civilization if we entered it." At the same time Wilson, informed of new U-boat incidents, told Lansing he did not believe the American people were prepared to go to war because a few Americans had lost their lives on merchant ships.[176]

The German memorandum about the illegality of arming merchantmen, rather than arousing Wilson's indignation, merely reinforced his earlier doubts. On January 24 he asked Lansing whether the procedures recently put into effect by Britain did not require a change in the American position; and as late as January 31, on the eve of the launching of unrestricted U-boat warfare by the Germans, he wrote his secretary of state that he thought the question extraordinarily complex, and that it seemed rather clear to him that the British had certainly gone beyond the spirit of the agreement which had been in force, and in some instances beyond mere defense as well.[177]

Are we to conclude that Wilson might have in the end reconciled himself to an intensified campaign limited solely to armed merchantmen—as Bethmann Hollweg hoped[178] —had not Germany brusquely burst into the situation with its declaration of unrestricted U-boat warfare? Such an outcome seems most unlikely. On January 31 Lansing, after long thought and some hesitation, presented to the president arguments in writing that were calculated to appeal strongly to his pacifist sentiments. If German U-boats began sinking armed merchantmen without warning, the Entente governments were bound to react with such deep resentment that peace talks with them would become meaningless. Besides, any concession to the Germans in the U-boat question would merely lend support to their view that Washington was afraid of war and that they might move on to sink any ship without warning, without risking a break with America.[179]

Wilson was not immediately convinced; but it is hard to envisage that he would have risked a break with the Entente governments over the U-boat issue on his own. It is quite true that Bethmann Hollweg's policy was more advantageous in a military sense than the German admiralty staff and the OHL were then prepared to admit,[180] but it did carry its own political risks; and a rupture of diplomatic relations could probably not have been avoided in any event. Still, American entry into the war might have been prevented or at least delayed, had the Germans practiced restraint. At the very least, world opinion would not have been challenged with the brutality inherent in the decision of January 9, which ordained that from February 1 onward all ships traveling to or from Britain and France would be sunk without warning.

Meanwhile talks concerning Wilson's peace mediation had continued. In Berlin Foreign Minister Zimmermann had for a while entertained the wishful hope that Allied rejection of the American peace note would infuriate Wilson to the point where he would persist in keeping the United States neutral, even should Germany launch unrestricted U-boat warfare. It was a foolish illusion.[181] The Allied note of January 10 was certainly a bitter pill for the president. Its territorial demands told him that the Allies, despite all their fine words, were certainly not simon-pure idealists fighting for the cause of freedom; but then, he had long since suspected as much. He had, of course, not the least idea that behind his back Lansing had recommended to the ambassadors of France and Britain much the same peace terms that were embodied in the Allied statement of January 10.[182] But Wilson did begin to dread total victory by the Allies and did not allow himself to be swerved in his peace efforts. This became startlingly clear in the talks Count Bernstorff, following his instructions, had with Colonel House on January 15 on the question of American peace mediation.

It will be recalled that on January 7 Zimmermann had instructed Bernstorff to turn down House's request for details on German peace terms, on the grounds that Germany wished to negotiate with the enemy powers directly, without the aid of a mediator.[183] This was not a particularly friendly attitude; but the ambassador carried out his order, which apparently reached him only after considerable delay, in his talk with Colonel House on January 15 in such a manner that House got the opposite impression—perhaps Bernstorff simply failed to mention the hard core of his message! At any rate, the colonel's report to Wilson mentions no German rejection of American peace mediation.

On the contrary, House was highly pleased with the German government's unexpected peace-willingness. Germany agreed to submit to a court of arbitration as a means toward the restoration of peace, to join a league of nations that would secure world peace, and to limit armaments on land and at sea. It proposed that Wilson submit a program for a peace conference, to which it gave agreement in advance. Lastly, as a token of goodwill, Germany was prepared immediately to conclude a "Bryan pact" with the United States, providing for arbitration.

As for German peace terms, they would be distinctly on the moderate side. Berlin had advised its ambassador that no part of Belgium was to be annexed. On his own Bernstorff had mentioned his belief that the Central Powers would want to create an independent Poland and Lithuania and that they would ask Serbia to cede only a narrow strip as a direct connection between Austria and Bulgaria, to open an unimpeded route from Berlin to Constantinople—something that House had always anticipated.

Nor did the Germans object to mutual restoration and indemnification, should Lloyd George propose such a thing. They might ask that Serbia and Montenegro be joined together under the Montenegrin dynasty, since the Serbian dynasty was thoroughly corrupt and stood in bad odor. "In my view," House added, "this is the most important communication we have received since the war began, and it provides a real basis for negotiations and peace."[184]

It will be seen that Bernstorff, contrary to his instructions, *had* discussed concrete peace terms with the American, scoring an excellent impression. House was so surprised that he asked Bernstorff to check whether the notes he had made during the discussion were accurate. Yet there can be no doubt— and this is confirmed in further correspondence—that House misunderstood the German. He took German agreement to the arbitration and league of nations issues to mean that the question of peace was to be submitted to arbitration at once or that as an alternative Wilson was to submit proposals for a conference promptly, to which Germany agreed in advance.[185]

On January 18 House wrote the president that on all the previous visits he had paid to Germany the Kaiser and his political advisers had more or less rejected the ideas of disarmament and a league of nations. A radical change of mind must now have occurred in Germany. Apparently the government was now entirely in liberal hands and its demeanor was as progressive as in any of the democracies. The Germans must now be taken at their word and peace made at once. "They agree with virtually everything that liberal public opinion in the democratic countries has demanded."

So enthusiastic was House that he proposed wiring the important news to London directly. He was even willing to go there in person.[186] After some initial doubts, Wilson eagerly entered into these plans. House was to draft appropriate telegrams to Balfour and Lloyd George at once but not to dispatch them until he had new and more definite assurances from Bernstorff. Since late December, moreover, Wilson had been planning to address the Senate on the issue of peace. He now wanted to get on with this and see what the effect would be.

All this seemed to open up highly favorable opportunities for German policy; and Bernstorff lost no time in reporting to Berlin—probably to the great surprise of the foreign ministry—that according to Colonel House Wilson regarded the message Bernstorff had been charged with delivering as "extremely valuable." It was quite certain, he said, that at the moment the president had no thought other than to make peace and that he would pursue this purpose with the utmost vigor and by every means available.187

This was certainly true. But great was House's chagrin when the ambassador, on inquiry, had to advise him on January 18 that the German government had given approval in advance only for Wilson's proposals to secure world peace *after* the war. These proposals were then to be debated at a general world conference. First, however, the war must be brought to an end by a conference of the belligerents, i.e., without American participation; and when House inquired whether the proposed Bryan pact was to apply to U-boat warfare, Bernstorff could, of course, only reply in the negative. Operations could not be broken off while a court of arbitration looked into the matter.

In this same letter of January 20, Bernstorff conveyed the distressing news that the sharp Allied response to Wilson's peace proposals had upset the situation in Berlin, where extremists were now again holding the upper hand. He was afraid his government might see itself forced to adopt "stern measures." It was unlikely that further communications on peace terms could be extracted from Berlin at present. Understandably, Colonel House was furious at this example of what he called German unreliability and "slipperiness"; but as will be shown, neither he nor Wilson on that account gave up their peace efforts.188

Bernstorff himself was in a mortal predicament. On January 19 he had been advised by Berlin that unrestricted U-boat warfare would commence on February 1 off the coasts of Britain and France. At the same time he was strictly enjoined to pass on this information to the American government only on January 31. He was asked to offer proposals as to what might be done by way of grace periods for neutral vessels or free passage for American liners bearing special identification marks, etc., to delay a break with America at least. He was also notified, however, that Germany was prepared to risk such a break, if necessary. What a dilemma for the ambassador! Unless he wanted to risk aggravating the situation, he could not break off his confidential talks with Colonel House; but if he continued them, he would appear as a hypocrite as soon as he made the bad news known.

On January 19 Bernstorff urgently asked Berlin at least to postpone the February 1 deadline for a month, to allow sufficient grace for Americans then on the high seas and to avoid thwarting Wilson's mediation effort, now at the climactic stage. Washington was bound to react to the announcement of intensified U-boat warfare on the very eve of its launching as though it were a declaration of war. On January 23, following Wilson's message to the Senate, he reported that the president had again urgently requested through Colonel House that the German peace terms be made known, publicly or confidentially. He, Wilson, would then immediately propose a peace conference, confident as before that it would indeed eventuate.[189]

This was directly after Wilson's famous Senate message of January 22, the president's second major effort to quench the great conflagration. He had been carefully preparing it since late December, leaving Lansing out of the picture, because he knew that Lansing would object. House, on the other hand, was a close participant. Wilson aimed at proclaiming his own peace ideals not merely to the governments but to the peoples of the world, and the message was wired to all American missions in advance, with a directive to give it the widest publicity. As the first in a series of similar statements during the ensuing years, this message has taken on special significance, and in some measure it anticipated the Fourteen Points of January 18, 1918. There was the unmistakable aim of convincing the powers that they had been wrong in rejecting the idea of a peace conference on January 10, of encouraging the Germans thereby to take part in peace talks, and of appealing to the world-wide longing for peace.[190]

All this was done in a very cautious way, however, and was capable of more than one interpretation. Wilson's style was reminiscent of a professorial prophet; i.e., he preached his ideals in very dogmatic terms, scrupulously avoiding any concrete demands that might have appeared as an unwarranted interference in European territorial controversies. This would have only further alienated the Allies and brought a new rebuff from Germany. Wilson, furthermore, knew full well that he lacked the military power to impose himself in the role of arbitrator.

The nub of Wilson's proposal was an idea that found instant and enthusiastic liberal approval throughout the world. He proclaimed that peace could endure only if all nations thought it just and reasonable rather than oppressive and rapacious. Peace must signify understanding, not force and power—it must be a "peace without victory." To the victory-bent Entente governments as well as to German nationalists this particular formulation came as a considerable shock. Wilson clung to it tenaciously, despite all the efforts of his advisers to eliminate it or water it down; and it established the fame of his message, which became anathema to militarists everywhere.

The other important principle enunciated in the message was self-determination, extended to domestic politics as well as foreign affairs. The Monroe Doctrine was to embrace all the nations of the world, large and small, but self-government too was to be introduced everywhere. There was approval for these noble principles in Britain; but there were also wry remarks that it was all very well for the president to make speeches, leaving it to the Allies to shed their blood for those principles. The ideals of humanity must be held high, wrote Lord Bryce, but how could one negotiate on them with a government waging inhumane warfare and trampling international law underfoot? There was a reluctance to treat the German enemy on a basis of equality. He continued to be viewed as a "war criminal" who must be punished.

Wilson nevertheless stuck to his guns—his faith that he could bring about a negotiated peace, if only the Germans showed themselves to be "reasonable"; but in the circumstances was this not a mere illusion? Some Germans were certainly pleased to learn that the only kind of peace Wilson would acknowledge as just was a "peace among equals," one that would reject vengeance and punishment. Regrettably, much of German public opinion failed altogether to grasp this central thought of Wilson's message but waxed indignant that he started out by comparing German reluctance to specify peace terms unfavorably with Entente willingness to do so. In a roundabout way, moreover, Wilson seemed to demand that Germany forego Alsace-Lorraine and that all Polish-speaking areas should be merged into a new and "independent" state of Poland.[191]

On that account Wilson's dictum about "peace without victory" was not taken seriously. Yet would German approval of Wilson's statement have changed the Entente rejection of peace talks in any way? Present-day American historians seem virtually agreed that the Germans here missed a major chance of saving themselves and attaining, with American help, the negotiated peace they so ardently desired. But even apart from the question of what such a peace would have been like, whether the German borders it specified in east and west would have materially differed from the terms put forward on January 10, 1917, and ultimately the dictated terms of Versailles, can anyone seriously believe that a speech by Wilson could have swerved the Allies from their iron determination first thoroughly to destroy "Prussian militarism"?

Wilson's most recent biographer, A. S. Link, thinks he has proved, from a study of British and American negotiations over war finances and needs, that without American aid the Western powers of Europe would have been unable to win the war, indeed that they would have scarcely been able to continue it beyond the spring of 1917 against America's will. If that were true, the president held immense power indeed; but was he not, on his part, also much dependent on good relations with the Western powers, in a psychological as well as an economic sense?

In October 1916 the British Foreign Office, on the basis of a thorough analysis of the situation, concluded that America could not risk a break with Britain and the British Empire without ruining its economy.[192] How far would Germany have had to go, what concessions would it have had to be prepared to make, to persuade Wilson to apply his strongest means of pressure on the Allies, the open threat of a break? It should be borne in mind that this could have been only a diplomatic break and on no account a declaration of war. It seems to us unjustifiable to blame only the obstinacy of the German government for the failure of the American peace initiative.

One thing is certain. Had America remained neutral, a military victory by the Entente would have been virtually impossible.[193] Except for the continuing hope that American aid would bring victory in the end, the Allied will to continue the war, especially in France and Italy, would have almost certainly flagged in the wake of the swift failure of the great Anglo-French offensive of the spring of 1917 (which Hindenburg and Ludendorff had so greatly feared), and the complete collapse of Russian fighting power with the March revolution. The great German chance of success lay in waiting out this paralysis, until then carefully avoiding anything that might bring America into the war and to this end, even at the cost of every possible concession, encouraging Wilson's hopes to score a great success as a peace mediator. This chance went aglimmering because of the hapless decision of January 9 and the stubborn German adherence to it.

The main reason was Ludendorff's iron will. The foreign ministry was not unreceptive to Bernstorff's warnings and exhortations. Nor was Zimmermann altogether unsuccessful in dickering with Holtzendorff about a period of grace for neutral merchantmen.[194] He also had to contend with very grave reservations on the part of Germany's Austrian ally. On January 12 Czernin said that the German government would be saddled with a fearful responsibility if the anticipated swift success did not eventuate or were delayed. A failure would hit Austria equally with Germany.

Ambassador Prince Hohenlohe showing himself too easily impressed by the German arguments, Czernin dispatched a special emissary, Baron Flotow, to Berlin for talks; and Zimmermann had to promise that the Vienna government would receive another hearing before the final decision were taken. In fact, it had already been taken at this time! Behind this hullabaloo was Emperor Charles's grave concern and sharp criticism of the German procedure. He was convinced Zimmermann was utterly wrong in expecting that Wilson, disappointed with the Entente response, would in the end remain neutral. If the president's friendly sentiments for Britain had really cooled, the last thing to do was to drive him back into Allied arms by virtue of the U-boat question! The emperor set a date of January 20 and insisted he should personally receive a representative of the German navy as well as the Austrian admiral Haus, rather than being simply passed over.

But all Flotow was able to bring back from Berlin were the military counterarguments with which we are already familiar—relating mainly to the great enemy offensive that threatened in the spring—together with Zimmermann's vastly optimistic predictions about the attitude of the neutral powers, especially America. He was assured that Germany would be able to establish no fewer than fifteen U-boat stations against Britain. Not even one ship could conceivably get through. As for naval traffic in the Channel, it was of no great importance, on account of the inadequacies of the French railway system! There would be such an effect of terror, moreover, that neutral vessels would scarcely venture out to sea any longer.

All this was meant to reassure the Austrians. Afterward Zimmermann admitted to them that he too had spent many sleepless nights over the matter. There was no positive assurance of success, he said. "Show me the way toward an acceptable peace, and I shall be the first to reject U-boat warfare. As things stand today, I and many others have already almost reached that point."

On January 20 Zimmermann appeared in Vienna, accompanied by Holtzendorff, to confer with Emperor Charles, Grand Admiral Haus, Czernin, and Tisza. The only news brought out at this crown council was that the German government had long since taken its decision. Haus was the only one on whom Holtzendorff's very optimistic report of the naval chances of success made any impression—Holtzendorff had inflated the number of available U-boats to 120! The Austrian admiral gave his unconditional approval.

Tisza and the Austrian politicians remained highly skeptical. They were surprised and incredulous that the OHL should suddenly be so pessimistic about the impending enemy spring offensive, but they were unable to change the German decision. The question now arose whether Austria should disassociate itself from the German plan or on its part launch unrestricted U-boat warfare in the Mediterranean. Czernin, with extreme reluctance, concluded that Austria could not avoid cooperating. Otherwise there would be an open split in the ranks of the Central Powers which was bound to become widely known; and the creation of a zone of greater security in the Mediterranean would endanger the success of the German U-boats.

Such a decision was indeed taken by the joint cabinet on January 22, with Emperor Charles presiding, after General Conrad and War Minister Krobatin had supported the proposal and confirmed the military apprehensions of the German OHL. It was done over the most serious political reservations, voiced especially by Tisza.[195] The decision was taken without the slightest enthusiasm or confidence in victory.

Bethmann Hollweg had encountered a similar mood of depression when he made the changed situation known to the foreign affairs committee of the federal council on January 16. He cited the arguments of the OHL and the naval high command, especially the need for cutting enemy supplies of guns and ammunition; but he made it plain enough that he had yielded to military pressure and the Kaiser's decision only with a heavy heart. As expected,

Weizsäcker, the prime minister of Württemberg, was most vocal in bringing out the doubts and reservations of the federal states.

First of all, in marked contrast to the uncertain calculations and statistics of the navy, Weizsäcker established the fact that even then there were no more than eighteen large U-boats available for action against Britain at one time. "It is on these eighteen U-boats, in other words," he said, "that the fate of Germany will depend." Would it really pay off to arouse opinion against Germany throughout the world, for the sake of 200,000 additional tons of shipping sunk per month? Would not Britain be able to make up for these losses by new construction? America, after all, had already doubled its tonnage during the war. It used to be said that the British would not buckle even if they lost 600,000 tons per month. Had this suddenly changed? Might not the navy be wrong? And what weight should be given to the political views of the OHL, which had been so grossly deceived in the matter of the Polish manifesto and then had done such harm with the deportations of Belgian workers?

"How shall we achieve peace at all," Weizsäcker said, "even if Britain were to acknowledge that its people did not have enough to eat? What is the basis on which we are to construct a durable peace, when through our U-boat campaign we send the whole world to rally round the British flag? " Did anyone really believe the OHL contention that morale in the trenches would be raised by the knowledge that America too was now in the enemy camp? True, among the people at home the great campaign might initially find support. But what if it did not succeed? Would not those who shouted loudest for unrestricted U-boat warfare slink away, indeed, be the first to reproach the government?

No one could have been blunter and more plain-spoken in his criticism than Weizsäcker. Evidently he registered a strong impression with the committee, especially its chairman, Count Hertling. Bethmann Hollweg's lame counterarguments did not carry the ring of conviction. Weizsäcker had said, among other things, that even if only the present fronts were held, a modest peace might in the end be won. The Chancellor replied that the OHL was not sure that the front could be held stable without U-boat warfare. "If army and navy insist that it must be so, who are we to say them nay? " This was his main argument, and it is typical of the situation that the whole committee, including Weizsäcker, dared not reject it and were in the end ready to reconcile themselves to the decision already taken. Even the federal council was not equal to the task of standing up to the military in wartime.[196]

On January 15 Bethmann Hollweg also confidentially informed the Prussian cabinet and several party leaders in the Reichstag. He told the ministers why he had decided not to resign at this time, a decision they approved. They agreed that his policy reversal was necessary, but they had little faith in the

new course. Recording his confidential talks with the party leaders, Bethmann Hollweg himself wrote that the "national-liberal and conservative loud-
mouths" were ecstatic, though Bassermann had been very apprehensive of the
danger of war with America. The democrats were ready to go along, and so
were the social democrats, though they were badly shaken. "They emphasized that they could do so only if I did not resign"—which was precisely
what Bethmann Hollweg had expected.[197]

When he made these notes, he was looking for still another peace effort by
Wilson, and this was indeed forthcoming. We have already heard of Bernstorff's dispatch of January 23,[198] in which he reported that Wilson continued to insist on a peace conference, which he was confident of being able to
bring about, if only the German peace terms were communicated to him. The
ambassador added that he saw no reason why this could not be done. To
avoid exciting German public opinion about their modesty, the German government might state that they had in the meantime been rendered obsolete
by the gruff Allied reply.

Three days later Bernstorff urgently requested that all further war measures be suspended at once, and on January 27 he supplemented this with the
news that Wilson, through Colonel House, had the day before officially offered to undertake an immediate confidential mediation effort with the Entente powers on the basis of his Senate message and without getting into
territorial questions, provided he was told the German peace terms—and not
on a confidential basis. In transmitting this offer, House had spoken of the
"impossible" peace terms of Germany's enemies, adding that since the Allies
had openly named their peace terms and the president had developed his own
program in direct conflict with them, Germany was under a moral obligation
to make its terms known, since otherwise it would appear to be insincere in
its peaceful intentions. Bethmann Hollweg had after all already let it be
known that Germany was putting forward a very moderate peace program
and was also prepared to consider taking part in a second peace conference,
to deal with a league of nations, freedom of the seas, and disarmament. Hence
Wilson hoped that his Senate message was in accordance with German wishes.
He would be particularly gratified if Germany were to issue an immediate
declaration that it was prepared to negotiate on the basis of his Senate message. He asked the Germans to trust him and expressed confidence in his
ability to organize both conferences—the peace conference proper and the
subsequent conference to insure that peace would endure. He thought it
could be done speedily enough to avoid needless bloodshed in a spring offensive. The Allied rejection of his peace note was mere bluff and need not be
considered seriously, in Wilson's view.

This was indeed exciting news. Unfortunately it was riddled with illusions.
The Entente reply was in no sense a "bluff," and there was no conceivable
German peace program that could have been reconciled with the publicly

proclaimed Allied peace terms, most of which represented treaty commitments. Germany's enemies, moreover, had made it plain more than once that they would in no circumstances sit down at the same table with an unvanquished Germany. It is hard to imagine that Wilson overlooked all this. What, then, was behind Bernstorff's dispatch?

His discussion with House was based on a letter by the president of January 24, in which Wilson had indeed told the colonel that "if Germany really wants peace, it can have it, quite soon too, if only it is willing to trust me and give me a chance." Bernstorff's last statements to House, however, had not been helpful. "It seems to me you might do well to talk to Bernstorff again. Tell him that this is the moment to do something, if those people [in Berlin] really and truly want peace; that the signs reaching us are such as to make us believe I might bring things about, with the help of a reasonable suggestion from their side." Otherwise, in view of the preparations Germany was evidently making for unrestricted attack on merchant ships, there was grave danger of a break in diplomatic relations between Germany and the United States. Yet neither here nor there was there hostility or resentment. "Do they really want my help? I have a right to know it, since I have a sincere desire to help and have now put myself into a position where I can do so without favoring either one side or the other."[199]

Wilson's request to House was, in other words, along familiar lines. The colonel was to make one more effort to persuade the Germans to accept Wilson as peace mediator and to that end supply him with "reasonable" proposals. House carried out the mission but apparently also added some views of his own. His communication, at any rate, mentioned neither "bluff" nor "impossible peace terms" on the part of the Allies, nor did they say that Wilson would refrain from interfering in controversial territorial questions. They did not speak of two separate peace conferences, nor of the Senate message as the basis for a new mediation effort, and most importantly they did not say that Germany should make its peace terms public.

How much of all this was House's own idea and how much stemmed from prior discussion with the president or from misunderstandings or exaggerations on the part of Bernstorff is impossible to tell with any precision, for the accounts of the two participants in the talk differ. According to House, the ambassador was deeply depressed over the OHL's political preponderance and the new U-boat offensive he hinted might impend "in the spring." Colonel House proposed that Germany at once provide Wilson "something definitive to work with." He suggested that the Germans should declare themselves ready to evacuate France and Belgium completely and to agree to mutual reconstruction, reparations, and indemnities. The ambassador had shrunk from the second of these demands—which he himself had said was acceptable as recently as January 15.

The colonel told Bernstorff that Wilson wanted to lay hold of something with which he might mobilize public opinion in the Allied countries, in order to force their governments to discuss the peace question. In an apparent effort at evasion Bernstorff remarked that the president's Senate message had made a good impression on German public opinion, especially what he had to say about freedom of the seas. After extended discussion agreement was reached, on Bernstorff's rather than House's suggestion, that the ambassador was to wire Berlin the next day, saying that the president would like to know Germany's final peace terms. If these were moderate, there was reason to believe that something could be done in the direction of bringing about an early peace.200 Let Bernstorff propose complete evacuation of France and Belgium to the German foreign ministry. In addition he should suggest that the German government declare its willingness to send representatives to a peace conference based on Wilson's Senate message.

According to House, Bernstorff added on his own the thought that the Chancellor, for his own protection, might find it necessary to make public the German peace terms in the form of a message to the president, in reply to the president's request. Such a definitive formulation would serve to calm down German public opinion much more effectively than a confidential communication. As House told Wilson, the fact that the president had asked Germany for its peace terms and had received them would facilitate his negotiations with the Allies; and since Bernstorff wanted it that way, he thought it best to let things run their course, i.e., to forego passing on the German peace terms to the Allies, initially in confidence. Whatever happened, the president was bound to figure as the originator of the whole effort.

There can be little doubt that House's account, written directly after the discussion, is trustworthy. It is not necessarily complete, however, and we may assume that House, on his own initiative but surely in keeping with the president's intent, added elements not specifically included in his instructions, notably the derogatory estimate of the Allied note of January 10 as mere bluff, which would have been very characteristic of Wilson's views. What Bernstorff did not mention in his dispatch were the demands that Belgium and France be evacuated and that "mutual" reparations were to be agreed on, the latter probably because he did not want to lead the German foreign ministry up the garden path. He also suppressed the fact that the demand for publication of the peace terms went back to his own proposal and was indeed opposed to the president's original intent.

Bernstorff's dispatch naturally threw the Berlin government into great confusion. If it were to consider Wilson's proposals, it would have to decide to cancel or suspend the U-boat offensive long since decided upon; but for just how long would it be delayed? Bernstorff counted on Wilson's plans quickly coming a cropper because of the obstinacy of Germany's enemies. In that case there need not be a long delay, and Germany would enjoy the immense advantage of appearing as the moderate and peaceful side, in contrast to the others, which would at the very least make it much more difficult for Wilson to enter the war against Germany solely on the grounds of the U-boat issue.

The reason why Bernstorff wanted to see moderate German peace terms made public was in the main his certainty that they would help dispel malicious rumors circulating abroad concerning German plans for conquest and world dominion—as he had seen in his talk with Colonel House on January 15. In the long run such publicity would create great difficulties for the war policies of the enemy powers; and as a diplomat posted abroad, Bernstorff probably thought this advantage would outweigh the lamentations of the nationalists at home.

But what if the enemy powers did consider Wilson's proposal, then rejected the German peace terms as insolent and arrogant, and dragged out negotiations forever? In that event, the U-boat campaign would come too late to bring the expected result. Since the ambassador even so had no faith in the success of the U-boat weapon, this prospect deterred him no more than did the great difficulties a peace conference would undoubtedly bring. The main thing was to get a conference, any conference, going. The enemy would not find it easy to pull out, once such a conference had started; and in his dispatch Bernstorff admitted that in his view Germany could in any event gain a better peace at the conference table than if the United States with its formidable resources joined the enemy camp.

On the other side, what would be the effect if Germany refused to consider the proposals and at once launched into U-boat warfare? Bernstorff correctly predicted that this would be considered a slap in the president's face and inevitably bring on war with the United States. At the time Secretary of State Lansing made an entry in his diary that was highly characteristic of anti-German sentiment in America:

> If our people only realized the insatiable greed of these German autocrats in Berlin and their sinister plans for world dominion, we would be already at war. . . . Sooner or later the die will be cast. . . . War is certain to come, but we must wait patiently for the Germans to do something that will cause general indignation and clearly show all Americans the dangers of a German victory. When that time comes, it will be on account of some German stupidity. . . . I hope these German fools will soon blunder into it, for without a doubt the Allies in the west are having a hard time of it, while Russia is making no progress, despite its masses.[201]

At the very time these lines were being written, Bethmann Hollweg and his staff were pondering how Bernstorff's telegram, which had arrived in Berlin at

4:15 P.M. on January 28, should be answered. Within three hours a first draft, making the German peace terms known to Wilson, was wired to Pless, and Grünau was ordered to discuss it with the Kaiser and the OHL.202 The Chancellor asked Helfferich to call on him at 10 P.M., and the interior minister found him in a state of unprecedented agitation. According to Helfferich's notes, Bethmann Hollweg had once again regained hope that war with America might be avoided and indeed that peace might even be within sight.

The latter, to be sure, can have been no more than a faint glimmer. Bethmann Hollweg could not possibly have counted on any willingness of Germany's enemies to enter into peace negotiations; and by his own subsequent testimony he was quite disinclined to entrust the fate of Germany willy-nilly to Wilson's hopes and hands.203 To make it difficult for the president to declare war on Germany, as Bernstorff suggested, was quite another matter. Germany risked nothing by gratefully and eagerly accepting his offer and thus meeting his desire and ambition to act as a peace mediator. It was quite safe to treat him as a special confidant and let him know the German peace terms, in as moderate a form as possible.

It was indeed along such lines that the Chancellor drafted his reply, including a carefully formulated list of German peace terms. Unfortunately, in the final version the message lost much of its value by declaring that it was meant exclusively for the president's own eyes. The peace terms, moreover, were stated to be only those on the basis of which Germany would have been prepared to enter into peace negotiations, had its enemies accepted the German peace offer of December 12, 1916. It had to be concluded, therefore, that they were now obsolete. It was also expressly stated that the German government by no means regarded the Entente reply of January 10 as a piece of bluff. The peace terms made public on that occasion were entirely in accordance with treaties concluded among the Allies, and as long as they were publicly upheld, publication of the modest German "shopping list" would be unacceptable to the Germans, since it would suggest a measure of weakness that did not in fact exist and therefore would merely serve to prolong the war.

The president was thus deprived of virtually any chance of influencing Germany's enemies in the direction of a negotiated peace; and German assurances that his offer was being gratefully accepted were bound to sound like the merest hypocrisy. It is not immediately discernible how this wretched compromise came into being. It does seem as though the Chancellor initially intended to afford Wilson a real chance for carrying out his peace effort. As late as the night of January 28-29 he traveled to Pless in the company of Zimmermann, in order to gain a temporary postponement of the U-boat offensive.

According to his own report, the admirals there told him categorically that delay was impossible, since a large number of the U-boats had already been dispatched and could not be reached for the moment. This does not seem very plausible. If there were indeed technical communication difficulties, surely this should have at worst resulted in only a handful of additional "incidents"; but it is possible that the OHL opposed the catalog of peace terms to be made known to the enemy, agreeing to it only if it were designated as "already obsolete."

We do not know the details; but the fact is that the Chancellor was unable to prevail with his postponement plans against the military men who were already champing at the bit over the great event.[204] In the end some phrases were added to the telegram to Bernstorff: Unfortunately it was too late, for technical reasons, to arrest the unrestricted U-boat warfare Germany's enemies had compelled it to launch; but Germany stood ready at all times to take America's needs into account to the fullest extent possible and would cease the U-boat campaign as soon as there were firm assurance that the president's efforts would lead to a peace acceptable to Germany.

A more misguided compromise could scarcely have been imagined. The hapless ambassador's quandary was unenviable, when he had to deliver this message on the afternoon of January 31, together with a declaration that unlimited U-boat warfare would begin the next day. One hand proffering the olive branch, the other, so to speak, brandishing a loaded torpedo tube, he had to face Lansing, who must have secretly rejoiced. Those clumsy German fools had really blundered right into it! Here at last was cause for general indignation over the German hypocrites and brutal militarists—the very occasion Lansing needed to push through American entry into the war for the purpose of "saving the freedom of the world."

It was August 1914 all over again. The impatient soldiers and their "technical difficulties" had once more done an expert job of fouling up the work of diplomacy; and the new phase into which the war was entering was proclaimed in terms as unfortunate as the wording of the war declarations against Russia and France.

Not even in Germany, however, was the proclamation received with anything like the general enthusiasm that might have been expected after the years of U-boat propaganda. Even Tirpitz, leader of the campaign, had begun to waver. Characteristically, he told Count Westarp in February—deeply shocking Westarp, by the way—that he feared the time for a successful U-boat campaign was already past. The statement was no doubt meant to provide the infallible prophet with an alibi, should the campaign fail;[205] and of course Tirpitz voiced such sentiments only to his intimates. In public his posture was one of supreme confidence, which was indeed the general attitude in Germany.

Viewed as a distant possibility, the U-boat campaign had seemed a tempting goal, but among those who had to share in the political responsibility it roused feelings of anxiety, now that it was upon them. A spirit of gravity and even depression rather than elation hovered over the federal council when it was advised of the new phase of the war on the morning of January 31, and this was true also of the Reichstag main committee, which assembled in the afternoon and discussed the issue for two whole days.

The new German challenge met with vigorous approval from the right, but the left was worried and critical, the South German democrat von Payer voicing qualms not unlike those put forward earlier in the federal council committee by that other South German, von Weizsäcker. Even sharper criticism of the admiralty staff calculations was expressed by the social democrats Ledebour, David, and Hoch; nor was there any lack of complaints that the Reichstag was once again confronted with a fait accompli.

Speaking for the government, Zimmermann and Capelle outdid each other in optimistic statements about the prospects for the U-boat campaign, [206] and even Helfferich surprised everyone by taking a view diametrically opposite to his earlier statistical calculations concerning Britain's economic situation, which he now interpreted in favor of the campaign rather than against it. The decision having been taken, he felt himself obliged to throw the weight of his economic expertise on the side of reassuring the German people.[207]

Capelle once again went so far as to insist that the effect of American entry into the war would be "zero"! American troops would not even be able to cross the ocean for lack of transport. Bethmann Hollweg did not find it easy to put a dignified face on his enforced switch, but even he was carried away into a rather extravagant final phrase: "We must, therefore we can! " He reiterated his earlier opposition to any "policy of desperation," but in point of fact what he now called necessity *was* desperation.

The Chancellor, however, had skillfully laid the groundwork in his discussions with the party leaders, and in the end all the parties refrained from offering open opposition to the new situation—the German note was actually handed to Ambassador Gerard while this session was going on! A small circle of Reichstag deputies and the leading members of the federal council were confidentially apprised as well of the peace terms Germany had sent to Washington.

This was the first official enumeration of peace terms to come to the knowledge of the Reichstag, and naturally a lively debate ensued. The right predictably said that too little was being asked, the left too much; but after several drafts the list had been shrewdly and cautiously concocted to rub neither Germans nor Americans the wrong way—such at least was the intention. It was unavoidably based on the agreement reached with the OHL early in November, and the peace terms of Germany's allies were merely stated to be "within moderate limits." Such questions as annexations, border rectifications, financial indemnities, colonies, and the future of Belgium were mentioned in such vague and general terms that the government retained, in effect, a completely free hand. It could move toward a peace of conquest or one of appeasement.[208]

Demands for freedom of the seas and a peace without barriers to trade were no more overlooked than a statement of German readiness to participate in Wilson's pet scheme, an international conference to establish world security on the basis of his Senate message; and as already shown, the whole peace program was tied to the German initiative of December 12, thus forfeiting its binding character and taking the wind out of the sails of the annexationists. Among the social democrats this could not but awaken the suspicion that Bethmann Hollweg, despite his earlier denials, was actually pursuing annexationist goals; but in the course of the debate it developed that at least the right wing of the social democrats, led by David and Südekum, was willing to acknowledge a distinction between "border rectifications" and "annexations." David was even willing to accept a "duchy of Courland."[209]

Thus Bethmann Hollweg, despite everything, had managed successfully to navigate the parliamentary shoals without losing his followers on the left; but how long would he now be able to retain their trust, with the preponderance of the military within the government so plainly visible?

The sincerity of Wilson's pacifist convictions is shown by the fact that even after the German note had been transmitted he needed another full two months to reach the decision to declare war on Germany. The sudden collapse of his hopes for peace came as a heavy blow to him. He told his friend House that he felt as though the world had suddenly begun to turn from east to west rather than from west to east, making everything topple.[210] He was at one with House and Lansing that the only dignified answer to the German challenge—which he felt indeed to be a "slap in the face"—was to break off diplomatic relations at once. In the *Sussex* note he had virtually committed himself to such a course.

Bernstorff was handed his passport on February 3, and Gerard was simultaneously recalled from Berlin; but Wilson, in his puritan obstinacy and idealism, clung for many weeks to the hope that war was still avoidable, despite the diplomatic rupture. Only four days after the German ambassador had been given his papers, the president was drafting a new plan for the organization of enduring peace. Lansing, to whom it was submitted for review, found it quite unrealistic.[211] Wilson hoped that the diplomatic break would bring the Germans to their senses at the last moment—they were mad and must be curbed! But when this result failed to materialize, and a message to the Congress threatening war if American ships and lives came to harm did no

better, he tried to give another turn to the diplomatic screw by inviting the
neutral powers to break off relations with Germany on their part. Except for
China, none of them followed him.

Not altogether unsuccessful was an effort on another front, an attempt to
drive a diplomatic wedge into the Austro-German alliance and persuade
Vienna to exert pressure on Germany. Count Czernin had sent the Austrian
declaration of unrestricted U-boat warfare to Washington in step with Zimmermann's note; but Wilson refrained from making the Austrian note public
and did *not* break off relations. There was, as a matter of fact, a newly
appointed Austrian ambassador in Washington, Count Adam Tarnowski von
Tarnow, who had not yet been formally introduced at the White House. On
February 5 Tarnowski was able to report to his minister that Lansing had
confirmed the president's reticence, coupling it with the hope that the Austrian U-boat note might be softened, apparently in the direction of not sinking any ships without prior warning. Czernin immediately expressed his warm
appreciation and implored Wilson to persuade the Entente powers to "follow
the Central Powers" in accepting the idea of peace without victory, as expressed in the president's Senate message—in other words, relinquishing their
proclaimed peace terms. These, he said, clearly threatened to break up the
Hapsburg Empire, and this Austria could never accept. For technical (note
well, not political) reasons, the U-boat campaign could not be modified—but
after all, if Wilson succeeded in making peace, that element would no longer
exist.

This message was communicated to Berlin only after it had been sent,
Czernin commenting naively that the Germans, after all, had agreed to halt
the U-boat campaign if Wilson could guarantee a peace conference! This was
certainly twisting matters a bit, for what the German note had really said was
that first there must be full assurance of an acceptable peace. There was a
hint in all this that the Austrians on their part might settle for less. Czernin
also suggested to Berlin that keeping the Austrian ambassador in Washington
might be useful to both the Central Powers, since he might encourage Wilson
to continue his peace efforts.

This was precisely the kind of diplomatic influence the president had
hoped Vienna would exert on Berlin. Berlin, however, became suspicious
immediately. Zimmermann said that Czernin's note misinterpreted German
willingness, adding that Germany had never accepted the idea of a peace
without victors and vanquished and could push through even its moderate
demands only if it were the winner. Austria's overfriendly attitude would
merely lead Washington to make a distinction between the two allies. "Wilson
is obviously out to make military difficulties for us. As a mediator he would
throw his whole weight in the balance against us." Czernin replied, reasonably
enough, that his conciliatory attitude forfeited nothing, and might serve to

deepen the differences between Wilson and the Entente powers and possibly keep America neutral.[212]

The German response to Vienna was curt and sharp. For Germany Wilson was no longer acceptable as a mediator. As it turned out, however, the Austrian minister's flexible attitude was the more successful. As a result of his reply of February 5, Wilson at once confidentially inquired of Lloyd George through Ambassador Page whether the threat of dismembering Austria, contained in the Entente note of January 10, might not be withdrawn, at least for the older units of the Hapsburg Empire. He said, probably with Bohemia and Hungary in mind, that these already enjoyed a sufficient degree of autonomy to guarantee a stable peace in that part of Europe. The future world organization, moreover, was to guarantee Austria free access to the sea—this evidently meant Trieste; and Austria could be appeased without impinging too greatly on the legitimate interests of the Balkan states.

Wilson said he knew that both the "Teutonic powers" urgently wanted peace, most of all Austria, about whose wretched food situation and growing discouragement he was thoroughly informed through his ambassador. Lloyd George should realize that the threat of radical dismemberment of their empire had convinced the Austrians that they were fighting for survival. If that nightmare were lifted from them, peace might be attained in very short order—a peace in keeping with the principles announced by America, which the government of the United States would never cease to support with the utmost vigor, even should it become embroiled in the war itself.[213]

This inquiry must have caused Lloyd George no small embarrassment. It was the first time the president had intervened so unequivocally and deeply in the settlement of European territorial questions, and he was doing so at the most sensitive point. As we have already seen, there was no inclination as such in Britain to destroy the Hapsburg monarchy; but Britain's allies—Rumania, Serbia, Italy—were all the more greedy. Once the Austrian problem came up for serious discussion, Britain's binding commitments under the treaties of alliance dating back to September 1914 were bound to come to light, with an inevitable deterrent effect on Wilson.[214]

The British prime minister therefore replied in extremely cautious terms. He said he was fully aware of Austria's troubles, of Emperor Charles's urgent desire for peace and his fear that in the event of a German victory Austria might become a mere satellite. Britain entertained no real hostility toward Austria, which "had never desired the war" [sic]; and the British did not object to the emperor retaining Hungary and Bohemia, though their allies had to be taken into consideration, on account of the regions with Slavic, Rumanian, and Italian populations.

Most important of all, the time was not propitious for a special peace with Austria, for the Allies could not yet spare Italy. The blockade must not be

broken on the Austrian side; and since Austria was now nothing more than a
grave burden for Germany, this burden should not now be lifted from Germany's shoulders. It would be best if the president were to make discreet
inquiries what concessions Vienna was now in a position to offer. At the
proper time one might then revert to these possibilities. According to Page's
report of February 11, Lloyd George concluded with words of almost exaggerated appreciation for America's inestimable aid. It was the only truly
unselfish great power, motivated by idealism; and its high-minded president
was bound to play a major role in establishing a new world order.

Such praise could scarcely gloss over Wilson's disappointment at the failure
of his hopes that his peace efforts, foiled by Germany, might still succeed by
way of an Austrian detour. By February 20, however, Page reported that the
British prime minister had changed his mind, apparently under pressure from
the army and navy. He was now ready to receive a formal proposal for peace
negotiations from Austria, provided it were kept strictly secret from the
Germans. Only two days later the American envoy in Vienna, Frederic Court-
land Penfield, was instructed to hold confidential talks with Czernin. America, he was to say, had been authoritatively informed that the Allies had no
intention of severing Hungary and Bohemia from Austria, unless circumstances were changed by a continuation of the war. Binding assurances to that
effect could undoubtedly be secured if the Vienna government really wanted
peace promptly and were willing to accept American mediation. Absolute
secrecy, however, must be guaranteed.

Czernin responded with ardent assurances of his willingness in principle to
make peace. He was convinced, he said, that peace would ultimately eventuate through President Wilson's good offices and that the Entente governments
were surely working toward that end in Washington even now.[215] Yet the
memorandum he transmitted on February 27 still insisted that Austria could
not enter into peace negotiations without the knowledge of its allies. Austrian
integrity, moreover, would have to be guaranteed and anti-Austrian propaganda in neighboring countries, especially Serbia, stopped.

Penfield gained the impression that this was not Czernin's last word; and
on March 3 he was instructed to suggest to Czernin that Austria was unlikely
to receive such a favorable offer again, while the progress of the war might
very well soon end opportunities for American mediation. Czernin thereupon
redoubled his assurances of undying gratitude for so much goodwill. He held
no fewer than four separate sessions with Penfield. On March 13 he even
transmitted a written statement that he no longer believed that either of the
two embattled groups could achieve final victory, hence wished to see the
slaughter ended as soon as possible by a peace that would be honorable for
all. He said he was only too willing to talk peace and proposed that an Allied
representative be dispatched to a neutral country to meet a spokesman for

the Vienna government. These discussions, however, must deal with a general peace, not merely a separate peace with Austria.216

Washington noted this open-minded attitude with deep satisfaction. Lansing urgently advised that it be exploited, refusing to take Czernin's rejection of a separate peace seriously – the man had to give the appearance of complete loyalty to Germany, if only to avoid drawing the vengeance of this mighty ally, should the secret leak out. Surely he must be aware that none of the Entente powers would dream of discussing a general peace with Austria alone, which was in no position to implement any commitments it made, as far as Germany was concerned. If Czernin was nevertheless offering secret talks, it must be from ulterior motives. A separate peace might be rejected, but it could be discussed, all the same. Lansing proposed that Czernin be asked if he had any objections to the president passing on the proposal for a secret meeting to the Allied governments. This would be done in a way to give the impression that the initiative came from Washington.217

Wilson apparently did not take this advice. At any rate, there was no further reply to Czernin.218 Yet by mid-March negotiations were fully under way in deepest secrecy between the Austrian emperor and agents of the Western powers on the subject of a separate peace. Czernin knew about this, though only quite sketchily. We shall learn more of this in Part 1 of Chapter 10.

In order to retain American goodwill, Czernin sought a middle way in the U-boat question as well. On March 2 he handed Penfield a wordy memorandum in which he sought to trivialize the Austrian proclamation of unrestricted U-boat warfare. It said that ships would not really be sunk without prior warning, such warning having been now issued in a general way, namely to keep away from the naval war zone! Austrian U-boat action, moreover, was confined to the Adriatic and Mediterranean and thus posed no threat to American interests.

Although Washington did not accept this view, the memorandum was unexpectedly well-received. Highly pleased with this reaction, Czernin added confidential assurance on March 22 that Austria would not pursue the U-boat campaign very vigorously and would certainly never molest American vessels.219 Czernin indeed thought that the danger of war with America was now over, and on March 14 he proposed that Germany should, "accidentally on purpose," spare two armed American ships that were then en route to Britain, i.e., *not* torpedo them. This would square Wilson with American public opinion; and it was certain that thereafter no further American ships would sail!

Czernin represented this as a "spontaneous" suggestion from Penfield, though offered "in accordance with instructions," but evidently the whole thing was his own idea.220 German headquarters, of course, instantly rejected it. Holtzendorff said Wilson would be "playing fast and loose with the destiny of nations" if he made the question of war and peace dependent on whether Germany closed an eye to the passage of individual American ships. William II added mettlesomely: "Once for all, no more negotiations with America! If Wilson wants war, let him get on with it! "

By mid-March there was no further thought of negotiations with Germany even in America. True, early in February there had been an effort to see what might be done to avoid incidents involving American passenger ships. This was done through the intermediary of the Swiss embassy in Washington, which represented the German interest there; but the effort failed, because Zimmermann, Holtzendorff, and especially the Kaiser would have no part of it unless diplomatic relations were restored.[221] Nor was there by that time and indeed until mid-March any acute problem, for no American ships had been sunk. This was partly chance, partly a result of the grace period for neutral vessels. Initially too American shipping companies dared not allow their ships to sail. Precisely this, however, troubled the American government, not merely on account of the economic loss it occasioned, but because of the damage to American political prestige. Charges were heard in Britain that America was spinelessly bowing to the German blockade, its pusillanimity depriving the Allies of badly needed supplies.

Indeed, the president's passivity was widely – even in Germany – interpreted as a sign of weakness and indecision. Wilson was said to be nervous and depressed, at a loss how to extricate himself from the dilemma he had brought on himself. Lansing saw with much concern that the widespread indignation over the German challenge was gradually fading, with peaceful tendencies once more coming to the fore. The president's advisers vigorously pressed him to arm American ships. He resisted for a long time, sometimes even flying into a rage; but on February 26 he yielded at last and asked the Congress for authorization. The House of Representatives approved, but in the Senate a pacifist bloc prevented a vote.

After protracted consideration, the president decided to act without Senate authorization; and on March 12 Lansing announced that American merchant ships would be armed. The decision was made much easier for Wilson, by virtue of a propaganda coup scored by Britain and transmitted to the U.S. government on February 24, the famous "Zimmermann telegram." On February 19 Zimmermann had instructed the German ambassador in Mexico to offer the Mexican government a military alliance against the United States in the event that country declared war on Germany. This war alliance was to hold out the prospect of regaining Texas, New Mexico, and Arizona, a truly fantastic proposal!

The artfully coded telegram had fallen into the hands of the British secret service. It had been deciphered with the help of a key that had long been in the possession of the British Foreign Office. Its publication on March 1 naturally created a furor, the more so since the German foreign ministry had routed the directive through Bernstorff, using official American wire facilities generously placed at Germany's disposal for purposes of negotiating peace mediation.[222]

Thus war now loomed more and more closely. Wilson, however, was firmly resolved not to be swayed by passion or sentiment but to be governed solely by what he thought to be his sacred duty. From March 7 to 19 he completely secluded himself in his study,[223] refusing to listen to the confusion of counsel and dropping not the slightest hint to those around him as to how he would decide. Meanwhile sinkings by the Germans kept rising, and more and more Americans lost their lives at sea. Ultimately there were only the alternatives of foregoing trade with Europe, i.e., submission to Germany's will, or war. As Wilson convincingly explained to a group of senators, "armed neutrality" in the face of U-boat attack was impracticable unless America took to the offensive at the same time.[224]

It was in these weeks that the decision was taken to let America emerge from its traditional isolationism, enmeshing its policies irrevocably with the confused relationships of the Old World. It was a decision that was to have vast and historic consequences; and Wilson reached it only with the greatest reluctance, for he had identified himself completely with the historical traditions of his people. It is probably not too much to say that even a league of nations was, for him and many of his fellow countrymen, a kind of wishful dream that was to make the radical break easier—it was to keep America from becoming entangled in a welter of bloody power struggles, of the kind it had been hitherto spared in its "splendid isolation"; but for Wilson, it would seem, American entry into the war also meant the surrender of the dream he had cherished, to lead the world into a fairer future as peace mediator, prophet, and founder of a better order.

But this was not really true—he was in fact renouncing nothing. Apparently Wilson's crucial reflection during these weeks was that he would be relinquishing America's prestige as a neutral, standing aside, even in "armed neutrality," and allowing others to fight to the death to "save freedom," without stirring a hand himself. None of the belligerents would listen to his voice any longer, once it came to ending the bloody strife and negotiating peace. He would be viewed as an unworldly dreamer with his notions of disarmament and a league of nations. America would remain a backwater on the stage of history.

All his letters and his speeches before Congress indicate that this was ultimately the decisive factor. It was a matter of political self-assertion, the need for a great power to retain its reputation as such—the very same motives, in other words, which, as we have seen, drove the great powers of Europe into war in July 1914, one by one, and which always ultimately tip the balance in the field of grand policy.

It has often been charged in Germany that what really moved Wilson was economic considerations—concern for American capital invested in the war industries of the Western powers; but there was no room in Wilson's mind for such thoughts, nor was there any hint of them among his circle of advisers. It would have been a foolish calculation, in any event, for the American economy would have flourished much better had the country remained neutral. War has always been an immensely costly and uneconomic undertaking. The Entente was already in incalculable financial difficulties; and closer study shows that during the early months of American involvement in the war, the sudden and total conversion of the American economy and way of life to its ends caused utter havoc. Virtually without experience in war, lacking a trained and seasoned bureaucracy, Wilson's administration was at times threatened with complete chaos by his decision to go to war.[225]

Nor did Wilson embark on war from fear that Germany might defeat the Entente unless America came to its aid. Concern along such lines certainly played a part, but neither Wilson nor any of the Allied statesmen were then as worried about this aspect as Lansing. Even so, both Wilson and Lansing then reckoned with an American volunteer force of at most half a million men rather than the army of two millions that had been moved to the battlefields of Europe by 1918.

Neither London nor Paris nor even the White House was inclined to place a very high estimate on American military capacity, and on neither side of the Atlantic was there any certainty that American troops would actually see combat before the war was over. As for the exaggerated fears Lansing is known to have entertained that the expansionist German power drive might reach all the way to the American continent, they were not shared by Wilson—indeed, on occasion he expressly rejected them.

It would be wrong, lastly, to insist that only the unrestricted U-boat campaign drew America into the war. This is true only in that the ruthless destruction of American ships and lives was more eloquent than any other factor in demonstrating to the president that American prestige and national honor were at stake. Another aspect, of course, was that but for the U-boat campaign it would have been difficult, if not impossible, to overcome American neutralist, isolationist, and pacifist sentiment and gain the support of the American people for entry into the war.

Soon after war was declared Lansing noted in his diary: "We would have had to come to the aid of the Allies, even if Germany had not violated our rights so seriously; otherwise the Kaiser might have become Europe's overlord, and this country might have become the next victim of his greed." [226] This was certainly not Wilson's opinion. It is true that in 1919, under cross-examination before a Senate committee, he said he "believed" or "hoped" America would have gone to war to defend itself, even if there had been no German U-boat attacks; but that was an uncertain reply, given in retrospect and under pressure from such political enemies as Senator McCumber, and we must not make too much of it.[227] When he spoke these words, the war had long since become a pure crusade for freedom and justice to Wilson, just as Lansing had always seen and preached it. Wilson first developed these war aims in his speech before Congress on February 26, 1917. He repeated them on April 2, when, following a cabinet decision of March 20 that had swept away the last reservations, he presented the war declaration to Congress.

This congressional message has become known as one of his most famous oratorical achievements. There was no more mention in it of "peace without victory," only of the subjugation of Germany, which was represented as the enemy of mankind, trampling humanity underfoot. The war was to serve the ends of peace, was indeed the indispensable prerequisite to enduring peace. It was a war to end war! It was to set the nations, including the Germans, free of tyrannical power and injustice. "The world must be made safe for democracy"—these words were in the true Wilsonian spirit. They were also thoroughly in the American tradition and they served to gain Wilson the enthusiastic support of his people.

But were they not in the sharpest possible contrast to the ideas of give-and-take, of a peace of reason in place of one of blood and retribution, which the same Wilson had proclaimed in his Senate message on January 22? Could he be sure that his new "associates"—as he deliberately chose to call them in order not to be bound too strictly to the "alliance"—were animated by the same lofty ideals he preached? [228]

Not long before his famous speech before Congress Wilson received a visit from a journalist who knew him well, Cobb of the *New York World.* Cobb movingly reported[229] that he found the president more depressed than he had ever seen him before. The war declaration, Wilson said, meant that Germany would be beaten—beaten so severely that there would be a dictated peace, a peace of the victors. This was what the Allies wanted, and the way was now open to a goal America had fought and hoped to block.

At this moment Wilson was indeed a prophet gifted with clairvoyance.

# 9

# Militarization of the Economy

## Part 1
## The Auxiliary Labor Act
## of December 1916

IF BETHMANN HOLLWEG believed that the decision of January 9 to launch unrestricted U-boat warfare had ended his differences with the supreme army command (*Oberste Heeresleitung,* or OHL), he was badly mistaken. The very next day, at a private audience, Hindenburg roundly asked the Kaiser to dismiss him. The Chancellor had shown such lack of resolution that he, Hindenburg, could no longer work with him.

Thus in the field marshal's view it was far more important that the Chancellor enjoy the confidence of the OHL than that of the Kaiser. Perplexed rather than indignant, William II asked Valentini to talk to the generals. The cabinet chief did so, first in a private meeting with Hindenburg, who was quickly persuaded that at this juncture, on the eve of the new U-boat phase, a change in the chancellorship would have a most unfortunate effect at home and abroad and that the continual attacks on the Chancellor by the extreme nationalists were malicious; but on this occasion too Hindenburg, despite Valentini's best efforts, was reluctant to reach a decision without the concurrence of his quartermaster general, and Ludendorff would not give an inch. The OHL, he told Valentini, would not insist on a change at this time, but in the long run it did not believe it could work with either Bethmann Hollweg, Zimmermann, or Helfferich. During the ensuing weeks, the head of the Kaiser's civilian cabinet was inundated by the OHL with a veritable flood of warnings, exhortations, and implorations, all originating with conservative and Pan-German politicans and calling for Bethmann Hollweg's dismissal. One day Valentini told the Kaiser about it, adding quite deliberately that Hindenburg had proposed Tirpitz as the new Chancellor. The Kaiser promptly gave the two generals a piece of his mind, but Valentini succeeded only in provoking their open enmity.[1]

As long ago as November Ludendorff had announced to General von Stein that the campaign against the Chancellor was out in the open: "Bethmann Hollweg will never be able to bring peace. He'll have to go."[2] Ludendorff created something like a special office for the purpose, run by Lieutenant Colonel Bauer, who since September had been head of operations section II (heavy artillery, ammunition, war industry, training). Bauer's office became the collecting point for newspaper clippings, political documentation, and simple gossip, all aimed at undermining the Chancellor's authority and available to Ludendorff as the need might be.

In his memoirs Bauer prides himself on having prepared a special report (probably in January 1917) in which all of Bethmann Hollweg's "sins of omission" were enumerated, together with their consequences. Ludendorff had shown this document to Valentini, who had rejected it, though he told both the Kaiser and the Chancellor about it.[3] There are many memoranda of this type among Bauer's papers, all purely political in content. Some of them are dated as late as August 1918, and they are all characterized by the same absurdly primitive political thinking found in his memoirs, displaying the arrogance of a typical militarist who insists on meddling in political questions from his narrow military point of view. Competent as a soldier but politically utterly unrealistic, Bauer, because of his political ambitions, seems to have functioned as something of an evil spirit in Ludendorff's immediate entourage.

He was, however, also Ludendorff's most important instrument in the efforts of the OHL to expand its authority over ever-wider spheres of public life, especially control of industry and of social conditions, always in the direction of military interest. The motivation was, of course, the army's manifest desire to increase war production and maintain the supply of manpower.

The First World War demonstrated clearly that sweeping militarization and central direction of the economy were an absolute necessity, and they have ever since been the very essence of modern totalitarian war. Even prior to 1914 there had been a law in effect in Austria, enjoining the populace to certain war contributions. In France war industry proper was militarized, the workers being tied to their jobs. In Britain the Munitions of War Act of July 1915 created the legal basis for far-reaching intervention in free enterprise.

Under this act strikes and lockouts were generally prohibited, though without complete success. War industry proper was placed under government control, its profits limited, wages and salaries regulated, all trade union privileges and agreements that stood in the way of increased production canceled. The minister of munitions was empowered to issue detailed regulations governing working conditions and to enforce them through inspectors. Workers in war industry could change jobs only by the employer's written permission, though the latter's right of dismissal went untouched. Similarly, war workers could be employed only if they were able to show proper papers. Special labor courts and compulsory arbitration for industrial disputes were introduced.

These measures succeeded in stabilizing war production while at the same time preventing wages and profits from rising excessively, a goal that was not attained in Germany. Ironically, the land of classic trade unionism and laissez-faire required the most incisive action in building up an efficient war industry from scratch; but when it was done, it was done with such success that it became the model for others. The Germans felt the impact during the Battle of the Somme in the summer of 1916 in the form of enormously increased arms production, especially guns and ammunition.[4]

Naturally the question arose at German headquarters as to what was to be done to counter enemy arms superiority and equip the German forces more effectively in order to meet the major offensive that inevitably impended on the western front in the spring of 1917. Every front-line officer at the time (including the present author) sensed that with the second succession in the supreme command these questions were being tackled with renewed and intensified vigor, which extended also to vastly better technical training of the front-line troops. In this sphere Ludendorff's tremendous energy undoubtedly accomplished wonders, making itself felt down into the lowest ranks. At the crucial centers, however, it soon led to serious friction, with the resultant danger of overstraining Germany's resources.

The friction originated in the first instance between the general staff of the field army and the Prussian war ministry, whose work Ludendorff acknowledged to have been excellent in the past but totally inadequate in the present situation. Scarcely two days in office, Ludendorff curtly demanded that by the following spring ammunition production be doubled, the production of guns and machine guns trebled. To effect this "Hindenburg program," as it soon came to be called, a whole new labor army composed of wounded war veterans, prisoners of war, women, and minors was to be trained and utilized.[5]

Lieutenant Colonel Bauer described himself as the father of the whole idea of this arms policy; and his papers do indeed show much evidence of his hand in formulating and subsequently implementing the Hindenburg program. Most of the OHL documents concerning it are probably from his pen. His style and spirit are shown especially in the comprehensive report Hindenburg dispatched on September 13 to the Chancellor and the war minister, which set off the whole subsequent debate about an "auxiliary service."

The report demanded nothing less than total militarization of German life. "Work for the general welfare," it stated, "is today the duty of everyone. No one has any right to special privilege in return for such work. On the contrary, our survival depends on it." A war labor bill was to be passed under which everyone capable of working could be drafted for war work, including disabled veterans, who were to be trained to that end on a large scale. Women were to be similarly drawn on.

> There are thousands of war widows who are nothing but a burden on the government. Thousands of women and girls are either simply idle or pursuing unnecessary occupations. . . . The dictum that 'he who does not work, neither shall he eat' was never more justified than in our situation, even in respect of women. Those who cannot work, on account of weakness or ill health, should be organized into special units and given proper treatment to return them to productivity.

As for nonessential businesses, from those already virtually shut down for lack of goods, department stores and the like, as many workers as possible were to be withdrawn and compulsorily transferred to war industry. Liability to military service was to be extended to the age of fifty (from forty-five), so that men capable of front-line duty could be relieved of garrison duty. Boys were to be intensively trained for military service from the age of sixteen and to this end appropriately excused from work as well as school attendance. Universities and other institutions of higher learning were to be closed, unless they were essential in training for professions necessary to the war effort, such as medicine.

Students of chemistry and other technical professions were to work in factories and elsewhere—not least in order that they and women students would not dispute the priority of war veterans, preempting places that should be rightfully theirs. "I do not doubt," Hindenburg said in conclusion, "that our people will willingly bow to these necessities, once the gravity of the situation is made clear to them, as must be done. If they do not, Germany would not deserve to win." Demagogy must be curbed, like the unworthy profiteering and amusement mania that prevailed in some parts of the country. "The whole German people must live only in the service of the fatherland. . . . The necessary measures must be taken immediately. . . . Every day is important."

It may be imagined that this product of true military thinking, one of the first in which the new OHL asserted its will, was received with very mixed feelings not only in the Reich chancellery but in the war ministry as well. The latter also received a second list of proposals, in which the compulsory labor service was set forth in greater detail. Working hours were to be apportioned in accordance with the workers' capacity and food rationing was to be adjusted correspondingly. Medical certificates were to take care of absenteeism and everything was to be watched over by a Reich labor office.

Actually, the war ministry had long since done everything in its power to bring able-bodied men to the front and reduce the number of exemptions by constantly "combing out" industry in an effort to replace the able-bodied with the less fit. Virtually everyone capable of work had already been mobilized and nonessential enterprises had either been curtailed or adapted to war production; but substantial arguments had been adduced against supplementing the existing war labor act by the introduction of compulsory labor, as proposed by the General Staff as early as July 1916.

"The workers," wrote deputy labor minister General von Wandel on July 31, "would regard such a measure as an undeserved response to the cooperative attitude they have taken." Unlike those in other countries, German trade union leaders, regardless of their politics, had persuaded the workers to enter spontaneously and wholeheartedly into war work. They had taken on and carried out a volume of work far in excess of peacetime standards. Compulsion would serve only to discourage performance, quantitatively as well as qualitatively. The government, moreover, instead of standing above the struggle, would be drawn into a highly dangerous responsibility for workers' welfare and especially income, and would become directly involved in the issues between conflicting interests. High wages and free labor agreements in Germany had proved superior to the kind of compulsion that prevailed in Britain and Austria, where it had led to numerous strikes and acts of sabotage, while in Germany the unions gave priceless help in maintaining labor morale and discipline.[6]

But soon after the change in the OHL, General von Wandel, who supported these liberal views, resigned. He had until then been the heart and soul of the war ministry in Berlin, since General Wild was always at headquarters, paying little attention to administrative detail, which he despised as petty. The new OHL, however, at once ordered Wild back to Berlin, which General von Wandel regarded as prejudicial to his own status.

The war minister did try to fall in with Ludendorff's demands, but he registered substantial reservations about Bauer's program of September 13, and to these we shall revert. He was not altogether unsuccessful in his counterproposals, but Ludendorff kept meddling across jurisdictional lines, often over General Wild's head. In the end the war minister could no longer tolerate this interference and protested, whereupon late in October he was relieved and transferred to the front.[7]

This may not have been a great loss for the ministry; but the choice of his successor was unfortunate. General von Stein was a General Staff officer in the old Prussian tradition of exaggerated military demeanor, totally lacking the skill and tact needed to deal successfully with Reichstag deputies, and without any personal knowledge of the affairs and staff of the war ministry, an agency employing some four or five thousand people.[8] It is true that to a certain degree he seems to have shared his staff's doubts of the wisdom of the

OHL proposals and reckless demands,[9] but he was not the man either to offer resolute opposition or to display any initiative of his own. Hence the innovations Ludendorff managed to push through came about through no discernible action or influence by the war minister.

Bethmann Hollweg's attitude was all the more important, as was that of his associates, among whom Helfferich was the most active, as secretary of the interior in charge of economic affairs. As long ago as August 1916 Helfferich had promoted a rise in munitions production, in connection with a petition submitted by the German steelmakers' association. He had sought to enlist Ludendorff's support on September 3, but he was horrified by Bauer's program of September 13. He urgently warned the Chancellor against abandoning the principle of voluntary cooperation, which had brought such admirable results. "Compulsion would crush the free structure of our body economic," he wrote in a memorandum. "An army will submit to command, but not a participatory economy."

Helfferich was formulating in almost classic terms the conflict between militarist and bourgeois-liberal thinking. He observed, moreover, that the OHL proposals were merely going over well-plowed ground. High wages in war industry had long since drained all useful manpower resources away from other branches of industry. All men over forty-five capable of working were already being utilized, and there were far more female job applicants than could be accommodated, etc. Helfferich concluded that the slight additional gains would not repay tampering with the sound structure of the German economy.[10]

Helfferich drafted the Chancellor's official reply of September 30 along similar lines, arguing that the contemplated compulsory measures would have very little practical effect while doing much political damage. Militarizing boys below the age of military service was described as a dubious expedient, the closing of universities and other schools of higher learning as impracticable and senseless. The Chancellor declared that only a few measures of limited importance were feasible—restriction of building construction not essential to the war effort, organized training of wounded war veterans for war work, early mustering of seventeen- and eighteen-year-olds for military service, possibly the extension of liability to military service to the age of fifty.

The concluding phrases of this reply are especially typical of the liberal economic ideals that animated the Chancellor: "Government directives handed down from above cannot substitute for our living and breathing body economic. Compulsory labor would pose a mortal danger, [reduce public confidence, and ultimately] destroy the already dwindling cadres we shall desperately need after the war to rebuild and maintain our economic life." Once again we see the statesman fighting against totalitarian war, against the military insistence that the national life must be harnessed to the military needs of the moment, without regard to the peace to come.

On October 14 the war ministry, then still under General Wild, said that in its experience a general compulsory labor act for both men and women was unnecessary and harmful. It pointed to a wealth of measures already in preparation within the ministry, in order to increase the production of arms and munitions.[11] Hence Ludendorff stood no chance of getting the Kaiser to approve Bauer's ill-conceived proposals. As a compromise and substitute, suggested in part by Wild, he proposed on October 23 that all males from the age of fifteen to sixty should become liable to military service, to the end of gaining an industrial army as well as reinforcements for the front.

It was another hastily formulated and ill-considered plan, as shown by the remarks it contained about young people and women. Students in the higher schools, it said, could well receive military training side by side with school attendance, if only some relief were granted in matters of final and qualifying examinations.[12] To introduce a formal service liability for all women would be a mistake, yet there was to be compulsory labor for women in nonessential occupations or who were not working at all! One must not, of course, overestimate the importance of female labor. "As before, virtually all intellectual effort as well as heavy physical labor will rest on the shoulders of men, together with all true production work and the entire running of the war." This should be plainly and publicly stated as an argument against the demand for equality for women in all branches of endeavor. "After the war we shall need women as wives and mothers." It would make no sense to keep the higher schools and universities open to them, since the scientific gain would be but slight and the net effect would merely be to nurture female competition with men.

There was scarcely a single tangible proposal in all this loose talk, for which Hindenburg as the signer expressly assumed responsibility in his role as "His Majesty's qualified adviser in matters of strategy." He urged the utmost haste and concluded with a kind of threat: "Should the Reichstag fail in the solution of these tasks, the identity of those elements that are closing their minds to the demands of national survival will be clear. At this point I am not called upon to discuss measures that might then have to be taken."

Crucial to the further course of negotiations was the fact that in mid-October the OHL entrusted them to General Wilhelm Groener, a military man who represented an unusual combination of technical, military, and political talents. Groener was head of the army rail transport service and since May a board member of the newly created war food agency. Ludendorff apparently sensed that he would get no further with Bauer's half-baked proposals and thought he could turn Groener into a kind of economic dictator. He was to become head of a *Kriegsamt* (war agency) that would be at one and the same time responsible for the procurement, utilization, and subsistence of war workers and for arms and munitions production. What Ludendorff envisaged was to combine in one hand the work of the war food agency with all of the other agencies the war ministry had in the meantime either instituted or planned—the agency for arms and munitions procurement (*Waffen- und Munitionsbeschaffungsamt,* or WUMBA), the agency for labor organization, the agency for the procurement of raw materials and clothing, the agency for export and import, the agency for surrogate materials, etc.

Dictators are always inclined to appoint plenipotentiaries for especially important missions, for they can then hold a single man responsible rather than having to negotiate at length with complex and slow-moving bureaucracies. Had the *Kriegsamt* come into being in the form originally contemplated, Ludendorff would have had in his immediate entourage a general through whom he could have, so to speak, commanded the country's entire economic life, transforming it according to military needs. His model was Lloyd George's ministry of munitions, though with even wider powers.

Integration of the numerous government procurement agencies was certainly a desirable goal. Besides WUMBA, for example, there were special agencies for the air force, the engineers, the army railroad service, post office and transport, the navy, etc. Things were made even worse by the fact that various military districts cut across the jurisdiction of the four independent war ministers under the cumbersome federal constitution, while labor and raw materials were growing increasingly scarce.

Yet both constitutional and political considerations kept the Chancellor from simply falling in with Ludendorff's plan. The Prussian war ministry with its huge staff of experienced specialists could not be swept aside, any more than the war ministries of Bavaria-Württemberg or Saxony. At the same time it could be turned into a Reich agency, to be incorporated into a *Kriegsamt,* only by constitutional amendment. Above all, how could this new agency be reconciled with the Chancellor's responsibility to parliament for broad areas of social and economic policy, especially if it had at its disposal the *stellvertretenden Generalkommandos,* the replacement commands or military districts, which under the so-called state of siege themselves possessed sweeping executive powers? 13

There were swift consultations, and the upshot was a compromise. The *Kriegsamt* was created by imperial edict on November 1, but instead of being superior to the Prussian war ministry, it was placed under that agency, at least in a formal sense. The *Kriegsamt* took over the Prussian war ministry's main section in the sphere of arms policy, but in actual fact it functioned as an autonomous central Reich agency, even vis-à-vis the Reich food agency, from which it abstracted responsibility for feeding workers in the war industry. The military districts served as its executive organs, though Groener had no direct command authority over them and therefore had to organize branch offices of the *Kriegsamt.*

The existing bureaucracies, in other words, were not incorporated into a single central military agency with dictatorial powers. What happened was simply that one more agency was created, with unresolved jurisdiction and a rapidly swelling staff running into thousands. It was an agency without any administrative tradition, and many of its staff members were untrained. The war ministry looked on it not without jealousy, charging it with unnecessarily complicating the course of work, especially the transfer of able-bodied workers to the army.[14]

It is not our job here to determine whether these charges were justified. One thing is certain, however: the creation of the *Kriegsamt* could not alter the fact that the available manpower resources were unequal to the needs of both the armed forces and the war industry. The army's appetite was insatiable. From January to October 1916 alone it had suffered losses of 1.4 million men who had to be replaced, to say nothing of the need for organizing new divisions. The war industry needed vast numbers of workers, especially skilled workers, to carry out the Hindenburg plan.

Ludendorff grew more and more impatient, but his exhortations, reproaches, and interventions were of no avail. The appointment of Michaelis as Prussian food commissioner separate from the war food agency under Batocki could not avert the consequences of the potato crop failure, which every survivor of the terrible "turnip winter" of 1916-1917 will remember indelibly; nor could the appointment of a "coal czar" keep coal production from falling.

This constant intervention on the part of the OHL did, however, greatly complicate the work of the head of the *Kriegsamt*, which needed a certain warm-up time to become successful. All in all the Hindenburg program, which had been greeted with enthusiasm not only by patriots generally but even by heavy industry, was in the light of subsequent events viewed by all the participants as having badly overstrained Germany's resources. It led to a precipitate construction program that soon had to be cut back, postponed, and even abandoned, on account of the disastrous lack of coal and transport facilities in the winter of 1916-1917. Helfferich reported that in the spring of 1917 forty new blast furnaces could not be put into operation.[15] The labor of thousands of workers went for nothing.

One reason why General Groener was unable to forestall these consequences was that the industrialists kept negotiating directly with Ludendorff—or rather Bauer. Groener actually had no ambitions to become an economic dictator; and privately he entertained the same reservations as did Helfferich, Bethmann Hollweg, and the war ministry about the principle of compulsory labor, which he had to support officially on behalf of the OHL. It was not merely his unusual combination of talents that distinguished this officer from Swabia from the run of his Prussian fellows. He was utterly different in character, completely lacking in class arrogance, and without the usual ties to the conservative political traditions of Prussian Junkerdom.

Groener took it for granted that the nation as a whole could be committed to compulsory labor service only if there were the closest collaboration with the trade unions, whether they were socialist or not in orientation. To work in opposition to them was unthinkable. Groener spoke a language the people could understand and his natural and unpretentious manner soon gained him a high degree of trust among trade union leaders. This was much in contrast to Helfferich, who was also shrewd enough to appreciate that cooperation was absolutely essential at this critical juncture. Helfferich too was prepared to make concessions to labor, but as former bank director, i.e., a "capitalist," he was politically suspect among the socialists; nor was he himself free of political distrust of the radical left.[16]

Despite these differences, the "Patriotic Auxiliary Service Act" of December 5, 1916, the very heart of the Hindenburg program, came into existence mainly through the close collaboration of minister and general. Initially Bethmann Hollweg was uncertain as to what he could do to alleviate the critical situation of German industry. In a letter to Helfferich, he described the OHL proposals of October 23 (which were discussed a few pages back) as unfeasible, but added lamely, in view of the Kaiser's determination: "We must somehow intervene and organize."[17]

Bethmann Hollweg would have probably preferred to proceed quietly by means of federal council decrees in accomplishing what little might still be done to find additional manpower and shift industry to war production; but Ludendorff insisted that the Reichstag must solemnly and unanimously proclaim the new law, as an impressive demonstration that Germany's will to win the war continued unabated. This, he expected, would make a big splash abroad; and oddly enough he also thought it would lead to a new nationalist upsurge inside Germany. It was for these reasons that he kept urging the greatest haste. The law must at all costs be passed before the Central Powers issued their peace offer, a kind of test of national strength. The Chancellor and the German foreign ministry, on the other hand, feared that passage of such a law directly before the peace offer would cast serious doubts on the sincerity of that offer.

Obviously a bill that would exact additional sacrifices from the people and limit if not terminate freedom of work required the most careful preparation in the federal council and the Reichstag's main committee, unless it was to lead to stormy and unedifying plenary debate, to be talked to shreds on the floor and probably to fail altogether. The first draft submitted by Groener met considerable opposition when it was discussed from October 29 to November 1 by a small circle of ministers and under secretaries. Helfferich would have no part of government-fixed working conditions, for reasons similar to those put forward by General Wandel in July. Bethmann Hollweg was afraid of military ambitions and wanted first to hold discussions with both employers and union officials in war industry.

On November 4 the Reichstag was adjourned. The Chancellor told the OHL that this provided a welcome breathing space. In reply the Kaiser wired him on November 6: "I command that the labor bill be brought before the Reichstag immediately and without the slightest delay. Its lead sentence is to read: 'Every German from the sixteenth to the sixtieth year is liable to war service for his fatherland.' "

The Chancellor was undismayed, replying that deliberations had been under full way for the past week. Important talks with industrial leaders impended. For the benefit of the OHL he added that upon hearing the requirements of the OHL he felt that it was his responsibility to do everything incumbent on the country's first minister to secure fulfillment of these requirements. "Nothing would be worse than an impractical and superficial draft lacking the kind of thinking that should go into a good strategic plan and incapable of being readily explained to the Reichstag."[18]

On November 7 and 8, 1916, Helfferich and Groener held their talks with the industrial leaders, with trade union officials, and with Reichstag party leaders. The idea of compulsory labor service had in the meantime been considerably softened. Every worker was to have the right, in the first instance, to pick the kind of job he liked—but all men had to engage in essential war work. The trade unions and the social democrats offered no objections; but as expected, they were opposed to precipitate action in the Reichstag, and their first concern was to see to it that the basic rights of the worker were safeguarded. They wanted all curbs on the right to organize removed, the right to strike maintained, the introduction of arbitration in wage disputes, adequate rehousing help when workers were transferred to other industries, etc.

The Prussian cabinet on November 10 debated these demands and the bill to be submitted to the federal council. Some of the ministers, led by the arch-conservative minister of the interior, von Loebell, utterly rejected any negotiations with captains of industry, let alone union leaders. They proposed that such people be dispatched to headquarters, there to be received by His Majesty and "enlightened" by Hindenburg and Ludendorff. Bethmann Hollweg was ably supported by Helfferich and Groener, but they were unable to write the right to strike and bargain collectively into the bill, though provision for conciliation in wage disputes was included. After protracted debate military training for sixteen-year-olds was dropped. Groener pledged that the new *Kriegsamt* would work harmoniously with the Reich and state authorities. On November 14 the modified draft, approved by the Kaiser, came before the federal council.[19]

But in the meantime Ludendorff had lost patience. On November 15 he persuaded Hindenburg to send a wire to the effect that he would have to decline responsibility for continuing the war, unless the country gave him the necessary support. "Months of discussion have gone by since my first proposal, while our enemies are proceeding in exemplary fashion." This telegram promptly reached the press, probably through Bauer's office, with the effect of pillorying the Chancellor in public.[20] And indeed, there was a note of considerable irritation in Bethmann Hollweg's reply. "I urgently request," he concluded, "that I be given sufficient time to prepare the bill properly and see it through smoothly and impressively. To force the issue is quite impossible, and I should not be in a position to accept the responsibility if this were tried."[21]

In a subsequent telegram[22] he suggested that the predictable political clashes among the parties could have been overcome far more readily if such unseemly haste had not been categorically demanded. The main burden of work fell on Helfferich's shoulders, and that during the turbulent weeks preceding the German peace offer. So indignant was Helfferich about the manner in which the whip was being wielded in Pless that he asked the Chancellor to submit his resignation to the Kaiser. He relented only when Bethmann Hollweg, in personal discussions at headquarters, managed to ease the tension temporarily, though gaining the impression that the men at Pless were already busily preparing his downfall.

On November 21 the bill passed the federal council. Two days later it came before the Reichstag committee, where it was debated for many days and nights. Helfferich was repeatedly irked by concessions General Groener made to the social democrats against his wishes. The Reichstag as a whole also held overtime sessions on the bill, which received its third reading as early as December 2. The vote was overwhelming but not unanimous, 235 to 14, with only the extreme left, the "independents," voting in opposition. Thus Ludendorff got something very close to the "national demonstration" he wanted, though only at the cost of concessions to the workers he did not relish at all.

There was not a word about conscripting workers' battalions, nor about women workers. The act made all male Germans from the seventeenth to the sixty-first year who were not serving in the armed forces liable to "patriotic auxiliary service," meaning just about any kind of work that directly or indirectly aided the common welfare in the war. The pertinence of the work within the meaning of the law was to be determined by the *Kriegsamt* and by local committees presided over by army officers but each also including two higher government officials as well as a representative of the employers and one from the unions.

At the highest *Kriegsamt* level too civilians played a decisive role. Legitimate private interests of those henceforth to be inducted into essential war work were jealously protected, and the preferred approach was volunteer service. There were even loopholes in the ties between worker and job, i.e., to some extent the worker could still pick and choose and move from job to job. He did require a discharge certificate from his employer if he wanted to move, but in the event of refusal he could appeal to a board on which workers were represented and which could decide against the employer "for good and sufficient reason." Section 3 of Paragraph 9 of the act provided that a worker's desire for better working conditions constituted such a reason, and thus the door was opened wide to luring scarce workers away with tempting offers of higher wages. In the wake of this controversial paragraph wages rose almost beyond all reason, a development favored by the fact that employers doing government work could, under their contracts, pass on their rising wage bills in full.

The act brought considerable social benefits to war workers. It not only confirmed the existing rights of assembly and association but introduced a major innovation. The larger plants were now required to accept shop-floor committees to handle grievances. Mixed arbitration boards were provided to settle wage disputes and working conditions. Even the Reichstag reserved a niche for itself. All enforcement regulations had to be approved by a board of fifteen deputies.[23]

It remains a remarkable phenomenon that under the whiplash of war a law was passed which the workers regarded as distinctly progressive in a social sense. The trade unions were happiest of all and called on their members to strain every fiber for war production. The employers, on the other hand, felt that the act went too far in curbing their rights, and some of them rebelled.

As expected, war production continued to lag behind the army's needs, and thus, inevitably, the high hopes that had been staked on the auxiliary labor act soon degenerated into bitter criticism. Employers' circles as well as the OHL began to blame the "Reichstag botch" for the political unrest and food shortages that agitated the workers, especially after the outbreak of the Russian Revolution.

General Groener had unhesitatingly negotiated face-to-face with Deputy Haase, leader of the radical left, persuading him to call off a strike; but employers in North Germany now began to call for "rolling back" the auxiliary labor act, and for the police to deal unmercifully with "trouble-makers."[24] Loudest of all was the voice of Ludendorff in decrying the "mess" the Reichstag had made of everything. He kept hammering away at the "irresponsible weakness" of the Chancellor and his associates in failing to oppose the trend.

The Prussian cabinet had met in between the final and crucial Reichstag sessions, and there Bethmann Hollweg's and Helfferich's ears had rung with complaints about the increasing arrogance of the workers; but their reply was irrefutable and convincing. The government was caught in a cleft stick. If the OHL insisted on Reichstag passage of the bill, Reichstag demands had to be met in full, for none of the parties except the conservatives dared oppose the demands of the workers openly.

The situation clearly revealed how times had changed under the influence of the war. Continuation of the class state had become impossible. The workers—precisely by their patriotic stand at home and in the field—had won the right to social equality; and the Russian Revolution, soon to come, was to strengthen their social and political claims even further.

Bethmann Hollweg, on his part, was quite willing to make the best of these developments, as a form of progress—at any rate, he refused to join in the moans of the conservatives. On one occasion he indignantly rejected the prediction of War Minister von Stein that after the war the act would vanish from the scene, leaving a strong government free to do as it pleased. After the war, the Chancellor said, the government would stand in even greater need of Reichstag consent. The war was bound to bring a complete political reorientation, and when it was over there would be no escape from shop stewards and mediation boards. The act could serve as a useful transition phase, in providing practical experience.[25]

As we shall soon see, Bethmann Hollweg's readiness to countenance political "reorientation" was to become one of the most important elements in his fall.

## Part 2

# The Deportation of Belgian Workers

IN NOTEWORTHY contrast to the kid-glove treatment accorded German workers, a brutal program was carried out in the occupied territories, above all Belgium, to conscript workers for German war industry. In terms of manpower utilization, it was a failure; but worse than that, it turned out to be a crude political blunder that could not be undone. This blot on the name and prestige of Germany as a civilized nation belongs to the darkest chapters of the war. Responsibility for it was by no means limited to shortsighted generals but falls in considerable measure on the shoulders of the politicians. Ludendorff was not even the principal author.[26]

The crucial impetus came rather from the Prussian war ministry, which had long been trying to achieve better utilization of Belgian industrial labor for German ends. There were limits to the degree to which Belgian industry itself could be made to work for the German war effort. International law stood in the way of doing this directly and Belgian workers and industrialists balked at it. Not least, however, it was German industry that fought against such Belgian competition. The issue gave rise to a major conflict between the war ministry and the German governor general in Belgium, von Bissing.

Colonel General von Bissing, rather like Beseler in Poland, was not just a professional soldier. He took an unusually keen interest in political questions. The principles by which he conducted the occupation are set forth in detail in a comprehensive report dating from February 1915, which shows him as a thoroughgoing annexationist. He saw his most important mission as preparing the incorporation of Belgium into the German Reich, in the form of a kind of permanent viceroyship, and this he sought to advance in theory, by studying Belgium's economic, social, and intellectual makeup, and in practice, by attempts to influence the people.

Bissing stated quite openly that he proposed to proceed with great ruthlessness and without any "obsequiousness toward insolent foreign nations." Germany's interests alone counted. Let the Belgians become used to the idea that their country would be used in some form to expand Germany's power. They would be taught law and order, brought closer to the German spirit, forced to acknowledge the advantages of a stricter regimen. Only in this way could Belgium become a serviceable outpost of German strength and power; but this authoritarian, indeed patriarchal governance was by no means to exclude autonomous administration by Belgians and Belgian institutions. First, however, the Belgians must be rendered pliable and taught the virtues of hard work.[27]

All this had a thoroughly militaristic ring. In practice, however, Bissing turned more and more into a protector of the Belgian economy against the efforts of the German army administration to exploit the country ruthlessly for its own purposes. Belgium with its large industrial centers and capital wealth was by far the richest territory Germany had conquered. It was also the most densely populated, creating its own heavy demand.

As the occupation administration grew familiar with the country, war-engendered havoc and human suffering with all their political consequences came into ever sharper focus. In his desire to bring the Belgians closer to the Germans, Bissing also wished to prevent the country from falling to Germany at the end of the war as a mere heap of rubble, utterly exhausted, sucked dry, haunted by human misery and boundless hate. As he put it to a conference of Belgian industrialists in Brussels on July 19, 1915: "I do not believe a squeezed lemon is worth very much—and you cannot get milk from a dead cow."[28]

Since Germany, on account of the British hunger blockade, was unable to feed the Belgians and North French from its own resources, the famous Belgian Relief Commission was agreed on with the enemy powers. Under the leadership of the American Herbert C. Hoover, the great humanitarian and later president, food, mainly from America, was imported by sea via Holland. Bissing saw to it that the distribution of these food supplies was run by an independent Belgian national committee formed under his predecessor, Field Marshal von der Goltz, with the occupation authorities keeping hands off. At the same time, in accordance with the agreement, the country's own agricultural output was essentially reserved to the Belgians.

Bissing also fostered the Flemish nationalist movement, which strove for equality with the French and Walloon elements in language, schools, and administration. This was in keeping with Bethmann Hollweg's wishes—as early as September 2, 1914, the Chancellor had advised the head of the civil administration in Belgium, von Sandt, to further this movement, and ever since then he had urged it time and again.[29]

True, Bissing's goal was not quite the same as the Chancellor's. Bethmann Hollweg seems to have been mainly concerned with gaining for Germany the status of Belgium's natural friend and protector, and with being accepted as such by a large part of the population. He wanted to undo the bad impression made abroad by German exploitation of Belgium, win sympathy, especially in Holland, and facilitate Belgian separation from the Entente, as was being attempted in the negotiations with King Albert. The governor general, on the other hand, wished to play off the Flemish "race" against the Walloons in a political sense, in preparation for subsequent incorporation into Germany, a goal never envisaged by the Chancellor. Yet even Bissing was in part motivated by the hope of appearing to at least part of the Belgian people in the role of friend and protector. In this respect his policy was not unlike that of Governor General von Beseler in Poland. But for many reasons it was even more illusory than Beseler's, and it failed utterly on account of the attitude of the war ministry and the OHL.

Bissing was intent on keeping Belgian industry alive, insofar as that were possible, and on rebuilding factories that had been destroyed. During the very first war winter, the war ministry seized and transported to Germany all Belgian machinery and raw materials that could be used by German war industry. After June 1915 the governor general managed in time to get seventeen plants going again, under military operation. He also kept the collieries going, with a payroll of about 157,000, and by 1916 they were producing 1.45 million tons of coal monthly, in part for export to neutral countries and Austria.[30]

In August 1915 Bissing had vainly tried to promote an agreement between Belgian industrialists and Britain, under which a certain quota of raw materials for Belgian industry would be exempted from the blockade, in addition to the food imports. When this failed, Belgian unemployment kept rising steeply, for the country was strongly industrialized. A factor in reducing jobs was the refusal of many industrialists to operate their plants for the occupation power, just as the Germans themselves were to do later on, in 1923, when the Ruhr region was occupied.

The estimate in 1916 was 400-500,000 workless males, and counting the families, this meant about a quarter of the population. The worst hardship, however, was averted because of the close network of charitable aid groups that spread over the country. Then too, the local communities instituted much emergency work. All this caused the governor general great concern, for he foresaw the danger of declining morale among the workers, with a corresponding growth of hatred for the occupying power. So close to the German front lines, this might pose a serious military risk, especially since the occupation forces were down to the barest minimum, for the most part older men. Bissing was willing to do anything that might provide employment for the Belgians in Belgium.

The war ministry in Berlin had rather different ideas. As unemployment in Belgium grew more and more threatening, hopes rose that labor might be recruited there for German war industry. As early as June 1915 a *Deutsches Industriebüro* was established to that end, initially supported by private industry, but subsequently enjoying official aid and even expansion. The results were disappointing, though the governor general, on his part, tried to help the endeavor by issuing a decree on August 15, 1915, that provided a prison term for anyone who refused to take a job without sufficient reason.

It would have been actually impossible to apply such penalties on a large scale; and indeed the whole scheme was primarily intended to exert pressure on the unemployed; but a further cause contributing to its failure was the fact that the Belgian Comité National now redoubled its efforts to provide support for the unemployed. One result of this was that acceptance of work in German industry was widely regarded as unpatriotic, if not tantamount to treason; for even when the jobs were not directly in war industry, every Belgian worker freed a German for front-line service—or so it was believed. By March 1916 no more than 12,000 Belgian workers had been recruited through the *Industriebüro*.

Military coercion was thus plainly shown to have its limitations. The military mind, however, was congenitally incapable of realizing this. The ministry in Berlin could see no farther than the irksome discrepancy between a surfeit of labor in Belgium and a shortage in Germany so severe that hundreds of thousands who might have served at the front had to remain behind.

As early as March 2, 1916, the deputy war minister, General von Wandel, scheduled talks with the chief of staff of the German governor general of Belgium on a totally unrealistic plan of having several hundred thousand Belgian industrial workers forcibly deported to Germany, where they were to free a corresponding number of German workers for front-line service.[31]

Bissing naturally protested, pointing out, among other things, that such brutal measures might halt American aid to the Belgians. He appealed to the Chancellor, only to get a halfhearted reply. Bethmann Hollweg had talked to General Wild, who had convinced him that intensified Belgian industrial activity would not advance the main goal of freeing German workers for front-line service. The Chancellor, before arriving at a decision, demanded to know whether more might not be achieved by means of intensified recruitment activities.

Colonel General von Bissing rather arbitrarily interpreted this inquiry as meaning that the deportation issue was dead. He pledged intensified recruitment but also urgently recommended that Belgian industry—the efficiency of which he praised to the skies—be used to relieve German war industry. To study these possibilities he proposed a meeting of all the interested parties with the governor general's staff.

In support of the recruitment campaign he issued another decree on May 15, 1916. The "work-shy" were now not merely to go to jail but to be transported to the ordained place of work by force, by judgment of German military rather than Belgian civil tribunals. The same day (and the next) saw the meeting with the war and economics ministries Bissing had proposed; and on the whole it went as Bissing wished. His representatives apparently cited the alleged desires of the Chancellor.

Agreement was reached that the use of naked force in augmenting the labor force was out of the question. Plans were put forward for improving recruitment methods and for drawing to a greater extent on Belgian industry for German war purposes. The economics ministry asked that an annual coal production quota of four million tons for export purposes be transferred to German pits, which would free 20-25,000 Belgian coal miners for work in German collieries. The war ministry went so far as to demand that all non-essential Belgian plants be shut down, so that the resultant unemployment might create a climate more conducive to Belgian workers taking jobs in German industry. The governor general's representatives did not immediately agree but promised to consider the matter. Thus forcible deportation was once again averted, though the Berlin government agencies did make it clear that in their view Belgian industrial health was not a consideration.

Increased recruitment activities were not attended by impressive success. By mid-September the total stood no higher than 26,000.[32] German industrialists whispered that the main reason was because the Belgian workers were better fed, on account of American aid; and the demand arose that stricter rationing should be introduced in Belgium.[33] The labor problem took on added urgency by virtue of the Hindenburg program; and on September 13 Ludendorff appealed to both the Polish and Belgian governors general to see to it that no employment was given within their jurisdiction to German workers, and to "make available" (i.e., initially to register) Belgian and Polish workers for employment outside it. If necessary local food rations, at least for the unemployed, should be reduced to the level of light workers in Germany. In view of the critical situation in Germany, considerations of social welfare and international law had to take second place.

Bissing instantly sensed a covert renewal of the war ministry's deportation program, which had been turned back with such difficulty only in May; and he hastened to reject the plan on the ground that all the agencies concerned had meanwhile acknowledged that any coercion in open conflict with the Hague convention must be avoided.[34] Bissing was plainly worried. He pointed out that his appointment expressly enjoined him to abide by the Hague provisions and said that unless he were empowered or instructed otherwise by the Kaiser he would have to refuse to carry out any policy that violated them.

He also insisted that the Chancellor be consulted. Complete registration of the 700,000-odd Belgian unemployed (he was apparently including women) he described as an impossibility, and large-scale deportation to Germany would be against international law. This would be even more true of forced labor on German fortified positions in North France. In either case the consequences were likely to be grave. Riots and open rebellion were distinct possibilities, and the thin occupation force would not be able to put them down.

The 15,000 Belgian workers employed on jobs for the German military would certainly down tools; and so, in all likelihood, would the 140,000 coal miners. The Relief Commission would instantly cease to function, with dire consequences. The neutrals, especially neighboring Holland, but Sweden as well, would be outraged by such a new German breach of international law, and all the malicious rumors about how Germany was running Belgium into the ground would be revived. Lastly, any such dubious methods were bound to fail. Civilized countries were not accustomed to using force on reluctant workers, hence such workers could never be depended on for highly skilled work. They would be just so many more mouths to feed, without providing an adequate substitute for German workers in short supply. Bissing said he was quite unwilling to assume responsibility for the consequences of such a policy.

This was certainly plain speaking, though the general must have feared that it would be fruitless in the end, for at the very outset he cited his decree of May 15, as well as a later one, under which the German *Industriebüro* was empowered to report to the regional Belgian authorities the names of all candidates who declined jobs even though they were jobless. The regional administrators were thus theoretically enabled to "take more effective action" and could be instructed to assemble small groups for relocation, as "a measure for the maintenance of order and security."

Bissing, in other words, immediately held out a compromise, and his plan subsequently became the subject of repeated discussions. What the plan amounted to was that the "work-shy" were to be treated as a species of prisoner. Defying a decree by the governor general, they were, so to speak, rebels posing a threat to public order and consequently liable to forcible "relocation." Since this could not be done on a large scale, it was to embrace, less conspicuously, only smaller groups, on the pretext of "security." The hypocrisy of the scheme is obvious. It was in contradiction, moreover, to Bissing's own statement that deportations—which could serve their purpose only if carried out on a large scale—posed a threat of riots, in other words of breaches of the peace, which were now to be prevented by small-scale relocations! In his concern to prevent the worst, the governor general himself pointed a way for circumventing international law.

Bissing was then seventy-three years old and suffering from heart disease; but he was worried enough not to shun the forty-eight-hour journey from Brussels to Pless, where on September 19 he pleaded his case in person. The OHL, however, proved quite unyielding, rejecting his dubious compromise as a half-measure; nor were they receptive to his argument that the contemplated forcible measures were unworthy of a civilized nation. As an OHL memorandum put it, "The whole war is unprecedented."

Bissing offered to resign, but the Kaiser insisted that he stay in office. In the end the governor general seems to have reached a verbal agreement with Ludendorff, under which only Belgians of military age and fitness would be affected. There would be no difficulty in registering them, and their deportation could be made to look like a purely military measure. No sooner was he back in Brussels, however, than Bissing retracted this concession. He had discovered that forced labor of the able-bodied in the arms industry was specifically outlawed under international law. The final decision was now to be taken at a conference in Berlin on September 28, with all the government departments concerned participating.[35]

The attitude of the OHL was almost certainly influenced in part by a conference which the war ministry had held on September 16 with leaders of heavy industry on the subject of the Hindenburg program. The industrialists, led by Privy Councilor Duisburg speaking for the chemical sector, insistently demanded that the "great human reservoir" of Belgium be opened up and that Belgian workers' rations be curtailed, so that those transported to Germany would not be tempted to run away, as was now happening. Walther Rathenau, head of the AEG, the huge German electrical firm, and also of the raw materials procurement agency (which played a major part in plundering Belgium), wrote a letter to Ludendorff the same day. The solution of the Belgian labor problem was supremely urgent, he said. "It can be solved only without regard to questions of international prestige, by making the 700,000

Belgian workers available to the home market, even at the risk of bringing American aid to a halt."[36]

Exposed to such powerful countercurrents, the governor general's position was hopeless from the outset. In his extremity, he appealed to the Chancellor, who so far had played no part in the affair. In a long and troubled letter he set forth his grave doubts about the planned mass deportations. They would inexorably trumpet the whole Belgian question to all the world once again, and the agitational effect would outstrip by far the damage already done since the Belgian invasion in 1914.

Bissing went considerably beyond his earlier letter in projecting the effects of the deportations abroad. The enemy camp would read them as a sign of military weakness as well as added proof of German brutality. Aid would cease; the neutrals would be outraged, especially America. Most important of all, the whole present policy of the government general in Belgium would collapse, the flames of hatred would be fed, churches and trade unions would be profoundly upset. Bissing dwelt especially on the havoc that would be wrought for the Chancellor's favorite Flemish policy, to say nothing of the Belgian response to German plans for economic integration. All that was to be risked for the sake of highly dubious economic gains, when in truth Belgian workers could be employed in Belgian factories and mines to the far more effective relief of German industry!

And what was the Chancellor's response to this appeal? One might have thought this was the time for vigorous and clear-headed statesmanship, for asserting the political imperatives against the arguments of the arms experts and profit-hungry industrialists, without regard to pettifogging legalistic interpretations of the Hague convention. Evidently Bethmann Hollweg lacked the firmness of will this would have taken, and perhaps also the necessary statesmanlike insight. In a marginal note on Bissing's missive he did express himself as "basically in agreement with the avoidance of forcible measures"; but he did not take very seriously the hazards Bissing pictured so eloquently, or at least he avoided seizing the initiative in this crucial question and failed to inject himself into the military consultations. The result, as in July 1914 and January 1917, was that the generals simply outmaneuvered him. Bethmann Hollweg was once again displaying the civilian's fatal hesitancy to tangle with military matters.[37] This time, indeed, one general, heading a major civilian administrative mission, showed greater political insight than the head of the Reich government.

Bethmann Hollweg waited until October 7 before signing the trickily worded reply to Bissing he had had drafted by a legal adviser in the foreign ministry. Bissing's carefully presented political reservations drew only an empty phrase—the Chancellor "fully appreciated" them. What was totally lacking was a firm rejection of deportations—the only pertinent statement was so self-evident as to be trite, namely that the Belgian labor manpower the German army had declared it must have should be secured by voluntary recruitment. For the rest, Bethmann Hollweg limited himself to a discussion of international law, an aspect on which the military had now focused too, to the exclusion of almost everything else.

Another meeting took place on September 28 between representatives of the OHL, the war ministry, the ministry of the interior, the Polish and Belgian governments general, and the foreign ministry. Rather than leading to any clear-cut results, it merely served to underline the differences of opinion more sharply. Actually, the question of whether sending Belgian workers to forced labor in Germany was economically feasible was not even discussed. The emphasis was on finding some legal pretext for the deportations that would not contravene the Hague convention too flagrantly.

One of the participants was General von Sauberzweig, who had already done much mischief by displaying a total lack of political sense as military governor of Brussels.[38] He now demanded 200,000 Belgian workers in the name of the OHL, to serve in the rear echelon areas behind the western front. His ostensible justification was the right of an occupying power to provide for "law and order" by deporting idlers to forced labor.

The foreign ministry representative, von Eckardt, wavered in his judgment but had no objection to the use of Belgian workers behind the front. Lieutenant Colonel Bauer and the war ministry man, Colonel von Wrisberg, fell in with Sauberzweig's demands, while the representatives of the governor general opposed them as being in violation of international law. The discussion grew somewhat confused, and the only point that emerged with any clarity was that there was no prospect of bringing the government general round to accepting the deportation of Belgian workers into areas directly behind the front. Deportation to Germany was discussed only casually.

It appears that the OHL subsequently decided to settle the rear echelon labor issue in the west on its own, without consulting the government general, let alone seeking its cooperation; for these areas were directly under army control and not subject to Bissing's jurisdiction.[39] Forced civilian labor, embracing even women and young girls, was actually employed to the end of the war in those areas with great ruthlessness, for fortification works and for road, rail, and barracks construction. In certain military districts it had begun much earlier; and in Lille and Roubaix, for example, this had at times given rise to near-riots.

Following the failure of the big Berlin meeting, Ludendorff tried to gain further headway in bilateral negotiations with the government general. He pressed Brussels for concrete proposals against the event that voluntary recruitment would not yield results that were good enough. Bissing steadfastly continued to oppose deportations to the rear echelon areas, but in the matter of deportations to Germany he allowed himself to be pushed more and more into a retreat. At any rate, in his replies he no longer mentioned groups of small size, being now apparently willing to countenance the shipment to Germany of large masses of the "work-shy," under his decree of May 16. The reason he gave was that they interfered with law and order in the occupied territories and endangered the security of the occupying forces, but this was palpably a legalistic fiction. At the Berlin talks his administrative chief, von Sandt, had but recently insisted that there was not a trace of any movement in Belgium that savored even remotely of rebellion.[40]

On his part, Ludendorff saw to it that the new talks on October 6 to which the OHL had dispatched two officers to Brussels would not again end inconclusively. This time his representatives asked for 200,000 workers, not for rear echelon service but for German industry. They rejected Bissing's notion that these workers might be deported to Germany as "detainees" under the decree of May 15. After a protracted tussle, in which Bissing again objected to rear echelon transports and emphasized that the issue was for him a question of conscience, it was agreed to wire the Chancellor for a decision on whether the deportees might be legally considered prisoners and thus held to forced labor, which Bissing himself thought feasible.

It was a curious way out of a legal dilemma, all the more strange since it was precisely Bissing who shrank from the brutality of mass deportations! One cannot help wondering whether the conferees really thought they could ship 200,000 "convicts" to Germany. Was the governor general intent only on getting out from under the responsibility and shifting it to the Chancellor's shoulders, where it rightly belonged? Or was he perhaps hopeful that Bethmann Hollweg's intervention would prevent mass deportations, so that he, Bissing, might get by with only small groups, sentenced to forced labor by courts-martial? As a weapon of terror, this might serve to push up voluntary labor enlistments.

The OHL men were convinced that the Chancellor would forbid forced labor in Germany and that this was what Bissing was hoping for. This, however, did not prevent them discussing with officials of the government general that same day certain details against the event of mass transports as well as for intensified recruitment. Both sides are likely to have been taken by surprise that the Chancellor's answer of October 9 was along purely legalistic lines. Privy Councilor Kriege of the foreign ministry's legal division had provided him with a masterpiece of legal dialectics. Bissing's prisoner plan was rejected, but a way was shown how "work-shy" Belgians might be deported without a court order and without flagrantly violating international law. The foreign ministry clung to this line of reasoning strictly ever after, and it was used also in replies to protests from abroad.[41] There was only a faint hint of political considerations:

The contemplated measures must be carried out with care, since similar measures in Lille brought representations from the pope and the king of Spain and also seriously prejudiced neutral and enemy opinion against us. It would be most welcome if the thing could be done without coercion, or at least with only a hint of coercion in the background. Perhaps the granting of higher wage levels would serve.

Bethmann Hollweg, in other words, instead of intervening vigorously to avert threatening disaster, recommended merely that the generals use "caution," at the same time offering them a legal subterfuge for their plan and expressing the pious hope that mass deportations could be avoided. What on earth could Ludendorff and Sauberzweig do with such guidance?

We need not here trace the further consultations that took place until late in October among the OHL, the war ministry, the ministry of the interior, and the chancellery. In a concluding session on October 22, Sauberzweig was able to state that all the departments were in agreement on the labor question. In Belgium only industries vital to the war were to continue to operate. The civilian populace was to be drawn on for certain army works. Belgian workers were to be recruited voluntarily to the greatest possible extent. If necessary, there were to be large-scale forced deportations to Germany.[42] General von Bissing no longer offered opposition and thus, on October 26, the mass deportations began. In the rear echelon area they had actually been under way since October 8, i.e., prior to the Brussels conference—in Bruges, of all places, the heart of Flanders!

Like all measures emanating from the OHL that winter, they suffered from excessive haste. To be successful, they would have required a considerable period of preparation. It would have been essential to select only able-bodied persons who could be proved to have been out of work for a long time, who were dependent on public assistance, and who were in some degree trained for the work they were to do.

In the event, the local Belgian authorities obstinately refused to supply rolls of the unemployed, in part because these did not exist, but preponderantly for patriotic reasons. Reprisals, such as the imprisonment of mayors and judges, were of no avail, and the Comité National was protected by international agreements. As a result, the deportations were carried out with great brutality in many places, under procedures that basically went back to the government general itself.

The local commandant of a town or district would call a "control assembly" at which all males from the age of seventeen upward were ordered to appear. Clergymen, lawyers, doctors, teachers, etc., were excused, as were those who appeared clearly unfit, and workers who could prove permanent employment, especially in enterprises working "in the German interest." The rest were requested to volunteer for work in Germany. Those who refused were immediately taken away and loaded into waiting freight trains, often cattle cars, and shipped to Germany under military escort.

Initially, some 8,000 men were to be picked up in this way each week, at the behest of Groener's *Kriegsamt.* Later there were more. They were shipped to assembly depots that were actually vacated prisoner-of-war camps. They were called shelters *(Unterkunftsstätten)* rather than concentration camps. Deportees who even now would not agree to voluntary work were daily escorted to and from work under military escort.

The whole scheme had the appearance of regular slave transports and slave markets, which mitigation by some well-intentioned local commandants could not alter.[43] The horrifying impression on the people need not be described, nor the despair of families left behind, often without leavetaking, nor the sufferings of the deportees who were shipped on endless journeys in freight or cattle cars during a particularly cold and wet winter, without proper clothing and on sparse rations. Illness ran rampant among them, and many reached their camp barracks in a wretched physical and mental state.

Deportees were selected with such haste that there were numerous blunders. They included men fully employed, occasionally even higher civil servants, many boys down to the age of fifteen, sometimes amputees, and, so it was said, more than a thousand employees of the American aid mission.[44] The report of a medico-military investigating commission of the war ministry after an inspection of the camps in March 1917 makes depressing reading. The camp officers were quoted as reporting that most of the deportees were in a wretched physical state from the day of their arrival, some of them totally unfit for work.

One of the reasons was that at the outset there had been no medical screening. When this was introduced, doctors in Brussels, probably acting also from humanitarian motives, passed only 360 of 1,200 men. By the time the deportations were halted on February 10, 61,000-62,000 men had been shipped off, of whom 17,433 (4,283 exempted and 13,150 unfit) were sent home. The death toll in the camps and factory hospitals ran to 816, mostly from pneumonia, heart failure, and tuberculosis.[45]

The material gain to German industry was trifling, compared to the political damage wrought by the deportations. The only successful aspect was that ultimately many Belgians did agree to sign "voluntary" work contracts, to escape the intolerable hardships of camp life and the wretched food.[46] Once out from behind the barbed wire and billeted with good-natured German families at good pay, many of these workers seem to have adjusted well to their new situation.

Under conditions of coercion, work performance was, of course, poor.

Indeed German employers from the very beginning did not relish going to the camps for reluctant foreign workers from whom they had to expect active resistance and even sabotage. One of the worst aspects was that a great many of the deportees had to be kept in the camps for weeks on end, because no work could be found for them. According to official reports, early in December 1916 only one-fifth of the 40,000 deported by then were working, the rest idling about the camps.[47] The *Kriegsamt* organization had failed miserably.

Not all of the dreadful consequences Bissing had predicted came true. There were no riots or general strikes and at first the American aid mission continued, though this was subsequently made very difficult, indeed almost impossible, because of the unrestricted U-boat campaign. Germany's good name was now completely destroyed, and the world found new corroboration for the specter of Prusso-German militarism.

There was a barrage of diplomatic protests from the neutrals—Spain, Switzerland, Holland, the papal see, above all America, whence a formal note soon followed verbal representations. It apparently took a considerable time for the Chancellor and the foreign ministry to realize the degree to which German-American relations had been damaged and with them the prospects of the peace effort contemplated by the Central Powers.

Bethmann Hollweg was, of course, in no position to disavow the generals, especially since he had had a hand in their measures. He was content to defend these measures as admissible under international law and necessary for reasons of military policy. He also recalled the Russian deportations of the people of East Prussia, against which no neutral nation had protested. There was a promise that the worst hardships would be remedied, and this was indeed done in time. The unfit were sent back to Belgium by the thousands. There was medical supervision of the selection process in Belgium. The Chancellor instantly agreed when the Americans demanded that a neutral commission should inspect the *Unterkunftsstätten*. He was powerless, however, to stem the food and coal shortages during the "turnip winter," which made camp conditions ever so much worse.

In Belgium popular indignation found many outlets—the Spanish envoy, Marquis Villalobar, for example, who was officially charged with looking after Belgian diplomatic interests and passing on Belgian complaints; many of the local authorities, who were not intimidated by reprisal arrests; above all the Catholic clergy and its bishops under the leadership of Cardinal Mercier, archbishop of Mechlin. Their petitions and church demonstrations naturally found papal support; but even the German episcopate grew restive, and Cardinal Archbishop Hartmann of Cologne voiced his concern to the Chancellor in person.

Vienna too was greatly worried, especially when the Austrian commissioner accredited to the government general, Baron Frankenstein, sent back highly critical reports about the "precipitate and ill-starred" German labor levies, behind which he suspected the "clumsy and amateurish" hand of General von Sauberzweig. Frankenstein gave a dramatic account of how indignation was mounting to fever heat in Belgium. The Austrian ambassador Hohenlohe protested to the foreign ministry, where he met with a sympathetic hearing but also found much vacillation in respect of the OHL, which it was felt must not be publicly put in the wrong.[48]

Colonel General von Bissing was badly shaken by the failure of his Belgian policies, and around Christmastime he contracted a severe case of influenza that limited his activities. He died in April 1917. In his place the head of his political section, von der Lancken, did his best to stem the tide. In January 1917 the newly established "Council of Flanders," concerned lest the deportations foredoom its nationalist goals, interceded with von der Lancken, pleading for their termination;[49] but discussions with General Groener, head of the *Kriegsamt,* were fruitless. The following month signatures were collected in Belgium for a manifesto of Belgian intellectuals, planned by Cardinal Mercier and other notables in order to protest before the forum of the civilized world against the Belgian "slave trade." Von der Lancken arranged that Villalobar should try to persuade the cardinal to change the manifesto into a petition to the Kaiser. The cardinal said he would agree, but only on condition that von der Lancken could give him assurance that the petition would not be rejected.

This German diplomat, with remarkable courage, thereupon set out for German headquarters to gain the initial approval of Ludendorff, which the foreign ministry had said would be indispensable. On February 20 he succeeded in gaining a personal interview with the omnipotent general, i.e., in the absence of any of Ludendorff's advisers, the headquarters "demigods." To his amazement, it proved relatively easy to convince Ludendorff that the great labor campaign was a failure and should be promptly called off—at least so runs von der Lancken's report. Actually, there is every reason for believing that the general had long since realized this failure.[50] In any event he now dropped the whole enterprise as quickly as he had done only recently in the case of the establishment of a Polish army. Indeed, the deportations had already come to a halt on February 10.

Just where the power lay at headquarters is shown by the fact that von der Lancken was able to depart at once with complete assurance. Without even having seen the Kaiser, he told Cardinal Mercier that by imperial order all persons unjustly transported to Germany would be able to go home at once, while further deportations would cease. The manifesto of the Belgian intellectuals was promptly redrafted, and von der Lancken himself submitted it to the Kaiser, with full success. In formal terms the resulting imperial rescript merely ordered an "investigation," pending which the deportations were to be suspended. In fact it was not merely the unfairly transported who were returned in the course of the next few months, but all the Belgian workers who had been deported and who did not wish to continue working in Germany.[51] The return shipments were effected in inconspicuous small groups.

An exchange between Bissing and Ludendorff following von der Lancken's interview with the latter forms a kind of epilogue to the whole tragedy. On February 22 Bissing expressed appreciation for his powerful antagonist's conciliatory attitude, at the same time reiterating his own autonomy. In a roundabout way he asked further that deportations to the rear echelon areas now be halted. In a lengthy reply dated March 3 Ludendorff maintained that the whole idea of mass deportations had been brought forward not by himself or the OHL but by the war ministry, and that it had been vigorously promoted by German industry, with which the government general itself had agreed on the numbers to be deported. The OHL had given general support to industry demands, but was responsible neither for the volume of the deportations nor for the haste with which they had been carried out and the blunders that had occurred. Even so, the increase in voluntary labor recruitment constituted a considerable measure of success.[52]

In other words, everything had been for the best. Ludendorff wasted not a word on the request for cessation of shipments to the rear echelon areas, where some 60,000 continued to do forced labor. Beginning in the spring of 1917, moreover, Belgian industrial activity was methodically cut back, all the equipment being taken away that might be useful to the Germans. In a letter to the Chancellor dated March 11, Hindenburg acknowledged that he had hitherto followed a policy of exploitation, in order to increase Belgian warweariness to the point where the government in exile at Le Havre would be forced to sue for peace; but in the face of Bethmann Hollweg's Flemish policy, this was no longer possible. Nevertheless, Belgium must continue to be economically weakened, to a greater degree than Germany was being weakened by the war. Only in this way could Belgium be kept in a state of dependence on Germany.[53] Here we have an example of militarism, pure and simple.

# 10

## Austria's Fighting Spirit Ebbs;
## The Affair of Prince Sixtus

### Part 1
### Emperor Charles and the Bourbon Princes

WHILE GERMANY endeavored to increase its fighting power still more by complete mobilization of all military and economic manpower reserves and to prevent industrial decline by ruthless exploitation of occupied territories, the fighting capacity of its allies rapidly faded.

This was most evident in Turkey. Since late 1916 the Ottoman Empire was having increasing trouble in staving off disintegration. After the failure of the Turkish push toward the Suez Canal in early August of that year, the British had been advancing step by step against Palestine, helped by rebellions of the Arab tribes and above all by bridging the desert with rail and water lines. In the summer of 1916 all of Armenia was lost to the Russians, and the subsequent fighting in Persia tied down a considerable portion of Turkey's Asiatic forces, preventing their timely intervention in the crucial war theater, Iraq.

In March 1917, the British managed to take Baghdad, which was of great political, economic, and military importance. This more than made up for their defeat at Kut El Amara the year before. On all the Asiatic fronts the Turkish defenders stood in painful need of replacements, equipment, and ammunition; and only by the incomparable hardiness, frugality, and valor of the Turkish soldiers was this thin front kept intact at all. Not least responsible for this situation was the fact that the Turkish high command had placed no less than seven well-equipped divisions at the disposal of its European allies for use on the Galician, Rumanian, and Macedonian fronts.

The main motive was political. Istanbul realized clearly that the real decision on Turkey's fate must be sought on the battlefields of Europe rather than Asia. When the danger rose to its peak with Rumania's entry into the war, Turkey sought to bolster the tottering Austrian and gravely threatened

Bulgarian fronts. Above all it was at pains to place the Central Powers under as strong a moral obligation as possible.

Turkish military aid was the occasion for a supplementary treaty of alliance, concluded on September 28, 1916, under which the two countries not only pledged themselves not to make peace separately, but—in rather cryptic language—pledged to make available to each other any advantages that would accrue to them when peace came. In effect this meant that Germany was to use the large enemy territories it had occupied as bargaining counters to gain the return of lost Turkish territories that could not possibly be reconquered.[1]

Turkey, in other words, had thrown in its lot completely with Germany, firmly trusting that country's ultimate victory and pledged to continue rejecting any offers of a separate peace from the Entente. In return, however, Turkey wished to share in its ally's apparently impressive victories and the "territorial hostages" Germany had taken.

In the critical situation in the fall of 1916 the German government was willing to enter into such obligations toward the Turks, though soon afterward, once the Rumanian crisis was over, it rejected a similar course of action in respect of the Austrians, as we learned in Chapter 7 (Note 7). True, the German commitment was vaguely worded and carried the mental reservation that it might be declared impossible of fulfillment.[2]

The Turks, however, took the treaty seriously. They remained steadfast even when the British, beginning in late April 1917, sent out various peace feelers. Now that they were so sorely beset by the German U-boat campaign, the British were desperately trying to reduce their own military commitments that required traversing the Mediterranean route. Various British agents in Switzerland and France and diplomatic representatives managed to convey tempting offers of a separate peace to the Turks. Not only were these all rejected, but the Turks immediately reported them to their two allies, in the expectation, of course, of being rewarded for these demonstrations of loyalty. What they wanted more than anything else was support against the insatiable greed of the Bulgarians. Nor did the Turkish attitude change when Russian fighting power began to fade in the summer of 1917.[3]

In the wake of the great successes of the Serbian and Rumanian campaigns, Bulgaria was in the fortunate position of having gained every conceivable military goal. Under its treaty of alliance it was assured of big territorial gains, and it was actually interested in continuing in the war only insofar as a victory by the Central Powers was essential to cashing in on Bulgarian war aims. The excessive character of these aims, especially the claims to Serbian and Rumanian territory, stood in the way of any negotiated peace and was bound to result in friction later on; but it also made any defection of this ally by virtue of Entente offers unlikely—at least as long as Bulgaria remained under threat from Entente expeditionary forces in Salonica. Ludendorff remarked on one occasion that the Allies were doing Germany a favor by their Salonica expedition, which kept Bulgaria from defecting.[4]

In contrast to the attitude of Germany's two weakest allies, the loyalty of Austria, the main ally, began to be seriously weakened in the spring of 1917. The crucial reasons were not so much economic difficulties and military weakness but rather the political worries and ambitions of the Austrian ruling class. Toward the end of the "turnip winter," the economic situation of the Austrians was naturally very bad, worse even than in Germany, because of poor administration and (until the spring of 1917) a ruthless embargo on agricultural produce from Hungary, which was much better supplied.

The hardships, at any rate, cut more deeply in Austria, nor was there any lack of regular bread riots. In the end, however, the crisis was overcome by imports from Hungary and Rumania. We have already heard how military discipline began to crumble in many parts of the multilingual Austrian army with its many organizational and logistic weaknesses. The replacement problem, for example, was much more serious than in Germany, after the enormous Austrian losses on the Russian fronts in the summer and fall of 1916. On the other hand, by 1917 the Austro-Hungarian front was no longer under serious threat at any point. With the fall of the czar on March 15 and the progress of the revolution, Russian army morale disintegrated more and more. As for the Italian army, its own commander, General Cadorna, expressed himself with great skepticism concerning its internal problems. After long hesitation and urging by the Allies, he launched a tenth breakthrough offensive on the Isonzo river. Like all its predecessors, it failed.

Emperor Charles had long before initiated secret peace negotiations with the Western powers, without breathing a word to his German ally. Even his own foreign minister, Count Czernin, was given only the sketchiest information.

Charles was the royal dilettante par excellence. A young cavalry officer, he had reached his high office without any training or experience in politics and administration. His self-confidence was nevertheless supreme, and he was quite willing to do without experienced advisers, who might make him ill at ease because of their expert knowledge, or because they had minds of their own.

He replaced most of the high officials in his government during the very first months of his reign. He took personal command of the army, dismissing Archduke Frederic in rather cavalier fashion. Actually, he lacked both the capacity and the application to manage so unwieldly an institution successfully and army affairs soon got out of hand. Charles regarded General Conrad, the chief of staff, as obstructive and transferred him to the front late in February 1917. Conrad's successor was General Arz von Straussenberg, a

competent officer without great talent, but a much more pliant man, who
stuck strictly to his technical military responsibilities.

The prime minister, Ernest von Koerber, an able man with a mind of his
own, was also retired, to be replaced by a swift alternation of ministers who
were courtiers rather than statesmen. The last man of stature and independence in the government, Count Stefan Tisza, was dismissed in May 1917,
also to give way to a swift succession of incomparably lesser men.

From the time he ascended the throne, the youthful ruler had but one
ambition, to win popularity as a humanitarian and a peacemaker—he wanted
to end the war as soon as possible. It must be admitted that Charles, reigning
over a multinational empire, had good reason for pursuing this goal, for the
Entente reply of January 10 to Wilson's peace initiative publicly proclaimed
the "liberation" of the non-German nationalities under Hapsburg sway as one
of the Allied aims, which meant in effect the dissolution of the empire.

The methods, however, by which Charles pursued his goal were amateurish
and frivolous. Even before a reply had been received from the Entente to the
peace offer of the Central Powers on December 12, he dispatched the German
liaison officer at the imperial court in Vienna, General Cramon, to Pless with
a second peace proposal. Both William II and the OHL rejected it, of course,
which greatly incensed the emperor and the ladies of his entourage, as a
demonstration of German militarism.[5]

Charles was lacking in character, and he was dominated in large measure
by his wife, Empress Zita, of the house of Bourbon, and by his mother-in-law,
the duchess of Parma. In higher officer circles it was jestingly said that all
major government and military decisions were now made in the boudoir of
the palace at Baden. At times these feminine influences led to orders that
were as unthinking as they were well-meant, like a prohibition against dropping aerial bombs behind the enemy front without the emperor's special
permission or against fighting enemy aircraft with incendiary ammunition.
Most importantly, they led to a decision to offer peace to France and Germany in secret, through the emperor's Bourbon brothers-in-law, who were
officers in the Belgian army and ardent French patriots.

A major factor in this decision was jealousy of Germany's superior power,
together with the desire to end Austria's dependence on Germany. Charles
had discussed these matters with his Bourbon brothers-in-law in August 1914,
when he was still only the successor to the throne. At that time the outbreak
of war had overtaken the two princes while they were traveling through
Austria. It was agreed then that only an alliance with France held out the
promise of freeing Austria from the "Prussian" grip and giving it the necessary freedom of action.[6]

Charles had apparently never abandoned this view, even after he became
emperor. In a communication to Czernin in May 1917 he protested vehe-

mently against the idea of tying Austria more closely to Germany through trade agreements—in other words, against the kind of *Mitteleuropa* plans we already know, from Chapter 4. Such plans, Charles maintained, were merely Hohenzollern efforts to place Austria in a state of abject dependence. Bismarck had known very well what he was doing when, not content with throwing Austria out of Germany, he had concluded the Triple Alliance, including Italy. Bismarck had wanted to strengthen Austria's mortal enemy, Italy, force Austria to tolerate Germany's disruptive influence on "our" Italians, threatening Austria's great-power status, and bring Austria totally under German thralldom, whether by peaceful means or through a common war. In a military sense, Germany was still intent upon making Austria subservient, hence the larding of "our magnificent army" with Prussian officers, while supreme command of the allied armies rested in the hands of the Kaiser.

Abroad, the emperor went on, all this had created the impression that Austria was totally under Prussian influence, and this certainly did not contribute to hastening peace. A dramatic German military victory would spell Austria's doom. Austria had no choice but to seek a negotiated peace on the basis of the status quo, which would leave a remnant of amity with the Western powers, who were not really Austria's enemies. This must be Austria's goal, and while not imitating the example of Italy, Austria must leave nothing undone to win the kind of peace suggested, even against Germany's will.[7]

Charles's meaning was clear. The alliance with Germany must not be openly breached, as Italy had done, but peace must be brought about, if necessary against Germany's will. Whether to call this goal a "separate peace" was purely a question of semantics. In any event, it implied a willingness to make peace even if Germany went on fighting. Charles's Bourbon brother-in-law, Prince Sixtus, never placed any other interpretation on the emperor's intentions or negotiated with him along any other lines. He left no doubts that the Western powers, if they were in a mood for peace at all, would conclude it only with Austria, while fighting Germany to the bitter end. This did not swerve the emperor from his purpose.

The first contacts with the two princes seem to have been at the instance not of Charles himself but of his mother-in-law, the duchess of Parma, who had been trying to arrange a meeting with her sons Sixtus and Xavier in Switzerland since early December. As recently as January 12, at a session of the joint Austro-Hungarian council of ministers, Charles himself had proposed that an understanding with Russia be sought, since there was scarcely a chance of contact with the Western powers.[8]

He must have changed his mind rather quickly, for when the duchess, on January 29, met her sons in Switzerland—then the arena for countless agents, spies, negotiators, and politicians from the belligerent countries—she was able to extend to them an urgent invitation to come to Austria for secret peace talks. Without troubling to discuss the matter with any Western statesmen, Sixtus sent a tentative basis for such discussions back to Vienna. It bore all the marks of amateur diplomacy in high places. Sixtus simply set down such French war aims as were known to him: the return of Alsace-Lorraine, within the borders of 1814, i.e., including the Saarland and Landau, to be effected without compensating Germany with colonies or other territory; the restoration of Belgium, which was to keep its Congo Colony; the restoration of Serbia, possibly to be enlarged by the addition of Albania; and lastly the cession of Constantinople to Russia.

These four points continued to form the basis for the discussions. Evidently the prince was not in on France's treaties of alliance, or else he would have scarcely failed to mention at all Italy, Rumania, Poland, and the German eastern borders to come. His first briefing session at the French foreign ministry took place only on February 11, at the hands of its secretary general, Jules Cambon. If the report by the Bourbon prince is correct, Cambon told him a pack of lies to the effect that a secret German peace offer had been received meanwhile, under which Germany was willing to betray without compunction Austria's interests in Italy, Russia, Rumania, and Serbia, in order to spare itself further sacrifices on the Western front. Hence Charles would have to hurry to anticipate his disloyal ally. Let him tell the Kaiser that he would down arms by a certain date. The Entente would respect his signature— probably meaning even without ministerial countersignature! —but Alsace-Lorraine must be returned to France in toto and without colonial reimbursement. None of the Allies, moreover—and this presumably included Russia! —would agree to any peace without the consent of the others.

Actually, this was not a briefing session at all, nor a proposed basis for negotiations, but rather a crude maneuver to spur Charles on and to sound out to what extent he might be used as an instrument in French hands to blackmail Germany into returning Alsace-Lorraine, under the threat that Austria would otherwise defect. Sixtus, however, refused to go along and immediately went much further. He handed two documents to his brother-in-law's emissary, Count Erdödy, a wholly minor figure. Charles was to sign either one, as he pleased. One was a draft proclamation to the peoples of the Austro-Hungarian Empire, announcing a separate peace; the other the draft of a secret treaty with the Entente. Both implied immediate cessation of hostilities on all the Austrian fronts and unconditional acceptance of the four Allied war aims mentioned above. The second document stated that the emperor might confidently anticipate that agreement would soon be reached on the questions of Poland, Galicia, Rumania, Serbia, and Italy. There was no mention that the Entente might offer any quid pro quo, such as guaranteeing the territorial integrity of the Austro-Hungarian Empire. In effect, the emperor was simply being asked to capitulate, though at the surrender only of territories of his ally.

In the face of these demands, the imperial couple apparently began to waver after all and preferred now to consult the foreign minister, though informing him but very incompletely.[9] Czernin was not told that the initiative came from the emperor—he suspected rather that the talks had something to do with the activities of Joseph Caillaux, the former French premier;[10] nor did he get to see the documents sent on by Sixtus, which would have surely deterred him from any further negotiations.

Czernin's advice was to invite the two brothers-in-law to come to Austria in secret, for face-to-face talks, so that swift progress might be made and any indiscretions on Swiss soil avoided. He also set down a general outline for further negotiations, for the benefit of emperor and empress. They were to say, first of all, that a separate peace with Austria was out of the question, and they were to discuss Austrian peace terms along the lines Czernin himself had followed during those very days with the Americans (see Chapter 8, Part 5), as laid down in a crown council of January 12. The line was slightly softened, however. Serbia was not to be destroyed but restored. There would be close economic cooperation with it, but Serbian propaganda to undermine the Hapsburg monarchy must be uncompromisingly halted. Rumania too would escape destruction, though it would continue to be occupied for the time being, to insure full restoration of Austrian territorial integrity—in other words, the return of the territories that had been lost. Belgium was to be restored; and lastly, Austria would agree to the return of Alsace-Lorraine to France, provided Germany was prepared to forego those provinces. Emperor and empress were to emphasize further that Austria was not engaged in a war of conquest, that it was not under German political tutelage, as was believed abroad, hence could negotiate as an autonomous participant at any peace conference,[11] and that it was unaware that any of the nationalities under its sway enjoyed special privileges. Austrian Slavs—this was presumably a reference to the Czechs—enjoyed full equality with German-speaking Austrians, stood in no need of "liberation," and were thoroughly loyal to empire and emperor.

This enumeration clearly shows that Czernin must have completely misread the nature of the Bourbon princes' mission; and if the emperor hoped that his talks might bring tangible success, it was certainly very naive of him to give his intermediary Erdödy in Switzerland a copy of Czernin's catalog, which then reached the French government by way of Prince Sixtus. We know, of course—from Doumergue's negotiations in St. Petersburg (Chapter 8, Part 2)—how Paris then envisaged peace; and it was a foregone conclusion that when Sixtus had his first interview with Poincaré on March 5, the Frenchman declined even to discuss Czernin's terms.

The only thing that made any impression on Poincaré was the prince's assurance that his brother-in-law had declared himself ready, verbally, through Erdödy, to accept the four French conditions; and commenting in writing on Czernin's notes, he said: "We shall support France and exert pressure on Germany by all available means. We feel the deepest sympathy with Belgium and know that that country has suffered a great injustice. . . . We are very definitely not at Germany's beck and call—we have not, for example, broken off relations with America, against Germany's will."

This sounded indeed as though Austria were ready for a separate peace—but how could Austria guarantee the restoration of Alsace-Lorraine, over which it had no authority? Poincaré talked the matter over with Briand, and his suspicions grew. Against all this, however, Paris was afraid of an impending joint Austro-German offensive against Italy, which probably could not withstand such an onslaught. Could this perhaps be prevented, if the emperor were told that peace talks could be held only if Austria ceased all hostilities against Italy?

On March 8 the French president advised the prince that the French government was prepared to negotiate with the emperor, but not with Germany, provided the emperor were to formally and unreservedly accept the four conditions and be ready for an armistice on all fronts. His peace offer would then be forwarded to the Allied government for further consultation. Italy was bound to put forward major demands, but Austria might find compensation in Germany, say Silesia.

Sixtus was highly gratified by the success of his endeavors; and in a long letter of March 16 he tried to persuade his imperial brother-in-law to sign an appended declaration as soon as possible. Among other things, this document pledged that Serbia should receive a large territorial increment, in the form of Albania, as a way of access to the Adriatic, but in return it pledged that the Allies would come to Austria's assistance, if that country were embroiled in a conflict with Germany. Sixtus sought to reassure the emperor on the Italian issue—on no account must this mortal enemy become the target of offensive action at this time, but the Allies almost certainly would not insist that Austria surrender Trieste.

Here, in other words, was a direct challenge to Austria to break its treaty with Germany. This time the two princes came to Vienna in person to deliver it, and there were long talks with the emperor and empress in strictest privacy. According to Sixtus's report, the emperor did not immediately accept the idea of a separate peace. He felt obliged, he is supposed to have said, to exert one last effort to make the Germans see reason, i.e., to accept the four points, though he did not believe he would be able to dissuade them from the idea of a peace with victory. If, however, the Germans remained recalcitrant, he was quite unwilling to offer up Austria to the folly of its neighbor but would make peace himself at once.

General agreement was reached on the four points, including the necessity of restoring Alsace-Lorraine with the Saar region to France. On the other hand, neutralization of the left bank of the Rhine was for the time being treated only as the prince's personal desire. The question of Russia's borders and the Straits was to remain open until Russia's internal situation had become clarified. Serbia, on the other hand, was to be restored and enlarged with "the entire Albanian coast." The only difficulty was Italy. Charles knew very well that he would forfeit all his popularity, indeed draw universal obloquy in Austria, if he left to the Italian arch-enemy the regions that country had been unable to take in offensive after offensive: South Tyrol and Trieste. Charles's way out was to refuse to negotiate with Italy directly. He was willing to make peace with France, Britain, and Russia. Together with them, the question of peace with Italy might then be tackled.

Toward the end of the talks Czernin put in an appearance; and on the following day he had a separate meeting with the princes. Exactly what he said to them is obscure, for Czernin was a cautious and taciturn man. Apparently he was at pains to give the French agents the impression of confidence rather than anxiety. He did, however, according to Sixtus, say more than once that the alliance with Germany would terminate if the Germans prevented Austria from concluding a "reasonable" peace; and since they would never give up Alsace-Lorraine, this would probably be the rock on which the Dual Alliance would fetch up.

It must be regarded as at least doubtful that Czernin was so lacking in diplomacy as to speak in this fashion of the alliance with Germany. It should be kept in mind, after all, that he expressed himself with great reserve on the question of Alsace in his directives for the emperor and empress. Yet some hint must have been dropped that Austria was not prepared to allow peace to founder in these shoals.[12] It remains strange, nevertheless, that he failed to break off the talks when the two Bourbon princes told him unequivocally that France did not wish any peace negotiations with Germany. The only likely explanation is that Czernin envisaged the possibility of Austria negotiating on behalf of both the Central Powers, deputizing for Germany, so to speak, and hoping that Germany might be persuaded after all to make major concessions on its western borders, to bring France to the peace table. We shall see later that this was the precise line he was following at the time.

Emperor Charles at once went much farther. If Czernin hoped that he could keep the youthful monarch from venturing on a slippery slope by injecting himself into Charles's talks with his brothers-in-law, he was badly mistaken. On March 24, behind Czernin's back, the emperor wrote a letter to Sixtus in his own hand, very probably from the latter's draft or at his dictation.[13] It was meant to be passed on to Poincaré and to serve as a token of Charles's determination to make peace.

This important document subsequently achieved notoriety as the *Kaiserbrief,* made public by Clémenceau in April 1918. Charles vainly denied that he was its writer, but his mendacity was so obvious that his prestige suffered a serious blow, and Czernin had to resign.

The letter began with fervent protestations of Austrian sympathy for France, with which the Hapsburg Empire had no serious conflicts of interest, and then gave assurances that the emperor would support with his full personal influence and all the means available to him the "just French demand for the return of Alsace-Lorraine." The other points presented by Sixtus were also accepted, subject only to certain verbally agreed limitations, i.e., a moratorium on the Russian question and no action at all in the matter of Italy. The prince was asked to sound out the French and British views of this offer, and thus lay the basis for official peace negotiations. There was no mention of consulting or otherwise involving Germany, though important questions of German territory were at stake.

Naturally enough the prince represented this letter to President Poincaré as an offer of a separate peace when it was delivered on March 31, and Poincaré immediately so understood it. Briand had fallen in the meantime, and the president confided in his successor, the aged Ribot, an old political warhorse who was always intent on appearing to support the war with the greatest ardor. This was to protect him from his political rivals, mainly Clémenceau, "the tiger," and from Clémenceau's scandal sheet; and in consequence his horizon in the sphere of foreign policy was rather limited.

Ribot agreed with Poincaré that these latest overtures must first of all be discussed with France's allies, including the Italian premier, Sonnino—to which Sixtus strongly objected, from fear of an Italian leak. Sixtus was in fact terrified that the secret might come to German ears. He insisted that the Germans would not shrink from assassinating Emperor Charles when they learned of his defection. Poincaré and Jules Cambon, however, declared firmly that there could be no thought of peace negotiations unless Italy were consulted. They proposed that Austria cede South Tyrol and compensate itself with Silesia. As Sixtus bitterly commented, this meant trading a firm possession against a province still to be conquered.

Apparently Sixtus did not even dare put forward his brother-in-law's desire to make peace with the Western powers first and then to negotiate with Italy *à trois.* He had good reason for this. He felt it was hopeless to try to persuade Italy's allies to play such a game behind Italy's back. The treaties of alliance specifically prohibited any separate peace and violation of these treaties was bound to provoke Italy's defection from the coalition. The Italians had long since grown weary of the war, and the political position of Sonnino, who was an ardent advocate of war, was already shaky enough.

There was, it would seem, a notable lack of enthusiasm in the French response to the Austrian offer.[14] France did not face Austria directly on any front and consequently could expect no immediate relief if Austria quitted the war. It was more than doubtful that Austria could exert pressure on Germany to return Alsace-Lorraine. Indeed, French patriotic sentiment was, as we have already seen, not particularly in favor of achieving this goal by negotiation unless Prussian militarism was first unequivocally and definitively put down. This alone would explain why the statesmen in Paris repeatedly and firmly told Sixtus that they rejected any peace mediation with Germany and preferred to continue the struggle against this arch-enemy.

America's entry into the war on April 2 confirmed the French in their attitude. Poincaré's expectations in respect of the prince's activities as an agent had been fulfilled. Sixtus had brought back assurances from Emperor Charles that there would be no attack on Italy so long as the peace talks continued. It was thus advisable to continue these talks for the time being. Yet it was quite unlikely that Austria would be in a position to satisfy Italy's boundless greed for territorial aggrandizement—which was always a thorn in Poincaré's flesh—and what the prince had to say on this question made it seem even more unlikely.

Ribot, lastly, did not even think it was to France's advantage if Italy made its peace with Austria, for in that event it could be counted out of the Allied front, already materially weakened by the failure in Russia. If the Italians made peace with Austria, it was very unlikely that they would continue the war against Germany. There was also an element of jealousy involved, at least in Lloyd George's judgment. The French begrudged the Italians the outrageous territorial gains they might make in a war that fell more heavily on France than Italy.

Both Poincaré and Ribot had their doubts whether Emperor Charles's offer had any practical value, in view of the stand taken by his minister in early April. For reasons still to be discussed, Czernin had stated publicly that the Central Powers were in complete harmony on the question of peace. Indeed, he showed clear signs of wanting to appropriate the slogans given out by the Russian revolutionaries: peace without annexations and indemnities, peace with neither victor nor vanquished. Both in France and Italy the politicians hated these slogans like the plague. Ribot, moreover, took a jaundiced view of a peace offer under which the only territories to be surrendered did not even belong to the emperor, and he found the whole thing irreconcilable with France's treaties of alliance. Might not this whole peace initiative be a camouflaged German maneuver intended to sound out the degree of French peace sentiment?

In the event, Lloyd George proved to be the only Western statesman to warm up to the idea of a separate peace with Austria. Sinkings were mounting to a peak during April,[15] and this built up strong pressure to put a swift end to war in the Middle East. Lloyd George reckoned that Austrian defection would cut off Bulgaria and Turkey from Germany, as well as cutting off Germany from Rumanian imports. It should also put an end to U-boat warfare in the Mediterranean. Lloyd George thought that the French politicians—including even Paul Cambon, who had long been ambassador in London—were shortsighted not to realize this. He had not abandoned hope that the Italians might sign a moderate separate peace with Austria, which would cede the latter Trieste in return for South Tyrol and firm pledges of a major share in the Turkish booty in Asia Minor—say Smyrna (Izmir).

Lloyd George was mistaken. Sonnino, Ribot, and Lloyd George met on April 19 in St. Jean-de-Maurienne, where the Italian proved so obstinate and greedy in his claims to territory in Asia and Africa that his partners soon gave up trying to talk peace with him. Instead, a protocol was signed in which a separate peace with Austria was expressly rejected as a danger to close Allied cohesion. In accordance with the Bourbon prince's wishes, Sonnino was never told who initiated the peace offer.

For the time being, therefore, Sixtus's peace effort failed, and he was so advised. The French government actually felt there were certain hazards to continuing the talks with Lloyd George, who hoped for Austrian concessions to Italy. The reason was that Count Czernin's behavior was arousing profound distrust in Paris.

## Part 2

# Czernin and the Bourbon Peace Effort

CZERNIN WAS a much nimbler spirit than his predecessor Burián. Clearheaded in his estimate of the situation and well aware of Austria's internal weaknesses, he was imaginative but at the same time capricious and of nervous temperament, lacking steadfastness in the pursuit of his goals.

The Germans at first welcomed his appointment, for he was accounted a loyal supporter of the Dual Alliance.[16] Disillusion ensued when Czernin, like Burián before him, obstinately refused to give up the occupation area of Lublin and leave Poland to Germany.[17] At the time, the German ambassador, Count Wedel, suggested to him that Austria should look to Rumania for compensation in place of Poland. He told Czernin on January 11 that Rumania might be carved up among Russia, Bulgaria, and Austria in such a way as to give Walachia to Austria; and Walachia would be a plum.

Czernin said that his first reaction was to reject the proposal, lest the balance of nationalities be shifted in Hungary.[18] The idea must have impressed him, nevertheless, for thenceforth it recurs again and again in his reports and political statements in various forms, as his own demand. The first time was at the crown council session of January 12, when the Polish question and Austria's war aims in general were discussed.

This was two days after the Entente reply to Wilson's peace proposal, a reply that seemed to hold a serious threat to Austria.[19] Perhaps under pressure of this threat and in the belief that all peace efforts had now failed, the Austrian war aims catalog turned out to be quite moderate—more so, at any rate, than it had been in Burián's time. In the main, Czernin was content with the restoration of Austrian territorial integrity—though this, of course, meant the reacquisition of large territories that had been lost and could be regained only with German aid. Beyond this there were to be only a few "military border rectifications," at the expense of Montenegro, Serbia, and Rumania—without Serbia, however, being carved up. Czernin thought that the Entente would not allow the Balkan states to be destroyed. In any event, the South Slav movement had such momentum that it was bound to prevail, either with Austria or against it.

In the economic sphere there was, therefore, need for a conciliatory attitude toward Serbia, either by conceding it an Adriatic port or better yet by an official trade rapprochement. Chopping up Rumania along the lines proposed by Wedel was not mentioned, but Czernin did suggest that the Entente would approve "cutting back" that country, in retribution for its failure as an ally. He also proposed that Moldavia be offered to Russia, as bait to conclude a separate peace.

Both Tisza and Emperor Charles approved the idea, but Conrad insisted on Walachia for Austria, which Czernin rejected, since it would make peace more difficult. Moderate demands (including a renunciation of indemnities) were to give the Entente, especially Britain, the "false impression" *(vortäuschen)* [sic] that the groundwork was being laid for a peace without victors or vanquished.[20]

Since Czernin prevailed in the main with his proposals, he apparently felt himself to be in a position to launch a new peace initiative on his own—indeed, it was his ambition to outdo his predecessor and put Austria in the forefront in the peace question. His first step was to seek contact with Britain, and in mid-February he asked Count Mensdorff, the former Austrian ambassador in London, to make such an effort in Scandinavia, where he had been sent to give official notice of Charles's ascent to the Austrian throne.

In his talks Mensdorff was to say that Austria was ready for a "mediated peace" without conquests, though border rectifications in favor of Austria were to be reserved and the Polish question was to be left open. He was to refuse any cessions of territory, but cautiously hint that Moldavia might go to Russia. He was to exude confidence and strongly emphasize the inviolability of the alliance with Germany. This was, of course, the program of January

12, which had virtually no chance of success. Indeed, things did not even reach the stage of a discussion with a British diplomat, though Lloyd George dispatched an emissary to Scandinavia for that purpose.[21]

As we have already seen, Czernin expressed himself along similar lines to the emperor and empress in mid-February, when he outlined a policy for negotiations with the Bourbon princes. His response to the American mediation offer was also similar. On both occasions he rejected the idea of a separate peace. He worked all the harder, however, at bringing about a general peace, if such a thing should be possible. He must, of course, have known— and the reports by the emperor on the discussions with Prince Sixtus would have confirmed it—that France would enter into no discussions except on the basis that Alsace-Lorraine would be ceded. Czernin, however, greatly overestimated the scope of the discussions with the Bourbon princes, believing that the impetus came from France, and he now did his utmost to win over the German government to large-scale concessions to France. Beginning in March, he pursued this goal with the greatest energy for months on end—so much so that the alliance with Germany was subjected to the severest strain and came close to the breaking point.

Czernin was, of course, in no position to breathe even a word to Bethmann Hollweg of the discussions between his emperor and the Bourbon princes. Instead he frantically sought parallel contacts with France by way of Switzerland, where individual French agents, some of them on semiofficial missions, had for months been trying to approach Austrian diplomats in efforts to sound out political trends and peace sentiment in Vienna.[22]

On March 10 the Austrian envoy in Switzerland, Baron Musulin, reported that one of these agents, a man named Haguenin, had sent word to him through a Polish intermediary, Count Rostvorovsky, that a certain M. Moysset, the Quai d'Orsay's expert for Polish questions, would shortly visit Switzerland. Rostvorovsky intimated that Moysset might seek political talks with a trustworthy Austrian. There were also reports that a pro-Austrian mood prevailed in Paris, where the desire had been expressed that the government in Vienna might try to serve as a mediator between France and Germany.

Musulin himself thought very little of these reports;[23] but to his surprise he was immediately instructed to spin out this gossamer thread with the greatest caution. At the same time a wire was sent to Hohenlohe, the Austrian ambassador in Berlin, announcing the impending visit of Kajetan Mérey von Kapos-Mérey, an Austrian foreign ministry official of ambassadorial rank. Mérey was to talk with the Chancellor and the German foreign minister about a suggestion allegedly emanating from the French side, under which trusted negotiators, one each from France and Austria, should talk peace in Switzerland.

Mérey did have this meeting, on March 14, in Berlin, but did not name

Mensdorff as the negotiator whom Czernin planned to send to Switzerland. The Germans were, of course, surprised and skeptical, the more so since the German foreign ministry had been through some unpleasant experiences with Haguenin and knew very well that he was a confidant not of Briand but of Jules Cambon, who was bitterly anti-German.

Could Czernin himself really have believed that Haguenin could open up a useful line to Paris that might be exploited with success? Could he have imagined that an obscure M. Moysset, whose intentions were only a matter of conjecture and whose visit was not even certain, would create a better basis for Franco-Austrian peace talks than. was possible by way of the Bourbon princes? Such a thing is quite improbable. Yet on March 18 he did have a wire sent to Berne expressing his "abiding interest" in seeing the contemplated meeting between Mensdorff and Moysset brought about.

The reason is not hard to find. Czernin needed a red herring to divert German attention from the real negotiator, Prince Sixtus.[24] His real purpose was to pressure the Germans into binding commitments by citing the supposed French peace feeler. He wanted to know how far the Germans were prepared to go in making concessions to the enemy and what was their absolute minimum, and if possible he wanted to lower that minimum even further. Oddly enough, he coupled this endeavor with a substantial expansion of Austria's own war aims.

All that Mérey achieved in Berlin was to gain reluctant German agreement to the dispatching of an Austrian negotiator to Switzerland. The Germans insisted that he should be a private person rather than an official, so that the secret talks would be unofficial in character and could be denied in the event of a leak, for the German foreign ministry stood in great fear of the OHL and German public opinion. Any demand for the cession of Alsace-Lorraine must be rejected out of hand. The most that could be considered in that direction was the surrender of a small portion of Lorraine in return for part of the French ore basin.[25]

Two days later Bethmann Hollweg came to Vienna with Under Secretary Stumm, and there was a long consultation on the question of peace terms, in which the two ambassadors participated—this will be discussed further on. After much hesitation, the Chancellor gave his agreement to the dispatching of Mensdorff as negotiator, but only if Mensdorff acted as a private person, and on the terms already outlined. Mensdorff was to be entirely passive and on no account to commit Germany to any minimum program. In effect this would have foredoomed his mission if, indeed, the point of actual negotiation had been reached; but as Musulin had feared from the start, weeks went by—and no negotiator from Paris. Haguenin's project was only a pipe dream.

Musulin did succeed, with the aid of the French embassy, in recruiting a highly placed international society lady who tried to open a line to Paris, whence she obtained many interesting reports. But while Briand had been willing, Poincaré and Ribot held out firmly against any secret talks with Mensdorff. These, they felt, would merely lead the Central Powers to believe that France was running out of steam—besides interfering with the talks between Prince Sixtus and Emperor Charles, which should be taken more seriously.[26] In the circumstances, Mensdorff's situation in Switzerland soon grew awkward. Ultimately even Zimmermann complained to Hohenlohe about this, and Czernin whistled back his emissary on April 7, complaining bitterly of German arrogance. Adding to his discomfiture, the Germans explained that they had contacts of their own in Switzerland that led to French politicians.[27]

Of greater importance than this pseudo peace effort were the talks on peace terms between Czernin and Bethmann Hollweg in Vienna on March 16 and 17. A marked change had come over the Austrian minister since the crown council of January 12. He had then firmly rejected the idea of major territorial gains for Austria and described the very thought of taking over Walachia as an obstacle to peace. In his directives for the emperor and empress in mid-February he was still speaking of only a temporary occupation of Rumania—that country was not to be destroyed but used as a bargaining counter to insure restoration of Austrian territorial integrity. Now it seemed that the most important Austrian concern was not to lose out on its share, compared to Germany and Bulgaria, when it came to dividing up the war booty.

Czernin told Bethmann Hollweg bluntly that Austria, bleeding from a hundred wounds, could not afford to emerge from the struggle empty-handed, let alone diminished, while Germany and Bulgaria walked off with the lion's share.[28] To allow this would risk the most serious danger for Austria. He was now after not only Walachia but also the western parts of Moldavia between the Carpathians and the Sereth, while offering only the eastern part to Russia and letting Bulgaria have that part of the Dobrudja which it had lost since 1913. The remainder of the Dobrudja was to form a tiny state of Rumania, under international control. This, of course, would have amounted to total dismemberment; and even Ambassador Mérey, who was present, raised objections. If the Russians were to be allowed to advance so far into the Balkans, it could serve only to stir up the Slavic peoples of the Balkans all over again. If any Rumanian territory were to be annexed, he argued, it must be a large area, for only in this way could irredentist plots be prevented.[29]

This is very curious, for in a report which Mérey prepared for Czernin soon afterward, he took a diametrically opposite position. For Austria, he said, the war was purely one of defense; and contrary to Germany and Bulgaria, Austria was not out for conquest, even should the war end in its favor. No one wanted additional territories—what, indeed, would Austria do with them? For a multinational empire they could not but be indigestible and conducive to further internal trouble. In the event of victory, Austria should rest content with a fair share of any war indemnities, and on this point agreement had already been reached with Germany.

Even Austria's German ally, however, could not look for large territorial gains. At best there would be a minor exchange with France in the west and a German protectorate over Poland and Lithuania in the east—nothing more. Yet Austria had no cause for jealousy. "We can scarcely deny," Mérey went on, "that in both an absolute and relative sense Germany has done more than Austria," militarily, economically, organizationally. Hence the Germans could justly make greater claims. If Austria were now to annex large parts of Rumania, it would be virtually compelling Germany to put forward even greater claims and thus utterly spoil any chance for a negotiated peace.[30]

This memorandum had been specifically requested by Czernin, as a review of notes he apparently made soon after his Vienna meeting with Bethmann Hollweg. It was to serve him as a position paper for a crown council scheduled for March 29. Since Mérey was here writing for internal use only, it is likely that this memorandum expressed his real views. Apparently he had taken a different stand at the talks on March 16 only because he felt obliged to come to the aid of his minister against the Germans.[31]

It is possible, of course, that his doubts did not rise until later. This is hard to say; nor is it easy to determine why Czernin shifted so rapidly from the status quo as his goal to putting forward very large claims to territory. The only reason he gave his opposite numbers has already been mentioned. Austria was not to be outdone by its ally. Bethmann Hollweg and Stumm had replied quite reasonably that Germany planned no large-scale annexations, nor were any such in prospect.

It is difficult to reconcile Austria's sudden leap in territorial claims with the unsparing description of Austria's critical internal situation with which Czernin opened the discussion—indeed, he had already belabored the Chancellor with it all morning. Austria-Hungary, he said, was at the end of its strength. Typhoid fever already raged in some districts, aided by malnutrition. The harvest was bound to keep getting worse, and even in Rumania crop yields were so low that there would be no surplus for the Central Powers.

The raw material situation was equally bad, and the manpower situation even worse, all reserves having been already exhausted. Realistic evaluation and calculation had shown that Austria could continue the war at best only until the coming fall. The peace feeler stretched out from France must be taken up at once; and the two Central Powers must promptly agree on an appropriate peace program. Yet when it came to discussing the Austrian share in such a program, there was no mention of concessions to Italy and Russia, only of carving up Rumania and regaining East Galicia and the Bukovina, provinces that had been lost to Russia; and to this end, Czernin preferred, as before, to hold on to the occupied Lublin area as a bargaining counter.

What is one to make of this strange combination of pusillanimity and exaggerated expectations? The most likely explanation is that while Czernin was very worried, he was at heart not so despairing as he pretended. He meant to exploit the supposed mission of Prince Sixtus in Austria's favor to its very limits. For the moment the main goal was to persuade the Germans to forego Alsace-Lorraine and Belgium. To this end they had to be thoroughly frightened by the spectacle of a half-starved ally on the verge of collapse and drained of all courage.

Such a shock would put them in fear of Austria's defection, despite all assurances to the contrary, and this apprehension would be deepened by mention of top secret peace talks with unnamed French agents. Czernin probably hoped that Berlin would then concede Austria almost any territorial gain it coveted in the Balkans, Rumania, already suggested by Count Wedel, being the likeliest target. Czernin's exposé for the crown council, already mentioned, shows how temptingly this goal now beckoned.[32] In it Rumania was described as an objective worth billions, but to export thence would mean carrying coal to Newcastle—this was undoubtedly a reference to Rumanian oil resources. Nevertheless, that was the only place where Austria could compensate itself.

If this was indeed Czernin's tactic, it was not entirely without success. It is true that the Germans were visibly taken aback by the plan to carve up Rumania. They said that the German people and particularly the OHL would be unlikely to find such a disproportion in war gains acceptable. They also had grave reservations about apportioning Moldavia to Russia. Bethmann Hollweg at once looked for a compromise—perhaps it would be sufficient to offer the Russians only the northern part of Moldavia, and Austria might find it possible to content itself with West Walachia. Germany itself sought only economic advantages in Rumania. The whole matter would have to be studied further in Berlin.

Czernin was shrewd enough to come up with a flexible compromise formula, to which Bethmann Hollweg agreed: (1) Russian and Balkan territories occupied by the two Central Powers must not be relinquished until the return of enemy-occupied Austrian territory was assured; and (2) any acquisitions made by Germany and Austria must be brought into a certain proportion, in both territorial and economic respects. This came close to the "solidarity agreement" Burián had vainly promoted, though it was now somewhat softened by an Austrian willingness to settle for fully restored territorial integrity—achievable, of course, only through German fighting power! —provided Germany too would be content with the status quo.

Beyond question this was a considerable diplomatic triumph. Czernin's efforts to pin down the Germans to minimum peace terms also bore some fruit. With respect to the east in particular, the Chancellor was extremely moderate in formulating his aims. He did, of course, cling to an autonomous kingdom of Poland under German protection but said that Germany would claim no Polish territories or "border strips" but rest content with strategically necessary acquisitions in Courland and Lithuania (Grodno and Vilnyus), their extent depending entirely on the military situation at the time of peace. He even went so far as to say that if worse came to worst a return to the status quo was a possibility. If Germany were forced at the time of peace to return Poland to Russia, it would be satisfied with mere rectifications along the Silesian and East Prussian borders.

Where Czernin failed was in gaining any concession in the question of Alsace-Lorraine. The Chancellor merely repeated what he had but recently told Mérey in Berlin was the German goal (see p. 387), firmly rejecting any thought of surrendering the two Reich provinces; nor was he willing to evacuate the occupied parts of France and Belgium without further ado—they were to be his bargaining counters to insure the return of the German colonies.

In terms of practical politics, the German stand was virtually useless to Austria. Without the return of Alsace-Lorraine and the evacuation of France and Belgium, there was no chance of even talking with Paris. Yet how else could Bethmann Hollweg have reacted? Germany had not suffered the loss of morale that afflicted Austria-Hungary. German spirits were still high, especially at supreme headquarters, which the German negotiators expressly mentioned. At this very time, in mid-March, news of the Russian Revolution transpired, and this was bound to have a strong influence in relieving pressure on the eastern front. U-boat sinkings in February had exceeded the most optimistic estimates by one-half. The Germans evacuated the threatened Somme salient and fell back on the well-prepared and much shorter Siegfried line, leaving an utterly devastated area to the enemy, who did not even detect the maneuver. The major offensive the Germans feared so much was delayed for many weeks, its best chance of success gone before it began.

Was this the moment for the kind of German capitulation envisaged by Emperor Charles and his minister? The main consideration should have been that the German people in every walk of life were totally unwilling to relinquish the two Reich provinces voluntarily. Only final and irrevocable defeat could force their hand; for Alsace-Lorraine had become a "national treasure" to the Germans even more than to the French, part of their heritage and symbol of their proudest hour.

It must have been a dismaying experience for Bethmann Hollweg to realize suddenly that Germany's major ally had grown not only enfeebled and dispirited but politically unreliable as well. It was most disquieting to have Austria press for concessions that not only would have precipitated the gravest conflicts with the OHL and German public opinion but would have been taken abroad as a certain sign that Germany too was at the end of its tether and willing to resign politically.

The story that went the rounds in Vienna court circles was that the Chancellor had simply lost his composure at the end of the second day, following an official dinner given by the Kaiser at which Czernin complained over and over about the disastrous situation inside Austria.[33] Quite possibly Czernin had been looking for such an occasion and exploited it to the hilt with defeatist talk. At any rate a remarkable passage occurs in his crown council exposé: "I am convinced that the key to the situation lies in the west. If Germany were to relinquish France and Belgium, and perhaps something more, it would mean peace. The Chancellor promised me this sacrifice in the strictest secrecy." What sacrifice? This was kept purposely obscure. Czernin, however, now decided to roll up bigger guns in his further negotiations with the Germans.

In his crown council exposé we read: "Telling the Germans that we shall not surrender those parts of Poland we have occupied until they have incorporated Rumania into Austria is a likely means to our end. We shall leave 'our' Poland voluntarily only as part of a sales transaction." Berlin would understand such tactics, he added. Czernin, in other words, was now ready to drop for good and all the "Austro-Polish solution" to which he had hitherto clung so fiercely—but only against compensatory gains in Rumania. That Austro-Polish solution was even so virtually unattainable, and the constant tug-of-war with Germany over Poland was "an utterly impotent maneuver."

Czernin airily dismissed the fears voiced by many that the Polish Galicians were bound to form an irredentist movement that would press for union with the new kingdom of Poland. Irredentists were ubiquitous, he remarked, and Austria-Hungary merely had a particularly colorful spectrum of them. Any country with a powerful army not embroiled in war—and after the current slaughter surely there would not be another war for a very long time—need not fear irredentists.

Nor was Czernin put out by the initial muttering of "Vienna beer garden politicians and Hungarian desperadoes" over the incorporation of Rumania. As for the danger of Russian encirclement in eastern Moldavia, had the Rumanians been any better and safer neighbors than the Russians? The arguments were threadbare, it will be seen, and Mérey at once protested, but they are typical of the glib and easygoing way in which Czernin constructed his plans; once they were under way, Czernin wanted not only to reduce Serbia in size but to take it into the Austro-Hungarian customs and trade union and force it to seek its future destiny in the closest integration with Austria.

The ultimate meaning of the whole plan was not revealed until the exposé's last sentence: "Only by looking to the Balkans and selling Poland to Germany can we expect that the idea of a partial cession of Alsace-Lorraine will take shape"—only under Austrian pressure, of course. In other words, leaving the Polish protectorate entirely to Germany was to be a quid for Germany's quo in foregoing at least part of the Reich provinces. At the same time, the Austrians were to get Rumania, conquered very largely with German and Bulgarian blood.

The whole plan seems almost too fantastic for an experienced career diplomat, yet Czernin was in bitter earnest, and henceforth it formed the guideline for his policy. At the crown council on March 22 he did not yet dare—if the minutes may be relied on—to suggest that Germany might relinquish parts of Alsace, only that it should forego unspecified conquests in the west. For the rest, he arranged to have the policy position he had taken on March 16 confirmed, and exacted authority to saddle Germany—if that were possible—with a kind of liability for insuring Austria's territorial integrity—in other words, Burián's old solidarity pact.[34]

That same evening Prince Sixtus of Parma and his brother turned up in Vienna. The following evening and on March 24 they talked with the emperor and empress and Czernin; and then they departed Vienna, in their pocket the so-called *Kaiserbrief* of which we have already heard. It pledged France Austria's firm support in its "just claim" for the return of Alsace-Lorraine. Czernin had also given them verbal assurances that Austria would not allow any peace effort to fail on account of the issue of Alsace-Lorraine (see above, p. 381).

As a next step, Czernin again went to Berlin on March 26, for the main purpose of telling the German government that Austria was prepared to forego Poland, against the event that the main part of Rumania would fall to Austria. He also wished to press further for major German concessions to France.[35] To enhance the generosity of his Polish offer, Czernin said: "If it were ever to transpire in Austria that I were willing to surrender Poland, my position would become quite untenable." He carefully glossed over the fact that the crown council had already decided this issue. He brazenly claimed that the gains Austria stood to make from the wreckage of Rumania were only moderate and blandly insisted that the Magyars would be vehemently opposed—though Tisza, at the recent crown council, had reached out with both hands and quarreled with the Austrian premier over this plum.

To demonstrate Austria's magnanimity, Czernin said that though he had not yet spoken to anyone about the matter he was personally prepared to get the Serbs a port on the Adriatic and accept them into the Austro-Hungarian customs union. Possibly this might diminish Entente interest in Rumania. What was not mentioned was that this was—as we have already seen—a demand put forward by Prince Sixtus, besides being proposed to the crown council by Czernin himself.

To spur on the Germans, he painted the situation in Austria in the gloomiest colors, suggesting that the workers among the non-German nationalities in the Austrian Empire were on the point of rising in rebellion. How long Austria could still hold out was only a matter of weeks—it could scarcely be beyond August or September, though even that was not certain. Should Mensdorff (meaning, of course, Emperor Charles!) meet with the French negotiator again, it would be well if he had something of substance to say—to wit, about favorable peace terms offered by the Central Powers.

But the Germans were not so easily taken in and they kept their nerve. When told about the grave food shortages in Austria, the Chancellor replied coolly that it would not be easy to convince the OHL, which kept hearing that there was a surplus in Hungary, from German officers and dignitaries who went there on official business. When Czernin asked that Bulgaria be allowed to participate in the alleged Swiss negotiations—which he did in order to strengthen his own position—he was told that this was hazardous and not necessary. When he warned the Germans that according to his intelligence sources, the Turks might make a separate peace, this was refuted from recent diplomatic exchanges. When he complained of OHL conduct in Poland, it was proved to him that this was a thing of the past.

Zimmermann was highly skeptical of Count Mensdorff's activities in Switzerland and warned against pressure tactics. The enemy should be allowed to come forward on his own—his situation was certainly far from rosy. Czernin was particularly worried that the German foreign ministry might press for acceptance of a somewhat mysterious Italian offer received in February by the German embassy in Berne, which was a hotbed of rumor and espionage. It apparently came from the Italian General Staff and said that the king of Italy was prepared to conclude a separate peace with Austria, if he got assurances about the cession of South Tyrol and a position of dominance in Istria. The whole thing may have been no more than a tactical maneuver by Cadorna, to forestall an attack by Austrian and German troops to be launched from Tyrol, which the Italians then considered an alarming possibility.[36]

Bethmann Hollweg had already mentioned this matter to Czernin in Vienna, though taking care not to recommend acceptance and especially not the cession of South Tyrol, for this would almost certainly have brought on still more Austrian compensatory demands, in the form either of a piece of Silesia[37] or of German relinquishment of part of Alsace-Lorraine. At the same time, however, Bethmann Hollweg had steadfastly refused to offer any guarantee that the Austrian territories occupied by Italy would be returned.

Czernin now worked hard to get such assurances. He insisted that the present Italian line, less than five miles away from Trieste, was quite unacceptable, nor could the port of Vlonë be left to Italy. Emperor Charles had said he would rather perish than surrender a single square foot of his empire to Italy; but Czernin's German partners were unmoved, and their attitude hardened even more when he came out with his most important request: Would Germany be ready under certain circumstances to cede part of Alsace-Lorraine to France?

Bethmann Hollweg gave a curt and ironic reply: "Count Czernin has just told us he could not cede even a square foot of Austrian soil to Italy, yet he expects us to give a piece of Reich territory to France!" This time too he would not be pushed into anything more than a new formulation of moderate German war aims in east and west;[38] and Zimmermann for the first time announced that Germany was interested in Rumania's oil. Czernin's diplomatic offensive, in other words, was beaten back. The alliance began to show the first cracks, as seen from the manner in which the two allies kept citing statistics on the sacrifices and losses they had suffered. Mutual confidence plainly had been shaken.

To avoid returning from Berlin empty-handed, Czernin secured a written record and elaboration of the agreements made verbally in Vienna on March 16. He had brought with him a draft in the form of an exchange of letters between himself and the Chancellor, which was to commit both governments formally to the agreed program; but the German government was unwilling to accept this. The upshot was a "résumé" signed by Czernin and Bethmann Hollweg, a considerably watered-down document that actually modified the Vienna agreements.

The "commitment" had turned into a mere intention of the two powers to use the enemy territories they had occupied for purposes of restoring the status quo, and even this was qualified rather than unconditional. The important thing was that the status quo was to be restored not merely in Austria-Hungary, but, for both powers, in east and west. If Austria, in other words, were to insist on German territorial concessions in the west, this might lead to Germany revoking the whole agreement.

Restoration of the status quo was described as a minimum program, and the second paragraph did not refer to new acquisitions outright, only in the event the war ended "favorably." In that eventuality "the territorial acquisitions of the two powers would have to be brought into correspondence with the contributions on either side." Indirectly but nevertheless quite clearly, this implied a higher priority for German ambitions. Yet Czernin could take comfort from the concluding sentence, which said: "For Germany this would mainly mean the east, for Austria-Hungary Rumania." Insertion of the word *mainly* suggested, however, that the possibility of German acquisitions in the west—for example, Briey—was kept open.[39]

The German foreign ministry at once sent a report on the Berlin talks to supreme headquarters for Ludendorff's information.[40] Czernin, on his part, was by no means prepared to accept the meager outcome, which was of no use whatever in further discussions with Prince Sixtus. Directly on his return to Vienna, he sent on to the major Austrian diplomatic missions abroad a report only just received from Musulin in Berne. That ambassador said his impression was hardening that the issue of Alsace-Lorraine was the crucial obstacle to peace. The French had retreated from the demand for "the destruction of German militarism" and become more reasonable. In the matter of Alsace-Lorraine, nevertheless, their vanity must be satisfied in some measure, since otherwise they would be quite unwilling to attend any peace meeting.

Ambassador Hohenlohe was charged with apprising the German government of this report to the best possible effect.[41] In a second wire he was instructed to reiterate to the Chancellor that territorial concessions to Italy were out of the question and that Austria would be ready to conclude a separate peace with Italy only on the basis of the status quo. This probably went back to an order from Emperor Charles.[42]

Germany professed not to understand how such obstinacy was compatible with a simultaneous dispatch from Count Wedel, the German ambassador in Vienna, quoting Czernin and Clam-Martinitz, the premier, as stating that for internal reasons Austria could not possibly continue the war for longer than six weeks, hence had to make peace at any price. This was a bit too much even for Prince Hohenlohe. He warned his minister not to push the alarm button too often, since this brought disrepute on Austria, whose plaintive cries were already believed to stand in the way of the struggle for a sound peace. There would be a day of reckoning when the peace conference actually came about.[43]

But Czernin knew very well what he was about. He intended to keep hammering away at the German statesmen along the lines of his peace initiative. On March 28, directly after his return to Vienna, he agreed with Emperor Charles on a major coup. Charles was to pay a personal visit to Homburg to make good his promise to Prince Sixtus embodied in the *Kaiserbrief*, i.e., to use every possible means at his disposal to persuade William II to conclude a "peace of renunciation."[44]

On the eve of the departure Czernin told Count Wedel just how he envisaged this action. He hoped to persuade the German government to cede the greater part of Alsace-Lorraine, without Briey as a quid pro quo. If it were a question of general peace, Austria was instantly ready to cede Galicia or South Tyrol—after all! [45] At the palace in Homburg Czernin went even further. He proposed that Germany forego all of Alsace-Lorraine in return for a claim to Poland plus Galicia.

Actually, there were no formal discussions on this point, for the meeting of the two emperors was more in the nature of a family affair than a working conference, large entourages having been mustered on both sides. Czernin managed only one private talk with the Chancellor, and later with Ludendorff, to whom he vainly tried to justify Austria's need for peace. The formal meeting of the ministers and generals broke up after only ten minutes, when Czernin and the Chancellor were summoned before the two emperors.

If Czernin had indeed staked his hopes on Emperor Charles using this occasion to besiege the Kaiser with arguments in favor of his peace plan, he must have been bitterly disappointed. The young Austrian monarch was politically naive and of limited intellect. In the presence of so lively a personality as William II, Charles was all but helpless. Apparently he did not even dare state his own case, leaving it to Czernin once again to paint a picture of Austria's crisis in the blackest colors. General Arz, the new Austrian chief of staff, was similarly charged, but he too was no match for that supremely confident pair, Hindenburg and Ludendorff. Charles's weak-kneed attitude may be gauged from the reply he gave to the Kaiser's question whether Czernin had not drawn too gloomy a picture of the situation. "Count Czernin always exaggerates," he said.[46]

Somehow the Polish question must have come up between the two emperors, however; for the Kaiser offered to summon Archduke Charles Stephen as regent of Poland, later to become king. Agreement was ultimately reached that "far-reaching annexationist velleities" must not be allowed to stand in the way of opportunities for a prompt peace, and that international integration of revolutionary movements over the heads of existing governments must be prevented. There was to be no new peace offer, though whatever "peace talks" were already under way should be continued, the two allies keeping each other fully informed. More importantly, any concessions that would have to be made should be borne by the two countries in common, in an equitable proportion.

The Homburg meeting was in reality a total failure, but Czernin drew comfort from this smooth and reassuring-sounding résumé.[47] The failure was a foregone conclusion, even had the renunciation of Galicia, improvised at the last minute, met with the approval of the joint Austro-Hungarian cabinet, and had it been possible to persuade the Entente to approve giving Austria Rumanian territory by way of compensation. At the Berlin talks on March 26, Bethmann Hollweg had already made it clear that the Germans would never understand why their country should surrender not only all the occupied territories in the west but part of Alsace-Lorraine to boot, in return for an irksome new Polish neighbor, while Austria would emerge from the war intact, indeed possibly enlarged with Serbian and Rumanian territories.

The real weakness of Czernin's proposal, however, was not this disproportion in gains but the fact that he had not the slightest assurance that German willingness to give up Alsace-Lorraine would immediately result in an "honorable" peace. By early April the spurious character of Mensdorff's mission had long been apparent, and Czernin was not even permitted to discuss the alleged peace offer of Prince Sixtus.

Asked for his opinion, Ludendorff rightly told the Chancellor that a German peace offer on the eve of the anticipated enemy spring offensive would be a blunder, in both a military and a political sense. Count Wedel remarked, equally reasonably, that developments on the Russian revolutionary front should first be awaited. Quite possible the whole idea of buying peace with major concessions in the west—rather than foregoing dubious annexations in the east and making attractive offers in St. Petersburg—was a mistake at a time when the Russian enemy was faltering, while American entry into the war was breathing new life into Western hopes of victory.

Count Czernin thought of himself as a shrewd realist, in contrast to the wrong-headed German militarists, and he had good reason; but the plan he proposed in Homburg was unrealistic, built on sand, amateurish—the foreign ministry in Berlin used the term *grotesque*. Under Secretary von dem Bussche recalled overhearing Czernin say on one occasion: "The Germans brought about the present war by their annexation of Alsace-Lorraine in 1870. It is now up to them to make a concession."[48]

As will be shown, however, Czernin did not stake everything on the supposed French peace feeler. Indeed, he may have been pursuing his "grotesque" plan of swapping Poland-Galicia for Alsace-Lorraine in only low gear at Homburg, precisely because in the meantime an altogether different peace perspective had appeared on the political horizon.

# 11

# The Russian Revolution of March 1917 and the Plan for a Peace Without Annexations

## Part 1
## Germany Stakes Its Hopes on Revolutionary Chaos in Russia

THE DAYS from March 12 to 15, 1917, when the czarist regime in Russia collapsed resistlessly, mark a historic turning point the enormous significance of which is becoming fully clear to us only now. The chaos begotten when the March revolution in St. Petersburg destroyed all old authority gave rise, in a matter of months and under pressure of the military crisis, to a new species of government that completely transformed the old Europe—totalitarian democracy, the one-party state. In Russia it was the creation of a single inspired man, a demoniac fanatic of irresistible will; but it was also the inexorable development of a process set in motion within all the countries of Europe that took part in the First World War—the first instance of total war. The political and social forms of the bourgeois-liberal age were being converted to twentieth-century mass democracy. A new era in history dawned in 1917.

Naturally none of the participants in the workers' and soldiers' rebellion in St. Petersburg in March 1917 had the slightest inkling of the sinister consequences the abrupt collapse of all public authority in the ancient czarist state would bring on. Everyone thought this was merely an improved, i.e., more radical repetition of the revolution of 1905. Foreign observers had even less of an idea of what was actually happening. The bourgeois-liberal politicians of the West believed naively that they were at last rid of the anomaly that had irked them since the war's beginning: fighting for liberal-democratic ideals side by side with a reactionary autocracy.

At the historic session of Wilson's cabinet on March 20, 1917, when war against Germany was decided on, Lansing argued that this was the right moment to proclaim a crusade for democracy and against absolutism; for autocracy had fallen in Russia, and encouragement should be given to the young Russian democracy.[1] This kind of thinking was common in the West, and there was a barrage of congratulatory messages to the provisional government in St. Petersburg, dispatched not merely by representatives of the socialist parties but also by the parliaments and governments of the Allied powers.

Yet these expressions of pleasure and sympathy were quite misplaced, if their senders looked on the Russian Revolution as a starting point for intensified military activity on the part of the Russian people. The mutinous garrison of St. Petersburg and the workers in Russian war industry were rising, not to increase war effort and sacrifice still further, but to put an end to the whole misery of war as swiftly as possible. Only the curious fact that the tiny liberal bourgeoisie, politically organized on the left as the so-called "Duma bloc," initially got the upper hand in the chaos of revolution, temporarily concealed the unequivocally antiwar character of the revolutionary mass movement.

The liberal democrats who organized the provisional government of Russia appointed as their foreign minister the historian Milyukov, most radical of all the chauvinists; but from the beginning the split in the revolutionary leadership was apparent, for beside the provisional government stood the St. Petersburg soviet (or council) of workers and soldiers, which regarded itself and its executive as direct organs of the popular will. Except for the mediating role of the social revolutionary Kerensky, who entered the government as the sole representative of the radical left, that government could not have prevailed at all; and the conflict of opinion between it and the soviets was assuaged only by concession after concession.

It was on these clashes that the Central Powers staked their hopes when the revolution broke out. The German government had been trying for years to foment the revolutionary movement in Russia along lines that would favor international understanding rather than the Russian nationalism methodically encouraged by the Entente. In pursuit of these goals the Germans used all manner of agents, and among these the romantic figure of the Russian socialist Dr. Alexander Parvus-Helphand was particularly prominent. The German method was methodical subversion of morale in the army and among the people; and to this end they used extreme leftist, pacifist, and internationalist slogans, of the kind featured particularly at the socialist conferences in Zimmerwald and Kienthal during the war.

The ultimate goals of these movements were the overthrow of bourgeois government and the union of proletarians everywhere to bring about world peace—in other words, world revolution. At first blush it seems rather strange that the German monarchist government should not have shrunk from maintaining clandestine contact with these forces of upheaval; but over the years sums running into many millions went to sustain Russian émigrés and their illegal propaganda work. The Germans knew very well that they were playing with dynamite; but since all the efforts, already reviewed, to reach a separate peace with the czarist government had remained fruitless, they felt they had to arrange themselves with the forces of revolution. Under pressure of a war situation that was growing more and more hopeless, any means of breaking out of the enemy ring of iron was deemed permissible.

General Max Hoffmann put it in military language: "I fire shells on the enemy's trenches and blow poison gas in his face. By the same token, as a belligerent, I have the right to use the weapon of propaganda on his men."[2] Actually, there was no way of knowing—certainly not from the vantage point of Germany—just how support of Russian revolutionary propaganda would work out. The Germans were merely guided by the pressures of the day, waiting impatiently for enemy morale to collapse. To accelerate that day, they made deals with any and every Russian agent they could find, reconnoiterers from the ruling class and arch-enemies of czarism alike.

Headquarters for liaison with the revolutionaries were the German embassy in Copenhagen under Count Brockdorff-Rantzau, and the embassy in Berne, where Freiherr von Romberg, the envoy, had many contacts among the Russian émigrés in Zurich, who were centered on Lenin. These émigrés were very broad-minded in accepting German financial subventions,[3] and apparently this did not exclude even Lenin, though Lenin took great care to avoid any direct contact with German agents, especially Helphand. According to a report to the Kaiser which Kühlmann rendered on December 3, 1917,[4] a good deal of money from German sources continued to flow into Lenin's pockets even after his return to St. Petersburg, enabling him to expand his party paper, *Pravda,* and his other propaganda activities on a large scale. Lenin, of course, would not have dreamed of trying to be useful to imperial Germany in the slightest way and used the German funds solely for conducting his activities on behalf of world revolution. These, however, did include immediate and radical de-escalation of the war, by inducing the proletariat to rise against the "imperialists" of all countries, including Russia.

By the same token, German diplomacy looked on the Russian Revolution solely from the viewpoint of the chaos it might wreak in the enemy camp, which would serve the German purpose. To make the mischief even worse, the Germans also supported separatist movements in the Ukraine and the Baltic provinces. Brockdorff-Rantzau reposed great confidence in the effectiveness of these methods, evidently under the influence of Helphand, whom he kept recommending to Berlin as a confidential agent. "Victory will be ours," he wrote in December 1915, "and the prize will be world leadership, if we succeed in revolutionizing Russia in time and thus in disrupting the coalition."[5]

These hopes had been frustrated time and again; and it was actually neither German nor British subversion that unloosed the uprising of March 1917.

Its cause was the profound weariness throughout the country and the resentment felt by all classes, including the bourgeoisie, against the czarist bureaucracy, which was universally regarded as incompetent and corrupt. Its collapse was greeted with the same sense of relief in Berlin and Vienna—not least at German headquarters—as in the Entente capitals, where a renewal of the Russian war effort was hoped for. The Germans and Austrians, of course, hoped for the opposite, that the Russian fighting spirit would now fade completely. They looked to the workers' and soldiers' soviets rather than to the provisional government, formed as a committee of the bourgeois Duma bloc under the chairmanship of Prince Lvov. The urgent question now was what should and could be done to help the active opponents of continuing the war, i.e., the Russian defeatists and deserters, carry the day. On this point there were differences among the politicians and the generals, and more importantly, between the governments in Berlin and Vienna, differences that struck a heavy blow at the alliance of the Central Powers.

The eastern high command was now under Prince Leopold of Bavaria, with General Hoffmann as his chief of staff. When the news from St. Petersburg reached that headquarters, the straightforward response was to prepare for a few powerful offensive strikes to give the coup de grace to Russian military morale. Such an action was indeed carried out on a favorable occasion at Toboly on the Stokhod on April 3, 1917, with great military success. On the other hand the political effect was that the assurances by German intermediaries that Germany sought peace with the Russian people forfeited a good deal of their credibility, as did similar sentiments proclaimed during German socialist demonstrations. In a political sense, therefore, this partial victory was a liability, and for the time being the supreme army command forbade any further attacks of this kind. Even Ludendorff realized that such successes did more harm than good. Actually, because of the overextended situation on the western front, he lacked the forces that would have been required to carry out a major offensive.[6]

In Hoffmann's judgment, moreover, the Russian front had not yet crumbled to the point where German forces could conceivably advance without encountering resistance. Furthermore, the social revolutionary party, which had enjoyed the strongest support from Russian workers and peasants since 1905, was not devoid of patriotism or nationalist sentiment, unlike the extreme Marxist followers of Lenin. Officers and government propagandists still found it possible to convince the ordinary Russian muzhik that the new-won freedom must be defended against German reaction, and that the Germans must not be allowed to shift large contingents of troops from east to west to prevent an Allied victory. Even the Bolshevists Stalin and Kamenev, prior to Lenin's reappearance in St. Petersburg, opposed the defeatist "down with the war" policy of simply abandoning the front.

What could be done to undermine this patriotic attitude? In March and April Envoy von Romberg and Ambassador Count Brockdorff-Rantzau discussed this problem at great length with Russian émigrés. Brockdorff advised a policy of covertly deepening the split between moderates and extremists, and of supporting the latter by every possible means short of overt intervention. This would wreak such havoc that within a matter of months the German army could walk in and seal the doom of Russian power.[7]

The man who seemed the likeliest candidate to implement this kind of agitation was Lenin, with his followers. Lenin was the most uncompromisingly radical of all the Russian revolutionaries, and Bethmann Hollweg had known since 1915 that his revolutionary program included an immediate peace offer, leaving France to one side—though Germany would be expected to forego annexations and indemnities. Lenin's very first draft of revolutionary theses, the basis for his campaign against the provisional government beginning in March 1917, contained a plank considered perhaps the most important, namely that all the belligerents were to be promptly and openly challenged to agree to an immediate armistice, to be followed by a peace based on the complete liberation of all colonies and all countries that were in a state of dependence or enjoyed less than complete equality. Although the proposal was not exactly realistic, it had a strong radical ring. The fourth of Lenin's subsequently famous "Reports from Afar," dated March 25, bitterly opposed as "routine philistinism" the policy of "peace with honor" which Maxim Gorki had just proclaimed, and outlined a peace program that amounted to a manifesto for world revolution.[8]

The Germans knew enough of what was going on to conclude that Lenin was counting on the extreme war-weariness of the Russian masses, hence decried as petty bourgeois every sign of "patriotism," even in the socialist camp. No sooner had the Russian Revolution broken out than Bethmann Hollweg agreed or even suggested[9] that Romberg take up contact with Russian revolutionaries who had been living in Switzerland and among whom Lenin was the most prominent, holding out to them the prospect of returning to Russia by way of Germany or Sweden.

As we know, these negotiations swiftly bore fruit. The first group of Russian émigrés, including Lenin, was able to depart Zurich by April 12, enjoying safe-conduct across the borders and Germany. All the agencies concerned in this operation went to work with a will and without the slightest hesitation—Bethmann Hollweg, the Kaiser, the German foreign ministry, the OHL, the German embassy in Berne, even the Swiss authorities, the socialists, and their trade unions.[10]

Other groups of Russian émigrés were to follow; and with the Germans setting a precedent, the Allies found themselves obliged to follow suit in allowing the revolutionaries who had found asylum with them to return. This included even so important a figure as Trotzky, who came back from America. Neither in Germany nor elsewhere did anyone have an inkling of the sinister consequences that were to flow from this remigration. The political needs of the day were all that mattered.

But even viewed from the aspect of such concerns, allowing Lenin passage turned out to be a miscalculation. In his first proclamation after his return he did inveigh against the Lvov government as the hired lackeys of the British and French imperialists and protest bitterly that millions of Russian peasants and workers were being sacrificed in order that War Minister Guchkov might lay hold of Constantinople, while Syria was abandoned to the French and Mesopotamia to the British capitalists. He demanded, further, that all secret treaties of alliance be made public at once.

But Lenin did not succeed, of course, in launching the immediate civil war he wanted in order to topple the government and create a Soviet dictatorship. Indeed, his immoderate revolutionary demands antagonized many of his oldest followers, and he was at first far busier with his domestic program than with propaganda for peace. He could not afford to preach total defeatism, if only because he knew he was rumored to be a paid German agent. He had never looked for a Russian offer to conclude a separate peace, for his principal goal, world revolution, could be attained only if socialists throughout the world rose up to demand peace.

Lenin actually spoke out against a separate peace after his return, as did the provisional government and ultimately the majority of the soviets. Kerensky had in the meantime mounted a tremendous propaganda campaign and succeeded in rekindling a degree of fighting spirit at the front. A new offensive was launched in Galicia on June 30, but even after it fetched up on a German counteroffensive and failed, Lenin did not yet get his way. The Bolshevist-inspired rally of soldiers and workers against the provisional government came to nothing, for the leaders of the soviets refused to join in. Publication of certain documents proving that Lenin's party had received German subventions, moreover, created a furor in the army ranks. The government was able to order Bolshevist leaders arrested, and some of them actually were. Lenin himself had to go into hiding. He fled to Finland and was able to return to St. Petersburg only late in October, in secret.

It took over half a year, in other words, together with the most painstaking nationwide propaganda and organizational effort, before Lenin's hour struck. The November revolution did prevail then with a policy of peace at any price; but Lenin's party could not have put this over but for the rising hardships of the war, the fear of a fourth war winter, the complete extinction of morale in the trenches, and the desertion of millions of peasant soldiers, who wanted a share in the redistribution of the big estates. All this made continuation of the war senseless.

To go back a bit, once it was clear that the war with Russia would not be brought to a sudden halt by fomenting chaos in Russia, the alternative was to try for an understanding with such Russian elements as showed themselves to be inclined toward peace; and this was indeed the goal now pursued by the Central Powers with the greatest vigor. The first impetus was a declaration by Russian socialists in Copenhagen on March 25, stating their party's desire for immediate peace without territorial gains or indemnities, while at the same time vigorously resisting any German effort to hinder the Russian Revolution or support the old regime in any way.[11]

Bethmann Hollweg and Czernin, meeting in Berlin, agreed the very next day to answer this appeal affirmatively; and the Chancellor did so in his Reichstag speech of March 29. He assured his listeners that none in Germany dreamed of "restoring the czar's rule over his enslaved subjects," nor of interfering in any way in Russia's domestic affairs. All that the Germans wanted was to live again in peace with the Russian people as soon as possible—in a peace that would bring honor to all concerned.

Two days later a German social democratic demonstration emphatically confirmed this declaration.[12] Czernin, in an interview in the *Wiener Fremdenblatt* of March 30, went even further. Rather at odds with his private sentiments, with which we are already familiar, he displayed much confidence in victory but proposed that a peace conference of all the belligerent powers be called at once—indeed, this might be done even if there were no armistice to begin with. In the matter of peace terms, Czernin followed the Central Powers' offer of December 12, 1916.[13]

The Bulgarians were even more eager to exploit the new situation in Russia. Czar Ferdinand, in particular, recommended that the Central Powers not stop at declarations of neutrality toward the revolution but offer the new government the most favorable peace terms possible.[14]

But the first, peaceable declaration of the returned Russian émigrés was followed as early as March 27 by an appeal from the St. Petersburg soviet to proletarians of all nations—primarily, of course, Germany and Austria—to rise against their annexationist governments, to cast off the yoke of autocracy, to refuse armed service for kings, landlords, and bankers and thus bring to an end "this monstrous war." As in a flash, the menace of what was happening in St. Petersburg became clear and German military censorship acted at once to suppress the proclamation. The monarchial governments of the Central Powers sensed that since czarism had fallen in Russia and President Wilson had solemnly declared war on autocracy, a great wave of democratic opposition and reform was rolling their way from their own peoples.

It was during these days that Bethmann Hollweg decided to proclaim the electoral reforms in Prussia on which the Prussian cabinet had been sitting for years. This was to be done in the form of a solemn "Easter message" from the

Kaiser. Bethmann Hollweg had every reason to think of ways of countering the threatening radicalization of the social democrats, whose left wing was slated to form a breakaway "independent" party during the Easter season at a session to be held in Gotha, April 9-11.

The German government, moreover, feared a dangerous rash of strikes in mid-April, when food rations would again have to be cut. The fear proved to be only too well-founded. Even the Vienna government found itself obliged to make some concessions to popular wishes. Despite the certainty that the imperial council for Austria (as distinct from Hungary), which had been adjourned since the spring of 1914, would serve only to exacerbate irreconcilable national differences, it was decided to reconvene this forum for a thousand and one complaints.

Highly contradictory reports on the attitude of the Russian leaders on the peace question were received during these weeks. The first of these came from Matthias Erzberger, the ever-busy amateur diplomat, who had gone off directly after the upheaval to sound out peace possibilities. He went to Stockholm with the approval of the foreign ministry and at the invitation of a former Russian state councilor, Kolyshko, who had been living there as a writer since the outbreak of the war. Indeed, Kolyshko had discussed German-Russian peace possibilities with Hugo Stinnes the preceding summer.[15]

During long discussions on March 26, this liberal intermediary, who apparently lacked any official credentials,[16] assured Erzberger that the new Russian government wished to be on friendly terms with Germany, provided Germany forewent large-scale annexations in favor of mere border rectifications (though still of respectable scope). An understanding would have to be sought on the Polish question, as well as German support for certain Russian claims in Turkey.

Erzberger reported this "success" and others to the Chancellor in portentous and neatly turned language that showed his optimism. A critical moment in history had been reached, he wrote, a moment for "touching the hem of the robes of providence," to speak with Bismarck. Time was of the essence, or it would be too late. Erzberger urgently advised an immediate peace offer to Russia on moderate terms. He announced that he planned another meeting with Kolyshko on April 20 to continue the discussion; and he was convinced that a separate peace was within sight, even though the Russian had spoken only of general peace.[17]

A few days later, on April 5, the new Russian foreign minister publicly and expressly upheld the war aims of the Entente. His statement also expressly rejected a return to the status quo, i.e., a peace without annexations and indemnities, proclaimed anew by the St. Petersburg soviet only three days earlier. Such a peace, the minister said, would be wholly in the German interest. There was, of course, not even a suggestion of a separate peace.

The Soviets vehemently opposed this stand, and on April 9 the provisional government felt obliged to publish another statement on the question of peace terms. With much circumlocution, it attempted a compromise, emphasizing the determination of the Russian people to "defend the national heritage at any cost," to chase the enemy from the country, and to act always in close agreement with the Allies. At the same time, it pledged that there would be no attempt to expand Russian power and subjugate alien peoples. The right of all nations to self-determination would be respected, as had only just been shown in the proclamation of independence for Poland (March 29). That new state was to embrace all territories with a Polish majority, including those in Germany and Austria!

## Part 2
# Czernin, Bethmann Hollweg, and the Soviet Peace Formula

MILYUKOV'S DECLARATION was a sobering reply to Erzberger's naive optimism; and the everlasting tug-of-war between the provisional Russian government and the soviets made it clear that the time was past when the Germans could still hope to get anywhere in St. Petersburg through the mediation of well-meaning émigrés and one-time czarist officials. All in all, the declaration by the Lvov cabinet sounded more like an appeal to the Russian people for a greater war effort than a message of peace.

Berlin and Vienna nevertheless tried to read a veiled peace move into the rejection of annexations. Czernin, in particular, was impressed with the news from St. Petersburg. On April 7, after the Homburg talks, he had strongly pressed Berlin to "purchase peace by large-scale concessions on the western front." He still thought, in other words, that peace would be made in the west. Two days later, when a dispatch arrived from Copenhagen suggesting that the soviets had said they were ready for a peace without annexations and indemnities, he instantly proposed an identical declaration by the two Central Powers, completely renouncing annexations in the east.[18] Berlin replied that the view was shared there that Russian desire for peace should be encouraged to the greatest possible extent; but with whom was one to deal, so long as it was not known who held the real power in St. Petersburg? Each dispatch seemed to contradict the one before, and while such chaos continued, any statement would be pointless.[19]

These delaying tactics did not last long. On April 13 Bethmann Hollweg summoned Prince Hohenlohe and expressed his willingness to join in a common reply to the declaration by the Lvov government. The reasons he gave were based mainly on domestic considerations—there was already so much trouble in the two countries that the proposal for a peace without annexa-tions must not go unanswered, even though it would be inadvisable to make any commitment to a peace entirely devoid of annexations. Accepting the proposal too eagerly would only serve to stiffen the Russian attitude, while in France and Britain such acceptance would be jubilantly greeted as a sign of complete German collapse. Bethmann Hollweg proposed a reply that would express general agreement with the principles of the Russian declaration, adding that the Central Powers, as before, were ready for a peace that would bring honor to both sides.[20]

This was a palpable evasion, a way of assuaging public opinion rather than a serious diplomatic step. What could have motivated Bethmann Hollweg? On April 12 Erzberger had spent many hours in an effort to persuade the Chancellor, Helfferich, Zimmermann, and Under Secretary Stumm not to let the favorable occasion of a probable peace feeler from the provisional govern-ment pass. Realizing that a direct answer was scarcely feasible, Erzberger proposed that the Kaiser should write the Chancellor a letter for publication, along the lines of the "Easter message," formally empowering Bethmann Hollweg to open peace negotiations.

As usual, Erzberger was overeager. He lost no time in sending Admiral von Müller, for submission to the Kaiser, a draft of the letter he had in mind— with the result that the OHL protested.[21] The Kaiser was persuaded to reject also a draft for a joint declaration by the two emperors, which Bethmann Hollweg (seeking to meet Czernin's wishes) had submitted on April 12. This statement would have expressed readiness for a moderate peace. The degree of suspicion engendered at headquarters by the peace rumors flying about may be gauged from a letter to the Chancellor over Hindenburg's signature, dated April 5, which stated that immediate consultations with Austria were necessary to set the peace terms that were to be put to Russia. Prior to this, however, very prompt agreement would have to be reached among the numer-ous German agencies concerned, some of which were unfortunately pulling in different directions.[22]

The OHL, in other words, was unmistakably putting forward its claim to be heard in the matter; and there could be no doubt whatever that it would cling with the utmost tenacity to its eastern goals, especially in the Baltic region, Ludendorff's "fief." The Chancellor was thus caught in a cleft stick from the outset—Austrian desires and domestic needs on the one hand, the OHL's thirst for conquest on the other. The difficulties at headquarters were the main reason why the Chancellor went no further in meeting Czernin's wishes.

Agreement was ultimately reached that an article should be published in a semiofficial newspaper. On April 15 the *Norddeutsche Allgemeine Zeitung* insisted that the Central Powers had no intention of violating the honor and freedom of the Russian people, nor did they wish to meddle in Russia's internal affairs. It was not they who were preventing peace, but the Entente powers, by their exaggerated goals of conquest, openly proclaimed.

This was, of course, a hint to Russia to cast loose from its allies, though the effect was greatly weakened by the phrase, added probably on Erzberger's advice, that the world expected Russia to "remain true to its obligations," which would have meant that hecatombs still had to be sacrificed for the attainment of Allied war aims. Czernin had angrily protested this addition. On the day before, April 14, he had caused the Austrian press to carry a statement calling much more unequivocally for a negotiated peace.[23]

But the differences between the two governments already went far deeper. Like Bethmann Hollweg, Czernin naturally anticipated OHL opposition to any renunciation of annexations in the east. It was for that reason that he addressed a special report to his emperor on April 12 on Austria-Hungary's situation, intended to shake severely the OHL's confidence in victory. It was to be passed on to the Kaiser, and it was to have serious consequences.

The report did more than merely describe Austria's desperate food crisis and manpower shortage, as had been done in previous documents. In ominous but carefully calculated language—"Your Majesty is familiar with the secret reports from the governors!"—it spoke of the immediate threat of revolutionary unrest, of the "deep rumbling heard from the broad masses," of the powerful and immediate effect the Russian Revolution had exerted especially on the Slavic populations, of the imminent danger of the monarchy crumbling. The tensions had reached a point where disaster could strike at any moment.

In Berlin too, the report went on, responsible political elements were well aware that Germany, like Austria, was at the end of its strength; but military circles there still seemed to labor under certain illusions. They pointed to the undeniable, indeed admirable U-boat successes, yet two and a half months after the onset of unrestricted submarine warfare, it was clear that any breakdown on the part of Britain was out of the question; and in politics nothing was more dangerous than wishful thinking.

At best, the campaign might bring Britain to the peace table a few months earlier than would be the case otherwise—but only if the Central Powers were prepared to build golden bridges. Before it was too late, and before America could intervene actively, it was essential that the Central Powers make another detailed peace proposal, in which they did not shrink from offering major and difficult concessions, if necessary.[24] Czernin struck a tone of great passion and sincerity in this appeal to the conscience of the two sovereigns. He concluded by hinting that in certain circumstances the people might well decide to make peace over the heads of their rulers.

The concessions that might have to be made were nowhere specified. Czernin probably continued to think of Alsace-Lorraine, but in the short run he was undoubtedly concerned with foregoing annexations in the east. His report reached German headquarters at the height of the great defensive battles that had begun in early April on the western front; and since the report did not call for immediate action, mentioning only peace negotiations after the major fighting in France was over, it went unanswered for the time being. Bethmann Hollweg replied to it in detail only in early May. His answer, to which we shall revert, was notably optimistic.[25]

In the meantime OHL pressure on the Chancellor's conduct of political affairs had greatly increased. Beset on all sides, Bethmann Hollweg vainly tried to maintain his freedom of political action; and his struggle during the crucial weeks of April makes an absorbing spectacle. On April 16 he rejected as premature and pointless the OHL demand for departmental consultations on peace terms. He said he had been aware since the preceding December what the General Staff and the admiralty had in mind by way of war aims.

Obviously Germany must build golden bridges for the first one of its enemies who was ready for peace; hence formulation of firmly defined maximum and minimum demands, as a program to which Germany must unalterably cling, would be inopportune at this time. Bethmann Hollweg hinted, further, that he, the statesman, alone had ultimate jurisdiction in political questions, though he put this claim forward only in weakened and circumscribed form:

> It must be our endeavor to attain the absolute maximum of those demands that aim at increasing our military security. Accordingly, the war aims to be pursued from a general political and economic approach, the determination of which is incumbent on me in carrying out the mission entrusted to me by the emperor, must take second place.[26]

This sounds as though Bethmann Hollweg were acknowledging the priority of the sword over the scepter; but in the very next sentence we read:

> Our guiding thought must be to disrupt the present enemy coalition and bring one or another of our enemies over to our side. This aspect will have to be taken into account in determining the extent of annexations we should envisage. Hence I see no possibility in reaching final conclusions on this point either at the present time.

As he had done from the beginning, Bethmann Hollweg was intent on keeping his hands free at all costs for the moment of peace, and he did not wish to commit himself to the military on the question of annexations. At the same time he was quite clearly reluctant to precipitate a conflict with

Ludendorff by speaking firmly and clearly. His caution is understandable in the light of the situation in which he found himself at the time.

Ever since he had unambiguously set a new course for German and Prussian domestic policy in the Prussian chamber of deputies on March 14, the campaign of vilification against the Chancellor as a "henchman of the Jews and social democrats" had reached new heights; and the OHL had long since become the center of opposition to him, as the Reich naval office had once been under Tirpitz. By emphasizing "maximum military security" and speaking of the annexations that should be envisaged, the Chancellor was undoubtedly seeking to appease the generals once again. What, then, was his true opinion? Except for pressure from the OHL, would he have been prepared, as Czernin wished on April 10, to forego all annexations in the east, in order to build golden bridges for the Russians?

Bethmann Hollweg himself has testified so often and unequivocally to his unwillingness to allow peace to fail over the question of annexations, that no doubt on that score is possible.[27] It was an altogether different matter to commit himself publicly to a policy of renunciation even before concrete negotiations were in prospect. Appeasement of this character meant different things to Germany and Austria. In the event of a general peace without annexations and indemnities, Austria-Hungary would be ahead. The provinces it had lost to Russia and Italy would be returned, while there were no conquests to be relinquished in return, apart from the Austrian share in Poland, the autonomy of which had long been promised by the Central Powers, while the Russian government on March 29 had declared Poland to be a free nation.

For Germany, on the other hand, to forego annexations meant to surrender large territories it now held as bargaining counters that might help it gain a reasonably favorable peace. To relinquish them without any assurances that the enemy was ready to talk peace on a basis of equality and calm political reason would have been irresponsible. It is true that the nationalist right went rather too far in banking on a policy of holding territory with which to bargain; yet actually to express agreement in principle with a peace without conquests did not necessarily imply that occupied territory had to be evacuated at once.

It was quite clear that Berlin had to use greater caution than Vienna in taking a stand on the question of peace. Berlin, moreover, was far more realistic in assessing the chances of a separate peace with Russia. In point of fact, until the Russian Revolution of November 1917 there never was any such tangible possibility. Neither the Duma government of Prince Lvov nor the ensuing socialist coalition governments were ready to make a separate peace with the Central Powers. What the Russians did instead, from April to October 1917, was to keep on vainly trying to persuade their Western allies to revise the war aims agreements along the lines of the soviet policy of peace without annexations and indemnities. The blame for their failure rests with the Entente rather than with the Central Powers. It was Ribot who displayed the greatest fear and revulsion of the soviet policy, while Sonnino was guilty of outrageous hypocrisy in glossing over Italy's plans for conquest.28

Viewed in this light, there was little practical significance to the quarrel between Berlin and Vienna, which was rapidly heating up. Peace manifestos, no matter how unambiguous they sounded, could scarcely gain the kind of swift separate peace with Russia Germany needed. Vienna was fond of over-looking, moreover, that the numerous soviet peace slogans included "the right of self-determination," which played an especially important role among the most radical wing, the Bolshevists. Its application to Austria-Hungary was bound to have the most disastrous consequences there. Hence there is never any mention of such a thing in Czernin's peace declarations. His policy can-not be said to have been cleverer than Bethmann Hollweg's. It was only less cautious, more nervous, and given to improvisation.

But acceptance of the idea of peace without conquest and indemnities was not merely a matter of assessing its diplomatic chances. In 1917 the problem of peace was more than a matter of traditional diplomacy—it was a question of political morale. All the peoples of Europe were thoroughly weary of the hardships and sacrifices of war and cheered the Russian revolutionaries who seemed to strike a chord of liberation, just as Wilson's appeal for "peace without victory" had found a sympathetic echo before.

It was the socialists everywhere who became the spokesmen of this popu-lar mood. Even the "social patriots" dispatched from France and Britain to St. Petersburg to seek liaison with the soviets returned brimful with the spirit of peace. Directly upon their return, two socialist ministers, Thomas in Paris and Henderson in London, recommended that their governments drastically overhaul their peace terms. Emissaries from St. Petersburg had been visiting the countries of the West, moreover, and so great was their impact that the Western governments were reluctant to grant their socialist members pass-ports to attend an international socialist conference in Stockholm organized by the Second International, with the soviets subsequently joining in.

The very calling of this conference was a symptom of the popular desire to take the business of peacemaking out of the hands of governments, not yet by revolutionary upheavals, but by irresistible pressure of public opinion. True, in France only a small minority could be mustered behind the demand of the radical socialists for revised peace terms (e.g., a plebiscite in Alsace-Lorraine rather than outright annexation). Yet there too the debate over participation in the Stockholm conference was stormy, the majority of the national council of the socialist party voting in the affirmative on May 28, overruling their executive.

There were disorderly scenes in the chamber about the secret war aims treaties among the Allies. Major strikes with a political tinge soon broke out, especially in Paris; and after the failure of the great Anglo-French spring offensive there were serious mutinies involving more than half the French army. The Third Republic came close to paralysis.

The Labour party in Britain was split on the peace issue. Attempts by radical pacifists like Snowden to get the House of Commons to agree to a peace without annexations and revise the peace terms proclaimed on January 10 remained without the slightest success; but March and April saw serious strikes and unrest in British war industry, reflecting the events in Russia and causing deep concern to Lloyd George. At a mass meeting in Leeds on June 3 organized by left extremists, the soviet peace formula was endorsed and a "French" peace à la Ribot rejected.

In Italy there were debates in the chamber, in which the socialist leader Turati pressed the government for a moderate statement on war aims. There were also sympathy demonstrations for the soviets, etc., but nothing more serious to begin with. There too, however, unrest mounted in the course of the summer. On July 12 the socialists introduced a resolution calling for immediate initiation of peace negotiations; and in August there were serious revolutionary riots in Turin, with the erection of barricades and the proclamation of a general strike, followed by a mass petition calling for immediate peace.

All in all the impression might arise that had the Central Powers openly and unequivocally declared their willingness to make peace on the basis of the status quo this might have greatly increased at least the internal difficulties of the Entente powers. Such a peace would have indeed amounted to a virtual victory on the part of the Central Powers—and at this point their enemies backed up. They were absolutely determined to prevent this, so soon after America's entry into the war.

Even if the question of the impression registered abroad is left open, there was another compelling reason for the Central Powers to declare themselves unequivocally in favor of a peace without conquest; for only by doing so could they maintain the confidence of the broad masses of their own people, who were bound to lose heart completely, once they suspected that they were expected to continue to bleed and suffer solely for certain territorial war aims set by their leaders and by bourgeois chauvinists.

The political truce concluded in Germany at the outbreak of the war was based on the willingness of the socialists to vote regularly for war appropriations and to preach and practice the duty of defending the fatherland in the same way as the bourgeois parties. This decision was facilitated if not made possible by the fact that the war was directed against the czarist empire, most reactionary of Europe's major monarchies.

Now the czar had fallen and the world's first socialist state seemed to be developing in Russia. For the German social democrats this meant an altogether novel situation; and nowhere did the Russian Revolution find so fervent an echo as among them and their Austro-Hungarian fellow partisans. They were bound to look on this event with the highest hopes for the future and to follow the peace efforts of the soviets with the warmest interest and sympathy. It was only natural that they should do everything in their power to establish liaison with their Russian fellow partisans and seek an understanding on the issue of peace.

Bethmann Hollweg's government gave vigorous support to these efforts. The very first message of greetings addressed to the revolutionaries on March 21 by the German parliamentary social democratic party was dispatched with the warm approval of Secretary of State Wahnschaffe at the Reich chancellery.[29] First personal contact was established via Copenhagen early in April with the support of the foreign ministry, through the Danish socialist Borbjerg, who gave the soviets a highly favorable report on the attitude of the German socialists. Indeed, preparations for the Stockholm conference were assisted with such zeal by the German embassies in The Hague, Berne, and Stockholm that it is not too much to say that German diplomacy had a considerable share in bringing about this international event.[30]

Yet the German majority social democrats, especially Ebert and Scheidemann, vigorously supported German vital interests. For example, they courageously and skillfully defended the rights of Germans in Alsace-Lorraine, while the independent social democrats under Haase favored a plebiscite in the Reich provinces.[31] Even this radical group, however, experienced no difficulty in obtaining passports for Stockholm. On March 29 Noske said in the Reichstag that German political and constitutional reforms had become essential, now that Germany was surrounded by democracies and could not possibly withdraw into isolation. The Chancellor was in full agreement, having already declared that a new domestic course was required in the interests of foreign affairs as well.

Had this course been pursued consistently, along the lines of some kind of "imperial democracy," such as Friedrich Naumann had long preached and certain noted intellectuals like Friedrich Meinecke and Max Weber had demanded in their wartime writings, the shared hardships of the war might have given birth to some degree of unification in German political life, superseding the old party conflicts that had seemed irreconcilable. This was Bethmann Hollweg's great hope, and in his last Reichstag speeches he defended it with all the oratorical warmth and passion of which he was capable. Unfortunately it became apparent almost at once that the ossified structure of Prussia-Germany's class and authoritarian state stubbornly resisted any real reform. In the sphere of foreign policy the issue was one of clinging to the conquests of territory on which the militarists insisted. At home it was a question of preserving the Prussian "Junker parliament" with the help of the three-class franchise.

The Chancellor's whole policy stood and fell with his confidential relationship with the Kaiser. He could cope with the opposition offered him by both his military and feudal-reactionary adversaries only so long as the ultimate decisions of the "All-Highest" went his way. His attitude in the spring and summer of 1917 would have made no sense at all, had he not believed that when the crunch came—i.e., when it was a question of really sitting down at the peace table—the Kaiser could be won over to a policy of a negotiated peace on moderate terms. (The Pan-German propagandists, by the way, had begun to dub this a "Scheidemann peace," in contrast to the so-called "Hindenburg peace.")

Bethmann Hollweg also counted on the Kaiser's consent to electoral reform in Prussia; and on both scores he had good reason for optimism, for at heart William II was not really the fire-eating braggart he liked to appear to his generals and in his notorious marginal notes. Deep down he was afraid for the fate of his throne. As he said to Admiral von Müller on April 26, 1917, he was fighting for his crown.

The Kaiser's frame of mind, however, was not calculated to offer strong support to the Chancellor, beset from many sides. It was Bethmann Hollweg's serious misfortune that neither he nor Valentini nor Admiral von Müller succeeded, despite their best efforts, in luring the Kaiser away from headquarters to Berlin for any length of time, even though he actually played only a pseudo role at the OHL. The Chancellor could count on only brief interludes, a day at a time, during which the Kaiser was directly exposed to his influence, which waned more and more after Ludendorff's appointment.

This was particularly true in respect of the peace question. Writing to his successor Hertling in January 1918,[32] Bethmann Hollweg said that it had been his intention in May 1917 to accept the Russian formula for a peace without annexations and indemnities "without a quibble," but that this had failed because of the opposition of the OHL, which enjoyed the Kaiser's support. Documents dating from May 1917, with which we shall yet be concerned, provide no reason for questioning this assertion; but they fail to suggest that Bethmann Hollweg was convinced at the time of the necessity for *publicly* professing his staunch adherence to a policy of peace without annexations. At any rate, he put up no fight. True, an imperial chancellor fighting for a peace of "appeasement" by the side of the social democrats against the godlike OHL—such a spectacle would have required a thorough reversal of public opinion on the matter of war aims and peace expectations, and also a radical change in the relations of the government and the political parties.[33] We shall see such changes heralded in July 1917, accompanied by such frantic confusion, however, that the Chancellor's doom was sealed.

The great weakness of Bethmann Hollweg's position vis-à-vis the OHL was that at no time could he point to any concrete, tangible possibility of peace, an opportunity that might have justified foregoing all annexations on principle. Thus he was bound to drift more and more in the wake of the OHL, certainly more than he wished and more than accorded with his own political insight. He was compelled to follow a course of continual compromise. In our view this was virtually the only course he could follow, since he dared not risk an open conflict. Yet this stand not only undermined the faith his parliamentary followers had in him, but earned him the reputation of vacillation and character weakness that to this day darkens the image he presents to history.

## Part 3

# Bethmann Hollweg's Peace Policy Caught in a Cross Fire

THE QUEST FOR a just assessment dictates that one eschew speaking glibly of Bethmann Hollweg's "weaknesses" unless one first gain a clear picture of the forces that pushed him down the path of compromise in the peace question. These counterforces leaped into instant action when the new slogan, peace without annexations and indemnities, first appeared on the horizon.

William II, wholly under the spell of the military, had a wire sent to the Chancellor on April 17, saying he had lately noted that there was talk in the neutral countries, and in socialist circles, of a peace that would involve neither the acquisition of territory nor financial compensation. He asked the Chancellor to oppose this trend and to try to persuade the social democrats to maintain at least a limited semblance of support for indemnities in return for the sacrifices that had been made.[34]

Bethmann Hollweg replied that public debates on peace terms would be most unwelcome at this time. He said he was nevertheless prepared to recommend a "reasonable middle way" in his press directives—no call for peace at any price, but neither any demand for territorial gains, which represented but one of many peace problems, and not even the most important. They would have to be de-emphasized as much as possible.

He would endeavor to arouse sympathy among the broad masses for restoration of economic relations with other countries, a goal of considerable importance to the worker and the little man. This might well involve the return of the German colonies. To this end the "bargaining counters" Germany had acquired would have to be used with great firmness. It was essential to maintain iron nerve and not to stumble into the kind of trap the Entente might prepare by suggesting unconditional renunciation of any indemnities on both sides. Their purpose would be to prevent Russia from making a separate peace. Attempts would be made, he added, to influence the deputies of the left in this direction.

On the other hand, it would have to be made clear to the right and to the Pan-Germans that Germany's situation held out little immediate prospect for a German-dictated peace. Germany would have to create the conditions for a negotiated peace favorable to it, before American intervention could become effective. The situation of Germany's allies made it quite impossible to "run one's head through the wall at every point." Exaggerated demands would only deter the enemy from seeking an understanding, while fanning the flames of conflict at home.[35]

It was a labored effort by the Chancellor to put his policy of moderation in the most favorable light for the benefit of the Kaiser and the OHL. Actually, Bethmann Hollweg made no effort whatever to influence the deputies of the left as he said he would. It is extremely unlikely that he anticipated an offer of peace without annexations from the Western powers, and he would certainly not have regarded it as walking into a trap if he could have made peace with them on such a basis.

But all Bethmann Hollweg's efforts to dissemble were fruitless. The suspicions of the OHL were ineradicable, and they were probably only increased by news of the exploratory talks Erzberger and more recently the Bulgarian envoy Ritzov were conducting with Russian emissaries in Stockholm and Christiania (Oslo), with the support of the German foreign ministry.[36] Hindenburg wrote the Chancellor on April 20 that he deeply regretted the rejection of provisional consultations on peace terms. The current negotiations with Russian leaders, like the propaganda being meanwhile conducted in the trenches, would be pointless unless German war aims were agreed upon.

On the question of what those terms should be, Hindenburg expressed himself with military precision and assurance: "For military reasons I do not propose to entertain the kind of peace based on the status quo put forward by Herr Ritzov." The golden bridges for Russia might be built by offering in return for Courland and Lithuania, which had to be "unavoidably" annexed, the occupied parts of East Galicia and the Bukovina, Austria being possibly recompensed in Serbia or Walachia. In any event, he went on, he naturally expected that the Chancellor would keep him in the picture, as far as government policy was concerned, since the closest cooperation was necessary with regard to political and military measures.[37]

Worse was yet to come. On April 19 the social democratic leadership in Prussia and Germany had issued a proclamation on the peace question, in which they were joined by a delegation of Austro-Hungarian socialists under Viktor Adler. This statement firmly demanded domestic political reforms after the war and rejected any foreign intervention (e.g., by Wilson) into internal German affairs. At the same time the parties welcomed with the "most fervent sympathy" the victory of the Russian Revolution and its peace aspirations. They expressed agreement with the Russian program, only recently reaffirmed by a soviet congress, of peace without annexations and indemnities, "on the basis of the free national development of all peoples." They went on to say that it was the duty of socialists everywhere to fight against greedy chauvinist ambitions, urge their governments to forego all dreams of conquest, and bring about definitive peace negotiations on such a basis as soon as possible. The socialist party organ *International Correspondence* directly challenged the German government to state officially that it was ready to forego annexations.

The socialist peace manifesto, clearly and beautifully worded, was published on April 20 in the *Vorwärts,* at the height of the great Berlin munitions workers' strike. On the next morning Hindenburg read it to the Kaiser, who lay ill abed, and demanded Bethmann Hollweg's instant dismissal, since the Chancellor quite evidently could no longer keep the social democrats under control. Valentini, swiftly summoned, was able to allay the storm once more; but it was repeated on April 22, when War Minister von Stein presented the same demand, using the same arguments, on behalf of Ludendorff and in the name of the army. Again Valentini was able to calm the waves, for the Kaiser invited the Chancellor and Zimmermann to come to headquarters at Kreuznach on April 23. The war aims discussions the OHL had pressed for were at last to be held, but the meeting was also to decide what could be done to counter the "arrogant" socialist declaration.[38] When Bethmann Hollweg got this summons, he rightly suspected that Ludendorff would now try either to trip him up or to commit him to the peace terms of the OHL.

It was against this tense background that the much-cited Kreuznach discussions took place on April 23.[39] They could scarcely be termed a formal conference, and no minutes were taken. Ludendorff presented well-prepared maps on which were shown the new borders he regarded as necessary, "for military reasons." Bethmann Hollweg and Zimmermann were apparently able to have some of the more outrageous demands eliminated, but realized that no reasonable program had any chance of prevailing and consequently simply took note of Ludendorff's statements as representing the viewpoint of the military.

On the evening of April 21 the Chancellor had consulted with a small circle of Prussian ministers in an effort to find a compromise that might avoid the annexation of Courland and Lithuania without affronting the OHL—even though Hindenburg had told him only the day before that these annexations were "absolutely essential." At the same time the group was looking for ways of protecting the German-speaking Baltic regions from the chaos in Russia;

and they also wished to avoid using the ambiguous term *border correction,* which Erzberger had liberally employed in his negotiations with Kolyshko.

At the suggestion of the minister of agriculture, Schorlemer, agreement was reached on demanding "autonomy" for the Baltic regions, in other words self-determination, in keeping with the Russian revolutionary slogans. These regions were to have no Russian garrisons and were to enter into close economic ties with Germany.[40] At Kreuznach, however, Bethmann Hollweg did not even mention this proposed compromise. Instead, he apparently joined Zimmermann in bringing up the matter of simply foregoing all annexations. This was, of course, instantly rejected by Ludendorff.[41]

In the afternoon, with the Kaiser presiding and Holtzendorff participating, a war aims program did begin to take shape. It did not actually become known until 1929, when it created considerable consternation, and at the time of its conception even Admiral von Müller and Valentini regarded it as "childish."[42] It called for enormous annexations in the east, reaching almost to Riga on the Baltic coast; the territorial exchange—Galicia and the Bukovina in return for Walachia—which Hindenburg had projected on April 20; military occupation and control of Belgium for an indefinite time, or until the country were politically and economically ready to enter into a mutual assistance pact with Germany; permanent possession of Liège and the Flemish coast, including Bruges, the region of Arlon, suspected by the OHL to hold mineral wealth, Luxembourg, and the Longwy-Briey basin; and certain "border rectifications" along the Franco-Alsatian border. It was announced that there would be further discussions about the Balkans, Asia Minor, the German colonies, and the naval bases wanted by the German admiralty.[43]

The OHL prepared several copies of this program and a few days later sent them to the participants for their signatures. On the accompanying letter by Grünau, Bethmann Hollweg made a note for the foreign ministry files. During the discussions, he wrote, he had repeatedly and expressly emphasized that he regarded these terms attainable only if Germany were able to dictate the peace. "I agreed only with that proviso."

Zimmermann applied the same reservation to the Belgian terms—Britain would first have to be completely subjugated, and both the OHL and the admiralty had admitted as much. Bethmann Hollweg wrote a more detailed minute for the chancellery files. He mentioned his suspicions about Ludendorff's ultimate purpose, already discussed, and added:

I joined in signing the record of the discussions only because it would be absurd for me to quit over pipe dreams. For the rest, I shall certainly not let this document bind me in any way. If the slightest chance of peace opens up anywhere, I shall pursue it; and I wish this specifically to be made a matter of record in these files.

Lastly, Bethmann Hollweg wrote Hertling at length on January 26, 1918, that he had never committed himself to any fixed war aims program; that the Kreuznach protocol merely recorded what the OHL wanted; and that for him that document constituted neither a basis for further German strategy, nor the basis for any further peace offer Germany might make.[44]

These reservations are clear enough. Bethmann Hollweg was not merely "covering" himself—he was rejecting the whole approach. On the other hand, his signing of the protocol was meant to be a mere tactical maneuver. He saw no reason to take Ludendorff's "pipe dreams" seriously, since he thought that for the time being there was no chance of peace negotiations, not even with Russia. He felt sure, moreover, that he would be able to draw the Kaiser over to his side, once there were the slightest chance of peace. In the event, he underestimated the practical significance of this Kreuznach program, established under the Kaiser's own chairmanship. Ludendorff at once began to use it as a powerful weapon in the struggle of sword against scepter, virtually paralyzing Bethmann Hollweg's freedom of action.

This was to be shown during the very next few days, in the "Erzberger affair." On April 23 that centrist deputy had returned from his second meeting with Kolyshko, triumphantly brandishing in the faces of foreign ministry officials a draft armistice that both he and his opposite number had signed. He immediately forwarded this document to supreme headquarters through Admiral von Müller; and he was particularly proud of having extracted agreement to "border rectifications," insisting, optimistically as always, that this must be interpreted by Russian standards of magnitude—i.e., that considerable territory might be involved.

In terms of practical politics the whole incident was of negligible value, merely the private pastime of two well-meaning amateur diplomats without any official standing whatsoever. Indeed, Kolyshko was soon afterward arrested in St. Petersburg as a "German agent."[45] The German foreign ministry was nevertheless pleased with Erzberger's news, if only because it might be a barometer of favorable trends in St. Petersburg. As for Bethmann Hollweg, he probably never for a moment viewed the document as heralding serious peace negotiations,[46] and he did not follow it up.

But at headquarters the draft caused a furor. Hindenburg complained volubly to the Kaiser of this unheard-of meddling by the Chancellor in military matters. The very idea of armistice discussions without OHL consultation enraged him. He was bitter about what he called Bethmann Hollweg's shilly-shallying in allowing his supposed emissary even to mention the status quo.

The Kaiser himself was indignant about the "impossible and hair-raising" terms laid down in the supposed agreement and at once drafted a bristling wire to the Chancellor, the dispatch of which Admiral von Müller was able to prevent only with the greatest effort. Zimmermann tried to clear up the misunderstanding by wire himself, but only half succeeded. In the end the Kaiser ungraciously ordered the foreign ministry henceforth to supply its intermediaries with "absolutely binding instructions" approved by himself. Any peace feelers were subject to the same directives that applied to propaganda in the trenches. German offers must stick to the line ordered on April 23 under the Kaiser's chairmanship.[47] Obviously the generals were using even the semblance of any deviation from this line as an argument for undermining the Kaiser's confidence in the Chancellor.

A far more serious direct consequence was that the Kreuznach decisions made it virtually impossible to carry on any fruitful propaganda in the trenches—even though this was the alleged OHL motive in insisting on clarifying and fixing German war aims. This curious form of propaganda, initiated in mid-March from the eastern high command with the dropping of Russian-language leaflets and soldiers' newspapers, originally aimed only at demoralizing the Russian troops. They were told they were being frivolously butchered for British ends and must not trust their provisional government, which was subservient to the British. They were reminded that they might go empty-handed unless they were present at the impending large-scale redistribution of land back home.

Undoubtedly this propaganda caused much mischief and served to undermine Russian troop morale even more seriously than the soviet revolution had already done; but it also led to fraternization scenes, especially at Eastertime, and to lively exchanges of letters across no-man's-land between the front lines. In the long run it threatened German and even more Hungarian troop morale, and there were second thoughts at headquarters. On the other hand, German military intelligence soon found chances for establishing liaison with Russian troop leaders and exploring possibilities for armistice negotiations that might bring on far-reaching political consequences.

It was General Seeckt, the chief of staff of the army group under Archduke Joseph on the Carpathian front, who late in April called attention to the dangers of trench propaganda and "wildcat" negotiations. The OHL and the foreign ministry thereupon agreed on a five-point program that was to serve as a basis for any further discussion with Russian staff officers. It pledged nonintervention in Russian affairs, good offices in settling the Dardanelles question, close economic ties, financial aid in the reconstruction of Russia, and renunciation of indemnities, but in return demanded that any "border rectifications" that might accrue to Germany would have to come out of Lithuania and Courland. Ludendorff's annexationist demands, in other words, were artfully trivialized. Zimmermann had had a difficult time of it in prevailing with this cautious formulation; and the OHL soon afterward changed it in favor of naked aggressive goals.[48]

Hence Russian distrust of the German proposals was well-founded. In a letter late in May General von Seeckt expressed himself very critically on this point. Confusion had certainly been created among the Russians, he wrote, but also a great deal of uncertainty that could only react unfavorably on the Germans.

> The trouble is our people want to retain Courland and Lithuania. I have never seen the need for this, on the contrary, I think it worsens our geographic situation. In my view we ought to say we are willing to forego it. . . . The OHL is poorly advised in these political questions and insists it always knows best.[49]

From the lips of this high officer, whom we already know to be opposed to Bethmann Hollweg,[50] this is a surprisingly objective judgment. Seeckt tried repeatedly with success to propose improvements in front-line propaganda; but of course he too was unable to change Ludendorff's annexationist plans in any way. Even so, he did submit a peace formula that would have expressly avowed the principle of "no conquests and no indemnities"; and he sought to make the inevitable "border rectifications in Lithuania and Courland" more palatable by reserving them to some form of agreement rather than demanding them outright.[51]

Bethmann Hollweg was apparently reluctant even to use the ambiguous term *border rectification* at all. He knew it implied the annexation of the two Russian provinces, which he sought to avoid. When a report from the front on May 7 held out the prospect of serious peace talks with Steklov, a representative of the St. Petersburg soviet, he dusted off a proposal discussed at a meeting of the Prussian ministers on April 21, under which Courland and Lithuania were to become autonomous states, though militarily, politically, and economically integrated with Germany. Ludendorff agreed, but the expected talks never materialized, for the Soviet negotiator never showed up.

The incident shows rather clearly that at the very first sign of a peace prospect—even though an illusory one—Bethmann Hollweg did not have nearly as much freedom of action as he had envisaged in his notes about the Kreuznach program. Once again he was constrained to enter into a dubious compromise. The day before, Ludendorff had expressly demanded that the Chancellor, in his impending Reichstag speech, must not transcend the directives given the front-line negotiators—which Bethmann Hollweg readily granted. Almost directly afterward Grünau explained what was actually meant: Headquarters expected Bethmann Hollweg to express an unmistakable disavowal of the "Scheidemann peace."[52]

Peace talks from trench to trench were thus made much more difficult by virtue of Ludendorff's annexationist plans. Their effect on the state of the alliance between the two main Central Powers was even more serious. On

April 23, while the Kreuznach talks were on, Czernin had dispatched an inquiry that must have filled Bethmann Hollweg with consternation. Czernin contended that the socialist declaration about a peace without annexations must not go unanswered. He himself was prepared to tell the Russians publicly that he would accept it without reservations. What did Berlin think?[53]

At almost the same moment when Ambassador Hohenlohe was presenting this inquiry, an annexationist group, the "Independent Committee for a German Peace," issued a public declaration calling on the government to take an unequivocal stand against the social democratic manifesto. In the circumstances, the hapless Chancellor had no choice but to perform a diplomatic "egg walk," as he himself described it in a note. On April 25 he launched an article in the semiofficial *Norddeutsche Allgemeine Zeitung,* in which doubt was expressed that the socialist document would have any effect, in view of the determination being shown by Germany's Western enemies, and their "insane" peace terms. The article, however, studiously avoided any outright rejection of "peace without annexations" and refrained from joining in the furious chorus of condemnation raised in the rightist press. All it really said was that the German government had nothing to add to its earlier peace offers. Hohenlohe had advance notice of the piece; and on the day of publication he tried to convince his minister that a declaration by the Central Powers on the peace issue at this moment would be premature and superfluous, since the pro-Entente Lvov government was bound to fall soon.

His advice came too late. Still on the same day, the *Wiener Fremdenblatt* published a Czernin-inspired "Answer to the Social Democrats," welcoming their declaration and giving assurances that Austria was pursuing no aggressive plans of any kind and had no intention of enlarging its territory at Russia's expense. Contrary to the policy of the Entente, both Central Powers had, after all, given crucial support to the socialist congress in Stockholm.

Evidently this was an attempt to outmaneuver the German government. In Czernin's view it would welcome being committed by its ally in this way, providing a pretext for defying the generals. He was quite wrong. Chancellor and foreign minister were greatly irked; indeed, Zimmermann said that Bethmann Hollweg's position was being made untenable by such escapades. The Austrian statement was a virtual invitation to the German political parties to resume their unhelpful debate on peace terms. Czernin was virtually "buttering up" the social democrats and encouraging them to broadcast further declarations, which would only call forth furious right-wing counterdeclarations, undermine the political truce, and cause the Chancellor grave embarrassment—the more so since Germany could not forego its territorial bargaining counters as airily as Austria. The end result would be to give the public the impression of disunity between the allies.

Czernin's reaction was no less strong. He flew into something like a rage

over another difference that blew up at the same time, concerning new mediation efforts by the Bulgarian envoy, Ritzov.[54] He wrote Hohenlohe that their
ally's everlasting reservations led him to the conclusion

> that Germany does not wish peace with Russia without mutual annexa-
> tions and indemnities. I ask myself again and again with amazement
> whether these gentlemen still do not see the full gravity of the situa-
> tion, whether they are really willing to accept responsibility for allow-
> ing a possible separate peace to fail because of the annexationist ambi-
> tions.

To give Bethmann Hollweg a jolt, he wired Berlin that serious hunger riots
had broken out in a small Moravian town. The military had had to intervene
and there had been twelve dead (later rising to twenty-one) and numerous
other casualties. Czernin grew so agitated that he sent no fewer than four
directives to Hohenlohe on a single day. He pointed out that there was no
Pan-German movement in Austria to serve as a counterpoise to the social
democrats, who now commanded the loyalties of all Slavs in the Hapsburg
Empire. He was compelled to cooperate with them, because of the seriousness
of the situation. Most of the troops behind the lines were unreliable, and a
mutiny of any size was bound to have disastrous consequences, reducing
Austria's value to Germany to nil. As their price for cooperation, the social
democrats demanded that the government come out for peace without annexations.

This gloomy estimate of the situation in Austria was sharply at odds with
the reassuring reports the Reichstag deputy Erzberger was at that very time
receiving from prominent figures in Vienna. They assured him that there was
no serious danger of strikes or revolution.[55] Czernin wired in turn that he
would regret it very much if the Chancellor did not believe him and failed to
do his part in enabling the Austrians to hold out. He indignantly rejected
representations made to him by Ambassador Count Wedel and disavowed any
responsibility for the discrepancies, adding that he found it impossible to
follow the incomprehensible vacillations of German policy.[56] He was all in
favor of harmony among the allies, but that did not mean that Austria always
had to endorse the German stand unconditionally.

This came close to an outright challenge, and Hohenlohe's efforts to restore
concord initially seemed quite unpromising. He tried to explain Bethmann
Hollweg's difficult position to his minister and to make clear the reasons for
the Chancellor's dismay at Czernin's statement in the press.[57] At the same
time he urged Bethmann Hollweg on his own to issue an unequivocal statement on German intentions in the east, arguing that earlier declarations in the
Reichstag on the future of the Baltic regions were now outmoded by the fall

of czarism. Why now hesitate to release these countries, when they had been given assurances of self-determination even before the revolution? Was he so afraid of the Pan-Germans as to pass up the chance of a separate peace with Russia?

It is painful to follow the Chancellor's squirmings in the face of such arguments, his inability to let the ambassador into his confidence about the reasons for his reluctance, especially his dilemma arising from the Kreuznach program. In the end he did agree to a statement that he "was ready for peace negotiations with Russia at any time and would not allow them to fail on account of annexationist goals, excepting military border rectifications." This could be stretched to fall within the Kreuznach program, and Bethmann Hollweg promised to back his offer even against Pan-German and military objections, if that became necessary.

But Bethmann Hollweg was unwilling to issue a formal public declaration, as proposed by the Austrians, not even in the form of an ex post facto endorsement of Czernin's statement in the *Wiener Fremdenblatt.* Too many manifestos, he remarked, would only create the impression that the Germans were at their wit's end. He suggested an attempt to advise the workers' and soldiers' soviet in St. Petersburg in confidence–a hopeless and misguided plan. The time for secret communication of artfully equivocal peace terms was past. What was called for now was to come out openly with a simple and clear-cut peace formula. That Bethmann Hollweg was unable to do.

Czernin next tried to bring about a solemn joint declaration by *both* governments, which would vehemently deny the existence of any political differences between the two allies. It would say that Austria was willing to forego any annexations of Russian territory, and that Germany would not allow any chance of peace with Russia to go by on that account, but would content itself with only "such border rectifications as were necessary to secure its borders against Russia." This would still not have been a politically effective and popular peace formula, but it would have at least openly committed Germany.[58]

To get this draft accepted in Berlin, Czernin secured the help of Count Hertling, whom he had invited to Vienna on April 24, with the intention of mobilizing him as a South German battering ram against the Pan-German and militarist truculence in Berlin. Observing protocol, Hertling had advised the German foreign ministry of his trip beforehand, and then wired Czernin's proposal to the Chancellor, recommending that it be accepted; nor did he fail to explain to the Austrian minister Germany's desire for certain "border rectifications," for the purpose of safeguarding East Prussia.[59]

Despite the Bavarian endorsement, Czernin's plan met with strong aversion on the Chancellor's part, and once again there was a sharply worded exchange of messages between Berlin and Vienna. Bethmann Hollweg's and Zimmermann's objections were initially purely on the tactical side. To solemnly emphasize unity would sound like a protest and merely arouse suspicion; and to say anything about border rectifications in public would convince many that this was merely a cover for annexationist goals. The effect, in other words, would be the precise opposite of what was intended—and here Bethmann Hollweg was undoubtedly right.

Again, Germany could not dream of publicly renouncing annexations. Such appeasement would not be confined to the east, and it would be utterly irresponsible to relinquish all the western "bargaining counters" as well, without any concrete peace prospects. The only remaining possibility was to seek an understanding sub rosa. The foreign minister had only just made this clear to the deputies of the Reichstag main committee with some difficulty, and he could not now disavow his own words. The objective content of the Vienna-inspired declaration was acceptable enough, but these things could not be said in public.[60]

Bethmann Hollweg thus clung tenaciously to his established line—no public statements about peace terms until negotiations had actually started, a free hand until that moment!

What was ultimately behind the Chancellor's reluctance? No unequivocal answer can be given, for during these weeks tactical considerations severely curbed his utterances. It was certainly not the mere desire to avoid further clashes with the OHL—though he must have clearly foreseen just what Kreuznach would do to him if he publicly proclaimed a peace of appeasement, arm in arm with the "defeatist" Czernin. He was probably more worried that a new public debate on peace terms might be unleashed, which would negate any public declaration and only deepen party and class conflict. To put it another way, Bethmann Hollweg may have felt that the German people had not reached a stage of development that could have mastered such conflict—the stage to which Bethmann Hollweg aspired as the ideal. Well, if the discord could not be overcome, he would at least cover it up as much as possible!

It does seem, however, that Bethmann Hollweg was not quite untouched by the optimism that then prevailed at supreme headquarters, where a victorious end to the war was expected "about the end of July," in the wake of the great initial U-boat successes, the failure of the Anglo-French breakthrough offensive (which was evident by late April), and the crumbling of the Russian front. We have already heard about the long report with which he responded in early May to Czernin's gloomy forecast of April 12. Among other things, it cited a wire of April 9 from the Italian ambassador in Paris, intercepted by OHL intelligence, which mentioned Ribot's grave apprehensions. Providence, it said, must have arranged American entry into the war, for "we are moving toward a state of exhaustion."[61]

Bethmann Hollweg was here opposing to Czernin's pessimism a highly optimistic estimate of the over-all situation. To overemphasize German willingness.to make peace would not only be fruitless at the moment but do outright harm, as a confession of weakness. The proper moment for a vigorous peace offensive would come in two or three months. Until then, the thing to do was to show no undue alacrity in the face of Russian peace feelers, but never to allow the thread to break.

Before the foreign affairs committee of the federal council he expressed similar sentiments, in a more subdued manner, on May 8. He gave a report on the Kreuznach agreements, reiterating his familiar reservations and saying that if necessary he would content himself with the absolute minimum, which was really no farther than the line of the Narev. Creation of a buffer state in Courland and Lithuania was something to be considered, i.e., not necessarily essential. Germany must not allow peace to fail on account of strategic and economic considerations—to that extent he was willing to go along with Austria. Von Weizsäcker, the prime minister of Württemberg, calm and shrewd as usual, encouraged the Chancellor to seize any chance of peace at once, since Germany would be in a very bad way if the British and Russian opportunities went unexploited. Bethmann Hollweg did not dispute him, nor did he try to disarm the Württemberg politician's doubts of the utility of Baltic buffer states and of the very possibility of creating them.

When he was challenged by the arch-conservative representative of Saxony, von Vitzthum, Bethmann Hollweg did emphatically disavow Scheidemann, whom he was eager to "get off his back" but could not, on account of Austria. His own notions of peace differed radically from Scheidemann's, he said, and were inclined to go rather too far on the incautious side, as far as the east was concerned—this was probably an oblique reference to "autonomous principalities."[62]

As always, Bethmann Hollweg was once again moving "on the diagonal." He cautiously sought a middle way between the extremes and tried to retain a free hand. He did not succeed in convincing the men in Vienna—either on the score of the favorable military situation or on the possibility of making headway in St. Petersburg by means of confidential peace feelers.[63] In time his policy of subterfuge put him in danger of losing the confidence not only of the Austrians but of the majority socialists as well.

Czernin was past understanding his German colleague. Why this resistance to a joint declaration, now that even Ludendorff, in his directives for front-line propaganda, was speaking in terms of border rectification rather than annexation? The effect in Austria-Hungary would be disastrous. Already the non-German elements were beginning to say that the German craving for annexations was plunging the monarchy into perdition. Czernin was bitter about Bethmann Hollweg's "unreasonable obstinacy," which he attributed solely to fear of the Pan-Germans.

Once again there was a flood of agitated messages to Hohenlohe, urging him to urge on the German Chancellor. By way of reinforcement, Admiral Holtzendorff was enlisted. During a visit to Vienna, the admiral also engaged in political talks, during which he freely agreed with Czernin's strictures on Bethmann Hollweg's policy. Holtzendorff undertook to make representations to Bethmann Hollweg and Zimmermann and indeed did so, exaggerating and distorting Czernin's statements.

He said he had been told in Vienna that further discussions in Berlin were utterly useless and that it would be better to negotiate with the OHL direct-ly—Holtzendorff claimed he was asked to inform Ludendorff accordingly. This, of course, merely aroused the Chancellor's ire. Bethmann Hollweg brusquely rejected any military interference with his authority, and his tem-per was not allayed by additional intelligence indicating that Czernin was seeking direct contact with headquarters by other means, in order to lodge complaints about Bethmann Hollweg with Ludendorff and the Kaiser via military channels. Some of these dispatches were based on misunderstandings, as it turned out. Still, the German foreign ministry filed a vigorous protest in Vienna.[64]

In the end the constant harassment got to be too much even for the Austrian ambassador. On May 4, in a long report, Hohenlohe told his minister he had hitherto understood he was to do all he could to keep the Bethmann Hollweg government in power as long as possible. For three years he had been reporting that any change could only be to the disadvantage of Austria. To incite the Bavarian prime minister and the admiralty chief (a political ignora-mus), and through them the OHL against the Chancellor meant deliberately working for his fall. The only possible successors were Falkenhayn, Tirpitz, or the aged Hindenburg, each with some smart under secretary beside him. He, Hohenlohe, had done everything in his power to put over the joint declara-tion in Berlin. Zimmermann had assured him he was not afraid of locking horns with the military; but the kind of public declaration Czernin wanted would bring such vocal protests in the conservative and national-liberal press and so furious a dispute over the peace terms that domestic tranquility would be at an end and political disunity flaunted before the whole world, thus negating the intended effect. Hohenlohe thought that this line of reasoning, put forward also by Bethmann Hollweg himself, was utterly sincere.

Czernin was quite evidently shaken up by these remonstrations.[65] He came back with alacrity, insisting that Vienna continued to be very much concerned that Bethmann Hollweg remain in office. He persuaded Emperor Charles to make a point of so stating to Count Wedel. As to the various missions with which he had charged Hertling, Holtzendorff, and others, Czernin now made light of them, and in the end he agreed to forego the joint declaration.

He did, however, propose a substitute: Let the Chancellor send him a congratulatory telegram on the occasion of the award to him of the grand cross of the order of St. Stephen; and let the message emphasize the conformity of German and Austrian war aims and the complete harmony prevailing between the two countries on all questions. Such a wire was indeed dispatched the same day. It was couched in warm terms, but did not include "conformity of war aims," a phrase Bethmann Hollweg wanted to save up for his Reichstag speech, only "common work and fullest understanding." Czernin used the same words in his reply, as public testimony of his confidence in Bethmann Hollweg.

All the same, even this elegant circumlocution did not commit Germany to Austrian war aims; and the Austrian statesman now adopted stronger means of pressure. Most dubious of these methods were attempts to exert direct influence on leading Reichstag deputies, a crude form of intervention in internal German policy aimed at mobilizing a parliamentary opposition to the German government on the peace issue. There was already a permanent link to deputies from Berlin that could be utilized. During Erzberger's visit on April 22, Czernin had arranged for messages to be carried back and forth by his friend the Ruthenian deputy Baron Vassilkov, who often made the trip. Vassilkov was well-connected among German parliamentarians.[66]

Erzberger had visited Vienna at the behest of the German foreign ministry, to find out whether rumors that Austria was seeking a separate peace were well-founded and also to combat the pessimism that prevailed in the Austrian capital. To prepare him for this mission, the foreign ministry had shown him Czernin's secret report for the Kaiser, dating from April 12. The upshot of the trip was, however, that Erzberger was himself in some measure infected with the Austrian pessimism.

Emperor Charles granted him a private audience during which he handed the German a copy of the report, telling him he could use it as he saw fit. Charles did not breathe a word of this to his minister; and later on, when the report had become known abroad, he brazenly denied having passed it on. Erzberger's precise responsibility for this faux pas is in doubt. He did read the report to a meeting of fellow party members late in July, but insisted he had done so only in confidence. He insisted further that many copies of the report had been sent from Switzerland to Germany, one of them actually reaching Britain.

However that may have been, both the author and the emperor intended the report to be something of a political bombshell; and this was indeed the effect it had—whether Erzberger read his friends the full text or merely gave them the general sense. Obviously outsiders and others in no position to form a judgment of their own were bound to be deeply affected by statements from a responsible statesman with access to all secret information, to the effect that Austrian strength was completely drained, that revolution might break out any day, that U-boat warfare had already failed, and that the war could at best be continued for only a few months of the summer.[67]

That was not enough, however. Bethmann Hollweg had to be given a good scare that Austria might really defect. For this purpose an epilogue, in itself unimportant, to the mission of Prince Sixtus was employed. The Bourbon prince had been deeply frustrated by the failure of his mission. Could it perhaps be continued, if he succeeded in persuading his brother-in-law to make certain concessions that might be offered to Italy? Lloyd George had thought the Italians might be content with South Tyrol or some of the Dalmatian islands, without insisting on Trieste.

Without authority from anyone, Sixtus passed such suggestions on to Vienna, only to be instantly invited to Laxenburg castle, where he met Emperor Charles on May 8. He had been picked up in Switzerland by Count Erdödy, who assured him—or so at least Sixtus reports[68] —that emperor and empress were ready to make peace with the Western powers. Czernin, he said, was prepared to go along and requested that, in the event of peace, the French officers stationed at the Russo-Austrian front should be transferred to the Russo-German sectors. Austria would allow grain purchased by the Entente in Russia to traverse its territory en route to Switzerland, but still would want crops planted by Germany in Rumania and Turkey to reach that country, with which it did not desire war.

These are extraordinary and improbable details to have been discussed even before such a meeting! The suspicion obtrudes that they were meant merely to lend greater credence to the purported Austrian willingness to make peace, by creating the impression that Vienna had already made elaborate preparations. To make all this even more palatable to the prince, statements were made to the effect that riots and peace demonstrations were expected in German munitions plants as soon as the separate peace with Austria became known and that the defection of Bulgaria and Turkey was also anticipated. To give at least the appearance that Italian opposition was not insurmountable, a mysterious peace offer by an Italian General Staff officer, dating back to February,[69] was dusted off and exhibited to the prince as alleged proof that the Italians were not nearly so immune to negotiations as they pretended. One must doubt whether Vienna really believed this would make an impression on the Entente. Perhaps it was merely a matter of encouraging the prince to make another effort, even though belief in its possible success was half-hearted. Perhaps the purpose was merely to lure the prince to Vienna once more.

Doubts of the sincerity of the talks at Laxenburg are not dispelled when their course is examined. Czernin took part almost from the beginning. The spirit was one of joviality, and none even inquired as to whether Sixtus had any credentials from the Entente governments, or what their views were. The main topic of discussion was Italy. Charles now agreed to cede South Tyrol to Italy, but not a square inch more, and that only if Austria were indemnified by territory other than German!

Prince Sixtus made the fanciful proposal that some African colony, say Somalia, be given in return for South Tyrol. Count Czernin took soundings to see whether his wishful dreams about Rumania had any chance of fulfillment, but got no answer. He insisted on guarantees for maintenance of the status quo for the monarchy, as a prerequisite for any concession, emphatically declared that Austrian policy was not dependent on Berlin, and expressed the desire that the talks be continued with authorized career diplomats in attendance. He then withdrew in an almost unseemly hurry, before anything had been decided.

The next day Charles gave his brother-in-law a letter that was intended to summarize the meeting, though it actually consisted of only a few noncommittal phrases and made no mention of the supposed Italian peace offer. Its opening coincided word for word with a draft Sixtus had brought with him from Switzerland, except that all mention of political concessions had been cut. Charles also handed his brother-in-law a note from Czernin, written in German, as requested by Prince Sixtus. It shows clearly that the minister never contemplated a separate peace behind Germany's back. It made four points:

1. There were to be no territorial cessions without compensation of equal value.
2. The Entente would guarantee that in any peace negotiations the integrity of the Austrian monarchy would be respected.
3. Austria would not even consult its allies in the matter, unless these demands were answered in the affirmative.
4. Austria stood ready, however, to continue the discussions now initiated, "to work for peace with honor and thereby to pave the way for world peace."

The term "peace with honor," if this were to be a preliminary stage to world peace, could only mean a separate peace; but so vague an assurance was, of course, quite unsuitable to serve as the basis for serious diplomatic negotiations, and it was probably not even intended to be that. To present it to Poincaré and Ribot at all, Sixtus had to falsify it into an offer of a separate peace in his translation. Naturally this was of no avail. Following some inconclusive consultations with Lloyd George, the Bourbon initiative was finally laid to rest.[70]

The main purpose envisaged by the Austrians, however, had been attained. No sooner had Prince Sixtus departed when Bethmann Hollweg was invited to Vienna for urgent talks about an enemy peace offer, as well as about the

Chancellor's impending Reichstag speech. The Chancellor appeared on May 13 and learned in deepest confidence from Czernin's and Charles's lips that Britain, France, and Italy had made Austria an offer of a separate peace, against cession to Italy of South Tyrol and an island or two. Such a separate peace would constitute no disadvantage for Germany, the minister added hypocritically, for Austrian troops released on the Italian front could take over the eastern Austrian front, while the German forces now stationed there could then be thrown against the west. The blockade in the Adriatic, moreover, would cease, and food imports from that side could be conveyed to Germany, as needed–though goods coming from Russia would have to be transported to Switzerland. Czernin said he had replied to this offer with the statement that it would have to be discussed with Austria's allies first of all. The retort had been that this was taken for granted. The offer of a separate peace was entirely "legitimate."

It is almost inconceivable that Czernin could have counted for even a moment on Bethmann Hollweg believing this tissue of lies, let alone that he would agree to the plan. His assurances of loyalty to the alliance were undoubtedly sincere–for the moment! –for he could not have failed to realize that Prince Sixtus had not come with a commission from the Western governments, in other words, that there was no peace offer to begin with; nor could he have been foolish enough to ignore the devastating consequences such a separate peace would bring for both the Central Powers, unless it directly merged into a general peace, which was not then in the mind of any Western statesman.

What would these consequences have been? The successful U-boat campaign in the Mediterranean would have ceased; Bulgaria and Turkey would have been cut off from German arms and munitions shipments; the troops in those countries probably would have been interned as well, eliminating them as effective allies; the Entente would have had free disposal of the Balkans and been able to settle the future of Rumania, Serbia, and the Adriatic coast; the German eastern front, an almost inextricable tangle of German and Austrian units, would have dissolved completely; the German people, and the German-speaking Austrians as well, would have smoldered with moral indignation over the treachery displayed by the very ally whom Germany had taken the field in 1914 to save; last but not least there would have been disastrous repercussions among the broad German masses, especially in war industry, as Erdödy had repeatedly pictured to Prince Sixtus, with incalculable revolutionary dangers for both monarchies.

But Czernin was not really intent on a separate peace at all. He wanted only to deal a jolt to German confidence in victory, to coerce Bethmann Hollweg into paying greater heed to his wishes. Informed by Wedel that the prince had turned up in Vienna, the Chancellor surmised correctly that Sixtus was the negotiator from Paris, though Czernin did not identify him.[71] Bethmann Hollweg gave no sign of his suspicions, merely observing that the alleged Entente offer sounded very vague and suggesting that U-boat pressure, failure of the western offensive, and the Russian Revolution had persuaded the Entente to move toward a general peace or make an attempt to disrupt the alliance of the Central Powers. He said he must first of all consult the Kaiser, to whom he immediately sent a report.

Czernin did conclude, however, that he had succeeded in his main purpose. He got the impression that Bethmann Hollweg was inclined to bow to Vienna's wishes in his impending Reichstag speech by showing himself conciliatory to Russia and making a sharp distinction between that country and the other enemy powers. Czernin instructed Hohenlohe to follow up with Bethmann Hollweg at once, but the Austrian ambassador was unable to carry out this mission, for the Chancellor had returned from Vienna tired and worn-out and declined to see him.[72]

The next day Bethmann Hollweg delivered his last Reichstag speech. He had assured the Kaiser that he had no doubts whatever of Austria's loyalty to the alliance, but he must have been deeply depressed over his experiences in Vienna. At the very least they showed that Austria was not really interested in continuing the war and sought to gain security for itself as soon as possible.

Directly on Bethmann Hollweg's departure from Vienna, Czernin endeavored to place the German ambassador, Count Wedel, under pressure, in which he succeeded very well. He let Wedel know in the friendliest form that impatience and distrust of Germany were growing at the Vienna court, not least under "Roman influence." It was feared that all of Austria's interests would take a back seat if Germany won—in Poland, Galicia, the Bukovina, Serbia, South Tyrol, Rumania. Wedel reported that the Entente, because of its well-known connections at the Vienna court, was indeed in an enviable position to make tempting offers of a separate peace with which Germany could not compete. "In politics one cannot stake everything on loyalty and gratitude." Berlin would do well, he advised, to present Czernin—who wanted to visit supreme headquarters on May 17—with satisfactory perspectives about Austrian war goals. Even among influential circles in Austria opinion was divided and vacillating; hence it was important to give backing to reliable upholders of the alliance, of whom Czernin was one.

It will be seen that the Austrian shrewdly played his cards along two different lines in support of his policies: his own loyalty to the alliance and his emperor's unreliability. Charles had in fact that very day written him the vengeful letter about German policy and the need for a separate peace of which we already know.[73]

In the circumstances, the Chancellor understandably found it desperately hard if not impossible (as he told the federal council committee on May 8) to make any public statement on German war aims. Vienna was besieging him to accept the Russian peace formula, and the latest news from St. Petersburg was an added incentive—Milyukov seemed about to fall and the peace party to gain the upper hand.

On the other side, there was a barrage of exhortatory and minatory wires and letters from headquarters, demanding the precise opposite. On May 9 the Kaiser sent word by telegram that in view of the splendid U-boat successes the foreign ministry must on no account display any eagerness in the peace question. It should fall in with Ludendorff's wishes and organize a movement in Livonia and Estonia that would seek integration with Courland and hence Germany. Spirits at headquarters were high, the message said. A sharp disavowal of the Scheidemann peace was looked for in the impending Reichstag debate.

A few days later the Kaiser complained that after three years of war he still had not seen a war aims program—and this despite Kreuznach! He was therefore compelled to assemble one according to his own ideas and those of "his" armed forces. He did indeed compile a list more fantastic than anything the OHL had put together since 1916; and he added the threat that "every further week of war will raise the price"—namely that German demands would be steadily increased.

At the chancellery and the German foreign ministry such occasional outbursts of imperial spleen were not taken very seriously. (It was known that on this occasion the message had been provoked by the visit of a notorious loudmouth.[74]) But Ludendorff was also heard from. He was furious over a story in the *Bayerische Staatszeitung* in which foreign ministry sources had quoted him as favoring an accelerated peace. This was not the case, he insisted. Time was on the side of the Germans, and the OHL definitely wanted nothing to do with "modest" peace terms.[75]

The Chancellor was being driven more and more into a corner. The social democratic majority in the Reichstag put a formal and unequivocal question to him. In the light of the Austrian and Russian peace demonstrations, what did he propose to do to bring about agreement among all the governments concerned so that the peace to come could be concluded on the basis of mutual understanding without annexations or indemnities? An attempt to sidetrack the question failed, since the conservatives filed a similar one: Was the Chancellor prepared to provide information about his stand on the socialist proclamation calling for peace without annexations? From both extremist wings Bethmann Hollweg was being besieged to state openly just where he stood. Things were to come to a head in the Reichstag session of May 15, which threatened to become the most crucial of his whole political career.

To gain backing, the Chancellor called in the parliamentary leaders of the moderate parties, whom he managed to convince that at this point in time any unequivocal statement for or against peace without annexations would be fruitless abroad and disastrous at home, because it would fan the flames of the war aims debate to white heat. He persuaded them to issue a joint declaration of confidence in him and approval of his reserve.[76] The only one who seems to have been less than satisfied was Erzberger, who had unsuccessfully recommended an impossible compromise to the Chancellor.[77]

At the last moment, by the way, Bethmann Hollweg does seem to have tried to get the Kaiser's approval for a peace formula that was at least meant to resemble the Russian one closely. On his return from Vienna on May 15 at noon, he had found a wire from the legation in Berne. A reliable informant, the socialist Dr. Adolf Miller, it said, had established by thoroughgoing inquiries that if the Chancellor wanted a separate peace with Russia, he would, in his Reichstag speech, have to accept the Soviet peace formula without reservations. Such a step was also favored by Federal Councilor Hoffmann, head of the Swiss foreign affairs department.[78]

This wire was at once transmitted to headquarters, where that night the Kaiser discussed it with his three cabinet chiefs and Grünau. The Kaiser quoted Bethmann Hollweg as being prepared to accept the formula, judging from a note in Admiral Müller's diary.[79] If this were true, the Chancellor must have declared his willingness by telephone during the day. In any event, Ludendorff objected, as was to be expected. He was willing to accept only some meaningless compromise formula—an "understanding based on the safeguarding of mutual interests." That sealed the fate of the Chancellor's effort—we shall never know how seriously it was intended. The ultimate decision in questions of such import had long lain with the OHL.

Actually, Bethmann Hollweg did not tie himself down to any peace formula. His Reichstag speech of May 15, awaited with great expectancy, was a masterpiece of diplomacy. It avoided a clear commitment for or against peace without annexations, but also the appearance of half-hearted weakness. It was firm and manful in asserting that Germany would follow its own way, and rose to heights of statesmanship in deflating emotionalism and extremism. Neither threats nor criticism would deflect him to a wrong course, he exclaimed, such as a policy of conquest or of premature renunciation. Both would bring disastrous consequences, at home and abroad. He was beholden to no party, but only to the German people. For purposes of dissociating himself from the radical left, he skillfully exploited a menacing-sounding phrase of Scheidemann, who had hinted of the danger of revolution if the war were continued solely to secure annexations.

He was even more pointed, however, in defending himself against crude accusations by the arch-conservative agrarian, Roesicke, off whom he scored by citing the Kaiser's Easter message, to the great satisfaction of his social democratic supporters. Supreme headquarters was pleased with Bethmann Hollweg's statement that Germany's military situation had never been more favorable. Czernin too got his sop. At the very outset of his speech, Bethmann Hollweg vigorously denied that there were any differences between the Central Powers on the issue of peace. What was calculated to please Czernin even more was that a sharp distinction was drawn between Germany's enemies in the west and its Russian neighbor. It was only in respect of the former that Bethmann Hollweg currently regarded any understanding as hopeless. As for the Russians, it was self-evident that Germany wished to create an enduring and peaceful life side by side with them. Nothing must be allowed to interfere with the development of such a relationship. Germany must put forward no claim incompatible with the freedom and will of the nations concerned, nothing that would merely sow the seeds of new hostility among the Russian people. All thought of coercion must be eliminated. No sting, no resentment must be allowed to fester. This formulation avoided outright acceptance of the Russian peace formula, while still stating its essence in circumlocution–self-determination and the renunciation of forcible conquest.

Bethmann Hollweg could not say more, and most probably did not wish to. The immediate oratorical success was very great. The parties of the middle unmistakably closed ranks behind the Chancellor against the extremists on the right and left. The Chancellor's last Reichstag speech deserves to be described as the brilliant conclusion of a brilliant series of addresses.

The Austrian ambassador, in particular, was deeply impressed. He reported to his ministry that Bethmann Hollweg, worked up over the attacks on him from right and left, had delivered his best speech.[80] Unfortunately, oratorical successes seldom last. The social democrats were not really satisfied, and the rightist parties persisted in their hate campaign. Although it came close to cynicism, the Chancellor, mindful of the Kreuznach program, had found it possible to say that there was full agreement between himself and the OHL on the question of war aims. This, of course, brought thunderous applause on the right; but the acclaim soon turned into enhanced distrust. The deputies on the right were not certain of Bethmann Hollweg's sincerity–could the statement not be read in two different ways? And the left was even more uncertain.

Neither side of the Reichstag was willing to be kept dangling much longer. As Hoetzsch put it in the *Kreuzzeitung,* both desired "political influence on the course of the war," now that the arbitrament of arms was dragging on without an end in sight. Calls rang out for political leadership and initiative, and the callers gave little thought to the question of whether there was even the slightest chance that Reichstag declarations could in any way affect the inexorable course of Germany's war destiny.

Part 4

# Czernin and the OHL's Balkan Program (May to June, 1917)

LUDENDORFF had in the meantime become more and more politically active—so much so that the war files almost create the impression that a separate foreign ministry had grown up within the OHL, while the chief of staff himself apparently had unlimited time to work on political questions.

His immediate aim was to commit Germany's Austrian ally firmly to his annexationist policies in the Baltic area. To this end he exploited statements by the Austrian army high command in late April, to the effect that front-line propaganda had progressed to the point where concrete peace terms had to be submitted to Russian negotiators. The Austrians wished to reach an understanding with the OHL on this issue.

Dispatching two telegrams in a single day, Ludendorff proposed that a war aims catalog be promptly agreed on with Austria, on the basis of the Kreuznach program. Zimmermann protested in vain that Czernin was nervous and unstrung, and wished only to conclude a separate peace with Russia, preserving Austria's territorial integrity and foregoing all annexations. Hastily staged conferences on the Courland issue were bound to be fruitless, merely resulting in arguments that would breed bitter resentment. The only chance was to allow the seasoned ambassador, Count Wedel, to prepare the Austrians gradually and cautiously for the OHL demands.

Zimmermann had barely dispatched this wire when Grünau reported he had heard through a Bulgarian liaison officer, Colonel Ganchev, and through Lieutenant Colonel von Massow, that Ludendorff was already engaged in preparing a conference of the Central Powers, including Bulgaria, which was to be convened in Berlin in mid-May. Zimmermann was horror-struck in anticipation of the preposterous terms the Bulgarians were likely to propose. How could Germany cope with such a situation without risking displeasure all round? [81]

Zimmermann proceeded to brief Wedel on the Kreuznach talks and asked him to try to persuade Czernin by and by to accept the agreements there reached: leaving East Galicia to the Russians against indemnifying Austria in Serbia and Rumania, an idea that Hohenlohe on his part had not rejected out of hand.[82] As usual, Ludendorff was in a raging hurry; and he cited, among other things, an alleged request, conveyed through General Arz, asking that Ludendorff urge the German foreign ministry to lose no further time in taking up closer liaison with Czernin on the war aims question. (When inquiries were made, it soon developed that no such request was ever made![83])

Ludendorff blandly said he foresaw no trouble in dealing with Austria. Germany's ally would have to be bluntly informed of German war aims in the east and equally bluntly told to look to Serbia and Montenegro. Austria would then surely be willing to forego East Galicia, to compensate Russia. Not a soul in Austria would really dream of sacrificing even a single life in order to reconquer that wretched country, East Galicia. Besides, Austria's real interests lay in the Balkans. Outright acquisition of part of Serbia, with the remainder forming a Neo-Serbian satellite state, would fully repay Austria, indeed strengthen the dual monarchy.

Serbia, after all, would have fallen into Austria's lap as a ripe plum, Ludendorff insisted. Having helped conquer Serbia, surely the German army need not forego its reward in Courland-Lithuania! The prestige of the house of Hohenzollern would suffer, unless peace brought Germany Courland-Lithuania.

As for rewarding Austria with parts of Rumania, as Czernin devoutly hoped, Ludendorff demurred. For Germany to pull out of Rumania altogether went too far and was not in accordance with the Kreuznach protocol. He would rather install Prince Cyril of Bulgaria as ruler of Rumania—Cyril would make a stout German ally. In that way too, the question of the Dobrudja, which had become a bone of contention between Berlin and Sofia, might be most simply solved.[84] To clear up this matter and other controversies (including some that involved Greece and Turkey), Ludendorff wanted Ferdinand of Bulgaria to visit the Kaiser; and against this event, he had already prepared detailed proposals.

Clearly the OHL was pursuing its own Balkan policy, trying to force the foreign ministry into its wake, if not actually using it as a mere instrumentality. Ludendorff insisted inflexibly that a Central Powers conference on peace terms be held, and that a complete program for reorganizing the Balkans be drawn up even before it convened. To this end, on May 12, two OHL officers, Colonel von Bartenwerffer, head of the political section, and Colonel von Oldenhausen of the rail transport section, met with representatives of the foreign and interior ministries.

At this meeting lines of negotiation with the Austrians and Bulgarians were carefully laid down, on such subjects as Rumania, the Dobrudja, pre- and postwar Bulgaria, Serbia, and shipping on the Danube. Germany was to have large-scale economic privileges in Rumania, and also in Serbia (inclusive of parts of that country to be incorporated in Bulgaria), and in respect of Danube shipping. French and Rumanian mines were to be expropriated, rail lines and mineral rights acquired, and above all a German oil monopoly established in Rumania.

All this was justified on the basis of Germany's overwhelming share in the conquest of both Rumania and Serbia, and the enormous financial subsidies Germany had paid and was still paying its allies. The OHL had obtained an exact accounting of these amounts. Difficulties were, of course, anticipated, and for that reason Ludendorff was prepared to hold back some of the German claims for the time being and to exempt Austria's share of Rumanian territory from the German economic monopoly, provided that share were limited to Little Walachia.

All in all, however, this heralded a new era in German war policy, already foreshadowed in the Kreuznach draft of April 23. It was to be dominated by the spirit of Ludendorff, who was as serious about projecting vast plans of conquest as he was about his military tasks, and who felt equally qualified for both.[85] There was not the slightest sign here of peace without annexations and indemnities.

How seriously the OHL approached its Balkan plans may be seen most clearly from the fact that even before the conference, and without saying a word to the foreign ministry, it sent its military attaché in Constantinople, von Lossow, an eight-point program on Balkan questions, similar to the one it had presented at Kreuznach in April, instructing him to discuss it with the Turkish government. Ambassador Kühlmann and the foreign ministry heard about it only afterward, and it took many inquiries and considerable confusion to learn the details of this arbitrary step. German diplomacy was now under the unwelcome necessity of telling the Turks about the secret German-Bulgarian treaties, and later about the Kreuznach agreements as well.[86]

We can only make a guess about Bethmann Hollweg's views on the OHL's ambitious Balkan program. He probably shared Zimmermann's skepticism— Zimmermann thought the program stood no chance whatever and was therefore of no practical importance.[87] Bethmann Hollweg probably also shared Zimmermann's doubts that agreement among the allies on so many controversial questions was possible and his fear that the alliance would only be further shaken.

Czernin did indeed initially respond with vehement opposition. He wanted no part of the cession of East Galicia and the Bukovina, merely to make it easier for the Germans to acquire the Baltic provinces; and the German hints about Austrian gains in Rumania and Serbia he described as "vague promises."[88] But the Austrian minister learned almost immediately that it was not merely the Germans who were thinking of territorial aggrandizement. On May 12 the Bulgarian chargé d'affaires complained about Czernin's piece in the *Wiener Fremdenblatt.* Public opinion in Bulgaria was quite upset about it, he said, and it was feared that Austria was about to force its ally to accept a peace without annexations. In the light of the promises anchored in treaties this was tantamount to a breach of the alliance. Czernin had his hands full to reassure the government in Sofia, which he told, not very credibly, that his article did not refer to the Balkans at all but was merely designed to calm the Slavic elements within the Hapsburg Empire.[89] Whether because of this objection or the persuasive Count Wedel, Czernin now said he was ready to participate in the war aims conference that was to take place on May 17 and 18 at headquarters in Kreuznach, with Bethmann Hollweg, Zimmermann, the OHL, Holtzendorff, and Capelle in attendance.

At that meeting, however, Czernin did not at all commit himself to the German "swap" and the renunciation of East Galicia. At the outset he actually planned a new "solidarity pact" in the style of the agreement of March 27,[90] under which the vast occupied territories in Russia were to serve primarily to regain East Galicia and the Bukovina for Austria.[91]

What was actually achieved at Kreuznach was not an agreement but a mere memorandum that held little more than parallel declarations of intention by the two partners, who on occasion contradicted each other. Austria-Hungary, it said, insisted on the complete territorial integrity of the dual monarchy and in addition demanded Mt. Lovčen as well as the reorganization of Serbia, as we already know. Germany wished to see the Balkans reorganized in a different way and Italy removed from Vlonë, which was evidently meant to become a German naval base. Austria was also to grant Germany a free hand in exploiting the natural resources of Neo-Bulgaria.

This was to be the subject of further negotiations, and Czernin did not give his formal approval. He did score a great success in that the German side agreed to leave all of occupied Rumania with the exception of the formerly Bulgarian part of the Dobrudja and a border strip south of the Czernavoda-Constantzaline to Austria as a "separate state." This fulfilled, indeed exceeded the Austrian minister's wishful dream with which we are already familiar.

The Germans did insist on retaining the lion's share in the ownership and exploitation of Rumania's natural resources, on which there was to be further consultation; but why did they make this big concession in the first place? Only to persuade Austria at least to tolerate the conquest of Courland and Lithuania and the long-debated association of Poland with Germany—though none of this was formally acknowledged in the draft. According to the German declaration, however, Austria was to get Rumania only if Germany were to prevail with the acquisitions just mentioned.

The tenacity with which Czernin fought against the Baltic annexations and the sacrificing of Poland may be gauged from the fact that he was now being offered far more than Walachia, the only prize he had once coveted. More than that, he was promised that the German military administration in Rumania would try to win over that country to the cause of the Central Powers, and beyond that that the territorial acquisitions and economic advantages gained on either side should be kept in an "appropriate proportion."[92]

The conflict between the two allies cannot be said to have been completely eliminated with this draft agreement. Czernin was of course highly gratified at his success in securing substantial prizes for his country in the event of victory, without foregoing East Galicia; but he remained skeptical as to whether any of these agreements would ever come to fruition—it was a case of sharing out fish not yet caught, as he put it to Wedel. Above all, he was suspicious of German economic goals in the Balkans, with good reason. He thought that the Austrian interest might be entirely pushed aside, the meat of Rumania falling to Germany, with Austria having to make do with the bones.[93]

There happened to be a cabinet crisis in Hungary, and it took a long time, in fact until June 18, before Czernin could report to Bethmann Hollweg that the two prime ministers of the dual monarchy had agreed, though only with strong reservations. Only future negotiations, it was stipulated, could settle Germany's economic role in the Balkans. Only in the event that Courland and Lithuania did not fall to Germany would Austria rest content to enjoy the same advantages in Rumania that accrued to Germany in Poland. The agreement over Poland, it was added, would have to remain strictly secret, else it would become invalid! It took a lengthy exchange to persuade Czernin to settle for the right to deny the existence of the agreement over Poland, if anything about it transpired publicly.[94]

Above all the Austrians continued to worry that the OHL's obstinate adherence to its Baltic plan of conquest would spoil any chance of a separate peace with Russia. There was good reason for this concern. Late in May a Swiss socialist of the Zimmerwald persuasion, National Councilor Grimm, who happened to be in St. Petersburg, told the Germans that he was willing to transmit a peace program to the local revolutionaries that would encourage their pacifist tendencies. Federal Councilor Hoffmann, the Swiss foreign minister, went so far as to offer his official line to St. Petersburg for purposes of transmitting such an offer.

Zimmermann took advantage of this opportunity, and the message he sent was couched in the most conciliatory terms. On the most delicate issue, the future of Poland and the Baltic regions, he offered a "friendly understanding." But the established fact of German territorial demands could only be glossed over. It was still there and so the whole project failed. To make matters worse, the Russian government intercepted, deciphered, and published the dispatch, which created a most serious quandary for Federal Councilor Hoffmann, indeed forced him to resign; and National Councilor Grimm was expelled from Russia.[95]

In time the Russian attitude stiffened more and more. Talk of peace at the front faded out when Kerensky began to prepare his great offensive with much publicity. Austrian military circles were naturally inclined to blame

German annexationist ambitions. Captain Fleischmann, the Austrian liaison officer at eastern headquarters already known to us,[96] reported to Vienna what Czernin had long prophesied. Arrogant German demands for the annexation of Courland and Lithuania had caused a change in mood at the Russian front. In its communications with the Russians, moreover, the OHL ignored the agreements with the Austrians. This led to a furious scene between Czernin and Count Wedel. Fleischmann was charged with delivering to the Kaiser a handwritten message from Emperor Charles, voicing bitter complaints about German behavior. There was no doubt, Charles wrote, that Russia would definitely cease hostilities if it were sure that Germany as well as Austria were willing to accept the status quo. Unfortunately German demands for substantial territorial gains had rekindled the war spirit in Russia. That was intolerable to the peoples of the Hapsburg Empire, especially the Slavs. They were slowly realizing that there had been a chance of settling with the Russians, but that German demands had now made this impossible. An offer of peace on the basis of the status quo should be promptly sent to St. Petersburg.

This message from Emperor Charles marks a first climactic point in the estrangement between the two allies. Its weakness was that it rested on mere conjecture, unprovable, and that it wrongly estimated Kerensky's political intentions as well as his readiness to make a separate peace—he had, in fact, never been ready to do such a thing. Hence the German foreign ministry was quite right in persuading the Kaiser to ask urgently for proof of Fleischmann's assertions in his reply to Charles of June 22. In a political sense, however, it was no longer a matter of whether the Austrian reproaches were well-founded. One of the difficulties was that they were now put forward in such brusque terms. Between the lines, Charles's letter revealed a strong degree of personal resentment. Evidently the Kaiser and his advisers were struck with dismay over this.

Bethmann Hollweg was already troubled by the Russian situation. On June 9 he made a note for the benefit of the foreign ministry. Too many people, he wrote, knew that the OHL wanted Courland and Lithuania. If the impression spread that Germany had missed peace with Russia on account of the annexation issue, the country would collapse.[97] It had now become unavoidable to issue a public declaration to counteract such an impression. This was done on June 16 in the *Norddeutsche Allgemeine Zeitung,* in the form of an article rejecting a recent declaration by President Wilson about American war aims. The article concluded by stating that the Russian formula about peace without annexations and indemnities

> constituted no obstacle of any kind to a peace between Russia and the Central Powers, who had never demanded annexations or indemnities from Russia. Rather did the Central Powers and their allies seek to

create a situation, by means of a free and mutual understanding with Russià, that would guarantee them peaceful and neighborly coexistence in perpetuity.

These sentences had been formulated and reformulated with the greatest care, as a result of discussions Bethmann Hollweg and his foreign minister had had to hold at headquarters, in order to secure the consent of the OHL, King Ferdinand of Bulgaria, and his prime minister, Radoslavov. At the same time, Czernin's agreement was to be sought, which was not quite easy in view of his quarrel with the German annexationists; and steps were to be taken to see to it that the rightist press did not break out into superpatriotic wailings, thus spoiling the effect the article was expected to have abroad.

In a letter to the foreign ministry and to Count Wedel of June 13 Zimmermann emphasized that the purpose of the article was to "finally invalidate the charge that we have made peace with Russia impossible through our attitude. The pursuit of our wishes in respect of Courland and Lithuania has been by no means abandoned." For the war press office he added: "Please notify press representatives immediately and see to it that blunders are avoided, in the patriotic interest. This is the express wish of the supreme army command as well."

There can scarcely be any doubt that the weakening addition to the effect that Germany had not given up its intentions with respect to Courland and Lithuania was also due to "an express wish of the OHL"; for scarcely two weeks later Ludendorff protested to the foreign ministry that Czernin had told the Bulgarian colonel, Ganchev, that the final sentences of the article actually meant that Germany was willing to forego Courland and Lithuania. He demanded that the Austrian minister be promptly informed that there was no such thought in Germany.

From Vienna, however, Ludendorff got the reassuring news that Czernin had merely expressed his regret to the German ambassador that the German declaration did not contain an express renunciation of Courland and Lithuania. This view, by the way, was shared by the entire Vienna press. Yet Ludendorff remained suspicious. He said he gained the personal impression in Vienna that Czernin and Hohenlohe did indeed believe in German willingness to forego the Baltic provinces.[98]

Obviously the controversial declaration had still been deliberately couched in ambiguous terms. It was meant only as a palliative—neither to proclaim territorial gains in Russia as a German war aim nor to exclude them, if by any chance they should prove to be within reach. This, however, was the limit of what the German political leadership was able to wrest from the OHL, unless it wished to risk open conflict.

That conflict, nevertheless, proved impossible to avoid.

# 12

## Political Confusion Inside Germany;
## The Reichstag's Peace Resolution;
## Fall of Bethmann Hollweg;
## Triumph of the Generals

### Part 1
### The Kaiser's Easter Message
### and Its Repercussions

T HE EFFECTS of the Russian Revolution were not confined to changing the situation at the front and raising peace hopes in Central Europe. It also set political forces in motion inside Germany.

Within the German social democratic party it gave powerful impetus to the radical left, which had long opposed the majority's conciliatory stand and its willingness to cooperate with the moderate bourgeois parties and the government. In April 1917 the "Independent Social Democrats" formed a separate party, which still could not be described as a truly revolutionary party. Despite the threatening words of its leaders Haase and Ledebour, revolutionary fervor was limited to a small group of extremists, the so-called "Spartacus League," and every effort to expand the hunger strikes of April 1917 into revolutionary mass action swiftly failed.

Yet once the czarist monarchy had fallen and "workers' and soldiers' soviets" had made their appearance in Russia, radical agitation in Germany stood a much better chance of success than before. The majority socialists found it increasingly difficult and even dangerous to preach patriotism to the masses. The fall of reactionary czarism had disposed of one of the major party slogans of 1914, as already discussed in the last chapter.

In other words, the party truce of 1914, the national unity front, finally disintegrated. This, however, was not merely, nor even primarily, a consequence of the Russian Revolution, but stemmed from the increasing exhaustion of the German people by virtue of the hardships and sacrifices entailed in a seemingly endless war. The dreadful casualties were bad enough—scarcely a family had been spared by now; but what really depressed the mood of the people in this third war year was the British blockade, the impact of which was growing more and more severe.

The noose was drawn tighter month by month and in the end even the last neutral import sources that had remained open until 1916 were blocked. Germany's unrestricted U-boat campaign was actually as much of a menace to neutral as to enemy shipping, and the neutral nations now also began to feel the pinch. During the turnip winter of 1916-1917 there was widespread famine, draining the working capacity even of workers in heavy industry, and this continued until the following harvest. The drought during the summer of 1917 promised not only no improvement, but worse to come.

Among the reasons for the steady decline in morale and the rise in dissatisfaction were the shortage of raw materials, of labor for civilian needs, and of fuel; the breakdown of transport; the increasingly wretched living conditions; and the fear that the war might drag on into a fourth winter. This unrest went hand in hand with lack of confidence in the government and in those who remained better off. The bureaucracy was charged with mishandling food rationing, and with failing to act against black marketeers and profiteers. The affluent were said to live in luxury, at the expense of the poor, by means of the black market; big business was said to be filling its pockets, supporting annexationist war propaganda, and thus helping to prolong the war.[1] The close links between the rightist parties and the East Elbian Junkers on the one hand and industry on the other lent a sharp political tinge to social rancors.

With characteristic militarist blindness, Ludendorff and his propagandists believed they could counteract this disaffection by appeals to patriotism and discipline. Down to September 1918 this misjudgment did a great deal of mischief, as will be shown in the next volume of this work. Rumbling stomachs and political distrust were not to be assuaged with promises of victory and statistics on sinkings. The generals talked of a victorious "Hindenburg peace" that would insure good pay for workers, while an ignominious "Scheidemann peace" would bring widespread misery; but such patriotic verbiage not only failed to restore the national unity front—it actually wrecked it even more.

The issue was joined. Could the constitutional monarchy on which Bismarck had indelibly left his stamp surmount the crisis of this third war year, adapt itself to changing conditions, show its capacity to survive even defeat? The first war year, the era of supreme confidence, had not shaken its authority. The people continued to look up to their leaders. When faith began to waver at the end of the second year, Bethmann Hollweg had found it necessary to use Hindenburg, the hero, to buttress it. By the end of the third war winter it had become clear that this had only made matters worse rather than better for the political leaders.

Men like Hindenburg and Ludendorff were quite useless in counteracting war-weariness and political distrust. There was really only one approach that would have worked. The people's representatives had to be given a greater share in the increasingly heavy political responsibility; and an end had to be made of provocative Prussian traditions like the three-class franchise of 1849, the obsolete state-of-siege law of 1851 with its sharp military restrictions on civil liberties, press censorship, protective custody for political suspects, anti-union restrictions on the right of association, etc.

The Russian Revolution certainly helped inspire demands to that effect, as did the charges hurled by Wilson against the grip of autocracy from which the Germans must be liberated. The staunchly monarchist bourgeoisie responded with indignant protests, embodied in countless resolutions, telegrams, and petitions that were organized by various meetings, groups, and communities.[2] But the voices from abroad were not without effect on the workers. From the spring of 1917 onward, both moderate and radical social democrats joined in a rising chorus of complaints in the Reichstag about bureaucratic evils and suppression of civil liberties by the military.

Bethmann Hollweg grew more and more concerned with the problem of securing a loyal Reichstag following for the government, in order to beat back the constant and increasingly vehement attack on it from the left and the right, and thus to revive faith in the government despite all the war-weariness. His sovereign's confidence in him, subject to constant attack by the Kaiser's military entourage, no longer afforded him sufficient protection, though he always counted on it and fought for it again and again, on increasingly frequent trips to supreme headquarters.

It was shown now that the Bismarckian constitution, based entirely on the personal authority of a popular monarch and his successful Chancellor, was simply not good enough in the critical situation of total and protracted war. Yet in the middle of such a war it was quite unthinkable to change that German constitution along the parliamentary lines that were alone regarded as democratic in America and Western Europe. It would have been a dangerous experiment, in any event, in view of the federal structure of the Reich.

Bethmann Hollweg had to resort to various expedients. From the beginning of the war he had been at pains to woo support for his policies in confidential discussions with party leaders. The rightist parties—the conservatives and national liberals—disappointed him time and again. Thus he was pushed more and more into close contact with the leftist parties—the center, the progressives, the majority socialists; and the more that party unity fell apart, the less possible it was to assert the traditional stand of the government as being "above party."

Bethmann Hollweg's government was inevitably pushed in the direction of seeking backing, preferably from a particular party grouping. In principle he was prepared to acknowledge and reward such support by appointing individual party leaders to cabinet posts—as full-fledged ministers or ministers without portfolio—or to form them into a permanent advisory council; but rather than bringing success, his efforts only contributed to his fall, for at the crucial moment the OHL intervened and managed to undermine Bethmann Hollweg's personal standing with the party leaders so thoroughly that in the end he was simply dropped. When that happened, Ludendorff, most radical of the militarists, gained virtually unlimited political power. His triumph was complete.

As long ago as March 1915 the minister of the interior, then Clemens Delbrück, had announced in the Reichstag that German political life was to be markedly liberalized—though only after the war! Even before that statement Bethmann Hollweg, in December 1914, had instructed the Prussian ministry of the interior to prepare proposals for reform of the three-class franchise. The conservative minister von Loebell, however, was reluctant and opposed, and work proceeded at a leisurely pace, report following long report. The upshot was a bill that instead of providing for "one man, one vote," still left certain groups of voters with more than one vote. Even so, Bethmann Hollweg intended to announce electoral reform in the speech from the throne in January 1916, but his arch-conservative colleagues presented such strenuous opposition that he could offer only vague promises for the future.[3]

In the spring of 1917 the Chancellor breathed new life into these slow-moving reform activities. Responding to President Wilson's libertarian challenge in a Reichstag speech of February 27, he spiritedly developed his own favorite ideas about the new society into which the war was to forge the German people. He quoted the working-class poet Bröger, who had said that Germany's poorest sons were its most loyal. The monarchy must sink its roots deeply and widely among the people and draw its strength from the love of free men.

In an improvised speech in the Prussian diet soon afterward he was more outspoken. Challenged by the Junkers, the chamber was debating the fate of its upper house.[4] Bethmann Hollweg stated unequivocally that despite every resistance there would be deep changes in German political life. The Prussian electoral law in particular would have to be reformed to enable the broad masses to take their rightful place in public affairs. Labor law would have to be revised to wipe out class conflicts and the diet itself would have to be reorganized, especially in respect of the upper house.

> Woe unto the statesman [he exclaimed dramatically] who fails to read the signs of the times, who thinks he can simply pick up where he left off, after a cataclysm such as the world has never seen before. . . . There have been doubts that I will suit my actions to my words . . . but I earnestly assure you that I shall do my utmost to carry these plans into effect.

As in all his speeches, Bethmann Hollweg made a deep impression on this occasion. The right took his words to express an outright challenge, and the campaign against him now drew added strength. The immediate effect on the left was increased respect. None dared question the sincerity of his reformist zeal. Yet there were doubts, only too well-founded, whether the Chancellor would succeed in prevailing. The Prussian diet he was addressing had a conservative majority and would never assent to any thoroughgoing reform of the three-class franchise, let alone to the socialist demand for extending the method by which the Reichstag was elected to the Prussian legislature. Even those with otherwise decidedly liberal leanings shrank from such a step, some because they opposed such radical equality on principle, others because they clung to the view that Prussia retained a special role as the bastion of conservative monarchial tradition.[5]

Yet comprehensive coordination of Prussian and Reich electoral law was long overdue. The tug-of-war between the two legislatures meeting in Berlin and the conflict in government authority pertaining to them was growing more and more intolerable. In the course of the war it had become an outright menace, subjecting the Kaiser to contradictory influences and paralyzing the Chancellor's freedom of action.

In this central issue of his work of reform, Bethmann Hollweg was beyond any doubt pursuing a radical solution rather than half-measures. He wished Prussian electoral law to be fully democratized. He repeatedly told Wahnschaffe that it would be pointless to write a new electoral law that was actually less than democratic, yet was to be represented as a democratic achievement. The only solution was one man, one vote.

If he nevertheless moved only slowly and gropingly toward this goal, it was not from weakness or uncertainty but because the situation inexorably hemmed him in. To have dissolved the diet and called new elections on the basis of the old franchise would have brought only highly equivocal results while risking the bitterest party struggles. Bethmann Hollweg was reluctant to take this chance in wartime, with so many electors in the trenches; and in his speech to the diet he said that the bill would be introduced only after the war, precisely to avoid such strife. But would the parties of the left wait as long as that? Would the government's willingness to initiate reforms outlast the war? Indeed, would Bethmann Hollweg himself still be in office?

The day after his diet speech came the news that the revolution had been victorious in St. Petersburg. The effect on the social democrats was immediate. On March 19, in the *Vorwärts,* Scheidemann demanded immediate introduction of the Reichstag-type franchise in Prussia. In discussions at the Reich chancellery he proposed that William II, as king of Prussia, should do so simply by decree, withdrawing the order-in-council of 1849 on which the three-class franchise was based. Another plan, supported by some moderate politicians as well, proposed that Reich electoral law simply supersede its Prussian counterpart.

In the Reichstag session of March 29 speakers from the left, supported on this occasion by Stresemann, implored the Chancellor to implement his reform speech of March 14 now and not wait until after the war before abolishing the three-class franchise. They were bitterly disappointed when he refused to take their advice and once again tried to justify his hesitancy with the unimpressive argument that while the war was on every effort must be concentrated on it. They scarcely listened to his assurances that he would "dearly love to institute the reform tomorrow," that he was tempted to grant the current political impetus such a triumph, just as they ignored his repeated and carefully worded explanation that he was not convinced of the wisdom of doing so now, that it was not in the nation's interest, and that he must therefore hold off until he was so convinced.

What was behind it all? For one thing, Bethmann Hollweg was in no position to give the assurances that were demanded until he had the Kaiser's authority; and he knew there was not the slightest chance that the OHL would assent to either a royal Prussian decree or a Reichstag act. Either plan would be seen as an attempt to do violence to traditional Prussian home rule, a right that was just then being passionately upheld in the upper chamber. As the Kaiser's Chancellor, Bethmann Hollweg could not mention this obstacle, for that would have meant drawing the sovereign's person into the debate.

No, he had to find another way, and this he did, as we shall see; but meanwhile his stand was incomprehensible to the parties of the left in their ardent zeal for reform. For the first time in the war the leftist press was unanimously against him on a domestic issue. They spoke of dilatory declarations that were no longer good enough, of lack of leadership and initiative. Distrust of the Chancellor grew—was he the right man in the right place, strong enough to prevail against the reactionaries, lucid enough in his aims? This lack of confidence never ceased until his fall.

As matters stood, however, wisdom was more important in the franchise issue than willpower. Bethmann Hollweg would have spoiled his every chance of success in advance if he had tried to force the Kaiser's hand by public declarations, or if he had angered his sovereign by excessively radical proposals. His own goal was actually much closer to that of his critics than they believed. At a meeting on the evening of March 31 he told his closest associates, including a representative of the Prussian interior ministry, that he planned reforms in the direction of Reichstag electoral law, i.e., one man, one vote, but also timely changes in the upper house, to strengthen its authority as a counterpoise to radical trends in the lower house. Having secured their assent, he left the next day to meet the Kaiser in Homburg, for the purpose of submitting his reform proposals.

There was a method for winning over the Kaiser to a cause he initially disliked. This was to persuade him that it would cast him in the role of high-minded and far-seeing ruler. Bethmann Hollweg always knew how to do this in masterly fashion. On August 4, 1914, he had fed the Kaiser the famous line: *Ich kenne keine Parteien mehr, ich kenne nur noch Deutsche!* [ Freely translated as "From this moment on I shall no longer countenance political parties—we are, all of us, Germans and nothing more! ] This had effectively overcome the old slander describing the socialists as "a rabble without a country."

Now he conjured up for the Kaiser the image of the "people's emperor" who held all his subjects equally dear and refused to recognize class distinctions; and he succeeded in persuading the Kaiser to issue a solemn proclamation promising reform of Prussian electoral law and the upper chamber of the diet, though without immediately defining these reforms in detail. While Bethmann Hollweg secured authority for consultations with the Prussian cabinet, his attempt to commit the Kaiser immediately to the principle of one man, one vote did not succeed, and he felt it to be the better part of wisdom not to press the point.[6]

Actually, Bethmann Hollweg had every reason to congratulate himself on kindling the Kaiser's enthusiasm for the idea of a solemn message "To My People" which, in William's mind, harked back to the message his grandfather had issued on enactment of the labor laws in the last century. Indeed, the Kaiser pressed for haste—the message must be made public on Easter Day. He was in strong measure influenced by Batocki, the Reich food commissioner, who had been suggesting to him that it was far better for the crown to anticipate pressure from below rather than allowing itself to be shunted from pillar to post.

Armed with this imperial authority, Bethmann Hollweg had his under secretary, Wahnschaffe, work out a draft of the Easter message in which a comprehensive program of reform was developed. The armed forces were to be transformed into a true people's army. All citizens were to receive the free, equal, and secret vote. The upper house was to be reorganized to include representative figures from every walk of life. The exempt status of certain groups in political and economic life was to be eliminated. German policy in the eastern provinces was to be revised, as were labor law and the law of master and servant. There were to be changes in general administration and the administration of justice and greater emphasis on home rule.

The major portions of this comprehensive program were to be tackled at once and dealt with with such dispatch that the required bills could be presented to the legislatures concerned during the current year. Bethmann Hollweg, in other words, seriously intended to go beyond the reservations he had voiced in his Reichstag speech on March 29. The Prussian diet was still not to be coerced into accepting the general franchise and reform of the upper house, but it would be given the chance to debate the bills as soon as possible, without waiting for the war to end. In the circumstances, this was the strongest pledge of his intentions Bethmann Hollweg could have given.

But as expected, he met stubborn resistance within the Prussian cabinet, on the part of such arch-conservative ministers as Loebell and Schorlemer, von Stein, the war minister, and above all the minister for education and religious affairs, Trott zu Solz, who viewed the reform proposals as the beginning of the end for old Prussia. The motion to introduce a universal suffrage bill immediately was carried by only one vote, and that only because Helfferich and Count Roedern joined the voting as Prussian ministers without portfolio.

An ominous complication was the arrival, during these deliberations, of a wire from Valentini at supreme headquarters, reporting that Ludendorff, in private conversation, had expressed brusque opposition to the introduction of universal suffrage. Valentini added the urgent warning: "Foresee severest crisis unless formulation leaves open possibility of compromise."

For the Chancellor this stand by the Kaiser's civilian cabinet chief was particularly alarming, for Valentini had hitherto been his most dependable supporter in that quarter. On more than one occasion his intervention had averted the Chancellor's dismissal, demanded by the generals. In domestic politics, however, Valentini stood to the right of Bethmann Hollweg—he was a classmate of Loebell, whose reservations about the franchise he seems to have shared, at least initially.[7]

For the time being, therefore, it seemed hopeless to bring the Kaiser around, on the basis of so tiny a majority within the Prussian cabinet; nor did Wahnschaffe's advice seem any more promising—he wanted Bethmann Hollweg to reshuffle the cabinet by replacing some of the ministers. If all were not to be lost, there was nothing left but to temporize once again. The draft of the Easter message was watered down in several passages. Universal suffrage went out the window and there was now mention only of abolishing the three-class franchise and of "direct secret ballot." The bill was no longer to be introduced forthwith but only "after our boys come home." In this modified version the Easter message was unanimously approved by the Prussian cabinet, signed by the Kaiser on April 7, and at once made public.

Even so it had a reassuring effect on the German public, and it raised new hopes in many of the liberals—mingled with new doubts of the Chancellor's capacity to take a full step forward. As for the parties of the left, they were now resolved all the more to act without making too many allowances for his difficult situation. On March 29 the Reichstag had created a special committee to consider constitutional reforms, and early in May this group met under the chairmanship of the social democrat Scheidemann to tackle a whole series of complex constitutional questions at once.

To Bethmann Hollweg's dismay, the moderate parties also put forward a resolution under which all officer appointments would have to be counter-signed by the responsible war minister. It soon developed that the proposers did not intend this bill to serve as a serious criticism of the work of General von Lyncker as chief of the Kaiser's military cabinet, nor was it meant to detract from the Kaiser's command power. They were motivated by certain legal considerations, and they also wished to do away with obsolete traditions from the age of absolutism.

The constitutional struggle during the 1860's has already shown us (Volume I, Chapter 7) the leading role traditionally played by the military cabinet in defending the crown's military prerogatives. Above all, the Kaiser's most sensitive point was his monarchial pride in his direct relationship with the officer corps, which was in theory totally exempt from intervention by any minister, let alone any elected representative—even though the army's swollen numbers had long since turned this into a mere formality.

Hence it was extremely clumsy politics to open up this ticklish question at the very moment when the Chancellor was painfully trying to lay the ground-work for greater trust between the monarchial and democratic elements in the government, and to convince the Kaiser that the new domestic course held no danger. William was greatly upset and included the Chancellor in his ire. The Chancellor, in his view, should have pounded the table and instantly put a stop to the goings-on in the Reichstag. For the time being there was not the slightest chance of making further progress along the lines of the Easter message, by appointing suitable parliamentarians to ministerial rank, for example, as Bethmann Hollweg had planned. One of the reasons was the vehement opposition now offered by Valentini, who locked horns with Bethmann Hollweg on this issue.[8]

But even before these developments, the Easter message had become a rallying point for the Chancellor's enemies, especially the conservative Old-Prussians. Colonel General Plessen, commandant at imperial headquarters, refused any longer to shake hands with him. Loebell, behind Bethmann Holl-weg's back, tried to commit the majority parties in the Prussian diet against universal suffrage and in support of his own compromise proposal. The campaign against the Chancellor's alleged "slackness" reached a climax in a speech which the conservative leader von Heydebrand delivered at Herford on May 17. The road was leading into the abyss, he said, and a halt must be called. Prussia was facing ruin. "Who now rules the German Reich? Is it our emperor and king, or does Herr Scheidemann run the world? " If matters went on in such fashion, Germany would end up as a republic.[9]

But of course the Chancellor's bitterest enemies were ensconced at supreme headquarters. We have already heard (p. 418) of the effort to unseat Bethmann Hollweg in mid-April, put forward by the OHL and its loyal hench-man, the war minister, von Stein. Ludendorff characterized the Easter mes-

sage to Wahnschaffe as "kowtowing before the Russian Revolution." The
munitions strikes in April he regarded as a proletarian challenge to policies
dictated by fear.[10] The imperial proclamation had laid bare Germany's weaknesses to its enemies, showing them the country's fear of revolution. Where
there is smoke, the enemy was bound to conclude, there must be at least
some glowing embers.

In the matter of electoral law as such, Ludendorff was probably interested
as little as the bulk of the army and even the people. Both were, in his
opinion, quite indifferent to it.[11] Ludendorff regarded all steps in the direction of democracy and parliamentary government as wretched expressions of
weakness and refused to acknowledge that there was any real danger of
revolution.[12] In his memoirs he insisted repeatedly that problems of internal
politics were always quite foreign to him; but in the spring of 1917 that did
not keep him from meddling in that sphere with an intensity at least equal to
his preoccupation with foreign affairs, of which we already know.

Reading the documents that deal with these activities during the month of
April, one might conclude that even while the battles raged in France there
were far too many people in Ludendorff's entourage with little to do that was
really useful. Questions of food, grain shipments from abroad (sometimes
mediated by military attachés), nitrate and coal production, transportation,
and drying plants for potatoes and feed were dealt with in great detail; but
beyond these urgent day-to-day needs, plans of very doubtful value were
made for the future.

In a comprehensive memorandum of April 3, for example, Ludendorff set
forth his ideas on demobilization at the end of the war. Wartime organization
with its centrally guided economy had to be maintained as long as possible,
he opined, for the German economy must retain its striking power, so that it
could instantly shift to war conditions again. Stockpiles of war material must
be accumulated. Exports and ship construction must be fostered on a large
scale. Without stringent and continuing state control of the economy the goal
of keeping up the German war potential could not be attained. "Military and
economic demobilization can only be guided by the same principles. Hence
both must remain in the hands of the military, preferably the *Kriegsamt.*"

In his reply of April 17 Bethmann Hollweg vainly explained that this
question and many others had long been under study by the executive branches concerned. He enclosed a printed list of the studies that had already
been completed and added that to leave all these matters to the military
authorities would mean dissolving the whole executive branch of the government. It would also be incompatible with the Chancellor's constitutional
responsibility for running the government.

Ludendorff stubbornly came back on May 5. The Reich office of the
interior, he insisted, was unsuited to such tasks. Top direction by the military

must be preserved, since only the military had the requisite perspective and expertise. On May 11 he went even farther. After the war raw materials and food supplies for "fortress Germany" must be stockpiled with such speed that Germany would never again be under duress from wanton British attack. The stockpiles must be measured by the present war, i.e., there must be enough to last at least three years. A prerequisite, the letter went on, was that German industry and agriculture should soon stand entirely on their own feet. It was not enough to make sure of the necessary imports by treaty. At war's end Germany must command a very large tonnage, the enemy powers as little as possible. That meant that the peace treaties must turn over much British and American tonnage to Germany, with many more vessels temporarily conscripted, to the end of enforcing fulfillment of the treaty provisions. This would give the German economy a major advantage over the enemy powers during the reconstruction period.

Bethmann Hollweg apparently stopped replying to these fatuous vaporings, unworthy of even an ensign. He was content to reject out of hand the added powers for the *Kriegsamt* that Ludendorff had demanded.[13] His vitriolic marginal notes on Ludendorff's letter of May 5 bespeak his resentment. Perusal of these documents is particularly important, because they illustrate so dramatically the character of militarist thinking. Ludendorff's messages were presumably drafted by that same Colonel Bauer whom we already know, from Chapter 9, as his adviser in matters affecting the war economy and as organizer of the anti-Bethmann Hollweg cabal. It was he who in July was to play the main role in the well-laid military plot that led to the Chancellor's fall. Thus it may be useful to examine one of the political reports Bauer wrote in the spring of 1917 for his chief Ludendorff and for the crown prince.[14]

At the outbreak of war, it begins, German morale was high and all antimonarchist sentiment forgotten. "When political questions again pushed to the fore, the government could easily have kept the people in line, by enlightening them and keeping them busy on the home front." Instead, it left this to the social democrats and the trade unions who initially, in order not to lose their followers, had departed from their anti-monarchist ways. Now they were back at their subversive work, while the government stood by idly. Their followers were still few [sic], but were growing in numbers, in the face of government inactivity. There were two parties in Germany now, a small one and a large one. The former consisted of the social democrat and Jewish liberal leaders who aimed at a republic and based their propaganda on food shortages, the promise of universal suffrage, and the demand for an immediate peace without annexations. This small but very active group was opposed by the large party of the monarchists which reached from the conservatives to the mass of the workers. They wanted a vigorous monarchy and a peace based on strength. They comprised the larger and better part of the people. They were dissatisfied with the Bethmann Hollweg government, which was supported solely by the small group of unswerving social democrats and Jewish liberals. What were the reasons for their discontent?

There was first of all the toleration of anti-monarchist tendencies and the granting of sweeping legal privileges under an auxiliary labor law that went much too far. Secondly there was the lack of clarity concerning goals. The government did not lead, but was merely yielding to popular moods, while the people wanted a strong hand and clear direction. Third came the serious deficiencies in food policy—impunity for profiteers, blundering distribution, and failure to increase production. The result was general unrest and mutual distrust. The fight against usurious prices, black marketing, and food hoarding was not waged with sufficient vigor. The Chancellor's speech in the Prussian diet on March 14 had destroyed the last remnants of domestic unity. Fourth came the failures in foreign policy. Whether or not the Chancellor was to blame, the fact was that the whole world now stood against Germany and this shook public confidence in Bethmann Hollweg's leadership. It was a grave fault to allow men like Scheidemann, Erzberger, and their ilk to puff themselves up as representatives of the people without let or hindrance. The fact that the social democratic peace proclamation of April 20 was allowed to be published had caused deep resentment which did not halt even before the throne. An added factor was that the Chancellor had aroused distrust throughout the world as long ago as 1914, by his foolish characterization of the Belgian neutrality treaties as "a scrap of paper." It was inconceivable that any government would seriously negotiate peace with such a man.

What were the remaining prospects? The Germans might soon receive a peace offer with an internationalist and social democratic tinge, which would lead to vehement internal strife. The war "must be carried to full victory, irrespective of peace, hardships, and internationalist trends." To that end Germany needed strong leadership, or there would be a "republic of internationalist coloration." Hence a new Chancellor was needed *now*. Even after the conclusion of peace Germany faced serious problems in reconstruction and social policy and these must be considered now. The Chancellor had done nothing in this respect on his own initiative. Attention had to be given to sustaining morale against new crises and hardships. That too called for a new strong Chancellor.

On the subject of who that new man was to be, Bauer's memorandum was silent. He is on record, however, as having stated quite clearly what he envisaged—military dictatorship. In his memoirs he says that this would have been the best solution, since "nothing could be done with the Reichstag as it was constituted." Ludendorff shared this view. He did, however, disappoint his followers with a statement that he aspired to no political office—

Hindenburg expressed himself similarly; but Ludendorff found the idea of dictatorship quite plausible.15 And indeed, he became dictator once he had succeeded in ousting Bethmann Hollweg, with the help of the Reichstag. The monarchy thereafter degenerated to a mere shadow institution.

In any event, we now know how Bauer, Ludendorff's political adviser and closest associate, pictured the political realities. Crown Prince Rupprecht of Bavaria, who came to know him at headquarters in those days, called him a "dangerous fanatic" and regarded his influence on Ludendorff as baleful, as he did that of Colonel Bartenwerffer, who headed the political section of the General Staff.16 Among the greatest oddities of the war years is the fact that this fanatic not only had access to well-known Reichstag party leaders and seasoned politicians, but actually enjoyed their confidence. It is a fact that casts a curious light on the political immaturity of Germany's elected representatives at the time.

## Part 2

# The July Crisis

BY EARLY MAY Bethmann Hollweg's position was already so shaky that the Bavarian war minister, von Hellingrath, sent word to Munich from headquarters that even his friends were giving him up as lost—"His days are numbered."17 Von Hellingrath regretted having to make this report, for throughout the South German governments the campaign against the Chancellor was being followed with close attention and deep indignation. The Austrian ambassador, Hohenlohe, was also much perturbed, and Czernin persuaded Emperor Charles of Austria to express with considerable ostentation his confidence in the besieged German statesman.18 Bethmann Hollweg himself was sometimes assailed by a sense of hopeless resignation. It would be much easier to be in the trenches, he confessed to Weizsäcker on May 8, during a confidential talk. There at least one could court a bullet. In his dreadful situation he could do nothing of the kind.19

He held it to be his duty, in other words, to stay on the job and struggle forward step by step, despite every obstacle. The Easter message had given him a breathing space; and on May 15, in his last Reichstag speech, already discussed, he managed once again to rally the moderate parties in support of his policies. Adjournment then brought him another breathing space.

But new danger loomed. The current appropriations to finance the war were exhausted before their time, and early in July it became necessary to summon the Reichstag to vote more money. Foreseeably, the parties of the left would insist on domestic reform with even greater determination than in March and April, and the social democrats would be even more vocal in their demand for a negotiated peace on the basis of the Russian peace formula. War-weariness had increased in the meantime. The people were afraid of a fourth war winter and new food shortages, in view of the summer's drought. It seemed, moreover, that the U-boat campaign had passed its peak in May, while there was no sign of famine or peace sentiment in Britain.

In late July Bethmann Hollweg got a lucid and reliable report on this subject, from the Danish state councilor, Andersen, already known to us as the carrier of German peace feelers in the first year of the war.[20] Andersen had just spent a week in London, where he witnessed a German air raid. According to him Britain had ample food supplies for an extended period, indeed, was virtually flooded with Danish butter and fat. Morale had hardened and was more determined than ever. In financial, political, and psychological terms, American entry into the war was of crucial importance. There was not the slightest chance of compromise.

The London air raids were having a disastrous effect. They strengthened morale infinitely and embittered even pacifist circles.[21] In other words, all expectations that the U-boat campaign would settle the war had proved erroneous. The Chancellor immediately transmitted these observations to the Kaiser, with whom he pleaded for an end to the senseless air raids.

All the while supreme headquarters continued to cling doggedly to its mood of victory. Holtzendorff said that stories that the U-boat campaign was a failure were mere rumors and challenged Bethmann Hollweg to set them right in the Reichstag. At his insistence the Kaiser, on April 4, sent the Chancellor a directive to tell the deputies in no uncertain terms that the U-boats would carry the day. On June 19 Hindenburg sent a message to Bethmann Hollweg in which he said: "One thing is certain—we shall await our triumph with serenity. In a military sense we are and shall continue to be secure. Our food situation is probably no worse than that of our enemies." The most important thing was to maintain internal unity and the will to stick it out. "I don't think our problem is as difficult as all that if only everyone is made to realize that time is on our side and that we are in a better position to last through the winter than our enemies." If the Germans stopped complaining about hopes gone awry and talking about peace, the enemy would soon see that his efforts were fruitless.[22]

This was precisely the kind of militaristic talk that had come to infuriate the parties of the left. The great military venture having failed, the politicians were given the "simple" task of maintaining internal unity and morale among the masses, which Ludendorff airily viewed as merely a matter of "strong leadership." Bethmann Hollweg vainly tried to make the OHL see that its expectations were illusory, to make it understand the policy he wished to follow. There were to be no more predictions of U-boat success, no promises of a "fat peace" that could not be kept, no discussion of peace terms that would merely deepen the gulf between the right and the left, no scornful statements about a negotiated peace. The element most destructive to morale, both at home and among Germany's allies, would be the impression that the war was being continued solely for conquest. What should be done instead was to continue with the internal reforms announced in the Kaiser's Easter message. Their political importance was grossly underestimated by the OHL. It was extremely dangerous to lend further credence to the idea that the opponents of reform enjoyed the kind of strong support that might ultimately prevail.

The OHL, in its reply, made pointed charges about alleged government failures, along lines with which we are already familiar from Bauer's report: deficiencies in food and coal rationing and above all in keeping a firm hand on public opinion. Britain would never agree to a negotiated peace. Sooner or later it would have to yield, if only Germany stood fast and stuck it out. Air raids against London were useful and necessary. The Chancellor was requested to provide the names of British statesmen who had been inclined to peace before the last great German air raid, but were now opposed.[23]

There was no effective communication. Bethmann Hollweg's reply was merely used by Hindenburg to denounce him to the Kaiser as an appeaser. Understandably enough Bethmann Hollweg was in a profoundly depressed mood when, on June 27, he listened to a report from the social democrats Scheidemann and David, who had just returned from the socialist conference in Stockholm. Meeting their party comrades from abroad, the two men had the full horror of Germany's situation in the world brought home to them. There was not even a glimmer of compromise in the enemy camp. There had not been a single French socialist with whom a German comrade was able to reach agreement on German war aims.[24]

Bethmann Hollweg listened closely and was particularly shaken by this last item of news. An even more important conclusion was that all attempts to make a separate peace with the Russian socialists were bound to have an opposite effect. The Russians instantly and quite correctly sensed that behind such efforts stood the desire to free troops in the east in order to overwhelm the French and the British. The two social democrats now thought that the Chancellor's earlier statements addressed to the Russians had been a mistake.

There was only one way to make further progress. Instead of another peace offer (which was not even mentioned), the German government should make a declaration subject to no possible misinterpretation, stating that it was prepared to conclude a general peace without annexations and indemnities. This would not only strengthen the peace forces in Russia but have a reassuring effect at home; for the bulk of the German people could now be kept in line only if they were certain they were not being asked to fight and endure hardships only for the sake of conquest. This also required visible progress along the lines of domestic reform announced in the Easter message. The main goal should be modification of the Reich constitution in the direction of government issuing from and supported by the representatives of the people, together with immediate introduction of the equal, direct, and secret ballot in Prussia.

The two socialists put forward these demands with great firmness and drew a very gloomy picture of morale on the home front. Bethmann Hollweg could not but conclude that this time further war appropriations could be secured only at the cost of far-reaching concessions. The time for dilatory and ambiguous declarations was past—indeed, the two socialists said so unequivocally, speaking for their party's central committee.[25] According to Scheidemann's testimony, the Chancellor agreed with them on almost every point, admitting that their stand was entirely consistent and, from their point of view, probably the only correct one. He hinted, however, that he must expect serious problems at headquarters and he requested a written record he might take along and use in evidence. This was done in the form of a comprehensive memorial signed by the heads of both the party as such and the parliamentary party, which drew an impressive picture of Germany's critical situation while at the same time putting forward demands in no uncertain terms.[26]

The political crisis that ultimately put an end to Bethmann Hollweg's chancellorship began with this memorial rather than with Erzberger's inflammatory address to a Reichstag committee, still to be discussed. There is no reason for doubting that Bethmann Hollweg personally agreed with the views of the two right-wing social democratic leaders—on the peace issue as well, at least in principle. Addressing the Reichstag on May 15, he had still believed, as did Czernin, that it was enough to meet the Russians halfway, while taking an attitude of watchful and aloof waiting toward the Western powers; but all hope of a separate peace in the east had vanished in the meantime.

Peace propaganda in the trenches had long since ceased, and on June 30 Kerensky's great offensive under General Brusilov was launched. On June 25 an all-Russian congress of workers' and soldiers' soviets had come out strongly for a general negotiated peace on the basis of the familiar soviet program. It expressed itself with equal firmness, however, against any thought of a separate peace or even an armistice with the Central Powers. This stand supported in every way the report of the two social democrats. Any effort to shorten the war by public declarations would have to appeal to the Entente as a whole.

It is highly improbable that the Chancellor and his foreign minister retained any faith in this approach. On June 20 the Turkish government proposed that all the enemy powers be advised of the readiness of the Central

Powers to conclude peace on the basis of the status quo, foregoing all annexations. Russia was to be given a time limit of one month within which to
persuade its allies to accept these terms. The German foreign ministry rejected the proposal as futile.

Talaat Pasha, the grand vizier, had hoped that it might at least create a
split in the Entente ranks.[27] But although it represented only a modification
of the offer of December 1916, Bethmann Hollweg must have been inwardly
opposed as well. As he told the main committee of the Reichstag on July 7,
such an offer would be received in the Western camp only with scorn and
satisfaction, as a sign of incipient collapse.

Now a declaration on the basic nature of German war aims–that was
something altogether different. As will become clear, Bethmann Hollweg was
prepared to discuss such a plan. As always, however, he placed greater faith in
confidential contacts and mediation efforts on the part of a neutral. When an
opportunity of this nature came his way just then, he reached for it with both
hands.

On June 26, the day before the two social democrats rendered their report, the new papal nuncio, Monsignor Pacelli, later to become Pope Pius XII,
had appeared in Berlin to present his credentials. He was armed with a letter
from Pope Benedict XV that spoke of papal efforts aimed at restoring peace.
He had also been charged with sounding out, in the strictest confidence, the
matter of German peace terms, and his questions were formulated with such
precision that the Chancellor suspected the seasoned and cautious papal diplomatic service of having already established contact with Britain. He felt
justified in assuming that there might be a chance for an understanding,
provided that Germany's terms were moderate.

The circumstances turned out to be rather different. The papal secretary
of state, Cardinal Gasparri, subsequently made it quite clear that the Holy See
had acted entirely on its own. Yet Bethmann Hollweg's response shows clearly that he was prepared to drop his former demand for ironclad guarantees
that Belgium would not become dependent on the Western powers. He was
content to pledge full restoration of Belgian sovereignty without any restrictions, adding only that this would be incompatible with domination by Britain
and France. He also expressed a willingness in principle to accede to arms
limitation and international arbitration; and he gave assurances that Alsace-
Lorraine need not be an obstacle to peace if France were in a mood to
negotiate. A way could be found in the form of certain mutual border rectifications, he said.

This was apparently as far as any German statesman could have gone at
this time, and it coincided entirely with what the German social democrats
had said in Stockholm. On the question of German war aims in the east,
however, the Chancellor declined to make any statements, naturally enough,

since he did not wish the well-known OHL demands to spoil any chances of peace. He plausibly justified this reticence with the continuing chaos in Russia, and the nuncio declared himself to be well-satisfied. He thought the way for the pope's peace efforts was now clear. The chief concern of the Holy See had always been the future of Belgium.[28]

Meanwhile, at supreme headquarters, the Kaiser was besieged anew by those who were intent on Bethmann Hollweg's dismissal. All the parties now wanted his ouster, the Kaiser was told. In corroboration Hindenburg and Colonel General von Plessen summoned the arch-conservative governor of East Prussia, von Berg, who spent many hours on June 24 vocally belaboring the Kaiser in the presence of his entourage. Berg, by the way, had been picked to succeed Valentini, though that did not eventuate until January 1918. Plessen had written Berg that Valentini's removal was an indispensable prerequisite to the Chancellor's fall.[29]

On June 29 Bethmann Hollweg came to secure the Kaiser's backing for his concessions to the parties of the left, but in the circumstances these discussions were highly disagreeable. It was the Chancellor's last effort to bring about an understanding by face-to-face talks with the OHL. To his dismay he saw that even the Kaiser had begun to waver and was seemingly content to do no more than appeal to the generals to display a conciliatory attitude.

Hindenburg actually did so, but only when he was alone with Bethmann Hollweg. Averse to open conflict and uncertain in political questions, he had repeatedly shown himself willing to reach agreement with the Chancellor. Yet he now declined to call in Ludendorff—indeed, Ludendorff seems not to have talked with Bethmann Hollweg at all on this occasion. Instead he announced his opposition quite openly to Wahnschaffe, head of the Chancellor's office. Bethmann Hollweg, he said, simply did not know how to fire the people's imagination with golden dreams of Belgian and Baltic prizes.

Ludendorff not only withheld his support but declined to desist from his campaign against the Chancellor. Valentini gained the impression that Bethmann Hollweg was already fighting his last battle and felt that everyone had abandoned him; but the chief of the Kaiser's civilian cabinet seems actually to have helped deepen this impression. He balked at bringing parliamentarians into the government, though Bethmann Hollweg had apparently obtained the Kaiser's consent to such a step.[30] The Kaiser himself, however, was beginning to feel isolated within his military entourage. His demeanor was nervous and restless. That evening he complained to Valentini that both Bethmann Hollweg and Hindenburg had asked leave to submit their resignations in the course of this stormy day.

The Chancellor traveled back to Berlin in a mood of deep depression. The one prop on which he had been able to depend, the Kaiser, showed signs of failing him. The empress of Germany had long been opposed to him, and a recent letter from the crown prince confirmed that the heir to the throne must be counted among his enemies.[31] For the first time he would now have to depend on firm Reichstag support if he wished to prevail against the forces of political reaction and militarism. But in that direction he was about to face the bitterest of all his disappointments.

On June 30 Helfferich, supported by Wahnschaffe, held a preliminary discussion with the party leaders in the Reichstag. Even then Scheidemann and David put forward their demands with extreme forcefulness. They wanted clear-cut peace terms—i.e., a declaration accepting a peace without annexations—and reform of Prussian electoral law. What particularly alarmed Bethmann Hollweg's associates was a remark made by Scheidemann: "I hold a high opinion of the Chancellor, but if he went tomorrow it might also facilitate peace. I am assuming that we should have to have someone better."[32]

In the light of the many confidential talks Bethmann Hollweg had consistently held with the social democratic leaders—indeed, even more frequently of late—this was a most unexpected turn. The trend of events was soon to become apparent. The activists of the left were no longer content with making representations and voicing their wishes. They wanted an actual hand in foreign policy. They were planning a Reichstag peace manifesto and they had begun to think that it might have a much greater impact abroad if the Reichstag demonstrated its political power by forcing a change of government.

In a sense they were anticipating the parliamentary form of government that was as yet nonexistent in Germany. They figured that a Chancellor summoned with the confidence of the Reichstag might demonstrate to the world more plausibly than the present one that things were changing in Germany. Bethmann Hollweg, after all, would merely emphasize that he had always been ready for peace. What the left wanted was a radical break rather than continuity.

But was there someone at hand who could command the confidence of the Reichstag, "someone better"? Scheidemann and his followers clearly knew of none. During the critical weeks that ensued they failed to put forward a single name; and on noon of July 11, before the Prussian election issue had been settled to their liking, they like the representatives of the progressive party told Vice-Chancellor Helfferich that they were no longer interested in a change in the chancellorship.[33] In the joint caucus of the parties of the left in the Reichstag Scheidemann actually opposed precipitate introduction of the parliamentary system, which, he said, would only cause confusion. He recommended a well-thought-out gradual program. Apparently what he had meant on June 30 was that the left did not feel itself tied to Bethmann Hollweg, particularly if he were hesitant and evasive, that it would make its own foreign policy, and that it would not be swerved.

Yet hesitancy and evasion seemed precisely to be Bethmann Hollweg's tactics when he first met with the party leaders after his return from Kreuznach. Apparently he opposed the view that acceptance of the Soviet peace formula should be allowed to appear the result of profound pessimism about Germany's situation and that of the world. This could only have a pernicious effect abroad. Bethmann Hollweg, in other words, was warning against panic reactions—and for the time being he said nothing about continuing the internal reforms.

A mood of panic had already blown.up, however, and the majority socialists were chafing for action and would not be restrained. They stood in fear of losing their followers, unless their campaign brought some visible success. This impatience is reflected most vividly in the diary of the otherwise moderate deputy David, who now described the Chancellor as a "shilly-shallying bureaucrat clinging to office for dear life" and found it intolerable that he should forever shuttle back and forth between the Reichstag and headquarters, with its political plotting.[34]

David had had his own experiences with representatives of the OHL during discussions on the peace issue.[35] Like all the other deputies of the left, he could be under no misapprehension as to why the Chancellor was compelled to keep going to and fro and where in truth the root of the evil was to be sought—at the OHL with its politicking. The historian finds it hard to understand why it did not occur to a single one of these deputies, then pressing for decisive action, to tackle the evil at the root and protest first of all against the continuous meddling by the General Staff in political decisions, which had long since become a public menace.

The French chamber offers a striking contrast. The French deputies were far less reluctant to criticize the generals, almost certainly going too far in some instances—the fall of Lyautey, the charges against Nivelle; but then, the French generals lacked the glamour of great military triumphs that enveloped the victors of Tannenberg. Yet it is fair to say that the predilection of German politicians from the left to the right for decrying the Chancellor's "pusillanimity" rather than straightforwardly coming to his aid flowed from the traditional German awe of military demigods who held them spellbound.

We shall have repeated occasion to ponder this question in the course of our report. Evidently the problem of militarism in Germany also had its parliamentary aspects. On the other hand, equally thought-provoking is what Bethmann Hollweg himself said during that ill-starred meeting on July 2, when doubts were voiced of his capacity to stand up against opposition at headquarters. He referred to the complaints about OHL intervention in political matters in his concluding words; but, he added, war and politics were always cheek by jowl, and especially now. It had been no different in 1870-1871, as those appreciated who were familiar with Bismarck's report on the subject. He must object to the imputation, however, that his policies were influenced by the OHL. "His Majesty the Emperor takes the decisions, and never without me. In major questions no decisions have been taken over my objections so far." When Scheidemann thereupon remarked that the Chancellor had voted for the unrestricted U-boat campaign against his convictions, Bethmann Hollweg replied: "I spoke quite openly on the subject and explained on January 31 [in the Reichstag] why I then favored it."[36]

Why this disavowal which was actually less than the whole truth? Was Bethmann Hollweg fighting against being regarded as an impotent figurehead whose assurances no one was any longer taking seriously? Was he trying to encourage the party leaders to trust his word, despite everything? Or was he protecting the Kaiser against contempt of the imperial authority? And a last possibility, was he, the Kaiser's Chancellor, perhaps reluctant to move against the OHL at the head of a leftist opposition? Whatever the reason, he was now wresting from the hands of the parliamentarians the one weapon he might have used to save himself and his policies.

It is true that at this time the parties of the left had evidently not yet formed a solid front—not even in the matter of a peace initiative.[37] In consequence Bethmann Hollweg underestimated the impatience and frustration in their ranks. He kept out of the discussions and let Helfferich conduct the negotiations, in a more or less dilatory and placatory way. It was only Erzberger's notorious speech before the main committee on July 6 that brought on a kind of political explosion. It was planned as a great surprise coup, taking even most of the members of the parliamentary center party unawares, though it had been preceded in June by certain warnings to members of the government. Its effect was essentially based on the circumstance that Erzberger was a member of the moderate center party rather than a social democrat. In fact he was known as a former supporter of an annexationist policy and a man in the confidence of the foreign ministry. Yet this bourgeois politician now painted Germany's military and economic situation in such gloomy colors that the only way out seemed to be an immediate peace initiative by the government, based on a declaration by the Reichstag. Erzberger's pyrotechnics were given even greater impact by the proof he adduced from his own statistics that naval command forecasts had been in error. He was lending voice to what countless others sensed to be true but dared not say openly.

The shock effect on those who listened to this speech was extraordinary— and that meant hundreds in the committee of the whole. An immediate and enduring result was that the previously scheduled talks among social democrats, progressives, centrists, and national liberals now promptly led to the formation of a left bloc in the Reichstag. While the national liberals never actually became firm members of this bloc, it nevertheless succeeded the "national unity front" of the early war years and endured to war's end as the "peace resolution majority." Its immediate unifying organ was a joint caucus, organized mainly by the Swabian democrats Haussmann and von Payer. The fact that Bethmann Hollweg failed to gain the confidence of this caucus played a major part in his fall.

Why did he fail in this? The original basis for the new bloc was Erzberger's proposal for a Reichstag resolution on the question of peace and war. From its first draft, written on July 6, this resolution was anything but a new peace offer, nor was it even an echo to the Russian peace formula. It was instead a declaration by the Reichstag—not the German government—that the German people, now and always, were waging war not for conquest but in defense of their freedom and independence and for the integrity of their borders. It rejected acquisition of territory by force—in the first draft also "violence to the right of other nations to freedom and self-determination"—as well as enforced indemnities and other economic reprisals (the German term used was actually *rape*). Later versions spoke of political, economic, and financial ravishment and failed to mention indemnities altogether. Some statements were added opposing economic blockades and favoring economic peace, freedom of the seas, and reorganization of international law as goals for the future. The declaration ended with the affirmation that the German nation would continue to fight so long as Germany and its allies were threatened with conquest and violation.[38]

Quite obviously there was no reason why concord between the parties of the left and the Chancellor should have come to an end over this peace resolution. Bethmann Hollweg discussed the draft with a multiparty delegation on the evening of the day on which it was drafted; and on July 7, before the main committee, he stated his views at length. As was his duty, he urgently warned against falling from one extreme into the other—from hyperbolic faith in victory into fainthearted despair. He said that in his view another peace offer, which certain deputies were demanding, would be ill-timed during the current Kerensky offensive, but he also opposed continuation of any propaganda for extravagant war aims.

> The right approach [he said] is to let the world know even without an explicit peace offer that if they are prepared to sit down at a table with us we shall not refuse and that we shall then maintain the principle that we are fighting solely for our right to exist and for a secure future.

Such a day would never come, he went on, if the Germans now grew dispirited and dropped their hands to their sides. Yet neither should they be under any illusions, after three years of war. He was well aware of the gravity of the situation; hence he clung to the view that Germany's readiness for peace, already documented, must be maintained, though without a formal peace offer. He would welcome any helpful action by the Reichstag in specifically endorsing such a stand. Such a declaration would greatly contribute to promoting war-weariness in other countries. The ultimate goal of the war, after all, was solely to bring the enemy to the peace table. The best way to reach that goal was to start negotiating without publicity rather than to exchange peace formulas. [39]

What Bethmann Hollweg was trying to do was to harmonize the Reichstag peace action with his own policies while at the same time stemming the mood of panic Erzberger had engendered; but the parties of the left had already embarked on a course that rendered them incapable of heeding the voice of caution and reflection. The war minister read a propitiatory letter from Hindenburg to the committee and Capelle feebly tried to discredit Erzberger's naval statistics; but this only served to irritate Scheidemann, who reiterated Erzberger's warnings and proposals with great vigor. Unlike the skeptical Chancellor, he predicted that the contemplated Reichstag resolution would have a tremendous effect abroad. The Russian government would challenge its allies: Why continue the war when Germany and its allies are in basic agreement with us? The moment the Reichstag reached a clear-cut decision, the French and British governments would face the greatest difficulties. The German people, at the same time, would have received reassurance that the war was not being continued for conquest. To provide this reassurance, Scheidemann called for a declaration of and by the popularly elected Reichstag entirely on its own rather than a government manifesto approved by the Reichstag. [40]

The new joint party caucus shared this attitude. It was a bustling body, with a fervent belief that a new era of effective parliamentary activity had dawned. At the same time, it was pervaded with deep pessimism about the war situation, naively overestimated the chances for its approach to succeed, and lapsed into utter confusion when discussing the immediate tasks that were to be done. [41]

It was plain from the first day that the caucus was determined to run its own show; and as Scheidemann had hinted on June 29, a change at the top would underline that. The trouble was that there was no agreement on which post was to have a new occupant or on who he was to be. Haussmann and Payer did not wish to topple Bethmann Hollweg—on the contrary, they wished to support him. The social democrats too, including even David, were convinced that he could be won over to the peace resolution. They did not call for his resignation at this juncture, for they counted on his ability to extract Prussian electoral reforms from the Kaiser.

Helfferich, on the other hand, was highly unpopular and there was wide agreement that Zimmermann and Capelle were gravely compromised and should go. [42] But the debate soon transcended these limited targets. It was no longer a matter of personalities—the whole system was to be changed. Introduction of the parliamentary system was discussed with much heat, though most of the speakers were at a loss to explain precisely what the term meant and how such a thing could be done in wartime. Oddly enough, it was the right wing of the caucus, the national liberals, that pushed this matter rather than the left. The national liberals' initial participation in the caucus—later abandoned—had a most confusing effect. That the debate did not drift away into global reform projects was largely due to the shrewd and cool-headed Swabian democrats and the common sense of Ebert and Scheidemann.

There was internal dissension among the national liberals. This party had always been one of the main rallying points for militant nationalism, though in the immediately preceding weeks it had once again become more mindful of its liberal tradition. Stresemann was among the most zealous advocates of domestic reforms along the lines of the Easter message and the constitutional committee. If there were to be liberal democratic innovations, the national liberals wanted their share of the credit—some of their members, indeed, aspired to ministerial posts. The peace resolution, however, caused grave misgivings in their ranks, even though Erzberger's illusion-shattering speech had sent these fervent advocates of "peace with victory" into the most profound depression.[43] Some of them were afraid that the resolution might once again strengthen Bethmann Hollweg's position, since it accorded with his over-all political approach.[44] The national liberal spokesmen tried to push the joint caucus into giving the highest priority to a change in leadership. They demanded a government of the parliamentary majority, for the time being without a common program.

In this they did not prevail; but they did much to enhance the sense of independence in the caucus, and to foster distrust and dislike of Bethmann Hollweg. Airily, indeed almost naively, they swept aside all the constitutional problems that loomed in the way of the reorganization they wanted. Deputy von Richthofen declared on July 6 that the whole thing could be settled by an order-in-council. "We must go and say that we intend to take the government into our own hands. It is the only course open to us"; and Stresemann boldly asserted: "The Reichstag can do anything it wants to do."[45]

No means were shunned to undermine confidence in Bethmann Hollweg. The man who did most in this respect was Stresemann, who had always been one of the most uninhibited propagandists for the anti-Bethmann Hollweg cabal. Only recently he had been one of the main figures in an ambitiously organized conference of business leaders that had met in the Hotel Adlon, Berlin, on February 25. The plan was to push through a resolution at this meeting demanding the Chancellor's recall, but owing to a skillful countermove in the press by Haussmann it failed.[46]

Stresemann, on July 9, took advantage of the restive mood in the Reichstag to deliver a highly aggressive speech before the main committee, a comprehensive indictment enumerating every possible failure, problem, and frustration that had bedeviled German policy during the war. He placed every single count exclusively at the Chancellor's door, in an effort to demonstrate Bethmann Hollweg's incompetence. Stresemann even had the effrontery to mention the U-boat campaign in this connection—in rather cautious terms— even though he had been its most determined advocate. Indeed, as Zimmermann bitterly remarked, only the preceding December Stresemann had rejoiced over the torpedoing of a ship, because he thought it made the rupture with America inevitable. [47]

Still an avowed annexationist himself, Stresemann described Bethmann Hollweg as unfit to carry out a policy of self-imposed moderation, because his prior policies had made him a marked man abroad. With oratorical brilliance he swept aside the obvious argument that the OHL rather than Bethmann Hollweg had to accept responsibility for certain blunders such as the precipitate Poland manifesto and the Belgian labor deportations. "There is no such thing as a Chancellor submitting to coercion," he said. "A Chancellor must have the ability to assert his will. If he cannot do that he must accept the consequences."

The statement as such was undoubtedly true; but from the lips of a politician who kept complaining that the OHL and the government were being played, one against the other, it was, to say the least, devious, especially since Stresemann himself had done so much to enhance military authority at the expense of political power. An even graver charge was that at this very time Stresemann was working on behalf of the OHL, with which he was in close contact. Among the social democrats Stresemann had long been regarded as "Ludendorff's young man"[48]—and not without reason. Here we reach the darkest point of the whole parliamentary campaign.

During these days the Reichstag was almost under siege from Ludendorff's liaison officers, who kept him informed of everything that took place. In addition to Colonel Bauer, they included Lieutenant Colonel von Haeften, who will be remembered from the events in 1915. On July 6, directly after Erzberger's flamboyant speech, War Minister von Stein wired Ludendorff to come to Berlin at once with Hindenburg, and he requested an audience of the Kaiser, to enable the three to render a report on Erzberger's proposals from the military point of view.

The two generals promptly appeared in Berlin on July 7—but reporting to the Kaiser was not their only errand. Colonel Bauer arranged a meeting for them with Stresemann and Erzberger. In the evening Ebert and Scheidemann were invited to a separate meeting with Ludendorff in the Hotel Excelsior.[49] OHL meddling with political questions could have scarcely taken on more open form. Hearing of the contemplated audience, Bethmann Hollweg barely managed to intercept the Kaiser, who was arriving from Vienna, and to explain to the monarch the enormity of what was in the wind. Hence the two generals met a very cool reception. The Kaiser declined to discuss the Reichstag debate with them and suggested that they get back to their posts as quickly as possible. Subsequently, however, they were bidden to attend the Kaiser at dinner and had to cancel the meetings Bauer had arranged—of which, of course, not a word could be breathed at court. They then traveled back to Kreuznach. 50

The hopes of the deputies for a meeting with their two heroes were thus frustrated. Erzberger and Stresemann had to spend the evening in Colonel Bauer's company alone. They suspected, of course—quite wrongly—that the Chancellor had foiled the meeting to which they had looked forward. Stresemann's anger, very probably fed by Bauer, was still plainly evident in a speech he delivered on July 9. The next day Erzberger vented his fury in the joint caucus. The Chancellor, he said, had cheated the Reichstag parties of an invaluable encounter. The two generals had been quite ready to provide information. Bethmann Hollweg still had not grasped the seriousness of the situation, which he was playing down to the Kaiser. Confidence in the Chancellor had received a body blow. 51

In his later accounts Erzberger used the incident to provide a plausible reason for his defection from the Chancellor's cause. It seems incredible, however, that a responsible politician should have changed course so completely and ominously over a mere trifle, which could have been cleared up by a simple telephone call at that. Was all the sound and fury genuine? And if so, why? What were the important matters to be discussed with the generals by the two deputies, who, by the way, had already met early in the morning to talk about what was to be done with Bethmann Hollweg?

Few are likely to believe that they wanted military information from the generals. Even less plausible was Stresemann's complaint in his speech—that a wonderful opportunity had been missed to hear from Hindenburg's own lips whether the OHL really shared responsibility for the Poland manifesto and the Belgian workers' deportations, and whether or not it had really opposed the Easter message, as was rumored. Stresemann was a frequent visitor at headquarters, and he must have known in advance what would be Ludendorff's replies to such questions. The whole thing was nothing but camouflage. The two deputies almost certainly had the same intentions as Colonel Bauer and his chief. They wanted to concert a plan for bringing about Bethmann Hollweg's fall.

Stresemann's role is easier to understand than Erzberger's. He had always wanted to topple the Chancellor and his motivation was the same as Ludendorff's. He wished to clear the way for the OHL in the political sphere. The only surprising element is that while he knew of Ludendorff's opposition to the Easter message and the introduction of the parliamentary system, he took no offense at it. Perhaps he counted on Bethmann Hollweg pushing through Prussian electoral reform and the summoning of a few parliamentarians to high executive office before he was ousted; or he may have expected that von Bülow, the candidate of the nationalist cabal, would accomplish this—Bülow had never stinted on promises. The Machiavellian Ludendorff, moreover, had instructed his young men in Berlin to spread word that he was by no means an enemy of the parliamentary system.[52] Erzberger's attitude is much more puzzling. It is quite incongruous that he should have allied himself with the Pan-German Stresemann and Ludendorff's confidant Bauer while he was at the same time working for the Reichstag to adopt a peace declaration that was in effect tantamount to Scheidemann's "peace of appeasement."

Equally puzzling is his transformation from a sweeping annexationist to an advocate of a negotiated peace. Erzberger had a keen sense of publicity and was highly responsive to changing popular moods. He knew what the masses wanted and it was only natural that by 1917 he should no longer be trying to ride the former tide of patriotic enthusiasm. As long as a year and a half ago he had become suspicious of admiralty forecasts and statistics[53] and he had always kept his own counsel in technical matters. From his own far-flung intelligence sources abroad he had gleaned too many sobering facts to give any credence to the talk about Britain's economic plight.

As we have already heard, moreover, Czernin's pessimistic report of April 12 about Austria's desperate situation had left a deep impression on Erzberger. In his memoirs Czernin virtually boasted that he was the real originator of the German Reichstag's peace resolution. He said that through his friend Baron Vassilkov he put into the hands of Erzberger and Südekum a peace program that became the basis for the resolution.[54]

This can scarcely be true. There is no evidence that Vassilkov had any influence on these two deputies; and Austria's plight played only a subsidiary role in Erzberger's crucial speech. As for Czernin's peace program, allegedly passed on by Vassilkov, it does not at all coincide with the Reichstag resolution which Erzberger, by the way, had little share in drafting.[55] Czernin, furthermore, never really gave up the idea of annexations for Austria—especially annexations in Rumania—nor did he believe that the Entente would accept any new peace proposal offered by the Central Powers. Czernin's only interest in the Reichstag resolution seems to have been his hope that it would sow confusion in the ranks of the Entente, split away Russia if possible, and most important of all commit Germany to unconditional relinquishment of Belgium. He wanted to realize the "solidarity principle" for which he had so long fought in vain—the principle under which the territories occupied by Germany were to serve as bargaining counters to insure the return of all the territories Austria had lost. Czernin actually thought that the Reichstag resolution was ill-timed, right in the middle of the Kerensky offensive.[56]

For Erzberger, on the other hand, considerations of diplomatic tactics were quite irrelevant. His dominant concern was almost certainly how the wretched war might be brought to an end; and these worries were of course intensified by the jeremiads issuing from Vienna. Erzberger simply seized the first opportunity that offered itself during the Reichstag session to voice his fears as vocally as possible. The fact that this might smash the delicate balance the diplomats were building up did not trouble him in the least.

Not only a born optimist but also a loyal Catholic, Erzberger harbored still another major hope, the pope's peace action. He had been confidentially put in the picture about Pacelli's mission, which he wished to support by the Reichstag resolution, hoping for swift success, as was his wont. He told his friend Müller-Fulda on July 2 that Germany could have peace if it really wanted it; and he assured his party committee on July 7 that Russia would come over to the German side in a matter of weeks. The day before he had said: "I am convinced that some form of parliamentary government and such a declaration could bring peace this year." 57

In the circumstances, he went on, he suspected that a man with as spotty a record as Bethmann Hollweg's should be dispensed with as soon as possible. He told the party committee quite openly on July 6 who had inspired his thinking. It was Prince Bülow and the recently retired ambassador Wolff-Metternich, both of them former diplomats whose disgruntlement was exceeded only by their ambitions. Wolff-Metternich had said meaningfully that no matter what Germany did, it would get peace only if it changed its system of government. Just in case the hint was lost, the ambassador had followed up with a typical morsel of diplomatic gossip. Bethmann Hollweg had handled Wilson so clumsily that the president had in the end virtually kicked out Bernstorff. 58

The reader need scarcely be told that this was extremely foolish talk. We are already aware that Bethmann Hollweg's continual struggle with the OHL was a familiar story abroad, especially in America, and that he was generally known as a man of moderation who simply lacked the necessary powers to prevail over the military and the annexationists. Hohenlohe's reports to Czernin during the July crisis reveal the despair with which the Austrian diplomat followed the parliamentary intrigues that were undermining the Chancellor's position—and these observations were offered at a time when there had only just been serious differences between Vienna and Berlin.59 Similar views were held at the courts of South Germany, where there was bitter resentment of the events that were taking place in Berlin. On July 4 the Bavarian war minister Hellingrath wrote to Count Hertling that it was high time that General Ludendorff were banished from the political scene and devoted himself exclusively to the soldier's trade.60

But Erzberger had long since succumbed to the glittering personality of the great intriguer, Prince Bülow, who had repeatedly received him in his sumptuous residence in Switzerland. The centrist politician came from modest Swabian origins and had enjoyed only a limited education. He could scarcely have been expected to perceive that there was little behind Bülow's wit and charm, as is amply apparent to us today, from the insipid and untruthful talk in the last volume of his memoirs. Erzberger was delighted at being taken seriously by the prince—at the foreign ministry this rather schoolmasterly busybody[61] was not a great hit, indeed quite often a source of irritation.

At any rate Erzberger was full of admiration, much in contrast to Scheidemann, who subsequently had only scorn and contempt for the aging and ambitious Bülow's sycophantic solicitation of social democratic aid for his candidacy for the chancellorship when Michaelis resigned.[62] Ever importunate, Erzberger had already tried early in 1917 to persuade Bethmann Hollweg and Zimmermann to use Prince Bülow as a peace negotiator. He tried to whip up support in Bavaria as well.[63]

Erzberger's efforts on behalf of Bülow coincided with Stresemann's. Like many Pan-German opponents of Bethmann Hollweg, Stresemann swore by Bülow.[64] The OHL, as represented by Colonel Bauer, also shared the views of Stresemann, who succeeded in winning over the brother of the empress, Duke Ernst Günther of Schleswig-Holstein, to Bülow's candidacy. The duke was to bring pressure to bear on the empress, and she did indeed work on Bülow's behalf. The duke is believed to have actually submitted a special memorandum on the subject to the Kaiser.

The arch-conservative Prussian ministers also supported Bülow, including Count Augustus Eulenburg, the Kaiser's house minister, who was influential in matters of appointments. There was thus a kind of united front on the candidacy of Bülow among the conservatives and the national liberals, and it was very active during the July crisis.[65] Erzberger joined this front and managed to persuade the other deputies of his party that Bethmann Hollweg was impossible as a peace negotiator. On July 11, without authority from his party, he went to Valentini and vainly tried to effect Bülow's appointment to succeed Bethmann Hollweg.

Strange indeed! For extreme nationalists like Stresemann the name of Bülow may have retained a certain glamour, for Bülow had already been Chancellor once, during a time when Germany shone in the councils of the world. Yet it seems almost grotesque that a leading politician participating in the new left bloc formed for the explicit purpose of putting into effect an anti-imperialist policy should have proposed as Chancellor an unprincipled opportunist and imperialist like Bülow. Could Erzberger really have imagined that such a man was better equipped to restrain the power-hungry OHL and institute a consistent policy of self-imposed moderation and reason than

Bethmann Hollweg, a man of character whose life was marked by a deep sense of responsibility? Incredible as it seems, such a conclusion is almost inescapable and it puts Erzberger's judgment as a politician in a bad light. Competent and hard-working in many respects, he remained a man of little stature; and that he became the key figure in the July crisis was nothing short of disastrous. His misjudgment of Bülow must have played an important part, for he would have scarcely promoted Bethmann Hollweg's fall with such zeal—initially the only one of his own party and indeed all the parties of the left to do so—had he not believed there were a more qualified successor.

Erzberger's latest biographer[66] suggests that his motives for aiming at a change in the chancellorship were purely tactical—he wished to draw the national liberals over into the new left bloc to create an overwhelming majority for the peace resolution. Judging from the man's over-all attitude this seems extremely improbable. Even if it were true, it would constitute anything but a justification; for the effort was foredoomed from the start, as the social democrats and democrats quickly perceived. Erzberger should have known, moreover—and Valentini told him so plainly on July 11—that the Kaiser, still harboring a deep grudge over the events of 1908, would have indignantly refused to reappoint Bülow as Chancellor. More than that, such an appointment would have severely shaken the alliance with Austria. Hohenlohe regarded Bülow as a mere "charlatan"[67] and like Czernin had no confidence in him whatever. He was still deeply resentful of the policies Bülow had pursued as ambassador in Rome in 1915, when he was accounted throughout Austria as one-sidedly pro-Italian. A Bülow candidacy was not only hopeless, it would have been a serious political blunder.

Another fault weighs much more heavily in the balance, Erzberger's uninhibited participation in the intrigues of the OHL. This too had begun many months before, apparently in March 1917, when General Max Hoffmann of the eastern command, during a journey to headquarters, had presented a very gloomy picture of the over-all military situation to Erzberger and a national liberal deputy, von Richthofen. Hoffmann was a cynic, much given to nonplussing people he talked to. He apparently impressed Erzberger, who had never met a military man of this type before.

Hoffmann's talk was naturally larded with the customary invective against the government, which he said was doing nothing to correct the people's illusions and to prepare them for a protracted war. The same key was struck by Colonel Bauer, with whom Erzberger had a long talk on June 10. Bauer went to extraordinary lengths in painting the prospects of the war on land black-in-black, especially in terms of the ammunition situation. Bauer overdid his prophecies of doom to such an extent that Ludendorff subsequently reproved him for the defeatist statements the Chancellor had reported back to headquarters.

Understandably enough Erzberger was shocked by this concerted shattering of illusions, which was further reinforced by figures on world tonnage he was receiving at the same time. What were the positive aims Bauer was actually pursuing? Erzberger mentions that they had talked about organizing a "psychological food agency," a kind of propaganda office to prepare the people for the impending war winter.[68] But was bad news the proper method to achieve such an aim? The OHL itself, after all, was constantly issuing statements in a spirit of supreme confidence, speaking of victory by the fall at the very latest.[69]

The conclusion is inescapable that Bauer was deliberately inciting Erzberger into delivering an alarmist speech in the Reichstag, a speech that would sow such confusion that government authority would be further undermined. The OHL would then profit from the resultant chaos and succeed in overthrowing Bethmann Hollweg. Whether Erzberger was aware of it or not, his course of action is susceptible to the interpretation that it was part of a carefully laid plan by military wire-pullers. On June 26, i.e., sometime before the Reichstag crisis began, Erzberger telephoned Colonel Bauer to say that his patience was wearing thin and that he too now favored a change; and during the meetings with the colonel and Stresemann on July 7 he confidently predicted that by the following Tuesday (July 10) Herr von Bethmann Hollweg would have been "taken care of."[70]

Prince Hohenlohe described Erzberger as a "vain mountebank," explaining his fulminating speech from the simple desire to play a major political role, the centrist deputy having the feeling that of late he was no longer being taken seriously.[71] These are harsh words, but there is no question that Erzberger was an uncommonly ambitious man, fond of giving himself the air of being in the confidence of highly placed people, of knowing things others could not even guess at. When introduction of the parliamentary system was mentioned in the very first session of the joint caucus of the left, Erzberger, with the mien of one who was "in the know," said that such thoughts were by no means foreign to the OHL, which viewed such a development as being potentially useful even in a military sense. Indeed, a committee of defense might well be formed by an order-in-council; and on July 9 he said with his wonted optimism: "We could have a parliamentary government by tomorrow night. Think of it, by tomorrow night! Surely this must be known in the places that count!"[72] He was apparently quite unconcerned over the likelihood that once the obstacle of Bethmann Hollweg was eliminated the OHL would outmaneuver the Reichstag, install its own Chancellor—not necessarily Bülow—and have its own way. The important thing was that he felt himself to be at the center of events. On July 13 he still considered it inconceivable that any new Chancellor unacceptable to the party caucus could be appointed.[73]

Erzberger's conduct helped to bring about great political misfortune in

Germany, the final triumph of the OHL over civilian authority. Yet other forces played an important part.

Bethmann Hollweg did not stand by idly while these negotiations were going on in the Reichstag. He took full advantage of the rare opportunity of having the Kaiser on hand in Berlin, away from the General Staff. On July 8 he persuaded the Kaiser to summon a crown council for the following day, to consider the question of Prussian electoral reform; and in a preliminary meeting with the Prussian ministers he said he would resign unless the crown decided in favor of universal suffrage. The session on July 9, presided over by the Kaiser in his capacity of king of Prussia, lasted almost four hours. The electoral problem was discussed very thoroughly from all sides, but no definitive settlement was reached, the Kaiser reserving to himself exclusively the right of decision.

That the OHL knew precisely what was going on all the time is seen from the fact that while the council was still in session a telephone call arrived from the crown prince who insisted that Valentini brief him and that his father should on no account take a decision in the electoral issue without consulting Hindenburg. The chief of cabinet thereupon persuaded the Kaiser to postpone his decision and summon the crown prince himself, and this was done that very night.

Waiting on the Kaiser the next morning, July 10, Valentini found him in a state of great agitation. He complained of having spent a sleepless night and of having been severely reproached by the empress over the course the crown council had taken. Early in the morning the arch-conservatives Loebell and Augustus Eulenburg had already besieged him with representations. Loebell had pressed him to hear members of the Prussian diet. The conservative reactionaries were thus already mobilizing, and as on July 8 the question of Bethmann Hollweg's successor was discussed with the chief of cabinet and the house minister. No suitable name turned up immediately, since the Kaiser would not hear of Bülow.

The discussion with Valentini took place in the park of Bellevue palace and while it was still on the Chancellor arrived. A highly dramatic confrontation with the Kaiser then ensued, lasting two hours. Bethmann Hollweg said that it would be beneath the dignity of the crown to receive spokesmen for the Prussian diet. He explained to the Kaiser that his position was now threatened from two sides, the conservative and Pan-German opposition and the hostility of the OHL. He described the latter in detail and told the Kaiser he was quite willing to resign since he did not wish to create the impression that he was asking for the universal franchise only to save his own skin. He added that any Chancellor who succeeded him would have to offer the same concessions to the left, and the Kaiser admitted that this was true. Valentini was a witness to the rest of the discussion and his account of it is so vivid that it is here cited verbatim:

Bethmann's voice was trembling with emotion as he continued without interruption from anyone. He made a magnificent case for the role of the emperor in a popular democracy. With deep fervor he mentioned the overwhelming achievements of the people in the war. Any remnants of distrust should be swept away, and there was no further justification for withholding full democratic rights from them. His advocacy of equal and universal suffrage stemmed not from any momentary crisis but from his firm conviction that the Prussian people had reached the necessary maturity for it. The franchise, freely granted by the crown now, would strengthen the monarchy beyond measure rather than weaken it. The sweep of Bethmann's words and whole personality, the strength of his character, the utter sincerity of his convictions, quite carried the Kaiser away, and after the Chancellor left, at about two o'clock, he said to me: "And that is the man they want me to dismiss! He stands head and shoulders above all the others! "74

What Valentini did not report was that Bethmann Hollweg had seized the Kaiser's favorable mood to read him the draft of the Reichstag's peace resolution, remarking only that possibly some minor corrections should be made in the direction of making it breathe a spirit of greater resolution. He succeeded in gaining the Kaiser's consent, together with authority to transmit it to the Reichstag. William, however, still reserved his final decision on the electoral issue. It would seem that only an ensuing audience he granted Hohenlohe drew him wholly over to the Chancellor's side. The Austrian ambassador had requested this audience for the express purpose of warning the Kaiser against dismissing his chief minister, and he did this with the greatest emphasis and success. It was apparently only during this discussion that the Kaiser fully realized how highly Bethmann Hollweg was regarded among Germany's allies, despite the political differences we know he had with Czernin.

The next morning the crown prince arrived in Berlin and the Kaiser told him that Bethmann Hollweg was indispensable, if only for Austria's sake. Universal suffrage would have to be conceded, to keep him. This was scarcely the way the Chancellor would have wished it put. Valentini advanced a more effective argument in favor of electoral reform. He reminded the crown prince of the impassioned resistance the Prussian conservatives had put up against Bismarck's great reforms in 1866 and 1870-1871. How much better it would be, he said, if the crown now took such a step voluntarily rather than being forced to do so by revolutionary unrest! "One would have to be stupid not to see that," came the reply—and the way was cleared for the new electoral law.

The final consultation took place that afternoon at a session of the Prussian cabinet, where Bethmann Hollweg submitted the draft of an order-in-council that would empower him to prepare a bill providing for the secret, general, and equal ballot in Prussia. It was to be introduced in time to allow the next elections under it. Since the decision had already been taken, the dissenting ministers had no choice but to submit their resignations; and in order to facilitate cabinet reorganization, the remaining ministers also re-signed. The royal order-in-council was made public on the morning of July 12, to be followed by an immediate protest demonstration staged by the conservative party.

The entire chapter was a great personal success for Bethmann Hollweg—a surprising success in the light of all that had gone before. The crisis over the chancellorship seemed happily laid to rest.

But appearances were deceiving. The Chancellor's success, instead of bring-ing on salutary consequences, merely served to accelerate his downfall; for the OHL now marshaled all of its resources to keep him from reconsolidating his authority. The prime agitator was, of course, Colonel Bauer, who saw to it that rumors were spread among all the parties in the Reichstag. "High officers at supreme headquarters," it was said, reported that Hindenburg and Luden-dorff refused all further cooperation with Bethmann Hollweg in any circum-stances. Ludendorff held that the war was lost unless there were a change in the chancellorship. This served to intensify the general unrest, to a level that Valentini described as hysteria. Helfferich, as vice-chancellor, vainly endeav-ored to speed the constitutional reforms the leaders of the left wanted. He held many meetings with them in an effort to establish procedures for closer liaison between government and Reichstag. He and other ministers were quite willing to make way for the appointment of deputies in their stead, but it soon developed that few of the parliamentarians showed any inclination to take on high executive office at so critical a juncture, and no firm commit-ments were immediately forthcoming.

In the end a "Reich Council" was proposed as a kind of liaison organ for the government, the Reichstag, and the federal council. In addition to the Chancellor and his ministers it was to comprise trusted representatives of the major parties and an equal number of members of the federal council. This body was to receive regular briefings and to be heard before any important decisions were taken at home or in foreign affairs. Quite evidently this was no more than a makeshift and would have rendered the already complex federal structure of the government even more cumbersome. Yet the proposal is noteworthy as a first step in remodeling the Reich constitution along parlia-mentary lines.

Naturally there was also further discussion on the peace resolution, which continued to be debated in the joint party caucus of the left; but in this area the Chancellor was reticent in his statements to the parties, for no final draft was as yet available. This caution was, of course, dictated by the continuing OHL intrigues. Bethmann Hollweg was content with general exhortations against making the resolution too "weak-kneed." [75]

In the end it was all in vain, for interest among the deputies centered more and more single-mindedly on the personalities concerned. Crown Prince William had clearly come to Berlin at the behest of the OHL, specifically charged with forcing the dismissal of Bethmann Hollweg.[76] On the evening of July 11 he dined with his former political adviser, Freiherr von Maltzahn, one of the leading spirits in the anti-Bethmann Hollweg cabal. On Maltzahn's suggestion—and probably with the Kaiser's approval—he invited a number of deputies to his palace for the next forenoon, for the purpose of sounding out their views of Bethmann Hollweg's fitness as Chancellor, surely a procedure without precedent in the history of the crown. The list—Count Westarp, Stresemann, Mertin, von Payer, Erzberger, David—was deliberately chosen to insure an outcome unfavorable to Bethmann Hollweg. Colonel Bauer kept a record of the discussion in an adjoining room.[77]

The sharpest attacks on the Chancellor's policies naturally came from Stresemann and Erzberger. The latter charged that Bethmann Hollweg "had missed every opportunity" and was thus responsible for preventing peace. He was reluctant to take responsibility, according to Stresemann, who further charged Bethmann Hollweg with being unimaginative and given to "let things slide." "Bethmann Hollweg has always been a weak customer," Stresemann concluded.

As for David, instead of supporting the Chancellor's policy of reform, he chose this occasion to lecture the heir to the throne at length on the goals and ambitions of his party. None of these politicians seems to have been concerned with the effect of his words on the Kaiser, from whom Bethmann Hollweg had only just wrested assent to electoral reform with such effort. The only one to favor Bethmann Hollweg remaining in office was von Payer, who found it humiliating, if not absurd, that Reichstag deputies should be required to line up on the dot like a group of raw recruits to undergo cross-examination. Actually it was the dignity of the crown that was violated even worse than that of the deputies; and the whole scene can only be described as marking a historic turning point.

It was indeed a juncture for the Chancellor, whom von Payer immediately informed. Only the day before, i.e., prior to Bethmann Hollweg's victory in the electoral issue, a majority in the joint caucus had been ready to cooperate with him further, if he were prepared to accept the peace resolution. The center party had joined in, though with certain reservations; and as already mentioned, Erzberger had gone to Valentini over the party's head. But the dramatic reception staged by the crown prince now overshadowed everything else, even the important announcement that universal suffrage was to be introduced in Prussia. The public got the impression that the crown itself was wavering and, not surprisingly, so now did the popular representatives, the more so since Stresemann brought back as a major piece of news the alleged certainty that Ludendorff would resign if Bethmann Hollweg remained in office. The center party promptly lost its nerve; and in the afternoon the national liberals and conservatives sent word to Valentini that the crisis could not be solved unless Bethmann Hollweg went. The Chancellor no longer commanded a majority in the Reichstag.

Everything now depended on the stand the Kaiser would take. Despite all his wavering, his confidence in Bethmann Hollweg remained unbroken by the evening of July 11 – at least he expressly assured Count Lerchenfeld, whom he repeatedly summoned during these days, that he wished to keep the Chancellor and for that reason had conceded him universal and equal suffrage. He seemed virtually to be pleading for support for the Chancellor within the federal council and made this plain to the Bavarian representative. He was full of praise for Bethmann Hollweg's high-mindedness, strength of character, and lofty bearing. When Lerchenfeld on one occasion remarked that the Chancellor was unfortunately lacking in a certain decisiveness, the Kaiser admitted that this was true, but added that this was solely due to his great sense of scruple.[78] He described himself as deeply impressed that, according to all the reports from Vienna and Hohenlohe's statements, Germany's allies would regard Bethmann Hollweg's departure as a disaster. He voiced bitter resentment over the political meddling by the generals, especially Ludendorff, citing outrageous instances to the Austrian ambassador.

The wind changed suddenly only on the afternoon of July 12. What part the crown prince's report on his discussion with the deputies played is hard to say. Following that discussion the crown prince had called on the Austrian and Bulgarian ambassadors, Hohenlohe and Ritzov, to hear their views of Bethmann Hollweg. Both had emphatically expressed sympathy, indeed admiration, for the Chancellor; and Hohenlohe took the occasion to warn the crown prince against the charlatan Bülow and the inveterate intriguer Tirpitz – Austria would find both of them intolerable. This does seem to have made an impression on the crown prince, which Valentini, in an ensuing discussion, did all in his power to strengthen. He did not shrink from telling the crown prince that it would be extremely harmful to the position of the crown if he officially challenged the Reichstag party leaders to demand that the Kaiser dismiss his principal minister.[79]

Yet the crown prince is bound to have reported that the Chancellor's parliamentary following had dwindled to a minimum, and this must have severely shaken the Kaiser. Was this all that had happened as a result of the sweeping political concessions to the parties of the left, which he had so painfully and reluctantly conceded? What a bitter disillusionment! And that very afternoon the OHL swung back into action. War Minister von Stein wired Kreuznach that the OHL must instantly make representations to the Kaiser by wire against the Chancellor assenting to the planned Reichstag peace resolution. It would be interpreted as a move toward a peace of appeasement that would do great damage and have a very bad effect on the army. The desired protest from Hindenburg promptly arrived. Though he did not even know the text of the resolution, Hindenburg voiced the gravest reservations, since the resolution was bound to increase the unrest that already prevailed in the army. Hindenburg pleaded "with the greatest humility" that the government be instructed to prevent such a declaration from being adopted.[80]

In consequence the Chancellor found that the atmosphere had turned peevish and unfriendly when he called at Bellevue palace in the evening. He was reproached with the contention that the electoral concessions had been in vain. Although the Kaiser had assented to the peace resolution only two days before, he would not hear of it now. When Bethmann Hollweg read him the text once again, he insisted on having Hindenburg's opinion. The text was thereupon transmitted to Kreuznach by telephone. The response came within half an hour: Hindenburg missed any expression of gratitude to the army. Furthermore he wished to cut precisely those sentences that alone carried political significance—they would undermine army morale and discipline. The Kaiser agreed at once and instructed Bethmann Hollweg to notify the parliamentarians. In the meantime, however, another report had arrived from Kreuznach. Hindenburg and Ludendorff had dispatched their resignations, since neither of them felt able to work with the Chancellor any longer. The representative of the military cabinet, von Marschall, added that Ludendorff had stated he would insist on having his way, regardless of consequences.

This came as no surprise to Bethmann Hollweg. He knew of the resignations by the circuitous route of the Bavarian military commissioner at headquarters, who was the first to learn of them, and perhaps also through word that had been spread by Stresemann. The Chancellor had realized since the morning that he was a forlorn figure on the political stage, deserted by everyone. As for the Kaiser, he flew into a rage at his highest officers whose outrageous breach of discipline had placed him in such a quandary. Hindenburg and Ludendorff were instantly summoned to Berlin, where the Kaiser (at Lyncker's suggestion) wished to challenge them and decline to accept their resignations.

Unfortunately this did not help Bethmann Hollweg's position. He could not have believed for a moment that the Kaiser was man enough to break Ludendorff's obstinacy; and without Ludendorff Hindenburg could not be kept in line, for without his "chief" the hero of Tannenberg was nothing. At bottom, however, it was of little account whether the generals stayed or went. It was foreseeable that if they went there would be a storm of popular disapproval that would render all the Chancellor's political efforts illusory and sooner or later force his fall, with the result that the two popular heroes would soon be recalled.

Not a single hand had stirred in the Reichstag to support the sorely pressed Chancellor against the all-powerful OHL. On the contrary, everyone seemed hypnotized with the belief that the two inspired soldiers might yet save Germany if every obstacle were cleared out of their way.[81] And the Kaiser's attitude on the peace resolution had only just shown that he was not to be relied on, despite the Easter message and the latest electoral decree. If the two generals remained at their posts it was therefore certain that the Chancellor would have only the alternatives of playing the role of their willing tool or of wearing himself out in renewed and continual conflict with them.

In any event, the policies Bethmann Hollweg regarded as correct had lost all prospect of success. On July 11 he had still counted on being able to deliver a major speech in the Reichstag within a matter of days, in which he would announce the dawn of a new era in German and Prussian politics. He would welcome the peace resolution as the overture to a foreign policy of understanding, and proclaim the introduction in Prussia of a Reichstag type of electoral law and the appointment of parliamentarians to high executive office and the newly created *Reichsrat.* This would set the stage for constitutional reform in both Prussia and the Reich, aimed at doing away with entrenched class and party conflicts, which would insure prompt approval of new war appropriations. Now his whole edifice had collapsed in the space of a single morning.

On the morning of July 12 Bethmann Hollweg had a brief talk with Count Hertling, who had hastened to Berlin at Lerchenfeld's request. The Chancellor gained the impression that the Bavarian premier was prepared to assume his succession. That night, with the Kaiser, he lost little time discussing his situation and his intention to resign but took his leave with the brief remark that Hindenburg's and Ludendorff's dismissal was of course out of the question.[82]

He had long since made up his mind. He had had enough. Deputy von Payer soon afterward brought him the final version of the peace resolution which, according to the party leaders, the Chancellor was expected to endorse without change or addition and without any reference to his own peace policies; but Bethmann Hollweg refused to quibble. He simply handed von Payer Hindenburg's response, remarking that he regarded it as the authoritative expression of the army's views. This could only mean acceptance of the fact that supreme political authority now lay with the OHL. Bethmann Hollweg suggested that von Payer deal with Hindenburg and Ludendorff directly.

He made his own views on the peace issue clear soon afterward during his farewell audience of the Kaiser. His final urgent request was that any opportunities for peace that might arise not be passed up for lack of strategic guarantees represented as essential, even though they might well prove illusory in the face of technical advances in warfare.[83]

Bethmann Hollweg gave another earnest of his consideration and loyalty on the morning of July 13 by handing Valentini his resignation at a very early hour, so that the Kaiser could see it before the generals arrived. He wished to spare his sovereign the embarrassment of a confrontation that could end only with the Chancellor's submission to the will of the OHL. The Kaiser was indeed greatly relieved at being able to tell the generals when they arrived that the whole matter was settled. Bethmann Hollweg had already submitted his resignation of his own free will. This enabled the Kaiser to speak his mind to the two without incurring any risks. He assured his entourage that he had minced no words.

From Hohenlohe's report, however, it would appear that he had not really grasped the full gravity of the political situation. The Kaiser summoned the ambassador early on July 13 and took a walk with him in the gardens of Bellevue palace. According to Hohenlohe, the chancellorship crisis was scarcely mentioned. The Kaiser was in a good humor and merely said in passing how glad he was that the whole affair was back to normal; but at ten o'clock that evening he called up Hohenlohe on the telephone to tell him that disaster had meanwhile struck quite unexpectedly. With a heavy heart he had had to agree to accept Bethmann Hollweg's resignation.[84]

The only likely explanation is that when Bethmann Hollweg failed to ask to be relieved of office on the evening of July 12, the Kaiser seriously believed he might somehow be able to make peace between the OHL and the Chancellor when he talked to the generals face-to-face. Evidently he had not the slightest inkling of how deep the conflict went and how much was at stake. Further plausibility is lent to this interpretation by the brisk pace at which the question of the succession was settled.

Hertling immediately declined. He rightly felt that he was too old and worn-out for so heavy a burden, and he was also deeply resentful of the stand the OHL had taken. There was a good deal of perplexity. In view of the new situation in the Reichstag an arch-conservative was scarcely indicated. Valentini proposed Count Bernstorff, but the Kaiser naturally raised objections and was prepared to accept Bernstorff only if Hindenburg approved. Valentini refused to discuss Bernstorff with Hindenburg, and when General von Lyncker, chief of the military cabinet, was asked to undertake the mission, he too immediately and indignantly rejected Bernstorff.

In the end the vitally important question of who was to become the new *Reichskanzler* was settled by the generals themselves. On Plessen's nomination and with Ludendorff as an eager second, the choice fell on Georg Michaelis, under secretary in the Prussian ministry of commerce. Michaelis was a competent administrator, virtually unknown, inexperienced, and uninformed in the political sphere. As he put it to Scheidemann a few days later: "I have been so busy that I have really done little more than jog along beside the ship of state."

When Michaelis took office, he knew neither the text of the peace resolution nor anything about the clash of opinions between the OHL and the Reichstag. He thought he owed his appointment to the fact that the two were in agreement. Actually, no one had even thought of consulting Gustav Stresemann and Matthias Erzberger.

Privy Councilor Riezler, Bethmann Hollweg's confidant and associate, cynically remarked to Haussmann of the democratic party: "I have always disputed you on the issue of the parliamentary system. Well, I am converted! It could not be any more confused than the system that now prevails."[85] He was right. This first sortie by the Reichstag into grand politics caused nothing but confusion.

True, there now was something like a majority bloc, with a left tinge. The baffling question was how such a left bloc could work with the new powers—that-be, i.e., with Ludendorff. The new situation had been created by an outright military cabal, to which the majority deputies had submitted almost without offering opposition. It was thus clear from the first day who would have the upper hand in the realignment of forces.

Things got off to an inauspicious start. On the afternoon of July 13 the leading deputies were summoned one by one to the General Staff building, for "military cross-examination," as Scheidemann scornfully put it. True, they did not meekly submit to being briefed, as was the general's intention, but set forth their views of the situation in no uncertain terms. Yet none of them seems to have considered the political significance of even appearing before the military to justify his political stand.[86] Even the social democrats were at pains not to irritate his Excellency, General von Ludendorff, by premature publication of the peace resolution—there were feverish nocturnal discussions on this subject and the general was even consulted by telephone. Behind all this politicking, however, one senses the exaggerated respect for the soldier's estate on which the Prussians were weaned.

Even less edifying was the attempt by the two generals to come to an agreement with the party leaders over the peace resolution in jovial exchanges that took place in the garden of the German office of the interior. While Bethmann Hollweg was still in power, the resolution had been decried as a piece of cowardly appeasement that would undermine army discipline. Now the generals, in Hindenburg's words, merely tried to inject "a bit more ginger." In the end they settled for an added word of praise for the army. There was one cut—a passage that might have been interpreted as implying OHL approval. All this was accomplished in docile discussion with the very Scheidemann who had hitherto been held up as the epitome of disloyalty.

Thus began the political triumph of the German supreme army command. It has long been a staple of German historiography to call Bethmann

Hollweg, the war Chancellor, a man pursued by misfortune, to describe his policy of maneuvering as a sign of poor leadership—these are, indeed, just about the words Stresemann used. Erzberger and the shrewd but cynical General Hoffmann were among the first to speak of "a policy of missed opportunities," though most of those who use this phrase nowadays fail even to hint at, let along specify, the favorable opportunities that were allegedly missed. The Chancellor is also often described as "weak-willed" and "incapable of making up his mind." Perhaps the commonest reproach was first voiced by Scheidemann in his memoirs: Bethmann Hollweg wanted to please all the parties and thus wound up sitting between all the chairs.

Our account has endeavored to steer clear of such generalizations and pick out in the fullest detail the motivations, prospects, and obstacles to Bethmann Hollweg's policies, and to comprehend those policies within the broadest historical context of the time. Rather than a weak personality who wanted to please everyone and ultimately lost the confidence of everyone, our story has revealed the moving tragedy of an estimable statesman of character desperately but never despairingly trying to disentangle himself from the fateful toils of war and to find a way out for his nation from a hopeless situation. His actions were never governed by the desire to please everyone. Invariably he sought to do what he thought reasonable and necessary, as the responsible head of the Reich government. It was precisely because he always acted in accordance with the dictates of his conscience that he incurred the enmity of those who thought he was doing either too much or too little.

What Bethmann Hollweg lacked was the charismatic power of the leader who is always sure of himself and his aims. He often seemed unsure in his judgment of alternative options and liked to consult experts—even military experts. This sometimes eroded his judgment even further and also served to undermine his authority. He was not lacking in realism, nor did the fault lie in the natural uncertainty that always afflicts political forecasts—an uncertainty immeasurably enhanced in wartime.

His opponents tagged him with the silly nickname, the "Philosopher of Hohenfinow"; but those who have read carefully this far are unlikely to have noted any signs of unworldly abstract thinking in Bethmann Hollweg, while they will probably agree that he displayed many signs of unswervingly lucid and objective insight into Germany's true situation. It was precisely this quality that his closest associates admired so much.

What Bethmann Hollweg's grasp of political realities showed him, in sharper focus than was seen by most of his fellow countrymen, was that Germany's position in the world was desperate and ultimately hopeless. Yet he did not allow himself to become discouraged, tenaciously fighting on. He was not the kind of man, however, who leaps over all doubts, problems, and dangers by taking swift and risky decisions. He always had to search his soul before making up his mind, cautious and conscientious to the point of awkwardness, ever full of concern, and lacking the saving grace of a sense of humor. Thus he did make an irresolute impression on some who were not close to him, while he occasionally exasperated his closest associates; but then again he would impress them with his unswerving strength of character under pressure, and in his Reichstag speeches the dramatic impact and sincerity of his moral message often swept his audiences off their feet.

Bethmann Hollweg, all in all, was no unworldly brooder but rather an intellectual lacking the ultimate instinct of power, and a bit too sensitive. At the same time he never fell victim to the demoniac blandishments of power. He never enjoyed power but merely regarded its exercise as his inescapable duty to the state and the hereditary Prusso-German monarchy. An aristocrat from Brandenburg, essentially an eastern region, he combined, by family tradition, a wealth of West German cultural tradition in his makeup. He was totally lacking in Junker arrogance. He was a high-minded humanitarian, and his outstanding characteristic was his utter truthfulness—confirmed in his unusually frank memoirs.

But these qualities also marked the limits of his capacity. He was far from weak-willed and pursued his goals with amazing tenacity, consistency, and courage, yet he was not a fighter by nature. He was not the kind of ruthless and assertive leader reaching for power without compunction and shunning no means to get it, including lies, cunning, and malice, if there were no other way. He was a worrier with a conscience and a thin skin. In conflict with so ruthless an opponent as Ludendorff this put him at a disadvantage; but what ultimately caused his failure was not his alleged weakness of will. The real reason was the problem that lies at the heart of this book—the problem of German militarism.

In wartime, politicians always have a hard time gaining and maintaining authority against successful generals. This has been the basic theme of our work from the first volume on, together with the reasons why the problem was particularly aggravated in Germany, and we need not repeat it here. Bethmann Hollweg's policy was one of moderation in war aims, and of party and class reconciliation at home; but to put this over against all militarist and nationalist opposition would have required the Chancellor to gain the support of a strong and united popular movement.

How could this succeed at a time when nationalist passions were inflamed, in the midst of a total war, with the exigencies that imprisoned the man who was at once Chancellor of Germany and premier of Prussia? We have considered the special problems of this situation at length from all sides. On May 8, 1917, in a discussion with Weizsäcker, Bethmann Hollweg defended himself against the charge that he was always backing and filling by remarking that Bismarck had once told him constant maneuvering was the only way in which he had been able to discharge his duties.[87] He expressed himself similarly in September 1917 in a letter to the editor of the *Preussische Jahrbücher,* Hans Delbrück. The German state, he said, was so constructed that every Chancellor had to follow a "policy of the diagonal." But the diagonal too, he added, was a straight line "and I think I have pursued it."[88]

The only alternative would indeed have been a consistently applied parliamentary system; and Bethmann Hollweg hinted in his letter to Delbrück that in the summer of 1917 he would not have objected to departing from the "diagonal" and seizing the opportunity then offered for the first time of governing with a firm party majority. Until then he had never controlled a firm majority—"or at best only one whose goals I found myself unable to accept."

It was only in the summer of 1917, following the rude shake-up that has been described, that things seemed to change and new possibilities open up. The reader of this book must judge who bears the responsibility for the failure of the effort.

It is difficult to say whether a Chancellor who was more of a fighter might have achieved more. One thing is certain, however: the end of the tragedy of Bethmann Hollweg also marked the tragic culmination of statesmanship in Germany. What followed was an era in which one can scarcely speak of a problem of militarism any longer, at least in the sense in which this term has here been used. Militarism was no longer a problem. It was harsh reality.

# Abbreviations

and Abbreviated Book Titles Used in the Notes

AA — Political archive of the foreign ministry *(Auswärtiges Amt)*, Bonn. (The subdesignation WW means World War.)

BA — Federal archive *(Bundesarchiv)*, Koblenz.

FR — *Papers Relating to the Foreign Relations of the United States.*
1915, Supplement: *The World War* (1928).
1916, Supplement: *The World War* (1929).
1917, Supplements 1 and 2: *The World War*, 3 vols. (1931).
*The Lansing Papers*, 1914-1920, 2 vols. (1939-1940). Not to be confused with Lansing's *War Memoirs*—see further on.

GLA — General state archive *(Generallandesarchiv)*, Karlsruhe.

GSTA — Secret state archive *(Geheimes Staatsarchiv)*, Munich.

HHSTA — Dynastic, state, and court archives *(Haus-, Hof-, und Staatsarchiv)*, Vienna.

HSTA — Main state archive *(Hauptstaatsarchiv)*, Stuttgart.

OHL — Supreme army command *(Oberste Heeresleitung)*.

RAW — Official war history *(Reichsarchivwerk)*, Der Weltkrieg 1914-1918, Vols. 5ff. (1929ff.).

Sch&Gr — A. Scherer and J. Grunewald (eds.), *L'Allemagne et les Problèmes de la Paix Pendant la Première Guerre Mondiale. Documents Extraits des Archives de l'Office Allemand des Affaires Etrangères*, Vol. 1 (1962); Vol. 2 (1964).

UA — Investigating committee *(Untersuchungsausschuss)* of the national assembly and Reichstag following the First World War (1919-1928).

UA I (= 15.UA I) — Stenographic transcript of public hearings, 15th Committee, Vol. 1 (1920). See also Chapter 8, Note 3.

UA II — Supplements to the stenographic transcript of public hearings, 15th Committee, 2nd Subcommittee: Documents on Wilson's peace efforts, 1916-1917 (1920). See also Chapter 8, Note 3.

UA III — Series III, Vol. 4, international law during the First World War (1927).

UA IV (Schwertfeger) — Series IV, Vol. 2, deposition of B. Schwertfeger (1925).

UA IV                       Series IV, Section 2 *(Der Innere Zusammenbruch),* Vol. 12, Part 1,
(Volkmann)                  deposition of Erich O. Volkmann, on questions of annexation in the
                            First World War (1929).
ZA Potsdam                  Central archive *(Zentralarchiv),* Potsdam.
ZA Merseburg                Central archive, Merseburg.


*Albert I of Belgium*  *Les Carnets de Guerre d'Albert I^{er} Roi des Belges,* ed. by General R.
                       van Overstraeten, Brussels (1953).
*Amiguet*              P. H. Amiguet, *La vie du prince Sixte de Bourbon,* Paris (1934).
*Asquith*              The Earl of Oxford and Asquith, *Memories and Reflections,
                       1852-1927,* Vol. 2, Toronto (1928).
*Bauer*                Colonel Max Bauer, *Der grosse Krieg in Feld und Heimat. Erinner-
                       ungen und Betrachtungen aus der Zeit des Weltkriegs,* Tübingen
                       (1921).
*Bergsträsser*         L. Bergsträsser, *Die preussische Wahlrechtsfrage und die Entstehung
                       der Osterbotschaft 1917,* Tübingen (1929).
*Bernstorff (1)*       Count J. H. Bernstorff, *Deutschland und Amerika. Erinnerungen aus
                       dem fünfjährigen Krieg,* Berlin (1920).
*Bernstorff (2)*       Count J. H. Bernstorff, *Erinnerungen und Briefe,* Zurich (1936).
*Bethmann Hollweg*     Theobald von Bethmann Hollweg, *Betrachtungen zum Weltkriege,* 2
                       vols., Berlin (1919 and 1922).
*Birnbaum*             K. E. Birnbaum, *Peace Moves and U-Boat Warfare. A Study of Im-
                       perial Germany's Policy towards the United States, April 18,
                       1916-January 9, 1917* (Acta Universitatis Stockholmiensis. Stock-
                       holm Studies in History, 2, Stockholm [1958]).
*Buehrig*              E. H. Buehrig, *Woodrow Wilson and the Balance of Power,* Bloom-
                       ington (1955).
*Class*                H. Class, *Wider den Strom. Vom Werden und Wachsen der natio-
                       nalen Opposition im alten Reich,* Leipzig (1932).
*Conrad*               Franz Freiherr Conrad von Hötzendorf, *Aus meiner Dienstzeit,* 5
                       vols. Vienna, Leipzig, Munich (1925).
*Conze*                W. Conze, *Polnische Nation und deutsche Politik im Ersten Welt-
                       krieg,* Cologne-Graz (1958).
*Cramon (1)*           A. von Cramon, *Unser österreichisch-ungarischer Bundesgenosse im
                       Weltkriege,* Berlin (1920).
*Cramon (2)*           A. von Cramon and P. Fleck, *Deutschlands Schicksalsbund mit
                       Osterreich-Ungarn. Von Conrad von Hötzendorf zu Kaiser Karl,* Ber-
                       lin (1932).
*Czernin*              Graf Ottokar Czernin, *Im Weltkriege,* Berlin-Vienna (1919).
*Deuerlein*            Ernst Deuerlein, *Der Bundestatsausschuss für die auswärtigen
                       Angelegenheiten 1870 bis 1918,* Regensburg (1955).
*Epstein,*             K. Epstein, *Matthias Erzberger und das Dilemma der Deutschen
                       Demokratie,* Berlin (1962).
*Erzberger*            Matthias Erzberger, *Erlebnisse im Weltkrieg,* Stuttgart (1920).
*Falkenhayn*           General Erich von Falkenhayn, *Die Oberste Heeresleitung
                       1914-1916 in ihren wichtigsten Entschliessungen,* Berlin (1920).
*Fester (1)*           R. Fester, *Die politischen Kämpfe um den Frieden 1916-1918 und
                       das Deutschtum,* Munich (1938).
*Fester (2)*           R. Fester, *Die Politik Kaiser Karls und der Wendepunkt des Welt-
                       krieges,* Munich (1925).
*Fischer*              Fritz Fischer, *Griff nach der Weltmacht. Die Kriegszielpolitik des
                       kaiserlichen Deutschlands 1914-1918,* Düsseldorf (1961).
*Gatzke*               H. W. Gatzke, *Germany's Drive to the West. A Study of Germany's
                       Western War Aims During the First World War,* Baltimore (1950).
*Gerard*               James Watson Gerard, *My Four Years in Germany,* London (1917).

| | |
|---|---|
| *Groener* | Wilhelm Groener (ed. by Friedrich Freiherr Hiller von Gaertringen), *Lebenserinnerungen. Jugend, Generalstab, Weltkrieg,* Göttingen (1957). |
| *Groos* | O. Groos (ed.), *Der Krieg in der Nordsee,* Vol. 2 of the official naval history, *Der Krieg zur See 1914-1918,* Berlin (1920). |
| *Hahlweg* | W. Hahlweg, *Lenins Rückkehr nach Russland 1917,* Leyden (1957). |
| *Hanssen* | H. P. Hanssen (ed. by R. H. Lutz *et al.*), *Diary of a Dying Empire,* Bloomington (1955). |
| *Haussmann* | Conrad Haussmann (ed. by U. Zeller), *Schlaglichter. Reichstagsbriefe und Aufzeichnungen,* Frankfurt (1924). |
| *Helfferich* | Karl Helfferich, *Der Weltkrieg,* 3 vols., Berlin (1919). |
| *Hoffmann* | *Die Aufzeichnungen des Generalmajors Max Hoffmann,* ed. by K. F. Nowak, 2 vols., Berlin (1929). Vol. 2 repeats the content of a work published in 1923, *Der Kreig der versäumten Gelegenheiten.* |
| *Hölzle* | Erwin Hölzle, "Das Experiment des Friedens im Ersten Weltkrieg 1914-1917," in *Geschichte in Wissenschaft und Unterricht,* Vol. 13 (1962), pp. 465-522. |
| *House* | Colonel Edward House, *The Intimate Papers of Colonel House.* Arranged as a narrative by Charles Seymour, Vols. 2ff., London (1926ff.). |
| *Hymans* | P. Hymans, *Mémoires,* ed. by F. van Kalken with J. Barthier, 2 vols., Brussels (1958). |
| *Janssen (1)* | Karl Heinz Janssen, *Macht und Verblendung. Kriegszielpoltik der deutschen Bundesstaaten 1914-1918,* Göttingen (1963). |
| *Janssen (2)* | Karl Heinz Janssen, "Der Wechsel in der Obersten Heeresleitung 1916," in *Vierteljahreshefte für Zeitgeschichte,* Vol. 7 (1959), pp. 337-371. |
| *Knesebeck* | L. G. von dem Knesebeck, *Die Wahrheit über den Propagandafeldzug und Deutschlands Zusammenbruch. Der Kampf der Publizistik im Weltkriege,* Munich (1927). |
| *Lafeber* | C. V. Lafeber, *Vredes- en Bemiddelingspogingen uit het erste jaar van Wereldoorlog 1. Augustus 1914-December 1915,* dissertation, Leyden (1961). |
| *Lancken* | Oskar Freiherr von der Lancken-Wakenitz, *Meine 30 Dienstjahre 1888-1918,* Potsdam, Paris, Brussels (1931). |
| *Lansing* | Robert Lansing, *War Memoirs,* New York (1935). See also FR, *The Lansing Papers.* |
| *Link* | Arthur S. Link, *Wilson,* Vol. 3, *The Struggle for Neutrality, 1914-1915,* Oxford (1960). |
| *Lloyd George* | David Lloyd George, *War Memoirs,* Vols. 2-4, London (1933-1934). |
| *Ludendorff (1)* | Erich von Ludendorff, *Meine Kriegserinnerungen 1914-1918,* Berlin (1919). |
| *Ludendorff (2)* | Erich von Ludendorff, *Urkunden der Obersten Heeresleitung über ihre Tätigkeit 1916-1918,* Berlin (1920). |
| *Matthias* | E. Matthias (ed. with R. Morsey), *Der Interfraktionelle Ausschuss 1917-1918,* Part 1 (Quellen zur Geschichte des Parlamentarismus und der Politischen Parteien. First Series, Von der Konstitutionellen Monarchie zur Parlamentarischen Republik), Düsseldorf, 1959. |
| *May* | E. R. May, *The World War and American Isolation, 1914-1917,* Harvard Historical Studies, Vol. 71, Cambridge, Massachusetts (1959). |
| *Meyer* | H. C. Meyer, *Mitteleuropa in German Thought and Action, 1815-1945,* The Hague (1955). |
| *Moltke* | Helmuth von Moltke (ed. by E. von Moltke), *Erinnerungen, Briefe, Dokumente 1877-1916,* Stuttgart (1922). |
| *Morrissey* | Alice M. Morrissey, *American Defense of Neutral Rights, 1914-1917,* Bloomington (1939). |

| | |
|---|---|
| *Mühlmann* | C. Mühlmann, *Oberste Heeresleitung und Balkan im Weltkrieg 1914-1918,* Berlin (1942). |
| *Müller* | Georg Alexander von Müller (ed. by W. Görlitz), *Regierte der Kaiser? Kriegstagebücher, Aufzeichnungen und Briefe . . . 1914-1918,* Göttingen (1959). |
| *Naumann* | V. Naumann, *Dokumente und Argumente,* Berlin (1928). |
| *Paléologue* | Maurice Paléologue, *Am Zarenhof während des Weltkreigs. Tagebücher und Betrachtungen,* 2 vols., Munich (1925). |
| *Payer* | Friedrich Freiherr von Payer, *Von Bethmann Hollweg bis Ebert. Erinnerungen und Bilder,* Frankfurt (1923). |
| *Pingaud* | A. Pingaud, *Histoire Diplomatique de la France pendant la Grande Guerre,* Vol. 3, Paris (1940). |
| *Pirenne* | H. Pirenne, *La Belgique et la Guerre Mondiale* (Publications of the Carnegie Endowment for International Peace. Economics and History, Vol. 124), Paris (1928). |
| *Poincaré* | Raymond Poincaré, *Au Service de la France. Neuf Années de Souvenirs,* Vol. 9, *L'Année Trouble (1917),* Paris (1932). |
| *Polzer-Hoditz* | Count A. Polzer-Hoditz, *Kaiser Karl. Aus der Geheimmappe seines Kabinettschefs,* Zurich, Leipzig, Vienna (1932). |
| *Ribot (1)* | A. Ribot, *Journal . . . et Correspondances Inédites, 1914-1922,* Paris (1936). |
| *Ribot (2)* | A. Ribot, *Lettres à un ami. Souvenirs de ma vie politique,* Paris (1934). |
| *Scheidemann (1)* | Philipp Scheidemann, *Memoiren eines Sozialdemokraten,* 2 vols., Dresden (1928). |
| *Scheidemann (2)* | Philipp Scheidemann, *Der Zusammenbruch,* Berlin (1921). |
| *Schulthess* | *Schulthess' Europäischer Geschichtskalender,* ed. by E. Jäckh and K. Höhn, New Series, Vol. 32ff., Munich (1921). |
| *Schwabe* | Klaus Schwabe, *Die deutschen Professoren und die politischen Grundfragen des Ersten Weltkrieges,* unpublished dissertation, Freiburg (1958). |
| *Scott* | James Brown Scott (ed.), *Official Statements of War Aims and Peace Proposals, December 1916 to November 1918,* pamphlet series of the Carnegie Endowment for International Peace, Division of International Law, No. 31, Washington, D.C. (1921). |
| *Seeckt* | Hans von Seeckt (ed. by Freiherr von Rabenau), *Aus meinem Leben 1866 bis 1917,* Leipzig (1938). |
| *Seymour* | Charles Seymour, *American Diplomacy During the World War,* 2nd ed., Baltimore (1942). |
| *Sixtus, Prince of Bourbon,* | *L'Offre de Paix Separée de L'Autriche,* Paris (1934). |
| *Smith (1)* | C. J. Smith, Jr., *The Russian Struggle for Power, 1914-1917. A Study of Russian Foreign Policy during the First World War,* New York (1956). |
| *Smith (2)* | Daniel M. Smith, *Robert Lansing and American Neutrality, 1914-1917,* University of California Publications in History, Vol. 59, Berkeley-Los Angeles (1958). |
| *Spender and Asquith* | J. A. Spender and Lord Asquith, *The Life of H. H. Asquith,* 2 vols., London (1932). |
| *Spindler* | A. Spindler, *Der Handelskrieg mit U-Booten,* 4 vols., part of the official naval history, *Der Krieg zur See 1914-1918,* Berlin (1932-1934). Vol. IV was printed in 1941 but not published. A photostatic edition appeared in 1964. |
| *Steglich (1)* | Wolfgang Steglich, *Die Friedenspolitik der Mittelmächte 1917-1918,* Vol. 1, Wiesbaden (1964). |
| *Steglich (2)* | Wolfgang Steglich, *Bündnissicherung oder Verständigungsfrieden.* |

|  | *Untersuchungen zu dem Friedensangebot der Mittelmächte vom 12. Desember 1916,* Göttinger Bausteine zur Geschichtswissenschaft, Vol. 28, Göttingen (1958). |
| *Stein* | Hermann von Stein, *Erlebnisse und Betrachtungen aus der Zeit des Weltkrieges,* Leipzig (1919). |
| *Suarez* | Georges Suarez, *Briand. Sa vie–son oeuvre, avec son journal et de nombreux documents inédits,* Vols. 3 and 4, Paris (1939-1940). |
| *Sweet (1)* | P. R. Sweet, "Austria, Hungary and Mitteleuropa: August 1915-April 1916," in *Festschrift für Heinrich Benedikt,* ed. by H. Hantsch and A. Novotny, Vienna (1957), pp. 180-212. |
| *Sweet (2)* | P. R. Sweet, "Leaders and Politics: Germany in the Winter of 1914-1915," in *Journal of Central European Affairs,* Vol. 16, No. 3 (October 1956), pp. 229-252. |
| *Tirpitz (1)* | Alfred von Tirpitz, *Politische Dokumente,* Vol. 2, *Deutsche Ohnmachtspolitik im Weltkrieg,* Hamburg-Berlin (1926). |
| *Tirpitz (2)* | Alfred von Tirpitz, *Erinnerungen,* Leipzig (1919). |
| *Trevelyan* | G. M. Trevelyan, *Sir Edward Grey. Sein Leben und Werk. Eine Grundlegung Englischer Politik,* Essen (1938). |
| *Umbreit* | P. Umbreit, *Der Krieg und die Arbeitsverhältnisse. Die deutschen Gewerkschaften im Kriege,* Publications of the Carnegie Endowment for International Peace, Economics and History, Vol. 104, Stuttgart (1928). |
| *Valentini* | Rudolf von Valentini (ed. by B. Schwertfeger), *Kaiser und Kabinettschef. . .* , Oldenburg (1931). |
| *Werkmann* | Karl Freiherr von Werkmann, *Deutschland als Verbündeter. Kaiser Karl's Kampf um den Frieden,* Berlin (1931). |
| *Westarp* | Count Kuno von Westarp, *Konservative Politik im letzten Jahrzehnt des Kaiserreiches,* Vol. 2, *1914-1918,* Berlin (1936). |
| *Wippermann-Purlitz* | *Deutscher Geschichtskalender. Sachlich geordnete Zusammenstellung der wichtigsten Vorgänge im In- und Ausland,* Vol. 32 (1916), Vol. 33 (1917), equivalent to *Der Europäische Krieg in aktenmässiger Darstellung,* Vols. 4-7. |
| *Wrisberg* | Ernst von Wrisberg, *Erinnerungen an die Kriegsjahre im königlich preussischen Kriegsministerium,* Vol. 2, *Heer und Heimat,* Leipzig (1921), Vol. 3, *Wehr und Waffen 1914-1918,* Leipzig (1922). |
| *Zeman* | Zbyněk A. B. Zeman (ed.), *Germany and the Revolution in Russia. Documents from the Archives of the German Foreign Ministry,* Oxford (1958). |
| *Zmarzlik* | H.-G. Zmarzlik, *Bethmann Hollweg als Reichskanzler 1909-1914,* Beiträge zur Geschichte des Parlamentarismus und der Politischen Parteien, Vol. II, Düsseldorf (1957). |
| *Zwehl* | H. von Zwehl, *Erich von Falkenhayn, General der Infanterie. Eine biographische Studie,* Berlin (1926). |

# Notes

*Notes to Chapter 1*

1. See Vol. II, Chapter 6, and my work, *Europa und die deutsche Frage,* cited there (Note 7), republished in 1962 by R. Oldenbourg, Munich, in different form under the title, *Das Deutsche Problem. Grundfragen deutschen Staatslebens gestern und heute* (Chapter 4, 3). On the early history of the First World War see also my essay, "Eine neue Kriegsschuldthese? " *Historische Zeitschrift,* Vol. 194 (1962), which deals critically with F. Fischer's contentions; also my article, "Bethmann Hollweg im Schlaglicht des Deutschen Geschichtsrevisionismus," *Schweizer Monatshefte,* Vol. 42 (November 1962); and my contribution, "Bethmann Hollweg und die Machtträume deutscher Patrioten im ersten Jahr des Weltkriegs," *Festschrift für P. E. Schramm* (1964).
2. Such statements are found in L. Dehio, *Historische Zeitschrift,* Vol. 194 (1962), p. 134 and *passim.*
3. Particularly persuasive evidence is found in a letter to the crown prince of November 15, 1913—he was then pressing for decisive action. "In any future war undertaken for no compelling reason," Bethmann Hollweg wrote, "it is not only the Hohenzollern crown that will be at stake, but Germany's future. . . . To engage in saber-rattling when there is no threat to the honor, security, and future of the land is not only rash but criminal." (Zmarzlik, p. 81.)
4. Vol. II, p. 135. See also my essay, "Der Anteil der Militärs an der Kriegskatastrophe von 1914," *Historische Zeitschrift,* Vol. 193 (1961). On Bethmann Hollweg's pessimistic fatalism see K. D. Erdmann, "Zur Beurteilung Bethmann Hollwegs," *Geschichte in Wissenschaft und Unterricht,* Vol. 15, No. 9 (September 1964), pp. 525ff. Riezler's diaries, there used and sensitively interpreted for the first time, are invaluable as evidence for the effect Bethmann Hollweg exerted on his immediate environment; and often they also reveal the Chancellor's secret thoughts and ultimate intentions. It is true, however, that these diary notes bear a strongly emotional tinge and on that account alone must be used with care. Riezler was not really a "political animal" and his sense of objective realism fell far short of Bethmann Hollweg's.
5. Evidence will be found, among other places, in Westarp, *passim,* esp. pp. 301ff. In its fight against the Chancellor, the conservative party was handicapped not only by its basic reluctance to "intervene in the privileges of the crown" (the appointment and dismissal of ministers), but even more by the fact that the Kaiser had

never forgiven it its failure as a bulwark of the throne in 1908. Bethmann Hollweg's most dangerous adversary, County Councilor von Maltzahn, political adviser to the crown prince, was relieved in June 1916, but did not give up his political activities.

6. There is very little direct evidence, but see Valentini, p. 162. William II's own memoirs, *Ereignisse und Gestalten* (1924), emphasize Bethmann Hollweg's warm human qualities as well as the high prestige he enjoyed among the governments of the German states and abroad, even during the war. But Bethmann Hollweg had first had to win the Kaiser's confidence. According to Valentini (p. 121), the Kaiser, in 1909, long resisted accepting Bethmann Hollweg as Bülow's successor – "He's always lecturing and knows it all." The Kaiser, in other words, found him too obstinate and lacking in humor. Yet the Kaiser unwaveringly set his face against reappointing Bülow.

7. Müller, p. 50. For the following, see *ibidem,* pp. 53 and 366.

8. House, Vol. 2, p. 139.

9. The papers of State Secretary Count Roedern were made available to me through the courtesy of Professor Heimpel and the Max Planck Institute of History, Göttingen. They are full of interesting recollections of the war years, written down in 1919. One can scarcely fail to be moved by the testimony of this conservative monarchist, who painfully reached the conclusion, after the upheaval of 1918, that the fall of the Hohenzollern dynasty was both necessary and unavoidable, its last representatives having failed so pitifully. The incident at Strasbourg is also briefly mentioned in Müller, p. 133.

10. *Ereignisse und Gestalten,* pp. 116ff. The Kaiser felt excluded from all military decisions. Müller (p. 68) quotes him as telling Prince Max of Baden on November 6, 1914: "If the Germans think I'm leading the army, they're mistaken. I drink tea and saw wood and take walks, and from time to time I'm told that such-and-such has been done, entirely at those gentlemen's pleasure." Only Groener, chief of the rail transport section, was nice enough, the Kaiser said, to keep him informed of all his plans.

11. See Janssen (1).

12. See Deuerlein, esp. pp. 189ff., 227. On the often helpful (though on occasion harmful) role of the federal council before the war, see Zmarzlik, Chapter 2.

13. Tirpitz (2), p. 23. In Tirpitz (1), p. 103, in a letter to Prince Henry of September 10, 1914, he said six to eight further years of peace would have been needed.

14. Westarp specifically mentions Tirpitz's son-in-law, von Hassell, as an intermediary, and Captain Löhlein, head of intelligence in the Reich naval office, the latter exercising great caution. There was also the arch-conservative county councilor, von Maltzahn. In a written statement to the foreign ministry of March 8, 1915, Löhlein denied that he engaged in any activities looking to Bethmann Hollweg's ouster, on behalf of Tirpitz (AA, Bethmann Hollweg's personnel file, Germany 122, No. 16, Vol. 8). On the subject of Bethmann Hollweg's distrust of Tirpitz, see, among others, Müller, pp. 76, 79, and *passim;* Haussmann, p. 25; Tirpitz (1), p. 96; Westarp, pp. 29, 304. For Bethmann Hollweg's efforts in October 1914 to remove Maltzahn from his post, see *ibidem,* p. 307. Tirpitz himself, in Tirpitz (1), p. 102, provides an astonishing example of his subtle technique of slander, in a letter to Prince Henry of September 10, 1914: "Rumors are rife in Germany that we are weak-kneed in our attitude toward Britain. I would regret it very much if there were any truth to this." Britain would have to be fought to a standstill, no matter what. Unfortunately, Germany was six to eight years behind in building its navy, for the Chancellor wanted a "weak navy" as a conciliatory gesture toward Britain, with which he sought an understanding, supported by pacifists, scholars, clergy, and businessmen. "There is a sinister feeling abroad in Germany that the attempt to conciliate Britain is to be taken up again. At any rate, banking circles are taking the lead. In the absence of sufficient evidence, I neither wish nor am entitled to pronounce judgment." Let the prince send a

confidant into the Reich naval office to secure information. According to Class, p. 320, an unidentified high officer in the Reich naval office established contact with him and the Pan-Germans at the very outbreak of the war. Class was a fanatical Bethmann Hollweg opponent.

15. Report on a discussion with Baron von Plessen of the German embassy in Rome, January 1, 1915, by the Bavarian envoy in Stuttgart, Moy (GSTA, Pol. A, VII, No. 30); Westarp, p. 304; Haussmann, pp. 12ff., 20 (statements by Rathenau), 24. Critical statements by the banking executive A. von Gwinner appear in Tirpitz (1), p. 65. One of the staples of Pan-German agitation against Bethmann Hollweg was the "utter failure" of German diplomacy in July 1914; see Class, pp. 301f., 310ff.

16. From documents published by Tirpitz himself in Tirpitz (1) and by Müller. Groos, p. 83, emphasizes, among other things, that the single-minded concentration on preparing for a naval battle stood in the way of every effort to harass the British troop transports. A report by Admiral Lenz that greatly disappointed Tirpitz threw light on the hopelessness of a naval battle—Tirpitz (1), pp. 85-89.

17. Tirpitz (1), p. 61.

18. Bethmann Hollweg, Vol. 2, pp. 8ff.

19. Tirpitz (1), pp. 109, also 42, 48, 79. See also Groos, pp. 81f.

20. It was all the cleverer, because the interview was deliberately submitted to the foreign ministry for censorship only with a delay. The announcement is reprinted in Tirpitz (1), pp. 621ff. See also Müller, pp. 76f., and Westarp, pp. 91ff. The text is truly amazing, not only on account of its blatant attacks on Britain (meant only for German readers), but for its heedless boasting of a weapons system that so far existed in only modest beginnings.

21. Müller, pp. 87, 89, and *passim;* Tirpitz (1), p. 80. At times Tirpitz entertained a weird plan under which the aged Hindenburg was to become Chancellor, chief of staff, and chief of the admiralty at one and the same time—see diary entries of January and March 1915, in Tirpitz (2), pp. 443, 457, 460f., 462, 466.

22. Westarp, p. 125.

23. Twenty letters to Dr. Wyneken, editor-in-chief of the *Königsberger Allgemeine Zeitung,* written from 1915 to 1919, printed in the appendix to the rather confused book by Knesebeck, pp. 151ff. The summer of 1916 saw the beginning of Ludendorff's change of mind in connection with Germany's yielding on the U-boat question. The files of ZA Potsdam relating to the Reich chancellery, Vol. 7, 4-6, include some letters exchanged between Bethmann Hollweg and Hindenburg from July 8 to December 7, 1915, in which there are constant assurances of mutual devotion.

24. AA (Germany), 122, 16, Vol. 6, Bethmann Hollweg's personnel file.

25. I have been able to listen to a recording, of rather good quality, of the Reichstag speech of February 27, 1917, unfortunately only a brief passage. It is in the sound archives of the German radio in Frankfurt. Surprisingly enough, one learns from Scheidemann (2), p. 33, that Bethmann Hollweg painstakingly memorized his very carefully prepared Reichstag speeches, in order to be able to deliver them without the use of a script.

26. Among Weizsäcker's papers is the record of a private talk of May 13, 1917, in which Bethmann Hollweg is quoted as saying that the sight of the conservatives sitting in chilly silence during his speech of August 4, 1914, was a dreadful moment in his life.

27. Letter from Haussmann to Weizsäcker in the latter's papers, in the possession of Freifrau von Weizsäcker, Lindau.

28. Westarp, p. 1.

29. BA, Haeften's papers, Portfolio No. 1. Delbrück had the draft reworked by Harnack, and then Bethmann Hollweg had R. Koser edit it again.

30. BA, *ibidem.* In the posthumously published work, *Die wirtschaftliche Mobilmachung in Deutschland 1914* (1924), pp. 128f., Clemens von Delbrück reports, appar-

ently erroneously, that the Chancellor rejected the proclamation. Nothing is known concerning the reception of Moltke's curious "military-political" demands of August 2, already discussed in Vol. II, p. 271. They represented an effort to remove the conduct of foreign policy from the Chancellor's hands.

31. See Note 32.

32. There is no need for another presentation of the flood of German wishful dreams and demands. This has already been done in great detail by Fischer, who interprets the war aims literature and Bethmann Hollweg's position as implying Germany's striving for world power. Fischer spares scarcely a glance for parallel developments abroad and does not even try for a historical analysis. Comprehensive studies by two of my students offer a wealth of largely unpublished source material: Klaus Schwabe's 1958 Freiburg dissertation and his lengthy essay, "Zur Politischen Haltung der Deutschen Professoren im 1. Weltkrieg," *Historische Zeitschrift,* Vol. 193 (1961); and Janssen (1), already cited (Note 11). See also UA IV (Volkmann); Gatzke; I. M. Geiss (a disciple of Fischer), *Der polnische Grenzstreifen 1914-1918* (1960); Paul Rohrbach, *Chauvinismus und Weltkrieg,* Vol. 2, *Die Alldeutschen* (1919).

33. Memorandum by Erzberger of September 2, 1914, with an accompanying letter to Bethmann Hollweg, received September 5, 1914, ZA Potsdam, chancellery file 2476, printed in Tirpitz (1), pp. 68-72. A draft of Bethmann Hollweg's very cautious reply is found in W. Basler, *Deutsche Annexionspolitik in Polen und im Baltikum* (1962), p. 29, note 22 (from ZA Potsdam, *loc. cit.*). It avoided any word of assent, merely stating: "We must at all costs hold out until Germany's future is fully secure. It is true that all possibilities must be considered, but our ultimate decisions are still entirely dependent on further developments." Westarp, p. 53, offers (from the chancellery files) another very amateurish war aims plan by Erzberger of June 28, 1915. Petitions to the foreign ministry by the Thyssen interests of April 28, 1914, citing Erzberger, are found in an AA WW file (15, secret, Vol. 1, memoranda on war aims). Even earlier, on August 28, Bethmann Hollweg had asked Delbrück to establish the extent of the Briey ore deposits. On September 3, von Dallwitz, the governor of Alsace-Lorraine, had sent him Röchling's proposals for the mines. Bethmann Hollweg now wished to hear further details from Dallwitz (correspondence of September 3, 9, 14, and 17). On November 17 Delbrück was asked to draw up a minimum and a maximum program of demands relating to Briey-Longwy (AA, peace treaties, No. 21, Vol. 1). The report of a discussion with Hugo Stinnes in the fall of 1914, given by Class, p. 327, throws a significant light on the political expertise of German "industrial leaders." Stinnes proposed that the hated Bethmann Hollweg be succeeded by the journalist Weiss of the *Frankfurter Zeitung!*

34. Class's pamphlet, written in September, was printed in an edition of not quite 2,000 at the behest of the leaders of the Pan-German group. By the time the police seized the pamphlet on January 12, 1915, many copies had been mailed and could not be retrieved—see Class, pp. 343ff., 345ff. A copy had gone to Jagow at the foreign ministry on December 23 (AA WW, 15, secret, Vol. 6, appendix). *Ibidem* (Vol. 1) the memorandum by the duke of Mecklenburg, sent in a privately printed edition to the Chancellor on July 7, 1915, to which he replied on July 17. There was a further memorandum, by Crown Prince Rupprecht of Bavaria, dispatched to the Kaiser on July 29. It met with the Kaiser's disapproval, and Treutler sent it on to Bethmann Hollweg. It is apparently identical with the one mentioned by Fischer, pp. 213f. Rupprecht expressed the hope that Holland and Luxembourg would voluntarily join the Reich as new federal states, if their territories were enlarged from the industrial regions of Belgium and France. France's northern border was to run from Etaples, south of Boulogne, by way of Arras-Soissons-Montmédy, to the level of Metz. In other words, the French were to surrender their chain of fortifications.

35. Valentini, p. 252.

36. For details, see the study by Klaus Schwabe, already cited. To my mind, the best and most substantial work of German World War I propaganda remains the collection edited by O. Hintze, Friedrich Meinecke, H. Oncken, and S. Schumacher in 1915 under the title, *Deutschland und der Weltkrieg.* Among other things, it contains a particularly interesting effort on the part of Meinecke to defend German militarism against its accusers. Hintze's discussion of how to abolish world hegemony also possesses considerable intellectual stature.

37. From a private letter to Jagow, AA WW, 15, secret, Vol. 6. Solf offered to provide headquarters with a whole "nosegay" of peace plans, some of them quite fantastic, that were floating about Berlin. Fischer, pp. 109f., merely hints that Solf was opposed to annexations in Europe, but gives all the more space to his plans for colonial acquisitions, to create an impression of unrestrained imperialism. On September 25 Solf repeated his warnings to Jagow, making fun of "rear echelon apostles of Germanization." He did, however, append proposals for the strategic improvement of Germany's western border, in the form of a map that indicated limited German territorial acquisitions *(ibidem).*

38. A similar notion is found in a comprehensive memorandum from Department II of the foreign ministry, headed "Proposals for a Peace Treaty with France" and dated in pencil October 1, 1914. Its author would incorporate Belgium "in principle," but administer it for the time being as an "external possession." The Franco-Belgian coastal region would continue under occupation, as a lever to exert pressure on Britain, but to be relinquished if that meant peace with Britain (AA WW, 15, secret, Vol. 1).

39. Memorandum of October 29 (AA WW, 15, secret, Vol. 6, 42 columns in the appendix, printed only in part in UA IV (Volkmann), pp. 187-193. A similar attitude toward Russia was publicly taken by the historian Otto Hoetzsch, who had some influence on the conservative party through Count Westarp and the *Kreuzzeitung,* though he was much closer to the Pan-Germans. See also Schwabe, Part 1, Chapter 4.

40. I am at a loss to understand how Fischer (p. 126) can insist that Loebell, in this memorandum, "expressed himself unmistakably as in favor of sweeping annexations in the east." He did not do so even in the accompanying letter of November 4 that went with his memorandum to Bethmann Hollweg (ZA Potsdam, chancellery file No. 2476). Elsewhere too (pp. 343f.) Fischer classes Loebell among the most extreme annexationists.

41. The word "probably" *(wohl)* was inserted in Bethmann Hollweg's own hand in Riezler's draft, presently to be discussed. Bethmann Hollweg, in other words, wished to keep open the option that Germany might be head of such a community.

42. Riezler had published a book in 1913, *Grundzüge der Weltpolitik in der Gegenwart,* under the pen name of Ruedorffer. In it there is much discussion of modifying conflicting power politics by international economic ties. We shall not know what share, if any, Riezler had as Bethmann Hollweg's political secretary in elaborating the European plan until scholars are given access to his diaries. The "September memorandum" was Riezler's personal conception, like part of the subsequent correspondence. It would seem that in terms of power politics Riezler's stand was far firmer than that of Bethmann Hollweg, who chafed under his responsibilities and considered the possibility of defeat as early as October.

43. Delbrück on his part evidently regarded the economic union as being based on common interest rather than coercion. He cautiously objected to the demands Bethmann Hollweg considered making of France, which we shall discuss further on. Delbrück said that the annexation of the Briey ore basin was unnecessary, and that if such an economic union came about, it would be most inadvisable to burden France with heavy reparations. (See Delbrück to Bethmann Hollweg, September 13, erroneously cited as a directive by Bethmann Hollweg in Fischer, p. 109, Note 14.) E. Zechlin prefers to view Bethmann Hollweg's *Mitteleuropa*

plan essentially as a tactic in the economic war against Britain, i.e., as a temporary measure (Supplement 20/63 to the weekly *Das Parlament*, pp. 14ff.). One reason why that does not appeal to me is that when Falkenhayn put forward such ideas to Bethmann Hollweg in 1915, the Chancellor rejected them as totally unrealistic (see Chapter 4, further on).

44. Bethmann-Delbrück correspondence in chancellery volume 2476, ZA Potsdam. Also to be found there is a letter from Bethmann Hollweg to Delbrück with "preliminary notes" on war aims, both dated September 9, 1914; and two more letters from Bethmann Hollweg, dated September 16 and October 22, together with letters from Delbrück, dated September 3 and 13. Zechlin, *loc. cit.*, pp. 41ff., has recently published the items of September 9, 13, and 16. The "directive" of September 9 is also found in W. Basler, *Deutschlands Annexionspolitik in Polen und im Baltikum 1914-1918* (1962), pp. 381ff. Uncovering the important exchange in the chancellery files is entirely to the credit of Fritz Fischer. He was kind enough to let me have the items of September 9, which I was able to supplement with photostats and file excerpts from the ZA, through the courtesy of its director, Dr. Lötzke. Fischer (pp. 108f.) traces back the idea of an economic union to suggestions by Rathenau (August 28 and September 7) and Arthur von Gwinner (September 3), but this is at odds with the following passage in Delbrück's accompanying letter of September 9: "Shortly after the outbreak of war [i.e., before Bethmann Hollweg's departure for Koblenz] we briefly discussed the economic program of a Central European customs union and found ourselves in basic agreement." Thus, if Delbrück himself, *loc. cit.*, pp. 124ff., describes Rathenau as the originator of the idea of such a union, this must be a slip of memory, possibly occasioned by the fact that he was writing only in 1917. Such a slip seems plausible, since on September 3 Delbrück sharply protested Rathenau's petition of August 28, calling for an immediate customs union with Austria. On September 16 Bethmann Hollweg thereupon suggested that perhaps a particularly close relation between the two allies might be possible within the economic community (ZA, *loc. cit.*). Rathenau's further submissions of September 7 and October 10 went unanswered. Thus the question of who provided the initial impetus remains open. From Gwinner Bethmann Hollweg could have scarcely received more than a general suggestion that Germany should establish economic predominance rather than an insistence on political annexations, while Rathenau probably convinced him that in an economic sense it would be impossible to wear down Britain, because of its worldwide connections. As always, Rathenau's ideas were a mixture of astute insight and near-fantasy. Citing Bismarck's Peace of Nikolsburg in 1866, he held that mild treatment after victory might wean France away from Britain and bring it into an alliance with Germany. See his letters, ed. by von Eynern (1955), pp. 118ff.

45. In the following, I base myself on the final version of the program.

46. Not eighteen to twenty years, as given by Fischer, p. 111.

47. This was stated at the Berlin conference with Czernin on March 26, 1917 (AA WW, 15, secret, Vol. 2). On Bethmann Hollweg's efforts to ascertain the real scope of German interest in Briey, see Note 33, above.

48. The governor of Alsace-Lorraine, von Dallwitz, had proposed this in a private letter of September 4, presumably under the impact of the French advances at Mulhouse. Bethmann Hollweg was at once interested and obtained maps for further study (September 9 and 14—see AA, Peace Treaties, No. 21, Vol. 1).

49. Accompanying letter to Delbrück of September 9. Bethmann Hollweg considered turning aside this demand by changing it into a cession of Lorraine steel works to German industry. Janssen (1), Chapter 1, pp. 30f., basing himself on South German sources, describes the annexationist exuberance of the Kaiser and various German federal princes.

50. In the discussion with Weizsäcker on May 13, 1917, cited in Note 26, above, Bethmann Hollweg said he had been under the necessity of speaking of Belgium in

this fashion, in order to win the social democrats to the patriotic cause.

51. See Vol. II, pp. 68ff.

52. Tirpitz (1), p. 65. On p. 68, *ibidem,* there is mention of a *couloir* (corridor) through Belgium.

53. Reply of January 15, 1915 (ZA Potsdam, chancellery file No. 2476). Fischer (p. 121) interprets this quotation as implying that Bethmann Hollweg was not really interested in the position of the navy but was for the first time committing himself in writing to a program of future German "world power." This is the kind of misinterpretation typical of Fischer.

54. There was, of course, the assurance that "the war does not disprove the soundness of a policy of taking risks" *(der Krieg ist kein Gegenbeweis gegen das Risikoprinzip).*

55. Even Colonel Bauer, Ludendorff's most zealous liege, acknowledged that—though only in July 1918! See draft headed "Thoughts on the Continuation of the War" among Bauer's papers, BA, Portfolio No. 2, Sheet 269.

56. Sources are given by Fischer, pp. 228ff. According to a note by Lerchenfeld (GSTA) he expressed himself in similar terms before the foreign affairs committee of the federal council, on April 7, 1915. See also Deuerlein, p. 281. According to Hölzle, p. 470, note 16, Belgium did try to have its neutrality status revoked in 1916. The historian Hermann Oncken, in a letter to H. Delbrück of June 28, 1916, reproduced in Schwabe, Chapter 1, p. 4, expressed concern that Belgium might seek vengeance. Helfferich was convinced that Belgian hatred would be enduring (minutes of a discussion at the chancellery on June 19, 1915, given by Fischer, p. 325).

57. See what is hopefully the last in the long series of polemics on the alleged Louvain atrocities, Peter Schöller's conciliatory pamphlet, *Der Fall Löwen und das Weissbuch* (1958), based on a study of both German and Belgian documents.

58. The semiofficial, excellent, and objective studies of the historian K. Hampe on the question of Belgian neutrality served the purpose of popularizing similar sentiments. Historical views also played a considerable part in the comprehensive report of February 1915 on the future of Belgium by Governor General von Bissing, which formed the basis for his occupation administration (copy in GSTA, Pol. A, VII, No. 56). On the attitude of the German intellectuals, see Schwabe, *Historische Zeitschrift,* Vol. 193, p. 610, and his book, Chapter 1, p. 4.

59. From Weizsäcker's private papers, see Janssen (1), Chapter 1, note 121.

60. Instructions to Delbrück and Under Secretary Zimmermann of October 18, and their comprehensive report of December 31, 1914, in AA WW, 15, secret, Vol. 6, appendix (reproduced in UA IV [Volkmann], pp. 193-199); Envoy von der Lancken (Brussels), February 7, 1915—Ballin to Bethmann Hollweg, February 8, 1915; also bank director Max Warburg, February 13, 1915—Riezler, February 15, 1915—all in the same file (which gives only a summary of Riezler's report). On the inquiry to Tirpitz, see Note 53, above.

61. Janssen (1), p. 35. Bethmann Hollweg's letter to Hertling appears also in AA, Peace Treaties, No. 21, Vol. 1.

62. Hoffmann, Vol. 2, p. 83. Bethmann Hollweg gave an identical explanation for his ambiguous attitude in the Belgian question in a letter to Professor Hans Delbrück of September 8, 1917 (in Delbrück's papers). It was certainly true, at least for the years 1914-1915. In another letter to Delbrück of August 12, 1918, he said that a pledge of full Belgian restoration would have been simply impossible—and how could one ask the impossible of a politician? On June 15, 1915, he told Admiral von Müller that peace with Britain was out of the question, so long as Germany clung to the Belgian coast. Müller adds (p. 109): "He asked me to think the matter over and write him about it."

63. He said, among other things, that their views did not diverge all that much from his, apparently having reference to the idea of a *Mitteleuropa,* which the two negotiators had mentioned. Fischer (pp. 117, 192, 226) deduces from this that there

was a far-reaching coincidence of aims between Bethmann Hollweg and the business groups, which were dominated by the Pan-Germans. He doubts that the words were merely spoken with a tactical purpose. In my view he displays prejudice and a regrettable lack of ability to understand Bethmann Hollweg's position. I find it to be evidence of palpable bias that he completely ignores the remainder of the discussion, which proves the opposite. Stresemann's record of this discussion was first published in English translation (from Stresemann's papers) by Sweet (2), pp. 244ff. The German text was published by E. Zechlin in Supplement No. 6 to the weekly, *Das Parlament,* June 14, 1961. In an immediately following discussion, Delbrück expressed doubt about any annexations, in east or west, and totally rejected Roetger's proposal to settle German war veterans in Belgium and the Baltic regions (see Sweet [2], pp. 247ff.).

64. See Bethmann Hollweg, Vol. 2, p. 17, for his own thoughts.
65. For convincing evidence, see W. Lipgens, "Bismarck, die öffentliche Meinung und die Annexion von Elsass-Lothringen 1870," *Historische Zeitschrift,* Vol. 199 (1964), pp. 31ff. I have shown in Vol. I, p. 254, that it was not aroused nationalist passions that persuaded Bismarck to annex Alsace-Lorraine and least of all any idea that Alsace was German in character. His reasons had to do with power and military policy, though they were reinforced by the impression of strong national conflicts. I did not know, however, that Bismarck himself did a great deal to bring the debate on Alsace-Lorraine into the press, indeed was mainly responsible for this happening. In this respect, therefore, my account requires correction, which will be made in the third edition.
66. UA I, session of October 23, 1919, pp. 182f. of the stenographic transcript.

*Notes to Chapter 2*

1. Zwehl. See also Groener, p. 187 and *passim.*
2. Wild von Hohenborn's papers, in the BA. Wild was at first quartermaster general on Falkenhayn's staff, then Falkenhayn's successor as war minister, but even in that capacity he remained at headquarters, and Falkenhayn continued to include him in strategic consultations.
3. See Falkenhayn. Estimates of Falkenhayn's military performance and of his quarrels with Ludendorff and Hindenburg, in military literature (including the official history), are largely dominated by the traditions of the Schlieffen school and by admiration—in my opinion exaggerated—of Ludendorff, not only as an organizer, but as a strategist. Apart from the Zwehl biography, the shrewd and detached memoirs of General Freiherr von Freytag-Loringhoven form an exception: *Menschen und Dinge wie ich sie in meinem Leben sah* (1923). Loringhoven himself was for a time quartermaster general on Falkenhayn's staff. My own judgment of Ludendorff was expressed in my article, "Ludendorff," in *Neue Deutsche Biographie.*
4. Lord Bertie of Thame noted in his diaries (Vol. 2, p. 59) that in the beginning Falkenhayn treated Bethmann Hollweg with open contempt (quoted by Sweet [2], p. 235).
5. Note for Wahnschaffe of January 7, 1915, in Haeften's papers, BA. He passed severe judgment on Tappen in a letter to Valentini of July 10, 1916—see Valentini, p. 236. A highly unfavorable judgment of Tappen is also found in Wild von Hohenborn's papers (BA). Wild said that Tappen never got beyond the dispatches of the day and had much too narrow a perspective. He loathed Ludendorff, and Wild held that after the war he would deserve a court-martial for his obstructionism. Other witnesses have testified that Tappen did much to increase the tension between Falkenhayn and eastern headquarters, with Wild playing the role of moderator. See also Groener's carefully considered judgment, in Groener, p. 178.
6. RAW, Vol. 5, pp. 11f. Groener, p. 179, thinks that Falkenhayn's strategy after the Marne retreat was a half-measure; but there is a very real question of whether his own proposals offered any chance of success.

7. Handwritten notes on a newspaper article by Reventlow, in which Bethmann Hollweg complains that he and the foreign ministry had vainly tried ever since October to get the generals to set a time limit after which (a) a decision should be sought in the east rather than the west, and (b) Northeast Serbia should be evacuated. They were told that no such dates could be set.
8. For his quarrel with Falkenhayn on the matter in January 1915, see Müller, p. 79.
9. For the following, see RAW, Vol. 6, pp. 2ff., 92ff., 254ff., 405ff.
10. This was the time, according to Fabeck (RAW, Vol. 6, p. 437), when he first mentioned an intention to resign to his intimates and expressed doubts of his fitness for the post, since he was "self-educated."
11. Plessen's and Colonel Tappen's diaries, RAW, Vol. 6, p. 93. It is noteworthy that despite his grave concern, the Chancellor did not dare make representations to the Kaiser about the needless bloodbath at Ypres, but successfully appealed to Adjutant General von Plessen. William II would have regarded any direct approach as "civilian interference" with the military command power.
12. Though the content of Bethmann Hollweg's report of November 19, 1914, had long been known (RAW, Vol. 6, pp. 406f.), it was first published in English translation by Sweet (2), pp. 231ff. It was given in German by Zechlin in the supplement to the weekly, *Das Parlament,* May 17, 1961, pp. 284f. Subsequently it was also published by Sch&Gr, Vol. 1, No. 13 (1962). RAW used the documents of the AA, as well as the files of the army archive, destroyed by bombing in 1945.
13. Bethmann Hollweg's directive of November 25 (Sch&Gr, No. 16) shows that Falkenhayn afterward had doubts as to whether Austria, which was failing more and more in a military sense, should be let into the secret at all. He now looked for ways of establishing contact without a formal invitation. Sweet believes that the idea of a separate peace with Russia was suggested to the general by Tirpitz, who had always favored an understanding with Russia against Britain. According to Tirpitz (1), pp. 166ff., the two men discussed this matter on November 15.
14. RAW, Vol. 6, p. 254.
15. According to Müller (p. 57), Bethmann Hollweg and Jagow offered "a sad spectacle of pessimism and irresolution" on September 13, 1914, after the failure of the Battle of the Marne; but as Müller himself later remarked, this was a general impression and a judgment from the military point of view, and its significance should not be exaggerated. Jagow seems to have been the more pessimistic of the two. According to an account by the envoy Romberg, communicated to me by Legation Councilor Dr. Ullrich (AA), Jagow told Romberg as early as December 1914 that the war was virtually lost. At a Prussian cabinet meeting on November 28, 1914, Bethmann Hollweg expressed himself in terms similar to those in his letter to Zimmermann of November 19. He said he would regard it as a great success if Germany were even able to maintain its position (Zechlin, in the supplement to *Das Parlament,* May 15, 1963, pp. 3f.).
16. Documents concerning this mission in AA WW, 2 secret, pp. 1ff. (Mediation Efforts), given in full in Sch&Gr. Lafeber gives a detailed presentation of all peace feelers and mediation efforts during the first year of the war, based mainly on German diplomatic documents. Andersen's effort is discussed on pp. 189ff. The first inquiry from Denmark was received on November 24. Bethmann Hollweg's draft of his reply to Andersen is dated November 30. The Kaiser, he said, was prepared to examine and evaluate peace proposals by the enemy powers (Andersen wanted to sound out London as well), in concert with his allies. The following sentence is crossed out: "The conditions must be of such a nature as to guarantee full indemnity for Germany and security against renewed enemy attack." Evidently Bethmann Hollweg was unwilling to slam the door on negotiations at the outset by insisting on preconditions. Sch&Gr (No. 20) give only the final draft, as, apparently, does Fischer (pp. 223f.)—at any rate, he does not mention the cut, and the manner in which he treats Bethmann Hollweg's conduct is nakedly biased. Did he expect Bethmann Hollweg to offer St. Petersburg the status quo

instantly, without even awaiting the issue of the heavy fighting around Lodz, and was he to forego guarantees of any kind in advance?

17. Paléologue, Vol. 1, pp. 184ff., audience of November 21, 1914. See also Smith (1), pp. 99f.

18. Memorandum of November 27, Sch&Gr, No. 17. Fischer gives the content at length (pp. 221f.), but tries to invest the memorandum with an "imperialist" meaning it does not possess and misapprehends its true purpose.

19. Bethmann Hollweg, Vol. 2, p. 44.

20. See Chapter 1, pp. 12f., above. Hoffmann thought the Chancellor "very shrewd . . . a clever man," but somewhat irresolute. He admitted, however, that Bethmann Hollweg was in a difficult spot. (Hoffmann, Vol. 1, pp. 64, 100.)

21. RAW, Vol. 6, p. 415, no source given. It is stated *ibidem* that Falkenhayn expressed himself in similar terms to Moltke a few days later, and similar statements are also found in a long report (165 typewritten pages) by Haeften about the Falkenhayn crisis during the winter of 1914-1915 (BA, Haeften's papers). This report was used by Zechlin (after I had finished writing this book) in the supplement to *Das Parlament*, May 15, 1963, pp. 26ff. Janssen (2), p. 340, mentions that Hertling, the Bavarian premier, also advised the Chancellor, early in December, to relieve Falkenhayn.

22. RAW, Vol. 6, p. 408. On the Kaiser's peace sentiments, see Sweet (2), after AA WW, 2, secret, Vol. 1 (November 25 and December 2, 1914). According to Sweet, even the Kaiser urged that steps be taken in St. Petersburg and offered to take the initiative himself.

23. RAW, Vol. 6, pp. 421f.

24. AA WW, 2, secret, Vol. 1 (December 1, 1914).

25. RAW, Vol. 6, pp. 310, 419; Mühlmann, pp. 80ff.

26. Note by Bethmann Hollweg for Wahnschaffe, January 7, 1915 (BA, Haeften's papers, on which the following is also based). Other quotations from this note are given in Note 5, above.

27. RAW, nearly always Ludendorff's and Hindenburg's partisan, virtually reproaches Bethmann Hollweg for not having insisted at the time on Falkenhayn's dismissal and Ludendorff's appointment (Vol. 6, pp. 440f.).

28. Moltke, pp. 395ff.; also Zwehl, pp. 105ff.

29. RAW, Vol. 7, pp. 11ff., 75ff.

30. The editor of Hoffmann's memoirs tactfully suppressed passages full of biting sarcasm, but they were published in the *Frankfurter Allgemeine Zeitung,* January 10, 1955. Hoffmann's papers, with typewritten excerpts from his letters to his wife, are in the BA.

31. Letter by Haeften to Bethmann Hollweg, January 12, 1915, among Haeften's papers in the BA. According to Haeften, he urged the field marshal to offer himself to the Kaiser as Falkenhayn's successor, but Hindenburg declined.

32. Direct report by Hindenburg to the Kaiser of January 9, 1915, RAW, Vol. 7, p. 11.

33. RAW, Vol. 7, p. 13.

34. Moltke, pp. 413ff. There had already been two direct messages to the Kaiser (on January 10 and 15), in which Moltke, along Ludendorff's lines, urged a strategic reorientation from west to east. There had also been a letter on January 12 from an unidentified general at court (probably Plessen), which was full of pointed anti-Falkenhayn sentiments.

35. Haeften belabored Marschall three times, for hours at a time, on January 7, 8, and 21.

36. Count Wedel of the foreign ministry cited an unidentified General Staff officer "fresh from the eastern front" in telling the Württemberg envoy Varnbüler of the optimism that prevailed there: Hindenburg was letting the ministry know that the diplomats would have to keep the vacillating neutrals on a string until late February. By that time Germany would have achieved such impressive military successes that the world could no longer doubt its final victory in the east.

(Varnbüler to Weizsäcker, February 15, 1915, HSTA, E 73, V 61, F. 12g.)
37. Falkenhayn, pp. 50f.
38. See, for example, Müller, p. 92, from reports from Helfferich in Berlin, February 19, 1915, and Janssen (1), p. 45, giving a letter from Lerchenfeld to Hertling, April 3, 1915. Within the General Staff during the summer of 1915 there was a widespread impression that Falkenhayn was preparing himself to assume the chancellorship. Trautmann, who held the eastern desk in the foreign ministry, said so to Jagow on June 10, citing confidential talks with "General Staff officers" (this probably meant the general replacement command in Berlin, known to be a hotbed of rumors). Trautmann added his own conjecture that Falkenhayn might well take advantage of the tension with America created by the *Lusitania* case to "realize his dreams" by taking a strong position (in contrast to Bethmann Hollweg's caution) and thereby winning public support. This would be entirely at odds with Falkenhayn's well-documented attitude in the U-boat question in 1915. Particularly during the Russian campaign Falkenhayn showed no inclination to risk a break with America and possibly other neutrals. (Notes by Trautmann, AA WW, 15, secret, Vol. 1 [Kaulmann, in Sch&Gr, Vol. 1, No. 102, is a misreading].) See also Groener, p. 239. It is true, however, that Bethmann Hollweg's suspicions caused him to consider Falkenhayn an aspirant to the chancellorship. In January 1916 General Wild discussed the matter openly with Falkenhayn, who told him that he did not wish to become Chancellor at that time. Wild got the impression, nevertheless, that Falkenhayn did not reject the idea for some future date. (Note dated January 20, 1916, in Wild's papers.) Crown Prince Rupprecht of Bavaria, who was not at all friendly to Falkenhayn, also suspected that Falkenhayn had ambitions to become Chancellor, but not until after the war. (Report by Legation Councilor Krafft to Hertling, February 21, 1916, GSTA, Pol. A, Vol. 7, p. 66.) On Seeckt's attitude see Chapter 3, Part 3, below. Rumors of this kind fed on the fact that Falkenhayn was extremely close-mouthed and almost unapproachable. According to Zwehl, however (p. 217), he firmly but vainly disavowed such ambitions during the summer of 1915.
39. UA IV (Volkmann), 54, from the army archive (since lost by fire). This is in agreement with statements by Count Westarp.
40. Valentini, p. 227.
41. Lerchenfeld to Hertling, March 6, 1915, from a report by Count Wedel, who had talked with Bethmann Hollweg (GSTA, Pol. A, Vol. 7, p. 50). A letter by Bethmann Hollweg to Treutler of March 14, 1915, indicates that Hindenburg's pessimistic statements were prompted in part by his reluctance to contribute divisions for an offensive in the west. He said this might cause the loss of all of East Prussia to the Vistula. (ZA Potsdam, chancellery file, Vol. 2, Section 8, p. 3; see also RAW, Vol. 7, p. 295, for demands for reinforcements in April 1915.)
42. Details in RAW, Vol. 7, pp. 323f. The voluminous correspondence between Falkenhayn and Conrad from December 27, 1914, to May 23, 1915, is printed in H. Wendt, *Der italienische Kriegsschauplatz in europäischen Konflikten* (1936), pp. 409-456. Of great interest are the skillful political negotiations Falkenhayn conducted with the Italian military attaché Bongiovanni on April 13, 1915. Bongiovanni reported on these to Cadorna, see Adriano Alberti, *General Falkenhayn. Die Beziehungen zwischen den Generalstabschefs des Dreibunds* (1924, translated from the Italian), pp. 108f. See also Zwehl, p. 129, and J. Stürgkh, *Im deutschen Grossen Hauptquartier* (1921), p. 117. Late in January, Falkenhayn told Stürgkh about his political aims, lashing out at the inaction of the diplomats. There is considerable exasperation with Falkenhayn in Bethmann Hollweg's letter to Valentini, cited in Note 5, above. Müller, p. 104, says that late in May Falkenhayn contemptuously brushed off Bethmann Hollweg's military proposals.
43. Falkenhayn, p. 55.
44. Mühlmann, pp. 86ff.

45. Conrad, Vol. 5, pp. 754ff, 811ff.; RAW, Vol. 6, pp. 370, 416. The reference last given describes Conrad's completely groundless perturbation–he was ignorant of the fact that the Vienna government had approved Andersen's peace feeler and suspected a sellout. Compare this with Fischer's account, p. 226. Sight unseen, Fischer supports Conrad and insists that Conrad had "quite correctly grasped Bethmann Hollweg's and Jagow's secret aims"! Actually there was no question of "Austrian counteraction." Count Stürgkh, the Austrian liaison officer, in his memoirs, p. 116, sharply criticizes Conrad. For the events of September 1914, and for the following, see my study, "Die Zusammenarbeit der Generalstäbe Deutschlands und Österreichs vor dem Ersten Weltkrieg," in the *Festschrift* for Herzfeld (1958), pp. 546ff., from documents in the Vienna archives. In a letter of October 20, 1914, to the chief of the imperial Austrian military chancellery, Baron Bolfras, Conrad severely criticized German operations in Poland (copy in the Vienna war archive [Conrad file]). He called the German desire to place the first Austrian army under Hindenburg a piece of "typically Prussian arrogance and tactlessness." On the ill-starred Austrian offensive in Serbia in the fall and winter of 1914, see RAW, Vol. 9, pp. 140f., 144ff.

46. According to a report by the Bavarian envoy in Stuttgart to Hertling of January 13, 1915, Baron Wolf von Plessen, for example, heard this from an "authoritative personage" in the Austrian foreign ministry (GSTA, Pol. A, Vol. 7, No. 30).

47. Crucial proof in HHSTA, secret war files, Vol. 47, 2b, 1914-1918, fasc. 1-17, which builds up into a dramatic picture.

48. Conrad, Vol. 4, pp. 476, 518ff., 537, discusses the controversy over the withdrawal of troop units from Serbia and over the fortification of the Italian border, in August-September 1914. On pp. 671ff. he deals with a quarrel about a foreign ministry liaison office at headquarters.

49. This did not always lead to tension. There was a regular and sometimes very extensive mutual exchange of information between the Austrian high command and the foreign ministry, as shown in the HHSTA, war series, Vol. 12 (information and instructions for the foreign ministry representative at headquarters).

50. Tisza to Berchtold, December 15, 1914; Tisza to the Austrian high command, January 18, 1915; the foreign minister to Conrad, January 12, 1915; the latter's tortured reply, with a sharp political attack, January 14, 1915–all in HHSTA, secret war files, Vol. 47, 2b 7 and 9.

51. Berchtold to Bethmann Hollweg, November 10, 1914; reply by Bethmann Hollweg and Jagow, November 23, Sch&Gr, Vol. 1, Nos. 9 and 15.

52. Memorandum by Baron Andrian, December 1914; comment by Ambassador Mérey, December 15, 1914; private letter by Ambassador Pallavincini to Count Forgách from Istanbul, December 16, 1914–all in HHSTA, secret war files, Vol. 47, 1c (memoranda). This repository also contains the memorandum by Count Forgách of January 10, 1915, discussed in the following.

53. Correspondence of the Württemberg envoys Moser (Munich) and Varnbüler (Berlin) with Weizsäcker, September 17, 1914, to June 12, 1915, in HSTA; correspondence of the Bavarian envoys Count Lerchenfeld (Berlin), Count Podewils (special mission to Vienna), and Moy (Stuttgart) with Count Hertling and State Councilor Dandl, January 9 to May 26, 1915, in GSTA, Pol. A, Vol. 7.

54. The evidence, from German and Austrian documents, is given by Zechlin, "Das schlesische Angebot und die italienische Kriegsgefahr 1915," in *Geschichte in Wissenschaft und Unterricht*, Vol. 14 (1963), pp. 533-556. Bethmann Hollweg hinted to Weizsäcker of his intention to facilitate Austrian surrender of South Tyrol by means of a small Prussian territorial concession, as the Bavarian envoy Moy wrote to Hertling on March 15. On the same day Lerchenfeld reported that no thought was being given at all in Berlin to offering the Austrians Berchtesgaden in return for South Tyrol, as was being rumored in Munich. Only Prussian territory was being considered by way of compensation. That deal was indeed being considered, with various parts of Silesia under discussion; but the decision

to do so would only be a last resort, and in view of the promise involving Sosnowiec and the beginning of negotiations between Vienna and Rome, the matter had been settled. (GSTA, Pol. A, Vol. 7, Nos. 30 and 50.) Conrad made a corresponding proposal as late as May 6, 1915. If Austria had to make any sacrifices at all, he said, let Germany indemnify it, for example, by turning over the county of Glatz, and Poland to the Vistula. (Letter to Burián, HHSTA, secret war files, Vol. 47, 2$^{bis}$-12).

55. A graphic picture of the intensity of German pressure for concessions and of the zeal with which Falkenhayn supported this pressure is drawn in a series of notes made by Burián on his negotiations with Bethmann Hollweg, Jagow, and Falkenhayn about the Italian and Rumanian questions (HHSTA, secret war files, Vol. 47, 3-16$^{bis}$). Bethmann Hollweg was always calling in Falkenhayn as an expert.

56. Conrad to Burián, April 2, 1915, HHSTA, secret war files, Vol. 47, 2b-11. See also RAW, Vol. 7, p. 340. Conrad also told Falkenhayn of his proposal to make peace with Russia, which Falkenhayn promptly passed on to the Chancellor, while he tried to talk Conrad out of the idea as hopeless. As recently as December 27, Conrad had told Falkenhayn that he regarded negotiations for a separate peace as hopeless (RAW, Vol. 7, p. 2).

57. AA WW, 15, secret, Vol. 1, contains a note by Bethmann Hollweg on his negotiations with Burián, with both chiefs of staff present.

58. German translation: *Die internationalen Beziehungen im Zeitalter des Imperialismus,* Series 2, Vol. 7, II, pp. 604-608 (1935).

59. The best survey is given in Smith (1). The documents, made public by the Bolshevists, appear in German translation in *Die europäischen Mächte und die Türkei während des Weltkrieges. Konstantinopel und die Meerengen,* Vols. 1 and 2 (1930); *Die Aufteilung der asiatischen Türkei* (1932). Smith (pp. 46ff.) also deals with Satzonov's twelve-point program of September 13-14, 1914—essentially on the basis of the Russian documentation (German: *Die internationalen Beziehungen im Zeitalter des Imperialismus,* Series 2, Vol. 6)—as well as the reaction of the Western powers. See also Isvolsky's report to Satzonov of September 13, 1914, In UA IV (Volkmann), Appendix 2, 3-5 (questions of annexation), and Hölzle, pp. 465-522. There was less than complete unity within the Russian cabinet on the future of the Prussian province of Poznan—see Conze, p. 76.

60. Details in Lafeber and Sch&Gr, Vol. 1, *passim.* A review was given by G. Wormser in a lecture before the French Academy: "Les sondages de l'Allemagne en 1915 et 1916 en vue d'une paix Separée avec la France," in *Revue des Travaux de l'Académie des Sciences Morales et Politiques,* Vol. 116, Series 4 (1963), pp. 255ff. On soundings in St. Petersburg, see also Zechlin, *loc. cit.* (Supplements 22-23, May 28, 1963), pp. 3-23. R. Stadelmann, in his important article, "Friedensversuche im ersten Jahr des Weltkriegs," *Historische Zeitschrift,* Vol. 156 (1937), put the beginning of the Andersen mission much too late, since he was at the time still ignorant of the German documents. Hence he erroneously charges German diplomacy with alleged deficiencies (pp. 541f.). Even so, it seems to me that Stadelmann goes too far, in that he overestimates the practical importance of the opposition offered by Witte and the "group of progressive Russian bureaucrats" (which Stadelmann hypothesizes), as he does Russian diplomatic concern about the future of the Straits and the possibility of a Russo-German condominium in Istanbul. Fischer's assertion (p. 277) that the Russians were afraid of sweeping German demands—a fear he seems to find justified—rests on nothing more than a casual remark by the agent Nobel that the Russians were afraid of the German Jews (meaning bankers), whom Bethmann Hollweg would consult in the matter of reparations. On Mme. Vassilchikova's clumsy efforts, almost certainly reflecting Jagow's instructions quite incorrectly, see also O. Becker, *Der Ferne Osten und das Schicksal Europas 1907-1918* (1940), pp. 52ff. Becker believes that an essential element in the czar's decisions was his fear of a

Japanese invasion of Siberia in the event of a separate peace between Germany and Russia; but this ill accords with the numerous efforts of the Japanese envoy Ushida in Stockholm from 1915 to 1917 to establish contact with German and Austrian diplomats in order to bring about a separate peace with the Central Powers or offer to mediate a separate peace with Russia. It is true, however, that in both Vienna and Berlin these efforts were regarded as highly dubious (HHSTA, war files, Vol. 25, p. 1; Sch&Gr, Vol. 1, p. xxxiii [where the documents in point are enumerated]). Jagow suspected that "the Japs tried to use negotiations with us for purposes of exerting pressure on Russia [in their negotiations over China]," *ibidem,* No. 270, note 3. Hölzle discusses Ushida's efforts at length in the *Festschrift* for O. Becker (1954), pp. 266ff. He views them as having held out the promise of a "restratification of the world system of states," the achievement of which was foiled by the hesitancy of German policy. In my view this interpretation is on the rash side.

61. Treaty of October 1-6, 1914, see Smith (1), pp. 23ff. On May 24, 1915, Varnbüler wrote Weizsäcker that Jagow had told him the Rumanians demanded all of Transylvania to the Tisza, a demand the Austrians could not be expected to accept. There was nothing for it but trust in the success of the Galician offensive (HSTA, E 73/61/129 II).

62. The most important of them are mentioned by Zwehl, pp. 144f. In its conclusions, the RAW (Vol. 8, pp. 622f.) cautiously leaves open the question of whether total annihilation of Russian fighting power would have been possible, but regards it as certain that a differently planned operation, advancing east of the Bug and by way of Vilnyus, would have brought greater success, especially in causing a precipitate and costly Russian retreat from Poland. Ludendorff's reserved judgment in his memoirs, written in 1919, probably stems from his strong desire at the time to allow no blemish to fall on the imperial army and its leadership.

63. Falkenhayn, pp. 107, 120ff.; RAW, Vol. 8, pp. 347ff.

64. He expressed this in memorable and dignified terms in a letter to Hindenburg of August 24 (RAW, Vol. 8, p. 350). None could share his grave and total responsibility, he said. He would deem it a crime to subordinate his honest and objective convictions to the views of anyone, no matter how exalted and venerable, "not because I think myself better than many others—I know my inadequacies only too well—but because in my office, which came to me . . . without my doing, there must, in my view, be no compromise on technical matters."

65. Stadelmann, *Historische Zeitschrift,* Vol. 156, p. 524.

66. Ludendorff wrote to Under Secretary Zimmermann on August 28, 1915: "Now is necessarily the time when we must offer something to the Lithuanians if we wish to achieve anything there. We shall not get a separate peace with Russia, nor do we need it, for we are strong. Now that Poland has been taken away from me [by the creation of the independent government general of Warsaw on August 24–GR], I must establish another kingdom for myself in Lithuania and Courland. Only give me political directives. Lithuania awaits a slogan." This is followed by a demand to separate the administration of the district of Lomza from that of Poland immediately, since the Narev border at Ostrolenka-Lomza-Ossowiecz must become German. (AA WW, 20c, secret, Vol. 1 [copy of A. S. 5422].)

67. See H. Meier-Welcker, "Die Deutsche Führung an der Westfront im Frühsommer 1918. Zum Problem der militärischen Lagebeurteilung," in *Die Welt als Geschichte* (1961), pp. 164ff.

68. Letters of July 8, August 5, 10, 18, and 27, and December 7, 1915, in ZA Potsdam, chancellery file, Vol. 7, p. 9.

69. To Valentini, August 22 (Valentini, p. 228); also letter from the chief president in Poznan, July 8, 1915 (ZA Potsdam, Vol. 7, p. 4). Prince Hohenlohe, the Austrian ambassador, sent home extremely vindictive reports about Falkenhayn, whom he described as an ambitious climber and jealous rival of Hindenburg. He com-

plained to the foreign ministry when he was invested with the order of the black eagle after the breakthrough at Tarnow-Gorlice, on the ground that the idea came from Conrad (HHSTA, war files, IVe [Germany, general]).

70. Fischer seems to suggest this to the reader (p. 232). The exchange of letters (both dated June 3) is found in Sch&Gr, Vol. 1, Nos. 96-97; see also RAW, Vol. 8, p. 604.

71. The offer was made by Mankiewitz late in July, according to the Russian envoy in Stockholm, Nekludov, in *Die europäischen Mächte und die Türkei. Konstantinopel und die Meerengen*, Vol. 4, pp. 333-337. Oddly enough, there is nothing in the political files of the foreign ministry about the much-discussed Mankiewitz mission. On preparations for it (agreements with Turkey, etc.), see Fischer, pp. 232, 234; Bethmann Hollweg, in *Preussische Jahrbücher*, Vol. 178, pp. 115ff., 178; and Lafeber, pp. 108f.

72. From a "reliable" but unidentified source that cannot be established from the material available so far. (The Chancellor to Falkenhayn, AA WW, 2, secret, Vol. 8 [final text].)

73. AA WW, 15, secret, Vol. 1 (June 14); Sch&Gr, No. 104; occasioned by the notes of eastern expert Trautmann (No. 102), already cited in Note 38, above. Trautmann's informants had told him about a report worked out within the General Staff on the basis of Schiemann's writings, according to which not only Courland was to become German, but Livonia with Riga as well. The only likely source of this memorandum was eastern headquarters. Trautmann on his part regarded a separate peace with Russia as out of the question, even should the Germans meet with still greater success. He also regarded a revolution in Russia during the war as impossible.

74. Bethmann Hollweg expressly attacked the published views of Th. Schiemann, a Baltic German, whom he blamed for the whole dangerous movement. Fischer manages to interpret even this document as evidence of Bethmann Hollweg's "reaching for world power" (p. 233). He cites only one sentence of little material importance, intended purely for the general, in which Bethmann Hollweg suggests that a basically anti-Russian policy of dominating the Baltic Sea was conceivable only if Finland and Sweden went along. Bethmann Hollweg's stand on the Baltic question, by the way, changed rapidly – see the next chapter.

75. Fischer, p. 225; Immanuel Geiss, *Der polnische Grenzstreifen 1914-1918* (1960), p. 73. Fischer suggests that the impetus came from Bethmann Hollweg, which seems doubtful to me. He might merely have asked Hindenburg to specify his desires more precisely with the help of maps.

76. Sch&Gr, No. 121. It is part and parcel of Fischer's approach to suggest that consultations on eastern questions by experts of the various ministries represented the Chancellor's ultimate intentions and war aims. He treats in the same way opinions from experts like the administrative chief of Schwerin and the agrarian politician Sering. Thus he accepts that the border strip was to be more than twice as large as Alsace-Lorraine, not including the region of Courland-Lithuania (conclusions of a meeting of July 13, p. 235, after Geiss, pp. 91ff.; see also the critique by H. Günther in *Aussenpolitik*, Vol. 12 [1961], p. 602; and Zechlin, *loc. cit.*, Supplement 22 [1963], pp. 16-21). The Baden Reichstag deputy Nieser reported on August 7 that Hindenburg had drafted a program of border security that amounted to the annexation of an area as large as Silesia (GLA; HSTA, Vol. 4, p. 35).

77. As is done by Fischer (p. 236). The quoted and paraphrased passages seem to me to show plainly that Bethmann Hollweg had as little confidence in total victory over Russia as did Falkenhayn.

78. Bethmann Hollweg to Falkenhayn, August 4 (two letters), Sch&Gr, Nos. 121-123. On July 22 Falkenhayn had forwarded a letter from Conrad that said that the proper moment for concluding a separate peace must not be missed (*ibidem,* No. 117; see also RAW, Vol. 8, p. 608). Bethmann Hollweg's reply to Falkenhayn is

also given in Sch&Gr, No. 119. It is couched in meticulously polite terms and concludes with a request for an opinion on the part of the military. Falkenhayn's reply of August 4 (with his resignation) is No. 122; Bethmann Hollweg's letter to the envoy Lucius, July 31, No. 120.

79. Hohenlohe to Burián, July 11 and 22, and August 9, 1915 (HHSTA, war files, IVa [Germany—general correspondence about German annexationism]). *Ibidem* (and Sch&Gr, No. 105) Bethmann Hollweg's notes of a talk with Tisza on June 18, 1915.

80. See the report by Nekludov of July 31, cited in Note 71, above (No. 337); also Andersen's reports of August 5 (through Count Brockdorff-Rantzau, Copenhagen) and August 9 (note by Ballin), in Sch&Gr, Vol. 1, Nos. 124, 127; also Bethmann Hollweg, Vol. 2, pp. 99ff.

81. Schwabe, Chapter 1, p. 4. Prince Hohenlohe's report of July 11, cited in Note 79, above, especially emphasized (possibly somewhat excessively) the role of Prince Hatzfeld in anti-annexationist circles, stating that he was seeking support from Hindenburg, not without success. In reply to a letter from Hatzfeld emphasizing the purely defensive character of the war, the field marshal had written that he entirely shared these sentiments. This agrees with the general attitude of eastern headquarters toward Bethmann Hollweg at the time.

82. He did, however, drop cautious hints late in May, of his hopes that the Russians might be ready for peace, in talks with social democratic deputies in which he also unequivocally expressed his own basic willingness to make peace. (Scheidemann [1], Vol. 1, pp. 346ff.) Scheidemann's book gives a graphic account of Bethmann Hollweg's awkward dilemma between right and left and clearly documents his endeavors to maintain liaison with the leaders of the parties of the left.

83. See Chapter 1, Note 59.

84. Correspondence between Hertling, Lerchenfeld, Bethmann Hollweg, and Legation Councilor von Schoen, March 21 to June 24, 1915, also notes by Lerchenfeld on the federal council committee session of April 7, 1915, all in GSTA. See also Deuerlein, p. 279. Louis III of Bavaria would have nothing to do with Hertling's proposals for a separate peace with Russia. Hertling on his part was horrified at the skepticism he encountered on the part of Stumm in the foreign ministry concerning such a separate peace. See Janssen (1), pp. 44ff.

85. Details in Zechlin, supplement No. 22 (1963) to *Das Parlament,* pp. 27ff.

86. Details in Chapter 5.

87. Fischer characterizes this speech as a "song of hate" against Britain (pp. 238f.). This completely ignores the political necessity for Bethmann Hollweg, amid the controversy of the U-boat campaign, to defend himself against the charge of being pro-British. Bethmann Hollweg naturally discussed his "war aims" at greater length and in a more positive vein than in his Reichstag speech in talks with the leaders of the right on May 13, in which he sought to persuade them to moderate their polemics (Fischer, pp. 229ff.); but this tells nothing of his ultimate intentions, nor of his estimate of the over-all situation.

88. See his highly skeptical response to a report on the seizure of the Belgian rail system, submitted to him by Groener on March 13, 1915, for transmission to the Chancellor (Groener, p. 277). In the spring of 1916, however, under pressure from the navy and its U-boat command, he did voice support for German domination of Belgium (letter to Bethmann Hollweg of February 13, 1916, Sch&Gr, Vol. 1, No. 199). He was nevertheless as certain in 1916 as he had been in 1915 that Germany's clinging to Belgium would make reconciliation with Britain impossible—but he hoped that the German U-boats would bring down Britain in 1916 (see Chapter 5, Part 3).

*Notes to Chapter 3*

1. RAW, Vol. 9, pp. 4, 20, and *passim.*

2. BA, Wild's papers, No. 2, note of November 1, 1915. Wild was strongly impressed with the personality of Bethmann Hollweg, whom he had met three times in Charleville. He said that Bethmann Hollweg listened attentively and was eager to be buoyed up by the optimism of the generals. His arguments were always stimulating and imaginative, but unfortunately he was too "thick-blooded."

3. A lucid and precise account is given by Mühlmann, based mainly on documents in the former army archives in Potsdam, lost by fire in 1945.

4. Mühlmann, pp. 101ff. The self-assured language of Falkenhayn's counter-reports in his correspondence with Bethmann Hollweg is noteworthy. For the exchange between Tschirschky and Jagow on a separate peace with Serbia, May 18 to 30, see Sch&Gr, Vol. 1, Nos. 84, 86, 87, 90, 91; RAW, Vol. 9, p. 152. Jagow's plan was based on Serbian resentment of Italy, which had been promised the entire Dalmatian coast in the London treaty of April.

5. AA Germany, 122, No. 16, secret (personnel file on Bethmann Hollweg). On efforts for a separate peace with Serbia, see Sch&Gr, Vol. 1, Nos. 142ff.

6. AA Germany, 128, No. 8, secret, and Greece, 61. I owe my knowledge of this correspondence to my assistant Gerd Lauruschkat, candidate for the doctor's degree in philosophy, who is preparing a study on German policy in Greece during the First World War.

7. Sch&Gr, Vol. 1, 143 and 149bis. The following is also based on documents in Sch&Gr (enumeration of items on pp. lviiiff.). The Austrian counterparts to this correspondence are in the HHSTA, war files, 25g. *Ibidem,* sub XLVII secret 3bis-10, very complete notes by Burián about his discussion with Bethmann Hollweg on November 10-11. Jagow was greatly taken aback by Burián's notion (soon dropped) of elevating King Nikita to be overlord of Serbia. The Baden deputy Nieser provided his government from January to April 1916 with rather precise reports on the Balkan negotiations with Austria and the Austro-Bulgarian quarrel, from sources within the foreign ministry (GLA, Berlin legation, fasc. 36).

8. There is much evidence of this, especially in Bethmann Hollweg's correspondence— for example, a letter to Hertling of July 2, 1915: "It's impossible to transact political business with Burián" (GSTA, Pol. A, Vol. 7, p. 53).

9. Burián at once interpreted the tentative agreement of the German foreign ministry as meaning that Germany had recommended him to let all of Serbia disappear from the map! (Directive from Burián to Hohenlohe, January 24, 1916 [see below], and Sch&Gr, Vol. 1, p. 261.)

10. Reports by Hohenlohe on talks with Bethmann Hollweg on January 20, 22, and 25, 1916; directives from Burián to Hohenlohe of January 21 and 24, 1916 (HHSTA, war files, 25k). *Ibidem,* report by Count Thurn from Pless, of January 27, which suggests that even the Kaiser was prevailed on to exert his influence on Austrian policy in Bethmann Hollweg's sense.

11. Bethmann Hollweg received with consternation a Havas dispatch that Nikita had broken off negotiations on January 18. He was at first unwilling to believe that Austrian diplomacy could have been clumsy enough to fail to build golden bridges for the enemy. (Lerchenfeld to Hertling, January 20, GSTA, Pol. A, Vol. 7, p. 50.)

12. To Ambassador Prince Hohenlohe, November 2, 1915 (HHSTA, war files, 25g).

13. Conrad to Burián, November 5, 26, and 28, December 17, 18, 21, 26, and 31, January 2, 24, 25, and 31 (some of these are undated and the date has been inferred); Burián to Conrad, December 25, 26, and 28, January 30—all in HHSTA, secret war files, XLVII, 2b 14-15.

14. Burián to Count Thurn, diplomatic representative with the Austrian high command, for Baron Conrad, January 30, 1916 (HHSTA, *loc. cit.,* fasc. 15).

15. Tisza to Burián, December 30, 1915, *loc cit.,* fasc. 14.

16. Conrad to Burián, December 31, 1915, *ibidem;* see also Conrad to Tisza, January 4, 1916, appendix to the minutes of the cabinet meeting of January 7 (HHSTA, political archives, XXXX, 292, session 526).

17. Falkenhayn, pp. 160ff. This account does not make clear how long Falkenhayn clung to the idea of an attack on Salonica.

*Notes to Chapter 4*

1. Helfferich, Vol. 2 (1919), p. 291.
2. Correspondence, Lerchenfeld-Hertling, October 27 and 31, November 2 and 3, 1915 (GSTA, Pol. A, Vol. 7, p. 50). Lerchenfeld had to be rather less than forthright to Hertling about his own definite agreement with Wedel's views. On November 2 he reported that the Kaiser, following a visit to Brussels, had once again "conceived a hankering for Belgium," and that even Hindenburg, who had always been opposed to annexations in the west and for prompt peace even without territorial gains—a view he had also expressed in writing—now "wanted to take as much as possible." On Falkenhayn's stand in the Belgian question, see Treutler's report of November 2, 1915, in Sch&Gr, No. 159. According to this document, Falkenhayn told the Kaiser that a line from Ostende to Metz (reconnoitered by the General Staff as suitable) was essential as a deployment line in future wars, though he did not actually commit himself. The end of the war had to be awaited, he said.
3. Prince Hohenlohe had proposed this to him as early as October 20, finding him not averse to it (Hohenlohe to Burián, October 21, 1915, HHSTA, secret, Vol. 47, pp. 3-10). But when Hohenlohe urged this course again on November 24, Bethmann Hollweg voiced doubts, since it might be interpreted as a sign of weakness *(ibidem)*. He had discussed the question of opening peace negotiations with Germany's enemies on August 7 with Admiral von Müller, remarking that the time for such an endeavor would have come as soon as the great attack on the Dardanelles was beaten back (Müller, pp. 121f.).
4. BA, Wild's papers, No. 2.
5. Falkenhayn (via Legation Secretary von Luckwald) to Bethmann Hollweg, November 29; Bethmann Hollweg's reply, November 30 (ZA Potsdam, chancellery file, II, supreme headquarters 21, Vol. 1—see also RAW, Vol. 10, p. 1). I cannot understand how Fischer (p. 258) reads a "monolithic German will for victory" into Bethmann Hollweg's letter. In a session of the federal council's foreign affairs committee on November 30, Bethmann Hollweg rejected the idea of a peace offer by the Central Powers at that juncture—i.e., during the Serbian campaign—since it would be interpreted as a sign of weakness (report by Varnbüler, HSTA, foreign ministry, IV, 3, B.A.V., 16; also a report by Nieser, GLA, Berlin legation, 35). Both reports suggest that Bethmann Hollweg was still quite uncertain of how the war would end and therefore refused to commit himself to any clear-cut "war aims."
6. Scheidemann (2), pp. 30ff. Internal and external party difficulties are graphically described in Scheidemann (1), Vol. 1, pp. 334ff.
7. Fischer, p. 259.
8. Falkenhayn to Bethmann Hollweg, November 4, reply, November 12; Bethmann Hollweg to Wild, November 29, reply, December 6 (ZA Potsdam, chancellery file, Vol. 7, p. 6; also BA, Wild's papers, No. 2). Falkenhayn asked Bethmann Hollweg to talk to the party leaders in an effort to prevent discussion of the food crisis on the floor of the Reichstag. Bethmann Hollweg said he did not need such an admonition. Wild had declared that Germany's manpower resources would not be exhausted until the fall of 1916. Falkenhayn retorted that they would last another three years, as would raw material and food resources. Questioned about these discrepancies, Wild said that for the time being it was impossible to give anything more than subjective estimates. For Falkenhayn's views on the war of attrition, see Sch&Gr, Vol. 1, p. 164 (August 30, 1915).
9. Müller, p. 144.
10. A very precise account is given in the excellent book by the American, Meyer,

Chapters 7ff. This book was still written without benefit of the German diplomatic documents.

11. According to Theodor Heuss, *Friedrich Naumann* (2nd ed., 1949), p. 336, 137,000 copies had been sold by 1917.

12. Sch&Gr, Vol. 1, Nos. 134, 135, 137, 139, 141, 147 (correspondence between Bethmann Hollweg and Falkenhayn from August 30 to October 13). See also BA, Wild's papers, No. 2; further documents in Sweet (1).

13. General Wild (papers, *loc. cit.*) surmised that it was Falkenhayn's brother Arthur, a privy councilor in the Prussian ministry of the interior, whom Riezler also met in November 1914 and found to be a particularly active exponent of the *Mitteleuropa* idea, together with Privy Councilor Reichenberg. From a file note signed "B," the foreign ministry suspected that the man behind it all was the diplomatic agent Ludwig Roselius who, on November 6, 1914, had tried to interest the king of Rumania in a great anti-Russian league of states (AA Germany, 180, secret, Vol. 1).

14. BA, Wild's papers.

15. Delbrück's papers, December 29, 1915.

16. Wild's papers, *loc. cit.* Wild says even Bethmann Hollweg acknowledged that the plan was imaginative. For Wild's own less glamorous proposals, see Sch&Gr, Vol. 1, No. 147, October 13, 1915.

17. Seeckt, pp. 258ff., letter of October 29; also discussion with Falkenhayn, on October 26, *ibidem,* p. 249.

18. Szögényi to Berchtold, August 11, 1914 (occasioned by a telephone call of Count Hoyos of August 10): Jagow was unwilling to issue a proclamation to the Polish people without first consulting Vienna. So far only copies of a military proclamation had been dropped from airships (HHSTA, secret, Vol. 47, p. 11). This repository also contains the documents cited in the following, which (in addition to other sources) are cited in Conze, pp. 5ff., who used copies made by W. Steglich for me.

19. Details in Conze, pp. 51ff.

20. The proclamation of August 16, by Grand Duke Nicholas rather than the czar, did promise reunification, but in addition only freedom of speech and religion rather than complete independence.

21. Telephoned instruction to Szögényi, August 18, *loc. cit.;* see also Berchtold to Conrad, August 18, in Conrad, Vol. 4, p. 480.

22. It is noteworthy that when Tisza had been asked about his war aims, in his talk with Bethmann Hollweg on June 18, 1915, he had said nothing about the acquisition of Poland but only that the coal mines of Sosnowiec would be most welcome, possibly in exchange for East Galician or Ruthenian regions (Sch&Gr, Vol. 1, No. 105).

23. With the directive to Hohenlohe of August 21 came the draft of a proclamation that said that the newly created kingdom of Poland was to be inseparably integrated with the states of the Hapsburg monarchy and administered autonomously and with national freedom, having due regard for the highest interests and needs of the monarchy. Hohenlohe shrewdly held this back, with Berchtold's subsequent approval.

24. Count Hoyos to Hohenlohe, August 28. Here is early mention of the suggestion repeated often later on, to the effect that Germany should create a buffer state east of East Prussia. The letter breathes concern about a quarrel with Germany over Poland and expresses willingness to be content at worst with German annexations in the coal region, which would have to be divided, however.

25. In a directive to Hohenlohe of October 13, 1914, there is a complaint that German troops were fostering national revolutionary movements in Congress Poland (presumably the one led by Pilsudski), without any control by the national committee in Cracow. Berchtold wrote Conrad privately on October 14, asking that these activities be curbed by dispatching a military governor to Russian Poland. (Both documents in HHSTA, *loc. cit.*)

26. Burián to Count Thurn, July 17, 1915, for the Austrian high command (HHSTA, war files, 11a). He said that all he knew so far was that Germany did not desire to incorporate any Polish territory, except for border rectifications, but that he would ask for binding declarations. (Correspondence Bethmann Hollweg–Falkenhayn, August 4, 1915, Sch&Gr, Vol. 1, Nos. 121-123.)

27. Chapter 2, above, Note 76.

28. Directive by Jagow to Treutler, July 19, with reply of July 23, in Zwehl, p. 168.

29. Sch&Gr, Vol. 1, No. 140, appendix.

30. Fischer, of course, views them exclusively in terms of German imperialism, bent on conquest. He insists that Jagow would not have returned Poland to Russia even in the event of a separate peace, but there is no hint of this in Jagnow's memorandum of September. Bethmann Hollweg and Burián, on the other hand, did agree to forego Poland if there were the possibility of a separate peace. This was during the extended conference on November 10 and 11 (Sch&Gr, Vol. 1, p. 220).

31. The Russian "nightmare" played at least as important a part in the thinking of Bethmann Hollweg and his immediate entourage–as early as July 1914, as shown by Riezler's papers–as it did within the General Staff. Riezler was beyond question deeply involved in Bethmann Hollweg's Polish policy in 1915–see Conze, p. 141; Bülow, *Denkwürdigkeiten,* Vol. 3, p. 249.

32. For example, Bülow, *Denkwürdigkeiten,* Vol. 3, p. 249.

33. Waldersee, *Denkwürdigkeiten,* Vol. 1, pp. 223, 230, 301, 303, 410, 412, Vol. 2, pp. 14, 81. Stadelmann, *Moltke und der Staat* (1950), pp. 330ff. On October 27, 1883, Bismarck told Chlodwig Hohenlohe that in a war in support of Austria against Russia, Germany would have to go all the way to the Dvina and Dnieper to restore Poland, though it would leave the re-creation of that country to Austria, which would proclaim an archduke king of Poland–if it had one to spare. This was no more than a semiserious notion. Bismarck evidently thought that such a necessity would bode no good and anticipated that a new Poland would soon be carved up again among its three neighbors (Hohenlohe, *Denkwürdigkeiten,* Vol. 2, p. 343). Waldersee was certain, however, that his Polish restoration plans met with Bismarck's approval.

34. Sch&Gr, p. 172 (to Bethmann Hollweg, September 8, 1915). This passage unequivocally refutes Falkenhayn's account in his memoirs, p. 233, in which he seeks to appear as a convinced opponent of Bethmann Hollweg's Polish policy–this was evidently overlooked by Conze, p. 139. The belief in Polish auxiliaries was, of course, shared also by Conrad, who even expected they would provide "a strong army of excellent soldiers" (minutes of the joint cabinet meeting of January 7, 1916, HHSTA, P.A. XXXX, 292).

35. Sch&Gr, Vol. 1, No. 141.

36. Details in Conze, pp. 85ff.

37. Notes by Bethmann Hollweg of August 13, in Sch&Gr, Vol. 1, No. 131. Notes by Burián of August 14, HHSTA, A. XLVII, secret, 3-9. Conze (pp. 80f.) knows only the latter source and therefore thinks that Bethmann Hollweg was more yielding than he was, in fact. It was not softness that then marked the Chancellor, but the conviction (discussed further on) that the Austro-Polish solution might after all be the lesser evil. Burián's visit had been preceded by discussion by Hohenlohe with the Chancellor and the minister, in which the ambassador, turned annexationist because of the latest campaign successes, opposed any thought of a separate peace with Russia, recommending instead a rapprochement with Britain and Polish union with Austria in a kind of ternary system, Poland occupying a position analogous to that of Hungary. He thought that Berlin might become reconciled to such a solution rather than to Polish incorporation into the far half of an Austrian empire divided by the Leitha. (Hohenlohe to Burián, August 9, 1915, HHSTA, war files, 4a.) Burián's own rather prolix account in his memoirs, *Drei Jahre meiner Amtsführung im Kriege* (1923), pp. 60ff., has all the earmarks of an apologia.

38. He had himself said very much the same thing in a directive to Lucius of July 31–Sch&Gr, Vol. 1, No. 120.
39. To Falkenhayn, Sch&Gr, Vol. 1, No. 140.
40. This is all the stranger since Jagow was invoking reasons of "nationalist sentiment," which Bethmann Hollweg had so sharply rebuffed on June 14. Jagow, however, also put forward a military argument: an autonomous Baltic duchy would offer Germany protection against the danger of an "eastern encirclement" (i.e., encirclement by an Austrian Poland). Fischer (pp. 245f.) manages to blur the manifest distinction between the views of Jagow and Bethmann Hollweg, which still existed on November 10-11 (see Note 48, below).
41. Details in Sweet (1), pp. 184ff., after the foreign ministry files, which include a copy with an accompanying letter from Friedjung, addressed to the Chancellor. According to AA Germany, 180, secret, the memorial was forwarded to Treutler for submission to the Kaiser, together with a copy of a letter to Falkenhayn of September 11 (see Sch&Gr, Vol. 1, No. 140).
42. Tschirschky to Jagow, October 29, Sch&Gr, Vol. 1, No. 150. For Jagow's note of October 25, see Fischer, pp. 248f. Tschirschky bore down heavily on maintaining the dominance of the German element in Austria and urgently warned against integrating Poland with Austria as a third state, since that would rapidly lead to the political emancipation of Poland from Vienna, running counter to German and German-Austrian interest.
43. September 16, 1915, Sch&Gr, No. 141. The draft (AA Germany, 180, secret, Vol. 1) is in Jagow's hand.
44. October 13, Sch&Gr, Vol. 1, No. 147.
45. In a letter of October 30 (not included in Sch&Gr) to the Chancellor, he said that an Austro-Polish solution would be acceptable in a military sense only if all the "verbally discussed" guarantees were put into effect. In another letter of November 4, he went further and asked for German control of those portions of Poland that would be left to Austria, if only because of the danger of subversive activities by Russia (AA WW, 20c, secret, Vol. 1a–see also Treutler to Bethmann Hollweg, November 7, in Sweet [1], p. 196). Judging from this, Falkenhayn was already foreseeing a struggle with Austria for dominance. General Wild held that the Polish problem was "basically insoluble"–the Germans had no use for Poland, but neither could they return it to Russia (note of November 1, 1915, in Wild's papers).
46. Minutes in HHSTA, political archives, XXXX/292, No. 524. *Ibidem,* secret, XLVII, 3-10, Stürgkh's draft constitution, with Burián's accompanying letter to Hohenlohe, dispatched on November 10 (several alternate versions). On September 6 (not October 6, as given by Conze, p. 143, following Kries) Conrad had pressed Burián for prompt settlement of the Polish question, along Austro-Polish lines. He professed to have confidential intelligence that the Germans, with a selfishness worthy of emulation," proposed to annex Poland themselves. They must be kept from that, while they were still dependent on Austrian armed aid (HHSTA, war files, 11º).
47. HHSTA, XLVII, secret, 3-10 (draft in Burián's hand, November 14, copy for the emperor). A much briefer note by Jagow of November 14 in Sch&Gr, Vol. 1, No. 167.
48. It is noteworthy that on this occasion too Bethmann Hollweg spoke of Russia's need of ice-free ports, avoided any precise commitment to East Prussian border rectifications while completely rejecting a "fourth partition of Poland," and displayed a perceptible disposition to frugality in his demands. He did say, before the federal council committee on November 30 (according to Nieser's report, GLA), that it would be to Germany's advantage to separate from Russia Poland, part of Lithuania, and Courland, but only if that could be done in such a way as to avoid giving Russia grounds for seeking prompt revenge. It was difficult, he said, to form any concrete ideas about this now.
49. Fischer's account (pp. 252ff.) seeks to create the impression that in essence the talks

failed because of the immoderate demands of the imperialist Bethmann Hollweg. He makes Burián appear quite moderate and ready to negotiate. Among other things, Fischer mentions that the Chancellor put forward demands regarding transport policy that would have made Poland into a German economic sphere. Burián's minutes speak only in general terms of "rail agreements, transport privileges, and agreements on waterways," which Bethmann Hollweg did not specify in detail and to which Burián raised no basic objections.

50. As might be expected, Fischer (p. 256) seizes on the phrase "eastern march of the German-speaking peoples" to characterize Bethmann Hollweg's whole *Mitteleuropa* plan as a kind of blueprint for conquest. The Hapsburg monarchy itself had become a German "war aim."

51. Confidential talks with leading federal council figures on November 13; meeting with the foreign affairs committee on November 30—both after reports by the Bavarian representative Nieser (GLA, HSTA, IV B 5).

52. Sch&Gr, Vol. 1, No. 168. Before the foreign affairs committee of the federal council, Bethmann Hollweg, on November 30, represented this reply as expressing willingness (report by Nieser, *loc. cit.*). Hohenlohe admonished the Chancellor not to consider the Austrian government's worries about the situation of the Germans in Austria when he transmitted the official reply, but he made no impression on Bethmann Hollweg. (Hohenlohe to Burián, November 24, HHSTA, secret, XLVII/3-10.) Late in November, while visiting Vienna, the Kaiser lashed into the Czechs (Sch&Gr, Vol. 1, No. 170), which was not very helpful to the German cause.

53. Details in G. Gratz and R. Schüller, *Die äussere Wirtschaftspolitik Österreich-Ungarns während des Krieges* (1925—part of *The Economic and Social History of the World War*, Carnegie Foundation, available to me only in the English version of 1928). The correspondence between the two foreign ministries on the beginnings of negotiations over a customs alliance (January and April 1916) is in HHSTA, secret, XLVII/3-10. It shows the German government on the offensive, the Austrian government hesitant and evasive. *Ibidem,* the printed record of the economic negotiations of April 20 and 25, April 27 to May 1, and July 20 to 26, 1916.

54. Fischer, p. 251, after H. Delbrück, *Ludendorff's Selbstporträt,* p. 71, cited from the original by Sweet (1).

55. Delbrück's papers, December 29, 1915.

56. Seeckt, pp. 208ff. (December 14, 1915).

57. Sch&Gr, Vol. 1, No. 192; also Zwehl, p. 169.

58. Sch&Gr, Vol. 1, No. 201; Sweet (1), pp. 204f. According to the latter, p. 211, Note 67, Tschirschky also expressed himself, on April 6, as opposed to an Austro-Polish solution.

59. This was shown even in the joint cabinet meeting of January 7, 1916, when the Serbian question was discussed (HHSTA, P.A., XXXX, 292).

60. Burián to Count Thurn (on behalf of Conrad), February 5, 1915, in reply to a report of February 3 (HHSTA, war files, 11⁰).

61. December 25, 1916, Sch&Gr, Vol. 1, No. 204. Bethmann Hollweg replied, via Hohenlohe, on February 29, and again on March 13. Burián to Hohenlohe, March 15, Hohenlohe's reply, March 16 and again April 6 (HHSTA, secret, XLVII/3-12).

62. Conze, p. 146.

63. Directive to Beseler, February 21, 1916, see Conze, p. 146.

64. Preparatory documents: Hohenlohe to Burián, July 6 and April 10, Burián to Hohenlohe, April 8 and 10 (HHSTA, secret, XLVII/3-12). Accompanying the last-named directive was a memorandum, going back to March 16, now printed in Sch&Gr, Vol. 1, No. 223. A German report on the talks (at which Jagow, Zimmermann, Hohenlohe, and the Austrian envoy von Ugron were also present) is contained in a message from Jagow to Treutler of April 16 (Sch&Gr, Vol. 1,

No. 227). On the Austrian side there are several accounts, some of them quite detailed: one by Ugron, in two versions (the second one a résumé); and hand-written notes by Burián of April 18, repeating Ugron's concluding sentences, printed in Werkmann, pp. 146ff. This was intended for the emperor. All three documents are in HHSTA, secret, XLVII/3-12.

65. Bethmann Hollweg to Treutler, April 10, Treutler's reply, April 12, Sch&Gr, Vol. 1, Nos. 221, 224. Falkenhayn had told Treutler on March 21 that his great difficulty in training Finnish volunteers had discouraged him. He was no longer interested in Polish recruits. None of his generals would be eager to command them (Zwehl, p. 171).

66. Such was the concluding passage in Jagow's report on the talks (Sch&Gr, Vol. 1, No. 277). Fischer (p. 295) insists that in this document Jagow described "the creation of an autonomous Poland under German suzerainty, to include Galicia" as a German war aim, but there is not a word of this. On the same page Fischer incorrectly reports Beseler's submission of April 22. Fischer suggests that Beseler simply demanded the inclusion of Galicia in the Polish buffer state. Instead, oddly enough, he hoped to achieve the voluntary surrender of Galicia by Austria, in return for appropriate compensation.

67. In contrast to Schiemann, Hoetzsch favored a peace of moderation with Russia, so that Germany's full attack could be mounted against Britain, and these views were very influential in conservative circles; but even Hoetzsch, in a printed pamphlet in December 1914, *Vorläufige Gedanken zur polnischen Frage*, demanded the annexation of parts of the province of Kovno, the Lomza district, Plock, Kalisz, Grodno, Polish Upper Silesia, and "perhaps" Courland. The Pan-Germans regarded this as a "soft line"—how much softer must Bethmann Hollweg's annexation plans have seemed to them! Even the group of intellectuals around Hans Delbrück, which opposed the manifesto of the annexationist Pan-German professors, left the possibility of broader annexations on the western border of Russian open, voicing only the reservation that annexations should not include "politically autonomous people, nor people used to autonomy." In time Delbrück himself drifted into an eastern annexationist program, though a moderate one. Even Adolf von Harnack, who was opposed to the Baltic plans of his compatriot Schiemann, would have welcomed it if Germany had clung to Courland, his homeland. See Schwabe, Chapter 4; also Gerhard Schmidt, *Die Stellung der deutschen Öffentlichkeit zum deutschen Ostkriegsziel 1914-1916*, unpublished dissertation, Jena (1938), with an excellent store of material.

68. Conze, pp. 151f.

69. This evidently meant going beyond the line of the Memel (Neman) river, which was still envisaged as the border on January 20. I cannot understand how Fischer (p. 295) arrives at a total area to be annexed of 90,000 square kilometers. He adds another Polish border strip of 30,000 square kilometers, but Bethmann Hollweg said nothing about this.

70. On German efforts, then under way, to incite to rebellion non-Russian peoples under Russian rule, see Fischer, pp. 290f.

71. See Chapter 8, below. Before the foreign affairs committee of the federal council Bethmann Hollweg declared on August 8, 1916, that Governor General Beseler, for strategic reasons, was asking for the incorporation of Polish territory to the Narev-Warta line. This area had a population of three million. Bethmann Hollweg admitted that he was at a loss how to react to this demand. The area could scarcely be Germanized, nor could it be allowed to remain Polish, on account of Poznan. In drawing a strategic border, he said, Germany had to limit itself to the minimum. The Suwalki region, lying directly beyond East Prussia, would, of course, have to become German. Apparently Bethmann Hollweg was once again willing to forego the Baltic countries. (Report by Weizsäcker, HSTA Stuttgart, E 49/51, foreign ministry, IV, Register 3, BA V/16.) Note that the federal council was the forum before which Bethmann Hollweg was accustomed to voicing his

ultimate political intentions more openly than anywhere else. On one further occasion, in the Reichstag main committee on November 9, 1916, following a hint from Count Westarp, he set forth his views on the Baltic question without any romantic embellishments. He said that his goal was to have German policy governed by reason rather than emotion. If it were possible, in pursuit of such a policy, to help the Baltic peoples, he would gladly take an interest in their destiny, but he was not in a position to have his policies governed by their interests. The most important consideration for him was that Germany should be served. (For the evidence, see Steglich [2], p. 129.) Steglich regards as a purely tactical maneuver the conflicting statements in Jagow's memorandum of November 21, 1916, on the question of a "solidarity pact," where he said that the ideal goal was to liberate Courland, the scene of the old Teutonic Order (see Sch&Gr, Vol. 1, p. 574). Note that Jagow was not as reserved as Bethmann Hollweg on the Baltic question—see Note 40, above, also Note 7 to Chapter 7, below.

Numerous consultations among Reich agencies took place during 1915 on the Belgian problem, some of them with the Chancellor presiding. The purpose was to arrive at the best method for integrating the Belgian and German economies, possibly going as far as a common currency, a customs union. and German control of Belgian communications. While the goal was German economic dominance Belgium was also to be benefited. Fischer (pp. 321-333) gives a very thorough account of these meetings, authoritatively documented. He creates a total impression of reckless German power striving, of a German desire to exploit Belgium to the utmost as a tributary state. He projects a "consistent" German policy in Belgium by throwing together demands and proposals by the German occupation authorities and Reich agencies with demands from German heavy industry, the German policy in Flanders, various annexationist proposals, demands by the military, and the brutal workers' deportations of the Ludendorff period. Fischer never touches on the one question that is central to any reasoned historical judgment: How much of all this represented serious German war aims, as against mere discussion, consideration, and clarification of technical possibilities, pros and cons? Nor does he come to grips with an even more important question: In view of Germany's over-all situation, what mental reservations did the Chancellor entertain in arranging all these meetings? To what extent did he agree with their proposals and how long did he stick to them? On p. 331 Fischer seems to suggest that Count Törring's negotiations with King Albert during the winter of 1915-1916, on behalf of the German foreign ministry, represented an attempt to "realize the preliminary work" he describes. Part 1 of Chapter 8, below, will show how wrong he is. On p. 332 Fischer roundly states that a draft treaty on Belgian integration, presented by the Reich agencies on February 9, 1916, remained the basis for German treatment of the Belgian question until the end of the war. It seems to me that a thoroughgoing and unprejudiced reexamination of German policy in Belgium is overdue. To deal with Fischer at length would transcend the scope of this book.

*Notes to Chapter 5*

1. All the statistics are from Spindler. For the reservations of the admiralty, see *ibidem*, Vol. 1, Appendices 2-5, text, pp. 37f.; also Tirpitz (1), pp. 286ff.

2. In July 1914, a memorandum from a Senior Lieutenant Blum was presented to Tirpitz. It maintained that effective economic warfare against Britain would require forty-eight blockade stations and 222 submersibles (Spindler, Vol. 1, p. 154).

3. Spindler, Vol. 2, p. 59. The most successful tour of the entire war was made by the U-38 from August 4 to 28, twenty-five days (Spindler, Vol. 2, p. 255). The normal duration was about seventeen days, of which twelve were spent coming and going.

4. Spindler, Vol. 3, pp. 77, 368. See also UA 1, minutes of the sessions of November 6/7, 1919, with particularly important statements by ex-minister Capelle and Reichstag deputy Dr. Struve, an expert. Struve (pp. 390f.) gave somewhat different figures on the total of large U-boats, but agreed that only two or three vessels could be on duty at the same time in the Irish Sea.

5. UA 1, 390. According to the diaries of Hanssen, p. 136, Capelle told the Reichstag budget committee on March 28, 1916, of three stations off the west coast of Britain, for each of which one to five U-boats were available. Hanssen, however, may not have got his figures right.

6. Spindler, Vol. 1, p. 6.

7. Spindler, Vol. 1, p. 83.

8. Opinion by Privy Councilor Kriege, foreign ministry expert on international law, of November 30, 1914 (Spindler, Vol. 1, pp. 42f.). *Ibidem,* p. 44, excerpts from Kriege's comprehensive report for the Reichstag investigating committee, which adopted it on May 30, 1923, printed in toto in UA III, pp. 121-181, with thirty-two exhibits of British and German proclamations of naval blockades and neutral protests. The controversy over the right of blockade and the illegality of the German U-boat campaigns is also treated at length in recent American literature on Wilson's policies. I have drawn on Seymour, an excellent work by the editor of the papers of Colonel House, available in Germany only in the state library, Munich; Smith (2), likewise valuable; Buehrig; Morrissey, highly critical of Wilson's policies; and May, a very objective work, in respect of German war policy as well, though it defends Wilson. Volume 3 of Link's great Wilson biography goes only as far as October 1915. Mr. Link was kind enough to make a Xerox copy of the complete fourth volume available to me. All the volumes have extensive bibliographies, including the major American sources, of which I shall here mention only House; and all seven volumes of FR, including *The Lansing Papers.* Considering the numerous memoirs, especially those by American diplomatists, the available American source material is more abundant than for any of the other countries that opposed Germany in the First World War.

9. Even in the American literature Germany's right to retaliate finds repeated acknowledgment, for example in Smith (2), p. 30. Even the fiercely anti-German Secretary of State Lansing, who was always fond of invoking international law, had doubts in February 1915 as to whether the exigencies of war did not compel the Germans to adopt their blockade policy. He seemed to realize that humane warfare was a practical impossibility (*ibidem,* pp. 43, 50; Buehrig, pp. 131f., partly from unpublished material in Wilson's papers and Lansing's diaries).

10. Spindler, Vol. 1, p. 98.

11. May shows (pp. 21f.) that Britain's allies, Russia and France, pressed as early as October 1914 for an intensified blockade, while Grey was more inclined to heed American protests. The early protests by the neutrals are printed in Spindler, Vol. 1, Appendices 13-15.

12. Report by Helfferich of October 6, 1916, UA 2, Supplement No. 167. It states that imports from January to August 1915 came to 5.248 billion marks (as against 11.638 for the entire year 1913), while from January to August 1914 they came to 4.222 billion, though at higher prices. Helfferich said that these imports consisted in the main of foodstuffs. Details in Helfferich, Vol. 2, 215ff. A. Skalweit's study, *Die deutsche Kriegsernährungswirtschaft* (1927, part of the Carnegie Foundation's German series on the economic and social history of the First World War) scarcely touches on neutral deliveries in 1914-1916 and gives statistics only for 1916-1918. The British government, by the way, occasionally cited in its notes statements by Bismarck and Caprivi, in which the treatment of foodstuffs as contraband was described as justified in certain cases (FR, 1915 Supplement, p. 142).

13. According to Buehrig, pp. 88ff., arms and ammunition accounted for only about 23 per cent of American exports to the Entente countries during the entire course

of the war. It is true, however, that a vigorous American arms industry developed during the very first winter of the war.

14. Even Lansing showed an understanding for this problem, as shown by his attitude in the question of armed merchantmen.

15. Spindler, Vol. 2, p. 184. From early May to late July 1915, ninety-four of 116 merchant ships were sunk by the law of prize and only twenty-two by torpedo, without warning. Of the latter, ten were neutral vessels sunk in error, for which indemnities had to be paid (*ibidem*, Vol. 2, p. 182). According to Vol. 3, p. 118, in March-April 1916, despite an official German navy directive to effect only sinkings without warning, sixty of sixty-eight vessels were still sunk by the cruiser rules, and only eight by torpedo without warning. By the summer and fall of 1916, German naval officers on combat duty, especially in the Flanders squadron, were opposing and even ignoring the obstinate stand of Scheer, head of the fleet, who insisted on unrestricted U-boat warfare or none at all. In the end they prevailed over the admiralty (Spindler, Vol. 3, pp. 242ff.).

16. UA 2, Supplements V, No. 190, report by Holtzendorff of December 22, 1916, p. 240 and *passim*. Note that tonnage sunk might have been increased, if the German government had applied for permission to sink without warning (as it considered doing) only to armed merchantmen, whom even Lansing regarded as illegal.

17. Spindler, Vol. 3, pp. 15, 93; UA 1, pp. 321, 323. Bethmann Hollweg reports what Holtzendorff told him in his *Betrachtungen,* Vol. 2, p. 117. Holtzendorff figured on only three U-boats per station rather than five, put down as standard the unusually long time of twenty-five days for each sortie, and put the number of torpedoes carried at nine rather than six or seven.

18. Tirpitz (1), pp. 492ff., 634ff. The information he gave the Chancellor on March 8, 1916 (pp. 494ff.), is a model of how the naked realities of a situation can be artfully concealed without falsifying the statistics.

19. Spindler, Vol. 1, p. 174, gives as the main reason for the conspicuously slow increase in the U-boat fleet the lack of skilled workers and Tirpitz's initial belief that the war was unlikely to last as long as two years. An added factor was the obstinate insistence on building up the battle fleet, as a result of which repair work often placed a great strain on the naval dockyards. A great deal of experimental work also continued, and standardization of vessels and equipment was adopted only at a late date.

20. Spindler, Vol. 1, Appendix 25, documents the enormous impact of the Wiegand interview in the German press. The statements by the professors are also given there (Appendices 19-24). The leading signer of the Berlin statement was the agrarian economist Sering, the others including Triepel, Wilamowitz, Kahl, Gierke, Schiemann, Harnack, and Schmoller, May (Chapter 6) offers a precise and detailed account of the early history and beginnings of the U-boat campaign, based in part on unpublished documents of the German foreign ministry.

21. A formal opinion by Kriege of January 1 had meanwhile put forward the theory of the retaliatory strike, to which the German government clung until 1918.

22. This is Spindler's interpretation (Vol. 1, p. 85). It is probably correct, for on February 20 Delbrück vigorously denied to Admiral von Müller (Müller, p. 92) what Bethmann Hollweg must have told Treutler (Tirpitz [1], p. 315), namely that Delbrück said the Germans would be able to continue feeding the Belgians unaided and could therefore risk the U-boat campaign.

23. Müller, p. 87.

24. Tirpitz (1), pp. 286ff., 300ff., 307. Tirpitz sharply criticized opening the U-boat campaign with fanfares and threats to the neutrals. He simply wanted to let it develop on its own, without public announcement or special directives to the U-boat commanders. This approach would have made Germany's breach of international law appear in an even more brutal light, for the neutral nations would not even have been warned against entering the newly proclaimed war zone.

25. Pohl said so openly on February 10. He would have welcomed British misuse of neutral flags. (H. von Pohl, *Aus Aufzeichnungen und Briefen* [1920], p. 109).
26. According to a German admiralty report of June 27, 1915, the navy agreed to this phrasing only because it had been assured by the foreign ministry that Britain would not agree to it (Tirpitz [1], p. 368). Evidently there had been talks on this mediation offer with the American ambassador, Gerard, even before February 20, during which the German navy had also discussed possible protective measures for American merchantmen (FR, 1915 Supplement, pp. 100, 116 [reports from Gerard]).
27. Seymour, p. 28, from Hansard, Parliamentary Debates 5, Series LXX, p. 600.
28. Tirpitz (1), pp. 319ff., for the discussion in Bellevue palace on February 28, 1915. For the exchange of notes, see FR, 1915 Supplement, pp. 118, 129, 140. According to Müller (pp. 92f.), there had been a discussion of the American offer (erroneously described as a note of reply by Müller) with the Chancellor on February 24, Müller, Tirpitz, Bachmann, Falkenhayn, Jagow, Delbrück, Wahnschaffe, and Zimmermann participating. It was then that Zimmermann and Falkenhayn had put forward the "senseless" additional demand, subsequently picked up by the admirals. After the meeting, however, Falkenhayn is said to have severely disapproved of Tirpitz's conduct. Even Admiral Capelle, Tirpitz's chief adviser, took Bethmann Hollweg's side against his chief, describing Bethmann Hollweg as the only possible Chancellor at this time, and indeed a good Chancellor. According to May, p. 142, who bases himself in part on unpublished sources, the proposal came originally from the pacifist American Secretary of State Bryan and linked up with the above-mentioned final phrasing of the German note of February 16, which Wilson had welcomed as holding out a ray of hope. Lansing was opposed, because he did not wish to put Britain in a position where rejection would worsen its moral stature. In Britain only Grey showed any inclination at all to consider the offer, but as shown in the British note of reply of March 13, he did not prevail. May (pp. 144f.) nevertheless conveys the impression that Germany rather than Britain was responsible for the rejection.
29. According to May (p. 205), even in the *Frankfurter Zeitung.*
30. One of the more unedifying examples of militarist and anti-British sentiment is an article by Matthias Erzberger, "Nur keine Sentimentalität," that appeared in the *Anklamer Zeitung* on February 18, 1915 (reprinted in Epstein, Appendix 4).
31. "Points to be noted," February 12, see Tirpitz (1), p. 308.
32. The best study of the *Lusitania* case, in my view, is the one by Thomas A. Bailey, "The Sinking of the 'Lusitania,' " in *American Historical Review,* Vol. 41 (October 1934), pp. 54-73. According to Bailey, the *Lusitania* carried more than 5,000 cases of ammunition, though the rifle cartridges in only 4,200 were actually charged with explosive. In terms of cost, about half the cargo consisted of war material. Bailey believes that the German government was probably right in asserting that the explosion of the cartridges was responsible for the incredibly fast sinking of the vessel, though this cannot be proved. It is certain, however, that the shipping company, the captain, and the passengers ignored prior warnings by the Germans or regarded them as mere bluff; that the captain omitted to take the precautionary measures that had been prescribed for his approach to the Irish coast; and that the Royal Navy took no security measures whatever. Sole trust was put in the vastly superior speed of the great liner. May (p. 135) lists further references about the *Lusitania.*
33. Müller, pp. 105f.; Tirpitz (1), pp. 344-350. Müller's notes on the talks in Pless on May 31 depart somewhat from Tirpitz's. According to Müller, Tirpitz, toward whom the Kaiser was not particularly well-disposed, was rather more cautious and ambiguous in his statements to the Kaiser than Tirpitz's own report suggests. Spindler (Vol. 2, p. 101) says erroneously that Bethmann Hollweg was present at Pless on May 31, but from the documents published by Tirpitz this cannot be true.
34. This view prevailed from the outset in the German navy, as shown by the ill-advised

bombardment of the British town of Yarmouth in early November of 1914, without prior notification of the Chancellor. Bethmann Hollweg vigorously forbade any repetition (Tirpitz [1], p. 151).

35. For a review of changing views during the 1920's and 1930's see Smith (2), pp. 166ff.

36. See Bernstorff (1), pp. 28, 60.

37. This is particularly true of the offer made by Ambassador Gerard on September 9, which mentioned making peace with France alone (Sch&Gr, Nos. 6-7. Colonel House's letter to Zimmermann of September 5 (*ibidem*, No. 3) was so devoid of content that Zimmermann had little choice in replying to it (*ibidem*, No. 20), which he did on December 3, saying that Germany would first have to know what the other side thought. Bethmann Hollweg replied to Gerard's offer on September 12 (*ibidem*, No. 7), saying that the German people needed a durable peace and guarantees of security and tranquility. He was probably still full of the victory hopes of the early war weeks.

38. For the diplomatic exchanges, see Sch&Gr, Vol. 1, Nos. 1ff.; also May, pp. 33ff., who cites the American sources; further, Link, pp. 191ff., at great length; House, Vol. 1, pp. 288ff.; Stadelmann, *Historische Zeitschrift*, Vol. 156, pp. 496ff. Fischer's account (pp. 220ff., 357ff.) fails to mention that neither in France nor in Britain was there the slightest readiness for a negotiated peace, so that the German government is put in the light of being the sole obstacle to an understanding. Trevelyan (pp. 394ff.) gives three noteworthy letters of the liberal, Grey, to Ambassador Spring-Rice, of September 3 and 22, 1914, and January 2, 1915. Grey stated as his personal opinion that only two conditions were necessary for peace, restoration and indemnification of Belgium, and a durable peace that would protect the Allies from future attack. What he meant by the latter term, however, is shown in his statements on "Prussian militarism," the victory of which would turn West Europe into an unlovely place and threaten freedom, humanity, and law. Grey wanted to see Germany defeated rather than destroyed, but defeat was to lead to democratization. At this early date he was already mentioning the idea of a league of nations, including America, for securing the peace. Initially Colonel House still rejected this.

39. House, Vol. 1, p. 299 (August 30, 1914).

40. Diary entries, November to December 1914, after May, pp. 77f.

41. Jagow developed and justified rejection of an international conference only in a message to Berchtold of November 23, 1914 (Sch&Gr, Vol. 1, No. 15), in reply to a communication from Berchtold of November 10 (*ibidem*, No. 9). From this it would seem that House submitted to the Austrian ambassador Dumba a concrete three-point peace program: no large-scale territorial cessions, mutual guarantees of territorial integrity among all the powers, disarmament. Vienna received the proposal eagerly but anxiously, but Berlin rejected it, regarding it as unrealistic. Oddly enough, nothing about this effort is found in House's intimate papers and letters.

42. May, p. 78. This work also contains the evidence for the following. See also Grey's memorandum for Asquith of February 24, 1915, in Trevelyan, pp. 397ff.

43. This idea had already been developed in writing by Grey in September 1914, see Note 38, above.

44. House, Vol. 1, p. 381 and *passim*. See also Grey's report to Asquith of February 24, 1915, in Trevelyan, pp. 397ff. Fischer (p. 359) seems to think that Count Bernstorff was the originator of House's great plan, to which Wilson and his advisers reverted after the sinking of the *Lusitania*. Grey's messages to Spring-Rice and Lord Crewe of June 14, 1915 (Trevelyan, pp. 401f.), show how deeply he was at times impressed with House's proposals. He thought of coupling "freedom of the seas" with protection against aggression of any kind from a hostile alliance, but also considered whether it might not be possible to allow food transports to Germany, if that country renounced submarine warfare. He very soon reached a

negative conclusion (memorandum for the cabinet of July 17, 1915, Trevelyan, p. 403).

45. Sch&Gr, Vol. 2, No. 46. See also House, Vol. 1, p. 377.

46. Gerard told House on February 15, 1915: "I am sure if a reasonable peace is prepared *now*–a matter of days, hours–it would be accepted." This urgency is perhaps explained by the fact that through the military attaché Langhorne he had a message from the German General Staff, hinting that leading German generals (possibly Falkenhayn himself) would still prefer it, if there were no need to declare U-boat war, as then impended, but in any event wanted to insure American neutrality. (House, Vol. 1, pp. 382, 396; FR, 1915 Supplement, pp. 9, 15, 17.) Gerard's memoirs (German ed., 1919, pp. 204f.) give only a confusing report and also mention a strangely secretive visit from Tirpitz, who may have wished to sound out the probable American reaction to the impending event. See Stadelmann, *Historische Zeitschrift*, Vol. 156, pp. 507ff., 515–the earlier reference gives a highly critical account of House's European trip. For supplementary information see Lafeber, pp. 174ff.

47. Sch&Gr, Vol. 1, Nos. 63, 68; House, Vol. 1, pp. 404ff. Fischer (p. 358) conveys the impression that the talks with House failed because of the inflexible German stand on the Belgian question. Birnbaum (p. 94) reports, from unpublished papers of Colonel House, that Gerard, on April 18, sent House in Paris German peace terms which House discussed with Delcassé. Delcassé regarded them as bait for a separate peace with France: a war indemnity for France, and the annexation of Liège, Namur, and parts of the Belgian Congo. Without knowing the text of Gerard's message, one cannot judge the ambassador's motivations.

48. Sch&Gr, Vol. 1, No. 107.

49. S. I. B. Moore, cited by Morrissey.

50. FR, 1915 Supplement, pp. 406, 415; Link, Vol. 3, pp. 392ff.–he does not believe that House was really serious in his efforts. Ambassador Page was reluctant even to submit the mediation proposal to Grey, lest the British cabinet be placed in the embarassing position of rejecting it, while the Germans accepted (House, Vol. 1, p. 452). The British cabinet was just then being reconstituted with the accession of conservative members of the House of Commons, which was bound to discourage the liberal Grey's more conciliatory attitude. Possibly connected with these wavering considerations of Wilson's was a rather mysterious dispatch from Count Bernstorff of May 29, received in Berlin on June 26, though advance notice had come on June 1, through a Swedish intermediary. Bernstorff professed to have heard from an unimpeachable source that Wilson, if the *Lusitania* incident were favorably settled, would "try to dissuade Britain from its interference with neutral trade, which was in defiance of international law." If he succeeded, he would bring together all the neutral states of Europe, propose a peace conference to the belligerents, and prevail on the neutrals to cut off from all imports of food, munitions, etc., all the belligerents who refused to attend the conference. Contemplated peace terms were: (1) the status quo in Europe; (2) freedom of the seas, i.e., neutralization of the oceans; (3) settlement of colonial questions. Jagow simply filed this curiously unrealistic proposal unanswered, with a note asking whether Wilson really imagined that Italy, at the start of a war of conquest, would be satisfied with its old borders. Fischer (p. 359) represents the whole proposal as Bernstorff's, though the Swedish transmission expressly stated that he did not wish to be associated with this proposal in any way, indeed did not even wish to be identified as its source! Fischer insists that Jagow rejected the proposal because he would not hear of the status quo, in other words was an annexationist. Fischer, by the way, gives a wrong identification for this document. It is found in AA WW, 2, secret, Vol. 8 (Film D. 956805/6). See also Birnbaum, pp. 29, 343ff. Birnbaum also regards the proposal as Bernstorff's notion, but fails to lend plausibility to this theory.

51. Bernstorff (1), pp. 157ff. Bernstorff apparently exaggerated to a considerable degree

both the danger and the reassuring effect of the efforts he undertook after June 2, entirely on his own (*ibidem,* pp. 148ff.).

52. He had demanded warnings against travel on the vessels of belligerent states, protests against the British blockade policy as well, arbitration in U-boat controversies, and prohibition of the arming of merchant ships.

53. See Lansing, p. 19, for a memorandum of July 11, 1915, outlining his basic policies; also Buehrig, pp. 134ff.

54. See Bernstorff (1), p. 151, for his report of June 2.

55. According to Buehrig, pp. 88f., U. S. foreign trade rose during the war from 3.4 to 9.7 billion dollars, i.e., by 284 per cent (not 184, as Buehrig wrote erroneously). Of the total, 23 per cent was in arms and munitions. On Bernstorff's error, see also Smith (2), p. 90.

56. Spindler, Vol. 2, p. 183.

57. FR, 1915 Supplement, pp. 453f., 457-462, Gerard's reports from June 24 to July 5; see also Tirpitz (1), pp. 375f. I cannot understand why May (p. 213) calls Gerard's proposals "fatuous." In his memoirs (p. 225) Gerard himself represents them as coming from Zimmermann. According to Smith (2), there were men even in Lansing's department who found the German proposal eminently reasonable (Johnson).

58. See Bachmann's notes on the talks of June 22, 1915, in Tirpitz (1), pp. 364ff.

59. *Ibidem,* p. 407.

60. *Ibidem,* pp. 372ff.; Westarp, pp. 107ff.

61. Helfferich, Vol. 2, pp. 319ff.; Tirpitz (1), pp. 385ff. The initial impetus came from a large transaction with American cotton exporters. May (pp. 215f.) believes he has shown that there was a semiofficial press campaign in support of Helfferich's proposals.

62. Pohl, *Aus Aufzeichnungen und Briefen während der Kriegszeit* (1920), pp. 130f. "I should not be at all displeased if U-boat warfare ceased, for then I could set the U-boats more against naval vessels, which would be more productive for me; but things will remain as they are—the U-boat campaign is far too popular. The German people will not do without this type of warfare. Every morning, when they pick up their newspapers, our worthy Germans want to read that once again so-and-so many ships have been sunk" (letter to his wife, June 5, 1915). Pohl's war letters, written aboard his flagship, give moving evidence of the German navy's desolate situation, arising from its enforced idleness.

63. Tirpitz (1), p. 401, falsely speaks of eight victims, including three Americans.

64. The report in Tirpitz (1), pp. 404ff., treats at length only Bethmann Hollweg's preliminary discussion with Tirpitz and Bachmann, dealing only briefly with the *Immediatvorträge,* the verbal briefings given to the Kaiser directly. Spindler, Vol. 2, pp. 274ff., gives further details about the main talks, probably from German admiralty records. A more recent presentation of these events, based on German foreign ministry files, is given in May, pp. 221f., but not all the details are correct.

65. An exchange between Bethmann Hollweg and Hertling on September 9-10, 1915, shows that Tirpitz's followers tried to enlist the king of Bavaria in support of the admiral and against Bethmann Hollweg (GSTA, Pol. A, Vol. 7, p. 591). Tirpitz himself at once tried to enlist the empress on his behalf, in connection with his attempted resignation (Tirpitz [1], pp. 416f.). The new chief of the admiralty staff found himself compelled to secure an imperial rescript, to counteract disaffection among the naval officers (Tirpitz [1], pp. 420, 431). The Kaiser's order of August 30, limiting Tirpitz's authority as naval minister, was softened on September 19 (Tirpitz [1], p. 437).

66. At any rate, Spindler (Vol. 2, p. 282), using the naval files at his disposal, says nothing about it.

67. Lansing, pp. 44ff. During the talks in Pless on August 26 the German admiralty had received a reassuring wire from the naval attaché, which it used successfully against Bethmann Hollweg.

68. This was accomplished only after a serious controversy within the British cabinet, during which the committed liberals (Grey, Runciman, McKenna, John Simon) opposed conscription with such vehemence that at times the coalition cabinet was in danger of flying apart. See Trevelyan, pp. 408ff.; Lloyd George, Vol. 2, Chapter 23.

69. *Mein Anteil am Weltkrieg* (German ed., 1933), 251ff. See also State Councilor Andersen's reports of December 1915 on inflamed war sentiment in Britain, Sch&Gr, Vol. 1, No. 174.

70. Seymour, pp. 138ff.

71. The *Lusitania* affair had been taken up anew and the German military and naval attachés (von Papen and Boy-Ed) sent home, at the request of the State Department, in November-December 1915 (House, Vol. 2, pp. 105ff.; May, p. 350).

72. We have House's own notes and letters about these talks (House, Vol. 2, pp. 140ff.), as well as notes by Bethmann Hollweg and Solf (UA 2, Supplements 193/194, both reprinted in Sch&Gr, Vol. 1, Nos. 195f.). Link (Vol. 4, Chapter 3) reproduces further reports by House to Wilson, from Wilson's papers. They show that House formed a correct estimate of Bethmann Hollweg's imperiled position and warned the president against rendering it untenable by putting forward demands in the *Lusitania* affair that went too far. Wilson understood the situation. Müller (p. 152) gives an account by the Kaiser of Bethmann Hollweg's verbal report to him on the talks with House. Coming at third hand, this account is virtually without value as evidence and suggests at best that Bethmann Hollweg, understandably, represented his stand toward House as being rather sharper than it actually was. Unfortunately Fischer (p. 361) uses only this dubious source, ignoring Bethmann Hollweg's own notes (which were known to him). He concludes that there was a formal British offer of peace, which the Chancellor rejected, in consequence of his war aims program of September 1914. Fischer also fails to mention that House's efforts failed in Paris and London rather than Berlin. His remarks about the so-called Grey-House memorandum of February 22 are without substance. House could have scarcely mentioned this memorandum in Berlin on January 28, for the simple reason that it did not then exist.

73. The disavowal, dated March 23, appears in Sch&Gr, Vol. 1, No. 212. For Gerard's very interesting report on a discussion of March 18, see FR, 1916 Supplement, pp. 207f. The press dispatch which Bethmann Hollweg disavowed actually said that he was ready to return to the status quo.

74. See Sch&Gr, No. 196, House to Bethmann Hollweg.

75. See Lloyd George, Vol. 2, p. 680. House's reports of his negotiations in Paris and London (in his *Intimate Papers*) are self-serving and fail to convey a clear picture. My own account is based, among other sources, on Link (Vol. 4, Chapter 4), who had access not only to the papers of House and Wilson, but to a wealth of unpublished material from French and British archives and from various private papers. A rather remarkable addition to our store of knowledge is Link's showing that House, on his return trip to London, stopped off to visit King Albert of Belgium in La Panne and proposed that the king advise the Germans of his willingness to sell them the Congo colony. House suggested that if Germany got this territory, with Portuguese Angola and a "sphere of interest" in Asia Minor, it would surely be prepared to return Alsace-Lorraine to France and cede certain German colonies in Africa to the Union of South Africa. King Albert's reply was that a treaty concerning the Congo could probably be arranged. It will be seen that the question of Alsace-Lorraine troubled the American mediator, whose estimate of it, however, was quite in error.

76. For example, by Asquith in an extended peace debate in the House of Commons on February 23, 1916. In addition to the full restoration of Belgium, Asquith demanded French security against attack (i.e., Alsace-Lorraine), independence for small nations, and total destruction of Prussian military rule. In the speeches of French ministers the return of Alsace-Lorraine had been demanded ever since November 1914.

77. The so-called Grey-House memorandum of February 22, 1916, appears in Grey's *Twenty-five Years,* Vol. 2, p. 123, and in House, Vol. 2, pp. 200f. See also Lloyd George, Vol. 2, p. 687.
78. Grey, *loc. cit.,* Vol. 2, p. 131; Seymour, p. 159.
79. The best evidence for these remarks is found in Seymour, pp. 149ff.; see also May, Chapter 17.
80. "The American terms were, it is true, not the terms that the Allies would regard as those of victory, but for Germany they were the terms of positive defeat. . . . It seemed to me inconceivable that Prussian militarism could look at such terms, while it was undefeated and hoping for victory" (Grey, *loc. cit.,* Vol. 2, p. 130).
81. Among others, with War Minister Wild von Hohenborn (see Wild's papers in BA); also Falkenhayn's "Christmas memorial" (Falkenhayn, pp. 176-184); further, RAW, Vol. 10, pp. 2ff.
82. Spindler, Vol. 3, p. 70, probably based on Tirpitz (1), p. 500. See also Bethmann Hollweg's memorandum of February 29 (Bethmann Hollweg, Vol. 2, p. 260), and Müller, p. 162.
83. RAW, Vol. 10, pp. 10ff. Ludendorff and his headquarters, always concerned with planning advances only in the east, had no sympathy for these worries. They simply regarded Falkenhayn as an "ignoramus." (Wild's papers in BA, diary entry of December 15, 1915.)
84. His uncertainty of the issue was shown rather clearly in a talk with Admiral von Müller on February 9. He remarked optimistically, however, that the Americans would probably swallow intensified U-boat warfare, since they had already swallowed the *Lusitania* affair without declaring war (Müller, p. 154).
85. Sch&Gr, Vol. 1, No. 199, previously printed in UA 2, Supplement 148, also appears in part in Spindler, Vol. 3, p. 92. Captain Widenmann worked on Falkenhayn at Tirpitz's behest (Tirpitz [1], pp. 473ff.).
86. Tirpitz (1), p. 459.
87. We already know (see above) that by February no more than twelve large diesel-powered U-boats were available, of which only two or three could operate off the coast of Britain at one time. In his memorandum of February 13 (UA 2, Supplement 147), Tirpitz spoke of thirty-eight U-boats, "including the Mediterranean." He said there would be fifty by April and from then on ten additional vessels each month, on the average. Widenmann (Tirpitz [1], p. 476) dreamed up 105 by September and 150 by December. Falkenhayn's uncritical attitude is all the stranger, since even an outsider like Ballin did not allow himself to be deceived about the inadequacy of U-boat strength (Tirpitz [1], p. 461).
88. From AA WW, 18, secret, Supplement 1, Vol. 1, published by Birnbaum, Appendix, II, 5, pp. 345ff.
89. Spindler, Vol. 3, p. 75. Holtzendorff had told the Chancellor that not until March 1 would sufficient U-boats be available.
90. He grew worried about the vague and fluctuating navy figures on available U-boat strength, and he was also impressed by foreign ministry apprehensions of war with the neutral nations. On January 20 he noted in his diary that the German army was buying all of its essential food staples and fat from North European and other neutral nations, at a cost of five million marks a day. How were these sources to be replaced? (Wild's papers, BA.) Yet during the crucial consultations Wild sided with Falkenhayn.
91. A rather detailed account of the press campaign is found in May, pp. 264ff. Bethmann Hollweg's countercampaign and censorship measures are also covered there.
92. Tirpitz (1), p. 484; see also Epstein, pp. 173ff. Epstein apparently failed to note the passage in Westarp (p. 116) where Erzberger (on February 1, 1916) appears as an outright warmonger. The attitude of the mercurial Erzberger was apparently not as consistent as Epstein makes it out to be. Erzberger probably did not find out the facts about U-boat inadequacy until February 1916. A letter from Lerchen-

feld to Hertling of January 26 (GSTA), cited by Epstein (p. 176), also speaks of some fluctuations in Erzberger's attitude. May (p. 271) maintains, without documentation, that Bethmann Hollweg personally was responsible for Erzberger's conversion. There is a remarkable report by Hohenlohe of February 20, 1916, addressed to Burián (HHSTA, Prussia III, 172), on a discussion with Jagow, in which Jagow spoke resentfully of the almost intolerable self-importance of the busybody Erzberger, who without the slightest credentials, had just told Austrian diplomats in Istanbul that he was on an official mission for the foreign ministry, which had vainly sought to dissuade him from this trip. "Unfortunately there is no way of interning Herr Erzberger, which we should otherwise gladly do." Hohenlohe vigorously agreed.

93. This was the way he himself justified his conduct to Lerchenfeld, who was one of his most loyal supporters, but who knew that only about ten U-boats were available for service against Britain and would have preferred it if Bethmann Hollweg had spoken more plainly to the party leaders. (Lerchenfeld to Hertling, February 26, 1916, GSTA.)

94. Hertling, in a message to Lerchenfeld of February 2, 1916, rejected any anti-Bethmann Hollweg intrigue and proposed convening the foreign affairs committee of the federal council in support of the Chancellor. Lerchenfeld, replying on February 5, said he did not quite believe that Falkenhayn wanted to oust Bethmann Hollweg. Lerchenfeld to Hertling, February 22: Even the Mecklenburg envoy had proposed that the Chancellor be supported against his enemies. Lerchenfeld to Hertling, February 26: He had advised Bethmann Hollweg of the federal council's stand against the navy's demand and offered to convene the foreign affairs committee (all in GSTA). See also Epstein, p. 176.

95. Tirpitz (1), pp. 492ff. (March 5, 1916), where we see how artfully Tirpitz managed to hide the true state of affairs. In the foreign ministry his statistics had long been treated with the greatest distrust. (Westarp, p. 117, discussion with Jagow, February 5.)

96. Exchange between Hohenlohe and Burián, February 27-28, March 6, HHSTA, war files, 4c. Further reports of March 15 and 20, *ibidem*, Prussia III, 172. Hohenlohe sharply criticized Tirpitz's political attitude before and after 1914. He said that Bethmann Hollweg, like Bülow before him, had left Tirpitz far too free a hand, instead of opposing him openly. Burián wanted the U-boat campaign put into effect, but passenger liners spared. If Tirpitz were really willing to back Hertling, he must be thoroughly deceived about Hertling's views on the U-boat question. On these rumors, see also May, p. 268, after Victor Naumann and Max Hoffmann.

97. Diary entry of March 9, 1916, in Wild's papers, BA.

98. A characteristic sidelight is an exchange between the two men on April 3-4, 1916 (ZA Potsdam, chancellery file, VII, 6), in which Falkenhayn ungraciously acknowledges a request from the Chancellor for military data for his Reichstag speech.

99. Westarp, p. 124. Müller (p. 115) reports an even more brusque rejection of anti-Bethmann Hollweg intrigues. If he should receive such a bid, Falkenhayn said in July 1915, he would simply throw it in the wastebasket. On the other hand, Falkenhayn would not agree with the Chancellor that the conservative effort in the Prussian diet on February 9 (see above) represented intervention into the privileges of the OHL (Tirpitz [1], p. 477).

100. Westarp, p. 125; Knesebeck, pp. 153ff. (Letter from Ludendorff to Wyneken, January 23, 1916).

101. Lerchenfeld to Hertling, February 5, 1916, with special reference to statements by Seeckt (GSTA).

102. Reproduced in Bethmann Hollweg, Vol. 2, pp. 260-273; UA 2, Supplement 149; Spindler, Vol. 3, pp. 94ff. Presumably Bethmann Hollweg was also impressed with a memorandum by Jagow of January 31 that painted a very gloomy picture

of the break with America, while on the other hand finding much encouragement in the land war situation as a result of the success of the year 1915 (Birnbaum, pp. 347f.).

103. Tirpitz (1), pp. 455f., 460; see also Spindler, Vol. 3, pp. 72ff. Erzberger (p. 213) assures us that Tirpitz told him early in January that the German U-boats would be able to force Britain to its knees within six weeks.

104. Compare, however, the discussion with Holtzendorff on January 8 (Spindler, Vol. 3, p. 75), cited in Note 89, above, and the note of January 10, in Birnbaum, pp. 345ff.

105. According to Müller, p. 158, the sparing of passenger ships was clearly to Bethmann Hollweg's credit, and not due to an independent initiative on the part of Holtzendorff, as Spindler believes (Vol. 3, p. 88).

106. Müller, pp. 146f. (January 10-12, 1916). The Kaiser seems to have been as much impressed by the inhumanity of sinkings without prior warning as he was afraid of war with America, which left him sleepless (*ibidem*, pp. 147, 149, 151).

107. Note that Wilson's second *Lusitania* note of June 9, 1915, had specifically recognized the right of U-boats to sink steamers that offered resistance, i.e., were armed.

108. Details in Bernstorff (1), pp. 210ff. For American policy during these months, see the recent American literature already cited, especially Seymour and May.

109. The main source on the talks of March 4 is a report by Bethmann Hollweg to Jagow of March 5, in Tirpitz (1), pp. 499ff., with further material, *ibidem*. Müller (pp. 160ff.) offers important supplementary information. Note that the failure to invite Tirpitz to this meeting goes back to a direct request by Falkenhayn. Tirpitz may have been Falkenhayn's powerful ally, but Falkenhayn found it difficult to put up with the arrogance and fatuous talk Tirpitz displayed during such consultations.

110. Late in March and early in April the Kaiser renewed his pressure for diplomatic preparations for unrestricted U-boat warfare. See the correspondence between Treutler and Bethmann Hollweg in Birnbaum, pp. 66f.

111. Diary entry of March 9, 1916, in Wild's papers, BA; see also Müller, pp. 1964ff.

112. Deuerlein, pp. 191-195, 284-287; Janssen (1), pp. 46f.; report by Lerchenfeld of March 15, GSTA. May (pp. 268f.) wrongly believes that the immediate danger to the Chancellor threatened from the side of the federal council committee—his was basing himself on Naumann's work, which tells of anti-Bethmann Hollweg intrigues in connection with Hertling. This is unequivocally refuted by the correspondence between Lerchenfeld and Hertling, already cited in Note 94. See also Weizsäcker's letter to Bethmann Hollweg of February 19, the reports of the Württemberg envoy Moser from Munich on March 9 and 20 (HSTA), and other documents. There were zealous efforts to support the Chancellor against his enemies, centering in both Munich and Stuttgart. For the press conference of March 13 see UA2, Supplement 152.

113. Müller, p. 169. Report by the Austrian ambassador, Prince Hohenlohe, to Burián, March 24, other long reports by the same, of March 8, 15, 19, 20 (HHSTA, Prussia, III, 172). Of course Hohenlohe writes as an anti-Tirpitz man, but he finds much fault with the weakness of the "philosophical" Chancellor, who should have long since fought his enemies with far greater vigor, and who lacked the physical and intellectual force—and above all the militant spirit—that were needed if he wanted to stay in power for any length of time.

114. A very lively account appears in the diary of the North Schleswig (Danish) deputy Hans Peter Hanssen, p. 134.

115. Westarp, p. 148, see also *ibidem*, pp. 127ff., 141ff. Further, Tirpitz (1), p. 484; Epstein, pp. 174ff.; Erzberger, pp. 214ff.; May, pp. 272ff., in part after a report by Erzberger to Hertling of March 18.

116. After Westarp, p. 144. Hanssen, pp. 136ff., gives a graphic and evidently true account, probably from notes written immediately after the event, of the sessions

of the budget committee of March 28 and 29. Unfortunately my request to the ZA Potsdam for details on Bethmann Hollweg's remarks from the committee minutes stored there was refused "for technical reasons." What May reports on the course of the sessions (p. 273) is found in neither Westarp nor Hanssen, both of whom he cites as sources. Possibly he was basing himself on press dispatches.

117. A motion by the extreme left did sharply oppose ruthless U-boat warfare and demand the initiation of peace negotiations.

118. May, pp. 191ff.

119. Müller, p. 170; FR, 1916 Supplement, p. 239 (Jagow, April 20), pp. 242ff. (Bethmann Hollweg, April 20, 24-25), pp. 253ff. (the Kaiser receives Gerard, May 3). Further details on Bernstorff's negotiations and the foreign ministry attitude in Birnbaum, pp. 72ff. For the following see Müller, pp. 171ff.; Tirpitz (1), pp. 527ff.; UA 2, Supplement 1 (documents on Wilson's peace effort, 119), Nos. 1-9; Gerard, pp. 324-345 (missing in the German translation); Helfferich, Vol. 2, pp. 341ff.; Falkenhayn, pp. 186f.; Bernstorff (1), pp. 238ff.

120. According to Birnbaum (p. 78 and Appendix III, 3), it is doubtful whether Holtzendorff's changed views were already voiced at the meeting of April 24—two days earlier, in a letter to Jagow, he had still rejected any concessions to America. Birnbaum's account does not make very clear just what the memorandum of April 27 from the navy files, which he cites there, contained. Apparently it was a meeting record rather than a memorandum. By April 26 at the latest, however, Holtzendorff took the position attributed to him in Spindler, Vol. 3, pp. 143f. The document used by Spindler cannot be a letter to Müller of April 30, for on that day both men were together in Charleville. According to Müller, p. 173, it was a set of notes intended for a direct report to the Kaiser. In this crisis too Hohenlohe asked and received authority from Vienna to intervene in the negotiations. He explained to Bethmann Hollweg, apparently on April 24, that Austria did not wish to be drawn into a risky war with America, by swashbuckling German naval officers. In this connection, Vienna had sent him a copy of a German memorandum, in which Kriege, of the German foreign ministry, around the preceding Christmas, had painted a gloomy picture of the consequences of such a war for the Austrians, to persuade them to adopt a conciliatory attitude in the controversy over the Ancona incident. (HHSTA, war files, 4c.)

121. He favored unrestricted U-boat warfare all around Britain, with safe passage for neutral vessels along certain routes, which Wilson had already rejected in 1915. A detailed account of the negotiations in Charleville, based on Bethmann Hollweg's exchanges with the foreign ministry, appears in Birnbaum, pp. 79ff., though Müller's war diaries (pp. 172ff.) were not yet available to him. On Falkenhayn's stand and his memorandum of March 10, see RAW, Vol. 10, pp. 306ff.

122. On April 1, 1915, he had emphatically assured Count Lerchenfeld that he would not voluntarily give way to such as Tirpitz and Falkenhayn (Janssen [1], p. 45).

123. See Note 120, above.

124. Gerard's report (FR, 1916 Supplement, pp. 253ff.) mentions no discussion of American intentions to mediate, which the Kaiser in a handwritten note of October 3, 1916 (UA 2, Supplement 2), insisted took place. Perhaps such a discussion took place only with Bethmann Hollweg. Gerard, in Chapter 17 of his memoirs, gives a very detailed account of the visit in Charleville, but says nothing of political importance that is not already in FR.

125. What the purpose was scarcely needs mention—to gain a political return for foregoing unrestricted U-boat warfare. Fischer's interpretation (pp. 361ff.) is that diplomacy was to be used for preparing unrestricted U-boat warfare. In a number of instances he uses the terms "intensified" and "unrestricted" interchangeably.

126. This reservation had also been requested in the resolution of the Reichstag committee.

127. UA 2, Supplements 1ff.

128. See Note 73, above.

129. According to Gerard's report (FR, 1916 Supplement, pp. 253ff.), Bethmann Hollweg told Gerard in conclusion that "he hoped the president would be great enough to take up peace, that Germany had won enough to be able to talk of peace without suspicion of weakness, and that this awful loss of life should cease. He said that he hoped Colonel House would take up the question and shall perhaps come here under the president's direction." See Bethmann Hollweg, Vol. 2, p. 147.

130. AA WW, 18, secret, Vol. 16 (not 17!), reprinted in UA 2, Supplement 7. Almost incredibly, Fischer (p. 363) manages, by means of abbreviated quotations, to turn this peaceable attitude almost into its very opposite. On May 5, Bethmann Hollweg himself drew up a round-robin dispatch to the German legations in Copenhagen, Stockholm, Berne, Christiania (Oslo), and Bucharest, which was intended to explain the renunciation of unrestricted U-boat warfare—it betokened a peaceful spirit rather than weakness. The neutral press was to be informed along such lines. Bethmann Hollweg added a note for the foreign ministry: mediation on the part of Wilson was at this time bound to encounter resistance from among the German people; but the pressure on Britain would not in any event bring immediate success, and in time, especially in the event of a worsening economic crisis, this German resistance would subside. Once Germany grew convinced that U-boat warfare would not force Britain to its knees, "it must eagerly seize on any opportunity to make peace." Fischer cites the quoted phrase, but finds it quite incompatible with the fact that "the Germans" (Bethmann Hollweg included by implication) did not wish Wilson to mediate. The Chancellor actually went so far as to express the wish that Danish diplomacy might be persuaded to support peace mediation by the president (AA WW, 18, secret, Vol. 15—Fischer's file reference is erroneous). See also May, p. 391. A few pages before the passage under discussion (p. 353), Fischer makes the astonishing observation that the reason that Bethmann Hollweg rejected a separate peace with Britain (a completely unrealistic idea in the first place) was that it "would have been tantamount to a general peace," which would mean foregoing Belgium. Bethmann Hollweg's thinking could scarcely be subjected to grosser distortion.

*Notes to Chapter 6*

1. The optimistic remarks about the military situation in this speech go back to Falkenhayn, whom the Chancellor consulted on April 3. Falkenhayn initially stuck to generalities, without volunteering any details, but when the text of the speech was submitted to him on April 4, he approved it (ZA Potsdam, chancellery file, VII, 6).

2. Falkenhayn to the press association, May 27; exchange between Bethmann Hollweg and Falkenhayn, June 4-8. Grievance petition by the Chancellor to the Kaiser of June 9 (sent to Valentini). On June 10 he replied to the press association that he could not yet approve a debate on war aims, but wanted censorship on this issue to be handled gently and was taking measures to that end. Opinion of the war minister, May 18. All these documents in ZA Potsdam, chancellery file, II, war files, X, 8. See also Wild's papers, BA. Wild tried to mediate, with the help of Lyncker, believing that Bethmann Hollweg was taking the matter too seriously. Falkenhayn, among other things, cited the fact that the head censorship office was an organ of the General Staff. He had not intended any political opposition. From such documents as have come to my notice, I cannot determine whether Bethmann Hollweg's petition of grievance was actually submitted to the Kaiser or withdrawn. Details on organization and operation of press censorship in Lieutenant Colonel W. Nicolai, *Nachrichtendienste, Presse und Volksstimmung im Weltkrieg* (1920), pp. 73-88; and W. Vogel, "Die Organisation der amtlichen Presse- und Propagandapolitik des Deutschen Reiches bis zum Beginn des Jahres 1918," in *Zeitungswissenschaft,* Vol. 16, Nos. 8-9 (1941).

3. An anonymous pamphlet by "Junius Alter" and a memorandum by the subsequent

putsch leader (in 1920), General Kapp, a high official in the ministry of agriculture. The latter responded with a challenge to a duel with pistols, and when the
Chancellor refused it, he engineered some further publicity on June 14 (see
Wippermann-Purlitz, Vol. 32, p. 1186), himself adopting the role of injured
innocence. He was officially reprimanded by the minister of agriculture, Schorlemer, but protested in writing on June 18. On June 20 the cabinet decided against
disciplinary proceedings and instead refused to confirm his reappointment on
July 1. (AA, 1A, Germany, 122, No. 16, secret [Bethmann Hollweg's personnel
file].) The Reich chancellery suspected (according to Westarp, p. 169) that
Junius Alter was either Count Höensbroech or one Hahn, head of the farmer's
league. According to Hanssen, p. 133, he was Baron Hans von Liebig, but this is
probably a confusion with Liebig's book, *Die Politik von Bethmann Hollweg,*
published in 1915. On this subject and the sometimes extremely subtle maneuvers of the pamphleteers to hide their identities, see Gatzke, pp. 126ff. Gatzke
thinks that Friedrich Sontag, editor of the *Alldeutsche Blätter,* may have been
the pseudonymous author. On June 20 Hohenlohe reported to Vienna on the
intensive but rather fruitless efforts by Bethmann Hollweg and the Reich authorities to charge the pamphleteers and their backers with unauthorized disclosure of
military secrets. On June 7 Hohenlohe had reported, with considerable satisfaction, the strong impression made by Bethmann Hollweg's attack in the Reichstag.
(Both reports in HHSTA, war files, 4a.)
4. Wild's papers, BA. Wild thought that as a result of this telegram the conservatives
   definitely abandoned any thought of putting Falkenhayn up for Chancellor.
5. Westarp, pp. 309ff., 328ff.
6. Reports to the Chancellor from Grünau on June 19 and 23 (AA 1A, Germany, 122,
   No. 16, secret). See also Müller, p. 192. As a significant sidelight, the crown
   prince had the audacity to tell the Kaiser that Bethmann Hollweg was a coward,
   because he had declined Kapp's challenge.
7. Details in Gatzke, p. 174. Prince Hohenlohe reported the establishment of this group
   in a rather skeptical vein on July 14, and the Austrian foreign ministry had the
   report printed for general distribution (HHSTA, war files, 4a). The report also
   dealt with the polemics in which Pan-German circles engaged, notably the quarrel
   between the national-liberal historian E. Brandenburg and the *Norddeutsche
   Allgemeine Zeitung.*
8. For Bethmann Hollweg's report to the Prussian cabinet of August 9, see Sch&Gr, Vol.
   1, No. 311; report of the Prussian envoy von Schoen from Munich, June 23, in AA
   WW, secret, Vol. 30, and Bavaria, 50; a note by von Schoen for Hertling (undated
   but probably late July), GSTA, Pol. A, VII; Bethmann Hollweg to Hertling, July
   29, *ibidem;* minutes of the audience of August 5, *ibidem;* Count Preysing (radical
   Pan-German) to Hertling, August 5, *ibidem;* Lerchenfeld to Hertling, August 9,
   *ibidem;* Württemberg envoy Moser to Weizsäcker, August 12 and 15, HSTA, E
   73, Register 61; notes by Legation Councilor Stengel on an audience of Professor
   Gruber and a visit by Hertling with Cardinal Bettinger, August 14, GSTA, Pol. A,
   VII. On the session of the federal council committee of August 8-9, see minutes
   of the Württemberg legation, HSTA, E 49/51, foreign ministry IV, Register 3, BA
   V-16 (very detailed and reliable); minutes of the Hanseatic legation in R. Koschnitzke, *Die Innenpolitik des Reichskanzlers von Bethmann Hollweg im Weltkrieg,*
   dissertation, Kiel (1951), appendix. This work includes (p. 305) the Pan-German
   petition to the Hamburg senate. The excerpts in Deuerlein, pp. 287ff., are quite
   brief. According to Bethmann Hollweg, Acting Vice-Admiral Thomsen, who was
   besieging Hertling, was one of his most vicious maligners (Sch&Gr, Vol. 1, p.
   444). May (pp. 277ff.) offers an account of domestic political developments
   during the summer of 1916, based on the press and Naumann.
9. Bethmann Hollweg had heralded such reforms as early as December 1914. The
   speech from the throne on January 13, 1916, mentioned them more plainly, and
   on May 1, 1916, trade union restrictions were eased.

10. RAW, Vol. 10, pp. 638f. (August 21, 1916).
11. RAW, Vol. 10, p. 405, gives figures according to which seventy French divisions of four regiments each (not three, as on the German side) were committed on the Verdun sector by late August. Total French casualties (dead, wounded, and missing) are put at 317,000, only about 12 per cent higher than the German figure of 282,000.
12. RAW, Vol. 10, pp. 304f., 319.
13. RAW, Vol. 10, p. 640 (August 21, 1916).
14. According to Müller, p. 200, this was the view of Artillery General Laufer, for example.
15. RAW, Vol. 10, p. 660. The character sketch of Falkenhayn that follows (pp. 670ff.) seems to me to miss the mark in several respects. I do not think he was capricious or lacking in logic and systematic thinking. There is much testimony to refute the view that he was lacking in self-criticism. It may be true that his emotional state was a bit precarious in the summer of 1916—this would be understandable, in any event; but it did not visibly affect his attitude as a soldier.
16. Exchange with Conrad, December 16, 1915, Falkenhayn, pp. 166ff. See also RAW, Vol. 10, pp. 571ff.
17. Telegram from Bethmann Hollweg to the Kaiser, August 16, RAW, Vol. 10, p. 637; Sch&Gr, Vol. 1, No. 306. Bethmann Hollweg thought the advance from Tyrol was intended to parallel the advance at Verdun, based on a common plan. See also his letter to Valentini of July 10, 1916 (Valentini, p. 236).
18. RAW, Vol. 10, pp. 441ff.
19. Detailed report to the Austrian foreign ministry by Section Councilor von Wiesner from Teschen headquarters, to which Wiesner had been assigned. Two copies are in the HHSTA war files, secret, XLVII, fasc. 17, undated and unsigned, but marked "top secret." They are in an envelope bearing the following notation: "I have the honor to submit to Your Excellency in the enclosure two copies of Herr von Wiesner's modified letter. Vienna, June 27, 1916—Rappaport." Perhaps the letter (apparently a private one to Burián—the copies show no addressee) was "modified" for submission to Francis Joseph or his military chancellery. A similar private letter from Wiesner to Burián of August 12 is in the same file. On Wiesner and his work, see General Baron Vladimar Giesl. *Zwei Jahrzehnte im nahen Orient* (1927), p. 278.
20. Ludendorff to Zimmermann, June 29, 1916, AA WW, 15, secret, Vol. 30.
21. According to a report by Hohenlohe of July 5 on a discussion with Bethmann Hollweg (HHSTA, war files, 4°), one may conjecture that this was due to complaints by Hindenburg about the fragmentation of the eastern front into autonomous army groups. The Chancellor was badly shaken by the success of the Brusilov offensive, but also complained that Falkenhayn had said that a new Russian offensive was impossible. In his arrogance and inadequacy, Falkenhayn thought he was equal to any challenge, the Chancellor said. He was apparently echoing complaints from the Ludendorff camp.
22. Valentini, pp. 226-239. On Jagow, see Janssen (2), p. 345. This competent article offers much other evidence.
23. Bethmann Hollweg to Baron Grünau (for Lyncker), June 23, 1916, ZA Potsdam, chancellery file, VII, 7. Grünau was also asked to inform General von Wild and Valentini. Lyncker, of course, was expected to present Bethmann Hollweg's thoughts to the Kaiser. Plessen had told Bethmann Hollweg in confidence that he would try to win even Falkenhayn over to vesting supreme command of the eastern front in Hindenburg.
24. Müller, p. 183, for Varnbüller; Janssen (2), p. 345, for Weizsäcker; Bethmann Hollweg to Jagow, July 21, ZA Potsdam, chancellery file, II, 2, supreme headquarters, 14, Vol. 1. See also Helfferich, Vol. 2, p. 102. Crown Prince Rupprecht (in *Mein Kriegstagebuch,* Vol. 1 [1929], pp. 496f.) noted on July 5 that the same view prevailed within the foreign ministry. See also Tschirschky to Jagow,

August 7, in Janssen (2), p. 365, Note 135: "In the light of the mood of the German people, we should not let Falkenhayn make the kind of peace that is now in sight."

25. Dispatch by Bussche to the German foreign ministry, July 12, 1916, Sch&Gr, Vol. 1, No. 283. Czernin proposed the territorial status quo, restoration and indemnification of Belgium, and general disarmament.

26. *Ibidem,* No. 310; Tschirschky to Jagow, August 19, 1916.

27. Dispatches by the German envoy in Sofia, Oberndorff, on discussions between the military attaché, Paul von Massow, and Czar Ferdinand and the crown prince on June 14 and July 18 (AA WW, 15, secret, Vols. 30, 31); Bethmann Hollweg to Jagow, July 20, on reports from the Bulgarian envoy, *ibidem,* Vol. 31, reprinted in part in Zwehl, pp. 208f. On October 9, 1916, the Kaiser complied with a request from Bethmann Hollweg to talk with the heir to the Austrian throne about reshuffling the Austrian cabinet by replacing Stürgkh and Burián (Sch&Gr, Vol. 1, No. 345).

28. Bethmann Hollweg to Jagow, July 24, 1916, AA WW, 15, secret, Vol. 31, and Russia, 104, secret; telegram to the Kaiser of July 23, AA WW, 15, secret, Vol. 32. Tschirschky had already reported similar statements by Andrassy on July 21 (See Item 7, Note 57, below). According to a report by Consul General Fürstenberg from Budapest on July 31, Count Apponyi had expressed himself in terms similar to those of Andrassy. Information on the attitude of Emperor Francis Joseph was rather vague. He was said not to be opposed to German supreme command, if the Kaiser told him that this was necessary (statement by General Cramon, from a note by Bethmann Hollweg of July 19; report by Tschirschky of July 24; report by Metternich of July 30 on talks with Ambassador Pallavicini; Jagow to Grünau on August 14, on his impressions in Vienna—all in AA WW, 15, secret, Vols. 31-32). According to a dispatch from Tschirschky on August 7, Francis Joseph subsequently agreed only grudgingly to placing part of the Austrian army under Hindenburg. "We were getting on pretty well as things were," he remarked (*ibidem,* Vol. 32).

29. Reports to the Kaiser of August 11 and 16, Sch&Gr, Vol. 1, No. 306. For the invitation, see correspondence with Tschirschky, July 24-26 (AA, Germany, 122, No. 16, Vol. 7).

30. See Note 19, above. On June 24 Conrad made embarrassed excuses to Burián for the failures in Italy and the disaster at Luck (HHSTA, war files, secret, $2^b$ fasc. 17).

31. These military considerations are here discussed at such length because in my view historians have hitherto paid far too little attention to them, allowing the personal rivalry of Falkenhayn and Hindenburg to overshadow the picture.

32. For details see Janssen (2). Bethmann Hollweg suspected that the OHL was keeping telephone traffic between the foreign ministry and the eastern command under surveillance and had Wahnschaffe and Zimmermann cautioned (*ibidem,* p. 357). The most important sources for the struggle for Hindenburg's supreme command and Falkenhayn's fall are the following: (a) AA WW, 15, secret, Vols. 30-32; (b) ZA Potsdam, chancellery file, VII, 7; (c) ZA Potsdam, chancellery file, II, 2, III, supreme headquarters, 14, Vol. 1; (d) ZA Potsdam, chancellery file, VII, 8. In the following, I shall use the further abbreviations AA; ZA R 1; ZA R 2; ZA R 3—adding the dates in each instance.

33. According to Wild's paper (BA), Falkenhayn did express doubts of Seeckt's competence on June 29: "His approach has often caused frustration in the Russian campaign." Did this mean that Falkenhayn thought Seeckt not aggressive enough?

34. RAW, Vol. 10, pp. 482ff., 489f.—Legation Secretary Luckwald to the foreign ministry, June 16 (AA).

35. Reports by Grünau to Bethmann Hollweg of June 23 and 25 on talks between Falkenhayn and Conrad in Berlin. Bethmann Hollweg's reaction was given in a telegram of June 23 addressed to Grünau but intended for Lyncker (ZA R 1).

36. Wild's role during these weeks was rather ambiguous. To Grünau he voiced sweeping criticism of the strategic planning and performance of his old friend and sponsor Falkenhayn, asking that it be kept confidential, as a "private and personal opinion." (Grünau's report of June 23.) Further, in order not to endanger his own position, he insisted on discussing the question of the supreme command with the Kaiser only when no one else was present. (Grünau's report of June 25.) According to his diary (BA) he repeatedly urged Falkenhayn, without success, to make greater use of Hindenburg (pp. 155, 159, July 2-3). In a talk on July 6 with the Kaiser (who was indignant over Lyncker's advocacy of the supreme command going to Hindenburg), Wild cautiously sought to mediate and recommend Hindenburg, but at the same time he pressed for the dismissal of "that dreadful grumbler" Treutler.
37. For sources see Note 38, especially Grünau's report of June 25.
38. Grünau's second report to Bethmann Hollweg of June 25 (ZA R 1). This report is not free of vindictiveness. Grünau describes Falkenhayn's military objections as a mere pretext, suppressing their most important point. A report from Lyncker of July 5, addressed to Jagow via Treutler, is in a far more objective vein (AA). A report from Treutler to Bethmann Hollweg of June 27 (ZA R 1) likewise covers the failure of Lyncker's efforts two days earlier and the hopes which the "conspiracy" put in the king of Bavaria.
39. Handwritten postscript in a letter to Grünau of June 25 (ZA R 1). Bethmann Hollweg based himself on a report from Schoen in Munich (Janssen [2], p. 348).
40. Details in Janssen (2), pp. 354ff.; see also Müller, p. 196. On Erzberger's abortive attempt to topple Falkenhayn with the help of the South German Catholic kings, see Epstein, pp. 177f.
41. It included a phrase to the effect that obviously there were as many advantages as disadvantages to the proposal (RAW, Vol. 10, p. 525).
42. Report by Müller, pp. 200f., who records what Lyncker told him about the audience of July 2. See also Lyncker's report to Bethmann Hollweg of July 5, already mentioned (AA and ZA R 1). Treutler reported to Jagow on July 1, 2, 3, and 5 (AA, Section 1, Germany, 122, No. 16, secret [Bethmann Hollweg's personnel file]). These reports bear witness to the zeal with which the envoy sought to change the Kaiser's mind.
43. Müller, pp. 201, 205.
44. Valentini, p. 235; *ibidem* for the following (July 7 and 10).
45. Bethmann Hollweg to Treutler (for Lyncker), July 4; Wahnschaffe to Treutler, July 5 (both in ZA R 1). On July 9, Helfferich personally reported back to Bethmann Hollweg on Ludendorff's military criticisms of Falkenhayn (Helfferich, Vol. 2, p. 100).
46. Hoffmann, Vol. 1, pp. 127f. According to RAW, Vol. 10, p. 526, Hindenburg did write to Lyncker on July 7, see Note 49, below.
47. [Missing in original.]
48. Details in Janssen (2), pp. 354ff.; see also Müller, p. 203, and Grünau's report of July 17 (AA). Appointed on July 1 to succeed Delbrück, the minister took advantage of his courtesy visits to the South German courts for the purpose of drumming up votes for Hindenburg being placed in command. Weizsäcker virtually implored him to see to it that the Chancellor "opened the Kaiser's eyes" (Helfferich, Vol. 2, p. 102). On July 21 Bethmann Hollweg told Jagow of similar appeals made to him by the king of Bavaria and the queen of Württemberg, as well as by Weizsäcker (ZA R 2).
49. On July 7 Hindenburg had written Lyncker, demanding unitary command over the entire eastern front "from Courland to the Bukovina," with full autonomy and a pledge of further reserves. Directly afterward Falkenhayn made his compromise proposal, gaining Hindenburg's assent (RAW, Vol. 10, p. 526). Conrad refused— notes by Hohenlohe for Bethmann Hollweg, July 15 and 17; Bethmann Hollweg to Grünau, for Falkenhayn, July 16 and 17; Falkenhayn (via Grünau) to Beth-

mann Hollweg, July 17; Falkenhayn to Bethmann Hollweg, July 18; Grünau to Bethmann Hollweg, July 17; Bethmann Hollweg to Falkenhayn, July 18 (all in AA).

50. The invitation of July 18 and Bethmann Hollweg's notes on the talks of July 19—the date should probably be July 20—are in AA.

51. Groener, p. 311.

52. Grünau to Bethmann Hollweg, July 18; Grünau to Jagow, same date; both in AA. Groener's adverse view of Ludendorff is especially noteworthy. He put no limits to his demands, Groener said, and he ignored jurisdictional problems, even with the Austrians: "If Ludendorff were only a bit more skillful in handling people— but no, he is so taken with his own power that he acknowledges no one over him" (Groener, p. 310, July 9, 1916).

53. Note by Bethmann Hollweg of July 19 concerning a frank talk with Cramon, follow- ing one with Falkenhayn (AA); Grünau to the foreign ministry, July 17 *(ibidem);* Jagow to Bethmann Hollweg, July 20, and Bethmann Hollweg's reply, July 21 *(ibidem).* The Chancellor was gratified over Falkenhayn's "concession" concern- ing the Alpine Corps, but requested that this be at once exploited politically in support of German over-all command. He immediately advised the Austrian ambassador, Prince Hohenlohe, of what he had learned through Falkenhayn about Conrad's opposition to German command, and Hohenlohe at once passed it on to Vienna (report of July 20, HHSTA, war files, 4a). Conrad, "as usual," had not even visited the Berlin embassy and according to a report by Count Thurn of July 20 *(ibidem)* had stated that the question of command was no concern whatever of the foreign ministry, but constituted a purely military matter.

54. The negotiations in mid-July over their employment, conducted with Enver Pasha, are a model for the discrepancy in military and political thinking. Falkenhayn asked Enver Pasha for this emergency aid of two divisions, to plug gaps in the front, and found the latter quite willing. But he met strong opposition on the German political side (Jagow, Ambassador Wolff-Metternich) and also from Gen- eral Liman von Sanders—troop shortages in Turkey, fear that such support might produce political counterclaims. To overcome these objections, he charged the military attaché, General von Lossow, to "clarify" them in frank discussion. This was done without the knowledge of the embassy and in such a clumsy form that the Turks conceived a deep distrust of their German ally. In the end, to calm their fears, further clauses in the treaty of alliance had to be negotiated on September 28, entailing certain political risks. Falkenhayn realized subsequently that he had gone too far. Details in Steglich (2), pp. 110ff., based on exchanges between Metternich, Jagow, and Falkenhayn from July 11 to August 6, 1916, in AA WW, secret, Vols. 31-32. See also the report by Margrave Pallavicini to Burián of September 29, 1916 (HHSTA, secret, XLVII/8b).

55. For details see RAW, Vol. 10, pp. 529ff., and Cramon, p. 67. Cramon had estab- lished that while the appointment of Hindenburg to command the entire eastern front would greatly please the Austrian people and the Austrian army, it would lead to Conrad's immediate resignation, and this must be avoided. The only feasible settlement would be one in which the operational authority of the Austrian high command would not be reduced, which meant placing the German commander-in-chief under Teschen headquarters. ZA R 2 contains notes and correspondence of July 22, showing that Bethmann Hollweg negotiated with the eastern command by telephone about still another proposal from Falkenhayn. This would have meant Hindenburg relinquishing his present command and tak- ing over the army group Linsingen, to overcome the Austrians' objections to being placed under the field marshal. Bethmann Hollweg advised Hindenburg to agree only if he were also put in charge of all frontal sectors north of the one in point—and this, of course, would have revived all of Conrad's earlier objections. Eastern command said they were ready for anything except "half-measures."

Bethmann Hollweg immediately wired Jagow at headquarters (July 22) that Hindenburg should at all costs receive command of the northern front as well. "General von Lyncker *must* now intervene without any further delay, or the whole game is lost." This was evidently a preliminary phase of the agreement ultimately concluded at Pless on July 27.

56. Groener, pp. 311f. The initial impetus came in a telegram from Bethmann Hollweg to Falkenhayn of July 21: "New Austrian defeat southwest of Luck bound to bring critical domestic repercussions unless Hindenburg factor fully utilized. All responsible owe crown and country prevention of this danger. Patriotic duty constrains me to say this emphatically to Your Excellency" (ZA R 2). Groener *(loc. cit.)* is highly critical of this wire. Falkenhayn's proposal actually went beyond Groener's. Groener wanted Hindenburg in charge of the Austrian left wing (army group Linsingen and Böhm-Ermolli), excluding the Southern army (Archduke Charles, heir to the throne, with Seeckt as chief of staff).

57. Following are the pertinent dispatches:

1. Bethmann Hollweg to Jagow, July 20—the Bulgars want Hindenburg in top command.

2. Personal report by Bethmann Hollweg to the Kaiser of July 23—already cited, deals with Andrassy's statements.

3. Bethmann Hollweg to Jagow, July 23—same subject (all in AA; last-mentioned wire also in ZA R 2).

4. Bethmann Hollweg to Jagow, July 21—king of Bavaria, queen of Württemberg, and Weizsäcker press for putting Hindenburg in charge (ZA R 2).

5. Bethmann Hollweg to Falkenhayn, July 21—Austrian defeat at Luck makes it even more urgent to appoint Hindenburg (*ibidem* and RAW, Vol. 10, p. 529).

6. Bethmann Hollweg to Jagow, July 21—impress the Kaiser with the gravity of the Rumanian question! Hindenburg the only salvation. Hohenlohe deeply depressed, querying whether any signs of yielding in Vienna. Can Falkenhayn be expected to yield?

7. Tschirschky to Jagow, July 21—don't be put off for prestige reasons, demand Hindenburg be appointed top commander! Hungary would be released from Austrian leadership!

8. In a similar vein on July 22.

9. Bethmann Hollweg to Jagow, July 22—gives the content of a wire to the Kaiser, reporting statements by Tschirschky that Andrassy had described union with Germany as Austria's only salvation and that Hindenburg's appointment would be greeted with relief (all in ZA R 2).

It was dispatch No. 9, received in Charleville on the evening of July 22, according to Müller (p. 204), that persuaded the Kaiser to go to Pless. Dispatch No. 2 (sent at 8 P.M. on July 23, received at 9:10 P.M.) and dispatch No. 3 (dated July 23, but sent the following day at 2:35 A.M. and received at 5:50 A.M.) only confirmed him in his decision.

58. Müller, pp. 204-206; Valentini, pp. 136ff.; diary notes of Wild von Hohenborn, July 24—the Kaiser reluctant to demand placing the Austrian front under the German OHL, Wild making proposals on how to sweeten the bitter pill for the Austrians—and July 26—Bethmann Hollweg entertaining the same reluctance, Wild describing Falkenhayn's proposal as "mad" and certain to provoke indignation in Germany; Bethmann Hollweg to Jagow, July 24 (ZA R 2)—he fears a belated invitation to Hindenburg to come to Pless. See also RAW, Vol. 10, pp. 531f., and the official Austrian war history, *Österreich-Ungarns letzter Krieg,* Vol. 5 (1934), pp. 120f.; Janssen (2), p. 362. It is noteworthy that as late as July 21 the Kaiser would not hear of a visit to headquarters by Bethmann Hollweg, changing his mind only as a result of Bethmann Hollweg's message about Andrassy.

59. Metternich to the foreign ministry, July 29; Tschirschky to the foreign ministry, July 30; Consul General Fürstenberg to the foreign ministry, July 31; Tschirschky to Jagow, August 7; all in AA.

60. Details may be traced in the eminently objective account in RAW, Vol. 10, pp. 536f., 558ff.
61. Groener, pp. 313ff., August 12-13. Groener tried to mediate by giving sensible advice.
62. She cautioned the Kaiser twice not to listen only to Falkenhayn, but to give a hearing to his opponents in the army, such as the duke of Württemberg and Crown Prince Rupprecht. She told Grünau about it, and he reported to the foreign ministry on August 9 (AA). She was almost certainly put up to this by the conspirators.
63. Foreign ministry to Bethmann Hollweg, August 11, about a telephone call from Ludendorff *(ibidem)*. During these months the diplomatist Grünau was extremely busy with military matters, functioning as a major participant in the cabal—see his wires to the foreign ministry of July 17 and 18, August 9, 12, 13, 15, 17, and 19 *(ibidem)*.
64. According to the account in RAW, Vol. 10, pp. 420ff., Falkenhayn talked to the army chiefs of the western front on August 14, instructing them to keep as much on the defensive as possible, in order to make manpower available for the east. Another directive of August 15 to the crown prince's army group urged the husbanding of manpower, but emphasized that any impression of Germany having entirely ceased the attack must be avoided. It asked for an opinion from the leaders of the two attack groups on whether certain positions, such as Fort Souville, might yet have to be taken to create a defense line that could be held. The two opinions were in disagreement, while the crown prince, counter to his own chief of staff, Knobelsdorff, demanded that all offensive action be foregone. On August 21, in still another and somewhat ambiguously worded directive, Falkenhayn left the final decision to the army group command, but at the same time he relieved Knobelsdorff, thus virtually siding with the crown prince. This, of course, did not mean that any of the thirty divisions committed at Verdun could be simply withdrawn.
65. Direct report to the Kaiser of August 16, 1916, printed in Sch&Gr, Vol. 1, No. 306, already cited in Note 29, above. For the following, see RAW, Vol. 10, pp. 560ff., 634ff., also Müller, p. 212.
66. Grünau to Bethmann Hollweg, August 17—gives a strongly colored version of the situation and the Kaiser's answer to Hindenburg of August 17, after Major von Bockelberg, an agent for Ludendorff; Grünau to Bethmann Hollweg, August 19—Ludendorff's resignation on the way (both in AA). A second dispatch on August 19 gave advance notice of Falkenhayn's report of August 21, describing his attitude as one of longing for Hindenburg's glory to fade (Sch&Gr, Vol. 1, No. 312). On the subversive activities of General Hoffmann on the staff of the eastern command—he too threatened to resign—see Hoffmann, Vol. 1, pp. 135ff., Vol. 2, p. 152. For Bethmann Hollweg's wire to Grünau (for Lyncker) of August 19, see ZA R 3, printed in WA, Vol. 10, p. 637.
67. This judgment is shared in RAW, Vol. 10, pp. 565f. For Falkenhayn's report, see *ibidem*, pp. 638-641. It has already been cited, in Note 13, above.
68. Bethmann Hollweg to Jagow, August 23 (AA); see also Janssen (2), p. 367, Note 153.
69. Valentini, pp. 139f. Lyncker probably used a letter from Crown Prince Rupprecht of August 21, which stated that Falkenhayn no longer enjoyed the confidence of the army—see Janssen (2), p. 368.
70. Diary note of August 28, in Wild's papers (BA).
71. See the treaty of August 17, 1916, between Britain, France, Italy, and Russia, UA IV (Volkmann), p. 183.
72. Groener, p. 316.
73. Erzberger's felicitations on August 30 were especially enthusiastic. "One may well say that a wave of jubilation passed across the whole German nation." Similar sentiments were voiced by Minister Breitenbach on August 30 and by Prince Max

of Baden on August 27 (all in ZA R 3). On Erzberger's alleged part in the appointment of Hindenburg as commander-in-chief on the eastern front late in July, see Janssen (2), p. 361. How deeply Bethmann Hollweg disliked Falkenhayn is shown by the sharp protest he lodged with Grünau on November 16, 1916, to the appointment of the general to succeed Tschirschky (recalled at Burián's request) as ambassador in Vienna. Falkenhayn almost certainly did not want the post, and the appointment had not gone beyond the discussion stage at headquarters. Bethmann Hollweg submitted that not only was Falkenhayn unpopular in Austria because of his alleged approval of the Tyrol offensive and on account of Verdun, but he also "failed as chief of staff" (Zwehl, p. 221).

*Notes to Chapter 7*

1. Müller, p. 217, August 30.
2. Bethmann Hollweg to the OHL, September 28; Grünau to Bethmann Hollweg, September 29 (initially approving); Grünau to Bethmann Hollweg that same afternoon (rejecting); Bethmann Hollweg's wire of reply, September 29; Grünau to the foreign ministry, September 30 (ZA Potsdam, VII, 9). At this time, at the urging of the parties, the budget committee *(Haushaltsausschuss)* was reorganized as the "main committee" *(Hauptausschuss)* and instituted as a continuing instrumentality, even during recesses, so that the government could be asked for information at any time as well as receive requests and complaints. This was much like the war committee of the Paris chamber and equally time-consuming for members of the government, which was a particular burden to Helfferich. There was discussion and concern about this in the foreign affairs committee of the federal council on October 30, 1916. Bethmann Hollweg, however, was intent on keeping in continual touch with the Reichstag and had regularly discussed important matters with the party leaders even previously.
3. For details, see RAW, Vol. 10, pp. 642f.; official Austrian war history, Vol. 5, pp. 263ff. (includes Conrad's submission of August 23). The documents are in HHSTA, war files, secret, XLVII, 13-3. See also Cramon (1), pp. 70ff. The agreement of September 15-19, 1916, between Germany, Austria, Bulgaria, and Turkey, was published in Curt Liebmann, "Die Entwicklung der Frage eines Einheitlichen Oberbefehls im Weltkrieg," *Wissen und Wehr,* Vol. 8 (1927), pp. 1ff., 65ff. Liebmann gives reasons why a uniform command had as little value in practice as all the earlier agreements concerning the eastern front. Friction with the OHL ceased only with the withdrawal of Conrad and his replacement by General Arz.
4. Cramon (1), pp. 68f.
5. Hohenlohe to Burián, September 13, 1916, HHSTA, Prussia, III-172. Tschirschky's comprehensive report of September 29, 1916, drew a desolate picture of political, financial, economic, and social conditions in the dual monarchy. He urgently recommended that the German government insist on changes of leading Austrian public figures. He favored Archduke Eugene as successor to the incompetent premier, Count Stürgkh (Sch&Gr, No. 332). Bethmann Hollweg thereupon, in a direct message of September 30 (Sch&Gr, No. 335), asked the Kaiser to make appropriate representations to Archduke Charles, heir to the throne, and urge particularly that Burián be relieved. Burián on his part had been trying since September 10, through Hohenlohe, for the replacement of Tschirschky, on the grounds that he was clouding the good relations between the two countries. Berlin was not very receptive—Burián to Hohenlohe, September 10; report from Hohenlohe, September 18 (HHSTA, Prussia, III-172). In a letter to Emperor Francis Joseph of October 28, the Kaiser sought to have Tschirschky's relief postponed until after the war. A reply of November 5 requested that he be immediately furloughed, on account of an operation, which should be followed by his recall without fail (HHSTA, war files, 25p). Tschirschky died on November 15.

6. A note by Hohenlohe, transmitted to the foreign ministry on July 4, led to inquiries at the OHL, the war ministry, the commercial section of the foreign ministry, and the Reich treasury, all of which expressed opposition to the Austrian request. By December 21, however, Hohenlohe had not yet received an answer, despite a reminder, as he stated in a "verbal note" of that date, which was in turn made known to the Reich naval office, the war ministry, the treasury, and the quartermaster general (all in AA WW, 15, secret, Vol. 2). My documentary material fails to show whether a written or verbal reply was ultimately made.

7. On the occasion of a discussion in Berlin on November 15-16, Burián handed Bethmann Hollweg an outline of his "desiderata" (Sch&Gr, Vol. 1, No. 382). A draft of November 21 in Jagow's hand (Sch&Gr, Vol. 1, No. 388) formed the first basis for the official reply of December 21 (Sch&Gr, Vol. 1, No. 428), in which the treasury also had a hand. Meanwhile Burián, through Hohenlohe on November 28, had submitted his request once again, in the form of a draft treaty. On December 3, 4, 6, and 16 Hohenlohe reported on unsuccessful representations to the Chancellor, the recently appointed foreign minister Zimmermann, and Under Secretary Stumm. For Burián's directive to Hohenlohe of December 5, see HHSTA, XLVII, 3-16, secret; AA WW, 15, secret; and Sch&Gr, Vol. 1, No. 400. See also the detailed account in Steglich (2), Chapter 10 and pp. 147f. Steglich's doubts (Note 372) on whether the memorandum of November 21 was originally the work of Bethmann Hollweg or of Jagow have been resolved by the finding of the handwritten draft (Sch&Gr, Vol. 1, No. 388). The passages concerning the Baltic accord entirely with Jagow's rather than Bethmann Hollweg's views. See Chapter 4, Note 70, above.

8. Hindenburg to Bethmann Hollweg, September 19 (AA, Germany, 180, secret, Vol. 4); Bethmann Hollweg's reply of September 29, *ibidem,* now published in Sch&Gr, Vol. 1, No. 333. On Falkenhayn's attitude, see Chapter 4, Note 14, above.

9. Grünau to Bethmann Hollweg (at the Kaiser's behest), November 6; Bethmann Hollweg's reply, same day; Grünau to Bethmann Hollweg (at the behest of the OHL), November 7; inquiry to the German embassy in Vienna by Jagow, November 7; the embassy's reply, November 8; Bethmann Hollweg to the OHL, November 10; letter from Grünau to Bethmann Hollweg, November 13, 1916 (all in AA WW, secret, Vols. 34-35).

10. Hindenburg to Bethmann Hollweg, November 15, 1916, about the auxiliary service act (Ludendorff [2], p. 85). This letter reached the press. Freiherr von Bissing, governor general of Belgium, let Hertling know through his son on November 17 that he was repelled by Ludendorff's audacity in reproving and instructing the Chancellor of Germany on nonmilitary matters. To deal with the highest Reich official on such matters was the privilege of the Kaiser and at best the federal princes. Hertling gave a reassuring reply on November 28. Lerchenfeld, however, clearly perceived the severity of the conflict, despite a reassuring article in the *Norddeutsche Allgemeine Zeitung* of November 22. He deplored the fact that when the new leaders of the OHL took office, Bethmann Hollweg had rejected as unnecessary the advice of friends to seek a clear demarcation of the respective jurisdictions, since Ludendorff was of a difficult and violent cast of mind and exerted a powerful influence over his chief (GSTA, Pol. A, VII, 62 and 51).

11. In a formal sense Jagow's resignation was occasioned by an insulting reprimand from the Kaiser over a trifling matter. Valentini's report of November 17 to Bethmann Hollweg (Valentini, p. 239) shows, however, that the OHL was behind the change. This is confirmed by Jagow's letter to Bernstorff of September 2, 1919 (Bernstorff [2], p. 118), and Hoffmann, Vol. 1, p. 149. Fischer (p. 374) offers an almost grotesque explanation for the replacement. He holds that Jagow was removed because he stood for an outright ("almost *völkisch*-racial") anti-Russian policy and was replaced by the reckless power politician Zimmermann who, like Ludendorff and Holtzendorff [sic], wanted a dictated peace and brought about a

kind of change of course in German policy. The only element of truth in this is that Zimmermann was on the whole much closer to the nationalist right than Jagow. The practical effect, as will be shown in Chapter 8, Part 4, was that he did not share Bethmann Hollweg's confidence in Wilson's peace mediation. Yet there can be no question of a change in course, if only because Jagow had shared Zimmermann's doubts about Wilson (see Chapter 8, Part 1, below). For the rest, Zimmermann's good relationship with Ludendorff did not long endure (see text, above). As early as January 1917, Ludendorff told Valentini (Valentini, p. 149) that in the long run he could work with Zimmermann no better than with Helfferich. That was the reason why Zimmermann, following Bethmann Hollweg's fall, was unceremoniously dislodged from his office. See also the next note.

12. Hohenlohe reported on November 23 and 25 at great length on the changes of personnel in the diplomatic service, some of which he had predicted on September 18. He regarded Jagow as a much cleverer man than Zimmermann and ascribed the former's fall to party criticism in the Reichstag and to the intrigues of Bülow, whom he had always believed to be a political charlatan. Because of his outspoken and jovial manner, Zimmermann might be better than Jagow in fending off OHL interference, and he was very popular with the Kaiser, the empress, and the crown princess. In conversation, however, the new minister expressed much concern over the conflict with the OHL that hung over him. As for Grünau, he carried little political weight at headquarters (HHSTA, Prussia, III, 172). Talking with Hohenlohe on November 28, Bethmann Hollweg seemed much depressed over Jagow's going (*ibidem,* war files, 4a). Lerchenfeld too reported to Hertling on November 24 and 30 on Jagow's withdrawal and what was behind it (GSTA, Pol. A, VII, 521).

13. My former assistant W. Steglich in 1956 copied an abundance of documents on the Polish question for me, from the Vienna archives (HHSTA, war files, secret, XLVII, 3, 12-16). Conze has already used some of them in his book. The most important documents from the files of the German foreign ministry (AA), especially series WW, 20c, secret, have now been published in Sch&Gr, Vol. 1 (see list of documents there, pp. xliiff.). Since Conze has dealt quite exhaustively with the background documentation of the Poland manifesto, I shall not, in the following, regularly cite references, but will limit myself to occasional mentions and supplements. The material Conze did not use still holds much interest, but to present it all would transcend the scope of this book.

14. Andrian to Burián, June 26 (HHSTA, *loc. cit.,* fasc. 12b). To judge from his reports and memoranda, Andrian was anything but pro-German. Colonel Paič, on the other hand, found the German claims to Poland fully justified and thought they should be encouraged, to divert them from the west, while he characterized as grossly unfair Austrian claims to gains in both the Balkans and Poland, considering the Austrian military record. This, at least, was what was reported to the Austrian foreign ministry on July 19 by Baron Hoenning, the ministry's representative at Lublin (HHSTA, war files, secret, XLVII, 3-12). According to a direct report to the Kaiser of July 23 (AA WW, secret, 32), Andrassy too thought that events had overtaken the "Austro-Polish solution."

15. Mutius, reporting on Beseler's views in a private letter to Jagow, June 23 (AA WW, secret, Vol. 30).

16. See Notes 34, 35, 45, and 65 to Chapter 4, above.

17. Sch&Gr, Vol. 1, No. 291, with Bethmann Hollweg's reply of July 20, *ibidem,* No. 292, and Bethmann Hollweg's earlier rejection, *ibidem,* No. 141.

18. Sch&Gr, Vol. 1, No. 288.

19. Details on the Russian events in Conze, pp. 173ff.; see also Paléologue, Vol. 2, pp. 157ff.; G. Buchanan, *Meine Mission in Russland* (1926), pp. 145f.

20. Burián was much disquieted by Austria's loss of ground with the Brusilov offensive. On August 4 he asked Count Thurn to admonish the Austrian high command to deal gently with the Poles in the Austrian zone of occupation, including Pilsud-

ski, since there was danger that the Germans were winning the popularity race. Conrad replied on August 15. (Both documents in HHSTA, war files, 11⁰.) The German foreign office anticipated that Tisza would support the German view, and he did in fact write to Burián on July 25 that since the Austro-Polish solution had become impossible, the protectorate over the Polish buffer state should be left to Germany alone. (Possibly he had in mind that this would divert Polish resentment to Germany!) This should be represented as a friendly act, in return for which other advantages might be sought. In no event should Austria allow a Hapsburg prince to mount the Polish throne, either as a puppet or as an enemy of Germany. Similar doubts about a dual protectorate were voiced on July 25 by Count Stürgkh, who hoped, however, that friction might be avoided by carefully delimiting the respective authorities and instituting a special coordinating agency. Burián replied to both ministers briefly on July 30, advising them that the emperor had meanwhile sanctioned his draft, minus the passage about a Hapsburg prince as king of Poland (HHSTA, secret, XLVII, 3-12). In discussion with Tschirschky Tisza thereupon declined to pursue his proposals further, in the face of Burián's plan, the difficulties of which he now minimized—Tschirschky to the German foreign ministry, August 5, Jagow's reply, August 7 (both in AA WW, secret, Vol. 32).

21. Conze, pp. 185f., where the statements in Falkenhayn's memoirs are corrected.
22. The minutes, approved by both sides, are given in Ludendorff (2), pp. 298ff. A committee of economists, appointed to study and forecast the consequences of union with Germany, presented a thirty-two-page report on September 6, but nothing further eventuated—Mérey to Burián (HHSTA, secret, XLVII, 3-12).
23. In his diary, Wild von Hohenborn says that Falkenhayn was angry because Bethmann Hollweg asked him, Wild, the war minister, to draft a military convention with Poland—that was no concern of the war minister and the whole incident was only another example of how Bethmann Hollweg wanted to bypass and oust him.
24. Bethmann Hollweg from Pless to Tschirschky, for Burián, August 23; Burián's reply to Hohenlohe, August 24—HHSTA, secret, XLVII, 3-12c. Urgent wires from Burián to Hohenlohe, August 15, 20, 21, and 23, *ibidem*. Thus Conze is mistaken in assuming (p. 188) that Falkenhayn had a more favorable view of the military situation in August, hence voted for adjournment. In a letter from the OHL to Conrad on September 7, Ludendorff was still giving full approval to postponement of the proclamation, in view of the military situation and the possibility of a separate peace with Russia (HHSTA, secret, XLVII, 3-12).
25. Sch&Gr, Vol. 1, No. 305. Notes 63-64 to the preceding chapter have already shown how Grünau exploited this directive to incite protest against Falkenhayn's allegedly "one-sided" western strategy.
26. It is worth noting that he expressed himself in a far more positive vein in a cabinet meeting on October 8, during which Beseler reported on the Poland manifesto (Sch&Gr, Vol. 1, p. 507). At the time its prompt promulgation had already been agreed to by the new OHL and had to be made to seem plausible.
27. Sch&Gr, Vol. 1, pp. 442, 446f., 454. Bethmann Hollweg's reserve in the Polish question is borne out by a message from Lerchenfeld to Hertling on August 21. The foreign ministry, he said, would prefer Russian rule over the new Polish state to German rule. The Poles would probably always be in opposition to the ruling country, and Warsaw would be far less attractive to German Poles, if Russia were the ultimate sovereign (GSTA, Pol. A, VII, 19-39).
28. Based on Lerchenfeld's just-cited report from the foreign ministry, which also tells of a very moderate peace program for the eventuality of a separate peace with Russia, drafted in the foreign ministry. See also Sch&Gr, Vol. 1, Nos. 272, 281, 295, 314, and 315. On the peace effort pursued by Consul Marx, see Wrisberg, Vol. 2, pp. 147-150. On Botkin's impending appointment, see Hohenlohe's report to Burián of August 21, relating remarks by Jagow (HHSTA, secret, XLVII, 3-12c).

29. See, for example, Jagow to Bethmann Hollweg, August 23 (Sch&Gr, Vol. 1, No. 315).
30. According to Bethmann Hollweg, speaking before the foreign affairs committee of the federal council on October 30, 1916, the OHL then thought that the Russian army might well be reorganized in the course of the winter.
31. Details in Conze, pp. 195ff., where it is shown that on August 17 Bethmann Hollweg thoroughly briefed the eastern command on the status of the Polish question. This refutes Hindenburg's subsequent attempt to deny any responsibility for the Polish undertaking.
32. Lerchenfeld to King Louis of Bavaria, August 18, 1916 (GSTA, Pol. A, VII, No. 9).
33. Statement of August 23, after Conze, p. 190, whose source fails to mention with sufficient clarity whether or not the "preliminary work" was for a volunteer formation, to be recruited soon after the proclamation of the new Poland. This is probable, however, since Beseler, during the Prussian cabinet meeting of October 8, spoke at length along such lines (Sch&Gr, Vol. 1, p. 496). Wild, the war minister, was more cautious—he counted on only one division (*ibidem*, p. 502). The figure of three divisions suggests that Beseler envisaged the Austrian Polish legion, of two divisions, each with twelve battalions (according to Conrad) —Conrad to Hindenburg, September 19, supplement to a report to Burián of September 22 (HHSTA, war files, secret, XLVII, 3-12[bis]).
34. The particularly outspoken message from the OHL of September 30 was, as Conze shows (p. 202), the outcome of consultations between Beseler and the OHL at supreme headquarters.
35. Hohenlohe to Burián, October 18, 1916 (HHSTA, secret, XLVII, 3-12). *Ibidem,* the exchanges between Hindenburg, Conrad, and Burián of September 2, 7, 11, 16, and 30 and October 1, on matters concerning the Lublin occupation administration. Negotiations between Burián and Tschirschky and Burián and Bethmann Hollweg, October 9, 10, and 13, *ibidem.* Burián to Thurn (for Conrad), September 13, *ibidem,* 12[bis]. Conze (p. 198) cites documents of the occupation administration to show that Bethmann Hollweg made a mediation proposal, under which Austrian administration would have continued under German suzerainty.
36. Zimmermann thought that rightist attacks on Jagow and Bethmann Hollweg had slackened of late, because it was realized that under a more resolute Chancellor the social democrats might refuse to go along altogether. This had become abundantly clear in Reichstag proceedings, especially in the discussions on the U-boat question before the main committee, September 29—October 10 (see Chapter 8, Part 3, below).
37. Conrad to Burián, September 26; note by Tschirschky for Burián, September 27; Burián's reply, September 29; a further exchange between Tschirschky and Burián, October 3 and 5; Burián to various agencies, October 6; note by Burián, October 9—all in HHSTA, secret, XLVII, 3-12. Conze (p. 202) is mistaken in believing that this was an attempt by Burián to retract the assurances given in Vienna.
38. Cramon protested to Conrad on September 21 against immediate publication of the measure in the press; Conrad to Burián, undated, probably September 22; exchange between Conrad and Hindenburg, September 19 and 21; Hohenlohe reporting to Burián on September 22 that Bethmann Hollweg and Jagow were greatly upset by publication; Count Thurn to Burián, September 25, reporting on discussions between the Kaiser and Archduke Frederic; Hohenlohe to Burián, September 27—all in HHSTA, secret, XLVII, 3-12.
39. Direct reports to the Kaiser by Bethmann Hollweg, October 2 and 3 (Sch&Gr, Vol. 1, Nos. 337, 338); Bethmann Hollweg to the OHL, October 10, *ibidem,* No. 344. According to reports by Hohenlohe of October 1 and 8, Jagow initially rebuffed the ambassador in the matter of prompt proclamation of the Poland manifesto on the grounds that the mixed military commission must first swing into action. Later on his excuse was that it would be better to await adjournment of the

Reichstag, in order not to give the Pan-Germans and Hakatists occasion for protest. Neither pretext was really valid. Bethmann Hollweg also favored postponement in the Prussian cabinet session of October 8. He said that the two occupation areas must first be amalgamated, since this could certainly not be achieved afterward (Sch&Gr, Vol. 1, p. 507).

40. Bethmann Hollweg's report to the Kaiser, October 2 (Sch&Gr, Vol. 1, No. 337); see also Conze, pp. 208f.; Bethmann Hollweg, Vol. 2, pp. 98, 106.

41. According to a report by Varnbüler of November 4, this possibility was strongly emphasized by Count Wedel, who cited the former ambassador in St. Petersburg, Count Pourtalès (HSTA, E 73, Register 61, fasc. 12h, III). For Bethmann Hollweg's message to the OHL of October 10, see Sch&Gr, Vol. 1, No. 344.

42. See his statements during the talks on October 17, in Conze, p. 212. In Berlin, he said, the prospects for recruitment were estimated to be rather poor. Deputy von Nostitz, from Saxony, reported on November 10 that he had heard from various sides, including officers and officials who had served in Poland, and even from Minister von Loebell, that there was much doubt whether volunteers could be mustered in any worthwhile numbers. Ludendorff, however, when questioned by rightist circles, had confirmed in a long letter that the OHL had indeed demanded both proclamation and recruitment (HSTA, Dresden, foreign ministry, 2078, XXVII, 2, 9a, 6a, Vol. 5).

43. I cannot follow Conze's interpretation (pp. 209f.) that this was merely an expression of irresoluteness, and an attempt by Bethmann Hollweg to shift the responsibility that was his alone.

44. Sch&Gr, Vol. 1, No. 346 (October 13).

45. Knesebeck, p. 159.

46. Minutes by Burián (HHSTA, *loc. cit.*); notes on the outcome by Jagow, October 18 (Sch&Gr, Vol. 1, No. 348); notes by Bethmann Hollweg (*ibidem*, No. 347, with a misleading date). The last refer only to Burián's proposal for a peace effort and were published in UA 2, Supplement 75. Conze (pp. 212ff.) also drew on slightly divergent notes by Major von Heynitz that covered the preliminary discussions among the German participants on October 17 as well.

47. Confidential discussion with Lerchenfeld, reported by him to Hertling on October 21 (GSTA, Pol. A, VII, 10-31).

48. Handwritten notes by Wahnschaffe on the proceedings (ZA Potsdam); a more detailed report by Nieser, October 31 (GLA, IV, Berlin legation, 37).

49. For further evidence see Steglich (2), pp. 49ff. Despite Bethmann Hollweg's statements before the foreign affairs committee of the federal council on October 30, I do not think it proven that Bethmann Hollweg originally wished to postpone the Poland manifesto still further, as Steglich believes. The Prussian cabinet remained very doubtful about the Polish plan, but there too, on October 24 and 27, Bethmann Hollweg emphasized the enormous pressure that was being exerted by the OHL. (Minutes in Sch&Gr, Vol. 1, No. 351, and ZA Merseburg, Rep. 90a B II 2b, No. 6, Vol. 165.)

50. At this session, to which members of the federal council had also been invited, Bethmann Hollweg first delivered a speech on the outbreak of the war, answering one by Grey on October 23 (see also Chapter 8, Note 87, below), which had been made public (*Kriegsreden*, ed. by Thimme, pp. 150ff.). During the subsequent executive session some serious doubts about German policy in Poland were voiced, not only by Ledebour of the extreme left, but also by the national liberals Schiffer and, of course, Count Westarp. In the view of von Nostitz of Saxony, however, the debate remained on a rather mild level, largely because a long letter by Ludendorff was circulating among the rightist opposition. In this letter Ludendorff gave his backing to the proclamation, "for military reasons." The Chancellor preferred to remain silent as to the character of these reasons. A number of deputies—von Payer, Noske, Gröber, *et. al.*—emphasized strongly that only a fundamental change in Prussia's Polish policy could create good relations

with a new Poland. All in all, the reception was cool, even anxious, Bethmann Hollweg himself displaying no enthusiasm. (Report by von Nostitz-Wallwitz of November 10, HSTA, Dresden, foreign ministry, 2078, XXVII, 2, 9a, 6a [Political Reports, Vol. 5]; report by Nieser, November 10, GLA, Berlin legation, 37.)

51. Hohenlohe wrote Burián on November 7 that Bethmann Hollweg had rejected Burián's proposal to postpone the recruitment appeal at least until November 16. The tremendous jubilation should be exploited immediately. Bethmann Hollweg had also rejected the immediate creation of a Polish national council (HHSTA, war files, 56a/1). Baron Andrian had predicted on October 27 that the recruitment effort would fail, in a dispatch remarkable for its anti-German tone. He advised the minister to receive Polish notables in Vienna and to encourage their aversion to the Germans (*ibidem,* secret, XLVII, 3-12).

52. My sources are reports by Andrian of October 27, November 11, and December 30 (HHSTA, secret, XLVII, 3-12, and war files, 56a/1).

53. Note by Czernin about a talk with the new German ambassador, Count Bodo von Wedel, on January 1, 1917 (HHSTA, secret, XLVII, 3-16). Wedel proposed, among other things, that a Saxon prince be installed as regent of Poland. Czernin demanded that if Germany indeed claimed territorial gains in the east, it should display a "reasonable" attitude in the west, i.e., forego Belgium unconditionally and make only minimal demands of France. Thus there was a sharp clash with the new foreign minister at the very first meeting! Minutes of these talks and Czernin's agreement with Bethmann Hollweg in Berlin on January 6, 1917: HHSTA, secret, XLVII, 3-17; AA 1A, Germany, 180, secret, Vol. 4 (E 569036-46). Czernin's message to Hohenlohe of January 16, conveying Emperor Charles's. agreement, *ibidem.* Minutes of the meeting of the joint cabinet of January 12, HHSTA, XXXX, 293, No. 530. Czernin remarked even then that since Germany had abandoned the plan of forming an army, the necessity for a Polish state no longer existed.

54. I have before me the enormous collection of Austrian correspondence on the oath question, from November 1916 to March 1917 (HHSTA, war files, 56c/3).

*Notes to Chapter 8*

1. Haussmann, p. 61 (May 9, 1916).

2. According to House, reporting to Grey on June 8, 1916 (Vol. 2, p. 290), this was the view Jusserand expressed to House.

3. House, Vol. 2, pp. 290ff.; Seymour, pp. 170ff.; May, pp. 358ff. The story of German and American peace efforts in 1916 has been very thoroughly told by Birnbaum and Steglich (2). Both have drawn so heavily on German and Austrian documents that I need to cite only a few of these in the following. By far the largest documentation appears in UA 2. Like all publications by investigating committees of the Weimar national assembly and subsequent Reichstag, these "supplements" are awkwardly designated in a bibliographical sense and, to make matters worse, there was a second edition in 1920, with differing pagination, from which Birnbaum quotes. Here the report of the second subcommittee (also called Committee No. 15) on Wilson's peace efforts in 1916-1917 precedes. I cite by document rather than by page numbers. Many of the pieces in this compilation also appear in Sch&Gr, Vol. 1, where additional ones will be found. The committee's hearing transcripts, often of great importance and cited in these Notes as UA 1, were published as *Stenographische Berichte über die öffentlichen Verhandlungen des 15. Untersuchungsausschusses der verfassunggebenden Nationalversammlung,* Vol. 1, (1920), unfortunately only incompletely, to November 14, 1919. Steglich's account is based mainly on the following files, of which I have copies: HHSTA, war files, secret, XLVII/13-1, and war files, 4a; AA WW, 24, secret, Vols. 1-13, WW, 23, secret, Vols. 2-5.

4. B. J. Hendrick, *The Life and Letters of Walter Hines Page* (1926), Vol. 2, p. 186.

5. Page to Wilson, June 1, 1916, *loc. cit.,* pp. 298f. and *passim.*
6. See letter to Bethmann Hollweg, April 29, Birnbaum, p. 98, Note 8; and of May 29, *ibidem,* p. 102. The Baden deputy, Nieser, also reported, on June 24, about foreign ministry aversion to Wilson's peace efforts (GLA, IV, 35).
7. See the round-robin message of May 5, Chapter 5, Note 130, above; also Bethmann Hollweg's statements before the investigating committee of the national assembly, UA 1, shorthand reports, p. 683, November 17, 1919.
8. Müller, p. 206, July 27, 1916.
9. Birnbaum (p. 126) juxtaposes Jagow's draft and Bethmann Hollweg's handwritten version.
10. Details about this political activist are given in Hymans, *passim,* esp. pp. 789-791. He presented his political views in a much-noted book, *La Belgique neutre et loyale.* He died in the early summer of 1916, victim of a traffic accident in London. For Törring's political attitude, see his moderate but rather unrealistic peace program of August 27, 1916 (Sch&Gr, Vol. 1, No. 317).
11. German documents in AA WW, secret, 20a, Vol. 1, published in Sch&Gr, Vol. 1, Nos. 129 (August 11), 132 (August 17), 152 (October 30), 169 (November 28), 172 (December 1), 183 (January 9, 1917), 205 (February 28), 206 (February 29), and 226 (April 14). The transcription of No. 205, which was apparently difficult to read, contains some errors.
12. The negotiations with Count Törring are not mentioned in the war diaries of King Albert I of Belgium.
13. Sch&Gr, Vol. 1, No. 183, Supplement 2. The "note" seems to have been agreed between the negotiators, and thus does not represent a personal statement by the king.
14. Not "insufficient," as Fischer erroneously states (p. 269).
15. In a note of January 1, 1916, probably meant to be discussed with Jagow (Sch&Gr, Vol. 1, No. 180), we read: "The best we could do would be a mutual assistance pact with political, military, and economic guarantees, the question of whether or not we are to annex Liège being left open." Bethmann Hollweg would also "strengthen our position in Belgium, to be based on such a defensive alliance, by vigorously fostering the Flemish." This, he believed, would make Germany appear as the benefactor of the Flemish, and he feared no unfavorable repercussions abroad. In the war aims catalog Bethmann Hollweg had communicated to Wilson confidentially on January 31, 1917, the annexation of Liège was eliminated and there was nothing about the Flemish.
16. Albert I of Belgium, pp. 102ff.
17. Fischer (pp. 262ff.) so represents them. Since the negotiations had to be broken off, it would have been a diplomatic blunder of the first order to hand Professor Waxweiler the list of German demands; but according to Fischer, Count Törring did not "dare" hand them over, because they were so immoderate!
18. Including Baron Beyens, after January 21, 1916, the foreign rather than prime minister—Fischer (p. 270) seems to regard him as the latter. Bethmann Hollweg was well-informed about the king's difficult situation, see, for example, Sch&Gr, Vol. 1, No. 350, Bethmann Hollweg to Ferdinand of Bulgaria, October 23, 1916.
19. Details in Hymans, Chapter 7 (pp. 152ff.), and pp. 883ff. (Nos. 23-30). On February 24, however, the cabinet decided there was no harm in at least listening to any offers from the enemy side—see memorandum by de Broquevilles in Suarez, Vol. 4 (1940), p. 226.
20. To rescue him from this position, some Belgian clergymen apparently concocted and submitted to the German government a fantastic plan, under which King Albert would have been taken prisoner by the Germans, "in circumstances of danger," i.e., presumably at the front. On February 25, Törring told Waxweiler about it, who as expected was highly amused and nothing more. It is characteristic of Fischer's approach that he instantly jumps to the conclusion that Bethmann Hollweg was responsible for this ludicrous proposal, on the sole "evidence" that

he wrote "What a pity! " in the margin of a brief preliminary report by Törring of February 28 on the failure of his mission (Sch&Gr, Vol. 1, p. 205). Had Fischer gone a few pages further in the files, he would have come on a more extended report by Törring (which indeed he actually used elsewhere! ). There Törring tells of Waxweiler's surmise that behind the proposal was a plot by Belgian extremists who in this way wished to try to compromise the king. Their agent, Waxweiler thought, was a certain Jesuit chaplain named Henusse, already known for similar antiroyalist intrigues (*ibidem*, p. 280).

21. The exchange between Hertling and Bethmann Hollweg in August 1915 (Sch&Gr, Vol. 1, Nos. 129, 132) was resumed in January 1916. Hertling proposed a meeting in Switzerland between the queen of Belgium and her mother, Duchess Charles Theodore of Bavaria, but Bethmann Hollweg vetoed this, since it would only serve to aggravate King Albert's difficulties. Lerchenfeld too was busy on this matter (GSTA, Pol. A, VII, 50, 53).

22. Fischer (p. 272) represents this admonitory proposal by Törring (which he recounts in somewhat distorted form) as expressing the views of the foreign ministry. It has now been published, as No. 226, in Sch&Gr, Vol. 1. On December 24 Count Törring once again offered himself to Bethmann Hollweg as a mediator (Sch&Gr, Vol. 1, No. 438).

23. Erzberger to Bethmann Hollweg, June 8, and subsequent correspondence between Jagow, Erzberger, and Gerlach, June 10-22, 1916–Sch&Gr, No. 268. Fischer (p. 272) says virtually nothing about this exchange, but presents at length some private opinions voiced by Erzberger in a letter to Gerlach of June 16, representing them as semiofficial.

24. Albert I of Belgium, p. 112f. Overstraeten gives further details in an article, "La Politique de Guerre du Roi Albert," in *Revue Générale Belge,* March 1964, pp. 15f. He says that Ulrich von Wilamowitz-Möllendorf, then rector of Berlin University, twice went to Brussels to see the banker Philipson, brother of the German historian of the same name, allegedly at the behest *(se disant interprète)* of the Chancellor. He said that Germany stood ready to concede full restoration of Belgian political, military, and economic independence, and suggested a meeting of trusted Belgian, French German, and British emissaries in Rotterdam, with the knowledge but not the authority *(engagement)* of their governments. The upshot of their consultations might then be submitted to their governments, to serve as a basis for official negotiations. In late August the same intermediary reverted once again to his mission, and Philipson was issued a passport for a trip to France, where he was to ask King Albert to submit this suggestion to the Allied governments, if he were ready to do so. These statements were confirmed by the American Hoover, head of the relief mission to Belgium and North France, who got the information from Philipson's own lips in Brussels. The Belgian financier Heineman, a friend of Helfferich, actually offered the same suggestion to Hoover directly. According to Heineman, Germany was ready to negotiate on the basis of restoration of Belgian political and economic independence, restitution of Belgian losses, and return of the occupied portions of French Lorraine, on condition that Germany should have a priority claim to five million tons of mineral ore from there. On the advice of the Belgian financier and politician Émile Francqui, then one of the leaders of the Belgian Comité National de Secours et d'Alimentation, Hoover visited the Foreign Office in London and told Sir Eustace Percy of the German peace feeler, with the result discussed in the text. I asked General van Overstraeten for his sources, and he assured me by letter that his statements were correct. Belgian historians have advised me that there seem to be no further Belgian studies on the stand taken by King Albert. On Lloyd George's position, see Part 2.

25. On March 21, 1916, the military attaché in Madrid asked the General Staff to support the king's request to be confidentially informed of German peace terms, for purposes of peace mediation (AA WW, 15, secret, Vol. 1). See also von der

Lancken's reports to the foreign ministry of December 3 and 8, 1916 (Sch&Gr, Vol. 1, Nos. 401, 414).

26. Albert I of Belgium, pp. 98f. The king was annoyed because Bethmann Hollweg, in his last Reichstag speech of June 5, had spoken of unequivocal German victory, citing the evidence of the front-line maps. Jagow's message to Bethmann Hollweg of August 22 seems to relate to a second discussion at La Panne (Sch&Gr, Vol. 1, No. 313). In late October Bethmann Hollweg bemoaned the fact that King Albert was so limited in his freedom of decision (*ibidem*, p. 522, Paragraph 2).

27. Bethmann Hollweg to Hertling, March 5, 1917 (GSTA, Pol. A, VII, 53). See also Steglich (2), p. 238, Note 537; and Sch&Gr, Vol. 1, Nos. 447 and 467. Statements in the rather unscholarly memoir by the Paris museum official A. Chatelle, *L'effort belgique en France pendant la guerra 1914-1918* (1934), p. 224, are worthless, because no sources are given, and furthermore are of little importance. They are repeated in the same author's *La paix manquée?* (1936), devoted to the familiar negotiations by von der Lancken in 1917. Bethmann Hollweg's strictures on Villalobar's efforts may be connected with the fact that the Spaniard, passing through Paris, expressed himself rather uninhibitedly about the German political leaders. According to a report by Isvolsky of December 23 (*Livre Noir*, Vol. 3, Part 1, p. 118) he told Jules Cambon—who was certainly far from edified by the news—about confidential talks he had just had in the foreign ministry in Berlin. He said that he had found Bethmann Hollweg a very moderate man, but Zimmermann, by contrast, *disposé de façon très irréductible*.

28. Hertling to Lerchenfeld, January 30, 1917; Hertling to Bethmann Hollweg, February 24, 1917; Bethmann Hollweg's reply, March 5, 1917—all in GSTA, Pol. A, VII, 51, 53. The papal effort probably went back to Erzberger's suggestion: Erzberger to Gerlach, November 11, 1916 (Sch&Gr, Vol. 1, No. 371). See also—on Hertling's attitude as well—E. Deurelein, "Hertling und die Annexion Belgiens," *Historische Jahrbücher*, Vol. 70 (1951), pp. 287f.; Sch&Gr, Vol. 2, Nos. 2, 9, 13, 15.

29. Hertling to Lerchenfeld, May 5; Lerchenfeld's reply, May 6 and 8; report of the Stuttgart envoy Moy, May 22, on a discussion between Weizsäcker and Bethmann Hollweg about whether German supplies would last until 1917. Bethmann Hollweg expressed the hope that there would be peace before that year (GSTA, Pol. A, VII, 50, 30).

30. Hertling to Lerchenfeld, July 24; Lerchenfeld's reply, July 27 (GSTA, Pol. A, VII, No. 51).

31. Poincaré, pp. 68ff.; Paléologue, Vol. 2, pp. 342ff.; Suarez, Vol. 4 (1940), pp. 132ff.; Smith (1), pp. 459ff.; detailed treatment of the background in Pingaud, pp. 291ff.; the correspondence between Pokrovsky, Satzonov, and Isvolsky from February 12 to March 11, 1917, was published in UA IV (Volkmann), pp. 84-86.

32. George Bonnefous, *Histoire politique de la troisième république* (1957), Vol. 2, p. 169 (chamber session of November 20, 1916).

33. Suarez, Vol. 3, pp. 413f.; Bonnefous, *loc. cit.*, pp. 160ff.

34. This is most clearly shown in his own memoirs. See also, among other sources, A. Fabre-Luce, *Caillaux* (1933). On the role of extreme left socialists in France and Britain, see the very detailed account by Arno J. Mayer, *Political Origins of the New Diplomacy 1917-1918*, New Haven (1959), Chapter 3, "Allied War Aims in Transition."

35. The statement was published in Suarez, Vol. 3, p. 419, but in juxtaposition with a letter of protest by the anti-annexationist industrialist Darcy, who was animated by lofty political sentiments.

36. Report by the Belgian envoy Baron Gauffin, January 31, 1916, Hymans, Vol. 1, pp. 159, 189f.

37. Poincaré, p. 4; see also Suarez, Vol. 3, p. 412, Vol. 4, p. 130.

38. Suarez, Vol. 4, pp. 128ff.; see also Hölzle, pp. 472ff., and for the following, *ibidem*, p. 475; also Pingaud, pp. 286f.

39. See Note 31, above.
40. The liberal deputy Dalziel, October 11, 1916–Schulthess, Vol. 32 (1916), II, p. 179.
41. A graphic account of how the liberal, pacifist, and neutralist press in Britain became converted to the "holy war" against militarism and Prussianism is given in the book by Irene Cooper-Willis, *England's Holy War. A Study of English Liberal Idealism During the Great War,* New York (1928).
42. Volume 4 of Link's great Wilson biography, soon to be published, will throw more light on this. In late November 1916, Wilson prevailed on the Federal Reserve Bank to warn American bankers against accepting short-term notes of the British treasury (A. S. Link, *Woodrow Wilson and the Progressive Era, 1910-1917* [new ed., 1963], p. 259).
43. See the memorandum he wrote for his colleagues shortly before a planned visit to St. Petersburg in December, as a kind of testament–*Twenty-Five Years,* Vol. 2, pp. 126ff.; see also Trevelyan, p. 408 (German ed.).
44. Lloyd George, Vol. 2, Chapter 30, p. 832 and *passim.*
45. Published in abbreviated form in Lloyd George, *The Truth About the Peace Treaties,* Vol. 1 (1938), pp. 31-50. The date is not given, but from the statements on p. 36, paragraph 3, it must have been before the declaration of war against Rumania, August 27, 1916, presumably during the earlier part of August.
46. See Part 1, above. According to Hölzle (p. 470, Note 16), who cites French documents, the Belgian government applied to the Western powers in the summer of 1916 for revocation of its neutrality obligations, though not going so far as to ask for a permanent alliance with them, since Paris and London seemed disinclined.
47. Remarkably enough, the only arguments the report puts forward (p. 47) for the allegedly aggressive character of the German government are that it wanted to acquire "additional colonies" belonging to other powers (this could probably relate only to Angola) and create "spheres of influence" through commercial penetration–in other words, the theme of "Reaching for World Power," quite along the lines of Fischer's book (Chapter 1).
48. See Vol. II, pp. 53f.; and also his detached judgment of Britain's military situation in late 1916, in Lloyd George, Vol. 2, pp. 898ff., and his report of August 31, *ibidem,* pp. 833-843.
49. Report by Cambon, September 10, 1916, in Hölzle, p. 470.
50. See the House of Commons session of August 21-22, 1916. The liberal member Byles cited statements by Zimmermann to the effect that Germany had repeatedly demonstrated its willingness to make peace, while the Entente, under British pressure, had never once done so. Byles also mentioned peace demonstrations by the German social democrats. Asquith and Cecil declared that no official peace offers from the German government had ever reached the British government, and only an official offer would have any significance (Schulthess [1916], p. 174).
51. Lloyd George, Vol. 2, pp. 853ff., where the account is somewhat fragmentary and muted (Schulthess [1916], p. 176).
52. Grey to Lloyd George, September 29, 1916–Lloyd George, Vol. 2, pp. 856ff.
53. Members Holt and Trevelyan in the House of Commons, October 11 (Schulthess [1916], pp. 178f.). Trevelyan cited Scheidemann's Reichstag declaration that Bethmann Hollweg sought no annexations, a statement that had never been disavowed. The end of the war was not yet in sight and it was by no means certain that the Allies were not continuing it to gain territory.
54. See Spender and Asquith, Vol. 2 (1932), pp. 243ff.
55. Asquith's speech in the House of Commons is in Lloyd George, Vol. 2, p. 891; see also Schulthess (1916), p. 178. Grey's speech in the Cecil Hotel is in the former, p. 893, the latter, p. 181. This speech supported the statements by Briand, Lloyd George, and Asquith, but sought to soften the repercussions of the "knockout" interview in America by adopting a milder tone, and by emphasizing America's

task of establishing a league of nations after the war that would secure the peace and of preparing for such an organization even now. In Germany this was wrongly interpreted as conciliatory, arousing false hopes among Bethmann Hollweg's liberal associates—see Prince Max of Baden, *Erinnerungen,* pp. 48ff.; also the discussion between Captain Boy-Ed and Riezler, November 5, in Birnbaum, p. 360. See also Note 89, below. Bethmann Hollweg discussed Grey's speech at a Prussian cabinet meeting on October 27, with cautious skepticism (ZA Merseburg, Rep. 90a, B III 2b, No. 6, Vol. 165).

56. Schulthess (1916), pp. 185f.; Spender and Asquith, Vol. 2, p. 241.
57. Prince Max of Baden, *loc. cit.,* p. 46.
58. Lloyd George, Vol. 2, pp. 888f.
59. The most plausible theory is that they were based on the Philipson effort, discussed in King Albert's war diaries, p. 112 (see Note 24, above). There were, however, many connecting threads, running by way of Belgium and Holland. As we have already seen, the Spanish envoy in Brussels, Count Villalobar, was particularly active. Hölzle says (p. 478) that he saw a note of December 30, 1916, by the director of the foreign ministry in Paris, de Margerie, according to which Villalobar told de Margerie that Bethmann Hollweg had held out the prospect of full restoration of Belgian independence and the return of Alsace-Lorraine. The latter sounds completely implausible, and one can only assume that de Margerie misunderstood Villalobar or that Villalobar was exaggerating. According to Hölzle, the French files failed to show that Villalobar's news had the slightest effect. It is noteworthy that Grey, in his "political testament" of December 1916 (*Twenty-Five Years,* Vol. 2, pp. 126f.), expected "tempting offers" from the Germans in the Belgian question, calculated to cause a split in the Entente.
60. Lloyd George, Vol. 2, pp. 877ff.; B. E. C. Dugdale, *Arthur J. Balfour,* Vol. 2 (1936), pp. 435ff.
61. Lloyd George, Vol. 2, pp. 862ff.; Asquith, Vol. 2 (1928), p. 138.
62. Lloyd George, Vol. 2, p. 874. *Ibidem,* pp. 873, 899ff., for Robertson's various reports. No statements by naval experts are given. For Grey's report of November 27, see Trevelyan, pp. 405ff.
63. Asquith, Vol. 2, pp. 147ff.; Lloyd George, Vol. 2, pp. 889f.
64. Lloyd George, Vol. 2, pp. 895f.
65. Bethmann Hollweg told the foreign affairs committee of the federal council that Falkenhayn and Holtzendorff were meeting that very day. "If Falkenhayn says that it is absolutely necessary for the struggle on our western front, what then? ... " (Report by Weizsäcker, HSTA, E 42-51, foreign ministry, IV v 3BA, V 116; see also Note 70, below.)
66. Unpublished report by Captain Grasshoff, used by Birnbaum, p. 140. The latter's account of the negotiations in Pless (pp. 133ff.) is based on Grünau's minutes (UA 2, Supplement 158), as well as on unpublished notes by Vice-Admiral Koch in the Reich naval archive.
67. Report by Weizsäcker, see Note 65, above.
68. Sch&Gr, Vol. 1, No. 318 (minutes).
69. Early part of Chapter 7.
70. Spindler (Vol. 3, p. 368) gives the figure of thirty-six as of December 20, 1916, but fails to say how many of these were in service against Britain. Before the investigating committee in 1919, Deputy Struve mentioned only twenty U-boats as of January 15, 1917, but said that another seventeen were added from February to May, and eighteen more by July. Elsewhere, however, he speaks of forty-one to fifty-three units "on mission" for the months of March to June, without, unfortunately, specifying how many of these were committed against Britain (UA 1, pp. 391, 393, 396). The comprehensive admiralty report of December 22, 1916, mentions no figures for vessels, but simply sticks to the earlier projection of 600,000 tons per month to be sunk. Spindler's tables (Vol. 4, p. 2) mention the following figures for U-boats of the high seas fleet, earmarked for service against

Britain: forty-six in February, increased to fifty-nine by July, but reduced to fifty-two by the end of 1917, by virtue of losses. The total figure for February is given as 105. On August 8, 1916, before the federal council committee, Bethmann Hollweg presented a detailed review of U-boat status, from a tabulation by the Reich naval office up to August 1 (see Sieveking's Hanseatic report, in R. Koschnitzke, *Die Innenpolitik des Reichskanzlers von Bethmann Hollweg im Weltkrieg,* unpublished dissertation, Kiel, 1951).

71. Birnbaum, in his otherwise excellent monograph, repeatedly suggests (pp. 149f., 169, 299, and *passim*) that Bethmann Hollweg hoped to be able to put the unrestricted U-boat campaign into effect without incurring war with the United States. This seems as improbable to me as it is unprovable. What is correct is that Bethmann Hollweg, in his comprehensive report of February 1916, was looking for forms of "intensified" U-boat warfare (including the sinking of armed ships without warning)—see Chapter 5, Notes 101ff., above—and that the Kaiser, in a circular of March 8, 1916, called for preliminary diplomatic steps with the neutrals for unlimited U-boat warfare, which Bethmann Hollweg thought pointless (*loc. cit.,* Note 108). Around the turn of the years 1916-1917, when all other prospects of avoiding unrestricted U-boat warfare seemed to have vanished, Bethmann Hollweg still clung to the hope that he might be able to reach agreement with Wilson on the sinking of armed merchant ships (see Part 4, below). He certainly did not regard or use peace initiatives by Wilson and the Central Powers—which, in fact, he welcomed—solely as a means for preparing for U-boat warfare, i.e., he did not in advance count on their certain rejection. The only passage capable of such an interpretation (his message to the OHL of October 1, 1916, UA 2, Supplement 162—see also Birnbaum, p. 169) fails to convince, because it was quite obviously a tactical move. To postpone the decision on limited U-boat warfare, Bethmann Hollweg had to find arguments that would appear plausible to Ludendorff. He would have made no impression whatever on Ludendorff by arguing that time must be allowed to see whether Wilson's effort met with success, for Bethmann Hollweg knew that Ludendorff discounted any such success. Hence Bethmann Hollweg argued that failure of Wilson's effort would greatly improve Germany's moral position in initiating a new U-boat campaign. I cannot see how else he would have expressed himself. Of course Fischer (pp. 369f.) regards this passage as "revealing the Chancellor's true intentions"—Bethmann Hollweg needed the peace effort (which he never thought would be successful) as an alibi for his own vicious purposes. At the same time he was naive enough to believe that he could protect himself diplomatically in such a way as to keep America out of the war, despite the U-boat campaign. In support of this theory Fischer cites Birnbaum, but Birnbaum had no doubts whatever as to the sincerity of Bethmann Hollweg's peace efforts. I do have an isolated objection to Birnbaum. He writes (p. 149): "Most political questions he [Bethmann Hollweg] judged primarily from the angle of home policy." Surely, if that were true, Bethmann Hollweg would not have undertaken the extremely unpopular attempt to mobilize Wilson as peace mediator. Note also his offer in 1915 to cede part of Silesia to Austria, discussed on p. 62, above, and made without regard to repercussions on the home front.

72. His first handwritten draft read "otherwise unrestricted U-boat warfare scarcely avoidable" (Birnbaum, p. 129). According to Helfferich (Vol. 2, p. 351, reporting a discussion of August 31), what Bethmann Hollweg meant by "conditional restoration of Belgium" was that Germany would settle its relations with Belgium after restitution in direct negotiation.

73. This is obvious to any discriminating reader of his reports. In Chapter 9 of his book Fischer—who takes no note of recent American sources—always takes for granted that Bernstorff's reports were absolutely in accordance with the facts, and he generally represents Wilson's policy in such a way as to leave the reader with the impression that Germany needed only to reach out to end the war as a draw, with America's help (p. 319); but Bethmann Hollweg who, according to Fischer,

had already, on June 5, publicly rejected a mediated peace with Britain, wanted total victory with the help of unrestricted U-boat warfare and feared nothing more than a status quo peace, which would have been the American goal. Virtually everything about this theory is erroneous, and the whole chapter is a chain of misinterpretations, in which the true state of affairs is almost turned on its head. I trust that its refutation is obvious from my account, so that I may by and large refrain from entering into detailed polemics.

74. Lansing, pp. 172f.; see also Buehrig, p. 138; Smith (2), pp. 146ff.
75. Details in Birnbaum, pp. 155ff. and Appendix VI, 2-3 (juxtaposing the draft instruction and its alterations); see also Sch&Gr, Vol. 1, Nos. 324-327, 330, 331, 336, 343. It is typical of the Kaiser, who often made an immature impression, that he prided himself before Bethmann Hollweg on the excellent English of his draft, complaining at the same time of the "atrocious" foreign ministry English. In line with the spirit of his military entourage, he reproached the Chancellor for entertaining "philosophical reservations," but immediately gave way when Bethmann Hollweg responded with a show of irritation.
76. Captain von Trotha, chief of staff to Scheer and an ardent admirer of Tirpitz; Captain von Levetzow, chief of the operations section; Captain von Bülow, admiralty representative at supreme headquarters. The higher naval echelons had also been very busy in Vienna since late August, drumming up support for their views. The HHSTA (war files, secret, XLVII, 3-15) includes an abundance of memoranda on the prospects for unrestricted U-boat warfare, addressed to both Burián and Czernin. In early September word came from Germany that the OHL and the foreign ministry had reached agreement on the necessity for intensified U-boat warfare, and the Austrians (including Conrad) were asked for their views. Conrad instantly replied: "In a situation in which our enemies' clear intention to destroy us has taken on such perfidious forms, I should regard any other course of action as a crime against one's own country." Burián tried, through the Berlin embassy, to keep abreast of Reich intentions in the U-boat question (see correspondence with Hohenlohe and Bethmann Hollweg after September 1, *ibidem*). The Austrian naval command shared the views of its German counterpart (memorandum by Musulin, September 4), but Burián warned against placing military considerations above political ones and circulated an extremely well-informed memorandum, by a Herr Molden, that discussed the grave hazards of antagonizing America (*ibidem*, Nos. 4990/91, 10, 10). All through the fall, of course, representatives of the German rightist parties kept pressing Hindenburg in the U-boat question. Hindenburg assured them that like them he was boiling with impatience to give the word that the campaign could begin (see Westarp, p. 134, on the visit to Pless on November 14).
77. It is worth noting that even General Max Hoffmann was quite hard-headed in judging the prospects of U-boat warfare. In his book he says (Vol. 1, pp. 124f., 130f.) that it might have been successful if Germany had had the U-boats it had now (June 21, 1916) at the outbreak of the war, when Britain had no organized defenses. Now it was too late, and even Ludendorff was highly skeptical as to whether there were enough U-boats. Tirpitz, whom his own subordinates called "the father of lies," must have been giving deceptive figures in the spring. On Ludendorff's attitude toward the navy emissary, see his report of September 10, in Ludendorff (2), pp. 302ff.
78. Bethmann Hollweg inflated this figure still further and spoke of 700,000 men. Varnbüler reported on October 7 that Kühlmann's remarks made a strong impression on Ludendorff and Holtzendorff, according to foreign ministry information (HSTA, E 73, Reg. 61/12h, III 169).
79. UA 2, Supplement 164, October 2, 1916.
80. Spindler, Vol. 3, pp. 244f., 350f. Spindler takes the period from mid-October to the end of January as equivalent to four full months, thus getting a monthly average of only 307,634 tons sunk, instead of 351,582.
81. Holtzendorff, on August 31, UA 2, p. 175.

82. See Haussmann, pp. 63ff. Haussmann got the impression that Bethmann Hollweg was "at a loss" *(ratlos)* even when he delivered his Reichstag speech of September 28.
83. Fischer, p. 370. A considerable stir was caused by a meeting in the Prussian diet building, on October 10, called by an "independent committee for a German peace." An OHL representative is said to have asked the audience to await Hindenburg's decision calmly. Reventlow, however, insisted in the press that Bethmann Hollweg must have misled Hindenburg, which created a new stir. Details in the dissertation by Koschnitzke, cited in Note 70, above.
84. See Haussmann, pp. 64ff.
85. On the exchange with Hindenburg that preceded this statement, see Westarp, p. 132. Hindenburg was reluctant to be drawn into political discussion, hence Bethmann Hollweg had to operate very carefully.
86. On the secret session of the main committee, Hanssen reports sketchily (pp. 144ff.). I have had no access to the minutes of that meeting, but a mediocre dissertation by Willy Bongert, *Die Zentrumsresolution vom 7. Oktober 1916,* Cologne (1937), is based on them, indeed this constitutes its chief value. See also Bethmann Hollweg, Vol. 2, pp. 127f.; Helfferich, Vol. 2, pp. 390ff.; Erzberger, pp. 217f. On the stand of the center party after August 1916 and its internal conflicts, see May, pp. 298ff.
87. Müller, p. 230.
88. Haussmann, pp. 72ff.
89. For British rumors, see Prince Max of Baden, *loc. cit.,* pp. 48ff.; for Riezler's talk with Captain Boy-Ed on November 5, see Birnbaum, p. 360. Birnbaum believes that Riezler was afraid of a British peace offer based on the status quo, and there is some confirmation in the fact that Bethmann Hollweg told the Prussian cabinet on October 27 (see Note 96) that Germany should anticipate a possible enemy peace offer based on restoring the status quo, since in any such offer the enemy would have the advantage. This, however, was almost certainly a subsidiary motive, and Bethmann Hollweg cannot have seriously counted on a British offer. Before the federal council committee on October 30 Bethmann Hollweg did cite alleged statements by Under Secretary Hardinge of the British Foreign Office, to the effect that a fair German peace offer would create great embarrassment in Britain. (Report by Nieser, GLA.) For Bethmann Hollweg's speech on November 9, see *Kriegsreden,* ed. by Thimme, pp. 151ff.
90. For exchanges between Bernstorff and the foreign ministry from October 11 to 20, see UA 2, Supplements 22-25.
91. See Chapter 7, Notes 46ff., above.
92. According to Helfferich, Vol. 2, pp. 355f., Grey's speech, already cited, and Helfferich's pleas provided the crucial impetus. Yet Berlin could not possibly have known the text of the speech on the 25th, and Helfferich's claim that the idea came from him is almost certainly unjustified.
93. Memorandum of November 8, 1916 (HHSTA, war files, secret, XLVII, 3-5; see also Birnbaum, p. 236).
94. This compromise probably goes back to proposals made in Berne in May 1916 to the foreign ministry, by Envoy Romberg, who was in constant touch with representatives of the French oppositional groups around Caillaux. In a report of November 27, however (Sch&Gr, Vol. 1, No. 397), Romberg said that changing public sentiment in France had rendered his proposals obsolete. He now demanded that all territorial exchanges and border rectifications be foregone and that Alsace-Lorraine be granted full autonomy as a federal state of the Reich, at the very least. Anything more would kill any chance of reaching an understanding even with French opposition circles. Romberg was disappointed with Zimmermann's reply, included in a report, dated December 13, by a legation member dispatched to Berlin (AA WW, secret, Vol. 2, unsigned copy). The minister insisted on cession of the Briey basin and some form of war indemnity, if necessary disguised as something else. Since certain assurances had already been given to

Bavaria, he was unable to give a firm pledge that the Reich provinces would receive full autonomy.

95. Fischer does not mention this. It is altogether incompatible with his insistence that Bethmann Hollweg pursued broad annexationist goals, never more stubbornly than in the fall of 1916.

96. It was Minister of the Interior von Loebell, whom we already know as an anti-annexationist (Chapter 1, pp. 27ff.), who supported Bethmann Hollweg's proposals most vigorously, in addition to Helfferich, of course. The only marked opposition came from Wild von Hohenborn and Minister of Commerce von Sydow (ZA Merseburg, Rep. 90a B III 2b, No. 6, Vol. 165).

97. Thus reads Wahnschaffe's draft outline (ZA Potsdam). The detailed report by the Baden envoy Nieser (GLA, IV, fasc. 37) reads: "If we come out of this with our development potential unimpaired we shall have won."

98. Before the federal council committee he emphasized, among other things, that he had deliberately avoided sharp language directed against France in his speeches and had repeatedly singled out French valor for praise. According to Wahnschaffe's notes he said: "Possible thought for French: Why keep on fighting with British? Then separate soundings."

99. Westarp, p. 79, discussion on December 23, 1916.

100. Sch&Gr, Vol. 1, pp. 583f. Romberg, writing to Bethmann Hollweg on November 27, 1916, mentions a discussion between Count Berchem and Marchetti, in which proposals were made that Romberg regarded as very noteworthy and with which he identified himself. He urgently warned against any border rectifications with France.

101. Bethmann Hollweg to Count Wedel, December 15; reply, December 18 (UA 2, Supplements 92 and 100).

102. Helfferich, Vol. 2, p. 358; Bethmann Hollweg, Vol. 2, pp. 152f; Sch&Gr, Vol. 1, No. 356. The message went on in the typically Wilhelminian style of boastful self-praise: "Such a deed calls for a ruler with a conscience, who feels himself responsible before God and whose heart beats for the enemy peoples as well as his own. . . . I possess that courage and I shall accept the risk, God willing." This letter was published in the *Norddeutsche Allgemeine Zeitung* in mid-January and also appeared in *Le Temps* on January 17.

103. Bavarian record of this meeting on December 11 (GSTA, MA, 1936, No. 2494/69; see also Steglich [2], p. 146).

104. This, approximately, is the basic interpretation of Steglich (2).

105. Sch&Gr, Vol. 1, No. 347, identical with UA 2, Supplement 75. In all the later versions it was carefully emphasized that the kingdom of Poland was created by "Germany and Austria-Hungary."

106. Meeting of the federal council committee on October 30 and letter to Hindenburg, November 4 (UA 2, Supplement 78; Sch&Gr, Vol. 1, No. 361).

107. Bethmann Hollweg was under continuing heavy pressure in the Briey-Longwy question, as shown in a message to Grünau of November 25, intended for Valentini. When the steelmakers' association heard a rumor to the effect that the Chancellor desired an understanding with France at any cost, even foregoing Briey, they decided at once to protest to Hindenburg (ZA Potsdam, chancellery file, VII, 10).

108. As might be expected, Fischer (pp. 402ff.) seeks to minimize the differences between Bethmann Hollweg's and Hindenburg's war aims programs, which he regards as being along the same line. One of his chief pieces of evidence is Bethmann Hollweg's apparently extreme willingness to give way after he had received Hindenburg's reply of November 5. I do not think that a detailed argumentation on this point would be rewarding.

109. According to Burián's report, this was also very clearly expressed in the Austro-German negotiations that took place in Berlin on November 15-16.

110. Among other things, he cited the contributions currently being exacted from Bel-

gium even then, with the effect that Hindenburg demanded a substantial increase in them (UA 2, Supplement 81).

111. The clauses covering Poland, Courland, Lithuania, and Belgium were returned to their original form. It was now stated that the Congo or part of it would have to be acquired by Germany. The incorporation of Luxembourg was described as necessary in the event that Germany were to acquire Briey and Longwy, which was thus left an open question (UA 2, Supplement 82).

112. This war aims catalog came into being only during the Berlin negotiations of November 15-16, about to be discussed. Bethmann Hollweg read them out on November 16 and handed them to Burián.

113. He thought that transmission of a peace note without enumerating terms—which seemed extremely modest to him, even in the form he himself desired—was virtually begging for peace in humiliating fashion. In other words, he wanted the terms stated and their rejection coupled with the open threat of ruthless U-boat warfare. He was skeptical of border improvements with Russia, now that Poland was no longer available for bargaining purposes. He wanted particularly to gain the port of Vlonë (Valona), allegedly indispensable against Italy, and to annex at least part of Montenegro and that part of Serbia that would not go to Bulgaria. He thus wanted to put into effect the old conquest program of February 1916, augmented by substantial border improvements against Rumania (November 9). Burián then inquired of Grand Admiral Haus as to the military value of Vlonë and the contemplated agreement on freedom of the seas and of shipping on the Danube. Haus said all this was quite worthless, describing a protectorate over Albania or that country's annexation as most undesirable. The only useful acquisition to his mind would be a Danubian strip along the Iron Gate (exchanges of November 12 and 15, HHSTA, secret, XLVII, 13-1). Burián's program of November 15 included a plan for dividing up Montenegro between Austria and Albania (UA 2, Supplement 85, Appendix 2).

114. Final agreement on the wording was reached only on December 8. This took Bulgarian desires into account as well.

115. Details in Steglich (2), pp. 81ff., 126ff.; and the early part of Chapter 7, above.

116. Complete documentation in Steglich (2), p. 93.

117. Birnbaum, p. 365, appendix, VIII, 3; House, Vol. 2, pp. 392ff. It is noteworthy that House described Count Bernstorff as the only diplomat of the belligerent nations who had retained a sense of proportion, free of chauvinism (p. 398).

118. Smith (2), pp. 146, 149.

119. Charles to Burián, December 5 and 6 (HHSTA, war files, secret, 25p). It is worth noting that Charles was also dismayed because the Kaiser showed himself to be completely uninformed about Germany's dismal economic situation and the undeniable war-weariness of his people. We can see why he was in such a hurry about the peace effort.

120. On December 12, 1916, Zimmermann told reporters that Germany had wanted to anticipate Wilson with its peace note; and on July 4, 1917, he repeated this before the main committee of the Reichstag, on both occasions for the sole purpose of influencing public opinion, which was hostile to American mediation. He wanted in particular to prevent attacks by Stresemann on government policy. He gave this as his motive when testifying before the investigating committee on November 4, 1919 (UA 1, pp. 201ff.). He then disavowed his former assertions, although he was quite frank that he personally had taken a more skeptical view of Wilson's mediation than Bethmann Hollweg. As our account has shown, his assertions in 1916-1917 were undoubtedly factually wrong. Bethmann Hollweg's fluctuating considerations become especially clear in his message to the OHL of November 27 (Sch&Gr, Vol. 1, No. 396). The upshot, however, was this: "Undoubtedly our situation will be better if the anticipated Entente rejection of all negotiation comes in reply to an offer from Wilson rather than ourselves. Hence the likelihood that a peace appeal from Wilson will be widely unpopular in

Germany must not determine our decisions." The only trouble, he went on, was that since Wilson's actions were so unpredictable Germany must not miss the right psychological moment for its own peace offer. (See also Birnbaum, pp. 242ff.) Fischer, of course, does not fail to use even this occasion (pp. 378ff.) for buttressing his misguided notion that the Chancellor and the foreign ministry were not seriously searching for peace, but merely wanted to prepare the U-boat campaign.

121. According to a report by Hohenlohe of December 11, Bethmann Hollweg and Zimmermann nevertheless returned from Pless well-satisfied, the latter particularly proud of having rebuffed Ludendorff's unjustified claims. Ludendorff had requested that military attachés be henceforth empowered to send their political reports to the General Staff without prior control by the ambassador. Hohenlohe voiced serious doubt, however, that Zimmermann would really be able to tame the rambunctious general in the long run (HHSTA, war files, 25p).

122. See Note 101, above.

123. See Note 120, above. Hohenlohe to Burián, December 16, 1916 (HHSTA, war files, 25p).

124. Report by the Württemberg envoy Moser on a reception given by Count Hertling on December 14 (HSTA, E 73, 61, fasc. 12i); report by Legation Councilor Schoen on a discussion with Zimmermann on December 27 (GSTA, Pol. A, VII, Nos. 10-80).

125. As Fischer asserts (p. 408). On p. 412 he goes so far as to speak of Bethmann Hollweg's "basic agreement," which he gathers from the program Bethmann Hollweg sent to Washington in confidence.

126. It is not known why this inquiry was made. We may conjecture, however, that in view of the impending colonial negotiations the Chancellor wished to be informed whether and how the kind of Central African colonial realm he envisaged could be rendered secure in terms of naval strategy. The ban on public discussion of war aims, by the way, had been lifted shortly before, on November 20.

127. Hindenburg to Burián, December 23 (Sch&Gr, Vol. 1, No. 435); second naval program, sent to Bethmann Hollweg December 24 (*ibidem,* No. 437); first program and previous items also in AA WW, 15, secret, Vol. 2; see also Steglich (2), pp. 155ff. According to Bethmann Hollweg's own report on his talks at Pless of December 29 (Valentini, p. 244), the OHL wanted Lithuania, Courland, and the regions of Brest-Litovsk and Bialowieza for Prussia.

128. For Bethmann Hollweg's report, see the preceding Note. On December 29 Zimmermann also briefed the OHL on the government's intentions concerning a Central African colonial domain, on which Ludendorff had requested information. To this end he probably used a brief note by Solf, for which Bethmann Hollweg had asked (AA WW, 15, secret, Vol. 2). Solf said expressly that while his earlier proposals had always met with the Chancellor's approval, this hurried compilation should be regarded as his private work rather than a government program. It does indeed go beyond any of Bethmann Hollweg's programs known to us, in that it calls for at least the demand, for prestige reasons, for the return of all Germany's former colonies, regardless of whether this was a realistic goal. Germany's colonial realm was to be augmented by other possessions—including those of Britain, if that were attainable. It was to be consolidated into a Central African domain and expanded westward as far as possible. These were rather vaguely formulated aims rather than a fixed program for negotiation.

129. UA 2, Supplements 118, 119.

130. Statement by Riezler on December 20, 1921, unpublished minutes in AA, a copy of which (XVIII, 461551-3) is in my possession. I am indebted to Steglich (1), available to me in manuscript form, for reference to this interesting testimony by Riezler, Helfferich, and other associates of Bethmann Hollweg.

131. Lloyd George, Vol. 3, p. 1,104. Similarly optimistic intelligence on Entente intentions, based in part on unsupported rumors, reached Berlin from Rome, via

Vienna (UA 2, Supplement 99; Sch&Gr, Vol. 1, No. 445). On the Vatican's fruitless efforts to establish details about the German peace terms and mediate an agreement with Belgium, if possible, see Steglich (2), pp. 168f., and Sch&Gr, Vol. 1, No. 470.

132. Envoy Nieser reported at length to Premier von Dusch after December 15 on reactions abroad, from foreign ministry intelligence (GLA, HSTA, IV, 37, pp. 403ff.). Press reports in Wippermann-Purlitz, Vol. 32 (II, 2), pp. 1,189ff., 1,192f., 1,194ff., 1,216ff., 1,239f., and 1,253ff.; also Lloyd George, Vol. 3, pp. 1,096ff. Various manifestos on the peace question after December 12, 1916, are to be found in Scott.

133. Such considerations were probably behind the failure of House's attempt, supported by a British attaché in London, to have all public declarations there banned until details about Germany's concrete war aims were known (House, Vol. 2, pp. 403ff.).

134. Hölzle, pp. 475ff. (for the following as well).

135. See Isvolsky's criticism of December 22 of the draft that emerged from consultations among Cambon, de Margerie, and Berthelot, and himself and Briand. He said that it must not contain any open calumnies (*Livre Noir,* III, 4, p. 117). For British objections, see Lloyd George, Vol. 3, p. 1,109.

136. This has now been convincingly demonstrated by Link, Vol. 4. He shows, further, that Wilson, far from being affronted by the German peace offer, was pleased with the comments on it from Bethmann Hollweg and really wanted the Allies to take it seriously.

137. Hölzle, pp. 477f., based on reports by Jusserand of December 20, 21, and 22. It is not clear whether Lansing's optimism was based on talks between House and Bernstorff or on news from Berlin. It does demonstrate how profound must have been the impression on the Americans of the German foreign ministry's willingness for peace. At the time, this was also confirmed to the government in Paris by Villalobar (see Note 27, above), though it had no effect there. (B. J. Hendrick, *Walter Hines Page,* Vol. 2, p. 207; Lansing, pp. 186ff.; *Livre Noir* Vol. 3, p. 120 [Isvolsky, December 24]; House, Vol. 2, p. 418 [discussion with Wilson on war aims]; Smith [2], pp. 150ff.)

138. Jusserand had proposed that this protestation be eliminated, since this was a kind of *annihilation politique.* He also preferred to do without the dubious *principe des nationalités*–reports of December 29 and January 5, Hölzle, p. 479. We are probably dealing with specifically British notions here. For the text of the notes, see Scott, p. 35, and FR, 1917, Supplement 1, pp. 6f. A documented account of the London negotiations on the notes of reply is given by Link, Vol. 4, Chapter 17. Interestingly enough, he shows that the list of peace terms corresponded approximately to what Lansing had discreetly suggested to the ambassadors of the Western powers.

139. According to Overstraeten, in the king's war diaries, p. 121. He mentions communications the king had received from Philipson and the Vatican. *Ibidem,* pp. 123ff., important diary notes and letters by the king. A. Chatelle, in *La Paix Manquée* (1936), mentions Villalobar's remarks, already mentioned (Note 27, above), and reproduces the decision of the Belgian cabinet of December 20 (p. 8). What was wanted above all was a knowledge of German peace terms. Apparently Jules Cambon did bring the Belgians news of this on February 24 (*ibidem,* p. 9), supposedly on the basis of the German war aims catalog sent to Wilson on January 31, which Cambon said he had obtained from Gerard. Most of this was slanderous invention.

140. Scott, pp. 38f.

141. UA 2, Supplement 178, identical with Ludendorff (2), pp. 315f., December 23, 1916.

142. Information from a dispatch by the Austrian ambassador Pallavicini of December 30, in Birnbaum, p. 257. That Bethmann Hollweg himself was no stranger to such

notions is shown by his message to the OHL of January 4, 1917 (UA 2, Supplement 119).

143. Birnbaum (p. 277) asks whether the Entente answer to the German offer may not have been more brusque than would otherwise have been risked, because of the negative German reply to Wilson's peace note. I think this quite unlikely, from both the background and the content of the reply to Germany, which was probably regarded as cautious rather than abrupt in Paris and London.

144. There is another possible explanation. The official message of December 24, to the effect that the reply of the belligerent powers might be given in confidence (see Note 123, above), was received in Berlin only after Zimmermann's note of the 26th had been dispatched. Wilson probably suspected as much. Perhaps he did not know that Lansing had informed Bernstorff. Gerard was actually able to transmit the communication of December 24 only at the turn of the year.

145. Sch&Gr, Vol. 1, No. 458. This war aims catalog should be compared with the message to Hindenburg of November 4 (UA 2, Supplement 78).

146. Birnbaum (p. 299) seems to me to greatly overestimate the chances of such cooperation—he thinks it might have reached a point at which there could have been unrestricted U-boat warfare without America entering the war, or perhaps merely that Bethmann Hollweg seriously considered such a possibility. I think there should be stronger proof of Bethmann Hollweg's blindness than passages in Zimmermann's draft suggesting that Bernstorff sound out House confidentially on whether there was a chance that Wilson would accept a U-boat blockade of the British and. French coasts. The reason that Bethmann Hollweg did not object to cutting these passages at the request of the OHL may have been his conviction that such soundings were pointless and that the military counterarguments were plausible (Birnbaum, pp. 301, 310f.).

147. Sch&Gr, Vol. 1, No. 463, identical with UA 2, Supplement 53.

148. Details in Birnbaum, pp. 310f.

149. Evidence for the following in Birnbaum, pp. 276-286, 304-309, 315ff. Most of these documents appear also in the UA 2 supplements, Helfferich, or Valentini. Birnbaum supplements these from the navy archives.

150. See Note 141, above. This wire was dispatched on the same day as the new war aims program of the OHL, discussed in Note 127, above.

151. A far more realistic estimate of these effects was given in a letter of November 6 by Privy Councilor Albert in New York, which Helfferich sent on to Zimmermann on December 18 (UA 2, Supplement 173).

152. Lloyd George, Vol. 3, pp. 1,126, 1,130, 1,159ff. Of considerable interest are Helfferich's figures on the enormous British shipping losses and the resultant supply problems, based on British admiralty publications, which he presented to the parliamentary investigating committee on November 14, 1919 (UA 1, pp. 535ff.). See also Lord Jellicoe's memoirs, *The Submarine Peril. The Admiralty Policy in 1917* (1934, German translation, 1938), and *The Naval War* (1920, German translation, 1937). They show, among other things, that until the fall of 1916 the British admiralty did not take the German U-boat menace very seriously and was poorly prepared to combat it. Spindler (Vol. 4, pp. 194ff.) gives figures on sinkings for February to May 1917, taking into account British and French naval tabulations. They are naturally somewhat below the figures made known in Germany in 1917. Initially a relatively large number of ships merely suffered damage, but later on this share sharply declined. See also Chapter 10, Note 14, below.

153. Holtzendorff to Müller, December 15, 1916 (Müller, pp. 242f.). The letter displays some personal resentment of Bethmann Hollweg, who had gone over his head to the General Staff, Holtzendorff thought. Friction between Scheer and Holtzendorff grew with the initiation of U-boat "cruiser warfare" and its unexpected success (*ibidem*, p. 233 [October 31], p. 236 [November 21]). According to Birnbaum (p. 305), Holtzendorff promised the high seas chief by letter on De-

cember 14 that unrestricted U-boat warfare would begin on February 1, 1917.

154. Birnbaum, p. 279, from admiralty files. His report on the talks between Bethmann Hollweg and the OHL on December 29 (pp. 283f.) is also based on new and unpublished material.

155. Birnbaum, Appendix 10, pp. 370ff.

156. RAW, Vol. 11, p. 461n–letter dated February 1927 by Lersner, addressed to the Reich archive. He cited Bethmann Hollweg and Helfferich as saying that they had to give way on the question of unrestricted U-boat warfare, since otherwise there would have been an open struggle between the OHL and the government. At the very least, this would have dealt a severe blow to Kaiser and country. To maintain domestic peace, they, as the weaker ones, had to set aside their own convictions. I must say that I very much doubt whether the two statesmen would have so openly admitted their willingness to capitulate completely in the presence of so very young a diplomat. So little did Helfferich, in fact, surrender that on January 10, when he was outvoted in Pless, he wanted to resign and was dissuaded only with difficulty (Helfferich, Vol. 2, p. 409). Bethmann Hollweg on his part gave in only on January 9, though he had certainly wavered before.

157. See text to Notes 145-148, above. On the talks with Czernin on January 6, 1917, see p. 231.

158. Notes by the Bavarian legation councilor von Schoen on January 9, 1917, on a discussion with Stumm (GSTA, Pol. A, VII, 11-10).

159. AA WW, 18, secret, Vol. 24, Sheets 19-21, Tel. No. 145 (L 118730-31), dispatched at 2:30 P.M. on January 4 in code by courier to the American embassy for transmission to Bernstorff. For his acknowledgment of January 9, see UA 2, Supplement 54. Bethmann Hollweg had not yet received this when he told Holtzendorff by telephone on January 8 that the note was being handed over (to Lansing) that day (UA 2, Supplement 212).

160. Note by Schoen, *loc. cit.*, Müller, p. 247.

161. See Note 147, above.

162. Minutes of the meeting of January 8, UA 2, Supplement 212.

163. Hindenburg, initially proposed by Holtzendorff, declined, saying that he could not speak in the Reichstag [sic] and naming the arch-conservative governor of Alsace-Lorraine, von Dallwitz. Ludendorff remarked that no one even knew whether Dallwitz favored U-boat warfare. Holtzendorff knew that the Kaiser would never appoint either Bülow or Tirpitz. Hence the gentlemen were at their wits' end.

164. Müller, p. 248; see also UA 2, Supplements 183, 213; Ludendorff (2), pp. 323ff.; Valentini, pp. 144f.; Bethmann Hollweg, Vol. 2, p. 137; Helfferich, Vol. 2, pp. 405ff.

165. Helfferich, Vol. 2, p. 405. Was it Scheer? –on the 8th the Chancellor had requested by wire that he be summoned to Pless (Müller, p. 248). But then, surely Bethmann Hollweg had long since been familiar with Scheer's role in the U-boat question.

166. Remarkably enough, Birnbaum overlooked this in his detailed account (pp. 325ff.), in which he charges Bethmann Hollweg with having failed to brief the generals on the latest news about American mediation efforts. Even Bethmann Hollweg pointed to the documents of December 23 and 27 in his letter to Prince Max of Baden of October 23, 1918 (Ludendorff [2], p. 771), refuting Hindenburg's notorious letter of October 10 to the same addressee (Ludendorff [2], pp. 345ff., also UA 1, November 18, 1919).

167. Roedern's papers (in the possession of his family), February 1917. There are no such emotional overtones in the reports of Valentini and Müller. Müller thought Bethmann Hollweg's presentation "somewhat discursive" and was particularly surprised about his apprehensions concerning Switzerland.

168. The fact that they were aware of this is not changed one way or another by certain temporizing measures. At the end of the talks in Pless the Kaiser asked the Chancellor to try to keep ·America out of the war by possible concessions in

respect of American sea passenger traffic (Müller, p. 249); Bethmann Hollweg himself had voiced a similar idea that morning (UA 2, Supplement 203); and even Ludendorff had discussed such a possibility with Holtzendorff on January 8 (*ibidem,* Supplement 212). For Bethmann Hollweg himself this possibility is certain to have meant no more than a last desperate hope in a situation from which there was no escape.

169. On the morning of January 9 even Bethmann Hollweg does not seem to have anticipated that American entry into the war would mean anything more than food supplies to Britain, financial assistance, the dispatch of airplanes, and a volunteer corps (UA 2, Supplement 213).

170. Bethmann Hollweg, Vol. 2, p. 136.

171. Helfferich, Vol. 2, pp. 410f.

172. Valentini's account (p. 146) was written down only in February 1918 and represents Bethmann Hollweg as a convinced opponent of U-boat warfare even on the evening of January 9; but Valentini evidently attributed some of his own convictions to the Chancellor.

173. Published in Ludendorff (2), pp. 329ff. The memorandum had been definitively agreed on between Bethmann Hollweg and Holtzendorff on January 4 (see Note 159, above). For the exchanges between the foreign ministry and Bernstorff, see UA 2, Supplements 51, 52, 54, 56. For the last item, see also Ludendorff (2), p. 328.

174. According to Link, Vol. 4, Chapter 17.

175. Helfferich, Vol. 2, p. 401.

176. House, Vol. 2, p. 415; Buehrig, p. 55 (after a diary note by Wilson) and pp. 76ff. (for the following).

177. FR, *The Lansing Papers,* Vol. 1, pp. 579ff. See also Page's report of January 5, 1917, inquiring whether America would object to British vessels being more strongly armed (FR, 1917, Supplement 1, pp. 546ff.).

178. This was already in his comprehensive memorandum of February 29, 1916 (see Chapter 5, Note 102, above), and was reinforced after the fall of 1916 (see Parts 3 and 4, above).

179. FR, *The Lansing Papers,* Vol. 1, pp. 581ff. The letter had not yet been finished when Bernstorff appeared in Lansing's office and handed him the announcement of unrestricted U-boat warfare. Lansing's appended memorandum, of considerable length, demonstrates, by the way, that the American secretary of state sought to justify virtually every resort to arms on the part of a merchant vessel. He thought even four six-inch guns, in any deck arrangement, perfectly justifiable.

180. According to British figures (Buehrig, p. 40), more than 300 armed British merchantmen were attacked in 1916, 80 per cent escaping by using their weapons.

181. Hohenlohe to Czernin, January 12 and 13 (Czernin, pp. 153ff.).

182. Link, *loc. cit.;* also Hölzle, pp. 477f.

183. See Note 147, above.

184. House to Wilson, January 15, 1917. Mr. Arthur S. Link was kind enough to send me copies of House's letters to Wilson of January 15, 16, 17, 18, 19, 20, and 26, 1917, and two letters by Bernstorff to House of January 18 and 20, all strangely enough omitted by Seymour in *The Intimate Papers of Colonel House.* All of these letters are among Wilson's papers in the Library of Congress, Washington, D.C.

185. Letter of the 18th: "They had proposed submitting the question of peace to arbitration, or, as an alternative, that you submit proposals yourself for a conference."

186. According to a diarylike note of the 18th (reproduced by Link, Vol. 4, Chapter 17), he was now indignant over the obstinate fighting stance of the British and the "horrible" French war aims. The president must now virtually force the Allies to make peace, in their own best interest and to prevent further slaughter. Even then he was developing some ideas about a just peace. Austria must have an ocean port as good as Russia's. When, on January 3, House consulted with Wilson

about a peace program the president might put forward in his Senate speech, planned even then, the two settled on the following points: a free Poland, on which Russia and Germany already seemed agreed, restoration of Belgium and Serbia, expulsion of the Turks from Europe, and possible Russian access to a warm-water port. They were still uncertain about Alsace-Lorraine (House, Vol. 2, p. 418). If Bernstorff, in accordance with his instructions, did tell House that Germany would on no account compromise on the question of Alsace-Lorraine, he may well have found House at least willing to listen. House, however, says nothing about this.

187. Bernstorff to the foreign ministry, January 16, 1917, received January 22 (UA 2, Supplement 59; Sch&Gr, No. 469).

188. In a letter of the 20th he wrote Wilson that despite everything he had not given up the belief that "at the moment liberal elements have control of the German government," although he suspected that the Kaiser might be secretly in league with the Russian autocracy [sic], or that the Germans might be merely maneuvering to prepare their unrestricted U-boat warfare, behind a camouflage of peaceful words that would enable them to disclaim responsibility. He further advised the British (through Wiseman, a diplomat close to him) to signify their willingness for a peace conference, if the Germans agreed to cease U-boat warfare in the meantime. Once started, a peace conference could not be halted, except with a peace treaty.

189. Sch&Gr, Vol. 1, No. 472.

190. I believe May to be in error in asserting (p. 369) that "the speech was addressed only to Germany."

191. For the text of Wilson's speech see Scott; Ludendorff (2), pp. 330ff.; Bernstorff (1), pp. 351ff.; also Wippermann-Purlitz. In Germany Wilson's demand for free access to the seas for all countries was evidently misunderstood. From House, Vol. 2, pp. 416ff., and Wilson's instructions to Page of February 8 (FR, 1917, Supplement 1, p. 40), it is seen that this did not primarily mean the conquest of West Prussia for Poland, but Russian access to the Mediterranean and Austrian access to the Adriatic (Trieste).

192. Link gives the evidence in Chapter 16.

193. See also the interesting article by Colonel Meier-Welcker, "Die Militärischen Planungen und ihre Ergebnisse 1917-1918," *Weltwende 1917,* ed. by H. Rössler (1964).

194. Ludendorff (2), p. 336. The OHL was kept currently informed of the exchanges with Bernstorff.

195. Czernin, pp. 153ff., 156ff., 161ff.; file notes of the Vienna foreign ministry of January 14 and 18; exchanges between Czernin and Hohenlohe, January 12, 14, 15, and 23 (HHSTA, XLVII, secret, 3-15; minutes of the joint cabinet meeting of January 22, *ibidem,* XXX, 293, No. 532).

196. Bavarian minutes of the meeting of the federal council committee of January 16, 1917 (GSTA, Pol. A, VII R, No. 58), supplemented by Bethmann Hollweg's report to Valentini, January 22 (Valentini, pp. 246f.). On his return to Munich Hertling gave a highly pessimistic account of the session to chargé d'affaires Count Brusselle. Only the navy, he said, seemed to be really in favor of intensified U-boat warfare (Brusselle to Czernin, January 19, HHSTA, war files, XLVII, secret, 3-15).

197. To Valentini, January 22 (Valentini, pp. 246f.); Westarp, pp. 152ff. Westarp said that until January 30 he was not informed, only told to throttle down for the time being the clamor for U-boat warfare in the conservative press, lest pending negotiations with America be prejudiced. Bethmann Hollweg was probably afraid of Westarp's radicalism, and indeed, on January 30 Westarp showed his dissatisfaction even with the announcement of unrestricted U-boat warfare, because it included an offer to spare individual American passenger ships.

198. See p. 323, above; UA 2, Supplement 67; Sch&Gr, Vol. 1, No. 472.

199. I am again indebted to Mr. Arthur S. Link for knowledge of this important letter as

well as of the complete text of House's report of the 26th (published in House, Vol. 2, p. 432, only in a quite incomplete version). Wilson's letter is among Colonel House's papers, and was used by May, p. 369. Bernstorff's report of January 27 is in UA 2, Supplement 69, also Sch&Gr, Vol. 1, No. 475.

200. "After much discussion it was finally decided, at his suggestion, that he send a dispatch tomorrow to his government telling them that you had requested a reply from them giving definite terms, and that you thought if their terms were moderate, there was reason to believe something might be done toward bringing about an early peace. He is to suggest to them that the terms include complete evacuation of Belgium and France. In addition to this he is suggesting that they make an offer to go into a peace conference on the basis of your address to the Senate" (not in *The Intimate Papers of Colonel House,* Vol. 2, p. 432). The report concludes with a request that Wilson wire any suggested changes that night in code. This renders highly improbable the theoretical possibility that the president amended his written instruction of the 24th by telephone.

201. Lansing, p. 208, note of January 28 (retranslated).

202. Steglich (2), p. 177 and Note 556. He cited, not Bernstorff's latest telegram, but the one of January 23, already discussed above (Note 189), which proposed that the terms should be described as obsolete even now.

203. On October 23 and November 18, 1919, before the parliamentary investigating committee (UA 1, pp. 154, 769). See also Bethmann Hollweg, Vol. 2, pp. 160ff.; Helfferich, Vol. 2, pp. 418ff.

204. Of particular importance with respect to the events in Pless on the 29th is Bethmann Hollweg's statement of November 18, 1919 (UA 1, p. 755). He said Holtzendorff was so emphatic in rejecting any delay that he never put his case to the Kaiser.

205. Westarp, p. 158; Tirpitz (2), p. 385.

206. In the federal council Zimmermann put the number of U-boats in service at 150 (120 large, thirty small), plus an additional 120 under construction. Directly afterward Capelle, before the Reichstag committee, said that the number of U-boats in service *and* under construction was 100! In view of the Atlantic stations, all these figures were inflated.

207. He used this justification himself before the parliamentary investigating committee on November 14, 1919 (UA 1, pp. 546ff.).

208. Fischer (pp. 414f.) naturally exploits this vagueness to read Bethmann Hollweg's entire "September program" into the document and thus demonstrate the "continuity" of Bethmann Hollweg's power politics.

209. Lerchenfeld to Hertling, January 31 and February 1, 1917 (GSTA, Pol. A, VII 11/24—reports on the federal council and main committee sessions). For Nieser's report to Dusch, January 31, see GLA, Berlin legation, fasc. 38, 84-92. See also Westarp, pp. 153ff.; Scheidemann (2), pp. 45ff.

210. Seymour, p. 201. Other sources used in connection with American policy from February to April were May, Chapter 19; Buehrig; Smith (2); Lansing and his papers (FR); and House, Vol. 2. Further details are given in Vol. 4 of Link's great Wilson biography.

211. Lansing, pp. 199ff.

212. Correspondence between Vienna and Berlin, February 5-8, 11, 1917 (UA 2, Supplements 215-218, 222-223). Czernin had to promise that he would instantly recall Ambassador Tarnowski in the event America declared war on Germany, and this was indeed done in April. On the other hand Czernin declined to allow himself to be used for purposes of protesting Wilson's policy. See Czernin, pp. 171ff.

213. Wilson to Page, February 8, 1917 (FR, 1917, Supplement 1, p. 40). Lansing strongly approved this action on February 10 (FR, *The Lansing Papers,* Vol. 1, p. 596).

214. Cross-examined in the Senate on August 19, 1919, Wilson insisted that only at the Versailles peace conference did he learn of the whole fiendish concatenation of secret Allied war aims treaties. Seymour (pp. 267f.) shows, however, that he must have been informed by April 28, 1917, at the latest, in a talk with Balfour.

After all, the Entente note of reply of January 10, 1917, had already outlined the program.

215. According to his memoirs (p. 192), he thought the offer came from the Russian side. For his note of March 5, 1917, see *ibidem,* pp. 381ff.

216. For the exchanges between Lansing, Penfield, and Page of February 5, 6, 8, 10, 20, 21, 22, and 27, and March 3 and 13, see FR, 1917, Supplement 1, pp. 38ff., 55ff., 62-65. In his memoirs, Czernin suppressed the content of his communications of March 13 about secret peace talks.

217. FR, *The Lansing Papers,* Vol. 1, pp. 24f., March 17, 1917.

218. Czernin, p. 193.

219. FR, 1917, Supplement 1, pp. 161, 178, 186. For the German text of the long memorandum, dated March 5, see Czernin, Appendix 2, pp. 381ff. It was handed to the press under the same date (Schulthess, 1917, Vol. 1, pp. 572ff.). Despite objections by the German ambassador, Count Wedel (UA 2, Supplement 230), it was transmitted to Penfield.

220. There is nothing of this in FR, which are otherwise very complete in reproducing the Vienna correspondence (exchanges with German headquarters, UA 2, Supplements 231-233).

221. UA 2, Supplements 219, 221, 227, 228 (February 8-21, 1917); Scott, pp. 72f. A comprehensive account appears in Link, Vol. 4, Chapter 18. Bernstorff, hiding behind a journalist, was secretly in on this. On December 10 he had himself wired the foreign minister, via Ritter, that Wilson wanted only protection for American shipping. By sparing American vessels, Germany might delay American entry into the war for a long time. Negotiations on this matter could be initiated at any time via the Austrian or Swiss embassies. On the 12th Lansing rejected the suggestion transmitted by Envoy Ritter, and this was at once made public. The result was a furor in the German press, over the impression that Germany was ready to compromise.

222. For detailed accounts, see Lansing, pp. 226ff., and B. J. Hendrick, *The Life and Letters of Walter Hines Page,* Vol. 3 (1926), pp. 330ff. Lansing was taken aback when Zimmermann at once conceded that the message was authentic, instead of embarrassing his opposite numbers by demanding proof. Barbara Tuchmann, in *The Zimmermann Telegram* (1959), treats the incident in minute detail. The wire had been dispatched to Bernstorff by three different routes and was intercepted by the British on each occasion.

223. He had caught a heavy cold and on March 7 took to his bed for several days.

224. To Senators Matthew and Hall, March 31, 1917 (Link, Vol. 4, Chapter 20).

225. A graphic account is given in Seymour, Chapter 6, "Diplomatic Speech of Coordination."

226. April 7, 1917 (Buehrig, p. 149).

227. UA 1, October 23, 1919, p. 106.

228. Link's findings from French files are of great interest (Vol. 4, Chapter 19). In March 1917, the French cabinet and foreign ministry were seriously worried lest American entry into the war might subsequently confer preponderance on that country in the peace negotiations. In that event it would be very difficult to divert the president from his notions of "peace without victory" and "restoration of the prewar political and economic balance." Unfortunately France had no choice but to seek American war aid. It would be one of French diplomacy's most difficult tasks to harmonize American policy with Allied plans and interests. Such sentiments appear, for example, in a memorandum written by Louis Aubert, in which the problems of Versailles in 1919 seem to have been foreseen.

229. Buehrig, p. 265, after J. L. Heaton, *Cobb of the World,* pp. 268ff. Cobb was under the impression that the interview took place just before the speech in Congress, but Link has shown that it could only have been on March 19.

*Notes to Chapter 9*

1. Valentini, pp. 146ff. According to the correspondence, *ibidem,* pp. 245ff., and

according to Müller, p. 250, the empress (whom Müller describes as Bethmann Hollweg's worst enemy) wrote the Kaiser in an effort to convince him that the Chancellor had suffered a physical collapse and should (as a first step) be given a leave of absence. Bethmann Hollweg sensed the intrigue and refused to be provoked.

2. Stein, p. 133.
3. Bauer, p. 123. The memorandum published on pp. 134ff. of this work, soon to be discussed, must be another document. Among the numerous letters of criticism in Bauer's papers (BA) is a report of February 3, 1917, by Captain Grasshoff of the admiralty political section which throws new light on the "controversy" between Hertling and the OHL in February-March 1917, described by E. Deuerlein in *Historische Jahrbücher,* Vol. 70 (1951), pp. 160ff. Grasshoff wrote that he had heard from Count Preysing about critical statements made by Hertling in confidence before the budget committee of the Bavarian chamber on the policies of the OHL in the Polish question and the Belgian workers' deportations. Grasshoff recommended that Preysing be consulted directly, so that "vigorous action" might be taken. Appended was a private letter from Count Bothmer to Preysing. Bothmer had heard from someone close to Bethmann Hollweg on January 30—and was highly indignant—that the Chancellor still doubted that U-boat warfare would meet with success. Thus Preysing was the informer vainly sought in Munich. On February 3 Grasshoff reported further rumored statements, in which Hertling said he hoped that the U-boat campaign would drive Wilson to peace mediation.
4. H. Wolfe, *Labour Supply and Regulation* (1923, part of the Carnegie work, in English). This book carries the text of the relevant laws, the effects of which are thoroughly and interestingly discussed in Lloyd George, Vol. 4, pp. 1,925ff. Apparently the whole system was in danger of breaking down in 1917, because of a serious wave of strikes. It was, however, shrewdly reorganized. A counterpart to Wolfe, A. Thomas, *L'organisation des industries de guerre,* was announced as part of the French Carnegie series, but seems never to have been published.
5. The OHL to the war ministry, August 31, 1919 (Ludendorff [2], pp. 63f.). *Ibidem,* further correspondence of the OHL on the Hindenburg program to November 26. I have excerpts from the ZA Potsdam (chancellery file, VII, 9-10), from that agency's documents, including relevant Prussian cabinet consultations; see also Bauer's and Wild's papers (BA); RAW, Vol. 11, pp. 32ff.; Groener, pp. 339ff.; Wrisberg, Vol. 2, esp. pp. 124ff. and Appendix 3, pp. 229ff.; Stein. The military, political, and economic effects of the auxiliary labor act have not yet been thoroughly studied. Umbreit's book limits itself in the main to the attitudes of the trade unions. I have been informed that a more comprehensive monograph may shortly be expected from America.
6. Wrisberg, Vol. 2, pp. 232ff. See the directives to the general replacement commands printed in the appendix to this work. The German trade unions had agreed in August 1914 that they would grant no strike pay during the war. There were strikes, nevertheless, and in the hunger year of 1916 they reached a total of 240 (Wrisberg, p. 116), which the war ministry still regarded as a "vanishingly small number" compared with peacetime.
7. Wild assumed that Bethmann Hollweg had a hand in his transfer, since he had offered the Chancellor determined opposition in both the U-boat question and the matter of the peace offer (Wild's papers, BA, esp. a letter to Professor Zorn of January 1, 1917).
8. Stein, p. 83; Groener, p. 347.
9. Wrisberg (Vol. 2, p. 101) offers an example. It is characteristic of Stein that he proposed (Stein, p. 109) that workers of arms-bearing age be given soldiers' pay, to equalize front-line and home service. He is critical of both the *Kriegsamt* and the auxiliary labor act in his memoirs.
10. Undated note, written between September 13 and 20 (ZA Potsdam, *loc. cit.*). On

September 17 Bethmann Hollweg sent the OHL a tentative reply in which he promised to consider the proposals of the 13th, but emphasized that some of the questions touched on were within his exclusive jurisdiction. Ludendorff's reply of the 20th was notably polite, mentioned that the OHL had put forward suggestions rather than demands, and admitted that apart from a few military measures all other questions were indeed up to the Chancellor. He expressed "sincere appreciation" that Bethmann Hollweg was willing to consider these matters and said he was at his disposal at any time for consultation. At this point Ludendorff was probably not yet quite certain of the Kaiser's attitude.

11. RAW, Vol. 11, p. 37.
12. The amateurish naiveté of the OHL in matters of higher education is shown, among other things, in a letter from Hindenburg to the Chancellor of January 24, 1918, asking that aliens (except from "dependable" allies) be barred from studying at German universities and industrial establishments. German technical superiority, he said, would have been greater in the war, but for German willingness to allow foreigners to share in the findings of German science. Under Secretary von Rado-witz made a marginal notation: "The Great Wall of China system," but sent copies to the Prussian ministry of cultural affairs and war ministry, and to the Reich economic office. All reacted negatively, the last-named reminding that Germany's flourishing foreign trade had been due not least to the fact that foreigners had been allowed to study in Germany (ZA Potsdam, chancellery file, VII, 11).
13. Bethmann Hollweg emphasized these factors in his reply of October 15 to the OHL proposal, which Groener had handed him on October 10. He carefully and shrewdly pointed out that if the *Kriegsamt* were given authority over the replacement commands, the imperial command power would be indirectly under the Chancellor, since his responsibility included the *Kriegsamt,* and also would be open to Reichstag influence. Hindenburg agreed in general on the 21st and appended a new version for an imperial rescript, which was then issued on November 1 (ZA Potsdam, chancellery file, VII, 9).
14. Wrisberg, Vol. 3, pp. 141ff. See also Groener's scathing criticism of the war ministry's slow-moving organization and methods (Groener, 553, September 16, 1916).
15. Helfferich, Vol. 2, p. 277.
16. The discrepancy between the popular Groener and the unpopular Helfferich is made quite clear in Umbreit's book, and also in the trade union proclamations of confidence in Groener.
17. ZA Potsdam, *loc. cit.,* October 26. See also reports by Hohenlohe to Burián of January 27 and 28 on a discussion with Bethmann Hollweg (HHSTA, war files, 4a). Hohenlohe complained of the Kaiser's rapidly increasing dependence on the OHL.
18. ZA Potsdam, chancellery file, VII, also for the following. For the exchange of telegrams with the Kaiser, see also AA WW, secret, Vol. 34.
19. Helfferich and Groener gave a preliminary and confidential briefing to the leading members of the federal council on November 9 (report by Nieser, GLA, IV, 37, pp. 310ff.). There was no opposition during these discussions.
20. The effects are also discussed in Chapter 7, Note 10, above.
21. November 17, 1916 (ZA Potsdam, *loc. cit.*). See also Bauer's papers (BA).
22. Of November 25, to Grünau and Valentini *(ibidem).*
23. For the text of the act and accompanying proclamation to the trade unions, see Umbreit, Appendix 2, pp. 239ff.
24. Groener, pp. 363f.; Umbreit, pp. 255ff. (demands by the iron and steel industry association, August 1917). On March 1, 1917, the president of the Deutsche Waffen- und Munitionsfabriken in Berlin addressed Ludendorff with a complaint that the auxiliary service act played into the hands of the workers for sabotage purposes. Conditions in the Berlin plants, he said, were worse than before, and he mentioned that he had also addressed the local military command, since the

official half-measures had become intolerable. The appended copy of this second message demanded that (a) factories and their shifts be placed under military surveillance; (b) refusal to work be made punishable by imprisonment; (c) minimum hours be fixed and regulated according to army needs; (d) maximum pay scales be fixed; and (e) freedom to relocate be revoked. Unless these measures were taken, the management declined to accept any responsibility for fulfillment of contractual arms deliveries. The letter was dispatched on the eve of the first large-scale strike in the Berliner Waffen- und Munitionsfabriken, in April. Groener (p. 362) regarded this strike essentially as a demonstration by wretched men, plagued by hunger and cold, resulting from still another recent cut in the bread ration. He added the text of a public message addressed to him by Hindenburg on April 19, in which the field marshal underlined the urgency of war needs. It concluded with the brusque admonition: "Anyone who goes on strike while our armies face the enemy is a contemptible knave." The trade union reply was a declaration of confidence in Groener, as well as appeals to workers that were not without success (Schulthess, 1917, Vol. 1, pp. 442, 460f.; Wippermann-Purlitz, VI, 2, pp. 785ff.). The OHL disagreed with Groener. On March 9 it forwarded Gontardt's letter, and another from Krupp, to the war minister and the Chancellor, commenting that the domestic situation posed a serious threat to army morale. Soldiers in the ranks were resentful of the munitions workers' continual pay rises. Their own pay came to pennies a day, while skilled workers earned more than staff officers, even though they bore far less responsibility. If officers' pay was cut, why not the wages of those liable to auxiliary service? Strikes must be stopped—they began as hunger strikes and invariably wound up with pay rises. The auxiliary service act was ill-conceived and had been turned into a weapon in the struggle for so-called "workers' rights." The strikers were totally lacking in any sense of duty. Agitators must be ruthlessly dealt with, the workers read the riot act, martial law applied. Wahnschaffe commented that it was industry itself that was agitating, in a most reprehensible manner. Basing himself on a draft by Helfferich, Bethmann Hollweg replied on March 15 that he entertained reservations of his own about the auxiliary service act but had suppressed them at the urging of the OHL. His fears had now proved well-founded, but it would be a grave mistake to revoke the law to please a few employers, or to restrict the rights that had been granted to the workers. The only result would be that well-minded labor leaders would completely lose their following. At best an attempt might be launched to modify paragraph 3 of article 9 of the act, by negotiation with the labor leaders. The sensible elements among the workers must be given support, so that they might propagate patriotic sentiments, but this meant certain sacrifices which employers must share, and it also meant foregoing coercive measures that would only provoke resentment. Bethmann Hollweg warned against misguided action in individual cases, which would cause justifiable unrest among the workers (ZA Potsdam, *loc. cit.*).

25. ZA Potsdam, *loc. cit.*, minutes of meetings of November 26 and December 1, 1916. Helfferich, in concert with Breitenbach, minister of public works, displayed remarkable energy in opposing the extension of workers' councils to the nationalized railroads.

26. The question of the Belgian workers' deportation (like the similar deportations from Poland, Lithuania, and Courland) really stands in need of renewed documentary study, which, as far as I know, is still entirely lacking on the German side. The difficulty is that the military files—of the government general, the Belgian rear echelon commands, the war ministry, the OHL, etc.—were probably all destroyed with the army archives. Apart from the deposition of Privy Councilor Kriege, there are very few relevant documents among those of the committee investigating matters of international law during the First World War (UA III). When the testimony was taken in 1925, a committee majority was intent on keeping strictly to the question of whether the deportations were sanctioned by international law;

and the social democrat Levi was the only one to read into the record a number of important documents dealing with the political implications. Ludendorff (2) is even poorer in documentation. A Belgian lawyer, F. Passelecq, working under official auspices, has written widely on the subject, his main work being *Déportations et travail forcé des ouvriers et de la population civile de la Belgique occupée* (1929, Belgian series of the Carnegie war study); but his work is based largely on wartime propaganda and press reports and deals almost exclusively with the situation as seen from the Belgian side. Besides the proclamations of the occupation authorities, it uses statements and recollections of eyewitnesses or participants, the reliability of which can no longer be checked in detail. The brilliant work by H. Pirenne, *La Belgique et la Guerre Mondiale* (1929, part of the same Carnegie series), seriously strives for objectivity—even though Pirenne himself was one of the victims of German occupation policies; but as to the deportations, Pirenne bases himself essentially on Passelecq and the book by M. L. von Köhler on the political occupation administration (German series of the Carnegie study).

27. Directive, dated February 20, 1915, to the chief of the civil administration, Dr. von Sandt. Together with the long memorandum on the future of Belgium, it is in the GSTA, Pol. A, VII, No. 52. *Ibidem,* No. 56, for Bissing's transmission of the memorandum to Hertling on November 8, 1915, at Hertling's request.

28. Pirenne, p. 172.

29. For details see Fischer, pp. 336ff.

30. Deposition by Kriege (UA III, 1, p. 205).

31. This passage and the following are based on the exchange published in UA III, 1, pp. 334ff.—Bissing to Bethmann Hollweg, April 12, 1916; Bethmann Hollweg's reply, April 17; Bissing's reply, April 28. See also the war ministry's complaint of March 1916 (day not given) to the field army General Staff, Wrisberg, Vol. 2, Appendix 4 (concerning the economic independence from the war ministry of the governments general in Warsaw and Brussels, export of rails from Belgium, and the labor question). It does not directly mention forced deportations, only improved recruitment methods and utilization of Belgian industry for important war purposes.

32. Bissing to the OHL, September 15 (UA III, 1, p. 341).

33. Helfferich to the Brussels government general, August 11 (*ibidem,* pp. 345, 383ff.). Bissing refuted this rumor in a message to the Reich office of the interior on August 15 (*ibidem,* p. 344—at greater length in a wire to the OHL, p. 347).

34. Under the Hague convention on the laws and customs of land war of November 18, 1907.

35. Lancken, p. 234. A date of September 19 is given in Groener, p. 553 (diary note). For the message from the OHL to Bissing, September 21, his reply, September 24, and undated OHL notes, see UA III, 1, pp. 345-348.

36. UA III, 1, pp. 382ff. *Ibidem,* pp. 360-365, Bissing's letter of September 26, discussed in the following.

37. When he testified before the national assembly's investigating committee on November 4, 1919 (UA 1, pp. 222ff.), Bethmann Hollweg expressed himself with marked uncertainty about the workers' deportations, details of which he did not recall. He emphasized his lack of power in respect of OHL wishes. "I was in no position to oppose the OHL contention that Belgian workers were needed to carry out the Hindenburg program. It would have been more than I could have answered for. I could not very well have said, 'No, I don't want that sort of thing.' I would only have been told that in that case our Hindenburg program would have to be abandoned."

38. Despite urgent representation by von der Lancken, chief of the government general's political section, he obstinately declined to pardon the British nurse, Edith Cavell, whom a court-martial had sentenced to death. Nurse Cavell was shot by a firing squad, providing the Belgian liberation movement with a martyred heroine re-

vered to this day. She had hidden many captured soldiers and helped them to escape.

39. During the Brussels talks of October 6, its representatives requested that no further recruitment for the rear echelon areas be conducted through the industrial bureau, since this situation would be settled separately. Unlike the situation in the government general, recruitment of workers for the rear echelon areas did not cease in March 1917. Details in Passelecq, Chapter 10.

40. *Loc. cit.,* p. 350.

41. This was the argumentation: Forced labor was permissible for work-shy elements that represented a burden on private as well as public welfare support. The Belgian relief mission was a semipublic agency. No appropriate work was to he found in Belgium. Forced labor in Germany was not necessarily and exclusively for war purposes, unless there was direct employment in arms plants. The compulsory character of the measures was based on the decree of May 15, 1916, but they were purely administrative rather than punitive and unnecessary hardship was to be avoided. Appropriate wages would be paid even to workers forcibly deported, but volunteers would receive higher pay (UA III, 1, pp. 368f.; date given on p. 308).

42. I mention the following further chancellery documents (ZA Potsdam, VII, 9): the war minister to the OHL, October 7, setting forth the ministry's stand on the workers' issue (published in Ludendorff [2], pp. 124ff.); the war minister to Bethmann Hollweg, October 10, transmitting the previous message and requesting support for it in Brussels; Wahnschaffe to Helfferich, undated (but prior to October 17), about intensified recruitment, but also calling for assembly camps for deportees and offering to take part in talks; Ludendorff to the foreign ministry, October 11, requesting participation in talks on the workers' issue at Pless on October 19; results of a preliminary discussion held on October 17 (printed in Ludendorff [2], pp. 127f.); conference on October 22 at Reich office of the interior (originally scheduled for Pless), presided over by Sauberzweig. It is noteworthy that much greater success with voluntary recruitment was attained in Poland, though there Loebell's opposition to the importation of large numbers of Polish-Jewish workers had to be overcome.

43. Passelecq gives many eyewitness accounts which show that the handling of the deportations varied greatly in detail. On the effect on morale, see among others diary entries by Auguste Vierset, chief administrative aide to the mayor of Brussels, in *Mes Souvenirs sur l'occupation allemande en Belgique* (1932), pp. 401ff.

44. Report by von der Lancken to the foreign ministry, January 11, 1917 (UA 2, Supplement 123).

45. This would mean that the estimate of 2,614 given by Pirenne, *loc. cit.,* p. 192 (after Mahaim), is much too high, though many may have died during the return voyage or afterward.

46. According to the report of March 31, 1917, just cited (UA III, pp. 374ff.), they numbered 33,000. Even Pirenne, who observed the apathy and revulsion of his fellow countrymen in the German factories, admits (pp. 196f.) that the terror tactics succeeded indirectly, by raising the number of voluntary work contracts.

47. Report by Nieser to Dusch, December 5 (GLA, IV/37). He remarked that even the OHL had begun to lose interest in the deportations. Lerchenfeld, in a message to Hertling of December 6 (GSTA, Pol. A, VII/51), remarked in his usual lucid and straightforward fashion that the deportations were a political blunder, but also described Bissing's policies in Belgium as unrealistic.

48. Hohenlohe to Czernin, February 22, 1917. See also Hohenlohe's report to Burián of December 13, 1916; Baron Frankenstein to Burián, December 6 and 13, 1916, February 16 and 27, 1917 (HHSTA, war files, 4f). For Cardinal Hartmann's exchange with Hertling of January 4 and 26, see GSTA, Pol. A, VII, No. 52; also E. Deuerlein, *Historische Jahrbücher,* Vol. 70 (1951), pp. 292ff.; Lancken's and Bissing's exchanges with the foreign ministry, October-November 1916, AA WW,

14b, Vol. 4; American protests and representations, FR, 1916 Supplement, pp.
299, 310, 312f., 319, 363, 366f.; Joseph C. Grew, *The Turbulent Era—A Diplomatic Record of Forty Years, 1904-1945,* Vol. 1 (1952), pp. 266ff.; the documentation for Kriege's report, UA III, 1, pp. 246ff.

49. Lancken, p. 234. In a letter to Grünau (for the Kaiser) of February 8, Bethmann Hollweg conveyed the desire of the newly formed Council of Flanders to be received by the Kaiser, which William II gladly approved on February 9. He voiced the outlandish desire that the Flemish might organize a great demonstration before the spring offensive, so that all the world might see that they looked to Germany for their liberation and thus rebuffed one of the main goals of the Entente (Sch&Gr, Vol. 2, Nos. 4-5). The Kaiser was taken by surprise by the Flemish development and this may have put him in a conciliatory mood with respect to the workers' issue.

50. See Nieser's report to Karlsruhe of December 5, cited in Note 47, above.

51. Umbreit (pp. 123f.) reports on efforts by a joint committee of the German labor unions to persuade the government and the Brussels administration to stop the deportations. Umbreit greatly exaggerates, however, when he asserts that the Belgian workers' deportations provided the social democrats with a reason for refusing to vote in favor of a war appropriations bill for the first time. The election reform issue rather than the deportations was the motive for their refusal. As far as I know, only Noske, on March 29, criticized the deportations on the floor of the Reichstag, though but briefly, for they had long since ceased. Bernstein did mention the matter in a declaration by the "independent" socialists on the emergency budget. On March 3 Scheidemann, speaking before the main committee, demanded the immediate return of the deportees (Scheidemann [1] [1928], Vol. 1, p. 420).

52. Ludendorff (2), pp. 131ff.

53. Fischer, p. 582.

*Notes to Chapter 10*

1. For the text of the treaty and details of its background, see Steglich (2), pp. 110ff. Another supplementary treaty, dealing with the revocation of the so-called "capitulations" and concluded on January 11, 1917, is given there on p. 118.

2. Statement by Jagow to Hohenlohe, October 1, 1916, and directive from Jagow to Kühlmann, November 20, 1916 (Steglich [2], pp. 115, 120).

3. These peace feelers are discussed in a long series of exchanges from late April to early August 1917 between the Vienna foreign ministry and its missions in Istanbul, Berne, and Berlin (HHSTA, war files, 25/21), of which I have copies. They were all launched in Berne and went very far in their offers, at least in the view of the Turkish diplomats: "(a) *Status quo ante bellum, mais certaines concessions économiques et navales aux Anglais dans le golf Persique;* (b) *Garanties de l'intégrité de l'Empire Ottoman par les pays de l'Entente et l'Amérique;* (c) *Payement de tous les sommes avancée par l'Allemagne à la Turquie;* (d) *Prêt des sommes nécessaires à la Turquie pour sa réorganisation économique. Au cas contraire ménace de l'annéantissement de la Turquie"* (report from the Turkish ambassador of June 23, at the Vienna foreign ministry). The German government was immediately informed of this in late April by Talat Pasha and the grand vizier and advised the Turks to pursue the British offers, but without any show of eagerness. (Exchange between Zimmermann and Oberndorff of April 30-May 1, 1917, AA WW, 15, secret, Vol. 3.) Britain's main agent was a certain Mr. J. R. Pilling; France's was Professor Haguenin, literary historian and propaganda chief, who was also an intermediary with Germany. Other French agents were the bankers Steeg and Villers, *et al.* The name of the American ambassador, Morgenthau, also turns up on occasion. A statement by the Turkish envoy that he was willing to help mediate peace with the Central Powers is said to have been well-received in

London, but nothing eventuated from it. If Istanbul failed to take all these offers seriously, it was probably because it was well aware of the secret treaties among the Allies, under which Turkey would have been carved up (notes of the Austrian embassy in Berlin, October 23, 1916, AA WW, 15, secret, Vol. 2, Russia, secret). The German foreign ministry staked its hopes on the deterrent effect during the Vienna talks with Czernin on March 16, when the Turkish stand was discussed (Sch&Gr, Vol. 2, No. 20, also Nos. 44 and 70 [further reports], and Nos. 122, 138, 141, 142, and 161).

4. RAW, Vol. 12, p. 520. See Birnbaum, p. 289, No. 3, on certain autonomy aspirations on the part of a satiated Bulgaria, with respect to its allies. On December 26, 1916, and January 15, 1917, Baron Wieden transmitted to Czernin secret intelligence from the Austrian military attaché in Sofia. Dispatches from the Bulgarian envoy in Berne suggested that he had sought and found contact with representatives of the Entente, to sound out the Allied stand on Bulgarian war aims. That stand was in part strongly negative—in respect of the Morava valley and traditionally Serbian territory—in part positive (HHSTA, war files, secret, XLVII/13 and 25p).

5. Cramon (2), p. 158. See also Cramon (1), pp. 98-115.

6. Amiguet, pp. 102f. The prince's own report on his role as a mediator remains the most important source. See also Poincaré, Vol. 9; Ribot (1); Suarez, Vol. 4; and Lloyd George, Vol. 4, pp. 1,983ff. (at great length). Czernin is naturally very reticent in his memoirs. The so-called memoirs of Count Erdödy, put together by P. Szmere and E. Czech under the title, *Habsburgs Wege von Wilhelm zu Briand* (1931), offer romantic embellishment of the venture rather than political information. Count Polzer-Hoditz displays a strongly exculpating bias, but presents many important details. A. Demblin, a section councilor in the foreign ministry, offers a carefully documented defense of Czernin, in his book, *Czernin und die Sixtus-Affäre* (1920). A number of the most important pieces of evidence are published (partly in German translation) in Ludendorff (2), pp. 374ff. The two books by Fester are so blatantly nationalist in orientation that they make difficult reading even today, but they do have the virtue of being the first to explore the circumstances with care and competence. Steglich (1) contains a new documentary account, but in many respects I find myself unable to accept his views.

7. Dictated text of a letter to Czernin of May 15, 1917 (Werkmann, p. 171). See RAW, Vol. 11, p. 486, for Charles's successful effort to revoke (by a secret supplementary agreement with the OHL) the Kaiser's supreme command, established in the fall of 1916.

8. The minutes are in the HHSTA, Pol. A, XXXX/293, No. 530.

9. Fester (2), p. 51, assumes that the crucial factor was the prince's insistence on the restoration of Karageorge dynasty in Serbia, while Charles supposedly demanded the creation of a large South Slav satellite state under an archduke—his only departure from Sixtus's program. This is possible but unproven. At the ministerial conference of January 12, to be discussed further on, Charles had expressed himself in favor of granting Serbia as much scope as possible for survival. In his account of the first meeting with the princes on February 13, Erdödy denies that political matters were discussed, as asserted by Prince Sixtus, p. 55. How sketchily Czernin was informed about the background of these negotiations is shown in a report he made to the deputy Baernreither, published by A. Kann in *Mitteilungen des österreichischen Staatsarchivs* under the title, "J. M. Baernreither und Graf Ottakar Czernins Darstellung der Sixtus-Affäre," and kindly made available to me in proof. Czernin's report was written only in 1920-1921 and was intended as an alibi. He confuses the talks with Sixtus in April and May, and his account must be taken with some caution.

10. Czernin to the Empress Zita, February 17, in K. F. Nowak, *Der Sturz der Mittelmächte* (1921), p. 419.

11. Czernin added that it was believed that France was entirely under British pressure.

This was, of course, said to encourage the French to emancipate themselves from British leadership; but it was most ill-advised, for it was the very opposite of the truth, especially in the question of peace, and was bound to create ill will in Paris.

12. According to Czernin's report to Baernreither (see Note 9, above), the minister said, among other things, that "Austria would not take part in a German war of conquest and eagerly anticipated word that the Entente too was prepared to end the war without conquest. If such welcome news came from Paris, Austria would commit its every resource to the common cause and 'go the limit.' "

13. Fester (2) suggests this (p. 71), and it is rendered very likely when the stylistic and political urbanity of this letter is compared with the rather awkwardly worded draft of May 15, mentioned above (Note 7). According to a statement by their cabinet chief Count Polzer to Baernreither, neither the emperor nor Empress Zita were able to write a letter in flawless French (Kann, *loc. cit.*). The reason for the letter form was that the princes were preserving strict secrecy even in France about their trip to Vienna and their discussions there.

14. For the following, see Poincaré, pp. 85ff., 111; Ribot (1), pp. 62, 64ff., 71f.; Lloyd George, Vol. 4, pp. 2,000ff., 2,027ff. After Clémenceau came to power, attempts were made to incriminate Poincaré and Ribot for the mere fact that they had allowed themselves to be drawn into these peace talks.

15. According to the official German account (see Wippermann-Purlitz, Vol. 2, p. 749), the total ran to 1,091,000 tons. According to Lloyd George, Vol. 3, p. 1,192, it was only 526,447. During a session of the Académie des Sciences Morales et Politiques on June 10, 1963, François-Poncet reported that the French foreign ministry was at the time very accurately informed about what happened to Allied vessels that had been torpedoed. Many of them that were reported sunk by the German navy were actually able to reach a port, where they were repaired and returned to service. François-Poncet and Massigli had actually written two anonymous articles on the subject for the *Neue Zürcher Zeitung*. Erzberger had read them when he was in Zurich and supposedly told the Reichstag that the German admiralty was misleading public opinion about its successes (*Revue des Travaux de l'Académie...* Vol. 116, Series 4[1963], p. 268; see also p. 557, Note 152, above).

16. The Bavarian envoy von Schoen wrote Hertling on December 27, 1916, how the Austrian change of ministers was received at the foreign ministry.

17. See Chapter 7, Note 53, above.

18. In a note of January 1, 1917, see preceding Note. According to Wedel's report of January 3, about this talk (AA WW, 15, secret, and 20c), the ambassador proposed that the Moldava region not be joined to Hungary but rather turned into a Reich province or a "second Bosnia" or a satellite state. Czernin later on reverted to this, as he did to Wedel's mention of the Russian attitude toward Rumania in 1877.

19. It is true, however, that the threat to dissolve the Austro-Hungarian union was less clear-cut in this answer than the Russian government had wanted, though it did quite plainly state the intention to grant autonomy to the non-German and non-Hungarian regions. For details see E. Hölzle, "Russland und die Entstehung der Tschechoslowakei," in *Bohemia*, Vol. 1 (1960), pp. 228ff.

20. Minutes of January 12, 1917, HHSTA, Pol. A, XXXX/293, No. 530. Emperor Charles actually hoped for an alliance with Russia!

21. Czernin's directives to Mensdorff of February 14 and 16, HHSTA, Prussia, III/175. Mensdorff's reports of February 18-28, 1917, are appended. See also Lloyd George, Vol. 4, pp. 1,987ff., where it is stated that rumors of Austrian peace tendencies had reached the British envoy Findlay in Christiania (Oslo) in January, the Austrian attaché, Baron Franz, having mentioned them to the king of Norway. When Lloyd George received further intelligence about Austrian peace agents in Copenhagen, he sent Sir Francis Hopwood to Scandinavia on February 1. Hopwood talked to a number of alleged Austrian agents, but never met Mens-

dorff. The farthest he got was some hints of Mensdorff's proposals dropped by the king of Norway. The king quoted Mensdorff as particularly deploring the threat to the Danubian monarchy in the Entente answer (see also Sch&Gr, Vol. 2, No. 27, March 22).

22. For reports of the Berne legation, from November 1916 onward, see HHSTA, war files, 25w. Especially singled out were Sauerwein, an editor of *Le Matin,* and Professor Haguenin, of whom we have already heard. Serving as intermediaries were the Polish count Rostvorovsky, a confidant of the Austrian *Evidenzbureau,* and Dr. Bader, a Polish journalist.

23. He wrote that Paris was presumably trying to gain concessions in the matter of Alsace-Lorraine through Austria. On March 12 he called attention to the fact that so far the only thing to go by was a hunch of Count Rostvorovsky.

24. This was a guess on my part, but I find it echoed in Polzer-Hoditz, p. 333.

25. Mérey to Czernin (via Hohenlohe), March 14, 1917, HHSTA, *ibidem.*

26. Poincaré, pp. 82f., 84f., March 22 and 28. The note given first also probably refers to the same lady, Mme. Alix Barton, whose comments on the changing moods in Paris soon became the sole content of Mensdorff's reports. For Mensdorff's and Musulin's reports of March 19 and April 15, see HHSTA, war files, 25w.

27. For the exchanges between Czernin and Hohenlohe, and Czernin and Mensdorff, April 6-16, see HHSTA, *loc. cit.* For the exchange between Romberg and Zimmermann, April 8-9, 1917, see AA WW, 15, secret, published in the *Münchner Neuste Nachrichten,* March 8, 1922. Among German efforts to establish liaison reported by Hohenlohe were a meeting between Lancken and Chamber President Deschanel, which never came off, and a discussion between Villalobar and the British envoy at The Hague, Tawnley. On talks with Haguenin, Sauerwein, etc., see Sch&Gr, Vol. 2, Nos. 22, 26, 46, 59, 124, 139.

28. In an exposé presented on March 20, shortly before the second crown council, Austrian jealousy came to the fore even more massively (see below). It would seem—so ran one passage—that Austria made its heroic sacrifices solely for the greater glory of Germany.

29. Minutes of the meeting of March 16, AA WW, 2, secret, published in the *Münchner Neuste Nachrichten,* February 23-26, 1922, and also in Fester (2), pp. 272ff., with supplements; also in Sch&Gr, Vol. 2, No. 20.

30. "Top secret" memorandum, dated March 1917, HHSTA, secret, XLVII/1c. Another memorandum, likewise undated, the work of a different unnamed author, is entitled "Comments on the Memorandum Concerning Austrian War Aims" *(ibidem).* It agrees with Czernin in principle, rejects peace without annexations, and expresses the view that annexations in the Balkans and in the direction of the course of the Danube would be sound and natural. Was only Germany to increase its territory? Was that what Austria fought for? The only question in that author's mind was whether Rumania could really be carved up.

31. Czernin challenged him directly at the meeting, as the minutes show. He was asked to disarm German opposition or at least take the edge off it. Mérey, by the way, must have been informed by Czernin about Prince Sixtus's mission, along the lines that this was a French peace feeler to be taken more seriously than those that went before; for he made remarks along such lines during the meeting, without of course identifying the prince, and he could not possibly have had reference to the vague maunderings of Haguenin and Rostvorovsky.

32. "War Aims and the Polish Question—Top Secret," undated but described on the cover as background material for Czernin's political exposé presented at the crown council of March 20, 1917, HHSTA, secret, XLVII/13. Published under a misleading title and wrong date in Nowak, *Sturz der Mittelmächte,* pp. 420-428.

33. Polzer-Hoditz (p. 334) says that Bethmann Hollweg suffered a spell of uncontrollable weeping on the evening of March 17, citing as his authority Baron von Marterer, head of the military chancellery.

34. Minutes of the joint cabinet meeting of March 23, 1917, HHSTA, Pol. A, XXXX,

293, No. 535. Among other things Czernin stated that Bethmann Hollweg had refused outright to give any guarantees for the recapture of territory lost to Italy. At the request of Emperor Charles, the problem of Serbia and Montenegro was left open.

35. Minutes of a meeting of Czernin, Hohenlohe, Bethmann Hollweg, Zimmermann, and Stumm on April 26, 1917 (AA WW, 15, secret, Vol. 2), published with many inaccuracies in the *Münchner Neuste Nachrichten,* March 1-7, 1922, more recently in Sch&Gr, Vol. 2, No. 33.

36. Details in Fester (1), pp. 40ff., Fester (2), pp. 59, 273ff. Through the good offices of Dietrich Schäfer, Fester had access to part of the files of the foreign ministry, in copies for the parliamentary investigating committee. See also Sch&Gr, Vol. 2, Nos. 34, 35, 37, 56, 58.

37. Thus Bethmann Hollweg surmised the secret Austrian goal, as had Poincaré and Jules Cambon, who commended it to Prince Sixtus.

38. Especially noteworthy is the reiterated assurance that Germany was quite likely to reach agreement with King Albert, "from all that we have heard about him during the war." The minimum claims Bethmann Hollweg sought to gain in Belgium were that Antwerp should not become a British commercial center and that if possible the country should be economically integrated with Germany. He said he would rest content with trade agreements, if the Belgian fortifications were razed and certain military guarantees given. More than that was probably beyond reach. "I dare say that if peace with Russia hinged on the return of Courland, we would give it up."

39. Résumé signed by Czernin and Bethmann Hollweg on March 27, 1917, published in UA IV (Volkmann), p. 200, and earlier in Ludendorff (2) under the misleading title, "Vienna Document." Steglich (2) printed the two earlier drafts he had found in the HHSTA (pp. 226f.), commenting on them on pp. 148ff. See also R. Neck, "Das Wiener Dokument vom 27. März 1917," in *Mitteilungen des österreichischen Staatsarchivs* (1953), pp. 7, 294ff.

40. Zimmermann to Lersner, March 28, 1917, dispatched March 29, the draft in Stumm's hand (AA WW, 15, secret, Vol. 2). Thus Ludendorff's complaint that he was insufficiently informed (Ludendorff [2], p. 374) was without foundation. He acknowledged receipt of this wire, adding that he found Czernin's pessimism exaggerated.

41. Musulin to Czernin, March 26; Czernin to Hohenlohe, March 28 (HHSTA, war files, 25w).

42. Polzer-Hoditz says (p. 340) that Czernin informed Emperor Charles of the Italian peace offer only en route to Homburg, on April 2, but Polzer apparently misunderstood a statement by Charles. Otherwise it would be hard to account for Czernin's wire to Hohenlohe of March 31, already cited, and another of April 2, to the Austrian high command, both saying that the Italian offer had been "declined" (HHSTA, secret, XLVII/13).

43. Hohenlohe to Czernin, March 31 and April 1. Tisza warned Czernin in similar tones on April 1 (Czernin, pp. 210f.). On March 31 Zimmermann complained to Vienna, via Count Wedel, of pessimistic talk by Ambassador Prince Schönburg in Switzerland. The prince was supposed to have said that Austria was at the end of its strength, and cession of Alsace-Lorraine was the only way of getting peace (*Münchner Neuste Nachrichten,* March 8, 1922; see also Sch&Gr, Vol. 2, Nos. 42, 43).

44. The preparations for the imperial visit to Schloss Homburg and the visit itself are described in Polzer-Hoditz, pp. 339ff., and Werkmann, pp. 221ff.

45. Wedel to the foreign ministry, April 2, 1917 (Sch&Gr, Vol. 2, No. 45). Wedel's report includes a curious proposal by the ambassador, to the effect that Austria, by way of a sacrifice of its own, should lease an Adriatic port to Germany as a naval base. It is quite likely that there was as much head-shaking about this in the foreign ministry as about Czernin's statements.

46. Cramon (1), p. 112; see also Ludendorff (1), pp. 350ff. Cramon's statement (p. 111) that he knew about Prince Sixtus's visit in Vienna even before the Homburg meeting and had reported it to the OHL is probably based on faulty memory. His report was not made until May, on the occasion of the prince's second visit to Vienna, and apparently only after considerable delay. (Report by Wedel to the foreign ministry, dated May 30, published in the *Münchner Neuste Nachrichten,* 1922, No. 107—but the visit actually took place on May 8-9!) It is inconceivable that the German side already knew the character of the alleged French peace offer at the time of the Homburg meeting.

47. HHSTA, secret, XLVII/3-16, undated, probably meant for Emperor Charles. To Ambassador Wedel Czernin conveyed the impression of being well-satisfied with the meeting (private letter by Wedel to Zimmermann, published in the *Münchner Neuste Nachrichten,* March 9, 1922—see also Sch&Gr, Vol. 2, No. 52). According to Polzer-Hoditz (pp. 343f.) spirits were badly depressed in the emperor's special train at departure, and Charles himself was visibly troubled. In his memoirs (p. 198) Czernin says that the Austrian offer was not unconditionally accepted at the talks, but neither was it rejected. It was simply laid aside for further consideration. This too must be based on faulty recollection. Czernin, by the way, has the meeting taking place in Kreuznach rather than Homburg.

48. Stumm to Grünau, for Bethmann Hollweg, April 2, 1917 (AA WW, 2, secret).

*Notes to Chapter 11*

1. G. F. Kennan, *Soviet-American Relations 1917-1920,* Vol. 1, *Russia Leaves the War* (1956), p. 15, from FR, *The Lansing Papers.* For the following see also R. D. Warth, *The Allies and the Russian Revolution* (1954); and A. J. Mayer, *Political Origins of the New Diplomacy 1917-1918* (1959).

2. Hoffmann, Vol. 2, p. 174.

3. In July 1915 the foreign ministry secured authority from the treasury to spend five million marks for such purposes and in December of the same year Helphand asked for twenty million rubles to organize a revolution in Russia. On April 1, 1917, the foreign ministry asked for another five million marks, a request that was granted. Control over the use of these monies was, of course, impossible. For documentation see Zeman, pp. 3, 9, 24 (this work is based on foreign ministry files). For further documentation see Hahlweg.

4. W. Katkov, "German Foreign Office Documents on Financial Support to the Bolsheviks in 1917," *Foreign Affairs,* Vol. 32 (1956), pp. 181ff.

5. Quoted in E. Hölzle, *Lenin 1917. Die Geburt der Revolution aus dem Kriege* (1957), p. 38. He expressed himself with similar optimism on August 14, 1915 (Zeman, p. 5), inspired by the hope that even the German social democrats, who had displayed such sterling patriotism during the war, could be won over to permanent and constructive support of the government.

6. Hoffmann, Vol. 2, pp. 168ff.

7. Report of April 2, 1917, Hahlweg, pp. 47ff.; Zeman, pp. 30f.

8. Draft of March 17, 1917, complete works of Lenin (German ed., 1928), Vol. 20, pp. 8ff., 53ff.

9. Confirmed by Bethmann Hollweg himself in a report to the Kaiser of April 11 (Hahlweg, p. 94), which rather abridged the circumstances. Erzberger's role in the whole affair cannot be precisely established. Perhaps he merely supported Helphand's suggestions in the foreign ministry (Epstein, p. 190).

10. It is nevertheless noteworthy that Ebert and Scheidemann protested the inclusion of the Swiss socialist Grimm, who had taken part in the Kienthal meeting and whose anti-German orientation they feared.

11. Schulthess (1917), Vol. 2, p. 671.

12. I think it unlikely that Erzberger was behind this declaration—as he asserts (p. 235) with his wonted complacency—if only for the reason that the declaration does not

in the slightest coincide with a draft of a speech Erzberger submitted to the Chancellor.

13. Schulthess (1917), Vol. 2, pp. 55f. Czernin instructed the Austrian foreign service to give as much publicity as possible to the interview. As the response showed, however, it had no effect. That the interview was agreed on with Bethmann Hollweg is clear from a wire from Czernin to Hohenlohe of March 29 (HHSTA, war files, 25x).

14. For two reports from Envoy Oberndorff of March 28 from Sofia and notes by Rosenberg on talks with Colonel Ganchev on March 30, see AA WW, 15, secret, Vol. 2. Concrete peace terms were actually discussed, like free passage through the Dardanelles and even the return of Poland. According to a report of March 24, Ferdinand asked that attacks on the Russian front be foregone, to which Ludendorff agreed (Sch&Gr, Vol. 2, Nos. 31, 32, 36, 39). Oberndorff's reports of April 28 are missing. For the exchange between the Kaiser and Czar Ferdinand of April 4 and 11, see *ibidem,* Nos. 51, 57. Ferdinand then opposed too many overeager peace declarations by the Central Powers.

15. Sch&Gr, Vol. 1, No. 272 (Stinnes to Zimmermann, June 17, 1916).

16. According to Erzberger, Kolyshko expected to be summoned to high office in the provisional government, but the summons never came. For Erzberger's reports to Bethmann Hollweg, see Epstein, pp. 186ff., and Sch&Gr, Vol. 2, No. 40.

17. In a dispatch of April 1, Musulin said that Erzberger had also immediately given a highly optimistic report of his successful Stockholm mission to Austrian diplomats in Switzerland. He admitted that the situation in St. Petersburg was still unresolved and that therefore negotiations with any one of the political parties were bound to be tentative. He did, however, think it dangerous to deal with the extreme radicals in Russia, since this would merely serve to encourage radicals in Germany (HHSTA, war files, 25t).

18. Czernin to Hohenlohe, April 9 (HHSTA, war files, 25w). Szechény, envoy in Copenhagen, to Czernin, April 9, and Czernin to Hohenlohe, April 10 (*ibidem,* 25t).

19. Hohenlohe to Czernin, April 11 *(ibidem).*

20. Hohenlohe to Czernin, April 13 *(ibidem).*

21. Epstein, pp. 189f. There is nothing on this in Müller, but Erzberger's draft is published in Sch&Gr, Vol. 2, No. 64. For the negotiations in Vienna, whither Stumm had been dispatched for that purpose, and for Bethmann Hollweg's proposals, see *ibidem,* Nos. 61-63, 65, 66; and Steglich (1), Chapter 2.

22. Hindenburg to Bethmann Hollweg, April 5, 1917 (Sch&Gr, Vol. 2, No. 49). On April 12 War Minister von Stein promptly fell in with Hindenburg's demand for departmental consultations, in which he wished his ministry to participate (Stein to Bethmann Hollweg, April 12, AA WW, 15, secret, Vol. 2).

23. *Norddeutsche Allgemeine Zeitung,* April 15; Austrian telegraph bureau, same date—see Schulthess; also Czernin's circular letter to Sofia and Istanbul, April 14; Czernin's protest to Hohenlohe, April 16; Hohenlohe's reply, April 17 (HHSTA, war files, 25t). For Erzberger's warning against a separate peace, see Epstein, p. 189. Hohenlohe thought it wrong that the German proclamation apologized, so to speak, for the successful attack on the Stochod. That attack had been no more than a local operation, not the starting gun for a general offensive.

24. Czernin, pp. 198ff.; Ludendorff (2), pp. 374ff., with Emperor Charles's covering letter for the memorandum sent to the Kaiser on April 14. This is given in Sch&Gr, Vol. 2, No. 68, with the Kaiser's marginal notes.

25. Czernin, pp. 204ff.; Ludendorff (2), pp. 379ff., dated May 4. According to Steglich (1), Chapter 2, Note 190, Bethmann Hollweg dated this memorandum May 9, but Sch&Gr, Vol. 2, No. 104, also puts the date at May 4. The Kaiser's covering letter of May 11, *ibidem,* No. 113. According to Sch&Gr, Vol. 2, No. 74, Zimmermann asked the OHL and the admiralty for countermemoranda as a basis for Bethmann Hollweg's reply to Holtzendorff's memorandum of April 18 (*ibidem,* No. 75). Ludendorff's reply of April 19, *ibidem,* No. 80. Characteristically, Ludendorff

insisted that the foreign ministry show him its reply to Vienna before it was dispatched. A further wire of similar character, dated April 23, via Grünau, was published in the *Münchner Neuste Nachrichten,* March 9, 1922.

26. The original draft, subsequently changed, spoke of "war aims to be pursued from political and economic aspects and to be established, in line with the Kaiser's commands, *solely by my own decision, to the exclusion of other agencies"* (italics mine).

27. Even Zimmermann told the German socialists quite bluntly when they set out for the Copenhagen peace talks in early April that the only thing that mattered now was to get peace with Russia, and that peace must not be allowed to fail on account of annexations (Scheidemann [1], Vol. 1, [1928], p. 422). He did say that border rectifications at the Narev were desirable, if there were such a possibility; and he actually mentioned the acquisition of Courland and Lithuania to the Bulgarian negotiator Ritzov (see below).

28. See Ribot (1), p. 228, where he expresses chagrin over the Russian government declaration of April 9; also Isvolsky's dispatch of April 25, 1917, in Adamow, *Die europäischen Mächte und die Türkei,* Vol. 2 (1930), pp. 429ff. Ribot told Isvolsky: "Even were Germany to agree to return all the occupied territories, this would scarcely advance the cause of peace"—since France could not rest content even with Alsace-Lorraine. On the over-all subject consult Robert D. Warth, *The Allies and the Russian Revolution* (1954); and Arno J. Mayer, *Political Origins of the New Diplomacy 1917-1918* (1959).

29. Scheidemann (1), Vol. 1, p. 421.

30. Envoy Rosen at The Hague said as much in a report to the foreign ministry of May 14 (AA WW, 15, secret, Vol. 3). Zimmermann, at least, doubted that support for the aspirations of German social democrats in Stockholm betokened a real interest in reviving popular peace sentiment with the aid of the Second International. In his exposé of May 4, intended for Ludendorff (Sch&Gr, Vol. 2, No. 102, marginal note), there is mention only of tactical considerations—the government should avoid the odium of reaction and autocracy that would follow if it refused passports to the delegates, etc. There was indeed mention of dangers arising from "contagion with international viruses" against which, unfortunately, the German social democrats could not be immunized. It is impossible to tell how much of all this was tactical maneuver and how much real conviction, nor what Bethmann Hollweg thought of it.

31. Fischer's treatment of the conduct of the majority socialists in Stockholm (pp. 503f.) is a masterpiece of synthetic reinterpretation along imperialist lines.

32. Bethmann Hollweg to Hertling, January 26, 1918 (AA WW, 15, secret, Vol. 5, and Germany, 122, No. 16, published in UA IV 2 [Schwertfeger], pp. 142ff.).

33. To become convinced of this, it is sufficient to read the detailed report which Colonel von Winterfeldt supplied to the OHL on May 24, 1917, concerning his talks with the Reichstag deputy Dr. David. David, a member of the extreme right wing of the majority social democrats, met with a truly astounding degree of incomprehension and political blindness on the part of high military figures, when he voiced his own political worries and reservations (Sch&Gr, Vol. 2, No. 132). Zimmermann tried vainly to make the OHL understand David's attitude (*ibidem,* No. 137).

34. Grünau to Bethmann Hollweg, April 17, at the Kaiser's behest (Sch&Gr, Vol. 2, No. 73). The text of the dispatch is so muddled that one can only surmise that the Kaiser did not comprehend what the OHL wanted of him. He tried to create the impression, however, that it was he who had mentioned these problems to Hindenburg, so that the field marshal might take an appropriate stand before his generals.

35. Bethmann Hollweg to Grünau, April 18 (Sch&Gr, Vol. 2, No. 76).

36. For documentation on Ritzov's mission (talks with the Russian envoy Gulkevich in Christiania on April 11), see Steglich (1), Chapter 2. Erzberger sent a report on his

Stockholm trip to Admiral von Müller as well, on April 12. Müller passed it up to Holtzendorff "through channels," and Holtzendorff read it to Hindenburg and Ludendorff on April 19. They received it well and promptly reproached Bethmann Hollweg with indecision in preparing for peace with Russia (Müller, p. 277).

37. Hindenburg to Bethmann Hollweg, April 20, 1917 (Sch&Gr, Vol. 2, No. 81). Apparently a directive by Zimmermann of April 22, probably addressed to Grünau (AA WW, 15, secret), already deals with the OHL proposal for exchanging territory. For the time being, he said, Germany must hold on to Rumania so that it would be in a position to indemnify Austria, if necessary, for surrendering East Galicia and the Bukovina.

38. Two wires from Grünau, April 20 (AA WW, 15, secret). Exchange of wires between the Kaiser and Bethmann Hollweg, April 21 (Westarp, p. 85). Bethmann Hollweg's file note to be discussed anon *(ibidem)*; see also Sch&Gr, Vol. 2, Nos. 82, 84. A report of the Bavarian military representative at headquarters of April 28, addressed to War Minister Hellingrath, gives a graphic account of the uproar at headquarters. As was to be expected, Bethmann Hollweg's weakness was blamed for the strike and the social democratic peace demonstrations. There was talk that the Alpine Corps would have to be dispatched to Berlin to conduct summary executions of a few hundred of the "troublemakers." Among those displaying the greatest agitation were Major Nicolai and Colonel Bauer (GSTA, Pol. A, VII/66).

39. No hint of this tension is conveyed to the reader by Fischer (pp. 449f. and 485)—as is to be expected he simply suppresses the enlightening file note in Westarp. So consummate is Fischer's skill in reinterpreting and doctoring the facts that he advances the farfetched conclusion (p. 487) that there were no concrete differences of opinion between the OHL and the Chancellor, only "differences in degree" on how dominion was to be exercised along Bethmann Hollweg's "annexationist line." Documented reservations are trivialized by suggesting (p. 452) that the Chancellor merely wanted to preserve tactical freedom of action and avoid any obligation to continue the war in any event, until the formulated goals were attained.

40. I am unable to decide whether any part was played by Bethmann Hollweg's older notions of freeing the Baltic regions of the czarist yoke, hinted at in his Reichstag speech of April 5, 1916. Unfortunately I did not have access to the minutes of this meeting (ZA Potsdam), which Fischer used (pp. 485f.). Fischer interprets the results of the meeting along the lines of the later negotiations conducted by Hoffmann and Ludendorff in Brest-Litovsk, i.e., as a veiled form of annexationism; and consequently he feels justified in revising all the previous estimates of Bethmann Hollweg's stand at Kreuznach.

41. He so advised Hohenlohe on April 29, as shown by Hohenlohe's report to Czernin of that date (HHSTA, war files, 25x). According to Hohenlohe, Bethmann Hollweg said that he knew nothing of the OHL taking the view that peace negotiations with Russia should be on the basis of the status quo. On the contrary, when he had last been at headquarters Ludendorff had been quite unreceptive to such a suggestion made by himself and the minister. In my view Steglich (1), p. 70, Note 80, goes too far in his conclusions from this bare hint. Since Bethmann Hollweg did not then seriously believe in the possibility of peace negotiations, he could have had in mind at best a German peace *declaration* along the lines of the status quo. More convincing seems to me Steglich's demonstration *(ibidem*, Note 202) that Bethmann Hollweg transmitted to Ludendorff only on May 7 his proposal to create "autonomous" principalities in Courland and Lithuania.

42. UA IV (Volkmann), Appendix 14, pp. 200ff.; Müller, p. 279.

43. A broader catalog of naval bases desired was presented by Holtzendorff on May 30 to Bethmann Hollweg, who had it filed as premature, though the Kaiser had approved it and Solf too had described it as useful and objective (Sch&Gr, Vol. 2, No. 129; UA IV [Volkmann], pp. 209f.).

44. File notes on Grünau's covering letter of April 24 (AA WW, 15, secret, Vol. 2). Further specimens *ibidem,* Vol. 3, with covering letter by Ludendorff, April 28. File notes for the chancellery in Westarp, p. 85. Letter to Hertling, *ibidem,* Vol. 5 (copy), original in AA, Germany, 122, No. 16, published in UA IV (Schwertfeger), p. 144; Sch&Gr, Vol. 2, No. 87.

45. Hugo Stinnes, acting at Ludendorff's behest, had before that time vainly tried to bribe him in the crudest fashion, in order to win him over to the war aims of the OHL. Details in Epstein, pp. 191ff.–though in my opinion Epstein is often not nearly critical enough of Erzberger's notes. Erzberger's report of April 24 with appendix now appears in Sch&Gr, Vol. 2, No. 85.

46. He asked Erzberger to say nothing about his Stockholm trip in Vienna, i.e., to arouse no false hopes there. He immediately criticized the fact that the "draft armistice" said nothing concrete about the real problem, the drawing of the borders. In the above-cited file note on the Kreuznach program he remarked that there were no current opportunities for peace negotiations; hence to set up a war aims program was superfluous.

47. Details of the exchanges in Fischer, pp. 488f.; Epstein; Müller, p. 279; Sch&Gr, Vol. 2, Nos. 88, 90, 92, 93, 94.

48. A war aims catalog of May 12 intended for General Dragomirov and probably transmitted to St. Petersburg demanded financial compensation for the maintenance of more than a million prisoners-of-war and further, quite brutally, integration of Lithuania and Courland with Germany, "since we need more land to feed our people" (Sch&Gr, Vol. 2, Nos. 114, 119, 125). In connection with the list of April 29, see *ibidem,* No. 98 (marginal note by Zimmermann), and a report by Hohenlohe of May 3 on a discussion with Zimmermann (HHSTA, war files, 25x). See also Ludendorff's statement to Consul Marx of April 19, in which he described the acquisition of the island of Sarema (Oesel) as indispensable (*ibidem,* No. 79). On trench propaganda, see RAW, Vol. 12, pp. 485ff., 492ff., also Sch&Gr, Vol. 2, No. 83.

49. Seeckt, p. 562, letter of May 29, addressee unidentified, probably his wife.

50. See Chapter 4, Note 17, above.

51. AA WW, 15, secret, Vol. 3, undated, written on the letterhead of the Austrian embassy, reception stamp of the foreign ministry dated May 30. See also Seeckt, p. 569–the editor, Rabenau, saw an elaborate proposal by Seeckt; further Steglich (1), Chapter 2, Note 248.

52. Grünau to Zimmermann, May 9 (AA WW, 15, secret, Vol. 3). For details of the Stecklov affair, see Steglich (1), Fischer, pp. 492ff., and Sch&Gr, Vol. 2, Nos. 107, 108, 110. According to Lersner's dispatch of May 7 (of which I have a copy), the intelligence officer negotiating with the Russians did not encounter unconditional opposition to annexations. Fischer, of course, interprets Bethmann Hollweg's stand in Machiavellian terms rather than as a reluctant compromise, to which end he makes the most of one of the Chancellor's phrases aimed at Ludendorff, namely that Courland and Lithuania must be dressed up *(frisieren)* as autonomous states. There was no conceivable means, however, by which Bethmann Hollweg could have compelled the OHL to allow its military negotiators to forego the Baltic countries completely. He probably planned to avoid the appearance of rigidity, once serious negotiations were under way. This is also shown in Zimmermann's extremely cautious formulation on May 14 of the peace terms to be proposed, in contrast to Ludendorff's undisguised annexationist demands of May 12. On May 9 he had insisted that the negotiators (Colonel von Winterfeldt, Envoy Rosenberg, and Deputy Dr. David) confront the Russians with a bill for at least two and a quarter billion marks for maintaining more than a million Russian prisoners-of-war, in the expectation that this would make them amenable to the cession of Courland and Lithuania! Fischer vainly seeks to play down the gulf between this kind of "diplomacy" and the approach of the foreign ministry.

53. Czernin to Hohenlohe, April 23 (HHSTA, war files, 25x). The motives behind Czer-

nin's inquiry are typical of the man: Austria needed a separate peace with Russia because of its critical food situation, which a peaceful Russia would be able to relieve—a conclusion strongly doubted in Berlin. I dispense with individual documentation here, referring readers to Steglich (1), Chapter 2, which goes into great detail on the source material that has been available to me, supplemented by further documents.

54. HHSTA, war files, 25t, April 26-28. Ritzov was to write to Maxim Gorki that the Central Powers were prepared to grant Russia peace without annexations or indemnities on either side and with the creation of an independent Poland. Bethmann Hollweg and Zimmermann, however, had been informed by a "confidential source" that the Russians did not trust Ritzov in the least and did not want him as a negotiator.

55. Epstein, pp. 194f. Count Wedel too reported on April 18 that Clam-Martinitz regarded Czernin's fears as exaggerated and did not believe that revolution threatened. Not even the Austrian socialists were thinking of such a thing (Sch&Gr, Vol. 2, No. 77).

56. The impression of "incomprehensible vacillation" had been created by a deliberately untrue assertion of Emperor Charles. The OHL liaison officer General Cramon, he had said, had told him that the OHL was presently negotiating with Russian military figures about a peace without conquest or indemnities. This led to misunderstandings and unsupported charges against Cramon, which took some time to clear up. See Cramon (2), pp. 168ff.

57. His detailed report on German newspaper statements about the question of a peace without annexations and about the article in the *Fremdenblatt* of April 28 shows that the entire bourgeois press, even the democratic *Berliner Tageblatt,* was dissatisfied with Scheidemann's declaration and that Czernin's article was causing the German government serious trouble. In discussion with Stumm Hohenlohe proposed that *mutual* border rectifications be agreed on with Russia, offering East Galicia for that purpose, evidently without authority. Stumm sensed a "feeler" behind this proposal. (Note by Stumm, April 29, AA WW, 15, secret, Vol. 2.)

58. The original draft also demanded complete restoration of Austro-Hungarian territorial integrity and corresponding modifications of the Balkan borders, but Czernin subsequently dropped this.

59. Details in Steglich (1), after official Bavarian files (also in my possession) and AA WW, 15, secret, Vol. 3. Hertling's wire to Bethmann Hollweg went by way of the German embassy, but was drafted or revised by Ambassador Mérey.

60. Hohenlohe's report of May 2, *loc. cit.* See also further correspondence in Sch&Gr, Vol. 2, No. 101.

61. Ludendorff (2), pp. 353, 380ff.; Sch&Gr, Vol. 2, No. 104—see Note 25, above.

62. Varnbüler's minutes, May 8 (HSTA, E-49-5, foreign ministry, IV, 3 BAV, 16).

63. On May 1 Bethmann Hollweg discussed Erzberger's Stockholm trip with Hohenlohe in terms that made it appear as a sweeping German peace offer. After some to and fro Zimmermann expressed his agreement with the plan that Ritzov should write to Gorki. Lastly—and only to reassure the Austrians—mention was made of von der Lancken's peace feeler with Chamber President Deschanel. On April 28, before the main committee, Zimmermann made a tortured attempt to justify the policy of silence, while trying to avoid the wrath of the social democrats, especially David (excerpts from the minutes in AA WW, 15, secret, and Germany, 122, 2c, No. 1).

64. Details in Steglich (1). The exchange between Czernin and Hohenlohe is in the HHSTA, war files, 25x. See also Zimmermann to Wedel, May 3 and 4, Wedel's reports of May 5 and 6, Czernin to Hohenlohe, May 3 (HHSTA, Prussia, III/175). Czernin sought to trivialize Emperor Charles's dispatching of Count Berchtold to German headquarters, and also the missions of Hertling and Holtzendorff.

65. Czernin was nettled by the ambassador's indirect criticism, but Hohenlohe settled this matter in a private letter of May 8.

66. Epstein (p. 194) so puts the matter, from Erzberger's papers. There is no mention of it either in Erzberger's official report to the foreign ministry or in his memoirs.
67. Czernin, pp. 211ff.; Werkmann, p. 176 (which tries to exculpate Emperor Charles and represent the transmission of the memorandum as a mere slip); Cramon (2), pp. 179ff. (reports on Charles's hypocrisy and lies); Ludendorff (2), pp. 390ff. (newspaper articles on the events by Count Wedel and Czernin, published in 1919); Erzberger, pp. 116ff.; Epstein, pp. 195, 229f. A report by Erzberger to Zimmermann of April 25 was published in the *Münchner Neuste Nachrichten* on March 10, 1922. A noteworthy feature of the report, repeated in substance in Erzberger's memoirs, is that Czernin said during the apparently brief discussion with Erzberger that he did not believe in the possibility of a separate peace with Russia, since Britain would always prevent such a thing, and that he was not minded to take any action in favor of peace for the time being. This seems to carry a note of resignation, but may have been meant merely to fend off the representations which Erzberger was charged with making in respect of Czernin's policies. Czernin was concerned, moreover, to encourage Erzberger to mount a Catholic peace initiative, an idea to which Erzberger responded positively. Epstein (p. 194) is wrong in believing that Czernin played down the threat of revolution. Rather the contrary was true, from Erzberger's report.
68. Prince Sixtus of Bourbon, pp. 159ff.
69. See Chapter 10, Note 36, above.
70. Prince Sixtus of Bourbon, pp. 165ff.; Lloyd George, Vol. 4, pp. 2,011ff. The discussion with Ribot on the 20th showed, among other things, that Ribot was not in the least interested in getting South Tyrol for the Italians, until and unless the French held Alsace-Lorraine. Ribot, moreover, regarded the Italian offer as more than dubious. Charles's letter and the draft by Prince Sixtus appear in German translation in Polzer-Hoditz, pp. 602f.
71. There is a hint of this in Bethmann Hollweg's direct report to the Kaiser of May 14 (Sch&Gr, Vol. 2, No. 118, with the Kaiser's marginal note). See also Bethmann Hollweg, Vol. 2, pp. 203ff. For the Kaiser's thoughts on the alleged Entente offer, see Sch&Gr, Vol. 2, No. 120. On May 30 Cramon wrongly reported to the ambassador and the OHL that the two princes had again appeared in Vienna. Wedel transmitted the news to the foreign ministry. On the margin of this dispatch Bethmann Hollweg noted that the princes were probably looking for an answer and that Czernin was likely to ask for information on what he should say. In that eventuality efforts should be made to initiate a dialogue with persons of substance. Discussions with irresponsible people could only do harm. This would mean that no official German stand had been taken by May 30. (Wedel to the foreign ministry, May 30, Sch&Gr, Vol. 2, No. 131.) At headquarters this alleged visit of the princes was associated with a trip by Charles to Feldkirch, where the empress's youngest brothers were attending school. The guess was that he wanted to meet Briand there—but Czernin deflated these rumors when he was questioned. The exchange of wires on June 4-6 was published in the *Münchner Neuste Nachrichten,* March 1922.
72. Czernin to Hohenlohe, May 13; reply, May 15 (HHSTA, war files, 25x).
73. See Chapter 10, Note 7, above. Wedel to the foreign ministry, May 15, Sch&Gr, Vol. 2, No. 121. That Wedel assessed the mood of the Austrian diplomats quite correctly is shown by a rather angry exchange of wires between Musulin in Berne and Czernin, May 4-8 (HHSTA, war files, 25x). Wedel's statements on the demeanor of Prince Sixtus in May, when he came alone, are so imprecise that little value can be ascribed to his subsequent assurances (before the parliamentary investigating committee of 1922) that Emperor Charles in 1917 did not want a separate peace—even though Steglich (1) gives great importance to them.
74. This was the former grain merchant Hermann Weil from Frankfurt, who for some years had drawn attention by statistical analyses of British food supplies. See W. Görlitz, in Müller, p. 286, Note 42.
75. Grünau to Zimmermann, May 9 and 13; Lersner to the foreign ministry, May 10 (AA

WW, 15, secret, Vol. 3). The dispatch of May 13 is in Sch&Gr, Vol. 2, No. 115.
76. Westarp, p. 87.
77. Erzberger proposed that there be no annexations and no war indemnities, but compensation for the occupied territories. (Epstein, p. 200, finds this formula ambiguous but, oddly enough, better than Bethmann Hollweg's "vague commonplaces.")
78. Romberg to the foreign ministry, May 13, published in Hahlweg, pp. 58ff. See also Steglich (1).
79. Müller, p. 287.
80. Hohenlohe to Czernin, May 15 (HHSTA, Prussia, III/173).
81. Grünau to Bethmann Hollweg, April 25 (two telegrams); Zimmermann to Grünau, April 26; Grünau to Zimmermann, April 27; reply, April 28 (AA WW, 15, secret, Vol. 2, also in part in Sch&Gr, Vol. 2, Nos. 89, 91).
82. Zimmermann to Wedel, April 28 (Sch&Gr, Vol. 2, No. 96).
83. Grünau to the foreign ministry, May 2 (Sch&Gr, Vol. 2, No. 103); Wedel to the foreign ministry, May 6 and 7; Grünau to the foreign ministry, May 8; note by Stumm, May 8 (all in AA WW, 15, secret, Vol. 3). Ludendorff apologized for having confused various dispatches. Even before, there had been two urgent wires from Ludendorff, via Lersner, April 29, *ibidem,* Vol. 2, also in Sch&Gr, Vol. 2, No. 100.
84. Bulgaria demanded the entire Dobrudja. The German foreign ministry was willing to concede it only the southern part, lost in 1913, in order to leave the Rumanians their only rail line to the Black Sea (Czernawoda-Constantsa) and avoid having all the routes of communication to Turkey in Bulgarian hands. Radoslavov, however, invoked an alleged verbal commitment—probably misinterpreted!—given by the Kaiser in December 1916. See Steglich (2), pp. 152ff., and Kühlmann, *Erinnerungen* (1948), p. 552. Zimmermann was no more concerned than the German envoy in Sofia over the possibility that the Bulgarians would be antagonized by Ludendorff's blunt rebuff to their wishes in the Dobrudja—foreign ministry to Lersner, May 4; Oberndorff (Sofia) to the foreign ministry, May 7; Lersner to the foreign ministry, May 10 (all in AA WW, 15, secret, Vol. 3).
85. Files on the Berlin conference of May 12 are in AA WW, 15, secret, Vol. 3 (partial copies also under other filing designations). On May 5 there had been a preliminary meeting with German interests, especially banks, concerned with the Serbian coal and ore deposits. This was at the Reich office of the interior (AA Bulgaria, 7). On May 6 Bethmann Hollweg agreed with the OHL on another meeting, to be held on May 17, before the arrival of King Ferdinand, with the OHL, the Chancellor, and Czernin participating. Answer from the OHL, via Lersner, May 7; Stumm to Grünau, May 9; Grünau to the foreign ministry, May 15 (Ludendorff asking and being promised information about the treaties with Turkey and the agreements with Austria concerning payment of subsidies). An exchange of wires between Zimmermann and Lersner, April 28-May 1 (Sch&Gr, Vol. 2, Nos. 95, 99, 102), leaves a curious impression of the foreign ministry's dependence on the OHL. Ludendorff was asked for permission, so to speak, to let the left socialist Ledebour go to the Stockholm conference, even though initially Ludendorff said that such purely political questions were not his affair.
86. Exchange between Kühlmann at the foreign ministry and Lersner, May 19, 21, 23, and 30, and June 1; Lossow to Ludendorff, June 6; Kühlmann to the foreign ministry, June 14 (transmitting Lossow's report for the OHL of June 6, together with the eight-point program and Enver's response); exchange between Zimmermann and Grünau, June 20 and 22—all in AA WW, 15, secret, Vol. 3. Ludendorff's instructions to Lossow are dated early May.
87. Zimmermann to Kühlmann, May 23, *ibidem.* Ludendorff on his part regarded the Kreuznach program as a firm agreement, which he cited, for example, when protesting Bulgarian recognition of Venizelist Greece—Ludendorff to the foreign ministry, May 30, *ibidem.*

88. Zimmermann to Grünau, May 5, about a communication from Hohenlohe (AA WW, 15, secret, Vol. 3); Wedel to the foreign ministry, May 4-6, *ibidem,* the last-named report also in Sch&Gr, Vol. 2, No. 106. General Arz was pressing for concrete directives for trench propaganda and seemed prepared to forego the Ruthenian areas of Galicia. For Czernin's directive to Hohenlohe, May 4, and Hohenlohe's reply, May 5, see HHSTA, war files, 25t.

89. Czernin to Count Otto Czernin (Sofia), May 12, reply, May 15 (two wires), HHSTA, war files, 25x; Czernin to the same, May 16, *ibidem,* secret, XLVII/3-8.

90. See Chapter 10, Note 39, above.

91. There are several different drafts by Czernin in the HHSTA, secret, XLVII/13. One is in the form of a treaty, another a letter to be addressed to Bethmann Hollweg and acknowledged by him. The former also mentions the return of at least most of the German colonies. Whether these drafts were submitted at Kreuznach cannot be established.

92. Notes with accompanying text: AA WW, 15, secret, Vol. 3, published in UA IV LVII/3-18). On pp. 202ff., identical with Sch&Gr, Vol. 2, No. 123. The notes were initially signed by Bethmann Hollweg, with Czernin adding "agreed to, subject to the agreement of the appropriate authorities [Faktoren]."

93. Wedel to the foreign ministry, May 23 (Sch&Gr, Vol. 2, No. 127); Czernin to Emperor Charles, May 18: "Negotiations proceeding satisfactorily, installation of a Polish regent unfortunately not gained" (HHSTA, secret, XLVII/3-18). On May 28 Clam-Martinitz received Ukrainian delegates and told them that Austrian surrender of East Galicia was out of the question—Wedel to the foreign ministry, May 30 (AA WW, 15, secret, Vol. 3).

94. Czernin to Bethmann Hollweg, June 18; Zimmermann to Wedel, July 5; Zimmermann to Lersner, July 6; Wedel to Zimmermann, July 8; Zimmermann to Lersner, July 11; Ludendorff to Zimmermann, via Legation Secretary Berckheim, July 10; Zimmermann to Wedel, July 26; Wedel's reply, July 31—all in AA WW, 15, secret, Vols. 3-4.

95. Details in Steglich (1), and Fischer, pp. 498ff. Fischer, in my view, greatly exaggerates the importance of the episode. It is neither probable nor demonstrable that publication of the war aims list burdened the German "government socialists" (i.e., Scheidemann and Ebert) in Stockholm with the odium of annexationism. Epstein (p. 201) suggests that Erzberger was active in this affair but offers no proof. See also Sch&Gr, Vol. 2, Nos. 133, 134.

96. See Vol. II, pp. 256ff., 261ff. For the following, see Steglich (1), Chapter 2, based on the Vienna files. For Emperor Charles's handwritten message of June 7, see Sch&Gr, Vol. 2, No. 136; the Kaiser's reply of June 22, *ibidem,* 2, No. 143.

97. Documentation in Steglich (1), Chapter 2, Note 260.

98. Zimmermann (at headquarters) to the foreign ministry and to Wedel, June 13 (AA WW, 15, secret, Vol. 3); corrected draft of an article, *ibidem,* 2, secret, Vol. 41 (photostat D 966 177-8); Ludendorff to the foreign ministry (via Grünau), June 26; Wedel to the foreign ministry, June 28; Ludendorff to the foreign ministry, July 4—*ibidem,* 15, secret, Vol. 4. Fischer (p. 468) says nothing about the background of Zimmermann's directive.

*Notes to Chapter 12*

1. The most dramatic account of these complaints and still others is embodied in the memorandum of the social democratic party and Reichstag leaders of late 1917, intended for Bethmann Hollweg, contained in Scheidemann (2), pp. 161ff. On the internal problems confronting the social democrats, see also H. Herzfeld, *Die deutsche Sozialdemokratie und die Auflösung der nationalen Einheitsfront im Weltkrieg* (1928). This book is written from a rightist point of view.

2. Bethmann Hollweg, Vol. 2, p. 189. On the complaints and abuses, see Helfferich, Vol. 3, pp. 86ff.

3. Bergsträsser, esp. pp. 95ff.

4. On the background of this speech, which Wahnschaffe and the press chief Deutelmoser had urged on Bethmann Hollweg, see Bergsträsser, pp. 117f.

5. See, for example, the stand of Meinecke and his Berlin friends during these months (F. Meinecke, *Politische Schriften und Reden,* ed. by G. Kotowski [1958], pp. 146ff., 171ff.). The latter reference gives F. Thimme's proposals for Prussian electoral reform of August 1916. See also the letter by Adolf von Harnack to his niece of June 23, 1917, in Fester (2), pp. 255f.

6. I do not feel I can echo Bergsträsser's charge (p. 133) that this was an error and a half-measure. Who can assess correctly today, years after the event, what was then possible and advisable in discussion with the Kaiser? Bethmann Hollweg did register a profound impression on the Kaiser with his remark that he would find it impossible to go before the country to advocate a bill under which an impoverished worker, decorated for valor in action, would be discriminated against at the polls as compared with an affluent shirker in the same district. These words continued to influence the Kaiser for a long time. See Bergsträsser, p. 140, Note.

7. See the telegram just mentioned (Bergsträsser, p. 153). At the very least it would seem that Valentini was convinced that universal suffrage could not be pushed through the Prussian diet. Still, the report in his book (p. 163) sounds rather different.

8. Bethmann Hollweg, Vol. 2, pp. 191ff.; Valentini, p. 153; Bergsträsser, pp. 154ff. Bergsträsser's criticism of Bethmann Hollweg's "policy of the diagonal" (p. 161) fails to consider whether in this situation Bethmann Hollweg had any alternative, i.e., whether table-thumping and threatening the Kaiser with his resignation would have brought him to the desired goal more swiftly and with greater certainty. On Bethmann Hollweg's initially vain efforts to dissuade Scheidemann and his constitutional committee from considering the question of officers' commissions, see Scheidemann (2), pp. 168ff. (discussion of May 7).

9. Schulthess (1917), Vol. 1, pp. 591f.

10. Bethmann Hollweg, Vol. 2, p. 191.

11. Ludendorff (1), p. 356. Ludendorff there discusses the ideal of a corporate *(berufsständischen)* electoral law, which he claimed was envisaged by Bismarck, but these thoughts probably stem from his postwar political activities.

12. See his letter to Minister Drews, December 8, 1917 (Ludendorff [2], pp. 291ff.).

13. The Chancellor to the OHL, June 6 (ZA Potsdam, chancellery file, VII, 11); the other pieces cited in the text, *ibidem.* The message to the OHL of May 11 was published in Sch&Gr, Vol. 2, No. 112.

14. What I am reproducing in the following is the gist of a seven-page memorandum, the draft of which is among Bauer's papers (BA), Portfolio 2, Sheets 169ff. This draft is undated, but seems to have been written soon after April 20, since it takes issue with the social democratic peace manifesto of that date. In content it overlaps the memorandum of March 1917 which Bauer published in his memoirs (pp. 134ff.). There are, however, contradictions and non sequiturs between and within the two memoranda.

15. Bauer, p. 159—see also the statement reported by Bergsträsser (p. 135). On June 29 the Bavarian legation councilor von Krafft, at the headquarters of Crown Prince Rupprecht, reported his impression from talks with Major Mende, the Prussian OHL liaison officer, that the General Staff wanted Ludendorff as Chancellor, or else Hindenburg, as Ludendorff's dummy (GSTA, Pol. A, VII/39).

16. Legation Councilor von Krafft to Hertling, March 13, 1917 (GSTA, Pol. A, VII/39).

17. Hellingrath to Hertling, May 3, 1917 (GSTA, Pol. A, VII/66). Hellingrath was a determined advocate of Prussian electoral reform, which he thought essential to army morale (Bergsträsser, p. 157). At headquarters, however, he was told that the Chancellor was an utter failure, had allowed the reins to drop from his hands, etc.

18. Reports by Hohenlohe to Czernin, February 26, May 6 and 9; Czernin to Hohenlohe,

May 9 (HHSTA, Prussia, III/173, and war files, 25x). Reports from South Germany (AA, Germany, 122, No. 16, secret). The Grand Duchess Louise of Baden, on March 1, wanted to congratulate Bethmann Hollweg on his last Reichstag speech.

19. Note by Weizsäcker of May 13 on a discussion that took place on May 8 (Weizsäcker's papers).
20. Chapter 2, Parts 1 and 2 (pp.47 and 68).
21. Bethmann Hollweg to Grünau, June 24, 1917 (Sch&Gr, Vol. 2, No. 145).
22. The OHL to Bethmann Hollweg, June 19 (Ludendorff [2], pp. 395ff.). Letter from Holtzendorff and the Kaiser (Spindler, Vol. 4, pp. 388f.).
23. Bethmann Hollweg to the OHL, June 25; reply, July 5 (Ludendorff [2], pp. 397ff.). See also Müller, p. 298.
24. In the matter of Alsace-Lorraine, however, the socialist minister Thomas did try, via some Scandinavian socialists, to reach agreement with the Germans on a plebiscite to be held after the war, under the ruling of an international court of arbitration. See Sch&Gr, Vol. 2, Nos. 149, 164n.
25. Matthias, p. xxv (introduction).
26. Scheidemann (2), pp. 160ff.
27. Details in Steglich (1), Chapter 2, Note 301. The Turkish ambassador handed his government's peace terms to the foreign ministry on June 21: no border changes, mutual evacuation of Persia, no war indemnities, readiness to arrive at a new settlement of the Straits question (AA WW, 15, secret, Vol. 3). They had already been transmitted in Vienna on June 12 (HHSTA, war files, 25t).
28. Bethmann Hollweg, Vol. 2, p. 210; Ludendorff (2), pp. 419-423 (article by Bethmann Hollweg in the *Deutsche Allgemeine Zeitung* of February 29, 1920). The accuracy of Bethmann Hollweg's statements was expressly confirmed by Gasparri and Pacelli (Steglich [1], Chapter 3, Note 16). Zimmermann repeated Bethmann Hollweg's declaration exactly, as had been agreed. On the discussion between Pacelli and the Kaiser, June 30, in the following, see Sch&Gr, Vol. 2, No. 157. For the Kaiser's reply to the pope, see *ibidem,* No. 165. The papal peace initiative as a whole will be discussed in Vol. IV of this work.
29. Valentini, pp. 153ff., also for the following. See also Bethmann Hollweg, Vol. 2, pp. 50f., 218.
30. Bethmann Hollweg, Vol. 2, p. 219. Müller, on the other hand, reports (p. 298) that the Kaiser refused to appoint the centrist deputy Spahn a minister. We already know Valentini's reluctance and this probably explains Müller's note *(ibidem)* to the effect that Valentini was greatly upset over the Chancellor's ineptitude and irresolution, though this does not square with the cabinet chief's memoirs. Valentini (p. 183) regarded parliamentary ministers simply as amateurs.
31. Crown Prince William to Bethmann Hollweg, June 24 (AA WW, 15, secret, Vol. 3), answered by a private letter. The crown prince sent along an article on Britain's war aims from the *Magdeburger Zeitung,* June 20 (No. 450). He thought the idea excellent of keeping Belgium with Antwerp, in order to deprive Britain of a bridgehead, secure land, render the German food supply independent of foreign sources, obtain coal and ore deposits, and above all disrupt the system of worldwide economic snares in which Britain was successfully trying to entangle Germany. The government must not allow itself to be intimidated by the threat of revolution but must find the courage to reject an inadequate peace, if that should be necessary. The people must be told that it would be far better to stick it out a few months longer rather than to have made all their great sacrifices in vain. It must be suggested to them that the domestic reforms desired would avail Germany nothing, if it were hemmed in from abroad. Such were the aspirations of a Prussian prince who wished to contribute to "Prussia and Germany emerging from the world war rich in glory and triumph, under the leadership of the Hohenzollern dynasty." Typical of the crown prince's political uncertainty is the fact that only a little earlier he had allowed himself to be impressed by the peace

plans of Czernin and Emperor Charles—see P. Herre, *Kronprinz Wilhelm,* pp. 83f.; Czernin, pp. 94-99. According to these sources, and also Bethmann Hollweg, Vol. 2, p. 209, the crown prince was ready in principle to agree to the cession of border districts.

32. Scheidemann (2), p. 83.
33. Helfferich, Vol. 3, p. 124.
34. Matthias, p. xxvi.
35. See Chapter 11, Note 33.
36. Note by Wahnschaffe (ZA Potsdam, chancellery file, VII/11).
37. Scheidemann (2), p. 84.
38. Matthias (pp. 110ff.) juxtaposes the various versions of the peace resolution for comparison.
39. UA IV, Vol. 8, pp. 120ff. (testimony of Bredt, with appendices).
40. *Ibidem,* pp. 115ff.
41. The debate can be reconstructed with considerable accuracy with the help of the source material, some of it new, compiled by Matthias.
42. Helfferich had drawn the ire of the left by his "capitalist stand" during the consultations over the auxiliary service bill in November 1916. He was furthermore charged with having changed his stand on the U-boat question too quickly and too thoroughly. Capelle was compromised on account of his erroneous predictions concerning the success of U-boat warfare, Zimmermann by the notorious Mexican telegram (see Chapter 8, Note 222) and because of a plot to bomb Norwegian ships in Christiania (Oslo), which had just become known (details in Sch&Gr, Vol. 2, No. 167). Actually the admiralty bore sole responsibility for the plot.
43. Payer, p. 31.
44. Haussmann, p. 103.
45. Matthias, pp. 6, 7, 11.
46. Stresemann wanted to talk on Bethmann Hollweg's policies under an innocent-sounding title at this ambitiously planned meeting of business leaders, presided over by Friedrich Duisberg of the Bayer company. A petition to the Kaiser, calling for Bethmann Hollweg's dismissal, was to be circulated and signed at the meeting. Haussmann, however, exposed this plot in the press so thoroughly beforehand that attendance at the meeting remained small and nothing came of it. Haussmann also discussed it on the floor of the Reichstag (pp. 87ff.). For an indignant report on the Adlon conference by Hohenlohe to Czernin, February 26, see HHSTA, Prussia, III/173.
47. Zimmermann to Haussmann, July 13 (Haussmann, p. 125). For Stresemann's speech see UA IV, Vol. 8, p. 125 (Bredt testimony). Scheidemann ([3], p. 88) thought Bethmann Hollweg's reply "uncommonly skillful"; Haussmann on the other hand (p. 103) thought it too defensive in tone and lacking mastery.
48. Scheidemann (1), Vol. 2, pp. 36f.
49. Scheidemann (2), p. 88 (the date is in error); Epstein, p. 217.
50. Valentini, p. 158; similarly, Bethmann Hollweg, Vol. 2, p. 229. Epstein's account (p. 217) would therefore seem to require correction. Bethmann Hollweg knew neither of the appointment with the generals nor of their sudden departure. Typical of Epstein's bias is his unfounded charge (p. 216) that the politically unsophisticated Bethmann Hollweg failed to appreciate the gravity of the crisis created by Erzberger's speech. In the first place, Bethmann Hollweg immediately distrusted Erzberger's sincere-sounding assurances given on the afternoon of July 6 (see Bethmann Hollweg, Vol. 2, p. 224, according to which the account of the talk accepted by Epstein is altogether erroneous); and in the second place, the situation report which he handed the Kaiser on July 7 was based on official information from Payer. See Matthias, documents, p. 19.
51. Session of July 8, see Matthias, documents, pp. 18f. Payer immediately denied Erzberger's charge that Bethmann Hollweg had misrepresented the situation to the Kaiser (see preceding Note).

52. Haussmann, p. 103; Bethmann Hollweg, Vol. 2, p. 232.
53. See Chapter 5, Note 92, above.
54. Czernin, pp. 212f.
55. Czernin says he made the following proposals, through Vassilkov: (a) no annexations or war indemnities; (b) complete and unconditional surrender of Belgium, politically and economically; (c) all territories occupied by Germany and Austria to be evacuated as soon as both countries had their own territories restored to them, including the German colonies.
56. See Czernin's negotiations in early July with Count Wedel and the Austrian ambassador to the Sublime Porte (Steglich [1], Chapter 2, pp. 108f.); also Wedel's report of July 16 (Sch&Gr, Vol. 2, No. 168). Czernin welcomed the Reichstag peace resolution but would have preferred to hear Germany declare that its goal was the status quo. This would do no harm, since the enemy would not accept it, but it would leave the Central Powers free to fight on and to demand high compensation for their losses. The Reichstag resolution called for peace without aggrandisement, even in the event of victory—and that might well cheat the Central Powers of victory. On July 18 Wedel supplemented Czernin's statement. A time limit might be put on the offer of the status quo, thus making it impossible for the Allies to accept, while the offer would still exert a fruitful effect at home. In the meantime Vienna had witnessed a great demonstration in favor of the status quo, laced with sharp speeches attacking Germany (AA WW, 15, secret, Vol. 4).
57. Matthias, p. xxix (introduction) and pp. 6 and 15 (documents).
58. Matthias, p. 6 (documents). For the story about the "spotty record" *(bekleckerte Weste)* see Bülow, *Denkwürdigkeiten,* Vol. 3, p. 265, after a story told by the crown prince.
59. Reports from Hohenlohe, July 10-16 (HHSTA, secret, XLVII/3-19).
60. Hellingrath to Hertling, July 4, 1917 (GSTA, Pol. A, VII/52-I); Lerchenfeld to King Louis III, July 7 and 12, on audiences of the Kaiser, *ibidem,* No. 60; Lerchenfeld to State Councilor Lössl on a talk with Valentini *(ibidem);* Varnbüler to Weizsäcker, July 10 (HSTA, E 73/61, 12 i II). Among Weizsäcker's private papers is an interesting letter from the noted publicist Professor Jäckh, of December 17, 1917, telling of a discussion with unnamed leading Bolshevists. They spoke of Bethmann Hollweg's policies with great respect. By his steadfast willingness to consider peace, he had prevented internal divisions in Germany, thus foiling revolution in Germany.
61. See, for example, his memorandum for the foreign ministry of December 1, 1916, which is almost comical in its pretensions to advise Chancellor, minister, and under secretary on how the impending peace negotiations should be prepared and organized (AA WW, 15, secret, Vol. 2).
62. Scheidemann (1), Vol. 2, pp. 111ff. On Stresemann's admiration for Bülow, see UA IV, 7, Vol. 2, p. 304.
63. Envoy Treutler from Munich to the foreign ministry, January 11, 1917; Bethmann Hollweg's reply, January 13 (AA WW, 15, secret). Hertling had reproached Erzberger for intriguing against Bethmann Hollweg. Erzberger replied that he wanted Bülow as peace negotiator, but would support Bethmann Hollweg until then. The Chancellor and Zimmermann allegedly agreed! When asked, the Chancellor told Hertling that he had listened to Erzberger's proposals in silence, while Zimmermann had commented only in a noncommittal fashion.
64. Hohenlohe reported on May 6 that he had attended a party of conservative and national-liberal politicians. They were all agreed that Bethmann Hollweg must go. Bülow was to succeed him and conduct the peace negotiations, and he in turn would be succeeded by a seasoned general who would revoke all the domestic concessions Bethmann Hollweg had granted (HHSTA, war files, 25x).
65. Bülow, *Denkwürdigkeiten,* Vol. 3, p. 115. Bülow asserts that for a brief time Eulenburg too had won the Kaiser over to the idea of summoning Bülow (Westarp, p. 354; Erzberger, p. 262; Valentini, p. 163).
66. Epstein, p. 216.

67. Report to Czernin, February 26, 1917 (HHSTA, Prussia, III/173). He used this expression to Crown Prince William as well, reproaching Bülow for having maneuvered Germany into a most unfavorable position, because of his frivolous diplomacy prior to 1908 (Czernin's report of July 12, 1917, HHSTA, secret, XLVII/3-19).
68. Our present information on Erzberger's talk with Hoffmann is very sparse—see the latter's memoirs, Vol. 1, pp. 157ff., 161ff., 166ff.; also Richthofen's testimony, UA IV, 7, Vol. 2, pp. 217ff. This is true also of Erzberger's discussions with Bauer (Erzberger, p. 252). Apparently Erzberger's papers include nothing of consequence, since Epstein (pp. 208f.) can tell us nothing essentially new.
69. Bethmann Hollweg was indignant when the OHL, in its letter of June 19, suddenly pretended that the notion that the end of the war impended emanated "from Berlin" rather than from supreme headquarters (Müller, p. 295).
70. Hoffmann, Vol. 1, p. 170; Helfferich, Vol. 3, p. 115. Erzberger's assertion (p. 262) that he stuck to Bethmann Hollweg during the July crisis "as long as the over-all situation permitted" is thus misleading.
71. Report from Hohenlohe, July 16, 1917 (HHSTA, secret, XLVII/3-19).
72. Matthias, pp. 7, 25 (documents).
73. *Ibidem,* p. 68.
74. Valentini, pp. 116f., requiring correction and supplementation from Bethmann Hollweg's own notes of July 11 and 14, UA IV (Schwertfeger), appendix, pp. 152ff., and from Helfferich, Vol. 3, p. 121. Valentini states that on the very afternoon of July 10 Bethmann Hollweg received the signed order-in-council on Prussian electoral reform, but this is in error.
75. Helfferich, Vol. 3, pp. 120ff., 127f.; Bethmann Hollweg, Vol. 2, p. 232; Haussmann, pp. 106, 110, 118f.
76. The Kaiser told Lerchenfeld on July 11 that the crown prince advocated Tirpitz as Bethmann Hollweg's successor—report by Lerchenfeld to Louis III, July 12, GSTA, Pol. A, VII/60.
77. Ludendorff (2), pp. 408ff.; Payer, pp. 31ff.; Bauer, pp. 141f. Bauer seeks to inflate his role in toppling Bethmann Hollweg, but is short on facts.
78. Reports by Lerchenfeld to Louis III of Bavaria, July 8, 9, and 12, GSTA, Pol. A, VII/60. On July 9 Valentini assured the envoy, at the Kaiser's request, that William had the fullest confidence in the Chancellor and would never drop him. Valentini nevertheless tried to sound out Lerchenfeld on whether Hertling might be available as a successor.
79. Reports by Hohenlohe, July 12 and 16, *loc. cit.;* Valentini, p. 165. Judging from Bethmann Hollweg's notes of July 14 (UA IV [Schwertfeger], p. 154), Valentini gave him a favorable picture of the crown prince's stand during the talks cited above, but Valentini's report was probably too rosy.
80. Ludendorff (2), p. 407. Ludendorff himself had already offered similar objections to Bethmann Hollweg and Zimmermann on July 8. He said he heard stories about a Reichstag resolution that forbade any conquests. This he would profoundly regret, from a military point of view. An offensive against the Russians was to begin in mid-July. Bethmann Hollweg replied the same day that the text had not been settled and that efforts were being made to improve it during the course of the day (ZA Potsdam, chancellery file, IX, 14; also AA WW, 15, secret, Vol. 4).
81. Strangely failing to understand the general situation in Germany in 1917, Epstein (pp. 222f.) feels called upon to reproach Bethmann Hollweg with "weakness" because he did not take up the struggle against Ludendorff at the head of a left Reichstag majority. This is his final judgment: "Responsibility for the fact that Bethmann recoiled before Ludendorff's ultimatum falls solely on Bethmann himself and cannot be laid at Erzberger's door. Indeed, in a way the Chancellor's weakness toward Ludendorff justified Erzberger's desire to see him removed from office." I am sorry to say that I regard this as an unpardonable misjudgment, bespeaking an apologist rather than a historian.

82. I am sure Valentini's memory deceived him when he wrote (p. 166) about Bethmann Hollweg's "inner struggle" that night and the "labored voice" in which he proffered his resignation—Valentini was writing in 1918. This is at odds not only with the Chancellor's own record, written on July 14, but with Hohenlohe's report, cited further on, about his talk with the Kaiser on the morning of July 13.
83. Helfferich clearly resented the miserable failure of the Reichstag members. He told Payer that the joint party committee's demand was equivalent to the "Caudine Forks" and that the Chancellor would never allow himself to be so yoked (Helfferich, Vol. 3, p. 128). For the final audience, see Bethmann Hollweg, Vol. 2, p. 19.
84. Hohenlohe to Czernin, July 16 (HHSTA, secret, XLVII/3-19).
85. Haussmann, p. 130.
86. Ludendorff (2), pp. 412f.; Scheidemann (2), pp. 92ff., 96ff.
87. Weizsäcker's papers.
88. Written from Hohenfinow, September 8, 1917. Among Delbrück's papers.

# Index

594

*Index*

China, breaks off relations with Germany, 336

Christiania, German-Russian meetings in, 417

Clam-Martinitz, Count Heinrich, Austrian prime minister, 396

Class, Henrich, Pan-German leader, 26

Clémenceau, Georges: attacks Briand, 288, 295; publishes Emperor Charles's peace proposals (1918), 382

coal miners, Belgian, 362, 363

Cobb, Irvin S., journalist of *New York World*, 34

Colard, General von, Austrian commander in Poland, 101

colonies, German: in annexationist schemes, 26, 28, 29; in BH's war aims, 33, 73, 91, 153; in Pact of London, 64; British dominions and, 138, 257; British foresee ransoming of Belgium by concessions in, 256, 257; in drafts of German peace offer, 277, 278, 282; naval requirements for defense of, 290-1; BH sees occupied France and Belgium as bargaining counters for return of, 391, 416

*Comité des Forges,* 251

common market, Central European, *see* customs union

Congo: in German war aims, 91; in Belgian peace feelers, 242, 298; in drafts of German peace offer, 282, 284; in Bourbon peace proposals, 378

Conrad von Hötzendorf, General Franz, Austrian chief of staff (1906-17), 41; relations between Germans and, 49, 51, 57-8, 59-60; and action against Serbia, 49, 78; amateur diplomacy by, 63, 85-6; and Poland, 112, 221, 226, 227; and offensive against Italy, 158, 185-6, 190; Teschen headquarters of, 189; and question of command in east, 195, 197, 198, 200, 210, 211, 215, 221, 223; and draft of German peace offer, 284; and U-boat policy, 326; transferred to front by Emperor Charles (Feb. 1917), 232, 375

conscription: in plans for *Mitteleuropa,* 98; introduced in Britain (1916), 150; Belgium refuses treaty requiring (1916), 243; for auxiliary war service (Germany), 276, 346-58; of workers from Belgium, 361-72

Constantine, King of Greece, 80, 89

Constantinople: threatened by Dardanelles campaign, 78; schemes for Russian possession of, 63, 64, 376

constitution of Reich, Bismarckian, 11, 15, 447, 477

convoy system, for British ships (from May 1917), 307

Copenhagen: Russian socialists in, 401, 405; German-Russian contacts in, 414

Courland: Ludendorff's operations in, 68; suggested German annexation of, 106, 108, 116, 227, 438, 443; German administration in, 115; naval demand for, 291; in drafts of German peace offer, 277, 278, 282, 283; suggested "duchy" of, 335; German strategic claim on, 391, 417; von Seeckt demurs at claim on, 422; suggested autonomy of, 418, 422, 427

Cracow, 102, 228

Cramon, General von, German liaison officer with Austria, 195, 198, 376

customs union: for *Mitteleuropa,* (proposed), 25, 30-1, 33, 94, (discussed with Austria) 107, 110, 111; French, Belgium refuses to join, 243; Austrian, Czernin wants Serbia in, 392, 393

Cyril, Prince of Bulgaria, suggested as king of Rumania, 438

Czechs: Bismarck and, 23; in Austrian army, 58, 186, 197; and *Mitteleuropa,* 96; in British peace terms, 255, 260

Czernin, Count Ottokar: as Austrian envoy in Bucharest, foresees Austrian defeat, 189; succeeds Burián as foreign minister, 231, 233; and Poland, 310; and U-boat policy, 325, 326, 336, 339; and separate Austrian peace moves, 338, 339; and peace moves of Emperor Charles, 375, 379, 380, 381, 383, 384, 430-1; gloomy reports about Austria from, 389-90, 394, 396, 397, 409, 424, 429; and Russian peace proposals, 405, 407, 409, 423-4; tries for joint declaration by Austria and Germany, 425, 427; congratulatory message from BH to, 428-9; alleges offer of separate peace from Allies, 432-3; and OHL's Balkan program, 437, 439-41; and Reichstag peace resolution, 471; has to resign (1918), 382

*Daily Telegraph* affair (1908), 13

Dakar, 291

Dallwitz, N. von, governor of Alsace, 14

Dalmatia, 64, 102

Danube waterway, 58, 78, 80; opened by conquest of Rumania, 94; shipping on, in OHL peace terms, 438

Dardanelles: Anglo-French assaults on, 58,

## DATE DUE

| 11/√ | | | |
|------|---|---|---|
| | | | |
| | | | |
| | | | |
| | | | |
| | | | |
| | | | |
| | | | |
| | | | |
| | | | |
| | | | |
| | | | |
| | | | |
| | | | |
| | | | |
| | | | |
| | | | |
| | | | |
| | | | |